WITHDRAWN FROM
THE LIBRARY
UNIVERSITY OF
WINCHESTER
KA 0124855 3

DICTIONARY
OF
LABOUR BIOGRAPHY

Volume VI

DICTIONARY OF LABOUR BIOGRAPHY

Volume VI

Edited by

JOYCE M. BELLAMY
Senior Research Officer, University of Hull

and

JOHN SAVILLE
Professor of Economic and Social History, University of Hull

First published 1982 by
THE MACMILLAN PRESS LTD
London and Basingstoke
Companies and representatives throughout the world

ISBN 0 333 24095 2

Phototypeset in Great Britain by
REDWOOD BURN LIMITED
Trowbridge & Esher

Printed in Hong Kong

Contents

Acknowledgements	vii
Notes to Readers	ix
List of Contributors	x
List of Abbreviations	xii
List of Bibliographies and Special Notes	xvii
Additions and Corrections Vols I–V	xix
Biographies	1
Consolidated List of Names in Vols I–VI	276
General Index	285

Acknowledgements

This present volume continues along the same lines and upon the same principles as the previous volumes. We have, however, compiled Additions and Corrections for the first five volumes and these immediately precede the biographical entries. We have also specialised to some extent on radicals of the pre-1850 decades and hope that this emphasis upon Chartists, Owenites and other individuals involved in the radical movements of these early decades will help to redress the balance of our previous coverage. We have continued the policy, initiated in volume five, of publishing Special Notes relating to aspects of general labour history. The three included here are first, a reprint of a feminist article 'Woman's Industrial Independence' published in 1848, and then two Notes: one on Boggart Hole Clough and Free Speech and the second on Ca'canny.

The research for this volume has been made possible by a generous grant from the Social Science Research Council. We are also especially grateful for the assistance we have received from many individuals and organisations. In particular we wish to express our thanks to our present research team: Mrs Margaret 'Espinasse and Mrs Barbara Nield in Hull, Mrs Vivien Morton for her work in London and Dr David E. Martin of Sheffield University who exercises meticulous care in reading MS entries and maintains a lively interest in all aspects of our work. We also wish to acknowledge the help given by our former colleague, Ms Ann Holt, who was involved in the earlier stages of this volume.

We are much indebted to Dr Philip Larkin and his colleagues of the Brynmor Jones Library, Hull University; to Mrs Peggy Williams and her staff in the University's Research Typing Service; to our contributors, and to all those individuals and organisations whose names are listed in the sources section of the biographies. Many librarians have assisted us but we would particularly like to record our debt to the British Library, London and Boston Spa, and the Newspaper Library, Colindale; the British Library of Political and Economic Science; Goldsmiths' Library, London University; Mrs I. Wagner and her staff at the Labour Party Library; Mr R.A. Storey, archivist, Modern Record Centre, Warwick University Library and Ms Janet Druker, formerly of the MRC; the staff of Dr Williams's Library and the Library of the Religious Society of Friends; Miss Christine Coates, TUC Librarian; Mr Roy Garratt, Librarian of the Co-operative Union; and Mr S. Tongue, archivist of the London Borough of Hackney.

We are also grateful for the information supplied by the staff of the General Register Offices in Belfast, Dublin, Edinburgh and London, the Registry of Wills at Somerset House, the PRO, the National Libraries of Scotland and Wales and the Institute of Historical Research. We have had less occasion, in the preparation of this volume, to seek the help of trade union offices but we would like to record the co-operation given to us by staff of the Amalgamated Society of Boilermakers, Shipwrights, Blacksmiths and Structural Workers, Newcastle and by Mr J.E. Mortimer, of the Advisory, Conciliation and Arbitration Service. The *Manchester Evening News* published two letters which brought us useful contacts.

We wish, also, to record our appreciation of the help given to us in various ways by Timothy Ashplant, Peter Drake, John Etor, Edmund and Ruth Frow, Mrs Margaret Gibb, OBE, Dr Marion Kozak, Dr K.O. Morgan, David and Naomi Reid and Dr Eric Taylor. Our thanks are also due to Mrs Thea Elliott, widow of Anthony Elliott, CMG, for permission to use her late husband's papers. We further acknowledge the help given in proof-reading by John Atkins, Jan Crowther, Dr David E. Martin, Barbara Nield, Sandra Taylor and the work on the index by Barbara Nield, assisted by V.J. Morris and G.D. Weston of the Brynmor Jones Library. Finally we wish to thank our publishers and in particular Mr T.M. Farmiloe in the London office of Macmillan and Mr A. Bathe and Mr T. Fox at Basingstoke.

JMB
JS

University of Hull
October 1980

While this volume was being prepared for the press we learnt of the death of Dame Margaret Cole in early May 1980. The origin of the *Dictionary of Labour Biography*, set out in the Introduction to Volume I began with a number of MS volumes which G.D.H. Cole had been collecting for many years and which Margaret Cole offered as a basis for our own work. The first volume was dedicated to her and to the memory of her husband, and throughout the many years of work which has gone into the making of this *Dictionary*, Margaret Cole was a valued contributor, and always helpful and generous with advice and suggestions. In the next volume we will try to make clear the great loss that we have suffered with her death, both in terms of her academic assistance and in our personal relations.

Notes to Readers

1. Place-names are usually quoted according to contemporary usage relating to the particular entry.
2. Where the amount of a will, estate value or effects is quoted, the particular form used is normally that given in *The Times*, or the records of Somerset House, London, or the Scottish Record Office, Edinburgh. For dates before 1860 the source will usually be the Public Record Office.
3. Under the heading **Sources**, personal information relates to details obtained from relatives, friends or colleagues of the individual in question; biographical information refers to other sources.
4. The place of publication in bibliographical references is London, unless otherwise stated.
5. P indicates a pamphlet whose pagination could not be verified. Where it is known, the number of pages is quoted if under sixty.
6. The *See also* column which follows biographical entries includes names marked with a dagger and these refer to biographies already published in Volumes I–V of the *Dictionary*; those with no marking are included in the present volume, and those with an asterisk refer to entries to be included in later volumes.
7. A consolidated name list of entries in Volumes I–VI will be found at the end of this volume before the general index.
8. In this volume there will be found between pages xix and xxxi additions and corrections to Vols I–V.

List of Contributors

Kenneth Brill Esq.	Crediton, Devon
Dr Kenneth D. Brown	Reader in Economic History, The Queen's University of Belfast
Michael Cahill	Research Student, Department of Social Administration and Social Work, York University
Dr David Clark, MP	London
Dr Stephen W. Coltham	Formerly Senior Lecturer in History, Adult Education Department, Keele University
Mrs Grace G. Cowie	London
Peter D. Drake Esq.	Social Sciences Department, Birmingham Reference Library
Mrs Margaret 'Espinasse	Formerly Reader in English Language, Hull University
Edmund Frow Esq.	Manchester
Mrs Ruth Frow	Manchester
Professor J.F.C. Harrison	School of English and American Studies, Sussex University
Mrs Barbara Hill	Lecturer, Hendon College of Further Education
Colin Holmes Esq.	Reader, Department of Economic and Social History, Sheffield University
Ms Ann Holt	Formerly Research Assistant, Department of Economic and Social History, Hull University
Dr Marion Kozak	London
David Large Esq.	Senior Lecturer, Department of History, Bristol University
Dr Alan J. Lee	Lecturer, Department of History, Hull University
Dr David E. Martin	Lecturer, Department of Economic and Social History, Sheffield University
Dr Helen Mathers	Liberal Studies Organiser, Chaucer Adult Education Centre, Sheffield
A.L. Morton Esq.	Clare, Suffolk
Mrs Barbara Nield	Research Assistant, Department of Economic and Social History, Hull University
Dr I.J. Prothero	Senior Lecturer, Department of History, Manchester University
Mrs Naomi Reid	Stockport
John J. Rowley Esq.	Lecturer, English and Liberal Studies, Dudley College of Technology

Dr Edward Royle	Lecturer, Department of History, York University
Professor James A. Schmiechen	Department of History, Illinois State University, Bloomington-Normal, U.S.A.
Richard Storey Esq.	Archivist, Modern Records Centre, Warwick University Library
Eric L. Taplin Esq.	Head of Department of Social Studies, Liverpool Polytechnic
Dr Eric Taylor	Senior Lecturer in Modern History, Wolverhampton Polytechnic
Dr Mavis Waters	Assistant Professor, Social Science Division, York University, Ontario, Canada
Professor Joel H. Wiener	Department of History, City College of New York, U.S.A.

List of Abbreviations

AACAN	Association of All Classes of All Nations
Abr.	Abridged
Add.	Additional
AEU	Amalgamated Engineering Union
AITUC	All-India Trade Union Congress
Amer. Hist. Rev.	*American Historical Review*
Anon.	Anonymous
App. (s)	Appendix (Appendices)
ASCJ	Amalgamated Society of Carpenters and Joiners
ASE	Amalgamated Society of Engineers
ASHDP	Amalgamated Society of House Decorators and Painters
ASLIB	Association of Special Libraries and Information Bureaux
ASRS	Amalgamated Society of Railway Servants
ASW	Amalgamated Society of Woodworkers
AUBTW	Amalgamated Union of Building Trade Workers
BAPCK	British Association for Promoting Co-operative Knowledge
BBC	British Broadcasting Corporation
BICSDW	*Bulletin of the International Council of Social-Democratic Women*
BL	British Library
Blackw. Edin. Mag.	*Blackwood's Edinburgh Magazine*
BLPES	British Library of Political and Economic Science, LSE
Boase	F. Boase, *Modern English Biography . . . 1851–1900* (Truro, 1892–1921; repr. 1965)
BPP	British People's Party
BPU	Birmingham Political Union
BSP	British Socialist Party
BUF	British Union of Fascists
Bull.	*Bulletin*
Bull. of CBCO	*Bulletin of the Central Board of Conscientious Objectors*
Bull. Soc. Lab. Hist.	*Bulletin of the Society for the Study of Labour History*
BWNL	British Workers' National League
C./Cd/Cmd	Command Paper
CFT	*Cotton Factory Times*
Ch(s)	Chapter(s)

CI	Communist International
CID	Criminal Investigation Department
CMG	Commander of the Order of St Michael and St George
CND	Campaign for Nuclear Disarmament
Coll.	Collection
Cont. Rev.	*Contemporary Review*
Co-op.	Co-operative
COPEC	Conference on Politics, Economics and Christianity
CP	Communist Party
CPGB	Communist Party of Great Britain
CSU	Complete Suffrage Union
Cttee	Committee
CVSL	Colne Valley Socialist League
CWS	Co-operative Wholesale Society
d	old pence
DLB	*Dictionary of Labour Biography*
DLP	Divisional Labour Party
DNB	*Dictionary of National Biography*
Dod	*Dod's Parliamentary Companion*
DORA	Defence of the Realm Act
EC	Executive Committee/Council
ECCI	Executive Committee of the Communist International
Econ. Hist. Rev.	*Economic History Review*
Econ. J.	*Economic Journal*
ed.(s)	edited, edition, editor(s)
Edin. Rev.	*Edinburgh Review*
EEC	European Economic Community
Engl. Hist. Rev.	*English Historical Review*
et al.	*et alia/et alii* (Lat.): and others
ff.	pages following
fl.	*floruit* (Lat.): flourished
Fortn. Rev.	*Fortnightly Review*
GFTU	General Federation of Trade Unions
GMWJ	*General and Municipal Workers' Journal*
GNCTU	Grand National Consolidated Trades Union
Hist.	History/Historical
HO	Home Office
ibid.	*ibidem* (Lat.): in the same place
idem	(Lat.): the same; author as mentioned in previous entry
IHR	Institute of Historical Research
IISH	International Institute of Social History
ILO	International Labour Office/Organisation
ILP	Independent Labour Party

imp.	impression
Ind. Rev.	*Independent Review*
Int. Rev. Social Hist.	*International Review of Social History*
Int. Rev. for Social History	*International Review for Social History*
ITF	International Transport Workers' Federation
IUP	Irish University Press
IWW	Industrial Workers of the World
J.	*Journal*
JP	Justice of the Peace
Jr	Junior
JRSI	*Journal of the Royal Sanitary Institute*
JRSS	*Journal of the Royal Statistical Society*
Lab. Mon.	*Labour Monthly*
LCC	London County Council
LDA	London Democratic Association
LDV	Local Defence Volunteers
LEA	Labour Electoral Association
LEL	Labour Emancipation League
Lib-Lab	Liberal-Labour
l./ll.	line(s)
LP	Labour Party
LRC	Labour Representation Committee
LRD	Labour Research Department
LSE	London School of Economics
LTC	London Trades Council
LWMA	London Working Men's Association
Mag.	*Magazine*
MESAC	Metal, Engineering and Shipbuilding Amalgamation Committee
misc.	miscellaneous
M of E	Minutes of Evidence
MP	Member of Parliament
MRC	Modern Records Centre, Warwick Univ.
MS(S)/ms.	manuscript(s)
NAC	National Administrative Council
NALU	National Agricultural Labourers' Union
NAPSS	National Association for the Promotion of Social Science
Nat. Rev.	*National Review*
NCA	National Charter Association
NCFS	National Community Friendly Society
NCLC	National Council of Labour Colleges
NCW	National Council of Women
n.d.	no date
NEC	National Executive Committee
NESWS	North of England Society for Women's Suffrage

NFWW	National Federation of Women Workers
19th C.	*Nineteenth Century*
NJ	New Jersey
NLP	National Labour Press
n.p.	no pagination
NPU	National Political Union
n.s.	new series
NSW	New South Wales
NTWF	National Transport Workers' Federation
NUC	National Union of Clerks
NUCAW	National Union of Clerks and Administrative Workers
NUDL	National Union of Dock Labourers
NUGMW	National Union of General and Municipal Workers
NUGW	National Union of General Workers
NUR	National Union of Railwaymen
NUS	National Union of Seamen
NUWC	National Union of the Working Classes
NUWSS	National Union of Women's Suffrage Societies
NUWW	National Union of Women Workers
NY	New York
NZ	New Zealand
Obit.	Obituary
OEP	*Oxford Economic Papers*
o.s.	old series
P	Pamphlet
p	new pence
p.a.	per annum
PC	Privy Councillor
PL	Public Library
PLP	Parliamentary Labour Party
PRO	Public Record Office
pt	part
Q.	*Quarterly*
Q(s)	Question(s)
QJE	*Quarterly Journal of Economics*
RACS	Royal Arsenal Co-operative Society
RAF	Royal Air Force
RAMC	Royal Army Medical Corps
R.C.	Royal Commission
RCA	Railway Clerks' Association
Ref.	Reference
repr.	reprinted
rev.	revised
Rev.	Reverend

Rev.	*Review*
RO	Record Office
RRA	Radical Reform Association
RSDLP	Russian Social Democratic Labor Party
s.	shilling(s)
Sat. Rev.	*Saturday Review*
S.C.	Select Committee
sc.	scilicet (Lat.): namely
SDF	Social Democratic Federation
SDP	Social Democratic Party
ser.	series
SFTC	Sheffield Federated Trades Council
SL	Socialist League
SLP	Socialist Labour Party
SNDC	Socialist National Defence Committee
Soc. Rev.	*Socialist Review*
Spec.	*Spectator*
SSLPL	South Side Labour Protection League
T & GW Record	*Transport and General Workers' Record*
TGWU	Transport and General Workers' Union
TLS	*Times Literary Supplement*
trans.	translated
Trans.	*Transactions*
TSSA	Transport and Salaried Staffs Association
TUC	Trades Union Congress
UCSRR	Universal Community Society of Rational Religionists
UDC	Union of Democratic Control
UN	United Nations
Univ.	University
vol.(s)	volume(s)
WEA	Workers' Educational Association
WIC	Women's Industrial Council
WIN	*Women's Industrial News*
WIRA	British Research Association for the Woollen and Worsted Industries
WLL	Women's Labour League
WSPU	Women's Social and Political Union
WTLC	Women's Trades and Labour Council
WTUC	Women's Trade Union Council
WTUL	Women's Trade Union League
WVS	Women's Voluntary Service
WW	*Who's Who*
WWW	*Who Was Who*
YFT	*Yorkshire Factory Times*

List of Bibliographies and Special Notes

Bibliographies

The subject bibliographies attached to certain entries are the responsibility of the editors. The entries under which they will be found in Volumes I–VI are as follows:

British Labour Party		
1900–13	**LANSBURY, George**	**II**
1914–31	**HENDERSON, Arthur**	**I**
Chartism to 1840	**LOVETT, William**	**VI**
Christian Socialism, 1848–54	**LUDLOW, John Malcolm Forbes**	**II**
Co-operation		
Agricultural Co-operation	**PLUNKETT, Sir Horace Curzon**	**V**
Co-operative Education	**HALL, Fred**	**I**
Co-operative Party	**ALEXANDER, Albert Victor**	**I**
Co-operative Production	**JONES, Benjamin**	**I**
Co-operative Union	**HAYWARD, Fred**	**I**
Co-operative Wholesaling	**REDFERN, Percy**	**I**
Co-partnership	**GREENING, Edward Owen**	**I**
International Co-operative Alliance	**MAY, Henry John**	**I**
Irish Co-operation	**GALLAGHER, Patrick**	**I**
Retail Co-operation		
Nineteenth Century	**HOLYOAKE, George Jacob**	**I**
1900–45	**BROWN, William Henry**	**I**
1945–70	**BONNER, Arnold**	**I**
Scottish Co-operation	**MAXWELL, William**	**I**
Guild Socialism	**SPARKES, Malcolm**	**II**
Mining Trade Unionism		
1850–79	**MACDONALD, Alexander**	**I**
1880–99	**PICKARD, Benjamin**	**I**
1900–14	**ASHTON, Thomas**	**I**
1915–26	**COOK, Arthur James**	**III**
1927–44	**LEE, Peter**	**II**
Scottish Mining Trade Unionism	**SMILLIE, Robert**	**III**
Welsh Mining Trade Unionism	**ABRAHAM, William (Mabon)**	**I**
New Model Unionism	**ALLAN, William**	**I**
New Unionism, 1889–93	**TILLETT, Benjamin (Ben)**	**IV**

Special Notes in Volume V

The Parliamentary Recruiting Committee and the Joint Labour Recruiting Committee in the First World War *see* **BOWERMAN, Charles William**

The 1917 Club *see* **HAMILTON, Mary Agnes**

The Mosely Industrial Commission *see* **STEADMAN, William (Will) Charles**

Special Notes in Volume VI

Woman's Industrial Independence (1848; reprinted) *see* **BARMBY, Catherine Isabella**

Boggart Hole Clough and Free Speech *see* **BROCKLEHURST, Frederick**

Ca'canny *see* **DAVIS, William John**

Additions and Corrections

VOLUMES I–V

These lists relate both to the text and to the bibliographies of volumes I–V and they refer to MSS, theses and printed materials to the end of 1979. Emphasis has been given to materials of especial relevance to the bibliographical sections but only exceptionally have general texts been included. For these, and for involuntary omissions, the accepted bibliographical sources should be consulted. We set out below the more important:

1. *Bulletins* of the Society for the Study of Labour History and the publications of the regional Labour History Societies.
2. Annual Lists of Publications on the Economic and Social History of Great Britain and Ireland published normally in the November issue of the *Economic History Review*.
3. C. Cook et al., *Sources in British Political History 1900–1951: compiled for the British Library of Political and Economic Science* 5 vols (1975–8).
4. *A Catalogue of Some Labour Records in Scotland and Some Scots Records outside Scotland*, ed. I. MacDougall (Edinburgh, 1978).
5. Information Bulletins and *Annual Reports* of the Modern Record Centre, Warwick Univ. Library. See also the following occasional publications of the Library: no. 2, R. Storey and J. Druker, *Guide to the Modern Records Centre, University of Warwick Library* (1977) and no. 5, J. Bennett and R. Storey, *Trade Union and Related Records* (1979) 30 pp.
6. The *London Bibliography of the Social Sciences* and the catalogues of the British Library, Library of Congress (Washington) and International Institute of Social History (Amsterdam).
7. ASLIB, *Index to Theses* (1950 to date) and annual *lists* of the Institute of Historical Research (for work in progress and completed theses).
8. *Index to the Diary of Beatrice Webb 1873–1943* (1978) [for microfiche edition].

In 1978 vol. I was reprinted with corrections (but not with additional material). In the present listing corrections which affect the content of the text have been repeated together with errors subsequently discovered.

NOTE. Corrections which refer to named people and/or matter of substance have been included in the index to this volume.

JMB
JS

PRELIMINARY MATTER

Acknowledgements I
xvii, *l*.18. *For* Eccleshall *read* Ecclesall
Abbreviations II
xiii, *l*.7 from foot. *For* International *read* India
List of Contributors III
x, *l*.5 from foot. *For* Anna *read* Ann; IV, x, *l*.6 from foot. *After* Studies *add* City of

BIOGRAPHIES

ABLETT, Noah III
3, **Sources:** (2) *Add* D. Egan, 'The Unofficial Reform Committee and The Miners' Next Step: documents from the W. H. Mainwaring papers, with an introduction and notes', *Llafur 2*, no.3 (summer 1978) 64–80.

ABRAHAM, William (Mabon) I
2b, last *l*. *For* Mabon' *read* Mabon's
4a, **Writings:** *Add* 'The Story of my Life',

Lloyd's Weekly News, 26 Mar, 2, 9, 16 Apr 1916.
4a, **Sources:** *Add* M. J. Duggett, 'A Comparative Study of the Operation of the Sliding Scales in the Coal-Mining Industry in Durham and South Wales, 1875–1900' (Wales PhD, 1977); Dr K. O. Morgan (letter, 3 June 1972) stated that Mabon took a considerable part in general Liberal activities, notably the Cymru Fydd (Welsh Home Rule) campaign of 1895–6; and also in the widespread protests against the 1902 Education Act.
4b, **Welsh Mining Trade Unionism:** *l.*7. *After* Miners' *add* Struggle'
4b, last *l. Add Merthyr Politics: the making of a working-class tradition*, ed. G. Williams (Cardiff, 1966); P. Stead, 'Working-class leadership in South Wales, 1900–1920' *Welsh Hist. Rev. 6* (June 1973) 329–53; D. Smith, 'The Struggle against Company Unionism in the South Wales Coalfield, 1926–1939', ibid. 354–78; D. H. Francis, 'The South Wales Miners and the Spanish Civil War: a study in internationalism' (Wales PhD, 1977); M. Barclay, '"The Slaves of the Lamp": the Aberdare Miners' Strike 1910', *Llafur 2*, no.3 (summer 1978) 24–42.

ACLAND, Sir Arthur Herbert Dyke I
8a, **Sources:** *Add* G. Sutherland, *Policy Making in Elementary Education 1870–1895* (Oxford, 1973); M. G. Jordan, 'The Educational Philosophy of A. H. D. Acland, 1847–1926' (London [King's College] Institute of Education MA dissertation, 1977); P. Gordon and J. White, *Philosophers as Educational Reformers: the influence of idealism on British educational thought and practice* (1979).

ALEXANDER, Albert Victor (Earl Alexander of Hillsborough) I
14a, **Co-operative Party:** *l.*7 from foot. *For* N *read* M

ALLAN, William I
18a, **New Model Unionism:** *ll.*17–18. *For* 'The Reform League ... to Secondary: *read* 'The Reform League, from its Origins to the Passing into Law of the Reform Act of 1867' (Oxford DPhil., 1961). (3) Other:

ALLEN, Reginald Clifford (Lord Allen of Hurtwood) II
10a, **Sources:** *Add* Lady Allen published her autobiography, *Memoirs of an Uneducated Lady* in 1975. She died in April 1976 (*Times* obit., 13 Apr 1976) and most of her papers are now at the MRC, Warwick Univ. (MSS 121).

AMMON, Charles (Charlie) George (Lord Ammon of Camberwell) I
22a, *l.*20 from foot. *For* Arthur *read* Alfred
22b, *l.*17. *For* Greek *read* Gerrard

ANDERSON, William Crawford II
15b, **Sources:** *Add* Records of War Emergency Workers' National Committee, Labour Party archives.

APPLEGARTH, Robert II
21b, **Sources:** (1) *Add* Mundella papers, Sheffield Univ. Library.

ARCH, Joseph I
29a, *l.*27. *For* (1948) *read* (1949)

AYLES, Walter Henry V
12, **Sources:** (1) *Add* Fellowship of Reconciliation records, BLPES; for No-Conscription Fellowship papers, see C. Cook et al. op. cit. vol.*1* (1975) 206–7.

BARKER, George I
37a, *ll.*18–19. From a ms. note written by Barker in his personal copy of S. and B. Webb, *The Decay of Capitalist Civilisation* (Fabian Society, 1923) there is some evidence that he went to China when he was thirty-five (i.e. about 1893) and stayed for over five years. He returned to China in 1903 but sources differ on details of his career before 1908.
37b, **Sources:** *Add* R. Lewis, 'The South Wales Miners and the Ruskin College Strike of 1909', *Llafur 2,* no.1 (spring 1976) 57–72.

BARNES, George Nicoll IV
14, **Writings:** *Add* 'Protection in the Staple Trades' in *Labour and Protection: a series of studies*, ed. H. W. Massingham (1903) 236–62.
14, **Sources:** (2) *l.*4. *For Revs 6 read Revs 33. Add* A. Carew, 'Rank and File Movements and Workers' Control in the British Engineering Industry, 1850–1914' (Sussex MPhil., 1972).

BARTON, Eleanor I
38b, *ll.*8–11. *For* 'Nellie' ... career. *Read* 'Nellie', as she was called by relatives, was

arrested following a free speech meeting at Ardwick Green in November 1893 [*Workman's Times,* 18 Nov 1893]. In the following year she married Alfred Barton [see *DLB 6*], who was a member of the Manchester Anarchist Group and secretary of the Free Speech Association.
38b, *l*.4 from foot. *After* Manchester *add* about 1897.
39b, last *l*. *Add* s to Organisation
40a, **Writings:** *Add The National Care of Motherhood* (1928) 11 pp. and *A New Way of Life* (1936) 7 pp.

BEATON, Neil Scobie I
43b, *l*.1. *For* 1964 *read* 1946

BELL, Richard II
38b, **Sources:** *Add* ASRS papers re Taff Vale and Osborne cases, NUR deposit, MRC, Warwick Univ. Library, MSS 127/AS [listed in Warwick Univ. Library occasional publications, no.3 *The Taff Vale Case* (1978) 28 pp. and no.4 *The Osborne Case* (1979) 48 pp.]

BESANT, Annie IV
30, **Biographical Works:** *Add* M. Cole, 'Annie Besant', *Women of To-Day* (1939) 191–232.

BLAIR, William Richard I
44b, *l*.5 from foot. *After* 1911. *add* In 1908 he was a delegate from Liverpool Kirkdale at the ILP Conference and in 1911 he represented Liverpool South East.

BLATCHFORD, Robert Peel Glanville IV
41, **Sources:** (2) *Add* L. J. W. Barrow, 'The Socialism of Robert Blatchford and the *Clarion* 1889–1918' (London PhD, 1975).

BONDFIELD, Margaret Grace II
41a, *ll*.15–16. *For* Women's Industrial *read* Industrial Women's
42a, *l*.26. as above

BOSWELL, James Edward Buchanan III
17, *ll*.4–5. Letter from Mrs Ruth Boswell [1 July 1976, *DLB* Coll.] noted that 'the year he spent in Iraq, 1943, was an extraordinarily fertile one. He drew extensively the army life there, painted strong, vivid scenes of the desert and reached what I believe to be the height of his satirical powers ... It was this period, not 'the early blitz years' that gave him new inspiration.'
19, **Writings:** *Add* (including graphic works) *after* **Writings:** also *add Boswell's London: drawings by James Boswell showing changing London from the thirties to the fifties* with an Introduction by W. Feaver (1978).

BOWERMAN, Charles William V
32, **Sources:** *Add* (1) MS: Labour Party archives: LRC 1900–6 and LP general correspondence; London Society of Compositors' records, MRC, Warwick Univ. MSS 28. (2) Other.

BRACE, William I
53b, *l*.23. *For* 1890 *read* 1891

BRAILSFORD, Henry Noel II
47b, *l*.35. *For* £500 *read* £1700
53a, **Sources:** (1) *Add* Original financial bond given to Lenin and Trotsky is in Institute of Marxism-Leninism, Moscow and copy in Museum of Revolution, Moscow.
53a, **Sources:** (2) *Add* A. P. Dudden and T. H. von Lane, 'The RSDLP and Joseph Fels' *Amer. Hist. Rev. 61* (Oct 1955) 21–47; A. P. Dudden, *Joseph Fels* (Philadelphia, 1971).

BROADHURST, Henry II
66b, *l*.10. *For* Kill *read* Will.
68a, **Sources:** (1) *Add* Mundella papers, Sheffield Univ. Library.

BROWN, William Henry I
57b, *ll*.19–20. *Delete* S. Webb, *The Place of Co-operation in the State of Tomorrow* [1920?] 20 pp.

BURNS, John Elliott V
39, *l*.25. *After* life. *add* He was also active in trade union affairs and a delegate to the 1885 ASE Delegate Meeting at the early age of twenty-seven.
46, **Sources:** *Add* Y. Kapp et al., *The John Burns A.E.U. Library* (Our History pamphlet, no.16: winter 1959) 21 pp.

BURT, Thomas I
63a, **Sources:** (1) *Add* Mundella papers, Sheffield Univ. Library, and (2). *Add* M. Gilbert-Boucher, *Étude sur les "Trade Unions". Un député ouvrier anglais* [i.e. Thomas Burt] (Paris, 1892).

BUTLER, Herbert William IV
50, *l*.9. *For* true *read* there

BUXTON, Noel Edward (1st Baron Noel-Buxton of Aylsham) V
54, *l*.21. *After* Germany. *add* He also visited

Hitler on behalf of the Quakers and a number of German politicians with a request, that was denied, that he and his brother be allowed to visit concentration camps [see M. Anderson, *Noel Buxton: a life* (1952) 127].

CAMPBELL, Alexander I
68a, **Writings:** *ll.*3–5. *Delete* from ; *Memoir of J. P. Greaves ... Combe* [1848?] and *insert* [includes a memoir of Greaves in vol.*1*]; Editor of *Life and Dying Testimony of Abram Combe in favor of Robert Owen's New Views of Man and Society* (1844) 24 pp.
68a, **Sources:** *l.*11 from foot. *For* J. *read* T.

CAPE, Thomas III
31, *l.*11 from foot. *For* but . . . sixties *read* this was due to a severe throat operation which prevented him from speaking in the House of Commons but 'he took the needs of his constituents direct to the minister concerned' [letter from his daughter, Mrs. E. Cain, n.d. Aug 1975].

CARPENTER, Edward II
91a, *l.*19 from foot. *For* January *read* June
91a, **Sources:** (2) *Add* N. Richards, 'Edward Carpenter', *Radical Humanist,* 18 Nov 1962, 534; S. Rowbotham and J. Weeks, *Socialism and the New Life: the personal and sexual policies of Edward Carpenter and Havelock Ellis* (1977).

CATCHPOLE, John I
70b, *l.*2. *For* Locoford *read* Lockoford

CHALLENER, John Ernest Stopford V
57, **Sources:** (1) *l.*1. *After* 1905 *add* part of TSSA deposit (MSS 55), MRC, Warwick Univ.

CHEW, Ada Nield V
64, **Writings:** *Add* 'Fighting Shy of Unions', *Yorkshire Factory Times and Workers' Weekly Record*, 29 Apr 1915, p.1.
64, **Sources:** *Add* J. Liddington and J. Norris, *One Hand tied behind us* (1978).

CLARK, Gavin Brown IV
61, **Sources:** *Add* J. Hunter, 'The Politics of Highland Land Reform, 1873–1895', *Scottish Hist. Rev. 53*, no.155 (Apr 1974) 45–68;

CLARKE, John Smith V
72, **Writings:** *Add* See *A Catalogue of Some Labour Records in Scotland* ... ed. I. MacDougall (1978) for additional writings by Clarke including pamphlets published by the Glasgow Proletarian School.

COLMAN, Grace Mary III
37, **Writings:** *Add* 'Women as Citizens', *GMWJ 22*, no.4 (Apr 1959) 104–5.

COOK, Arthur James III
44, **Sources:** *Add* P. Davies, 'The Making of A. J. Cook: his development within the South Wales labour movement, 1900–1924', *Llafur 2*, no.3 (summer 1978) 43–63; D. Hopkin, 'A. J. Cook in 1916–18', ibid. 81–8.
44, **Mining Trade Unionism, 1915–26:** (2) **Theses:** *Add* P. Davies, 'A. J. Cook: a study in trade union leadership' (Bradford PhD, 1979). (5) **Other Works:** *Add* G. W. McDonald and H. F. Gospel, 'The Mond-Turner Talks, 1927–1933: a study in industrial co-operation', *Hist. J. 16,* no.4 (1973) 807–29; M. G. Woodhouse, 'Mines for the Nation or Mines for the Miners?: alternative perspectives on industrial democracy, 1919–1921', *Llafur 2*, no.3 (summer 1978) 92–109. Among the many works published around the fiftieth anniversary of the 1926 General Strike were: Birmingham PL and WEA, West Midlands, *The Nine Days in Birmingham: the General Strike 4–12 May, 1926* (1976) 43 pp.; M. Morris, *The General Strike* (Harmondsworth, 1976); *Llafur 2*, no.2 (spring 1977); G. A. Phillips, *The General Strike: the politics of industrial conflict* (1976); J. Skelley, *The General Strike 1926* (1976); see also *Bull. Soc. Lab. Hist.* for 1976 and particularly no.34 (spring 1977) 86–7 where a specialised bibliography is included. M. W. Kirby, *The British Coalmining Industry, 1870–1946: a political and economic history* (1977).

COOMBES, Bert Lewis (Louis) IV
65, **Sources:** *Add* P. Norman, 'The Boy who escaped from the Valley of Witches', *Times*, 29 Dec 1979.

COWEN, Joseph I
85b, *ll.*22–3. *For* M. Dunsmore ... League' *read* M. R. Dunsmore, 'The Working Classes, the Reform League and the Reform Movement in Lancashire and Yorkshire'.
85b, *ll.*9 and 8 from foot. *For* J. D. Morrison, . . . (1879) *read* J. M. Davidson,

Eminent Radicals in and out of Parliament (1880)

COWEY, Edward I
88a, **Sources:** *Add* F. Rogers, *Labour, Life and Literature: some memories of sixty years*, ed. with Intro. and notes by D. Rubinstein (Brighton, 1973); D. Rubinstein, 'The Independent Labour Party and the Yorkshire Miners: the Barnsley by-election of 1897', *Int. Rev. Social Hist. 23,* pt 1 (1978) 102–34.

CRAWFORD, William I
94a, **Sources:** *Add* M. J. Duggett's thesis (see ABRAHAM, William above)

CROOKS, William II
112a, **Sources:** *Add* (1) MS: Labour Party archives: LRC 1903–6 and LP general correspondence. (2) Other: C. F. G. Masterman, *The Condition of England* (1909, and later eds) which gives a short but vivid account of Crooks as a speaker.

CURRAN, Peter (Pete) Francis IV
66, *l.* 2. *For* months' *read* weeks'
66, *l.*24. *After* 1898. *add* He resigned from the Council in July of that year consequent upon what he regarded as the growing oligarchy in the ILP leadership [Pelling, *Origins* (1965 ed.) 176].
69, **Sources:** *Add* (1) MS: Labour Party archives: LRC 1900–6 and LP general correspondence. (2) Other: article by D. Rubinstein on Barnsley by-election (see COWEY, Edward above).

CRAIG, Edward Thomas I
91a, *l.*21. *For Coventry read County*
92a, *l.*29. *After* 1894. His funeral took place at Hammersmith Cemetery.
93a, **Sources:** *Add* W. A. C. Stewart and W. P. McCann, *The Educational Innovators 1750–1880* (1967).

DARCH, Charles Thomas I
96a, *l.*22. *For* Education *read* Educational

DAVIES, Margaret Llewelyn I
99a, **Writings:** *Add* (with A. L. Martin), *Why Working Women need the Vote* (Kirkby Lonsdale, 1897) 19 pp.; 'The Claims of Mothers and Children' in *Women and the Labour Party* ed. M. Phillips (1919) 29–39 and (with others), *Co-operation and Labour Unrest* (1919) 8 pp.

DEAKIN, Arthur II
115a, *l.*25. *For* Edwards *read* Evans
117b, *l.*23 *For* Sholton *read* Shotton

DILKE, Emily (Emilia) Francis Strong, Lady III
67, **Writings:** *ll.*28–9. For *The Idealist* ... (1897) *read* 'The Idealist Movement and Positive Science: an experience' in *Littell's Living Age 215* (1897) 306–14.

DYE, Sidney I
108a, **Sources:** *Add* R. W. Johnson, 'The Nationalisation of English Rural Politics: Norfolk, South-West, 1945–1970', *Parliamentary Affairs 26* (Feb 1973) 8–55.

ENFIELD, Alice Honora I
113a, *l.*27. *For* 1927 *read* 1925

FINNEY, Samuel I
121a, *l.*25. *After* Wilson. *add* He was made a CBE in 1925.

FOX, James Challinor I
125b, *l.*7 from foot. *After* £1500. *add* According to a note on Fox's death certificate his name was just James Fox, a correction made by the registrar on 9 November 1877 on production of a statutory declaration signed Joseph Makin and Mary Street.

GALBRAITH, Samuel I
127b, *l.*8 from foot. *For* after the First World War *read* in 1917.

GANLEY, Caroline Selina I
129a, *ll.*11–8 from foot. *Delete* Mrs Ganley ... 1923.
129b, *l.*19. *After* Battersea. *add* At the LCC elections of 1922 she represented the co-operative women's movement, was endorsed by the Trades Council, and at that time, according to the *Morning Post*, 27 Oct 1922, was a member of the CP.

GOLDSTONE, Sir Frank Walter V
86, *l.*4. *After* Street *add* Council School, also in Sunderland.

GRAHAM, Duncan I
134a, last *l.* After Fraser. *add* He left an estate valued at £2126 (Scottish probate).

HALLAS, Eldred II
153a, *l.*16. *After* advancement. *add* In 1912 he informed the King's Heath ILP branch

that he was resigning as he had decided to join the BSP which he believed to be more in accordance with his views [ILP minutes, 7 Apr 1912, Birmingham Reference Library].

HALLIDAY, Thomas (Tom) III
94, **Sources:** *Add* A. Dalziel, *The Colliers' Strike in South Wales: its cause, progress and settlement* (Cardiff, 1872); see also thesis by M. J. Duggett listed in ABRAHAM, William above.

HANCOCK, John George II
160b, *l.*15 from foot. *After* (1923). *add* He supported the Conservative candidate at Belper in the 1924 general election.

HARRISON, Frederic II
170b, **Sources:** (1) *Add* Correspondence in Mundella papers, Sheffield Univ. Library. See also C. Cook and J. Weeks, *Sources in British Political History* ... vol.*5* (1978) for additional sources.

HARTLEY, Edward Robertshaw III
98, *l.*3. *For* 1907 *read* 1906.
98, *ll.*3–5 *For* He fought ... 1913 *read* Under ILP auspices he fought a by-election in Dewsbury in 1895 and was a candidate in Pudsey in 1900 but withdrew before the poll. Shortly after this (about 1903) Hartley joined the SDF. He fought Bradford East in 1906 and a Newcastle by-election in 1908 under the SDF label, Bradford East again as SDP in 1910 and a Leicester by-election in 1913 for the BSP.
98, *ll.*26–7. *For* He acted ... 1912; *read* He was appointed in 1901 as manager of the Clarion Van scheme;
99, **Sources:** *l.*2. *After* [portrait] *add* and 152

HARTSHORN, Vernon I
151b, *l.*24. *After* 1918. *add* In the same year he was awarded the OBE.
152a, **Sources:** *Add* P. Stead, 'Vernon Hartshorn', *Glamorgan Historian 6* (1969) 83–94.

HASLAM, James (1867–1937) I
156a, *l.*33. *After* 1937. *add* He left effects valued at £3066.

HAYWARD, Sir Fred I
158b, last *l. After* 1904. *add* In 1898 he was a delegate to the ILP Conference from Hanley and represented Burslem at the 1907 Conference.

HENDERSON, Arthur I
164a, **Writings:** *Add* 'Democracy and Christianity' and 'Character the Essential' in *Labour and Religion by Ten Labour Members* (1910) 20–36; *Legislation for the Workers* (1924) 18 pp.; *The Government's Attack on Trade Union Law* (Trade Union Defence Cttee, 1927) 23 pp.; see also *Labour Party Bibliography* [1967].
165a, **Sources:** (2) *Add* W. Purdue, 'Arthur Henderson and Liberal, Liberal-Labour and Labour Politics in the North-East of England, 1892–1903', *Northern History 11* (1976) 195–217; R. I. McKibbin, 'Arthur Henderson as Labour Leader', *Int. Rev. Social Hist. 23,* pt 1 (1978) 79–101.
165b, **British Labour Party, 1914–31:** (2) *For* last five lines and 166a, *ll.*1–4 *read* MSc.(Econ.), 1966); R. J. A. Skidelsky, 'The Labour Government and the Unemployment Question, 1929–31' (Oxford DPhil., 1967); R. S. Barker, 'The Educational Policies of the Labour Party, 1900–1961 (London PhD, 1968); W. Golant, 'The Political Development of C. R. Attlee to 1935' (Oxford BLitt., 1968).
166a, *l.*15. *For* D. W. Butler *read* D. E. Butler
166a, *l.*27. *For 1914–24 read 1917–24*
166b, *l.*2 from foot. *For* Schwarz (and in vol.*1* of *DLB* (repr. 1978) Swarz) *read* Swartz.
167a, *l.*4. *Add* R. Davidson, 'War-time Labour Policy 1914–1916: a re-appraisal', *J. of Scottish Labour History Society*, no.8 (June 1974) 3–20; R. McKibbin, *The Evolution of the Labour Party 1910–1924* (Oxford, 1974); idem, 'The Economic Policy of the Second Labour Government 1929–1931', *Past and Present*, no.68 (1975) 95–123; C. Howard, 'MacDonald, Henderson and the Outbreak of War, 1914', *Hist. J. 20*, no.4 (1977) 871–91; R. Eatwell and A. Wright, 'Labour and the Lessons of 1931', *History 63*, no.207 (Feb 1978) 38–53; R. Lowe, 'The Failure of Consensus in Britain: the National Industrial Conference 1919–1921', *Hist. J. 21*, no.3 (1978) 649–75.

HEPBURN, Thomas III
100, *l.*7 from foot. *Add* In 1922 or 1923 a play about Hepburn *The Pitman's Pay* by Ruth Dodds was produced by the Progressive Players in Gateshead, and during the General Strike was performed in miners'

halls in aid of the Miners' Relief Fund. Hepburn was included in the GPO Social Reformer Stamp series of May 1976 by the issue of an $8\frac{1}{2}$ *p* stamp.
101, **Sources:** *Add* J. Oxberry, *Thomas Hepburn of Felling: what he did for the miners* (Felling [1939]) 18 pp.

HICKS, Amelia (Amie) Jane IV
92, **Writings:** *Add* 'Legislation concerning Child-bearing Women' in *Women in Industrial Life* ed. Countess of Aberdeen (1900) 8–9.

HINDEN, Rita II
182b, **Writings:** *Add The Labour Party and the Colonies* (1946) 19 pp.

HINES, George Lelly I
175a, *l*.30. *For* Liberal *read* Conservative

HOBSON, John Atkinson I
178b, *l*.31. *For* Pethwick *read* Pethick

HODGE, John III
115, **Writings:** *Add* 'Labour and the Churches' in *Labour and Religion by Ten Labour Members* (1910) 13–18.

HOLBERRY, Samuel IV
96, **Sources:** *Add* B. Moore, S. Holmes and J. Baxter, *Samuel Holberry 1814–1842: Sheffield's revolutionary democrat* (Holberry Society for the Study of Sheffield Labour History, 1978) 26 pp.

HOLYOAKE, George Jacob I
186a, **Sources:** *Add* L. E. Grugel, *George Jacob Holyoake: a study in the evolution of a Victorian radical* (Philadelphia, 1976) and B. J. Blaszak, 'George Jacob Holyoake: an attitudinal study' (State Univ. of NY, Buffalo PhD, 1978).
188b, **Retail Co-operation–Nineteenth Century:** *l*.8. *For* Webb *read* Potter

HORNER, Arthur Lewis V
118, *l*.1 **Sources:** *Add* D. H. Francis, 'The South Wales Miners and the Spanish Civil War: a study in internationalism' (Wales PhD, 1977).

HOWELL, George II
195a, *l*.3. *For* 1–85 *read* 23–65

HUDSON, Walter II
199a, *l*.14 from foot. *Add* **Writings:** 'The Mainspring of all Reform' in *Labour and Religion by Ten Labour Members* (1910) 41–7.

HUGHES, Edward II
200b, **Sources:** *Add* T. McKay, 'Edward Hughes 1856–1925, North Wales Miners' Agent, 1898–1925', *Llafur 2*, no.4 (spring 1979) 38–53.

HUGHES, Hugh I
192a, *See also. Add * before* Edward

JACKSON, Thomas Alfred IV
108, **Sources:** *Add* V. Morton and S. Macintyre, *T. A. Jackson: a centenary appreciation* (Our History pamphlet no.73 [1979]) 27 pp.

JEWSON, Dorothea (Dorothy) V
120, *l*.16. *After* 1935 *delete* stop and *add* after Dorothy Jewson had refused the candidature.
121, *l*.8. *After* causes. *add* During the Spanish Civil War, Jewson spoke on the same platform as Emma Goldman. The meeting was arranged by the Norwich Freedom Group, the ILP, and the Labour League of Youth on 23 May 1937. Alex Rudling was in the chair.

JONES, Benjamin I
200b, *ll*.15–16. *For* A. Mann . . . (n.d.) *read* A. Mann, *Democracy in Industry: the story of twenty-one years' work of the Leicester Anchor Boot and Shoe Productive Society Ltd* (Leicester, 1914).
201a, *Add* to **Co-operative Production:** D. C. Jones, 'The Economics of British Producer Cooperatives' (Cornell PhD, 1974); idem, 'British Economic Thought on Association of Laborers 1848–1974', *Annals of Public and Co-operative Economy' 47* (Jan–Mar 1976) 5–36; K. Themistocli, *Industrial Cooperation: a bibliography* (Rome, Oct 1978).

JONES, Patrick Lloyd I
201a, *l*.2. *Insert* first *before* forename
206a, **Sources:** *Add* J. D. Osburn, 'The Full Name of Lloyd Jones: reflections of 19th-century working-class religion and politics', *Bull. of the Institute of Historical Research 46* (1973) 221–6.

KANE, John III
125, *l*.2. *After* code. *add* He left effects valued at under £450.

KENYON, Barnet I
208a, *l*.11 from foot. *For* 1896 *read* 1898
209a, **Sources:** *Add* M. Petter, 'The

Progressive Alliance', *History 58*, no.192 (Feb 1973) 45–59.

KNEE, Fred V
132, **Sources:** (1) *Add* Records of War Emergency Workers' National Committee, WNC/19/2/402, Labour Party archives [Fred Knee Recognition Fund (of the London Trades Council)].

LANSBURY, George II
222a, **Pamphlets:** *Add The Futility of the National Government* (1933) 8 pp.
223b, **Sources:** *Add* P. A. Ryan, '"Poplarism", 1894–1930' in *The Origins of British Social Policy* ed. P. Thane (1978) 56–83, N. Branson, *Poplarism 1919–1925* (1979).

LAWRENCE, Arabella Susan III
129, *l.*16 from foot. *Delete* 'In 1919 ... Council' and *substitute* She served on the executive committee of the LRD from 1919 to 1921. She was not elected to the Poplar Borough Council but like John Scurr (see *DLB 4*) was appointed an alderman in 1919 and held this office until she entered Parliament in 1924.
129, *ll.*15–13 from foot. *Delete* Led by ... twenty-eight and *substitute* Led by George Lansbury, the councillors did not refuse to collect the Poor Rate but they did decline to collect the rates for the central London bodies, i.e. LCC, Metropolitan Water Board, Metropolitan Asylums Board, and Metropolitan Police, and eventually thirty ... [information from Mrs N. Branson, letter of 24 Mar 1978].
132, **Sources:** *Add* to personal information: letter from Dame Margaret Cole [*DLB* Coll.]

LEE, Peter II
232a, **Sources:** *Add* J. Lawson, 'The Influence of Peter Lee' in *Mining and Social Change* ed. M. Bulmer (1978) 95–104.
234b, **Mining Trade Unionism, 1927–44:** *Add* D. Smith (1973) [see ABRAHAM, William above]; M. W. Kirby (1977) (see COOK, Arthur James above).

MACARTHUR, Mary II
260a, **Sources:** *Add* M. Cole, *Women of To-Day* (1938) 89–129; J. Morris, 'The Gertrude Tuckwell Collection', *History Workshop: a journal of socialist historians*, issue 5 (spring 1978) 155–62.
260a, *See also l.*2. *For* Bondfeild *read* Bondfield

MacDONALD, James Ramsay I
228a, **Sources:** (2) *ll.*1–2. *Delete* from G. Elton to (1921); 228a, *l.*9. *After* (1938); *add* G. Elton, *Life of James Ramsay MacDonald (1866–1919)* (1939);
228a, *l.*10. *After* Elton] *add* D. Marquand, *Ramsay MacDonald* (1977); M. B. McLeod, *The Parliamentary Speaking of Ramsay MacDonald: a study of his first Labour Government* (Mysore, 1978).
228b, *l.*17. *For* R. L. Lyman *read* R. W. Lyman;
228b, *l.*18. *After Government add 1924;*
228b, *l.*6 from foot. *For* Sep 1970 *read* June 1970.
229a, **Sources:** (3) *Add* R. Barker, 'Political Myth: Ramsay MacDonald and the Labour Party', *History 61*, no.201 (Feb 1976) 46–56; M. Callcott, 'Sidney Webb, Ramsay MacDonald, Emanuel Shinwell and the Durham Constituency of Seaham', *Bull. of the North East Group for the Study of Labour History*, no.11 (Oct 1977) 13–27.

McGHEE, Henry George I
229b, *l.*10. *After* death. *add* He was a member of the executive committee of the Parliamentary Pacifist Group in 1936, of the Labour Party Peace Aims Group after the outbreak of war in 1939, and he signed their manifesto calling for an Armistice. In November 1939 he urged a parliamentary secret session to discuss the continuation of the war. He was also associated in its early days with the post-war Victory for Socialism campaign—for a time as chairman.

McKEE, George William V
149, **Sources:** *l.*1. *For* NUS *read* MRC

MADDISON, Fred IV
122, **Sources:** (1) *Add* Mundella papers, Sheffield Univ. Library and (2) *l.6 For Revs 6 read Revs 33*

MANN, Amos I
231a, **Writings:** *l.*3. *After* Leicester *add* Anchor Boot and Shoe.
231a, **Writings:** *l.*3. *After* Society *add* Ltd

MESSER, Sir Frederick II
261b, *l*.15. *After* 1935, *add* was a member of the committee of the Parliamentary Pacifist Group in 1936, of the LP Peace Aims Group and signed the Armistice Manifesto in October 1939. At the 1945 ...

MITCHISON, Gilbert Richard II
267a, *l*.11. *Add* At the same election his wife was a Labour candidate for the Scottish Universities but was not successful.
268b, **Sources:** *Add* N. Mitchison, *You may well ask: a memoir 1920–1940* (1979).

MORGAN, David Watts I
246b, *l*.6 from foot. *After* Thomas *add* a miner

MURNIN, Hugh II
268b, *l*.17 from foot and *l*.15 from foot. *For* 1865 *read* 1861

NEALE, Edward Vansittart I
225a, **Sources:** (2) Last *l*. *Add* Baltimore *before* 1957
255b, **Sources:** (2) *Add* P. N. Backstrom, *Christian Socialism and Co-operation in Victorian England* (1974).

NEWTON, William II
276a, **Sources:** *l*.10. *For* 1868 *read* 1968

NOEL, Conrad le Despenser Roden II
277a, *l*.2. *For* Winchester *read* Wellington
277a, *l*.18 from foot. *For* 1893 *read* 1891
285b, **Sources:** (1) *l*.5 from foot. *Add* papers collected by R. Groves for his book on Noel, MRC, MSS 172.

NOEL-BUXTON, Lucy Edith Pelham, Lady V
166, *l*.23. *Add* Her daughter, Jane, recalled her mother's 'very strong sense of duty' in the years following the 1945 general election ... 'during late sittings other women MPs would say, When Lucy goes, we all go' [letter from Jane Buxton, 13 June 1978].

NUTTALL, William I
258a, **Writings:** *Add Co-operative Share Capital: should it be transferable or withdrawable?* [a paper read at Derby and Leicester Co-operative Conferences, 25 and 28 Dec 1872 and repr. from *Co-operative News*] (Central Co-operative Board) [1872?] 11 pp.

PARE, William I
262b, last *l*. *After* 18 pp. *add* and his biography, *William Pare (1805–1873): co-operator and social reformer* (Co-operative College Papers, no.16: Nov 1973) 56 pp.

PATERSON, Emma Anne V
170, **Sources:** *l*. 17. *For* (1965) *read* (1955)

PEASE, Edward Reynolds II
296a, *ll*.2 and 1 from foot. *For* he ... Parliament *read* went to the ILO in 1920

PENNY, John I
266b, **Writings:** *Add Socialism and Genius* (Sheffield n.d.) 16 pp. and *Co-operation: an economic and political force* (1920) 19 pp.

PICKARD, Benjamin I
270a, **Sources:** *Add* D. Rubinstein's article on the Barnsley by-election (see COWEY, Edward above)
270b, **Mining Trade Unionism, 1880–99**. *Add* J. Evison, 'The Opening up of the 'Central' region of the South Yorkshire Coalfield and the Development of its Townships as Colliery Communities 1875–1905' (Leeds MPhil., 1972); W. R. Garside, 'Wage Determination and the Miners' Lockout of 1892' in *Essays in Tyneside Labour History*, ed. N. McCord (Newcastle Polytechnic, 1977).

PICKARD, William I
271 a, *l*.23 from foot. *Add* In his evidence he revealed that he owned shares worth £365 in the Wigan Coal and Iron Company.
271b, **Sources:** *Add* T. C. Barker and J. R. Harris, *A Merseyside Town in the Industrial Revolution: St Helens 1750–1900* (Liverpool, 1954).

PICTON-TURBERVILL, Edith IV
140, **Sources:** *Add Times,* 18 Oct 1976 [for letter addressed to her by J. R. MacDonald, dated 25 Aug 1931, to which she added: 'I do not remember in all my life having so difficult and agitating a time when making a decision on the question. Finally I decided I could not honourably follow RM'.

POINTER, Joseph II
303a, *l*.8. *For* Pointer . . . 1910. *read* in 1910 Pointer became president of the Sheffield Clarion Ramblers and in the same year joined the Fabian Society.

303a, **Sources:** (1) *l*.4 from foot. *Add* H. J. Wilson papers, Sheffield Univ. Library

POSTGATE, Raymond William II
306b, *l*.11. *After* Colleges. *add* He served on the Plebs League executive and, according to J. P. M. Millar, played an influential part in ensuring that the League's work was handed over to the NCLC in order to defeat attempts made by Communist members to get control over the League [letter, 14 Jan 1976, *DLB* Coll.]
309a, **Writings:** last *l*. *For 1*, no.1, 5 Aug 1920 *read 2*, no.66, 5 Nov 1921.

POTTS, John Samuel II
312a, **Sources:** *Add Sheffield and Rotherham Independent*, 1 Oct 1897.

PURCELL, Albert Arthur I
276b, *l*. 11. *For* second *read* recent.
279a, **Writings:** *Add* (with J. Hallsworth), *Report on Labour Conditions in India* (1928)
279b, **Sources:** *Add* W. P. Coates, 'A Tribute to Albert Purcell' *Forward* [Glasgow], 11 Jan 1936.

RICHARDSON, Tom IV
147, **Sources:** (1) *After* LRC *add* and Middleton papers (JSM/RIC) for a file on the Richardson Fund.

ROGERS, Frederick I
292a, **Writings:** *l*.36. *For wait read Work*
292a, **Sources:** *Add* (1) MS: correspondence between F. Rogers and J. Middleton 1909–14, *DLB* Coll. and (2) Other: S. Charteris, 'Labour and the Church: an interview with Mr Frederick Rogers', *Treasury* (Apr 1907) 1–6; J. Middleton, 'Labour's First Chairman: an appreciation of the late Fred Rogers' [*DLB* Coll.]

SCURR, John IV
153, last *l*. *After* Union. *add* He stood unsuccessfully for the Poplar Borough Council in 1912 on the nomination of the export branch of the Dockers' Union. His election address referred to his membership of the BSP.
154, *ll*.12–13. *For* He was . . . alderman. *read* He was appointed an alderman of the Poplar Borough Council in 1919 although he had not previously been elected to the Council. Such appointments were for a six year term and Scurr served until 1925.
154, *l*.22. *After* Guardians *insert* on which he served from 1922 to 1925.
155, *l*.15 from foot. *After* Department *add* (from 1919 to 1921 and 1922 to 1924).
156, *l*.13. *For* 1910 *read* 1900
156, **Writings:** *l*.3. *For* [n.d.] *read* (1923) and *l*.4 *delete* question mark *after* 1923.

SHACKLETON, Sir David James II
336b, *ll*.13–15. *For* who had . . . 132] *read* had voted for Hardie [Morgan (1975) 155].
336b, *l*.6 from foot. *For* Monmouth *read* Newport
339a, **Sources:** *Add* K. O. Morgan, *Keir Hardie: radical and socialist* (1975).

SHANN, George II
340b, **Writings:** *Add* 'The Effect of the Non-Living Wage upon the Individual, the Family, and the State' in *The Industrial Unrest and the Living Wage* with an Introduction by Rev. W. Temple [1913] 87–105.

SITCH, Thomas I
299b, *l*.10. *After* England. *add* He pressed for the appointment of women to the Chain Trade Board in 1917 [PRO, Lab2/213/TB 5703]

SKEVINGTON, John I
300a, *l*.21 from foot. *For* 50 *read* 51
302a, *l*.8. *For* 1850 *read* 1851

SKINNER, (James) Allen V
200, **Writings:** *Add* 'The Labour Party Machine: an obstacle to Socialism', *Adelphi* (Oct 1934) 11–15.

SLOAN, Alexander (Sandy) II
347b, *l*.2 from foot. *After* War. *add* He voted against National Service in 1939, was a member of the LP Peace Aims Group and signed their Manifesto calling for an Armistice in October 1939.

SMILLIE, Robert III
173, **Scottish Mining Trade Unionism:** (4) *Add* G. M. Wilson, 'The Strike Policy of the Miners of the West of Scotland, 1842–74' in *Essays in Scottish Labour History: a tribute to W. H. Marwick* ed. I. MacDougall (Edinburgh, 1978) 29–64.

STANTON, Charles Butt I
312a, *l*.22 from foot. *For* N *read* M.
312b, **Sources:** *Add* (1) MS: Milner papers, Bodleian Library, Oxford and (2) Other: Dr

K. O. Morgan (letter 3 June 1972) noted that Stanton was arrested early in his career for firing a revolver during a strike. He was a founder member of the Aberdare Socialist Society, 1895–6; an early and very active member of the ILP, and president of the ILP and Socialist Federation formed in South Wales after the 1898 coal stoppage and lock-out.

STEADMAN, William (Will) Charles V
208, **Sources:** *Add* (1) MS: Labour Party archives, LRC 1900–5 and LP general correspondence.

SUMMERBELL, Thomas IV
166, **Sources:** *l.*2. *For Revs 6 read Revs 33*

SUTTON, John Edward (Jack) III
177, *ll.*9–10. *For* candidate ... 1892 *read* candidates in North East Manchester in 1885 and 1886, and in East Manchester in 1892 (where Arthur Balfour was the Conservative member) ...

SWANWICK, Helena Maria Lucy IV
168, *l.*16 from foot. *For* in 1864 *read* on 30 June 1864.
171, **Sources:** *Add The Suffrage Annual and Women's Who's Who* (1913) 372.
171, *See also For* BUXON *read* BUXTON and *before* Edmund *insert* *

TILLETT, Benjamin (Ben) IV
184, **Sources:** *Add* J. Schneer, 'Ben Tillett: the making and un-making of a British labor militant' (Columbia PhD, 1978).
187, **New Unionism, 1889–93** (5). *Add* P. M. Johnson, '"Old" and "New" Unionism in England during the 1890's', *North Dakota Q. 29*, no.4 (1971) 39–49.

TOYN, Joseph II
368b, *l.*1. *For* 1938 *read* 1838

TWEDDELL, Thomas I
324a, **Writings:** *Add Co-operators and the Disposal of Profits* (Inaugural address Co-op. Congress 14 May 1894, repr. Manchester, 1914) 16 pp.

VEITCH, Marian III
194, foot of page *add* **Writings:** 'Ruskin College', *GMWJ 20*, no.1 (Jan 1957) 4–6; 'Trade Unionism in Poland', ibid., *21*, no.2 (Feb 1958) 42–3; 'You never can tell' [with photograph], ibid., no.5 (May 1958) 134–5.

VINCENT, Henry I
333a, *l.*6 from foot. *After* Library *add* and correspondence relating to his lectures in H. J. Wilson papers, Sheffield Univ. Library, ref. 37P/45.
334a, *l.*5 from foot. *For 87 read 82*

WALKDEN, Alexander George V
225, **Writings:** *Add Railway Pooling Proposals and Joint Working Arrangements: the case for safeguarding railway employment* (RCA, July 1932); (with Sir W. Jowitt), *Employees' Case for Safeguards* (RCA, Nov 1932).

WALLAS, Graham V
226, *l.*8. *After* manqué *insert* quotation mark
231, **Sources:** *Add* P. Clarke, *Liberals and Social Democrats* (Cambridge Univ. Press, 1978).

WALLHEAD, Richard [Christopher] Collingham III
195, *l.*15 from foot. *For* about 1910 *read* in 1908
195, *l.*7 from foot. *Add* the following paragraph:
R. C. Wallhead's later prominence in the national ILP has tended to obscure his contribution to the Socialist movement in the Manchester area before the First World War. From 1903 he was a regular speaker at open-air meetings in Manchester and Salford, as well as in North Cheshire, the Potteries and Bolton. He spoke at unemployed demonstrations in Manchester between 1905 and 1908, and also did election work for Victor Grayson in Colne Valley in July 1907. While still living in Wilmslow, Wallhead joined Manchester Central Branch ILP on 20 September 1904, and served as its delegate to Manchester and Salford ILP Council in 1906. However, on 19 March 1907 he resigned from this branch. During a by-election campaign at Cockermouth in early August 1906 (where Robert Smillie was an ILP candidate), Theresa Billington-Greig and Christabel Pankhurst, both branch members, had spoken in a manner which Wallhead and many others believed to be detrimental to party interests. A group of WSPU sympathisers, however, retained power within Central Branch and the dissenters, who included Wallhead, broke away to form the

new City of Manchester Branch, for which Wallhead became a regular speaker in 1908. Before his involvement with the national ILP scouts, Wallhead had become one of the most active members of the organisation of Manchester Clarion Scouts which was re-formed in June 1905, and he served as president in the following year. In January 1909 he began to contribute the 'Our Scouts' column to the *Labour Leader*. Wallhead also put his artistic talents to the service of the local Socialist movement, and was responsible for much of the interior decoration at the Clarion clubhouse, Handforth, and Pankhurst Hall in north Salford.
198, **Sources:** *Add* Manchester Central Branch ILP, Minutes, 1904–8, Manchester PL; *Labour Leader*, 1903–12.

WARD, John IV
191, *l*.13. *For* Gasworkers *read* SDF
193, **Sources:** *for Revs 6 read Revs 33*

WATTS, John I
342a, **Sources:** *Add* J. Smethurst, E. and R. Frow, 'Frederick Engels and the English Working Class Movement in Manchester, 1842–1844', *Marxism Today* (Nov 1970) 344.

WEBB, Beatrice and WEBB, Sidney James II
377a, *l*.11 from foot. *For* four *read* six
389, *l*.25. *Add* 'The Diary of Beatrice Webb 1873–1943' 57 vols (Cambridge, 1978) [on microfiche] and *Index to the Diary of Beatrice Webb 1873–1943* (1978).
393a, Sidney and Beatrice Webb, (1) **Books:** *Add The Letters of Sidney and Beatrice Webb* 3 vols ed. N. MacKenzie (Cambridge Univ. Press, 1978).
393b, **Sources:** (1) *Add* correspondence in Mundella papers, and minutes of the Coefficients, June 1903–May 1905 in W.A.S. Hewins papers, Sheffield Univ. Library.
394a, (3) **Biographical Works:** *Add* M. Cole, *Women of To-Day* (1939) 261–89.

WELLOCK, Wilfred V
238, **Writings:** *Add War and the Workers. An Appeal to the Labour, Trade Union and Co-operative Movements and the Unemployed* (No More War Movement, [1934?]) 16 pp.

WELSH, James C. II
399b, *l*.12 *For* C in title *read* Carmichael

WHITEHEAD, Alfred I
345b, *ll*.22–20 from foot. *For* and indeed ... although *read* but an Alfred Whitehead was an ILP delegate from Manchester Miles Platting in 1907, 1908, 1911 and 1913 and ...

WILKIE, Alexander III
208, **Sources:** *Add* Labour Party archives: LRC 1900–6 and LP general correspondence.

WILLIAMS, Aneurin I
346a, *l*.8 *For* 1880 *read* 1883

WILLIAMS, John I
348a, **Sources:** *Add* J. E. Morgan, *A Village Workers' Council* (Pontypridd, 1951) 3 pp.; K. O. Morgan, 'The Gower Election of 1906' *Gower 12* (1959) 15–19; idem, 'The "Khaki Election" in Gower', ibid., *13* (1960) 20–5. The best general first-hand source for Williams is the local newspaper *Llais Llafur* (part of which was in English).
[The editors are indebted to Dr K. O. Morgan for these additions and also for his comment that Williams owed much in 1906 to the support of local Liberal stalwarts, including Rev. Gomer Lewis, the minister of his chapel, Capel Gomer, Swansea, who campaigned strenuously for Williams (letter of 3 June 1972)].

WILSON, Joseph Havelock IV
208, **Sources:** (1) *Add* Sunderland branch minute book, 1887–90 (ref. MSS. 175) and ITF files (ref. MSS. 159), MRC, Warwick Univ. Library; Labour Party archives: LRC 1901–6 and LP general correspondence.

WOOLF, Leonard Sidney V
246, *l*.4. *For* laying *read* lying
247, **Sources:** *Add* G. Spater and I. Parsons, *A Marriage of True Minds* (1977); *The Diary of Virginia Woolf* vol. *2*: *1920–1924*, ed. A. O. Bell (1978); J. Lehmann, *Thrown to the Woolfs* (1978); D. Wilson, *Leonard Woolf: a political biography* (1978); *Letters of Virginia Woolf* vol. *4*: *1929–31 A Reflection of the Other Person* (1978) and vol.*5*: *1932–1935 The Sickle Side of the Moon* (1979) both ed. N. Nicolson. OBIT. M. Cole, 'Leonard Woolf', *Fabian News 80*, no.8 (Sep 1969) 2.

CONSOLIDATED LIST OF NAMES

Volumes II–V
For MURNIN, Hugh (1865–1932) *read* (1861–1932)
For RAMSEY, Thomas *read* RAMSAY, Thomas
For SKEVINGTON, John (1801–50) *read* (1801–51)
For WELSH, James C. (1880–1954) *read* WELSH, James Carmichael

Volumes II–IV
For HUGHES, Edward (1854–1917) *read* (1856–1925)

Volume IV
For BOSWELL, James Edward Buchanan (1960–71) *read* (1906–71)

INDEX

Volume I
361a, Boards of Guardians. *For* Bedwelty *read* Bedwellty
362a, *after* Cardiff, 95–6 *insert* Carey, Rose, 117
362a, Carlile, Richard. *Delete* 51
362a, *before* Carpenter, Mary *insert* Carlyle, Thomas, 51
367a, *l.*9 from foot. *For Coventry read County*
370a, *delete* Haldane, J. B. S., 80–1 and *substitute* Haldane, John Scott, 80–1 and *below this*, Haldane, Richard Burdon (later 1st Viscount Haldane of Cloan), 7
371b, International, Second. *Delete* 276
372b, *l.*25 from foot. *Delete* formation of
380a, *ll.*1–2. *For* Confidence *read* Confident
382b, *l.*5. *For* 115 *read* 119
383b, *l.*2. *For* Miners *read* mines
384b, *l.*13 from foot. *For* Raynor *read* Rayner
388b, *l.*18 from foot. *For* Education *read* Educational

Volume II
422a, *l.*15. *For* 6th *read* 1st
429b, *l.*9. *Delete* Derby, Lord (17th Earl of), 23
430a, *l.*21. *For* Edwards, Sir Lincoln *read* Evans, Sir Lincoln
431a, *l.*14. *For* Freemantle *read* Fremantle
434a, *Below* Industrial Union *insert* Industrial Women's Organisations, Standing Joint Committee of, 41, 42
438b, *l.*26. *For* Mattinson *read* Mattison
444b, *l.*19 from foot. *For* 260 *read* 360
448a, *l.*27. *For* Seigfried *read* Siegfried
448b, *For* Shaw, Thomas, 337 *read* 338
449a, *l.*18 from foot. *For* Sydney *read* Sidney
452a, *Below* United Irish League *insert* Unity Manifesto, 50
453b, *l.*26. *Delete* Women's Industrial Organisations etc.
453b, *Below* Women's Suffrage Movement *add* Women's Trade Union Association, 397

Volume III
219a, *ll.*24–5. *For* Ship Platers *read* Shipbuilders
221b, *l.*11. *Delete* Richards
234a, Strikes and Lockouts, General Strike. *Insert* 40 *after* 39

Volume IV
221b, *l.*13. *For* William John *read* J.
225a, *l.*30. *For* 171 *read* 71
232b, *l.*3 from foot. *After* 90, *add* (1932–7)

Volume V
257b, *l.*6. *For* Amalgamated *read* Associated
264a, *l.*13. *For* Gallagher *read* Gallacher

ADAMS, Mary Jane Bridges (1855–1939)

SOCIALIST AND EDUCATIONALIST

Mary Bridges Adams was born on 19 October 1855 at Maesycwmmer, Bedwas, South Wales. She was the daughter of William Daltry, an engine fitter and his wife Margaret (née Jones). Nothing is known of Mary's early life. The first record of her career was her success in the University of London matriculation examination, where she was placed in the first division in 1881; and a year later, in June 1882, she passed the University of London's intermediate examination in Arts. She attended classes in English language and literature, English history, and French, Latin and Greek. Nothing further of her educational career is known, but it is likely that she became a teacher.

On 22 October 1887 she married Walter Bridges Adams, whose father, William Bridges Adams, was a well-known civil engineer, the author of *English Pleasure Carriages* (1837), a radical in politics who in the 1830s, and possibly later also, used the pen name of 'Junius Redivivus'. He had first married a daughter of Francis Place, then when she died Sarah Flower of the famous Unitarian family. When she, in turn, died, William married Ellen Rendall, who became Walter's mother. William died in 1872, but Ellen lived on until 1898.

Very little has been discovered about Walter Bridges Adams. He is referred to as a 'devotee of German opera' [Speaight (1971) 11] and as a tutor, although where or what he taught is not known, and even his date of death – in one source given as 1902 – cannot be firmly stated. There was a W. Bridges Adams among the signatories to the 1885 Manifesto of the Socialist League, and this may have been Walter or his brother William. Though neither took an active part in the League [Thompson (1955) 428], it was undoubtedly a political family that Mary Daltry had married into, since Walter's sister, Hope married Dr Lehmann of Munich, a well-known Bavarian Socialist, and both the Lehmanns were close friends of August Bebel [*Call*, 2 Nov 1916].

The earliest reference to any political activity on the part of Mary Bridges Adams is a minute of the education committee of the Royal Arsenal Co-operative Society, where it is recorded that she had agreed to chair one of a series of lectures the Society was organising together with the southern section of the Co-operative Union in 1894. From this time she became known as a left-wing Socialist, one who was especially interested in all educational matters. It was in the same year, 1894, that she stood unsuccessfully as a Labour candidate for the Greenwich division of the London School Board; she contested the election again in 1897, and this time was successful, holding the seat until its abolition after the 1902 Education Act. Her obituary in *The Times*, written by a friend, noted that 'under the influence of Kropotkin and William Morris she skirted Fabianism and became an uncompromising Socialist'; and Mrs Adams herself, wrote in later life that she had 'the blessing and good wishes of William Morris when she began her work for educational reform' [*Cotton Factory Times*, 21 Sep 1923, 2]. The ambience of his early home life is described by her son, William, as 'much more I.L.P. and S.D.P. than Fabian, where the word Bourgeois . . . was held to be outmoded, silly, and taboo; we laughed at people who used it' [Letter to John Moore quoted in Speaight (1971) 11].

Down to the years of the First World War Mrs Adams was a leading propagandist for educational reform within the labour movement. Her work on the London School Board gave her an important base in the movement, and her energies were concentrated on demands for free school meals, medical inspection of school children, and the creation of open-air schools for the sick and under-nourished. In November 1901, largely on her initiative, the National Labour Educational League was established, its purpose being the elaboration of a positive educational programme and policy for the whole movement, and especially for the unions. The League's original Appeal was signed by an impressive list of personalities: three Lib-Lab MPs – Bell, Burt and Fenwick; eight members of the TUC Parliamentary Committee; five LCC Labour aldermen; and Ben Jones with three other prominent co-operators [*Co-op. News*, 25

Nov 1901]. The League, however, never became a serious influence and it seems to have died by the end of 1902.

Mrs Adams always had strong support from the Royal Arsenal Co-operative Society and from other working-class bodies in south London. In the summer of 1899 she had been the main organiser behind a Loan Picture exhibition in Woolwich, backed by the Woolwich and District Trades and Labour Council and other local working-class groups. The names of the consultative committee read like a list of what later would have been called 'the stage army of the good'. Mrs Adams and Felix Moscheles were joint honorary secretaries and Walter Crane opened the exhibition on its first day.

She seems to have been continuously active in local affairs. In 1900 she was a member of a local committee which investigated housing conditions in Woolwich. In December 1902 she took a prominent part in a joint conference organised by the RACS education committee and the Co-operative Women's Guild on 'Why Women should join Trade Unions'. Gertrude Tuckwell, of the Women's Trade Union League, gave the main address, and in the discussion Mrs Adams announced that she was a member of the Gas Workers' and General Labourers' Union, and urged all the women in the audience to join. She became a close friend of the Countess of Warwick for a few years and at least in the winter of 1904–5 acted as her secretary. W.M. Haddow reports meeting her, with the Countess of Warwick, at the International Socialist Congress held in Amsterdam in August 1904. In February 1905 it was announced that the two women would tour the country campaigning for free school meals, and that they would visit every constituency with a Socialist candidate. Their initiative was not always welcomed. Mrs Adams helped Victor Grayson in his election campaign in the spring of 1907; and she was evidently encouraged in this by the Countess of Warwick. Whether she was still her secretary is not certain, and from about this time the two women seemed to have moved apart.

One of her successes was the establishment of the first 'Open Air School for Recovery' in Borstall Woods, which was owned by the RACS. The Open Air School was for tubercular children. It opened on 22 July 1907, but ran only for three months; thereafter, however, Mrs Adams remained a fervent advocate of the idea. In 1915, during the short period when Arthur Henderson was President of the Board of Education she offered to organise a national system of open air recovery schools, and although the proposal came to nothing she continued her agitation. Among her last writings in the late 1920s were articles on these schools.

In the few years before the outbreak of the First World War, Mrs Adams developed a new interest in independent working-class education. She went to Oxford a few days after the Ruskin College strike began in March 1909, and from then on her advocacy of workers' control of their own educational programmes and institutions was unceasing. It took two main forms. The first was her support of the Plebs League and the Central Labour College. At the August 1909 conference, which brought the Central Labour College into existence, Noah Ablett moved the resolution on 'The principle of independence in working-class education' and Mrs Adams seconded in a speech which *Plebs* described as 'a fighting speech of great power and force'. Later that year, in October 1909, she was billed to speak at the Stockport Labour Church on 'Oxford University and Working-Class Education', with special reference to:

> (i) Lord Curzon's impudent proposal for a "Poor Men's or Working-men's College", (ii) The oft-repeated demand of the Trade Union Congress for the restoration of the University and Public-school Endowments which have been stolen from the poor. This is the third visit of our comrade to Stockport. She is a stalwart on the Education Question; an uncompromising Social Democrat; believes that some of our Labour M.P.'s want watching on the so-called Working-men's college question; has repudiated the idea of Lord Curzon's, with respect to his scheme of a "Poor Men's" College. Mrs Bridges Adams is always sure of a large audience. We wish there were more men with the same pluck and enthusiasm.

George Sims wrote of her in *Plebs* in July 1912:

> For three years and three months (the whole time our movement has been in being) Mrs Adams has propagated, and propagated, and propagated, in Scotland, Wales, North, South, East and West of England she has carried the gospel of the Central Labour College educational programme, roping in helpers and funds, directly and indirectly, and while not sparing herself has insisted on more and more work from us. She has her reward in the affection and esteem in which we hold her and the knowledge of the success of her efforts. Now the men's side is well under way and occupying an assured position in the Labour Movement she has set out to accomplish the other half of the programme – a residential section for women workers.

It was early in 1912 that Mrs Adams began a campaign to establish a Working Women's Labour College. At a conference of the Central Labour College in September 1912 she reported on progress to date. She had taken a house – 96 Lexham Gardens – in Kensington, and renamed it Bebel House; and although the Women's College did not get established, Mrs Adams was still writing from the Working Women's College address as late as 1915 and continued to live at the same address until her death.

The second part of her campaign in support of an independent working-class educational movement was expressed in vigorous hostility to the Workers' Educational Association; then she became among the most vociferous of the Socialist critics of the WEA. Albert Mansbridge in his farewell address to the WEA on 20 November 1915 referred to her as 'the arch-enemy of them all'. Her criticisms were directed both against the content of what was taught and the absence of real working-class control. She always objected to control and interference from outside the labour movement.

The years of war, however, gave her political energies a new direction, without in any way submerging her continued interest in educational advance. There were in existence before August 1914 several large-scale relief organisations in France, Germany, Austria and Belgium, for the succour of the many Russian political exiles, most of whom were in Siberia. The outbreak of war made most of these organisations ineffective, and George Chicherin, later to become the Soviet Foreign Minister, who was then living in exile in London, conceived the idea of a London relief committee to help to fill some of the gaps that had now appeared. All the London *émigré* organisations supported him, and Mrs Adams became his assistant secretary. Maisky wrote of her in his memoirs:

> [Chicherin's] principal assistant was a woman, Mrs Bridges Adams, one of those English people who somehow fail to come to terms with life and so devote all their passion and determination to some 'cause' which fires their imagination or touches their heart. In the years before the First World War Mrs Bridges Adams was a fervent suffragette and smashed shop windows and attacked Members of Parliament. When she met Chicherin the heroic struggles of the revolutionary movement in Russia stirred her imagination. She was all fire and flame for this new 'cause' and became the moving spirit on the committee [Maisky (1962) 75].

It is necessary to remark that there is no evidence other than this comment of Maisky's that Mrs Adams was a militant suffragette. Indeed, her obituary notice in *The Times* speaks of her as a believer in universal suffrage but lukewarm towards 'the Votes for Women movement as a small "bourgeois" affair'. The organisation to which Maisky referred was the Russian Political Prisoners and Exiles' Relief Committee in London, which was formally constituted during the summer of 1915. Its stated aim was the collection of monies for relief, but under Chicherin's direction the Committee became an agitational body against Tsarism. The Russian Government early in the war had tried to secure the repatriation of certain of its citizens living in England and France, but the principle of the right of asylum was firmly upheld. It was then suggested that political *émigrés* should make their contribution to the war effort by joining the

British and French armies; and when conscription was introduced in Britain in 1916 the British Government became more pressing in its demands upon the *émigrés*. The activity of the Committee was therefore wholly engaged in a campaign to prevent their conscription. The *Call* founded in February 1916 by the anti-war group within the BSP, carried a fair amount of information, and Mrs Adams herself wrote at length in the *Yorkshire Factory Times* and the *Cotton Factory Times*. The details of the agitation are therefore abundantly available. The Committee's main helpers in Parliament seem to have been two Liberals: Joseph King in the Commons and Lord Sheffield (formerly the Hon. Edward Lyulph Stanley) in the Lords – the latter a personal friend of Mrs Adams. Lord Derby, Secretary of State for War made an outspoken attack on Mrs Adams in the House of Lords in March 1917. Part of his speech read:

> Mrs Bridges Adams first came under the notice of the authorities in consequence of a letter in the *Labour Leader* on November 4, 1915, which contained a plea on behalf of the Russian Political Prisoners and Exiles Relief Committee, and which referred inquirers for information to her as the hon. secretary. The noble Lord [Sheffield] quoted this as a perfectly harmless committee. I can assure him that this is not the view taken by the responsible people, who do not regard it at all in that light, and I may say that the lady herself, I believe, has described it as being one of a dangerous character. Whether she has done so or not is comparatively immaterial. The fact remains that those who are in authority have advised us that this society is one of a dangerous character whose actions must be closely watched. In consequence of her association with this particular committee it was considered desirable to keep observation on Mrs Bridges Adams, and it was found that she was closely connected with two men named Petroff and Maclean [*Hansard* [Lords], 7 Mar 1917, 411].

Mrs Adams's house was searched several times, and on one occasion (30 June 1916) she was arrested for distributing a pamphlet, *The Right of Asylum*, and detained for twenty-six hours. The matter of the Russian *émigrés* was largely resolved by the February/March revolution of 1917; although the later imprisonment of Chicherin led to further efforts on her part to have all the *émigrés* released who had been jailed for one reason or another. They included Peter Petroff, who had been arrested with John Maclean in the summer of 1916. In the end it was Trotsky's firmness with the British Government that ensured their release [Fischer (1930) vol. *1*, 25].

Mrs Adams's political engagement was of a practical rather than a theoretical sort. Indeed, she seems to have been of a notably untheoretical cast of mind. Her political pre-occupations apart from her remarkable efforts during the First World War on behalf of the Russian political *émigrés* – were centred upon education, and when she took up the cause of the arrested John Maclean and his comrades in 1916 it is interesting that she stressed their educational work rather than their revolutionary political attitudes. In day to day terms before 1914 she was sympathetic to both the ILP and the SDF although she seems to have found the latter increasingly congenial.

After the war ended Mrs Adams resumed her work for educational change with an emphasis upon international contacts between working-class movements. She constantly reiterated the emphasis she had always given to control by the working people of their own independent educational institutions [see, for an example, a long article in the *Socialist*, 23 Mar 1922]. She was naturally sympathetic to the Soviet State, and declared herself on one occasion as 'an unattached Communist' [*Cotton Factory Times*, 21 Sept 1923]. Earlier she had somewhat naïvely defended the Soviet Government against the widely-circulated accusations of 'Russian Gold' and the subsidising of Bolshevik propaganda in Britain [*Socialist*, 22 Dec 1921 and 12 Jan 1922]. She was, however, vigorously critical in her attitude towards the British Communist Party, and on issues such as their hostile approach to the Central Labour College she was vehement in opposition to them. R. Palme Dutt especially, she felt, was often unhelpful in his analysis and harmful in his political attitudes.

Mrs Adams continued to write for the *Cotton Factory Times*, mainly on educational matters, for the whole of the 1920s, and into the early 1930s. By this time she was over seventy-five years old. The last article that has been traced was published on 15 July 1932, and dealt with the Geneva disarmament conference. She died at Princess Beatrice Hospital, London on 14 January 1939, survived by a son, William, who was director of Shakespeare Festivals at Stratford from 1919 to 1934 and by a grandson, John Nicholas William Bridges-Adams, at present (1979) a Recorder of the Crown Court. No will has been located.

Mary Bridges Adams was a woman of great personality, abundant energy and a marked capacity for achievement. Margaret Cole remembers her at the end of the war as a rather *grande dame* of whom the young women intellectuals were somewhat shy; and the first question Chicherin asked Robin Page Arnot when the latter visited the Russian Foreign Office in 1926 was 'And how is my friend Mrs Bridges Adams?' Her obituary notice in *The Times* underlined the friendships she made, and the account which has been given here is evidence of the many contacts and relationships she had within the labour movement. But the *DLB* research group are unable to find anyone who could offer a detailed personal account of her. This short biography has therefore been built up almost entirely from secondary sources, and it is quite likely that some parts of her story have been left untold. Her life is hardly noticed even in the footnotes of works about the labour movement in the twentieth century – a melancholy illustration of how easily memories become dimmed and reputations are lost.

Writings: Mary Bridges Adams was a prolific writer of articles and letters especially to the *Cotton Factory Times*, between 1915 and 1932, and the *Yorkshire Factory Times* from 1915 until the paper ceased publication in 1919. She also contributed to trade union journals, in particular the *Railway Review and the ASE Monthly Journal and Report.* A selection of her writings is given below to indicate her specialist interests; further details are available in the *DLB* Coll. Letter on 'The Proposal for a Working Women's College', *Link 1*, no. 8 (Apr 1912) 16; 'Last Ditch of the Co-partnership Fraud', *Daily Herald*, 6 June 1913; 'The War and Free School Meals' [letter], *YFT*, 4 Feb 1915; 'The Solidarity of Working Class Motherhood and Rural Child Labour' [letter], ibid., 11 Feb 1915; 'Consumption in the People's Schools' [letter], ibid., 8 Apr 1915; 'A New Alliance with Russia' [letter], ibid., 20 May 1915; 'The Russian Political Prisoners and Exiles' Relief Committee in London', ibid., 15 July 1915; 'Attitude to the War', *CFT*, 6 Aug 1915; 'Starving Education' [letter], *YFT*, 30 Sep 1915; '"Reform" in Russia: value of recent political developments' [letter], *CFT*, 8 Oct 1915; Russia and the War: what is the censor concealing?', ibid., 22 Oct 1915; 'Why Political Prisoners?' [letter], ibid., 29 Oct 1915; 'The Russian Labour Movement', *YFT*, 16 Dec 1915; 'British and Russian Workers unite!', *CFT*, 17 Dec 1915; 'Towards Peace on Earth: strong influence of internationalism', ibid., 24 Dec 1915; 'Another Police Raid: Mrs Bridges Adams's house searched' [letter], ibid., 14 Jan 1916; 'The Two European State Groups', *YFT*, 10 Feb 1916; 'Looking beyond the War: development of capitalist imperialist policy', *CFT*, 11 Feb 1916; 'In Defence of my Propaganda: dangers of reaction during the war', ibid., 25 Feb 1916; 'Education, and the Youth of the New International', *YFT*, 2 Mar 1916; 'The Right of Asylum: shall a great tradition go by the board?', *CFT*, 24 Mar 1916; 'The Extradition Laws and the Case of Peter Petroff', *YFT*, 30 Mar 1916; 'Protection and Labour: what is the movement's policy?', *CFT*, 31 Mar 1916; 'The Arrests on the Clyde: five educational workers out of the way', ibid., 14 Apr 1916; 'The Sentence on John McLean: significance of attack on educationalists', ibid., 21 Apr 1916; 'The Approach of the Iron Heel: democracy swept back by tide of war', ibid., 28 Apr 1916; 'John Maclean and Working-Class Education', *Call*, 8 June 1916, 14; 'The Zimmerwald Message: growth of the international spirit', *CFT*, 9 June 1916; 'The Great International Alliance: international capitalism after the war', ibid., 23 June 1916; 'In the Hands of the Police', ibid., 14 July 1916; 'Smashing Right of Asylum: Home Office goes behind back of Parliament', ibid., 4 Aug 1916; 'Education as a Weapon: why workers must forge their own', ibid., 25 Aug 1916; 'Congress and Right of Asylum: adventures with leaflets at Birmingham', ibid., 22 Sep 1916; 'A Great Tradition in Peril: end of "voluntary" recruiting of Russians', ibid., 29 Sep 1916; 'Rothschild's Advice: refugees must join the Army or – !', ibid., 20 Oct 1916; 'The Revolution in Russia', *YFT*, 29 Mar 1917; 'A Great Russian Socialist Meeting in London', ibid., 5 Apr 1917; 'The Case of Mr George Tchitcherine' [letter], ibid., 18 Oct 1917; 'The House of Lords and George Tchitcherine' [letter], ibid., 14 Feb 1918; 'Mr Arthur Henderson and the Russian Soviet Government' [letter], ibid., 9 May 1918; 'British Labour and Allied Intervention in Russia' [letter], ibid., 29 Aug 1918; 'Education and the New International' [letter], ibid., 14 Nov 1918; 'Imprisoned Russian Subjects in Britain' [letter], ibid., 1 May 1919; 'The B.S.P. and C3 Clerical Schools', ibid., 22 May 1919; 'Koltchak – "The Man of the Hour"' [letter], ibid., 29 May 1919; 'The White-Washing of Koltchak' [letter], *CFT*, 13 June 1919; 'Consumptive Children' [letter], ibid., 20 June 1919; 'Labour Solidarity: proposed International Students' Union', ibid., 26 Dec 1919; 'Education and the Youth of the Red International', *ASE Monthly J. and Report* (Mar 1920) 59–60; 'Sectionalism in Schools: Mr H.A.L. Fisher's reactionary proposals', *CFT*, 23 Apr 1920; 'Unemployment and C3 Schools', ibid., 19 Nov 1920; 'Propaganda and "Russian Gold"' [letters], *Socialist*, 22 Dec 1921 and 12 Jan 1922; 'The Irish Labour Movement and Independent Working-Class Education' [letter], ibid., 23 Feb 1922; 'Russia and British Working-Class Education', ibid., 23 Mar 1922; 'Workers' Education: Communist attitude to independent control', *CFT*, 4 May 1923; 'The Communists: wanted, post-Revolution information', ibid., 21 Sep 1923; 'Political Prosecutions' [letter], ibid., 19 Dec 1924; 'The Workers' Children: need for open-air recovery schools', ibid., 11 Mar 1927; 'Obstacle to Peace in Industry: segregation in the field of education', ibid., 11 Nov 1927; 'A "Schools Front": tuberculous children in mining areas', ibid., 6 Apr 1928; 'The 1896 Congress: why not another international in London?', ibid., 5 June 1931; 'The War Experts and Geneva: futilities of the disarmament conference', ibid., 15 July 1932.

Sources: (1) MS: The William Bridges-Adams papers, University of Calgary, Canada contain some childhood letters to his mother but contain no details about Mrs Adams's life and career; Royal Arsenal Co-operative Society, Education Cttee minutes, 1894–1901, RACS, London; LP archives: LRC 8/8, 11/87–96, 24/125–39; *Link* (Apr 1912) p. 16 in ILP papers, Herbert W. Bryan Coll. section VII, Press Cuttings 1904–14, LSE R (Coll.) Misc. 314; Mansbridge-Zimmern correspondence [May 1910], Zimmern MSS Box I, Bodleian Library, Oxford; Mansbridge Farewell Address to WEA Central Council, 20 Nov 1915, Lectures and Addresses, Mansbridge MSS, BL; Correspondence, Mrs Bridges Adams to Bertrand Russell in relation to Russian Political Prisoners [1916], Bertrand Russell Archives, McMaster Univ., Hamilton, Ontario. There is a closed HO file on Peter Petroff; and undoubtedly, if still extant, a Metropolitan Police file on Mrs Bridges Adams; and there are some references to her in Foreign Office files in 1922–4 and 1927 for which see the Kraus/Thomson *Index to General Correspondence of the Foreign Office* (1969). (2) Other: *DNB 1* (1885) [for William Bridges Adams]; W.T. Linton, *Memories* (1895); 'The Newly-elected London School Board', *Illustrated London News*, 4 Dec 1897, 796 [photograph]; RASC, *Half-yearly Report* (Jan 1898); *Woolwich and District Labour Notes* (June and July 1899); *School Board Chronicle*, 25 Nov 1899, 559; *Comradeship* (Aug 1900), (Aug and Dec 1901), (Dec 1902); *Co-op. News*, 19 Dec 1903, 19 Nov 1904; Between 1903 and 1910 there are numerous references to lectures and speeches made by Mrs Bridges Adams, largely related to her campaign against the WEA, in issues of the *Clarion, Justice, Labour Leader* and *New Age*: details in *DLB* Coll.; National Anti-Sweating League, *Report of Conference on a Minimum Wage held at the Guildhall, London on October 24–26 1906* (1907); *Socialist Standard 4*, no. 48 (Aug 1908) 90; *Nelson Leader*, 8 Jan 1909; *Worker* [Huddersfield], 3 Apr 1909; *Railway Rev.*, 6 Aug 1909; correspondence between Mrs Bridges Adams and George Alcock of the ASRS, ibid. (Dec 1909) and (Jan 1910); *Plebs 1*, no. 8 (Sep 1909) 174; *Justice*, 27 Nov 1909, 4; *Clarion*, 25 Feb

1910, 6; G. Sims, 'A Tribute', *Plebs 4*, no.6 (July 1912) 131–2; 'Proposed Working Women's Labour College', ibid. *4*, no. 8 (Sep 1912) 176–7; 'Notes', ibid. *4*, no.11 (Dec 1912) 264; G. Tchitcherine, 'Russian Political Prisoners: an appeal' [letter], *CFT*, 9 July 1915; idem. 'The Liverpool Scandal' [letter], *Labour Leader*, 4 Nov 1915; 'Death of Dr Hope Adams-Lehmann', *Call*, 2 Nov 1916; G. Tchitcherine, 'Raid on Communist Club' [letter], *CFT*, 8 Dec 1916; *Hansard* [Lords], 7 Mar 1917 [debate on DORA]; 'Ex-Tsar's Secret Police', *CFT*, 24 Aug 1917; 'Tchitcherine and his Accusers', ibid., 7 Sep 1917; 'Is Internationalism Pro-Germanism?', ibid., 21 Sep 1917; 'Behind Closed Doors', ibid., 26 Oct 1917; 'An Ambassador in Gaol', ibid., 7 Dec 1917; C.H. Wright, 'Mr Tchitcherin and Mr Petroff' [letter], *Times*, 13 Dec 1917; 'Tchitcherine not yet released', *CFT*, 28 Dec 1917; 'Russian Subjects deported', ibid., 11 Jan 1918; *Hansard* [Lords], 30 Jan 1918 [debate on treatment of Russians]; 'Mazeppa', 'Views about Russia' [letter], *CFT*, 28 Mar 1919; Articles by Sir Basil Thomson [Director of Intelligence, 1919–21] on activities against Communists were published in *The Times* on 12, 14, 15, 16 Nov and 1–10 Dec 1921; *The History of the Royal Arsenal Co-operative Society Ltd 1868–1918* ed. W.T. Davis and W.B. Neville (Woolwich, 1922); J. Brown, 'Propaganda and "Russian Gold"' [letter], *Socialist*, 5 Jan 1922; S. Bryher, *An Account of the Labour and Socialist Movement in Bristol describing its Early Beginnings, Struggles and Growth* (Bristol, 1929–31); L. Fischer, *The Soviets in World Affairs* 2 vols (1930); E.S. Pankhurst, *The Suffragette Movement* (1931); W.J. Brown, 'Open-air Recovery Schools', *Comradeship and the Wheatsheaf* (Dec 1933) xvi–xvii; P. Petroff, 'George Tchitcherin', *Labour* (Aug 1936) 306; T. Gautrey, "*Lux Mihi Laus"; school board memories* [1937]; A. Mansbridge, *The Trodden Road* (1940); E.P. Thompson, *William Morris* (1955; rev. ed. 1977); E.F.E. Jefferson, *The Story of England's First Open Air School* (Leicester, 1957); W.P. McCann, 'Trade Unionist, Co-operative and Socialist Organisations in Relation to Popular Education 1870–1902' (Manchester PhD, 1960); *Who's Who in the Theatre* (1961); *WWW* (1961–70); I. Maisky, *Journey into the Past* (1962); W.W. Craik, *The Central Labour College 1909–29* (1964); R.K. Debo, 'George Chicherin: Soviet Russia's Second Foreign Commissar' (Nebraska PhD, 1964); B. Simon, *Education and the Labour Movement 1870–1920* (1965); M. Blunden, *The Countess of Warwick* (1967); S. Maclure, *One Hundred Years of Labour Education 1870–1970* (1970); *A Bridges-Adams Letter Book*, ed. with a Memoir by Robert Speaight (Society for Theatre Research, 1971) [letters of Mrs Bridges Adams's son, William]; I.W. Hamilton, 'Education for Revolution: the Plebs League and Labour College Movement' (Warwick MA, 1972); F.B. Smith, *William James Linton 1812–97* (1973); C. Cook et al., *Sources in British Political History 1900–1951* vol. *1* (1975); D.G. Clark, 'The Origins and Development of the Labour Party in the Colne Valley 1891–1907' (Sheffield PhD, 1978); biographical information: K. Blackwall, Archivist, Bertrand Russell Archives, McMaster Univ., Ontario, Canada; Edmund and Ruth Frow, Manchester; Colin Holmes, Sheffield Univ.; Local History Library, London Borough of Greenwich; T.D.W. Reid, Stockport Reference Library; A. Rothstein, London; L.P. Turnbull, Registrar, Bedford College, London; personal information: Mrs Jenifer Bridges-Adams, Fornham St Martin, Bury St Edmunds, grand-daughter-in-law; the late Sir Will Lawther. OBIT. *Times*, 25 July 1872 [William Bridges Adams, senior]; *Times*, 16 Jan 1939 [Mrs Bridges Adams]; *Cork Examiner*, 18 Aug 1965 and *Times*, 19 Aug 1965 [William Bridges Adams, junior]. The editors wish to express their appreciation of the assistance given by John Attfield, Bromley, and Professor B. Jennings, Univ. of Hull for information on various aspects of Mrs Bridges Adams's career; Mrs Naomi Reid, Stockport, for supplying material from several sources and Dr R. Challinor, Newcastle upon Tyne Polytechnic, whose earlier draft encouraged the editors to undertake further research. NOTE. There are variations in the spelling of Chicherin's name in English; in French it was Tchitcherine and in German Tschitscherin.

JOHN SAVILLE

ATKINSON, Hinley (1891–1977)
LABOUR PARTY AGENT AND ORGANISER

Hinley Atkinson, the only son of Robert Atkinson, stonemason, and Eliza Jane Hinley, was born on 24 September 1891 at Ingleton, Yorkshire. He was lame from infancy, possibly as a result of mild poliomyelitis: his left leg was short, and the muscles were underdeveloped. He always used a stick for walking; in later life he wore a calliper to keep his left leg straight. Nevertheless he was always physically active and both walked and cycled for pleasure. He was a tall man with grey eyes, fresh, fair colouring and open direct features. His only formal education was at the village school, but he read a great deal from an early age; in spite of their poverty his mother bought him good books, in the cheap editions which were by that time available.

Robert Atkinson was often unemployed in bad weather, and as the family was a fairly large one, they all knew poverty in their childhood. Hinley himself was unemployed in his youth. On one occasion he walked as far as Goole to look for work; but he found none, and returned to Ingleton, where he was eventually apprenticed to the local bootmaker, Tom Berry who was a member of the ILP and a crusader for its principles. Hinley Atkinson's active mind and his experience of hardship meant that he was receptive to the Socialist ideas expounded by Berry; he had also a strong idealistic urge to better the lot of his fellows. He had already rejected as hypocritical the institutional Christianity which he had encountered in the local Wesleyan chapel, and described himself as a humanist and an agnostic; but his brand of Socialism sprang more from Nonconformist than from Marxist roots. Encouraged by Berry he began to read works on social questions, and he absorbed the ideas of Shaw, Wells and other Fabians. He became widely read, but never thought of himself as an intellectual; indeed, he was one of those who suspected a Socialist whose origins and experience were not genuinely working class if he claimed to speak for that class.

By 1914, when he had set up his own boot-making and repairing business in High Bentham near Ingleton, he was a committed supporter of the Labour Party. He opposed Britain's entry into the First World War and was, for this period in his life only, a firm pacifist. His physical disability exempted him from conscription, and he was able to help friends who were conscientious objectors. In 1915 he married Jane Helen Holmes, who belonged to a local family. She supported all his activities, in spite of the disapproval of her relations. They had one child, a daughter, Joan, who was given the education through grammar school and Cambridge which was never possible for her parents, and who eventually became a grammar school headmistress in Reading.

After the end of the war Hinley Atkinson became increasingly involved in local politics; in 1925 he was elected a Labour member of the Settle RDC, and his talent for organisation led to his appointment as secretary and agent for the Labour Party in the Skipton division of the West Riding. In this period he associated with local Labour men like Philip and Tom Snowden, O.G. Willey (who contested Skipton in 1923 and 1924), Ramsay MacDonald, whom he then admired warmly, and Maurice Webb, one of Atkinson's young disciples. Well-planned campaigns in Skipton caused Head Office to send Atkinson in autumn 1926 to organise a by-election for Labour in Howdenshire, near Hull. Here he met Grace Taverner, one of the Labour women organisers, who had likewise been sent to help. She became a life-long friend.

In 1927 he was appointed organiser for Birmingham, but after the 1929 Labour Government had taken office he was promoted to chief organiser for London. His work in this capacity was immensely valuable to the Party, particularly in the years following 1931. In that year of crisis he opposed MacDonald and the National Labour Party – and much regretted the defection of old friends like Philip Snowden.

The Labour Party in the London region polled as catastrophically in the October 1931 general election as in the rest the country. Labour's thirty-six MPs fell to five. Herbert Morrison, who lost his seat at Hackney, returned to take up his previous position as full-time secretary of the London Labour Party. His assistant secretary was Donald Daines. With Atkinson, Morrison developed a close working relationship. As Morrison's biographers wrote:

> Morrison trusted him, and in turn Atkinson was his devoted servant, to such an extent that some felt that Atkinson was more Morrisonian than Morrison. He waged war against communists and disrupters within local parties and ensured that only reliable candidates were selected. He was tactful in settling disputes within local parties, where he always championed the Morrison line [Donoughue and Jones (1973) 181].

The local elections in November 1931 had gone just as disastrously as the general election, and in the London metropolitan boroughs the number of Labour councillors was reduced to 257, two below the 1922 figure and total votes were only 12,000 more than in 1919. All of which made Labour's recovery so very remarkable. One of the first indications of a new spirit was the Labour gain at the East Fulham parliamentary by-election in late October 1933, when John Wilmot turned a Tory majority of 14,521 into a Labour one of 4840. Atkinson was election agent; and the constituency received the most thorough Labour canvass it had ever had. In March of the following year the London Labour Party won control of the LCC, with thirty-nine more councillors than in 1931, and an overall majority of sixteen. It was a famous victory which greatly encouraged the Labour movement all round the country, and Atkinson's contribution was widely appreciated. The successes of the London Labour Party, and the fact that Atkinson was trusted both by Morrison and Labour Party headquarters, made for good working relations with the national party throughout the decade. The West Fulham parliamentary by-election in 1938 was another triumph for Atkinson, and the successful candidate, Edith Summerskill, put on record how 'he devoted himself to giving me the maximum encouragement and subsequently organising the election in a masterly manner' [letter, 4 Oct 1977]. The minutes of the London LP's EC show frequent congratulations to Atkinson on the results of county council or parliamentary elections.

Atkinson recognised very clearly the growing threat of Fascism and the need for rearmament; at the same time he vigorously opposed the Government's 'non-intervention' policy in regard to Spain and Chamberlain's policy of appeasement. But he regarded most left-wing opinion as wrongheaded at best and downright dangerous at worst. Like Morrison he fought hard against every sort of leftist influence and infiltration – particularly Communist – and he would have no truck with any movement, such as the United Front or Popular Front, that took from the Labour Party its central position in British politics.

When war came in 1939 Hinley Atkinson added the Party organisations in the Home Counties to his existing responsibilities. Herbert Morrison as Home Secretary gave him various tasks, including one in the Ministry of Information. Throughout the war and the bombings of London Atkinson did all he could to keep local party machines ready for elections whenever they should be resumed. He broke his hip in 1944 and Morrison, conscious as always of Atkinson's worth, went to Dr Edmund Hambly with an urgent plea to get Atkinson back at work as soon as possible. Hambly was a Harley Street orthopaedic surgeon who was a strong Labour supporter (he later became an LCC councillor); and Atkinson recovered in good time for the stirring events of 1945. Labour victories in London were especially sweeping. 1945 was undoubtedly the period of greatest satisfaction in his life.

His aim for society was to achieve an ordering of it which would give the highest possible quality of living to all its members. He believed that this could only be realised by a Labour majority in Parliament, and that the Party must always use the existing constitutional structure to reach its ends. His political position was on the right of the Party; his men were Morrison, Bevin, Attlee, Deakin, Citrine, and later Gaitskell and Roy Jenkins. He was critical of Cripps, Laski, Bevan and other men of the left, including Lansbury, since his sympathy with pacifism in 1914 had not survived into the 1930s.

In 1946 he felt that he had achieved all he could as a Party organiser, and he looked for new ground. He was never tempted to stand for Parliament, though he was often urged to do so. In the opinion of Lady Summerskill 'He would have made an excellent Minister in the House, with his loyalty and dedication to the Labour movement, his all round experience, his melodious speech and his shrewd Yorkshire common sense' [letter, 24 Oct 1977]. But whatever the other reasons he knew that his health would not have permitted it. He became an adviser and public relations officer to Odhams Press and worked for the *Daily Herald*, which he regarded as vitally important to the Labour movement. He stayed with the *Herald* until he retired in 1956. Even after that he took no other daily paper and continued to read it with great loyalty, if not always with pleasure, until its demise in 1964.

Hinley Atkinson was one of the original members of the Stevenage Development Corporation and he took a particular interest in the planning of new towns. But his chief interest after his retirement was in practising the crafts of the gardener and handyman. He moved from his home in north London to a cottage in Crowborough, Sussex, where he hoped to enjoy the countryside and these hobbies. He said later that he had deliberately cut himself off from most of his old colleagues when he retired. Perhaps to some extent he was disillusioned with the politics of the Labour movement, although he always refused to admit this. He enjoyed his gardening, but he became intellectually isolated and increasingly nostalgic about his early days in Yorkshire, which he loved to return to on holiday.

His final illness was a long decline. He died in Blagrave Hospital, Tilehurst, Reading, near his daughter, on 22 January 1977, aged eighty-five. He was cremated in Reading and his ashes were scattered, as he had asked, above the village of Ingleton, in sight of the cottage where he was born. His widow survived him by only fourteen weeks. He left an estate of £19,872.

Writings: 'West Fulham's Lead for Sanity', *London News* (May 1938) 1; articles for Party journals.

Sources: (1) MS: London Labour Party archives, Herbert Morrison House, London. (2) Other: C.L. Mowat, *Britain between the Wars* (1955); R. Heller, 'East Fulham revisited', *J. Cont. Hist.* 6, no. 3 (1971) 172–6; B. Donoughue and G.W. Jones, *Herbert Morrison* (1973); personal information: Miss J.H. Atkinson, daughter, Reading; Mrs M.H. Gibb, OBE, Cambo, Morpeth; Mrs Lucy Middleton, London; the late Rt. Hon. Lady Summerskill; R. Stanton, Walton on Naze, Essex; Miss Grace Tavener, London. The editors wish to acknowledge an earlier draft from Miss J.H. Atkinson on which this entry has been based.

JOHN SAVILLE

BARMBY, Catherine Isabella (1817?–53) and **BARMBY, John [Goodwin] Goodwyn** (1820–81)
CHARTISTS, FEMINISTS AND UTOPIAN SOCIALISTS

J.G. Barmby was born in 1820 at The Vines, Yoxford, Suffolk, the only son of John and Julia Barmby. He was christened, on 12 November, John Goodwin, but throughout his adult life preferred to call himself Goodwyn. His father, described as an Attorney at Law died in 1834, leaving Goodwyn, apparently, very much his own master. He attended no school and spoke of his boyhood having been spent roaming the fields and reading poetry. He seems to have modelled himself on Shelley, and was an omnivorous reader and a prolific writer. At seventeen he wrote a long poem, *The Madhouse*, but it cannot be claimed that any of his poetry has any particular merit. Suggested careers in the Church, in law and in medicine were early rejected.

While still in his teens he was attracted by both Owenism and Chartism, and the *Dictionary of National Biography* refers to him as addressing agricultural workers at the age of sixteen, though details of his activities only begin to appear in the local press (especially in the *Suffolk*

Chronicle) a couple of years later. The part of Suffolk in which he lived was one of the comparatively few rural areas in which Chartism made a substantial impact. On 23 November 1838 a meeting of a thousand people is reported at the village of Friston, leading to the formation of an East Suffolk Working Men's Association. On the Boxing Day following four thousand assembled on Carlton Green near Saxmundham, many marching in from surrounding villages. It is likely that Barmby had a hand in all this, and when an East Suffolk and Yarmouth Chartist Council was formed in September 1839 he claimed, with a characteristic absence of false modesty, 'all the credit due' for this achievement. In December the Council unanimously elected him as its delegate to 'the Convention at Newcastle, or any other Convention hereafter to be assembled'. In April 1841 he was similarly elected at a meeting of the National Charter Association in Ipswich. There is some uncertainty here. Barmby himself claimed to have attended a Chartist Convention, though he does not say which. Yet his name does not appear in any list of delegates nor any report of proceedings. On the other hand it does appear among twelve signatories to the Manifesto issued after the Convention held at Manchester in July 1840 at which the NCA was set up.

In June 1840 Barmby went to Paris with a letter of introduction from Robert Owen. He moved in radical circles and almost certainly met Étienne Cabet and possibly William Weitling. In the letters published in the *New Moral World* (1 Aug and 12 Dec 1840) he used for the first time in English the equivalents of a new French vocabulary: communist, communism, communitarian, communitarianism [Bestor (1948) 280]. When he returned to England he was still an enthusiastic Owenite. He published in the *New Moral World* (10 Oct 1840) a poem about a visit to Tytherley, and he further contributed articles on literature and drama, and on language reform – he was to be a keen advocate of a universal language. He also published at this time a critique of Fourier's system which he compared unfavourably to that of Owen; and although he soon ceased to regard himself as an Owenite occasional contributions continued to the *New Moral World*.

From 1841 he was living largely in London, with an address at 2 Wyndham Street, Bryanston Square, but continued references in the local press suggest that he spent a good deal of time in Suffolk where he still had his Yoxford house. In June 1841, at a meeting of the Ipswich NCA he was chosen as prospective Chartist candidate for the forthcoming election, being described as a 'moral-force, sensible Chartist' and 'the sweet little Suffolk poet.' However, he did not appear, even as a demonstrative candidate on the hustings at the election in the following month, and there is no further mention of him as a personality in Suffolk Chartism. He did not break with his old associates nor formally repudiate his political ideas but he was by now immersed in millenarian activity. Communism was to be the salvation of the world: a body of advanced ideas to be realised in sectarian communities.

On 13 October 1841 he formed the Central Communist Propaganda Society. The council of the Society met on 3 November to establish the Universal Communitarian Association which was to operate, at least initially, through five groups: London, Cheltenham, Ipswich, Merthyr Tydfil and Strabane, in Ireland. Barmby was chairman, Thomas Heaviside secretary and George Bird treasurer. The first periodical to appear, in November 1841, was the *Educational Circular and Communist Apostle*, edited by Henry Fry from Cheltenham and published in London by John Cleave and William Lovett. Its 'guaranteed' circulation was one thousand copies. The main article in the first issue was the 'Document on Marriage in the New Common World'. It was an important statement of principle, typical of the social millenarian writing of this period, with marked affinities to Owen's *Lectures on the Marriages of the Priesthood of the old Immoral World*. Barmby's 'Document' was an interesting essay in utopian thinking, from which he made 'the following practical deductions':

I. That from the education of the girl and boy in common, love will develope itself gradually and not pruriently, and that therefore marriages will become sacred and the children produced by them more perfectly generated than now.

II. That from the education of the married in infancy and youth together; from the fact of their being architectured entirely by love priorly recognized in each other during that education, and from the general arrangements of communization, marriages will be more permanent in the New Common World, and the promiscuity so frequently manifested in the old individualized world altogether unknown.

III. That from the facility of divorce if required, family quarrels will be ended and their unhealthy influence unfelt by children, and that from this facility of divorce, and from the prior education, and marriage for love of the communitarians, the married persons will be less likely to disagree than they would with the knowledge that they should be compelled to remain together during life [*Educational Circular and Communist Apostle* (Nov 1841) p.5].

In November 1841 Barmby came of age, and, presumably, now had full control of his inheritance. At any rate, from this date there seems to be an extension of his activities as well as a growing tendency to dominate, and to strike messianic attitudes. One sign of this was his adoption of the new Communist Calendar, in which 1841 became Year One. Another was his adoption of the form 'We' when speaking in the first person.

In January 1842 there was published the first number of the *Promethean; or Communitarian Apostle*. This was a substantial sixpenny monthly, almost entirely written by Barmby himself. Its contents illustrated his readiness to pontificate on almost any subject. They include not only 'The Outlines of Communism' in four parts, and 'Studies in Industrial Organisation' in three parts, but also 'An Essay Towards Philanthropic Philology', 'The Past, Present, and Future of the Stage' (two parts), 'The Amelioration of Climature in Communalization', 'Past, Present, and Future Chronology, an Introduction to the Communist Calendar', and 'Floral Accordancies, or a Companion Chapter to the "Language of Flowers"'. There were also several contributions from Salvador St Just of Vines Villa, Yoxford, who can hardly be anyone but Barmby himself. The *Promethean* also contains a programmatic document in the form of a list of forty-four 'Societarian Wants'. The first ten of these will give an adequate idea of Barmby's general standpoint:

> 1. Community of sentiment, labour and property. 2. Abbreviation of manual labour by machinery. 3. Organisation of Industry in general and particular functions. 4. Unitary architecture of habitation. 5. The Marriage of the city and country. 6. Economy through combination in domestics. 7. Love through universality in ecclesiastics. 8. Order through justice or abstract mathematics in politics. 9. Medicinally prepared diet. 10. Common or contemporaneous consumption of food.

After three monthly issues it was announced that the *Promethean* would in future appear as a shilling quarterly. Barmby explained with engaging candour that this was 'First, because we are engaged in perfecting the general view of our doctrine and system. Second, because the *Promethean* has not a sufficient sale; and Third, because we require some country air.' In June the magazine appeared for the first and last time in its new form.

In March 1842 Barmby was lecturing in the 'Communist Temple' at the Circus, Marylebone, on his theory of a community; and in the May issue of the *Educational Circular* he announced the proposed foundation of a 'Communitorium'. This was established in the following year, in a house at Hanwell. He had apparently already had some previous contact with James Pierrepoint Greaves of the Ham Common Concordium, and his own community – the Moreville Communitorium – strictly vegetarian and teetotal, was to be especially concerned with adult education, industrial training, and with 'juvenile education for both sexes' [Armytage (1961) 199]. The Communitorium was run jointly by Goodwyn Barmby and his wife Catherine (née Watkins) whom he had married on 4 October 1841 at Marylebone. She was about three years his senior and already a feminist and a socialist, well known to readers of the

New Moral World under the pen-name Kate. Her essay 'Female Improvement' [*NMW*, 13 June 1835] was a standard feminist argument for legal and educational equality, but a longer article in the issue for 25 May 1839 offered a more sophisticated insight into Owenite theories of psychology and education. Her writing style was vigorous and unadorned by comparison with that of Barmby's, and her essays were sprinkled with quotations from the Romantic poets, especially Shelley. She wrote some poetry herself, with indifferent results, if we may judge from some awkward verses she contributed to the *Gazette* of the Whittington Club in November 1849. Catherine Barmby followed her husband in and out of his different political and religious ventures, and she was a regular contributor to his publications. Her most ambitious essay 'The Demand for the Emancipation of Women, Politically and Socially' appeared as No. 3 of Barmby's pamphlet series, *New Tracts for the Times*. The *Tracts* were re-issued as part I of the *Communist Miscellany*, which included as part II the six issues of the *Educational Circular and Communist Apostle*.

Catherine Barmby's pamphlet was an eloquent statement for what she described as the 'total emancipation of woman': under three main headings. Political freedom could only be realised through universal suffrage, on the 'no taxation without representation' argument; and to the clauses of the People's Charter must be added general female suffrage, thus linking together the electoral rights of woman and man. Ecclesiastical freedom, the second main heading, involved the entry of women into the priesthood, but much more it meant a transformation in the social thinking of women themselves about themselves. Catherine Barmby does not phrase the matter in these words, but she was certainly centrally concerned with what modern feminists would describe as 'consciousness-raising'. The means for effecting the ecclesiastical emancipation of women 'appear to us' she wrote 'to consist in the formation of a "women's society" in every city, town, and village possible. In this society women might converse, discuss, and speak upon their rights, their wrongs, and their destiny; they might consult upon their own welfare, and that of the great human family, and thus prepare each other for the mission of the apostle in society at large, and for the right use of that influence which they must ever exercise'. The third area of emancipation – domestic – rested upon the economic independence of woman so that she would be free from 'mere household drudgery' and the tyranny of the husband. Catherine Barmby developed her ideas at some length about economic or 'industrial' independence in a later article in the *Apostle* which is reprinted in a special note below. She concluded the general argument in her pamphlet by emphasising the ways in which woman was not only oppressed by political institutions: 'she is also the serf of social regulations. Custom, even in her dress, tyrannises over her throughout all countries . . . This must not be in the future. The free woman must be adorned with a new dress; uniting freedom and delicacy, utility and grace. The emancipation of woman from the garb of her slavery will be the outward sign of her liberty' [pp. 38–9].

The same year that the Barmbys established the Moreville Communitorium a new paper was published, the *Communist Chronicle*, a threepenny weekly, noteworthy for the attention given to William Weitling's ideas. Weitling himself came to London in the summer of 1844. Barmby converted the Communitorium into a Communist Church and about this time was making contact with a group of 'White' Quakers in Dublin, led by Joshua Jacob and Abigail Beale. Jacob had been disowned by the Quaker meeting in Dublin in 1838, and had founded his sect in 1843. Barmby's first visit to them was in that year, and by the later 1840s the community numbered thirty persons, including children [*Howitt's J.*, 18 Sep 1847]. *Some Account of the Progress of Truth as it is in Jesus* (1843) gives at length the correspondence and statements between Barmby and the White Quakers during the first year of their encounter.

Early in 1845 Barmby began his collaboration with Thomas Frost, whose *Forty Years' Recollections* give the most intimate and detailed picture of Barmby which we have of his Utopian period. It must be remembered, however, that Frost was writing long after the events described and that their association ended with a bitter quarrel. Frost was a young man of Barmby's age and a similar history, who came from a middle-class background into the Chartist and Utopian movements. He was for a time at the Ham Common Concordium and had attempted, without success, to form a community of his own. He then planned a journal to cover all the activities of the socialist and communist groups. When he met Barmby they decided to re-start the defunct *Communist Chronicle* as a penny weekly. It was published by Hetherington.

Frost seems to have been impressed by Barmby's erudition and drive. He wrote: 'I found him a young man of gentlemanly manners and soft persuasive voice, wearing his light brown hair parted in the middle after the fashion of the Concordist brethren, and a collar and tie *à la Byron*.', (p. 57). Barmby was 'conversant with the whole range of Utopian literature' and he 'blended with the Communistic theory of society the pantheistic views of Spinoza, of which Shelley is in this country the best known exponent.'

The *Communist Chronicle* published as a serial Barmby's utopian romance *The Book of Platonopolis*, of which Frost wrote 'all that has been imagined by Plato, More, Bacon and Campanella, is reproduced, and combined with all that modern science has effected or essayed for lessening human toil or promoting human enjoyment.' Another feature was the prominence given to reports of revolutionary movements abroad, where information probably obtained from correspondents drawn from Weitling's European contacts, was put to good use. Late in 1845 and early in 1846 Barmby made a series of propaganda tours in the Midlands and North, forming branches of the Communist Church and sending back enthusiastic reports of successful meetings and the effect his lectures would have in increasing the circulation of the *Chronicle*. But no increase took place and his relations with Frost, who claimed to have met the costs of its publication, became increasingly unhappy. Frost commented: 'Neither in politics nor in religion were we in accord. He advocated the paternal system of government, I the democratic.' 'Neither democracy nor aristocracy', he wrote, 'have anything to do with Communism. They are party terms of the present. In future Governmental politics will be succeeded by industrial administration' [p. 71].

Frost had proposed starting a paper of his own, to be called the *Communist Journal*. He 'wished it to be conducted on broad unsectarian principles.' But Barmby 'regarded the title which I had chosen as an infringement of his copyright, and forbade me its use in a highly characteristic document, sealed with a seal of portentous size, engraved with masonic symbols, in green wax, green being the sacred colour of the Communist Church.' [p. 74]. Neither the *Journal* nor the *Chronicle* long survived this break between them.

The lack of a journal of his own was to some extent made up for by *Howitt's Journal*, to which Barmby now became a frequent contributor. In 1847 he was lecturing in Poplar and at the Farringdon Hall. In July he was one of the convenors of a meeting in the Literary Institute, John Street, to organise support for Cabet's attempt to found an Icarian settlement in Texas. The Communist Church continued to exist, with only minimal support. When the revolution of 1848 broke out Barmby went to Paris as its representative as well as a correspondent for *Howitt's Journal*.

Before leaving he had convened a communist conference at the Farringdon Hall, which he addressed on his return. Delegates from a varity of utopian organisations attended and passed a resolution demanding that the Government restore the church land taken by Henry VIII and use it for the founding of communisteries. This marked the end of Barmby's communist period. He had always been liable to abrupt changes of direction and was perhaps disillusioned by the failure of the 1848 revolutions. His move away from millenarianism coincided with the virtual demise of political millenarianism in Britain. He was not yet thirty.

Barmby now became a Unitarian minister, perhaps influenced by W.J. Fox, the anti-Corn Law orator, an old friend and a Suffolk man like himself. After short ministries at Southampton, Topsham, Lympstone and Lancaster, he went to Wakefield in 1858. There he remained politically active, if in a more orthodox style. He had been a member of the Council of Mazzini's International League and took part in movements in defence of Polish, Italian, and Hungarian liberation. He also seems to have joined the National Society for Women's Suffrage in the 1860s. Barmby took an active part in local affairs and politics in Wakefield. When Wakefield Liberal Association was founded in 1859, he was appointed chairman of the North Westgate ward committee; and in 1860 he was chairman of the full committee of the Association. He was also active in the Mechanics' Institute movement; founded and led the Band of Faith, a Unitarian religious order, and his Wakefield congregation included some interesting personalities: Thomas Todd, the Dewsbury Chartist and oil miller; Daniel Gaskell, Liberal MP for Wakefield in the 1830s, later friend of Kossuth and supporter of the infant educational reformer Samuel Wilderspin; and Henry Briggs, who with his sons introduced the principle of profit-sharing into manufacturing enterprise.

Barmby became well known in the Unitarian denomination. For several years he held the office of secretary of the West Riding Unitarian Mission, and he was always an ardent advocate of Unitarian missionary efforts. He wrote a number of Unitarian tracts, and was a regular attender at the annual meetings of the British and Foreign Unitarian Association. In 1867 Barmby organised a large public meeting to support the demand for parliamentary reform. From time to time he contributed to *Howitt's Journal*, the *People's Journal*, and other periodicals. In 1879 his health broke down and he retired to the house at Yoxford in which he was born. Here he died on 18 October 1881 and was buried at Framlingham. He left an estate valued at £1219.

Catherine Barmby died on 26 December 1853 aged thirty-six. She had one son named Morrville [which might have been spelt Moreville] Watkyns, born 27 April 1844 and a daughter, Maria Julia, born on 3 July 1846 and who died at the age of eighty-three in the summer of 1930 at Honiton, in Devonshire. Goodwyn married again on 30 July 1861. His wife was Ada Marianne Shepherd whose father was governor of the Wakefield gaol, and they also had a daughter, Mabel Katherine, who was born at Wakefield on 9 May 1865. Ada was living at Mount Pleasant, Sidmouth, Devonshire where she died on 5 February 1911. Probate was granted to the two half-sisters on effects valued at £2832. The younger daughter Mabel died at Honiton in the first quarter of 1945.

Writings: In addition to his editorial work, J.G. Barmby was a prolific writer of tracts, hymns, poems and periodical articles. A selection of his principal writings are given here; works by his first wife, Catherine, are also listed in addition to her article reprinted below. **J.G. Barmby:** *The Madhouse: a poem* (1839; repr. 1842); 'Journal of a Social Mission to France' [cont. as 'French Correspondence'], *New Moral World*, 11, 25 July, 1, 22 Aug 1840; 'Biographical Sketch of St. Simon', ibid., 3 Oct 1840; 'Queries on Fourierism' [letter], ibid., 21 Nov 1840; 'Inferiority of Fourier's Classification of Society', ibid., 5 Dec 1840; 'Mr Barmby's Reply on Fourierism' [letter], 12 Dec 1840; 'High-Church Socialism, or corrupted St Simonism', ibid., 23 Jan 1841; 'On what is Fourierism' [letter], ibid., 6 Mar 1841; 'French Report', ibid., 20 Mar 1841; 'An Essay towards Philanthropic Philology', ibid., 3 Apr 1841; 'The Man-power, the Woman-power, and the Woman-man-power', ibid., 1 May 1841; 'Select Translations from the Works of Charles Fourier', ibid., 12 June 1841; (with others), 'Declaration in Favour of Electoral Reform', ibid., 17 July 1841; *The Outlines of Communism, Associality and Communization* (1841) P; editor of the *Communist Miscellany* [1841–2?] which was in two parts. The first, *New Tracts for the Times* in which *inter alia* Barmby wrote 'The Best and Only True Way of gaining the People's Charter', *1*, no. 4 n.d. pp. 41–6 and the second, six issues of the *Educational Circular and Communist Apostle* in one of which he published 'Document on Marriage in the New Common World', no.1 n.s. (Nov 1841) 3–6; editor of the *Promethean; or Communitarian Apostle* (1842); various epistles and letters in *Some Account of the Progress of Truth as it is in Jesus* ed. J. Jacob (1843) [copy in Library of Religious Society of Friends, London which also has two handbills in Barmby's name: *A Testimony against the Parson-Class* and *A Testimony against the Trader-Class* (both undated)]; 'Military Agricultural Colonies', *People's J. 3* (1847) 31; 'Woe of Erin' [poem on Irish Famine], ibid., 82; 'The Recent American Communities', ibid., 196–8; 'Defence of Communism, on Religion, Family, Country, Property and Government in answer to Joseph Mazzini', ibid., 283–4; 'Emerson and his Writings', *Howitt's J. 2* (1847) 315–16; 'Letters from Paris' in ibid. *3* (1848) the details of which are: 'The Paris of the Revolution', 210–11, 'The Placards of Paris', 247–8, 'The Elections in France', 248–50, 'The Organisation of Industry', 267–9, 'The Pamphlets of Paris', 269–70, 'The Clubs of Paris', 300–2; *Hymns for Special Services and Missionary Use* (Wakefield, 1849); *The Poetry of Childhood* (1852) 29; *The Poetry of Home* (1853) 52 pp.; editor of *Special Services of Public Worship: for the use of the Churches of Christ* (Wakefield, 1859) 26 pp.; *The Return of the Swallow and Other Poems* (1864); *Aids to Devotion* (1865). He also contributed to the *Band of Hope Messenger* (1872).

Catherine Barmby: 'Female Improvement', *New Moral World*, 13 June 1835; 'Man's Legislation', ibid., 25 May 1839 [both articles signed 'Kate']; 'Invocation', *Educational Circular*, no. 4 n.s. (Feb 1842) 27; 'The Universal Communitarian Society' ibid., no. 6 n.s. (May 1842) 45–6; 'The Demand for the Emancipation of Woman, politically and socially', *New Tracts for the Times 1*, no. 3 [1841–2?] 33–40; 'Woman and Domestics', *People's J. 3* (1847) 37–8; 'Woman's Industrial Independence', *Apostle and Chronicle of the Communist Church 1*, no. 1, 1 Aug 1848, reprinted below.

Sources: (1) MS: Glyde Coll., Ipswich PL; ms. notes by Barmby in *The Communism of Christianity* n.d. and *The New Revelations of the Paraclete* (1856), copies in Dr Williams's Library, London. (2) Other: 'A Young Socialist', 'Remarks on Fourier's System' [letter], *New Moral World*, 28 Nov 1840; 'A Phalansterian', 'Reply to Mr Barmby's letter "On what is called Fourierism"', ibid., 1 May 1841; 'Amo', 'Mr. Barmby – "Phalansterianism"', ibid., 15 May 1841; idem, 'Mr Barmby and the Giants', ibid., 29 May 1841; Anon., 'A Day with the White Quakers', *Howitt's J. 2*, no. 38, 18 Sep 1847; *Examiner*, 30 Nov 1850; G.J. Holyoake, *The History of Co-operation in England*, vol. *1* (1875); T. Frost, *Forty Years' Recollections* (1880); *Boase 1* (1892); *DNB 1* [by W.E.A. Axon]; A.E. Bestor, jr., 'The Evolution of the Socialist Vocabulary', *J. of the History of Ideas 9*, no. 3 (June 1948) 259–302; H. Fearn, 'Chartism in Suffolk' (Sheffield MA, 1952); A.L. Morton, *The English Utopia* (1952); A.F.J. Brown, 'Working Class Movements in the Countryside, 1790–1850', *Amateur Historian, 3*, no. 2 (winter 1956/7) 49–54; W.H.G. Armytage, 'The Journalistic Activities of J. Goodwyn Barmby between 1841 and 1848', *Notes and Queries 201* (Apr 1956) 166–9; idem, *Heavens below: Utopian experiments in England 1560–1960* (1961); biographical information: Gail Malmgreen, Indiana State Univ.; Barbara Taylor, London: E. Frow, Manchester; J. Goodchild, archivist, Wakefield Metropolitan District Council; Library of the Religious Society of Friends, London; Dr Williams's Library, London. Obit. *Unitarian Herald*, 28 Oct and 11 Nov 1881; *Inquirer*, 11 Nov 1881.

A.L. Morton
John Saville

See also: Robert Owen; and below: Woman's Industrial Independence (1848; reprinted).

Woman's Industrial Independence by Catherine Barmby (repr. from the *Apostle and Chronicle of the Communist Church 1*, no.1, 1 Aug 1848)

The greatest want of woman is industrial independence. Our protestation is that throughout the world woman, in her industrial relations, is wrongly placed. We deem that industrial independence is, at least, as necessary for woman as for man. Until assured the means of living as the result of her independent labour, woman must ever continue a slave. While she is unable to obtain employment, it is not possible for her to be free. When industrial occupations which obtain remuneration are refused her, whether through prejudice, or the sharp-set severity of competition, she is ever exposed to the misery of bargaining herself for bread. Unless indeed woman is secured independence by her own industry Magdalene Asylums will increase, but still remain as now, entirely inefficacious in curing the disease, which they are benevolently, but not very wisely, instructed to remedy.

The subject of woman's industrial relations is involved in many apparent contradictions on the page of history. According to date or country, she presents herself in different employments. In no chronological or geographical position do we find her, however, entirely in that condition of industrial independency in which she should be placed. Among savage tribes she is portioned the drudgery of house, and of maize-plot, and even carries the canoe or arows [*sic*] of her husband, who reserves himself in idleness, except for the hunt or the fight. As the soft slave of the seraglio, her position may seem lighter, but consider the confinement, the monotony, the drudgery on dress, and recollect also, that in the harem there is still dependency – no enfranchisement through work – no independence by industry.

As a dweller in Christian countries is woman's condition improved? I fear, to the present time, but little. Change there has been, some for the better, but much has also taken place for the worse. Formerly, in savage life, man forced woman to do the drudgery of existence, now, in civilised society he competes with her in the commercial market; and in many departments of work forbids her a chance of industrial occupation. As also in feudal times leech-craft was valued in woman, and she was often the only surgeon of the wounded, and the sole doctor of the sick, so in later centuries even the exercise of midwifery is forbidden – so far as social convention is concerned, – to her who is in herself maternity, and therefore the fittest, as well as the most delicate agent to assist at the mother's couch. In fact comparisons are not all in favour of civilisation with regard to woman. To farther follow them, however, would extend our present paper beyond its intended limits.

Our chief aim is to point out that in the present competitive social state, the industry of woman is not independent, but in wrong relations. Competition itself places man in an antagonistic position to woman in the labour market. Even in departments of industry which are peculiarly adapted to her sex does man deprive woman of a chance of work. Not only in midwifery is this the case. Look at our drapery and haberdashery shops filled with effeminate young men, whose hands would be better employed with the spade or the plough than in winding up ribbons, sorting out silks, and thus preventing women from supplying their own sex with articles for their own wear. Recollect the many other instances of similar cases which might be adduced.

What then is the combined effect of all this? It is to "crib, cabin and confine" the industry of woman, and thus to destroy her independence through life. In the majority of cases it is to compel her as a daughter to remain at home, subsisting upon the support of her parents, or to enter into the sad slavery of domestic servitude. It is in most instances to force her to seek in a marriage, often without love, a fancied emancipation as to the reality of which she is too soon undeceived by experience. As a wife the isolation of domestic life, and that infinite division and parcelment which now prevails in affairs that only require combination and system to make them agreeable and easy, introduce her chiefly to household drudgery alone and the constant care of children. But too generally for food, for lodging, for raiment, she is entirely dependent upon the industry of her husband. Her industry, however toilsome it may be, gives her no independence. If she disagrees with her husband she has no legitimate resource. Their quarrels increase; they may perhaps separate, although divorce at present is not permitted to the poor. If she separate, however, what then is her chance of industrial independence? It is but little. Few are Mary Wolstonecraft's [*sic*]; few can write like George Sand. Man, moreover, has monopolised the labour market; or such departments as may be distasteful to her are only open. What then is often her end? Prostitution or suicide!

Is there no remedy for this? We who are friends of associative arrangements have of course one in view. Something better even in the present state could without doubt be effected for woman, – we wish it God-speed!

Under associative arrangements only, however, can woman's independence by industry be generally and fully guaranteed, as in association only can household drudgery be lessened, and the care of children rendered light. In the communitive life, with its associative household, with its common nursery, and with its organisation of industry adapted for both sexes, can woman's independence only be completely secured, and those injustices removed that now cause her misery, or now seduce her to crime. Let woman therefore assist in hailing the morning light of a better state of society.

BARKER, Henry Alfred (1858-1940)
SOCIALIST

Henry Alfred Barker was born on 25 February 1858 in Leonard Street, Shoreditch. His father, Charles Barker, who came originally from Colchester, was a self-employed builder and decorator and vestryman at St Leonard's, Shoreditch, and his mother Jane (née Selfe) came from a long-established farming family in Wiltshire. After an elementary education at St John's School in the neighbouring parish of Hoxton, Barker joined his father and brothers in the family business when he was fourteen.

His interest in progressive social movements developed in his late teens and he began to take part in open-air meetings, often speaking from a platform at the junction of Old Street and Curtain Road. During these years and in the early 1880s, he attended classes on hygiene and sanitation given by A.T. Burgess at the Regent Street Polytechnic, principally to improve the technical aspects of his work. He also attended classes on science at the National Secular Society's Hall of Science; these included classes on physiology given by Dr Edward Aveling. Subsequently he was awarded certificates in animal physiology by the Society, in 1882, 1883 and 1884, and he went on to teach a physiology evening class at St Mark's School, where Annie Besant was also a lecturer, in psychology. He continued with his studies especially in sanitary science and obtained an advanced certificate in hygiene in 1893.

It is probable that Barker became a member of the Hoxton Labour Emancipation League in 1885. The League, founded at the end of 1881 by Joseph Lane, Frank Kitz and others, was the first Socialist organisation in London with any real influence; and the Hoxton branch was to become a lively centre. The LEL sent delegates to the annual conference of the Democratic Federation at the beginning of August 1884; and among the decisions then taken were a change of name to Social Democratic Federation and an affiliation of the Labour Emancipation League to the new SDF. When the split within the SDF became irrevocable at the end of 1884, the leaders of the LEL and the majority of the membership went with Morris and the Socialist League. During 1886 Barker was secretary of the Hoxton branch and became an active outdoor campaigner as well as an indoor lecturer. Among the subjects he lectured on were 'The Poor's House', based on the evidence presented to the R.C. on the Housing of the Working Classes (1884-5), and 'Spiritual Consolation and Material Satisfaction'.

He was becoming well known in London labour and Socialist circles and on 20 December 1886 was elected national secretary of the Socialist League, a position he held until he resigned in May 1888. His immediate successor was Fred Slaughter of Norwich but in December of that year Frank Kitz, of the Merton Abbey branch, took over. During his association with the SL, Barker wrote and performed, with his sister Rose and his brothers, 'The Lamp: an extravaganza' to raise funds for the League. This was presented first during the Christmas period of 1887, and on several occasions early in 1888 at the Socialist League HQ in Farringdon Road. It was, evidently, successful.

Barker, as an official of the Socialist League, was involved in all the main public demonstrations during 1887. He was especially active in the Free Speech agitation. In May 1887, for example, at an anti-Coercion meeting in Victoria Park, Barker introduced the resolutions from the League platform, proposed by William Morris, seconded by Bernard Shaw, and spoken to by Joseph Lane and Sam Mainwaring. In October of the same year he helped to organise a public meeting at South Place Institute, to protest against the recent arrest of the Chicago anarchists, and to re-affirm the principle of free speech, and for a period in 1888 he managed *Commonweal*. But he disagreed with the attitude to be taken towards Parliament and parliamentary action – of central concern in the internal politics of the SL at this time – and he began in 1888 to dissociate himself from the work of the League. But throughout the debates and discussions Barker continued to address meetings of the Hoxton LEL and in November 1888 he addressed a Victoria Park rally to commemorate 'Bloody Sunday'.

This change in Barker's attitude towards the League was most probably due to his involvement with J.L. Mahon in the formation in 1888 of the Labour Union, the object of which was to unite workers of independent views. Only three months after his resignation from the secretaryship of the SL, Barker was joint secretary with Mahon of an organising committee of the Labour Union, with Thomas Binning as treasurer and seven other members including Robert Banner and A.K. Donald (formerly financial secretary of the SL). In August 1888 a circular letter was sent out which requested names of likely supporters and also financial help [Barker papers, BAR 3/1]. By 1889 the Labour Union was established and to a general statement of aims was added a series of immediate reforms, including Irish Home Rule, adult suffrage, triennial parliaments, payment of MPs, the eight hour day and the abolition of the House of Lords. A later version (August 1889) included Home Rule for Scotland and Wales. The central purpose of the Labour Union was stated to be the formation of a national independent political Labour Party; and the organising committee included former Socialist Leaguers who could no longer accept the anarchist influence in the League [Thompson (1955) 615–16].

In January 1889 Barker stood as a Labour Union candidate for the Hoxton division of Shoreditch in the first LCC election, but polled only 169 votes. He did, however, become a regular attender at the LCC, and contributed articles describing his impressions to the *Illustrated Weekly News* which he had helped to found under its first title of *Police and Public* in July 1889; (the name was changed on 21 Sep 1889, but the paper ceased publication three months later.) To this journal he contributed articles on a wide range of social questions. One of his main concerns was housing in the East End, and at one point he established a Fair Rents League to campaign against rapacious landlords. As a working builder his practical knowledge was a considerable asset. In 1892 he acted as agent for A.K. Donald when he contested Shoreditch for the Labour Union in the general election. In spite of an active campaign, including the circulation of pamphlets on the eight hour day, Donald polled only nineteen votes.

The political importance of the Labour Union at the end of the 1880s was not considerable, although it certainly had a nuisance value to William Morris and the Socialist League. But the Union's industrial record was disastrous. In September 1889 the Union made efforts to form an organisation of coal-porters, without success, and in October there was published the first issue of the *Postman's Gazette*. J.L. Mahon had become secretary of a Postmen's Union, with Binning, A.K. Donald and Barker among the executive. The Union, wrote the pioneer historian of the postal workers 'was hatched under the wing of the well-meaning but in this case misguided Labour Union leadership' [Swift (1900) 208]. A strike at the Mount Pleasant sorting office in London in July 1890 ended in total failure, with scores of workers being victimised. In the middle of 1890s Barker was active among London building trade unionists. He was chairman of the London District Organising Committee of the Amalgamated Society of House Decorators and Painters in 1893 which arranged meetings and demonstrations against 'Sweating Masters and Non-Unionist Painters' in parts of north and east London and, two years later, he offered himself as a candidate in the election for general secretary to the Amalgamated Society [Election Address of 8 May 1895, Barker papers, LP]. He was certainly on the EC as late as 1897 but in 1898 he was excluded from the Society for non-payment of a fine of £5 imposed by the EC on 21 October 1897 for bringing the Society into discredit and withdrawing £17 from the bank contrary to rule [ASHDP records]. In April 1896 he had been a delegate, on behalf of the London Building Trades Federation, to the London Labour Conciliation and Arbitration Board.

During the early 1890s the Labour Union actively supported the many attempts that were being made to found an independent Labour Party. Joseph Burgess, at this time editing the *Workman's Times* from London, and actively pursuing his campaign for labour independence, personally presided over the formation of the London ILP. This was on 13 June 1892, at a meeting at the Democratic Club in Essex Street. A provisional executive was elected, with Shaw Maxwell as secretary, and Barker and Tom McCarthy among its members. The first national conference at Bradford on 13 and 14 January 1893 was principally the result of the work of Burgess, Keir Hardie and W.H. Drew. Barker was one of the twelve delegates from London but it was a northern dominated affair: and Barker was wrong in a letter to the *Clarion* (8 Oct 1909) when he claimed 'that the North of London had as much, probably more, to do with the founding of the ILP than the North of England'. He himself, however, took a prominent part in the first discussion of the conference which concerned the name of the new party and it was his amendment – that its title should be the Independent Labour Party of Great Britain and Ireland – which was in the end accepted with the words 'Great Britain and Ireland' omitted [*Workman's Times*, 21 Jan 1893].

Barker continued to be active politically for many years, but he became increasingly afflicted with failing eyesight through iritis. He worked closely with Harry Quelch and Will Thorne during the preparations for the London Congress of the Second International, held during the last week of July 1896. As secretary of the Congress printing committee he organised all the literature for the 800 delegates, including programmes and agendas in three languages, and all the handbills and posters advertising the reception for Liebknecht and the Sunday demonstration.

From the time when Bruce Wallace established the Brotherhood Trust in January 1894 [Armytage (1961) 344], Barker was associated with the Brotherhood Church in Southgate Road, Islington. (He had been confirmed at the Congregational Chapel in Southgate Road before the Brotherhood Church was established there.) He was greatly influenced by Bruce Wallace and was a long-standing member of the Church Council and a trustee for some thirty years. When the First World War broke out Barker was greatly distressed at the political divisions which arose within the Brotherhood movement; at a time also when the Southgate Church came under violent attacks from jingoists and thugs. After the war he played a prominent part in its physical and spiritual regeneration. Many well-known personalities gave addresses and lectures – including Saklatvala and Maude Royden; and Maisky came to unveil a marble memorial commemorating the famous three-week congress of the Russian Social-Democrats held in the Church [Kendall (1969) 80–1]. The Southgate Road building, which had been erected in 1851, was demolished about 1934–5 and replaced by a factory.

Barker married Cecily Ruth (née Manning) in 1894. She had obtained a certificate in hygiene of the Department of Science and Art two years before. There were five children of the marriage, which was a happy one, his wife being an immense support to him during his periods of illness and increasing blindness. In his later life, too, one of his sons, Alfred, was a constant companion who shared his father's political outlook. Henry Barker loved walking, was a devoted follower of English cricket, and, outside politics, his main intellectual and emotional interest was poetry. His favourite authors were Shakespeare and William Blake, and he himself wrote much verse. He died on 12 January 1940 in Hackney Hospital in his eighty-second year. No will has been located.

Writings: 'Is the Miners' Union a Failure?', *Commonweal*, 10 Sep 1887; 'The Condition of the Working Classes', ibid., 3 Dec 1887; 'Free Combination', *Postman's Gazette 1,* no. 1 (Oct 1889) 1–2; 'The Rights of Labour', *Illustrated Weekly News, 1*, no. 12, 7 Dec 1889; 'Re the Origin ILP etc.' [letter], *Clarion*, 8 Oct 1909. It is likely that Barker wrote other articles, unsigned, in the *Illustrated Weekly News* and the Barker Coll. in the Labour Party archives contains miscellaneous writings by him. There is also some correspondence at the William Morris Gallery, Walthamstow, and in the Socialist League papers at the International Institute of Social History, Amsterdam.

Sources: (1) MS: ASHDP records, MRC; Barker papers, Labour Party archives; Socialist League archives, correspondence section K, IISH, Amsterdam; correspondence, Morris Coll. J 156, J 158, J 159, J 358–9, William Morris Gallery, Walthamstow; 'The G.O.M. of Socialism', ms. biography of H.A. Barker by his son, A.M. Barker [copy in *DLB* Coll.]. (2) Other: *Commonweal*, Mar 1886–Dec 1888; 'The Independent Labour Party: first general conference', *Workman's Times*, 21 Jan 1893; 'The International Socialist and Trade Union Congress', *Labour Annual* (1897) 69–75; H.G. Swift, *A History of Postal Agitation* (1900; rev. ed. 1929); H. Pelling, *The Origins of the Labour Party* (1954; rev. ed. 1965); E.P. Thompson, *William Morris* (1955; rev. ed. 1977); W.H.G. Armytage, *Heavens below* (1961); W.L. Arnstein, *The Bradlaugh Case* (1965); W.Kendall, *The Revolutionary Movement in Britain 1900–21: the origins of British Communism* (1969); E.D. Lemire, 'The Socialist League Leaflets and Manifestoes: an annotated checklist', *Int. Rev. Social Hist. 22*, pt 1 (1977) 21–9; biographical information: Greater London Record Office; R.A. Storey and C. Woodland, MRC, Warwick; S.C. Tongue, London Borough of Hackney Archives Department; personal information, A.M. Barker, Ballybunion, Kerry, Eire, son.

Barbara Nield
John Saville

BARTON, Alfred (1868-1933)

ANARCHIST, LATER LABOUR PARTY WORKER

Alfred Barton was born on 30 July 1868 at Kempston, Bedfordshire, the son of a foundry labourer, Henry Barton, and his wife Eliza (née Savill). Alfred Barton was largely self-educated; he became well-informed in philosophy and history, especially classical history, and had a reading knowledge of several languages. Little is known of his early days in Bedfordshire – his first job was in a public library at the age of twelve, and he left home around 1890 to go to Manchester. By this time he was already, evidently, a member of the Socialist League, with strong anarchist tendencies. He was first a clerk and then worked in Rylands Library. In 1894 he married Eleanor Stockton [see *DLB 1*].

Barton was very active in anarchist affairs in his Manchester years; and he was arrested on several occasions, mainly on the issue of free speech. He was prominent in the protest movement which followed the Walsall anarchist case, for which Joseph Deakin, among others, was sentenced to prison [see *DLB 3*, 58-62]. On the 17 April 1892 Barton, with David Nicoll, editor of *Commonweal*, Herbert Stockton and John Bingham addressed an audience of several thousand in Stevenson Square, Manchester, in protest against police provocation and the long sentences imposed on the defendants. Although of a very militant disposition Barton did not, however, belong to the extreme wing of the anarchist movement at this time. He wrote a revealing letter to *Commonweal* in July 1892 concerning the paper's support of the actions of François Ravachol [for which see Quail (1978) 140]. Barton ended his letter:

> . . . We do not want any English Ravachols in the sense of men who are ready to commit such actions; we do not wish to make Anarchy – which should be synonymous with peace, love and harmony – another word for bloodshed and violence. It is true, conditions often

> force such action upon us, but in that case it is an unfortunate necessity, not a matter for satisfaction. No doubt deeds speak louder than words, but the deeds should have some humanity and heroism about them. The true Anarchist is he who is as gentle and humane in all his dealings with others, as is consistent with a fierce and unflinching resistance to authority and oppression in every form [9 July 1892].

The Bartons moved to Sheffield in about 1897 (and not about 1894 as is stated in Eleanor Barton's biography [*DLB 1*, 38]). Barton took a commercial post and quickly became involved in the labour movement. He joined the ILP and made a name for himself as the 'Monolith Orator'. He was vigorously opposed to the Boer War, spoke constantly in public on anti-war platforms and faced bitter hostility. 'I have been mobbed again and again' he wrote later of this period [*Sheffield Guardian*, 25 Oct 1907]; and according to the same article it was about this time that he began to move away from his anarchism to more orthodox political trade union agitation and organisation.

Barton had several jobs in Sheffield, but it was as a member of the Shop Assistants' Union that he became a delegate to the Sheffield Federated Trades Council (SFTC), a Lib-Lab body in which in the early years of the century the ILP were playing an increasingly active role. The SFTC was dominated by representatives of the traditional Sheffield small workshop trades. Although the SFTC affiliated early to the national Labour Representation Committee, it proved reluctant to establish a local LRC in Sheffield, preferring to rely upon its own 'electoral committee' through which trade union Liberals had become elected to local authorities. But in 1903 it finally gave way to national and local pressures and convened a Sheffield Conference, addressed by J.R. MacDonald and G.N. Barnes, out of which emerged a Sheffield LRC with a deliberately vague constitution. Henceforth the political struggles between the Lib-Labs and the Socialists were to centre upon the local LRC. The story is told in detail in the *Sheffield Trades and Labour Council 1858–1958* [ed. Mendelson et al. (1958)]. The conflict was resolved with the exclusion of the SFTC from the Sheffield LRC, and henceforth Sheffield had two Trades Councils, a situation which lasted until 1920.

Alf Barton, as one of the leading Socialists in the city, had taken a full part in these internal dissensions; but he had also continued his active part in the development of the ILP as a political force. In 1905 he and others reorganised the branches of the ILP in Sheffield on a centralised basis, and a weekly paper was brought out, the *Sheffield Guardian*. The following year Barton became assistant secretary to the party, and in 1907 secretary, when he also gave up his job to take on the editorship of the *Guardian* whose financial fortunes were at a low ebb. There were factions within the ILP, and Barton was strongly identified with what was known as the 'SDF clique'. In the next few years he was involved in increasingly acrimonious disputes within the ILP which began to centre around Joe Pointer, following the latter's parliamentary election for the Attercliffe division in April 1909 [see *DLB*, *2*, 302]. Majority opinion inside the ILP was on Pointer's side, and in January 1911 Barton resigned both the editorship of the *Guardian* and his membership of the ILP. When the inaugural meeting of the Sheffield branch of the British Socialist Party took place in September 1911, Barton became vice-president. In the same year he published a pamphlet, *The Universal Strike*, which called for a general strike to achieve the 'Co-operative Commonwealth' [*Clarion*, 17 Nov 1911]. About this time he became an insurance agent, a job which gave him plenty of free time and wide contact with working people.

In local politics, Barton first contested Hillsborough ward (where he lived) in 1906 and was returned for Brightside ward in 1907. He lost the seat on standing for re-election in 1910, and the Labour Party refused to endorse another candidature in Brightside in 1911. He was forced to run as a Socialist candidate in Heeley ward, where he was defeated. The following year he demanded his old seat back with such vehemence that the official Labour candidate withdrew. He lost again, but was returned for Brightside in 1913, unendorsed by the Trades Council, but unofficially supported by many trades unions. Because of the suspension of municipal elections during the war he served from 1913 to 1920, and became a Labour Party councillor officially again in July 1914 when the BSP affiliated to the Trades Council. Barton as a city councillor was the scourge of both Liberals and Conservatives. He was a skilled filibuster and indifferent to the hatred he provoked through his tactics. It was the only means, he argued, by which Labour could put forward its policies, particularly on housing and unemployment, at a time when there were only two Labour councillors. In 1914 Barton was nominated unsuccessfully for the late Joe Pointer's parliamentary seat.

Unlike the Sheffield ILP, which was pacifist during the First World War, Barton was in favour of military intervention. In *The War: how it was made, who shall profit by it?* he argued that the war was an economic one for supremacy between capitalist states in which the workers of all the nations could have no interest. But since the capitalism of Germany ('Kaiserism') was 'hardened by Militarism' while Britain's was 'tempered by Democracy', the German system must be opposed.

At the 1918 general election Barton ran as Labour candidate for Park constituency, receiving 20.4 per cent of the poll. In 1920 he briefly joined the new Communist Party. His decision to resign from the CP after only a month seems to have marked a turning-point in his political career and in his life. He began to move away from militant Socialism and returned gradually to his earlier beliefs in a non-political 'ethical Socialism' but without an anarchist framework. He had already joined the Co-operative Party, in which his wife was deeply involved. (She was a Labour and Co-operative representative on the City Council from 1919 to 1922 and in January 1926 succeeded Honora Enfield as secretary of the Women's Co-operative Guild). He rejoined the ILP, became vice-president, and was again a delegate to the Trades Council. He began to study philosophy once more and in 1924 published a philosophical treatise in the style of Plato ['Philosophy and Kings'] which argued the case for 'educational' Socialism: that is the achievement of social reform through education and moral development. The same theme runs through two works of history: *A World History for the Workers* (1922) and *A Short History of Trades Unionism* [1926]. In the latter he rejoiced at the greater unity of industrial, political and co-operative sides of the movement in the struggle for the 'Co-operative Commonwealth'.

Barton stood again for Parliament at Harwich in 1924, but lost his deposit. He had also failed to be returned for the City Council in 1922, but was successful at Hillsborough in 1926 – the election at which Labour gained its majority on Sheffield City Council. He was immediately appointed chairman of the libraries committee and two museum committees and gave much effort and attention to the development of the libraries and museums of Sheffield in the last years of his life. In 1927 he prepared a draft paper for the finance committee on the taxation of land values – something he had long campaigned for. He was for some time a member of the education committee and chairman of the adult education committee. He changed ward to Owlerton in 1929, and was elected an Alderman in the same year.

In his last years he had become noticeably moderate in his views. He died a generally respected figure on 9 December 1933 at the age of sixty-five. His funeral took place at the City Road Crematorium on 12 December and he was survived by his wife, a son and a daughter. He left effects valued at £264.

Writings: Letter in *Commonweal*, 9 July 1892; Editor of *Sheffield Guardian*, 1907–11; *The Universal Strike* [1911] P; *Election Address* (Brightside ward, Nov 1912) 4 pp.; *The War: how it was made, who shall profit by it? A Book for Working People* (Keighley, 1915); *Burden of Interest, and how to avoid it* (1919); *A World History for the Workers; a story of man's doings from the dawn of time, from the standpoint of the disinherited* (1922); 'Philosophy and Kings', in *The Bermondsey Book* (Sep 1924) 20–3; *A Short History of Trades Unionism* (Sheffield, [1926]); 'Vers la Réalisation de la Réforme Foncière' [Extrait du Rapport concernant l'impôt sur la valeur du sol, présenté par le Conseiller A. Barton et adopté par le Conseil de la ville de Sheffield, le 3 Octobre 1928], *Terre et Liberté,* 5e annee no. 2 (Avril-Mai-Juin 1929) 38–41; *In Praise of Sheffield* [poem] (Sheffield, 1930) 8 pp.

Sources: *Commonweal*, 25 May 1889–4 Sep 1892; *Clarion*, 1 July 1893; *Workman's Times*, 7 and 28 Oct, 25 Nov and 23 Dec 1893, 13 Jan 1894; J. Carunada, *Twenty-five Years of Detective Life* (Manchester, 1895); *Labour Leader*, 7 Feb and 27 Nov 1897, 24 May 1902, 6 May 1910, 19 June 1919; *Reynolds's Newspaper*, 25 May 1902; *Sheffield Guardian*, 5 Oct 1906, 25 Oct 1907, 4 Nov 1910, 27 Jan and 27 Oct 1911, 2 Feb, 20, 27 Sep, 4, 11, 18 Oct 1912, 15 Aug and 7 Nov 1913, 4 Dec 1914; *Sheffield Forward* (July 1922); *Sheffield Co-operator* (Nov 1926); F. Thraves, 'Speech on Alfred Barton', *Edward Carpenter Memorial Service* (Sheffield, 1947) 9–10; M. Walton, *Sheffield: its story and its achievements* (Sheffield, 1948); J. Mendelson et al., *The Sheffield Trades and Labour Council 1858 to 1958* (Sheffield, [1958?]); N. Connole, *Leaven of Life: the story of George Henry Fletcher* (1961); B. Barker, 'Anatomy of Reformism: the social and political ideas of the Labour leadership in Yorkshire', *Int. Rev. Social Hist. 18*, pt 1 (1973) 16–18; *Minor Parties at British Parliamentary Elections, 1885–1974* ed. F.W.S. Craig (1975); J. Quail, *The Slow Burning Fuse* (1978); biographical information: W. Sellars, Sheffield; personal information: Dr J.W. Sterland, Sheffield. OBIT. *Sheffield Daily Telegraph* [portrait] and *Yorkshire Telegraph and Star*, 11 Dec 1933; *Co-operative News*, 16 Dec 1933.

HELEN MATHERS

See also: †Eleanor BARTON; †Joseph POINTER; Ernest George ROWLINSON.

BECKETT, John [William] Warburton (1894–1964)
LABOUR MP (LATER MOSLEYITE)

Born on 11 October 1894 at Hammersmith, London, the son of William Beckett, a master draper and his wife Eva Dorothy (née Salmon), his name was registered as John William Beckett. His father came from an old stock of yeoman farmers in Cheshire, and his mother's family were from the fishing community on the East Coast. He went to an elementary school and won a scholarship to the Upper Latymer Secondary School in Hammersmith. When he was fourteen he was apprenticed to a draper. His father's business collapsed about this time through ill-judged ventures on the Stock Exchange. John Beckett taught himself advertising and journalism through correspondence courses and night schools, and had begun working in these professions when war was declared on 4 August 1914. He enlisted on the same day [*South London Observer, Camberwell and Peckham Times*, 25 May 1929].

In the Army he was originally in the 9th Middlesex Battalion, from which he transferred to the King's Shropshire Light Infantry. He was, then, one of the 'front generation', whose souls were scarred by the Great War, and it is apparent from his later life and career that the war experiences exercised a considerable influence upon his later philosophy. Before the war he had been a Conservative and militarist, but after his discharge from the Army because of physical ill health in March 1917 he quickly moved into left-wing politics. He went to live and work in Sheffield, and a turning point in his life came when he heard W.C. Anderson, then Labour MP for Attercliffe, speak at a meeting of the local Ethical Society. The effect upon him was profound, and he began to take a serious interest in Socialism.

John Beckett joined the Independent Labour Party in September 1917. He was already active in the Sheffield branch of the Comrades of the Great War and was elected to the executive committee. He was invited to stand for the city council but his employers, affronted by his politics, dismissed him. Beckett then moved to London and settled in Hackney, joining the Hackney branch of the ILP. An association with Ernest Mander led to the formation of the National Union of Ex-Servicemen, and Beckett became its first chairman. The organisation existed for just over a year, but the Labour Party refused to support it financially; and when various ex-servicemen's groups amalgamated into the British Legion, there seemed little possibility of maintaining an independent political organisation, and it was subsequently dissolved.

By this time Beckett had met Ramsay MacDonald, and he did a great deal of speaking in Hackney and the London area in general. In November 1919 Labour became the governing party in Hackney, with a majority of two in a council of seventy. For its first mayor, in order to safeguard its tiny majority, the Labour Party chose someone outside the council; and when he died a year later, Herbert Morrison was brought in as mayor. Beckett had become a Hackney councillor two months after the general council election, and relations between Beckett and Morrison became increasingly strained and hostile; and as a result of the publicity he was receiving, Beckett once again found himself out of employment. But he was far from discouraged, and now began to move in the direction of full-time political activity. He was elected to membership of the London and Southern Counties divisional council of the ILP, and at the end of 1920 he accepted the position of full-time agent, at a salary of £6 a week, for Clement Attlee in Limehouse. He moved into the large house by the docks in which Attlee lived. By now he was beginning to accumulate political expertise; he became honorary secretary of the ILP divisional council, and was elected secretary of the London committee of the No More War Movement which had been founded on 24 February 1921.

With Fenner Brockway, Clifford Allen and Attlee he also served on the informal committee set up to work out a programme for the ILP; and their document was presented, and accepted, at the national conference of 1922. But his main work at this time was as Attlee's agent. He showed his entrepreneurial flair and journalistic talent by founding and running a monthly periodical – the *East London Pioneer* – which ran between 1921 and 1923. Attlee was returned for Limehouse in the general election of 1922, and Beckett then acted as his private secretary. The Parliament lasted only eleven months, and at C.P. Trevelyan's suggestion he allowed himself to be put forward as a candidate for North Newcastle. He was the first official Labour candidate to stand in the division, and he polled nearly 6000 votes, a few hundreds behind the Liberal. On the strength of his campaign performance, he received invitations for his name to go forward as prospective candidate for East and West Newcastle and for Gateshead. Eventually, he was selected for Gateshead where he was returned on the ILP ticket in 1924 with a majority of over 9000 in a three-cornered fight with Conservative and Liberal candidates, in an election which was notorious for its anti-Labour and anti-Socialist smears. He had just celebrated his thirtieth birthday, and he was to serve as ILP member for Gateshead until 1929. In that year he decided not to stand again for the northern constituency, for a variety of personal and political motives, and he was influenced by Hugh Dalton into becoming a candidate for the latter's old seat of Peckham. Beckett was duly elected and served until the general election of 1931.

Beckett's parliamentary career was full of incident. Soon after his arrival in the House he became known through his contributions at question time and began his first parliamentary campaign. Attlee told him of a peculiar incident he had come across at the War Office which he did not wish to pursue but which he thought might interest Beckett. During the War the Germans had discovered a new method of extracting nitrogen from the air, called nitrogen fixation. The British Government had also spent considerable sums on a factory at Billingham-on-Tees in an attempt to improve nitrogen production but the British method incurred far higher production costs than its German rival. Under the terms of the Armistice the British Government had the right to investigate any German secrets and a Commission of three Army officers was sent to Cologne to survey the nitrogen process. According to Attlee their original report was no longer in the keeping of the War Office and the three members of the Commission had retired into private life. Beckett discovered that the Government factory at Billingham had been sold for a trifling sum to a firm controlled by Sir Alfred Mond; that under Sir Alfred's auspices a new company had been formed to exploit the new method of fixating nitrogen from the air; that the senior officer on the Commission was now a director of the new company; that the other two officers were employed by the company and that the information contained in the Commission's report was placed at the disposal of the purchasers. The deal took place in 1920 when Sir Alfred Mond was a member of the Government.

It was this situation which Beckett began to inquire about on 3 March 1925. He took up the issue not out of a desire for parliamentary sensation, but because, as an ex-soldier, the thought of war profits produced in him an almost uncontrollable rage. It was such an anger against injustice and outrage which brought him into the Labour ranks, but it was a passion which the Party was unable to appease or satisfy, and which later was to lead him to seek political solutions elsewhere. In this first campaign he met at once with Government evasiveness and this led others, including Dalton and Maxton, to take an interest in the matter. In the end it became apparent that the sale of the factory had been by private treaty after advertisement but whether all interested parties knew that details regarding the German method of production would be included in the sale remained unclear and confusion also surrounded the existence and whereabouts of the Government records relating to the disposal.

The Synthetic Nitrogen affair was important in two respects. First of all, Beckett became regarded as a man with little respect for tradition: he was prepared to take up issues which others, more discreet souls, were inclined to avoid. At the same time, the incident affected his attitude towards the parliamentary system. He continued to raise issues, particularly those concerned with ex-servicemen's rights, problems of unemployment and the theatre (in which he had a considerable interest). But he was an impatient man, keen to get things done, and over time he began to show his disrespect for what he regarded as the stuffy traditions of the House: a disrespect which was indicated by a series of events in which he was involved.

His first press headlines in this connection came in December 1925 when he offered to provide the *Daily Herald* with details of a 'secret' session in the House which had followed the cry of 'I spy strangers', an action which had been indulged in to liven up proceedings. No disciplinary measures were taken against him for making his offer to the press. Following this in 1927, in the debate over the Trade Disputes Bill on 4 May 1927, he was suspended for the first time from the service of the House. In one session, Baldwin, while expressing his affection for the trade union movement, regretted that the control of some unions had fallen to the Minority Movement. This accusation aroused certain Labour members to protest but Baldwin showed no inclination to withdraw his statement or even to prove it. Beckett proceeded to rise on a point of order and asked the Prime Minister to admit that he had lied. This was regarded as a gross breach of parliamentary etiquette and at this point the Speaker intervened to protect Baldwin. Beckett was asked to withdraw his remark. He agreed to do so but only if the Prime Minister also withdrew his. As a result of his action Beckett was 'named' and his suspension was moved. It was carried by 321 votes to 88.

His second suspension came in 1930. This arose over an incident at question time on 17 July 1930 when Fenner Brockway, in an attempt to draw attention to the condition of political prisoners in Indian gaols, was suspended for refusing to obey the Chair. When Beckett saw Labour members trooping into the lobby to vote for Brockway's suspension, he seized the Mace, calling out to the Speaker as he did so, 'Mr Speaker, these proceedings are a disgrace to the House.' The Mace was taken from him by two attendants, and he was named by the Speaker. He left the House immediately. In retrospect Brockway felt Beckett's action 'smothered' the dignity of his protest about conditions in British India although he also added that he had a 'friendly memory' of the motive which led Beckett to run away with the Mace [Brockway (1942) 206]. The incident could easily be dismissed as a pointless and fruitless exercise. To be properly understood, however, it has to be considered not merely or mainly as the action of a publicity-seeking politician, as it was almost universally reported in the press, but in the light of Beckett's growing disillusionment with the parliamentary system, and in particular with the 1929–31 Labour Government which in his view was failing to implement the wishes of those who had put them in power. His faith in some individuals, however, notably John Wheatley, remained unshaken. Beckett had come into close contact with Wheatley after

1929 when he acted as unofficial whip to a small ILP ginger group.

Wheatley's death in 1930 increased his sense of isolation within the Labour ranks but what finally ended any respect he still had for the Labour Party came in 1931 when the Unemployment Insurance Anomalies Bill was introduced. The level of unemployment after 1929 placed a heavy burden on the Exchequer and pressure developed for a reduction in the level of expenditure in the social services sector. The Anomalies Bill had as its aim the prevention of the 'abuse' of unemployment insurance by four sections of the labour force – casual workers, short-time workers, intermittent workers and married women workers – and was one example of the Government's cut-backs in social policy. The measure was an indication of the pressures which were upon the Labour Government, and which were to lead in 1931 to the emergence of the National Government.

In the general election of 1931 Beckett stood as ILP candidate for his own constituency of Peckham. There were four candidates: National Government, National Labour, official Labour Party and Beckett. He lost the seat by 8241 votes to the National Government candidate, but he polled 11,217 votes against 1442 for National Labour and 1350 for official Labour. With this defeat at Peckham he was now in a quite new situation. His life since the end of the First World War had been given to political activity. In the course of the previous decade he had engaged in a certain amount of political journalism – for the *Bradford Pioneer, Lansbury's Weekly* and the *Daily Herald* among other papers – but he had no obvious trade or profession to which he could return. In June 1930 he had married the actress Kyrle Bellew, widow of Arthur Bourchier, actor and proprietor of the Strand Theatre, who had died in 1927. Beckett had first married in 1918, and was divorced in December 1929, an episode which led to a considerable furore in his Peckham constituency. The local Labour Party divided into two factions over the issue of a divorced member of parliament being allowed to continue to represent the constituency. The debate was brought to a close when the general management committee of the Peckham Labour Party gave Beckett a unanimous vote of confidence [*South London Press*, 27 June 1930].

His second marriage – at Gretna Green, [*Daily Herald*, 30 June 1930] – led to him undertaking the management of the Strand Theatre after his electoral defeat. But this involvement in the theatre did not mean Beckett had lost interest in politics: he was selected in 1932 by the Peckham branch of the ILP as prospective parliamentary candidate, although there is no evidence of an endorsement by the National Administrative Council of the ILP; and Beckett was never to stand again as an ILP candidate.

In March 1934, a year in which he was also declared a bankrupt, it was reported in the national press that he had joined the British Union of Fascists; and from this time his career requires only to be briefly summarised. Beckett had been impressed on visits to Italy by the achievements of the Mussolini regime; he was initially much influenced by the oratorical ability of William Joyce; and he was introduced to the Mosley circle by Dr Robert Forgan, an ex-ILP member of parliament, supporter of Mosley's New Party, and a founding member of the British Union of Fascists. During his years with Mosley, Beckett was closely involved in agitational work all over the country; he took his full share of rowdy meetings; he became Director of Publicity; and for two years, 1936–7, he edited both *Action* and *Blackshirt*. These activities brought him a number of court cases, mainly libel actions in which he was the defendant; but there was an early one in 1934 in which he was awarded £700 damages against the wrongful allegation that he had converted funds from the National Union of Ex-Servicemen for his own use. The two most important cases which as defendant he lost were the libel action brought by eight members of the EC of the Amalgamated Engineering Union in 1936 [Benewick (1972) 268–8] and the more sensational action, in 1937, brought by Lord Camrose and the *Daily Telegraph*. The plaintiffs alleged strong anti-Semitic statements and allegations. Lord Camrose was awarded £12,500 damages and the *Daily Telegraph* £7500 [ibid., 269–71].

By the time the trial took place Beckett had already left the BUF, and in court he was openly critical of Mosley. Beckett, together with William Joyce, and a number of others had been sacked by Mosley in the spring of 1937. Consequent upon this Joyce and Beckett founded their own organisation, the National Socialist League. They were joined by John Macnab, the former editor of the *Fascist Quarterly*, but the League could never claim more than a handful of members and it was never a viable organisation. In September 1938 Joyce joined with Viscount Lymington to form the British Council Against European Commitments. The Council was a co-ordinating body, to which the National Socialist League became affiliated, and Beckett and Lymington proceeded to publish a monthly journal, the *New Pioneer* which championed non-involvement in European affairs. The Joyce–Beckett relationship ended in 1939. Joyce let it be known that if war were to break out he would fight for Hitler; Beckett could never have followed this path.

By early 1939 the National Socialist League was effectively dead and in March of that year Beckett moved into a new organisation when he joined with Lymington and the Marquess of Tavistock in founding the British People's Party, which took as its slogan, 'Campaign against War and Usury' and which incorporated into its programme monetary reform (Tavistock had previously been associated with Social Credit), the protection of small shopkeepers against trusts, security of employment and electoral reform. Tavistock became chairman of the organisation while Beckett became the secretary, as he also did of another organisation which was spawned from the same source, the British Council for Christian Settlement in Europe. The BPP's activities were confined to holding meetings, issuing publications (it issued the *People's Post* and *The Truth about this War*), and contesting one by-election when H. St John B. Philby stood at Hythe. But Beckett's new orientation which this time had firmer financial foundations through Tavistock, was soon interrupted with the outbreak of war in September 1939. Beckett's position began to receive attention and on 23 May 1940 he was arrested under Regulation 18B.

Beckett spent his time as a detainee in prisons in Brixton, Stafford and the Isle of Man. In his fight for his release in April 1943, he made an ex-parte application for a writ of Habeas Corpus to be directed to the Home Secretary and the Governor of Brixton prison. His assertion was that the reasons given for his detention were political in character but when Germany had invaded Western Europe his views had completely changed and he had joined the LDVs (later the Home Guard). It was also questioned whether his continued detention was required under the scheme of classification which the Home Secretary had spelt out to the House in 1941. None of this impressed the three High Court judges who considered his application and the case was dismissed. He was eventually released on 29 October 1943.

After his release Beckett had to reside within twenty-five miles of London for the rest of the war and after spending some time with Forgan he moved into accommodation provided by his old political collaborator, the Duke of Bedford. Soon afterwards, in June 1945, the activities of the British People's Party were revived and in the immediate post-war years its meetings often took place against a background of violent protest. The Party was inextricably linked, in the minds of most people, with pro-Nazi sentiment and anti-Semitism, and encountered opposition on both counts.

For Beckett, the BPP marked the end of the political road. The connection with Bedford was doubtless useful and it remained until the Duke's death in 1953. After that Beckett became essentially a private person. His last recorded press comment was in 1961. He was then living at Rickmansworth and sending out a fortnightly stock market letter called *Advice and Information* in which he gave advice to small investors. From it he managed to make a living for himself and his family.

He later moved to London and died on 28 December 1964 at 187 Queen's Gate, S.W.7. His death certificate described him as 'journalist and writer (retired)'. As a result of his war-time experiences, and the succour he had received from a Roman Catholic priest, he became increasingly interested in Catholicism, and was received into the Church in 1952. On his death a requiem mass was held at Brompton Oratory. His passing went almost unnoticed with only a brief obituary notice inserted by the family in *The Times* of 30 December. There was no will.

Writings: 'The London County Council Elections', *Soc. Rev. 19* (Apr 1922) 188–92; 'The Problem of the Middle Classes', ibid. *21* (Apr 1923) 162–5; 'Labour and the Pensions Ministry: an immediate task', ibid. *23* (Mar 1924) 117–20; 'Fascism and the Trade Unions', *Fascist Q.* (July 1936) 327–36; Introduction to W. Joyce, *National Socialism now* (1937).

Sources: (1) MS: Most of Beckett's printed and personal papers have been lost or destroyed but there are still some papers, including an autobiography, written in 1938, in the possession of Mrs D.A. Beckett, London; C.C. Aronsfeld, 'Organised Anti-Semitism in Britain, 1942–1946' (1946) [typescript in Wiener Library, London]. (2) Newspapers: *Daily Herald*, 7 Aug 1925, 5 May 1927, 1, 18 and 30 July 1930, 10 Nov and 9 Dec 1936, 18 Mar 1937; *South London Observer, Camberwell and Peckham Times*, 25 May 1929; *Manchester Guardian*, 18 June and 24 July 1930, 9 Nov 1934, 24 Apr 1935, 10 Apr 1943; *South London Press*, 27 June 1930, 19 Mar 1937; *Daily Herald*, 30 June and 1 July 1930; *Daily Mail*, 13 Feb 1932, 11 Dec 1946, 25 Oct 1947; *Sunday Despatch*, 4 Mar 1934; *Morning Post*, 27 Apr, 14 May, 6 Nov 1934, 13 Apr 1937; *Daily Telegraph*, 15 Dec 1934, 16 Dec 1936; *Times*, 4, 5, 6, 10 Nov 1936, 16 Oct 1937, 18 May 1943; *Daily Express*, 17 Mar 1937, 24 May 1940; *Jewish Chronicle*, 7 July 1939, 17 Aug 1945; *People's Post*, 20 Apr and 23 May 1945; *Reynolds News*, 27 Apr 1946; *Evening Standard*, 7 Nov 1961. (3) Other: *Gateshead Labour Party and Trade Council Monthly Circular*, 15 Aug 1924; H.M. Swanwick, *Builders of Peace* (1924); *Hansard*, 1924–5, 1927, 1929–30, 1931; *Dod* (1925), (1929), (1931); *WW* (1931); British People's Party, *The Truth about this War* (1939; repr. 1940); M. Muggeridge, *The Thirties: 1930–1940 in Great Britain* (1940; rev. ed. 1967); F. Brockway, *Inside the Left: a political autobiography* (1942; rev. ed. 1947); idem, *Socialism over Sixty Years* (1946); R. Jenkins, *Mr Attlee: an interim biography* (1948); H. Dalton, *Call back Yesterday: memoirs 1887–1931* (1953); J. MacGovern, *Neither Fear nor Favour* (1960); C. Cross, *The Fascists in Britain* (1961); J.A. Cole, *Lord Haw-Haw – and William Joyce* (1964); R.J. Benewick, *Political Violence and Public Order* (1969; rev. as *The Fascist Movement in Britain* (1972)); B. Donoughue and G.W. Jones, *Herbert Morrison; portrait of a politician* (1973); biographical information: C. Cross, Shepperton; the late T.A.K. Elliott, CMG; Mrs I. Wagner, Labour Party librarian; personal information: Mrs D.A. Beckett, London; F. Beckett, London, son; Lord Brockway; the late Dr R. Forgan; Fr. B. Fox, London. Obit. *Times*, 30 Dec 1964.

Colin Holmes

See also: †William Crawford Anderson; †Herbert William Butler; Robert Forgan.

BENBOW, William (1784-?)

ULTRA-RADICAL REFORMER

Benbow, according to his prison testimony [HO 20/10, 1 Jan 1841] was born at Middlewich, Cheshire. Little is known of his early life except that he learned the trade of shoemaker, and at the age of twenty-four, in 1808, appeared in Newton, a suburb of Manchester as a dissenting preacher. In the closing years of the Napoleonic Wars he was among those who responded to the ideas of Major Cartwright favouring parliamentary reform, and by 1816 he had become one of the leading reformers in Lancashire. He was already, as he was to remain, a physical-force revolutionary: a man of great courage, radical doggedness and a larger-than-life presence, who, although quarrelsome, inspired many more of his fellows to devotion than to disdain.

Benbow became important in the radical movement at a time when there is evidence that a physical-force conspiracy was under way: 'inextricably inter-twined with the counter-conspiracy of Government provocateurs' [Thompson (1963) 650]. Benbow and Joseph Mitchell of Liverpool were appointed in December 1816 by the Lancashire radicals as missionaries to the West Riding and the Midlands; and they also went to London. In the capital Benbow made the acquaintance of Sir Francis Burdett, William Cobbett and Henry Hunt and was especially attracted to the group of Spencean revolutionaries led by Dr James Watson and Arthur Thistlewood. He was active in addressing meetings of the London trade societies; he defended radical reform against the more moderate ideas of Burdett; and he made a considerable personal impression on Cobbett. Benbow and Mitchell seem, from this time, to have become the Lancashire agents for Cobbett's *Register*.

In January 1817 a Convention met at the 'Crown and Anchor' tavern in the Strand, called by Cartwright and attended by delegates from reform societies in many parts of the country. Benbow represented the Manchester Hampden Club and took a leading part in the proceedings. He also attended the secret meetings of some of the delegates and London extremists at the Cock tavern in Soho. After the Convention broke up Benbow returned to Manchester and was active with Mitchell in organising a large number of petitions to be taken personally to Westminster by groups of men, each one provided only with a blanket. The result would be masses of men marching into London at the same time, a revolutionary situation. They succeeded in arranging the 'Blanket meeting' at Manchester in April which began the famous march. A revolutionary government was also to meet at Nottingham, and Benbow was to be one of the members. But before the meeting took place Habeas Corpus was suspended and warrants were issued for the arrest of many radical leaders, including Samuel Bamford, Mitchell and Benbow. Benbow spent two months on the run from the military authorities and decided to flee to America and join Cobbett. But he confided in a fellow-reformer who was also a spy. Though he sailed from Liverpool to Dublin, he was arrested there in May, and brought back to London where he joined a number of other radicals in prison. His letters to his wife were stopped by the authorities, at which he wrote violent letters of protest to the Home Secretary, Lord Sidmouth. In America Cobbett collected money for his relief and published letters to him in his *Register*. Late in December 1817 most of these political prisoners were released on agreeing to certain conditions as to future behaviour. But three refused such conditions – Benbow and the two Spenceans, Thomas Evans, father and son. All three thereby became radical heroes, and were released unconditionally. A fund was set up for the relief of the released prisoners, and the largest amounts went to these three, Benbow getting £75.

Benbow now returned to Manchester, opened a cheap shoe-shop and resumed his radical activity. In 1818 he published his first pamphlet, *Censorship exposed*. The writing was typical of an autodidact of limited formal education, but with great force and imagination. Benbow was quite unaltered in the militancy of his general opinions. He was the chief advocate in Manchester of a plan to flood the country with forged Bank of England notes to create a financial panic and a chance of revolution. But in June 1818, to the disgust of some radicals, he judged it prudent to flee again, and this time succeeded in joining Cobbett in New York. There he seems to have communicated the currency plan to Cobbett, for it was soon advocated in the *Register* as 'Cobbett's puff-out' and aroused great interest in radical circles. Cobbett also dedicated the first edition of his famous *Grammar* to Benbow. Benbow dug up the bones of Thomas Paine who had died in Manhattan, and he and Cobbett decided to bring them back to England and sell them. They boarded ship late in 1819, but Cobbett was not allowed to sail, since he had Paine's bones. He therefore followed in a later ship while Benbow arranged welcomes for him in Liverpool and Manchester. Benbow immediately plunged into radical activity in Manchester at a time when plans for insurrection were at their height in December 1819.

The two then went to London, where Benbow became Cobbett's employee and published his *Register* and other writings. He opened a large shop in the Strand and published a number of other tracts, including *A Peep at the Peers* and *Full View of the British Commons*, exhaustive analyses of the members of both Houses of Parliament and their positions and connections. But his main publications were a large number of bills and pamphlets in support of Queen Caroline, whose case convulsed London in 1820–1. When the Bill against her was dropped, his illuminated shop was the centre of demonstrations of triumph. Benbow had thus become one of the chief radical publishers in London. Though he and Cobbett quarrelled violently and split up in January 1821, his own publishing continued until he was arrested in May, at the instigation of the notorious Constitutional Association, for a caricature of the King. He spent eight months in prison without ever being brought to trial, his wife died, and his business was ruined.

Probably in 1821 he had started to publish a series of pamphlets directed mainly against the Church of England although there was also a denunciation of Methodists and dissenters. The second of these articles is signed 'W.B. King's Bench Prison, May 7, 1821'. In 1823 he brought them together in one volume under the title *The Crimes of the Clergy*. On his release from prison he opened smaller premises in Castle Street, Leicester Square, under the sign 'Byron's Head'. Here he published occasional tracts and pirated editions, especially works by Byron. Benbow at this time had a fierce quarrel with Richard Carlile, who was still in prison, over the publication of an edition of Paine's works [Carlile [1821] 14–20]. In February 1822 Benbow was prosecuted by Byron's publisher for pirating *Cain,* but the Lord Chancellor dismissed the case on the grounds that the immorality of the work deprived it of legal protection. In July of the same year Benbow was prosecuted by the Society for the Suppression of Vice for publishing obscenity in his *Rambler's Magazine* and for a translated French novel, but was acquitted. For the remainder of the 1820s he continued as bookseller and occasional publisher, and seems to have spent two more terms in prison in 1827. By this time his writings were showing considerable development. His 1825 pamphlet against Southey, *A Scourge for the Laureate*, has been described by Max Beer as written by a man 'with a trenchant style and with no inconsiderable literary knowledge' [(1920) 315].

By 1831 Benbow was running a coffee- and beer-house in the centre of London which became a meeting place for radicals. He was now an influential member of the National Union of the Working Classes; and although early in 1832 his business incompetence forced him to give up his shop, he moved his stock secretly, in order to avoid his creditors, and opened in Theobalds Road the 'Institution of the Working Classes'. This again became a main meeting place of the National Union, and also headquarters of one of the chief co-operative societies in London. His second wife also organised a radical women's society there.

Benbow was among the most militant speakers of the National Union. He denounced the Reform Bill as a fraud, supported Henry Hunt's stand in Parliament and made vigorous speeches exonerating the Bristol rioters of October 1831. He was in the chair at the weekly meeting of the National Union when it was decided to call a mass meeting in London on 7 November 1831, and at the same meeting he emphasised both the importance of local organisation, following the example of the Methodists and their 'classes', and his scheme for a 'month's holiday' or general strike [*Poor Man's Guardian*, 29 Oct 1831]. Benbow distributed staves in preparation for the 7 November assembly. When the Home Secretary, Lord Melbourne, banned the meeting, the committee of the National Union decided to cancel it against the opposition of Benbow. He still at this time had close contacts with Manchester. He addressed a meeting there in June, and when John Doherty came to London he was closely associated with Benbow.

In January 1832 Benbow published the pamphlet for which he is best remembered; indeed, much of his active radical career has often been over-shadowed by it and passed over. The pamphlet of sixteen pages, *Grand National Holiday and Congress of the Productive Classes*, argued that the people were oppressed by a few who were the '*jugglers* of society the *pick-pockets*, the *plunderers*, the pitiless *Burkers* – in fine, they are all *Bishops*! They exist on disease and blood: crime and infamy are in the breath of their nostrils' [p. 4]. The people were ignorant of their own power, and must take things into their own hands. They must unite, accumulate provisions for a week, take supplies from the rich, stop work for a month, and elect a congress to reform society:

> The grounds and necessity of our having a month's Holiday, arise from the circumstances in which we are placed. We are oppressed, in the fullest sense of the word; we have been deprived of every thing; we have no property, no wealth, and our labour is of no use to us, since what it produces goes into the hands of others. We have tried every thing but our own efforts... Our Lords and Masters have proposed no plan that we can adopt; they contradict themselves, even upon what they name the source of our misery. One says one thing, another says another thing. One scoundrel, one sacrilegious blasphemous scoundrel, says "that over-production is the cause of our wretchedness." Over-production, indeed! when we half-starving producers cannot, with all our toil, obtain anything like a sufficiency of produce. It is the first time, that in any age or country, save our own, *abundance* was adduced as a cause of *want*...
>
> Over-population, our Lords and Masters say, is another cause of our misery. They mean by this, that the resources of the country are inadequate to its population. We must prove the contrary, and during a holiday take a census of the people, and a measurement of the land, and see upon calculation, whether it be not an unequal distribution, and a bad management of the land, that make our Lords and Masters say, that there are too many of us. Here are two strong grounds for our Holiday; for a CONGRESS of the working classes...
>
> The object of the Congress; that is what it will have to do. To reform society, for "from the crown of our head to the sole of our foot there is no soundness in us." We must cut out the rottenness in order to become sound. Let us see what is rotten. Every man that does not work is rotten; he must be made to work in order to cure his unsoundness. Not only is society rotten; but the land, property, and capital is rotting. There is not only something, but a great deal rotten in the state of England. Every thing, men, property, and money, must be put into a state of circulation. As the blood by stagnation putrifies, as it is impoverished by too much agitation, so society by too much idleness on the one hand, and too much toil on the other has become rotten. Every portion must be made to work, and then the work will become so light, that it will not be considered work, but wholesome exercise. Can anything be more humane than the main object of our glorious holiday, namely, to obtain for all at the least expense to all, the largest sum of happiness for all [quoted from pp. 9, 13].

The idea of a general strike, a term which Benbow himself does not use (but soon to be found in John Doherty's *Herald of the Rights of Industry*, 5 Apr 1834), was not a new one when Benbow put it forward. Plummer noted a proclamation of Glasgow and district strikers in 1820 which appealed for support throughout the country [(1971) 123]; and Kemp-Ashraf has argued a correspondence between Benbow's National Holiday and the ideas of Thomas Spence [(1966) 286–7]. Benbow's pamphlet had a large circulation, a second edition appeared in May 1832, and it remained to exercise a considerable influence in the early years of the Chartist movement.

The idea of a congress or national convention went back to the radical movements of the 1780s, and implied a wholesale rejection of existing authority. The existing parliaments were unrepresentative and the people should choose their own convention whose authority would thereby have a greater legitimacy than the old. Benbow's ideas in general, in this pamphlet as in his other writings, must always be analysed in the context of their time. His understanding of politics derived from his early involvement in the radical cause: from the radicalism of Burdett and especially of Cobbett's *Register* and the *Independent Whig*. Like many radicals of his day, he spoke of the people against aristocracy or privilege, but while in the 1832 pamphlet he warned against hoping for support from the middle classes – and he elsewhere attacked 'shopocrats' – it was not wholly clear what he meant by 'working classes'. His analysis was in terms of political attitudes rather than of economic roles; and it is this which underlay the seeming ambiguity of many ultra-radicals, and later the Chartists, towards the 'middle-classes'.

In March 1832 Benbow took a leading part in the great procession in protest against the general fast called by the Government to avert the cholera epidemic. He, William Lovett and James Watson were all prosecuted, but triumphantly acquitted, partly because Benbow was able to expose the murky past of one of the police officers giving evidence. But Watson and Lovett then accused their colleague of a fraudulent claim for expenses, and when he was nevertheless re-elected to the committee of the National Union, they resigned.

This was not the only occasion when Benbow was accused of dishonesty, and historians have found difficulty in coming to a firm conclusion on the matter. Like many other working men within the radical and labour movements, Benbow was not particularly competent in managing many of the ventures he underook. He had difficulties, often, in personal relationships (he *was* quarrelsome) and apparently found it difficult to keep accurate accounts. But he has not been alone in this, and labour history is littered with examples of similar derelictions. In the case of Benbow it is true that he was not forthright and open about his mistakes and inadequacies, nor did he ever seek to make amends – he tried instead to brazen things out. Yet that he was crooked or unscrupulous in money matters may be doubted, and his commitment to the ideals of the movement was never in question. It must be accepted, too, that many of the complaints and accusations made against Benbow came from those who were strongly opposed to his ultra-revolutionary politics.

The opposition to Benbow in the National Union was led by Lovett, Watson and Hetherington. In part this was because his Institution was a rival centre to a chapel run by Watson, but much more because of ideological differences in the areas of tactics and strategy. Benbow's opposition to Owen, for example, was not because he was against the co-operative idea – his own Central Co-operative Association thrived for some time – but rather it was a denial of certain basic attitudes in Owen's approach, including the latter's refusal to recognise the class struggle, his undemocratic methods, and his patronising attitudes towards the working class and its capacities; and in this attitude Benbow would be supported by many working-class co-operators. Benbow was a delegate at the London Co-operative Congress in April 1832, and elected one of the missionaries for the London district. During the Congress he held his own festival in rivalry to that of Owen's, and afterwards published an attack on Owenism.

During 1832–3 Benbow continued to preach political sermons at his Institution. Immediately after the publication of the *Grand National Holiday* he published a monthly *Tribune of the People*, but he soon quarrelled with his printer, R.E. Lee, over money, and the fourth number was the last. In December 1832 Lee led a successful revolt against Benbow's leadership of the Central Co-operative Association although the society was soon to collapse; and in March 1833 the NUWC ceased meeting at Benbow's Institution because of the quarrels with Lee. By June 1833 the National Union itself was falling apart, and there was a general parting of the ways in its ranks. Benbow then helped to establish the Republican Association, which utilised, among others, the services of the Rev. Robert Taylor who held services at the Institution. At the end of 1833 Benbow began another monthly periodical, the *Agitator*, which demanded trade union support for radical reform, including a general strike, and also called for division and redistribution of the land and a statutory minimum wage. Only two numbers appeared. By the beginning of 1834, the Co-operative Association had broken up and Benbow was soon to quarrel with his partner in the ownership of the Institution. He was now unemployed and desperate, and he became a frequent associate of the equally bitter Thomas Preston, Thistlewood's old friend.

He seems then to have resumed shoemaking. In April 1834 he took part in protests against the convictions of the Tolpuddle labourers, and reissued his pamphlet. The London Committee that arranged the great demonstration of 21 April seriously considered calling a 'general holiday'. Later in 1834 Benbow and Cleave were reported as being at Manchester in connection with secret plans to hold simultaneous meetings over the country, and elect 'legislational attorneys' in place of the elected MPs.

Benbow was now about fifty years old, and while he still remained committed and active within the movement, he was never again to play a leading role. Between 1836 and 1838 he took part in the widespread agitation against the New Poor Law. In 1837 he was reported making a living as a fruiterer. In 1838 and 1839 he toured Lancashire in a horse and cart, making inflammatory speeches in support of the Charter, advocating a general strike and selling his pamphlet. He was arrested in mid-August 1839 in a house in Manchester by police from Colne. Stockport magistrates also had a warrant for him on a charge of sedition; and it was decided that he should be detained on the Stockport warrant. He pleaded not guilty and spent eight months in prison because no-one apparently was willing or able to provide bail. At his trial in April 1840 he made a ten-and-a-half hour speech in his own defence, but was found guilty, and sentenced to sixteen months in Chester Castle. A confidential report on him of January 1841 [HO 20/10], made by an Inspector of Prisons, noted that he was fifty-six years old, married with three sons; called himself a Baptist 'but really is of no religion. Pays the most marked disrespect at prison chapel by never rising from his seat'; was on the normal prison diet for most of his sentence to date (1lb of bread daily, 1 quart of gruel at breakfast, 1½lbs of potatoes at dinner, 1 quart of gruel for supper); had received about £12 from outside subscriptions; was locked up at 7 pm every evening, and allowed only *The Times* newspaper; occasional attacks of indigestion but otherwise in good health. The general observations of this Inspector on Benbow are worth recording:

> The name and character of this prisoner is familiar to all acquainted with agitation. The associate of Carlisle [*sic*], Hetherington and others, he is now 56 years old, and time seems to have abated nothing of his warmth in the cause of Republicanism. He seems to exercise some degree of influence over a portion of his companions, but he is much incensed against McDowall [*sic*] of whom he says 'As a surgeon I would not trust him with a dog's leg to cure – and as a Chartist his only principle is money . . .'

The Chartist prisoners in Chester were divided into two bitterly warring factions, one led by J.R. Stephens, and the other by M'Douall. Benbow backed Stephens, and on release kept up his attacks on M'Douall. The Manchester Chartists set up a committee to examine the charges, and found in favour of M'Douall.

By October 1841 Benbow was back in London, where he was a regular Chartist lecturer until 1845. He was an unsuccessful candidate for Finsbury in the election of delegates to the Birmingham Conference of December 1842; but he was elected by the Mile End locality to its local committee. He also took part in shoemakers' meetings and spoke at least once in the agitation over the Master and Servants' Bill. He is last mentioned in the *Star of Freedom*, 16 and 23 October 1852 when it was reported that the Finsbury Manhood Suffrage (late Chartist) Association had decided to call a meeting on the following Sunday to discuss the formation of a National Party which William Newton was suggesting. Benbow was among those invited, and with Julian Harney, Thornton Hunt and Leblond, he was among the speakers. In seconding the motion for a committee to be appointed, Benbow made a statement remarkable for its revisionist temper. After emphasising the failure of the radical movement for reform, and of the refusal of so many to continue to support the Charter, he concluded:

> He agreed with the proposal to agitate for Manhood Suffrage. If the people are to have a real movement they must lop off everything but the principle, and must agitate for one thing only, let them leave the details to a Manhood Suffrage Parliament. The people being free, their parliament would soon make arrangements for the equalisation of districts, payment of the members, and all the other modes of making the suffrage national [*Star of Freedom*, 23 Oct 1852].

Benbow was about 68 years old when he made this statement, and no trace of him afterwards has yet been discovered. For the benefit of future research workers into the life of Benbow the death registers at the GRO were searched from 1852 to 1867, but none of the details elicited seemed apposite. Inquiries were also made in the Shropshire area where many Benbows are still living, but again without success. A letter in the *Manchester Evening News* brought no replies relevant to his death but did, however, produce evidence of a marriage between a William Benbow, cordwainer and a Jane Meadow at Manchester on 9 June 1808. As Benbow was in the Manchester area at this time, and as his first wife's name was Jane, it is possible that this record relates to his own marriage. In *Notes and Queries*, 28 Apr 1877 a request was made for information concerning Benbow but no replies were apparently received.

William Benbow was a rather unusual personality in the British radical movement. He seems to have kept his revolutionary opinions right through his long political career, excepting the very last years for which we have only the one statement already quoted. He spanned a range of historical experience wider than any of his contemporaries and although he never was in the top rank of leadership his class-conscious approach to politics and especially his advocacy of the general strike made a considerable impact upon his own generation. He was, it is clear, a man of great presence and considerable political influence. He had strong religious beliefs in his earlier years and there is some evidence that he retained a degree of religious conviction throughout his life, albeit within a context of vigorous anti-clericalism and friendship and support for acknowledged freethinkers. In personal terms he remains, however, a somewhat shadowy figure, and it is to be hoped that there is much more about all aspects of his career to be discovered by historians.

Writings: *Censorship exposed: or letters addressed to the R.H.V. Sidmouth, and to Mrs Benbow*... (Manchester, [1818]) 11 pp.; *The Whigs exposed; or, Truth by Daylight addressed to the Reformers of Britain* (1820) 24 pp.; *The Crimes of the Clergy, or the Pillars of Priest-craft shaken; with an Appendix entitled the Scourge of Ireland* (1823); *A Scourge for the Laureate* [i.e. Robert Southey] [1825?] 20 pp.; *Grand National Holiday, and Congress of the Productive Classes* [1832] 16 pp. [a facsimile reprint of this with an Introduction by A.J.C. Rüter has been published in *Int. Rev. for Social Hist. 1* (1936) 217–56; also repr. in 1977 in Radical Reprints: series 1]; *The Delusion, or Owenism unmasked* (1832) [no known copy extant]; (with others), *Middlesex sess., May 16 1832: a correct report of the trial of Messrs Benbow, Lovett and Watson as leaders of the farce day procession* [1832] 40 pp.; *The Trial of William Benbow and Others* [1832] 8 pp.; *Agitator, or Political Anatomist* (Nov and Dec 1833).

In 1820–1 Benbow was Cobbett's publisher. He also published other works, of some of which he may have been the author. The chief ones were: *A Peep at the Peers*... (1820) 24 pp.; *A Letter to the King: shewing, by incontestable facts, the fundamental causes of our unexampled national distress* (1820); *Full View of the British Commons*... (1821) 50 pp.; *The Philosophical Dictionary* (2nd ed. 1822). He also published in 1820 *The Spanish Constitution*, 36 pp. and *The Queen's Trial*. The BL has five tracts published by him in support of Queen Caroline: *Kouli Khan: or, the progress of error* [1820?, several eds.] 24 pp.; *The Queen [Caroline] and the Mogul [George IV]: a play in two acts* (1820) 24 pp.; *Fair Play, or who are the Adulterers, Slanderers and Demoralizers*? (1820; later eds.) 32 pp.; *A Peep into the Cottage at Windsor: or "Love among the Roses": a poem founded on facts* [1820?] 16 pp.; *The Suppressed Poem. A Peep into W – r Castle, after the Lost Mutton* (1820) 24 pp. Seven others are known to have been published by him. There are many examples of his bills and placards in favour of the Queen in the BL, especially in the Place Coll. sets 18 and 71 and in the PRO, HO 40/14 and 44/8. In the early 1820s he pirated Byron's *Cain, Don Juan* and *English Bards and Scotch Reviewers*, and Southey's *Wat Tyler*. In 1822 he published the *Rambler's Magazine: or fashionable emporium of polite literature*. He is not known to have published anything after 1825 until 1832 when, in addition to his other writings he produced the *Tribune of the People* (June–July 1832), copies of which were lost during the Second World War.

Some verbatim reports of speeches by Benbow are to be found in HO papers, especially 64/14 and for intercepted correspondence of Benbow see HO 64/16. Many reports of his speeches are in the radical press of the early 1830s, especially the *Poor Man's Guardian* (1831-3), but also *Voice of the People* (1831), *Union* (1831), *Republican* (1832), *Working Man's Friend* (1833), *Man* (1833) and *People's Conservative and Trades' Union Gazette* (1834). For the Chartist period there are reports in the *Northern Star* (1839–46) and *Star of Freedom*, 16 and 23 Oct 1852.

Sources: (1) MS: The main sources are the Home Office papers from 1816 to 1840, especially series 20/8, 20/10, 40, 42, 44, 64 (intercepted corr. 64/16) and the Assize Book 61/9 (Chester), PRO; for the early 1830s *see* the Place MSS dealing with the National Union of the Working Classes and also the Broughton papers, Add. MSS., 36,459 and 36,460, BL. (2) Newspapers and periodicals: apart from those already listed, there is some information in *Cobbett's Weekly Political Register* (1817–20); the *Manchester Observer* (1818); *Black Dwarf* (1818); *Sherwin's* [*Weekly*] *Political Register* (1818); *Blanketteer, and People's Guardian* (1819); *Republican* (1822, 1826). There are reports of his court cases in *The Times* in 1822, 1823 and 1833. (3) Other: H. Hunt, *The Green Bag Plot* [1819] 16 pp.; T. Cleary, *A Reply to the Falsehoods of Mr. Hunt* [1819] 8 pp.; 'Correspondence between Mr Benbow and Mr Carlile' in R. Carlile, *Letters from Dorchester Gaol* [1821] 14–25; 'National Union of the Working Classes', *Poor Man's Guardian*, 29 Oct 1831; *Proceedings of the Third Co-operative Congress, held in London* . . . ed. W. Carpenter (1832); R.E. Lee, *Victimization, or Benbowism unmasked: addressed to the National Union of the Working Classes* [1832] 8 pp.; S. Bamford, *Passages in the Life of a Radical* 2 vols. (Middleton, 1839–41); W. Lovett, *Life and Struggles of William Lovett* . . . (1876; later eds); *Notes and Queries*, 5th ser. 7, 13 and 27 Jan and 28 Apr 1877; [H.S. Ashbee], *Bibliography of Prohibited Books 2* (1879; repr. NY, 1962), *3* (1885; repr. NY, 1962); L. Melville, *The Life and Letters of William Cobbett in England and America* 2 vols. (1913); M. Hovell, *The Chartist Movement* (Manchester, 1918; 2nd ed. Manchester, 1925); M. Beer, *History of British Socialism 2* (1920); N. Carpenter, 'William Benbow and the Origins of the General Strike', *QJE 35* (1921) 491–9; H.W.C. Davies, 'Lancashire Reformers 1816–17', in *Bull. of the John Rylands Library 10* (Manchester, 1926) 47–79; A. Plummer, 'The General Strike during One Hundred Years', *Economic History* (supplement to the *Econ. J.*) *1* (1926–9) 184–204; W.H. Wickwar, *The Struggle for the Freedom of the Press, 1819–1832* (1928); W.H. Crook, *The General Strike: a study of labor's tragic weapon in theory and practice* (Chapel Hill, 1931); A.J.C. Rüter, 'William Benbow as Publisher', *Bull. of the International Institute for Social History* no. *1* (Leiden, 1940) 1–14; *Notes and Queries 183*, 21 Nov 1942, 317–18; W.H. Oliver, 'Organisations and Ideas behind the Efforts to achieve a General Union of the Working Classes in England in the Early 1830s' (Oxford DPhil., 1954); E.P. Thompson, *The Making of the English Working Class* (1963; rev. ed. 1968); 'Selected Writings of Thomas Spence 1750–1814', ed. with an Introduction by P.M. Kemp-Ashraf in *Essays in Honour of William Gallacher* (Berlin, 1966) 267–354; D. Thomas, *A Long Time Burning: the history of literary censorship in England* (1969); J.H. Wiener, *The War of the Unstamped* (Cornell Univ. Press, 1969); P. Hollis, *The Pauper Press: a study in working-class radicalism of the 1830s* (1970); D.J. Rowe, *London Radicalism* (1970); A. Plummer, *Bronterre: a political biography of Bronterre O'Brien 1804-1864* (1971); T.M. Parssinen, 'Association, Convention and Anti-Parliament in British Radical Politics, 1771–1848', *Engl. Hist. Rev. 88* (1973) 504–33; I. Prothero,' William Benbow and the Concept of the "General Strike"', *Past and Present*, no. *63* (May 1974) 132–71; idem, *Artisans and Politics in Early Nineteenth Century London: John Gast and his times* (Folkestone, 1979); biographical information: J.D. Beckett, chairman, Manchester and Lancashire Family History Society; E. Frow, Manchester; Dr D. Goodway and J. Grossman, Leeds Univ.; Mrs Naomi Reid, Stockport.

I.J. Prothero

See also: Richard CARLILE; †Henry HETHERINGTON; William LOVETT, for Chartism to 1840; Robert OWEN.

BOWER, Sir Percival (1880–1948)
TRADE UNION OFFICIAL AND LABOUR ALDERMAN

Percival Bower was born about 1880, although it has not been possible to confirm the date and place from official records. He was the fourth son of a serving soldier, William Henry Bower. His father was then stationed at the School of Musketry at Hythe with the 2nd Queen's Royal East Surrey Regiment. Percival Bower attended the Hythe Church School but the death of both his parents within a year, when he was ten, meant that he had to find work. He started by selling newspapers on the street for 3*s* 6*d* a week, but then found general work and board at a local farm. After three years there he secured, through the influence of relatives, an apprenticeship with a blacksmith in London. Looking back on his early life, Bower concluded 'Few men in the Labour movement have been reared in circumstances more difficult than I. Those early days turned me to the Labour movement' [*Town Crier*, 7 Jan 1927]. It was in London that he first joined the ASE and the Hearts of Oak Friendly Society, and subsequently the Associated Blacksmiths' and Ironworkers' Society. He rose rapidly in the latter body, and in 1911 was appointed its full-time organiser for the Midlands, based in Birmingham.

Bower had joined the ILP in London and continued his involvement in Birmingham. But it was through his trade union activities that he began to make an impact on the public life of the city. He soon proved himself to be an effective negotiator. During the war he largely stood apart from the bitter disputes which divided the Birmingham Trades and Labour Council; instead he concentrated on administrative work. Among the committees he served on were the Birmingham Munitions Tribunal, the Advisory Committee on War Munitions, and the Birmingham and West Midlands Employment Committee. He was elected secretary of a co-ordinating committee in the engineering industry, the Birmingham and District Joint Committee of Engineering Trade Unions, which was active on the shop floor.

Bower's war work enhanced his reputation both within and outside the labour movement: he was awarded the OBE in 1920 for his war services, while he quickly became a major figure in the newly established Birmingham Borough Labour Party. In February 1919 he was elected as Labour councillor for Saltley, and within a year had become an alderman. He was also appointed an overseer of the poor and a magistrate. He was elected to the executive of the Birmingham Labour Party in 1920, and served as president in the following two years. His debating skills were appreciated on the City Council, where he led the Labour group in 1923 and 1924. When the group met in April 1923 to elect a nominee for the Lord Mayoralty, Bower was selected by a large majority. Later in the year the Associated Blacksmiths' and Ironworkers' Society added Bower's name to its parliamentary panel, and at very short notice he fought the Aston constituency of Birmingham at the 1923 December general election, polling 7641 votes in a three-cornered fight to come second to the Unionist Sir Evelyn Cecil.

Although there was some resentment within Labour circles in Birmingham at Bower's rapid rise to prominence, his election as Lord Mayor in November 1924 was seen to confirm the Labour Party as the principal opposition party to the Birmingham Unionists. Bower's first year as Lord Mayor was a great success. As one local paper afterwards recalled: 'He had that slightly portentous dignity which combined with much geniality seems to invest the office of first citizen with an added importance' [*Sunday Mercury*, 28 Jan 1944]. The City Council unanimously agreed to invite Bower to serve a second year, in spite of an agreement that he would only be proposed in exceptional circumstances.

The General Strike transformed Bower's political career. The potential difficulties of such a situation for a Labour Lord Mayor without a Labour majority on the Council became clear in

January 1926, when the Council set up a sub-committee to be responsible for the maintenance of supplies in the event of a general strike. The Lord Mayor was invited to join the sub-committee, and Bower accepted, explaining that he felt it to be his duty 'to prevent innocent and hapless members of the community being ground between the upper and lower stones of industrial conflict'. He kept to this position throughout the strike, retaining the confidence of the Unionists and local Unionist press. Behind the scenes he attempted to mediate between the police and the trade unions, and he did secure agreement on some picketing rights. After the collapse of the strike he threw his weight against any victimisation of Council employees. However, his public stance, which included an appearance as a prosecution witness in a trial of five Communists, infuriated many rank and file trade unionists, and there was widespread criticism that he had 'joined the bosses'. There were also demands that no future Labour politicians should accept the mayoralty without a Labour majority on the Council. Lasting bitterness had been generated between Bower and the Birmingham labour movement.

After his mayoralty Bower had intended to return to his trade union work, but in February 1927 he announced his resignation – ostensibly to seek a more remunerative post, but basically because of local feeling arising out of the General Strike. His critics in the labour movement were added to when he received a knighthood in the 1927 New Year Honours List. He began to distance himself from his Labour colleagues on the City Council, claiming a degree of independence because he was Deputy Lord Mayor. During his period as Lord Mayor Bower had joined the Concord Lodge of the Freemasons, and increasingly his personal friendships tended to be with those who were nominally his political opponents. By June 1928 he was being openly attacked in the Council Chamber by W.S. Lewis, who referred to him as 'a Socialist once'. Bower succeeded Neville Chamberlain as chairman of the Municipal Bank Committee, and began to acquire business interests.

The final break with the Labour Party came in 1932. The immediate cause was the granting of the Freedom of the City to Neville Chamberlain. Bower voted for this, in defiance of the Labour whip. An internal Borough Party committee of inquiry was set up, Bower refused to meet it, the committee recommended his expulsion, and in May 1932 the Erdington Divisional Labour Party duly expelled him. After a period as an Independent he formally joined the Aston Manor Conservative Club in August 1933.

Bower's service on two national committees in the 1930s – the Ray Committee on local government expenditure and the Hadow departmental committee on local government staff– established for him a reputation as a municipal administrator. He was elected to the board of several public companies and held various other administrative posts. He fitted somewhat uneasily into the ranks of Birmingham Unionism – as one leading Labour councillor recalled, 'his switch was more a marriage of convenience than a conversion to Tory principles'. After the Second World War some of the younger generation of Labour councillors in Birmingham came to admire his administrative knowledge and expertise, and to regret his loss to the labour movement.

Percival Bower married twice. His first wife, Alice Hare from Canterbury, died in 1933. They had married in 1904 and had a son and a daughter. Mrs Bower suffered from bad health for many years, which limited Bower's parliamentary ambitions. Their son Robert Dennis Bower was killed in 1941 while serving with the RAF. In the same year Percival Bower married Mildred Ogden from Derby, who survived him.

Bower died on 7 May 1948 at his home in Erdington, Birmingham, after a heart attack. The funeral at Erdington Parish Church was followed by cremation at Perry Barr Cemetery. His estate was valued at £30,109.

Sources: *Yardley Labour Torch* (Nov 1924); *Town Crier,* 7 Nov 1924, 7 Jan 1927; *Birmingham Mail*, 23 Aug 1933; *Birmingham Gazette*, 23 Aug 1933; *Sunday Mercury,* 28 Jan 1944; *WWW* (1941–50); R.P. Hastings, 'The Labour Movement in Birmingham 1927–1945' (Birmingham MA, 1959); J. Corbett, *The Birmingham Trades Council 1866–1966* (1966); Birmingham Public

Libraries and WEA, *The Nine Days in Birmingham: the General Strike 4–12 May, 1926* (Birmingham, 1976) 43 pp.; R.P. Hastings, 'Birmingham' in *The General Strike 1926*, ed. J. Skelley (1976) 208–31; M. Morris, *The General Strike* (1976). OBIT. *Birmingham Gazette, Birmingham Post* and *Evening Despatch*, 8 May 1948; *Town Crier*, 15 May 1948.

PETER DRAKE

See also: †Walter Samuel LEWIS.

BROCKLEHURST, Frederick (1866–1926)

SOCIALIST AND SECRETARY OF THE LABOUR CHURCH UNION

Frederick Brocklehurst was born in Macclesfield, Cheshire, on 1 February 1866, the son of Joseph Boulton Brocklehurst, a bookkeeper employed by James Swinnerton on the *Macclesfield Courier*. Fred's mother, Hannah (née Trafford) was the daughter of a Cheshire yeoman, who, although in general a staunch adherent of the Church of England, had lost all his money in fighting the Church on the question of tithes. So his daughter was obliged to begin work at about seven years of age; she became a piecer in a silk mill, later a winder, and then a weaver. Both Fred's parents held strong Tory views, and their son was brought up to share their religious and political opinions.

Fred Brocklehurst was later to remark that 'he was cradled in poverty, though he never had to go without a meal'. At the age of four or five he was sent to St George's Day and Sunday Schools in Macclesfield; but when his father died the boy, then in his tenth year, was obliged to begin half-time work as a piecer in a silk mill for 2*s* 6*d* a week. Two years later he left school altogether, and began earning 5*s* a week as a telegraph messenger. He later worked as a 'printer's devil' on the *Courier*, (which at some point referred to him as a bookkeeper), and it was then that he first became interested in trade unionism. He served only two years of his apprenticeship in the printing trade before transferring to Swinnerton's stationery shop, where his initial salary of 7*s* a week rose to the rate of £26 a year before he left, at the age of nineteen. During this period he continued to attend St George's Sunday School, where he became a teacher and took part in mission work, thereby acquiring considerable facility as a speaker. He also attended evening classes, and devoted much of his spare time to self-education. His ambition was now to enter the Ministry, and in 1885 he became a lay reader under the Rev. William Laycock, vicar of Hurdsfield near Macclesfield, which was then a populous district inhabited chiefly by mill workers. Two years later he moved, again as a lay reader, to Barrow-in-Furness, where he assisted the Rev. Edward W. Oak, in St Luke's parish. Here, among some of the town's worst slums, he began to realise that preaching and visiting alone could have little effect upon the prevailing social evils. Such doubts did not, however, deter him from his aim of further education, and in January 1890, financed by two scholarships and his own savings, Fred Brocklehurst entered Queens' College, Cambridge.

Brocklehurst's entry to the college had in fact been delayed for a term owing to ill health, which continued to hamper his later career. Nevertheless he took an active part in debates at Cambridge; and he became something of a radical. After passing the preliminary examination in June 1890, he won a college prize for New Testament Greek, and a pass in Honours in the first part of the Theological Tripos examination in June 1892. His intention was then to seek a quiet curacy, where he could read for the second part of the Theological Tripos. From several curacies offered to him, he decided to accept a title from a West Acton vicar for the Advent ordination of 1892. But his studies, together with his practical experiences in Barrow, were already causing him to modify his ideas on social and political questions and he abandoned his intention of taking Holy Orders, although he obtained his BA degree on 15 December 1892.

During the Easter vacation of 1892 he appeared on the platform of Ben Tillett, then parliamentary candidate for West Bradford, and upon returning to Bradford that summer, devoted considerable time to attending Labour meetings, and addressed several of these. He had also met John Trevor at the inaugural meeting of the Bradford Labour Church [*Labour*

Prophet, Jan 1893]. He had begun to fear that his advocacy of social reform might eventually conflict with the priesthood, but his dilemma was temporarily resolved by the offer of a post from John Trevor, founder of the Labour Church, at a weekly salary of £2; he entered upon his new duties in Manchester as secretary of the Church at the end of 1892 in succession to H.A. Atkinson. But the relationship between Trevor and Brocklehurst was not a peaceful one. Trevor, while condoning some philanthropy by Labour Churches, was 'afraid that social reform might become an aim which the Labour Church pursued heedless of its spiritual life' [Inglis (1958) 454]. Brocklehurst, on the other hand, 'wanted the Labour Churches to work in practical ways for social justice, especially by harmonising the different wings of organized labour' [ibid.]. Samuel Hobson, a Quaker who joined the movement, recorded that at meetings of the Labour Church Union – an organisation formed in 1893 with Brocklehurst as secretary and intended to draw the Churches closer together – his main task was to keep peace between the two men [Hobson (1938) 41].

Financial difficulties soon encountered by the Labour Church Union obliged Brocklehurst to resort to constant lecturing in order to earn a living but this was only possible after an agreement had been reached with the Church for whom he had been appointed to work full time. An appeal for funds to support the Union's secretary was made in the *Clarion* of 6 October 1894 by its treasurer, Sam Hodgkinson, who complained that due to 'thoughtlessness of the Local Labour Churches, who amidst the many calls that press upon them locally, forget the larger movement, and the obligations of the executive'. At the fourth conference of the Union held in Halifax on 16 November 1895, Brocklehurst and Hodgkinson refused to continue their offices of secretary and treasurer respectively.

Brocklehurst's role in the Labour Church, however, soon drew him into the political wing of the movement. He was elected to the executive committee of the Manchester and Salford ILP in January 1893, and attended the national party's first general conference as a delegate from Manchester Labour Church. He also played an active part in the formation of the ILP's Lancashire Federation, and subsequently served on its committee. During 1894, Brocklehurst was elected a vice-president of Manchester and Salford ILP, as well as a member of the NAC. He was to retain the latter position until 1897. In April 1894 he was adopted as ILP parliamentary candidate for Bolton, having also received invitations to stand for Blackfriars and Hutchesontown division of Glasgow, and for Hyde. Although the general election of 1895 found him at the bottom of the poll, with 2964 votes, Brocklehurst had by this time become president of Manchester and District ILP, as well as financial secretary of the national party, and secretary and treasurer of its parliamentary finance committee. During 1894 and 1895 he was a regular contributor to the *Labour Leader*. After the general election he also took part in an attempt to establish a Socialist Society in connection with the New Church (associated with the Swedenborgians), and undertook an extensive lecturing tour in the Midlands, including the Potteries, the London district, Southampton and Bristol. Much of his leisure time was devoted to cycling with the Clarion Club.

In the summer of 1896, Manchester and Salford ILP became involved in a struggle with Manchester Corporation's parks committee, to establish the right of public speaking in Boggart Hole Clough [for an account of which see special note below]. Brocklehurst was among ILP members who defied the prohibition on public speaking by addressing people on social and labour questions in a secluded part of the area on 14 June and was sentenced to a month's imprisonment. His experience in Strangeways Prison from 19 June to 18 July 1896, were to provide the material for a series of articles entitled 'I was in Prison', published in the *Manchester Evening News* (from 31 May to 4 June 1898) and a book, which appeared under the same title later in the year. His principal criticism of the prison system was that men imprisoned for political or conscientious reasons were treated as criminals.

Shortly after his release from prison, Brocklehurst served as a delegate to the International Socialist and Trade Union Congress held in London in 1896, and was elected secretary of its standing orders committee. Brocklehurst had been ill while serving his prison sentence, and after the London Congress, in November 1896 he travelled to the South of France and North Africa. Following two severe attacks of influenza, he was admitted to hospital in Algiers. He was also in need of financial assistance, which was provided as the result of an appeal in the *Labour Leader*. Leaving Algiers in April 1897, he sailed to Italy, North Africa and Rotterdam before finally returning to England. For some time he lived in London, where he collected material in the British Museum for a projected 'socio-religious study'. Nothing of this nature, however, appears to have been published.

Just before the municipal elections of November 1897, Fred Brocklehurst returned to Manchester, and became candidate for Harpurhey ward. He defeated, by 259 votes, George Needham, who as chairman of the parks committee had played a leading role in his prosecution. Brocklehurst served on watch, parks, rivers, sanitary and tramway committees of the Council, and he also became a member of the Mersey and Irwell Rivers Joint Board. Then in November 1897 he was elected to the Manchester School Board. Throughout this period he earned a somewhat precarious living by lecturing and in journalism.

In February 1899 Brocklehurst was adopted ILP parliamentary candidate for South-West Manchester. He withdrew from the NAC of the ILP at the Leeds conference in April 1899, but attended the International Congress committee held in Brussels in May 1899 and was also a delegate to the Labour Representation Conference held in the Memorial Hall, London, in February 1900. Just after this he aroused much hostility in the ILP by apparently supporting the continuation of the war against the Boer republics. Both H. Russell Smart and Keir Hardie called for his resignation, but after protracted correspondence in the *Clarion, Labour Leader* and *I.L.P. News*, and a statement of his views at the ILP's Glasgow conference in April 1900, he was able to convince members of his support for the party's anti-war policy, and put on record his past work for the Manchester Transvaal Committee. However, further criticism arose in the following month when he received his MA degree at Cambridge, and entered Lincoln's Inn in order to qualify for the Bar. The *Labour Leader* commented: 'He is already a Parliamentary candidate, a City Councillor, and a member of the School Board, etc. People in Manchester are thinking he is trying to do too much.' He was, however, defeated at the general election of October 1900 but retained his local offices in the November elections of that year, and served as an ILP delegate to the LRC in 1901. In May 1901 he and Mrs Pankhurst gave evidence on behalf of Manchester School Board before a committee appointed by the Home Office and Education Department to inquire into the employment of school children. Brocklehurst urged that the minimum age for street trading should be raised to twelve, while licences should be obligatory for all under the age of sixteen, and might be refused to girls, if the watch committee thought it necessary. Responsibility for the observance of the age limits should, he believed, be placed upon the parents. He wished to prohibit the part-time employment in other fields of children under the age of eleven and to extend the 'permit system' – which allowed street trading and other work out of school hours – to all children under fourteen, whose hours would also be regulated.

After further ILP criticism of Brocklehurst, on the ground that he had supported the Liberal candidate at a local by-election in Ardwick ward in 1902, he gradually withdrew from his party commitments. In February 1903 he announced that he did not intend to stand at the next parliamentary election. After passing his final Bar examination in May 1903, he was called to the Middle Temple, and he subsequently took Chambers in Manchester, joining the Northern Circuit. He did not seek re-election to his Manchester City Council seat in November 1903, and by the summer of 1905 he had changed his political allegiance to such an extent that he acted as counsel in a case against a Socialist councillor in Altrincham.

In December 1910 Brocklehurst stood, unsuccessfully, as Conservative candidate for the Prestwich division of South-East Lancashire. In 1919 he was appointed chairman of Salford Hundred Quarter Sessions, a position which he continued to hold until his death. His other activities at this time included membership of Manchester Statistical Society, in which he served as president, and membership of Manchester Press Club. For some years he was an officer in one of the local volunteer battalions. Towards the end of his life he lived in Stockport, where he was a member of Heaton Moor Conservative Club.

Fred Brocklehurst died on 4 July 1926 at the age of sixty, and was cremated. The funeral service was held on 7 July at Manchester Southern Cemetery. He left a widow and son, and was also survived by a sister. Mourners included members of the Bar and other members of the legal profession, together with representatives of political bodies and masonic lodges. He left effects valued at £700.

Writings: Articles on 'Education Reform' and 'Parish Councils', *Labour Leader* (1894) *passim*; 'I was in Prison', *Manchester Evening News*, 31 May to 4 June 1898 [repr. as a book in the same year]; 'Labour and Progress', *Manchester Evening News* (weekly on Saturdays in 1898); *A Socialist's Programme: an address delivered in the Hulme Town Hall, Manchester on February 27th, 1899* 16 pp.; two letters in the *Clarion*, 7 and 14 April 1900; 'Progressive News and Notes', ibid., June–Nov 1900; Evidence before Inter-Departmental Committee on Employment of School Children, *M of E* 1902 XXV Qs 7422–640; 'Recent Democratic Legislation', *CWS Annual* (1904) 185–208; he also wrote articles in the *Manchester Guardian* and *New Weekly*, and from 4 Oct 1894 to Sep 1895 he edited the *Bolton and District Independent Labour Party Pioneer*.

Sources: (1) MS : ILP, Minutes of NAC, 1894–1900, BLPES; Manchester Central Branch ILP, Minutes of meeting, 7 Oct 1902, Manchester PL, Archives Dept; LP archives: LRC 2/49. (2) Newspapers: *Workman's Times*, Dec 1892–Dec 1893; *Labour Prophet*, Jan 1893–Dec 1895; *Clarion*, 1893–1903; *Commonweal*, 20 Jan 1894; *Labour Leader*, 1894–1905; *I.L.P. News*, Oct 1897–Dec 1900; *Pioneer*, Mar 1900; *Daily Dispatch*, 25 Oct 1900; *Manchester: a monthly journal of the Manchester and Salford Independent Labour Party* (Nov 1900). (3) Other: ILP, *Annual Conference Reports*, 1893–1903; *Labour Annual* (1895), (1897), (1898); City of Manchester, *Index of Minutes of the Council . . .*, 1897–1903; *Manchester Faces and Places 9*, no. 11 (Aug 1898) 209–14; LRC, *Report of the Conference on Labour Representation. . .*, 1 Feb 1900 and *Report of the First Annual Conference. . .*, 1 Feb 1901; Slater's *Manchester, Salford and Suburban Directory* (1920); E.S. Pankhurst, *The Suffragette Movement* (1931); J. Toole, *Fighting through Life* (1935); S.G. Hobson, *Pilgrim to the Left: memoirs of a modern revolutionist* (1938); J.A. Venn, *Alumni Cantabrigienses*, Part II: *1752–1900* vol. *1* (1940); F. Williams, *Fifty Years' March: the rise of the Labour Party* (1949); K.S. Inglis, 'The Labour Church Movement', *Int. Rev. Social Hist. 3* (1958) 445–60; D.F. Summers, 'The Labour Church and Allied Movements of the Late Nineteenth and Early Twentieth Centuries' (Edinburgh PhD, 1958); S. Pierson, 'John Trevor and the Labour Church Movement in England, 1891–1900', *Church History 29* (1960) 463–78; K.S. Inglis, *Churches and the Working Classes in Victorian England* (1963); E. Shinwell, *The Labour Story* (1963); P.d'A. Jones, *The Christian Socialist Revival 1877-1914* (Princeton, NJ, 1968); S. Pierson, *Marxism and the Origins of British Socialism* (Cornell Univ. Press, 1973). Obit. *Manchester City News* and *Manchester Evening News*, 5 July 1926; *Cheshire Daily Echo, Manchester Guardian* and *Times*, 6 July 1926; *Stockport Advertiser*, 9 July 1926; *Law Times*, and *Manchester City News*, 10 July 1926. The editors are indebted to Professor Judith Fincher Laird, Denison University, Ohio, U.S.A. for an earlier draft of this biography.

Naomi Reid

See also: John Trevor and below: Boggart Hole Clough and Free Speech.

Boggart Hole Clough and Free Speech

In 1896 Boggart Hole Clough became a national symbol of the Socialists' struggle for the right of free speech, and of a campaign which involved many of the leading members of the ILP. Boggart Hole Clough is now an urban park in north Manchester, but in the 1890s it was an extensive open space, comprising 147 acres of rough grass, sandy slopes, fields and natural woods, located just north of the built-up city area. Moreover, 'some distance from the main road a cup-shaped hollow, open to the level on the brook side, makes a natural amphitheatre in the slope, capable of holding, perhaps, 30,000 people' [Rowe (1896) 3]. The North Manchester Fabian Society held meetings here in 1892, as the ILP did in succeeding years. At this time the Clough formed part of the Carill Worsley estate; but when, in 1895, it was acquired by Manchester Corporation, the summer propaganda continued, with the tacit sanction of the authorities.

In May 1896, however, the Parks Committee, under the chairmanship of Conservative Councillor George Needham, decided to put an end to the meetings of 'a certain party' [the ILP]. On the 10th and 17th of that month, the speakers and chairmen were ordered by the police to discontinue the meetings, and their names and addresses were taken upon refusal. The first summons was issued against John Harker, vice-president of Manchester and Salford ILP, who had, moreover, opposed Needham in the last municipal elections. Harker was fined 10*s*, on the ground that 'someone else might want to hold meetings in the same park and the result would be a disturbance' [*Labour Leader*, 30 May 1896].

There were at this time in other parts of the country prohibitions on Socialist meetings. The motives were, of course, political. When the two ILP members on the Manchester City Council – J.E. Sutton and Jesse Butler – tried to raise a discussion on the issue of the Clough meetings, they were ruled out of order. When Butler, at a Parks Committee meeting two days later, asked for a guarantee of no further prosecutions, this was also refused, and the committee endorsed the chairman's action in instructing that the summonses should be issued.

The summonses in question, all heard at the Police Courts on 3 June, amounted to twenty: two each against John Harker, the Rev. Conrad Noel, Harry Henshall, Joseph Nuttall, S. Smalley, G. Vowers, W. Cash, and W. Blunden, for nuisance and annoyance on 24 May, and two each against the Rev. Conrad Noel and William Tweedale, for like offences on 31 May. Dr Pankhurst appeared for the defendants. Mr Headlam, the stipendiary magistrate, ordered a fine of £5 with costs against Harker and Noel, and of 40*s* with costs against Henshall, Nuttall, Smalley, Vowers and Cash. The summons against Blunden was withdrawn. The second cases against Noel and Tweedale were adjourned. At a special meeting the following Saturday (6 June), the ILP decided that the Boggart Hole Clough meetings should be continued under the charge of the EC, and that members should be levied to provide funds until the question was settled. So the Sunday meeting was held as usual, with Leonard Hall addressing a crowd of some 2000, in spite of a downpour of rain. As a result of this meeting, Hall, Harker, Vowers, Charles H. Brierley, Smalley, Tweedale, Mrs Pankhurst, 'the veteran Chartist' Charles Moss, and John Hempsall (ex-Elective Auditor for Salford), all appeared in court on the following Friday (12 June). Prosecuting on behalf of the Parks Committee was Christopher Cobbett, grandson of William Cobbett. All the summonses except those against Brierley, Harker and Hall were dismissed, and according to Fred Brocklehurst, who gave an account of the defendants' activities in the *Clarion* (20 June 1896), evidence against them was flimsy. Harker, he claimed, was prosecuted for writing a note and passing it to the speaker; Brierley for holding an umbrella over his head when it rained; Smalley for helping a park attendant in keeping order; Vowers for 'nothing in particular'; Tweedale and Moss for standing quietly for ten minutes at the edge of the crowd; Hempsall for smoking a cigar within six yards of the speaker; Mrs Pankhurst for lending her umbrella for the purposes of the collection; and Hall 'for the unpardonable crime of opening his mouth'. Brierley, Harker and Hall were fined £5 each, with costs, or one month's imprisonment. Harker, 'much to his disgust', was set at liberty, and a distraint order served upon him. Brierley, on the advice of Fred Brocklehurst (who was then studying law), allowed the ILP to pay his fine, as imprisonment would have meant the loss of his means of livelihood. Leonard Hall was sent to Strangeways gaol, where he was treated as a common thief: he was denied books, paper, writing materials or visits, and limited to prison diet. His wife applied for him to be as a first class misdemeanant, but the request was refused.

The meeting at the Clough on 14 June again resulted in the prosecution of the speaker, Fred Brocklehurst. Upon his refusal to pay the £5 fine and costs, he joined Leonard Hall in gaol. Brocklehurst, conducting his own defence, stated that the police had confessed that he had violated no by-law. He also discovered from the parks superintendent that the latter had been instigated to take action by the chairman of the Parks Committee. Two of the collectors at that meeting, Philip M'Andrew and Patrick Gleeson, appeared in court, although their cases were apparently dismissed. Neither was a member of the ILP. Prominent among the collectors had in fact been Mrs Pankhurst, whose activities the prosecution ignored. On the following Sunday (21 June), she delivered the principal speech at the Clough, a well-chosen address on 'The Life and Times of William Cobbett'. Spectators crowded into the Clough in a long procession, and sang 'England Arise' to open the proceedings. After Mrs Pankhurst's address, the collection was taken, but instead of the usual practice of receiving contributions in an upturned umbrella, women and girls, including Christabel and Sylvia Pankhurst, went round with collecting boxes and received over £11.

The names of Mrs Pankhurst and of some collectors, for instance Mrs Mary Helen Harker and Mrs Agnes Smalley, were taken, but the Parks Committee now faced a dilemma. To prosecute and even imprison working men was one thing; to do this to the wife of an eminent local barrister was quite another. Needham declined to take responsibility for prosecuting the women. He duly consulted Cobbett, the Town Clerk and the Lord Mayor, with the result that a special meeting of the Parks Committee was held to consider the matter. An understanding was then reached, that there should be no further prosecutions until after the forthcoming Council meeting. As the *Labour Leader* (27 June 1896) remarked: '. . . and yet we are continually being told that social status counts for nothing.'

On 28 June John Bruce Glasier addressed a large meeting at the Clough, as a result of which he and four collectors, Mrs Pankhurst, Mrs Harker, Mrs Mary Ellen Mellor, and Mrs Lily Bennett, all received summonses. The City Council, voting as to whether an inquiry should be held into the whole affair, was divided, with 25 in favour, 36 against, and 43 neutral. In the absence of any decision, the ILP members finally appeared on trial on Friday, 3 July. The ILP's National Administrative Council, then meeting in Manchester, had adjourned so that members could attend the proceedings. Thus Tom Mann, Keir Hardie, Russell Smart, Pete Curran and France Littlewood were all in court, with Enid Stacy and Caroline Martyn sitting at the back. Still hoping to avoid sentencing the women, the stipendiary announced that the summonses would be adjourned for a week, with the outcome dependent upon what should happen on Sunday. That evening an estimated 12,000 people in Stevenson Square cheered as the NAC and 'prisoners' declared that 'There wasn't a member of the ILP that wasn't prepared to go to jail if necessary in defence of the sacred right of free speech' [*Labour Leader*, 11 July 1896]. Mrs Pankhurst, when interviewed by 'The Pilgrim' for the *Labour Leader* (4 July 1896), had announced that she was prepared to go to prison and had commented, somewhat prophetically, 'It wouldn't be so very dreadful, you know, and it would be a valuable experience. I could afford to go, too, better than most. I have had quite a number of offers of help in the housekeeping.'

The whole affair of Boggart Hole Clough was turning into a massive ILP propaganda exercise; and the non-Socialist press also expressed sympathy for the ILP's case. The *Manchester Guardian* asserted on 23 June that Hall should never have been prosecuted, and that the Parks Committee could have set aside a convenient place in the Clough for meetings. From the *City News* (27 June 1896) came another reminder that meetings had taken place in the Clough long before its acquisition by the Corporation, and that they were held far from any footpath. The by-laws did not provide power to prohibit meetings, and according to the *City News*, Councillor Needham had issued the prohibition order on his own initiative, and before consulting his colleagues. The Bradford division of East Manchester Liberal Association passed a resolution condemning the action of the Corporation in illegally imprisoning men for public speech under the pretext of annoyance, while A.J. Mundella, MP, in a letter to Sheffield ILP, described the action of Manchester Corporation as incomprehensible. Money flowed in to the Boggart Hole Clough Defence Fund from all over the country; on 26 September 1896 contributions totalled £271 *2s 7d*. Most important for the ILP was perhaps the fact that vast numbers of people, who otherwise might never have attended a Socialist meeting, all flocked to Boggart Hole Clough.

On Sunday 5 July Mrs Pankhurst took the chair for Keir Hardie at Boggart Hole Clough. Dr and Mrs Pankhurst and their children, Keir Hardie and Miss Goulden, drove up in an open barouche. Travelling along Piccadilly and Rochdale Road they passed, and were cheered by, crowds of people going to the Clough. Trams were packed, while the Clarion Scouts were out in force on their bicycles. Socialist literature sold well at the meeting, and the collection amounted to £20 *2s*. At the ninth meeting in the campaign, Katharine Bruce Glasier delivered the address, while on 19 July an estimated 50,000 people listened to Ben Tillett. Subsequent meetings were addressed by Enid Stacy, Shaw Maxwell and Dr Pankhurst.

Leonard Hall was released from Strangeways on 11 July, and Brocklehurst a week later. On each occasion an enthusiastic welcome was followed in the evening by a mass meeting in Stevenson Square. Hall immediately published an account of his experiences in the *Clarion* (18 July 1896), under the title 'For One Calendar Month'. Brocklehurst, having written a column 'In Prison and Out' for the *Labour Leader* (25 July 1896), later contributed a series, 'I was in Prison', to the *Manchester Evening News* (31 May – 4 June 1898), which he republished in book form.

Legally the situation was turning into a farce. Bruce Glasier, having twice refused to pay a £5 fine, remained at liberty, while Hall and Brocklehurst had been imprisoned for the same offence. The case against Hardie, Mrs Pankhurst and the women collectors was brought up again on 14 July, and adjourned first to 21 July, then to 6 August and 3 September. Hardie staggered the Bench by stating that he had 473 witnesses, including Liberals and Conservatives, to prove that the meetings were orderly and well-conducted. Meanwhile the Council turned its attention to a new by-law, passed at a special meeting on 28 July, which prohibited meetings and collections in the parks unless permission was previously granted by the Corporation. To the ILP this move by the Council appeared as proof that it had lacked such powers at the time of the prosecutions. The by-law was finally accepted by the Home Secretary in January 1897, 'in the confidence that the discretionary power of allowing meetings, which the by-law gives to the Council, will be exercised as to meet any reasonable demand.' Needham duly announced that the feeling of the Parks Committee 'was that they should not sanction the meetings of a certain Party' [*Labour Leader*, 16 Jan 1897]. But his later attempts in the Council Chamber to ban ILP meetings in the Clough proved unsuccessful, and in May 1897 North Manchester ILP opened its summer propaganda campaign there with an audience of 2000.

Thus, apart from the sufferings of Brocklehurst and the Hall family, the whole affair of Boggart Hole Clough had been a great triumph for the ILP. Part of the reward came in November 1897, when Councillor Needham lost Harpurhey ward in the municipal elections, to none other than Fred Brocklehurst. The local and national ILP had been united by a common aim, and the cause of free speech and the general publicity had drawn into the ambit of the ILP many people who might not have been attracted to routine Socialist meetings. After the Boggart Hole Clough affair, ILP meetings in Manchester generally remained free from interference; and in September 1913 Manchester and Salford ILP Federation celebrated its coming-of-age by holding a demonstration in the Clough, with Hardie as chief speaker, and Tom Fox in the chair.

Sources: (1) Contemporary: *Manchester Faces and Places 2*, no. 1, 10 Oct 1890, pp. 8, 10-11, contains a photograph and description of Boggart Hole Clough. Regular accounts of the free-speech campaign appear in the *Clarion, Labour Leader*, and *Manchester Guardian*, June-Aug 1896. Cuttings from other newspapers are contained in the Pankhurst Coll. Newspaper

Cuttings Book, Dr Pankhurst 1896 no. 7, International Institute of Social History, Amsterdam; these include: *Courier*, 23 May 1896; *Manchester Guardian*, 23 May, 4, 6 June, 10 July, 6, 10 Aug 1896; *City News*, 6 June, 8, 15 Aug 1896; *Evening News* and *Evening Mail*, 19 June 1896; *Reynolds's Newspaper*, 19 July 1896. The collection also contains a photograph (unlabelled) showing Hardie addressing a meeting, apparently at the Clough. A full illustrated account is contained in H.C. Rowe, *The Boggart Hole Contest* (Manchester, 1896) 18 pp.; F. Brocklehurst, 'I was in Prison', *Manchester Evening News*, 31 May to 4 June 1898 gives Brocklehurst's personal recollections. Later that year he published a book under the same title. Brief references to the campaign appear in the *Labour Annual* (1897) 199, and ILP, *Report of the 5th Annual Conference* ... (1897) 11 and 17. (2) Other: A. Woolerton, *The Labour Movement in Manchester and Salford* (City of Manchester Branch ILP Pamphlets no. 1: 1907) 20 pp.; W. Stewart, *J. Keir Hardie* (1921); E.S. Pankhurst, *The Suffragette Movement* (1931) [She states that Harker was imprisoned, but this is not mentioned in any other source]; S. Dark, *Conrad Noel: an autobiography* (1945); L. Thompson *The Enthusiasts: a biography of John and Katharine Bruce Glasier* (1971); I. McLean, *Keir Hardie* (1975); K.O. Morgan, *Keir Hardie: radical and socialist* (1975).

NAOMI REID

See also: Frederick BROCKLEHURST; *(William) Leonard HALL; Henry (Harry) HENSHALL; France LITTLEWOOD.

CARLILE, Richard (1790-1843)

RADICAL JOURNALIST AND FREETHINKER

Richard Carlile was born at Ashburton, in South Devon, on 8 December 1790. His father was a shoemaker and exciseman who died when Richard was four years old (some versions state that the father abandoned the family at this time). His mother supported Richard and his two sisters from the takings of a small village shop in Ashburton; and with the help of relatives, Carlile completed his primary education at the Bourne free school. At the age of twelve he went to work in a druggist's shop in Exeter but after a few months was apprenticed to a series of tinplate masters, with whom he served out his time. He first went to London in 1811, and then, after marrying a Dorset woman in 1813, he settled permanently in the capital city.

Until the winter of 1816–17 he worked at his trade, and took no part in politics or public affairs. It was the economic distress of the post-war years that propelled him towards an active radicalism. These were years of a great outpouring of radical journalism and political activity associated with the names of William Cobbett, Jonathan Wooler, William Hone and John Wade. In March 1817 Carlile became a hawker for Wooler's *Black Dwarf*, and almost immediately entered upon a business and political acquaintanceship with William T. Sherwin, a young Northamptonshire printer. The two men collaborated on *Sherwin's [Weekly] Political Register*, a major radical periodical which survived until August 1819, at which time Sherwin abandoned political journalism entirely.

The relationship with Sherwin, negotiated in April 1817, was a turning point in Carlile's life. Carlile undertook legal responsibility for publishing the *Register*, a not innocuous obligation given the frequent prosecutions of the radical press occurring at that time; in exchange, he was permitted to use a portion of Sherwin's publishing rooms at 183 Fleet Street and so, indirectly, to launch upon his career as a tract-seller and radical publicist. Carlile and Sherwin worked closely together between 1817 and 1819: they produced the *Register* jointly (with Carlile doing more of the writing than he took credit for); published squibs, tracts and pamphlets, most of them reflecting a position of extreme political radicalism; and commenced the cheap reprinting of controversial radical writings. In August 1817 Carlile reprinted three political parodies by Hone on parts of the book of Common Prayer: 'Wilkes's Catechism', 'The Political Litany', and 'The Sinecurist's Creed'. It was done without Hone's agreement, but both Hone and Carlile were prosecuted. Carlile remained in prison awaiting trial; Hone was prosecuted three times for blasphemous libel in December 1817, conducted his own defence and secured acquittal in each instance. Carlile was then released unobtrusively from prison, the charges against him being neither pursued nor struck from the record.

Carlile had read Tom Paine's *Rights of Man* in 1816 or 1817 – more likely the latter date; it was a landmark in his own progress towards radicalism; and while in prison he completed his education by reading the *Age of Reason*. His mission was now to lay bare the iniquities of kingcraft and priestcraft. He republished the *Age of Reason*, with Sherwin's collaboration, in December 1818; a successful second edition, from which Sherwin dissociated himself, followed shortly after. The initial sale was not great – the print was in two half-guinea volumes, but Carlile had also begun a number of other reprints in cheaper format: Paine's *Common Sense* and *Rights of Man* were issued in weekly parts along with *Sherwin's Political Register*; and other reprints were made available later in the *Deist; or Moral Philosopher*. Early in 1819 the Attorney-General as well as the Society for the Suppression of Vice began prosecutions. Following the Peterloo massacre of August 1819 – at which Carlile had been present – he published a bitter account of what had happened, and for this he was arrested on a charge of seditious libel. Carlile had taken over Sherwin's *Register* which he now called by its original name, the *Republican*, and it was in this journal as well as in the final number of *Sherwin's Register* that Carlile published his attack upon the Manchester magistrates and yeomanry. When, however, his trial was finally heard at the Guildhall in October 1819, it was the earlier blasphemy charges that were preferred. Carlile had become, in the previous three years, well acquainted with the leading personalities of the general radical movement; and many rallied to his defence, among them William Hone, Henry Hunt and Dr James Watson senior.

Though celebrated in the annals of nineteenth-century reform, the two trials, spread over four days, were a disappointment to his supporters and to the many curious onlookers who thronged the precincts of the Guildhall. Carlile lacked eloquence and had no legal training, and notwithstanding the efforts of Hone, 'Orator' Hunt and Leigh Hunt, he was decidedly outmanoeuvred by the presiding judge. His speeches were phrased badly; his attempts at flights of rhetoric trailed off into disconnected ramblings. The jury rejected his arguments and he was convicted on two counts of blasphemous libel stemming from his publications of Paine and Elihu Palmer's *Principles of Nature*. The harshness of the sentence shocked many: payment of a £1500 fine and three years' imprisonment in Dorchester gaol. Carlile was not to gain his freedom until November 1825 due to his inability to pay the large fine.

The *Age of Reason* had been withdrawn shortly after the trial for fear of another prosecution. But Carlile had spent a day reading it in court, and it could therefore be included in the verbatim reports of the trial. Ten thousand twopenny numbers of the *Mock Trials* were sold. His bookshop in Fleet Street was kept open, first by his wife Jane, and then, when she was arrested and sent to join her husband in Dorchester gaol, by Mary Anne, his sister. Carlile launched his first national appeal in October 1820. Little groups of sympathisers began to collect monies, and after Mary Anne was arrested (joining her brother and sister-in-law in Dorchester gaol in November 1821), volunteers started coming to London to serve in the shop, and to keep radical literature circulating. More formal organisation began in Edinburgh in December 1821, with the establishment of the Edinburgh Freethinkers' Zetetic Society, the leading figures in which were James and Robert Affleck. The idea of local radical or Zetetic clubs to support Carlile found modest support in the country, the greatest activity, outside Edinburgh and London, being in the West Riding, Lancashire and Cheshire. Support for Carlile was impressive: in the one year 1822 nearly £900 was sent in from fifty-seven localities throughout Britain. Membership of these pro-Carlile groups and Zetetic societies were mainly artisans and shopkeepers.

Those who suffered most from official persecution were the replacements for the shop in Fleet Street and the persistent vendors of radical tracts. The Stockport hatter, Joseph Swann, spent four and a half years in Chester gaol for attending a seditious meeting and for selling the *Republican* in Macclesfield (and he received another three months in 1831 for hawking the *Poor Man's Guardian*). This was an heroic episode in working-class history, and some of its activists deserve a closer documentation. James Watson, for example, a volunteer shopman from Leeds, became a pioneer of the unstamped press in the 1830s, while William Campion and Richard Hassell, to name only two of many obscure supporters, were untutored youths of great promise. It was an episode from which derived Carlile's reputation as a fearless champion of a free press. He provided funds, incessant propaganda and ample moral fervour, and so kept the cause alive.

In Dorchester gaol Carlile read widely in general radical literature and especially in religious history and theological criticism. The results of his study produced a shift in his ideas towards republican theories of government and to materialisic interpretations of religion. Morever, he slowly moved away from the political radicalism of Hunt, and his economic views were beginning to be influenced by Francis Place. For a time Carlile leaned towards classical political economy rather than to the co-operative or Owenite views of many of his working-class contemporaries. These changes in his thinking can be traced through the pages of the *Republican* which he continued to edit from his prison cell. Although the journal never reached a mass circulation – its peak figure was about 5000 – it was of considerable importance in the history of free thought, and it allowed Carlile to consolidate his reputation as an absolutist champion of freedom of expression. He also used its pages to conduct bitter disputes with other reformers – with Hunt and Cobbett for instance; but at the same time his sharp comments upon contemporary events were marked by a growing certainty as well as lucidity of expression. He was now moving away from Paine's deism to an acceptance of atheism. In his *Address to Men of Science* (1821) he proclaimed scientific knowledge to be superior to 'superstition' and 'priestcraft'; human reason was generated by 'the same laws as every other natural product'. But he still adhered to a sceptical materialism until he began to be influenced by the ideas of Baron d' Holbach, the French materialist philosopher. By 1822 Carlile began to expound the gospel of atheism (or infidelity, as it came to be called).

Carlile was released from prison in November 1825. Towards the end of his sentence he had become somewhat interested in Freemasonry, and he published a number of articles in the *Republican* and later reprinted them, with additional material, in a *Manual of Masonry*, which continued to be read long after his death. His return to London in January 1826 found him in considerable financial difficulties, largely because during his imprisonment there had been several distraints upon his property in attempts to recover the £1500 fine. His establishment of a Joint Stock Book Company was not a success although a number of interesting tracts were published, including a reprint of Shelley's *Queen Mab* and Peter Annett's *Free Enquirer* (for which Annett had been imprisoned in 1762). Of even greater historical importance was the publication of *Every Woman's Book; or, What is Love*? in February 1826. An earlier version of *Every Woman's Book* had appeared in the *Republican* (vol. *11*, no. 18) in 1825. The 1826 pamphlet evidently enjoyed a wide circulation, and slightly revised editions appeared in 1828 and 1838, the latter published by Alfred Carlile. There were also various abridged editions. There was no legal interference with those involved in the early birth control propaganda, and Carlile himself suffered no prosecution for this particular contribution to the struggle for a free press. It led, however, to a bitter quarrel with Cobbett.

In May 1826, with the discreet assistance of Francis Place, he purchased a house and shop at 62 Fleet Street, where he was to remain for the next ten years. The heavy costs seriously strained his resources, and for the remainder of his life he was never free from financial worries, although later Julian Hibbert, a wealthy London freethinker, gave him substantial support. The spy reports always described Carlile as desperately poor. He had one good year (1819) which carried him on for a time, but for most of his life he lived from hand to mouth.

In the years immediately after his release Carlile began to modify his atheistic views. He began in 1826 what was to be a close association with the Rev. Robert Taylor who by the time Carlile met him was preaching an allegorical Christianity. Taylor was a renegade clergyman who in 1824 had started in London the Christian Evidence Society, whose aim was to expose the fraudulent claims of Christianity to be grounded upon truth. Taylor propounded a 'pagan' theology based upon a universalist conception of sun worship. But it would be misleading to suggest that Carlile was wholly dominated by Taylor. The two men moved in tandem, constructing jointly an amalgam of ideas and symbols. Taylor nudged Carlile towards theological millennialism and their friendship grew steadily. It was strengthened when Taylor was successfully prosecuted for blasphemy, his prison sentence being spent in Oakham gaol during 1828. When Taylor was released in February 1829 he and Carlile went on an 'infidel mission' round the country. The most interesting response was in the towns of Lancashire where very effective propagandist activity had already been carried on by Rowland Detrosier.

Carlile had begun a new periodical, the *Lion*, at the beginning of 1828, and it was in the columns of the *Lion* that the tour was most fully reported. It was intended that there should be a second tour in 1830, but they were unable to raise sufficient money, and they had already begun to quarrel. In May 1830 Carlile and Taylor took over the site of the former Surrey Institution on Blackfriar's Road. The Rotunda, as it came to be known, was the centre of London working-class radicalism in the early years of the thirties. Carlile, with the financial assistance of Hibbert, refitted its two theatres, and Taylor – the 'Devil's Chaplain' as he was called by Henry Hunt – was one of the main attractions at the Rotunda; but it was also increasingly used by many radical groups – including the Radical Reform Association and the Irish Anti-Union Association – and later, for a time, it became the accepted meeting place for the National Union of Working Classes.

In response to the agricultural labourers' revolt Carlile published a supporting article: 'To the Insurgent Agricultural Labourers' in the 27 November 1830 issue of the *Prompter*, for which he was prosecuted by the Whig Government. After a hurried trial, marked by irregularities, Carlile was convicted and sentenced to thirty months' imprisonment, a fine of £200, and he was bound over in the sum of £1000. Carlile paid neither fine nor surety. This time he was gaoled in the Giltspur Street Compter, a good deal more conveniently situated for his journalistic work than Dorchester gaol had been.

The suspicion among his radical contemporaries that his prosecution had less to do with the agricultural disturbances than with his activities at the Rotunda was strengthened by the subsequent trial and conviction of Taylor in May 1831 for a Good Friday sermon. Gale Jones and Julian Hibbert did what they could to prevent the collapse of the Rotunda as a centre of radical activity, and in this they were assisted by Eliza Sharples, a disciple of Carlile whose discourses attracted large crowds to the Rotunda in the early months of 1832. In the spring of 1832, however, the Rotunda was given over to another tenant.

By 1832 Carlile had moved a long way from the uncompromising materialism of the early 1820s. As Taylor's influence grew Carlile began to alter his materialist conception of the world; his atheism became tempered increasingly by a universalist framework. Exposés of particular theological abuses came to concern him less than the abstract assumptions of religion. A further influence prior to 1832 was that of Rowland Detrosier, a Stockport deist, whose millennialist leanings reinforced those of Taylor.

The ambiguities and unresolved elements in Carlile's thought came together in a synthesis in 1832. The catalyst was Eliza Sharples. Sharples was the daughter of a Bolton textile manufacturer. She had attended the Carlile-Taylor meetings in 1829, was familiar with Carlile's writings, and had developed well-formed freethought and feminist ideas. Not deeply versed in theological disputation, she left Bolton in January 1832 and came to London to enlist in Carlile's crusade; and she rapidly became his most ardent disciple and lover. She was 'Isis', the eponymous heroine of the radical newspaper by that name (1832), whose discourses at the Rotunda and elsewhere were widely publicised. Sharples lived with Carlile after his release from prison and became his 'moral mistress', bearing him four children (his acrimonious marriage to Jane Carlile having led to a final separation in 1832). Carlile's stress upon the 'respectability' of this union notwithstanding, he was denounced politically and personally for his immorality. Contemptible aspersions were cast upon his liaison with Sharples, and he spent hundreds of contentious hours in defence of a principled liaison.

Sharples gave Carlile the final push in the direction of Christian millennialism. He had anticipated his conversion as early as 1827 in a Stockport sermon entitled *The Gospel according to Richard Carlile*, in which he had asserted the allegorical nature of true Christianity. Jesus, he contended, was nothing more than the universal 'principle of reason'; Christianity was 'as old as mankind', being a reworking of the Greek legend of Prometheus. The presence in 1832 of 'Isis' – the Egyptian goddess, 'waving the magic wand of intellect over the darkness of this land' [*Isis*, 10 Mar 1832] – gave meaning to his maturing vision. In revelatory imagery he proclaimed his conversion in May 1832: 'I am become a Christian in the highest, best, and purest sense of the word' [ibid., 5 May 1832].

His new faith represented a millennialist fusion of extreme rationalism (the 'moral allegory' of human life), Christian theology, and atheism; and freethinkers, predictably horrified, denounced him as a traitor to their cause. But in the eyes of orthodox religionists he remained an atheist, without qualification. Neither side was entirely wrong. Carlile's fundamental objective was to affirm his integrity, to give universal validity to a once hopeful career that now lay in ruins about him. His conversion to 'Christianity' enabled him to identify his person with that of Jesus, the heroic figure shunned and abandoned by all but the righteous in heart.

This doctrine, however, not only lost Carlile most of his remaining supporters; it obfuscated the language of reformism. Chartists and socialists were proposing alternative blueprints for reform with which Carlile disagreed; he countered with apocalyptic appeals for the construction of parish 'churches'. As he burrowed ever more deeply into the language of theology, his message became more incomprehensible. Metaphor replaced lucidity, and self-righteousness became a substitute for the plaudits of the multitude.

The final decade of Carlile's life was, almost inevitably, politically disastrous. He was imprisoned a fourth time for his opposition to church rates (1834-5), lived in Manchester for a short period (1837–8), and debated and preached endlessly with Chartists, socialists and orthodox churchmen. (In 1836 he qualified for a preacher's license in order to facilitate his standing as a public speaker). Many of his discourses were delivered out of doors for want of meeting place, and most of his opponents were of little substance. He condemned vitriolically all political and economic proposals for reform, the Chartist demands most strongly. Between 1836 and 1840 he spoke in almost every city and town of any size in England, criss-crossing Yorkshire and Lancashire several times, seeking vainly for converts to his 'Catholic Christian Church'. A few artisans and philanthropists were won over – notably Sarah Chichester, a translator of Fourier, who gave him modest financial support – but the financial returns were meagre.

Carlile quarrelled with nearly all of his former associates, including Taylor, and in the late 1830s his financial position plummeted to a new low. He continued to sell copies of his earlier tracts and was able to publish one successful unstamped newspaper, the *Gauntlet* (1833–4), but he could not generate the capital to publish much that was new. Among works that did appear were some Manchester penny tracts published and distributed with the aid of Abel Heywood (1838–9); a shortlived anti-Chartist periodical, *Carlile's Political Register*, produced with the aid of his sons, Alfred and Thomas Paine; and the *Christian Warrior* (1843), a journal published just before his death in which he attempted a final clarification of his views. Isolated politically, and very poor financially, Carlile retreated increasingly into experiments with mesmerism and vegetarianism.

He continued, however, to write prolifically in the final years of his life, but he did so anonymously and for payment. As editor of the *Durham Chronicle* (1840-1) and *Besley's Devonshire Chronicle* (1840-1), and as a weekly contributor to the *Bolton Free Press* (1841), he wrote with zest on a wide range of subjects and attempted, wherever possible, to insinuate his Christian allegory into his leaders.

During 1835 Carlile gave up his house at 62 Fleet Street and in the following year he abandoned his lecturing room near Temple Bar. One consolation was the leasing of a cottage in 1836 along Enfield Highway, north-east of London. This accentuated his physical isolation from the metropolis, and caused his 'moral marriage' to suffer. A final blow occurred at the end of 1842 when he had to give up the cottage and move back to Fleet Street quarters with his son, Alfred.

Carlile died, after a prolonged period of ill health, on 10 February 1843 in his lodgings in Fleet Street. Even in death, he continued to evoke controversy. *The Times* reported (15 Feb 1843) that the body 'of this eccentric man' had been removed two days earlier to St Thomas's Hospital for dissection, in accordance with Carlile's instruction; and that a Mr Grainger had lectured upon the body. On the next day *The Times* carried a further report that the Hospital Governors had expressed their disapproval of the lecture taking place, because of Carlile's religious views; and that Mr Grainger had publically 'asserted his opposition to Carlile'. Later in the month at the burial at Kensal Green Cemetery where several hundred mourners took part in a final tribute, Carlile's sons protested at the reading of the burial service, but to no avail [*Times*, 27 Feb 1843]. But the public's response to Carlile's death was muted, and later attempts to erect a monument to his memory proved abortive. The *New Moral World* of 17 June 1843 reported that Eliza Sharples and her three children had been left destitute, and that 'a few friends' had agreed to take the mother and her two daughers as residents of the Concordium, Alcott House, Ham Common, while Julian was placed in the Harmony Hall School. The *New Moral World* launched a financial appeal for the family's support. Emma Martin preached an eloquent sermon on Richard Carlile's death at the City Road Hall of Science on Sunday evening 26 February 1843; and her text was later published in pamphlet form. She was frank about the changes in Carlile's ways of thinking in his last years, but she insisted that these were 'minor points in which we may have discovered blemishes', urging her audience to consider 'those leading features in his life, which have honoured him and advantaged us'. She spoke with dignity of the moral values and beliefs of the atheist, and exhorted her hearers to continue to press the causes for which Carlile had struggled and suffered.

Jane Carlile died in the same year. Of three sons by his marriage (two children having died in infancy), Alfred and Thomas Paine became booksellers, and Richard migrated to the United States, where he became a member of the Wisconsin House of Assembly; he died in New York in 1854. Eliza Sharples died in London in 1861, in circumstances of extreme poverty. Her three surviving children migrated to the United States: Julian died during the American Civil War; Theophila, who married Colin Campbell (the first Socialist candidate for governor of Wisconsin) wrote a biography of her father and died in California in 1913; and Hypatia died in Chicago in 1923.

Richard Carlile remains a somewhat neglected personality in the history of the British working class. Yet his achievements were remarkable. It was Carlile, above all others, who established the traditions of Tom Paine in London, Sheffield and elsewhere in Britain, whereby Old Corruption meant kingcraft, lordcraft and priestcraft. Only republicanism and the end of priestcraft would free the people; and to the furtherance of these ideas Carlile brought an indomitable spirit and an assertion of independence that was of central importance in the emergence of a free press. That he was personally difficult, indeed unlovable in some respects in no way detracts from the contributions he made to the popularisation of freethought; to the courageous dissemination of birth control ideas; and to the emphasis he gave to rationality and reason. He was correct to write of himself in 1833: 'If I die today, I shall leave the aggregate man better than I found him.' He should have added 'woman', for his acceptance of a feminist position went back at least to 1819.

Writings: *A Letter to the Society for the Suppression of Vice on their Malignant Efforts to prevent* *a Free Enquiry after Truth and Reason* (1819) 13 pp.; editor of the *Deist, or Moral Philosopher* 3 vols. (1819–26; later eds.); *The Life of Thomas Paine* [written to bind with his writings] (1820; ed. and adapted by G. Aldred [Strickland Classics, no. 6: Glasgow, 1940, 22 pp.]; *An Effort to set at Rest some Little Disputes and Misunderstandings between the Reformers of Leeds* (1821) 28 pp.; *Observations on "Letters to a Friend . . . by Olinthus Gregory"* (1821); *An Address to Men of Science . . .* (1821) 48 pp.; *To the Reformers of Great Britain* [letters written from Dorchester Gaol in 1821] [1821]; 'Correspondence between Mr Benbow and Mr Carlile' in R. Carlile, *Letters from Dorchester Gaol* [23 Oct–25 Dec 1821] [1821] 14-25; *Every Man's Book; or What is God?* (1826) 47 pp.; *Every Woman's Book; or What is Love?* [abridged from *Republican*] (1826; rev. eds. 1828 & 1836) 48 pp.; *The Gospel according to Richard Carlile, shewing the True Parentage, Birth, and Life of our Allegorical Lord and Saviour, Jesus Christ* (1827) 32 pp.; *Richard Carlile's First Sermon upon the Mount* (1827) 16 pp.; *A New View of Insanity* (1831); *An Exposure of Freemasonry* (1831; rev. ed. as *Manual of Masonry* (1836) and in later eds. as *Manual of Freemasonry*); *A Form of Prayer on Account of the Troubled State of Certain Parts of the United Kingdom* (1831) 7 pp.; *The American Antitheistical Catechism* (1832) 16 pp.; *A Letter . . . to Charles Larkin of the Newcastle Press* (Newcastle upon Tyne, 1834) 12 pp.; *A Respectful Address to the Inhabitants of Newcastle upon Tyne and its Vicinity* (Newcastle upon Tyne, 1834) 16 pp.; *The Respectful Address . . . to the Inhabitants of Plymouth, Stonehouse and Devonport* (Devonport, [1834]) 12 pp.; *Church Reform: the only means to that end, stated in a letter to Sir Robert Peel* (1835); *The Letters of Mr Richard Carlile to the Inhabitants of Brighton, with a syllabus of his course of seven lectures* [1836] 8 pp.; *An Abstract, embodying the Evidences of the Lectures delivered . . . at Brighton and elsewhere in the Year 1836* (1837) 32 pp.; *Extraordinary Conversion and Public Declaration of Richard Carlile, of London, to Christianity* (Glasgow, 1837) 24 pp.; *A Dictionary of some of the Names in the Sacred Scriptures translated into the English Language* (Manchester, 1837) 38 pp.; *Carlile's Railroad to Heaven* (Manchester 1838) 8pp.; *Jesus Christ the only Radical Reformer* (Manchester, 1838) 8 pp.; *A View and Review of Robert Owen's Projects . . .* [1838] 16 pp.; *An Address to that Portion of the People of Great Britain and Ireland calling themselves Reformers* (Manchester, 1839) 16 pp.; *On going to Church* (Manchester, 1839) 12 pp.; *Unitarian, or Socinian and Social Catechism* (posthumously published NY, 1846) 14 pp.; *Jail Journal: prison thoughts and other writings by Richard Carlile* ed. G. Aldred (1913 as *Jail Jottings*; rev. ed. Glasgow, 1942).

Carlile's published works are too numerous to list. Many contained introductions or edited comments by him and included reports of his trials of 1819 and 1825. The periodicals which he published, however, include: *Republican* (1819–26); *Moralist* (1824); *Newgate Monthly Mag.* (1824–6); *Lion* (1828–9); *Carlile's Journal for 1830* (1830); *Prompter* (1830–1); *Union* (1831–2); *Isis* (1832); *Gauntlet* (1833–4); *Political Soldier* (1833–4); *A Scourge for the Littleness of 'Great' Men* (1834–5); *Phoenix; or the Christian Advocate of Equal Knowledge* (1837); *Carlile's Political Register* (1839); *Christian Warrior, or New Catholic Church Militant 1*, nos 1–4, 7–28 Jan 1843.

Sources: There is no major biography of Carlile. Information about him derives, therefore, from his own papers and writings and disparate references to him in the works of others. (1) MS: Carlile papers, Huntington Library, San Marino, California which are incomplete but useful for the mid–1820s and later 1830s; Brougham papers, University College, London; Holyoake papers, Co-op. Union Library, Manchester and Bishopsgate Institute, London; HO papers, PRO; Place MSS; BL. (2) Contemporary periodicals: *Cobbett's Weekly Political Register* (to 1836); *Sherwin's [Weekly] Political Register* (1817–19); *Bull Dog* (1826); *Poor Man's Guardian* (1831–5); *Cosmopolite* (1832–3); *Northern Star* (1837–1842); *Star in the East* (June–July 1838); *Besley's Devonshire Chronicle* (1840–1); *Morning Advertiser* (Apr–Sep 1840); *Durham Chronicle* (1840–1); *Bolton Free Press* (1841).
(3) Other: *Vice versus Reason: a copy of the bill of indictment found at the Old Bailey Sessions, January 16, 1819, against Richard Carlile, for publishing Paine's Age of Reason . . .* (1819) 15

pp.; *A Sketch of the Public Life and the Last Trial of Mr Carlile* [1831?] 3 pp. [copy in *DLB* Coll.]; *Trial of Mr Carlile for publishing No. 3 of the Prompter, Old Bailey Sessions, on Monday, January 10th, 1831* [1831?] 5 pp. [copy in *DLB* Coll.]; H. Hunt, *Memoirs and Correspondence* 3 vols. (1820–2; repr. NY, 1970); *New Moral World*, 17 June 1843, 426; G.J. Holyoake, *The Life and Character of Richard Carlile* (1849) 40 pp.; W.J. Linton, *James Watson: a memoir of the days of the fight for a free press in England and of the agitation for the people's charter* (1879); H.B. Bonner, *Charles Bradlaugh* 2 vols. (1894); T.C. Campbell, *The Battle of the Press as told in the Life of Richard Carlile* (1899); G.J. Holyoake, *Sixty Years of an Agitator's Life* (1906); G. Aldred, *Richard Carlile, Agitator: his life and times* (1923; rev. ed. Glasgow, 1941); N.E. Himes, 'The Birth Control Handbills of 1823', *Lancet*, 6 Aug 1927; W.H. Wickwar, *The Struggle for the Freedom of the Press 1819-32* (1928); T.W. Mercer, *Richard Carlile on Co-operation* (1929) 11 pp. [repr. from *Co-op. Rev.*]; N.E. Himes, *Medical History of Contraception* (1936); G. Aldred, *The Devil's Chaplain: the story of the Rev. Robert Taylor M.A., M.R.C.S. (1784–1844)* (Glasgow, 1942) 32 pp.; C.W. Brook, *Carlile and the Surgeons* (1943); G.D.H. Cole, *Richard Carlile 1790–1843* (Fabian Biographical Series no. 13:[1943]) 37 pp.; E.P. Thompson, *The Making of the English Working Class* (1963; rev. ed. 1968); P. Fryer, *The Birth Controllers* (1965); G.A. Williams, *Rowland Detrosier* (1965) 36 pp.; *La Presse Ouvrière 1819–1850* ed. J. Godechot (Paris, 1966); D. Thomas, *A Long Time Burning: the history of literary censorship in England* (1969); J.H. Wiener, *The War of the Unstamped* (Cornell Univ. Press, 1969); idem, *A Descriptive Finding List of Unstamped British Periodicals 1830–36* (1970); P. Hollis, *The Pauper Press* (1970); E. Royle, *Radical Politics 1790–1900: religion and unbelief* (1971); W.H. Oliver, *Prophets and Millennialists: the uses of biblical prophesy in England from the 1790s to the 1840s* (1975); A. McLaren, *Birth Control in Nineteenth-Century England* (1978); J.F.C. Harrison, *The Second Coming: popular millenarianism 1780–1850* (1979); I.J. Prothero, *Artisans and Politics in Early Nineteenth-Century London: John Gast and his times* (Folkestone, 1979); J.H. Wiener, 'Richard Carlile (1790–1843)' in *Biographical Dictionary of Modern British Radicals 1: 1770–1830* (Hassocks and NJ, 1979) 79–82; biographical information: Gail Malmgreen, Indiana State Univ., U.S.A. OBIT. *Times*, 15, 16 and 27 Feb 1843; E. Martin, *A Funeral Sermon occasioned by the Death of Richard Carlile* . . . [1843] 24 pp.

JOHN SAVILLE
JOEL H. WIENER

See also: John CLEAVE; †Henry HETHERINGTON; Emma MARTIN.

CHANCE, John (1804–71)

CHARTIST

John Chance was born in the village of Oldswinford, near Stourbridge, in 1804, the second of the eleven children of John and Nancy Chance, nailers. He was one of the three main leaders of the Chartist movement in the Black Country, but much less is known of him than of the other two, Samuel Cook of Dudley and Joseph Linney of Bilston. He began work as a chainmaker in 1811, and at various times worked in the other local metal industries, the manufacture of nails and spades. He also kept a beershop in Oldswinford from about 1850.

Several of the Chance family were involved in radical politics. Both John and his younger brother Charles were said later to have been active in the Reform movement of 1831 and 1832, although no definite evidence of their participation has survived. John Chance helped Samuel Cook to build the early Chartist movement in the area of Kidderminster, Stourbridge and Dudley in the years 1839 to 1841. At Stourbridge meetings were held in the Mechanics' Institute in Angel Street, where members included a number of Owenite Socialists. In 1841

Chance was one of the signatories of Henry Vincent's teetotal Chartist pledge; and in October 1841 a branch of the National Charter Association was established at Stourbridge, with John Chance and his brother James elected to the general committee. John was a strong supporter of Feargus O'Connor, and when a split developed between the NCA and the Christian Chartist group in Birmingham, Chance sided with the national body.

Chartist organisation continued in Stourbridge in 1842, although during the industrial crisis of the summer the branches at Wednesbury and Bilston in the centre of the coalfield came to dominate the area. In spring 1843 the Stourbridge branch was represented at a meeting which established a short-lived Birmingham and Midland Counties Chartist Association. From this time, however, Chance's energies were mostly channelled into encouraging union organisation in the nailing industry and campaigning against the effects of the truck system.

In February 1847 a branch of the Chartist Land Company was established at Chance's house in Oldswinford, and Chance and Joseph Linney represented the Black Country branches at the second Land Company Conference at Lowbands in the following August. In July 1848 Chance made a militant speech at Great Dodford, near Bromsgrove, in support of a demonstration of Land Company sympathisers from the Black Country; he described the meeting as 'surrounded by disguised bluebottles' and said that he had not come to seek persecution, since 'he had had that nine times already' [*Northern Star,* 22 July 1848].

From April to July 1850 Chance was prominent in a nailers' strike against the persistence of truck and a 10 per cent discount on nails; further strikes occurred in 1851 and 1852. This was a time when Chartist activity in the Black Country was at a low level; but the movement began to revive from 1855, and in the next two years Samuel Cook and John Chance led an attempt, based on co-operation with the middle classes, to promote renewed agitation for electoral reform. Chance attended two Black Country delegate conferences in June and July 1857, successfully moving a resolution that a Chartist conference should be held to which leading reformers of other viewpoints could be invited. He moved a similar resolution at a meeting in Dudley in September, and in December he was elected one of the Midland delegates to attend the long delayed (and largely unsuccessful) Chartist national conference, which finally opened on 8 February 1858 [Saville (1952) 66 ff.].

In August 1859 chainmakers in the Brierley Hill and Stourbridge areas formed a union and entered upon a twenty-week strike. Chance was again a leading speaker at strike meetings. This is, however, the last reference to his political activities which has been traced. On 9 February 1865 his wife Lydia died at their home in Heath Lane, Oldswinford, aged fifty-eight. After her death John Chance went to live in Corser Street, Oldswinford, with his younger brother George, a Post Office letter carrier, and his family. He died there on 8 February 1871, aged sixty-six, and was buried on 12 February in St Mary's Churchyard, Oldswinford. No will has been traced, nor have any obituary notices been located.

Sources: (1) MS: Census schedules 1841, 1851, 1861, 1871 – Township of Oldswinford and Upper Swinford; Parish Registers of St Mary's, Oldswinford. (2) Other: *Northern Star,* 1839–48; *Wolverhampton Chronicle,* 1839–59; *People's Paper,* 1853–8; *Dudley and Midland Counties Express,* 1857–8; *Dudley Weekly Times,* 1857–8; *Brierley Hill Advertiser,* 1857–61; H.E. Palfrey, *The Story of Stourbridge Institute and Social Club 1834–1948* (Stourbridge, 1948); J. Saville, *Ernest Jones: Chartist* (1952); G.J. Barnsby, 'The Working-Class Movement in the Black Country, 1815 to 1867' (Birmingham MA, 1965); ibid., 'Chartism in the Black Country 1850–1860' in *The Luddites and Other Essays* ed. L.M. Munby (1971); biographical information: Dr G.J. Barnsby, Wolverhampton.

JOHN ROWLEY

See also: Samuel COOK; Samuel Quartus COOK; Joseph LINNEY; Daniel WALLWORK.

CLARK, Thomas (1821?–57)
CHARTIST

Thomas Clark was born in Ireland in about 1821. Of his early life little is known; the only clues are provided by the 1841 Census of Stockport. Among the residents in Garnett Street, part of the town's Irish quarter, are listed Stephen Clarke, a fifty-year old labourer, Margaret (aged forty and presumably his wife), together with Maria and Thomas, both aged twenty. These four are described as having been born in Ireland, and the remaining inhabitants, two fifteen-year old boys Stephen and John, were listed as born in England. No details as to place are provided, only the fact that they were not born in Cheshire. The indications are that the Clark family had left Ireland in the early 1820s, but had not made Stockport their first place of residence. No details of family relationships are provided by the Census; but while Stephen and John were later described in the press as being Thomas's brothers, it is not certain whether Maria was their sister or Thomas's wife. Thomas Clark was married twice, and of his first wife the only certain information is that she died in 1848. Clark claimed from the National Co-operative Benefit Society, and received in August 1848, £10 on account of his wife's death. At the time of the 1841 Census, both Thomas and Maria Clark were cotton weavers, while Stephen and John were employed as piecers. The two younger brothers were also to become involved in the local Chartist movement; they appear to have been employed as Chartist lecturers in 1848.

One record shows that Clark was an active Chartist by 1839. In that year, according to a letter quoted by George Julian Harney in the *Democratic Review* of June 1850, Clark

> . . . came to Halifax in 1839, a poor, ragged creature, unfit to appear in public, until the people of Sowerby, Warley, and other places in the district subscribed and purchased him a suit of clothes in order that he might make a decent appearance. He was at that time a great physical force man, and went round the district with an old acquaintance of mine, to exhort the people to arm with all possible speed [p.35].

Apart from this isolated reference, there is no further record of Clark's Chartist activities until August 1840, when he took part in a meeting at Stockport. His principal political interest at this time appears to have been Ireland, for he expressed his concern that Ireland would not be incorporated with England in the work of national regeneration, owing to the influence of Daniel O'Connell. Clark attended Stockport Chartist meetings regularly during 1840. By the end of the year he had become both secretary to the local committee organised in support of the return of Frost, Williams and Jones (the Newport Chartists who had been transported), and an honorary member of the Birmingham Restoration Committee. In April 1841 he was nominated by his Stockport colleagues to the General Council of the National Charter Association, as sub-secretary. In the following June he received a further nomination from the town's Bamford Street branch.

From his earliest contact with the Chartist movement until 1848, Thomas Clark was a militant O'Connorite in political attitudes. He was an active campaigner against the Anti-Corn Law League; a strong advocate of unity between Chartists and Irish Repealers; a supporter of physical force policies; and, when O'Connor launched his Land Plan, an enthusiastic champion of the scheme.

In 1841 and 1842 he spoke regularly in Cheshire and Lancashire, and although he gave full support to the demonstrations, meetings and strikes of 1842 in the Potteries, he was not among those arrested. At the end of 1842 he was the Stockport delegate to the Complete Suffrage Conference in Birmingham. He was made a temporary paid lecturer for Cheshire in the middle of 1843 and at the Chartist Conference of September 1843, in Birmingham, he was appointed to the general executive of the Chartist Association. His salary was 30*s* a week, with travelling expenses when he went on lecture tours. Towards the end of the year Clark left London for what was to be the first of several lecture tours; in the West Country, South Wales, the North-

West. His meetings were well reported in the *Northern Star,* and he was obviously highly successful. The Truro Chartists, for example, wrote to thank the executive for sending among them, 'so able, straight-forward, and talented a lecturer, whose conduct has met with universal admiration.' On the last Sunday in September 1844 Clark arrived in Glasgow, where he held many meetings. He also visited Edinburgh, Perth, Dundee and Aberdeen. The Edinburgh Chartists reported that 'Mr Clark's tour amongst us has done wonders.'

Between late February and the end of March 1845 Clark undertook an extensive lecture tour of north Lancashire, and then returned to Birmingham shortly before the opening of the Annual Convention in London on 21 April. This was the meeting which inaugurated the Land Company. Clark, who strongly supported the Land Plan, was constantly to urge that the Company should be registered. As a member of the National Charter Association executive he was appointed *ex officio* a director, and from this time his agitational work was increasingly taken up with advocacy of the Land Plan. In September 1845, for instance, he joined Philip M'Grath and Christopher Doyle for a campaign in Lancashire, Cheshire and the Potteries. He played an active part in the Land Conference which opened in the Carpenters' Hall, Manchester, on 8 December 1845 and was re-elected a director. When, at short notice, a Chartist Convention was called, to meet at the same venue on 22 December, Clark attended as a member of the executive committee. He then left for London, where a new phase of his political life began. Up to now Clark had advocated causes which were of interest to the Chartists of Stockport. In London, however, he became involved in the international trends of the Chartist movement. In March 1846 he was present at a meeting in the Crown and Anchor in the Strand, called under the auspices of the 'Democratic Committee for the Friends of Poland'; and on 20 May 1846 he shared a platform with Ernest Jones and Carl Schapper at a Polish meeting. By June the organisation had been renamed 'The Democratic Committee for Poland's Regeneration'. Clark was not, however, losing touch with the affairs of the Land Company; he was to continue his peripatetic lecturing; and when Thomas Cooper criticised O'Connor's financial dealings, it was Clark above all others who vigorously defended O'Connor. At the August 1846 Chartist Convention in Leeds Clark was responsible both for fixing the location of the next Convention in London and for proposing resolutions against capital punishment and flogging in the Army. When he returned to London Clark became secretary of the reorganised Veterans, Orphans and Victims' Relief Committee. By now he was also an active member of the Fraternal Democrats. At the general election of June 1847 he became a parliamentary candidate for Sheffield, winning the show of hands at the hustings but ending up at the bottom of the poll with 326 votes.

1848 was the turning point in Clark's political career. He began the year, unchanged in his attitudes, as a director and corresponding secretary of the Land Company, a member of the Chartist executive, and a committee member of the Fraternal Democrats. He warmly welcomed the Continental revolutions in the early months of the year, attended the Chartist Convention of early April 1848 which was responsible for the Kennington Common demonstration, and expressed his conviction that despite the Government's proclamation, the procession to Parliament accompanying the third National Petition should go ahead. The subsequent dispute over the actual number of signatures contained in the Petition caused Clark to be appointed by the Convention to its own committee of inquiry. He had, however, already expressed his belief that an error had been made in the number of signatures, and that the Chartists should acknowledge this.

When the National Assembly met on 1 May 1848 Clark represented Sheffield, but he was not then appointed to the provisional executive. At this time Clark said that while not disposed 'to offer any factious opposition' to middle-class reformers who were campaigning for a narrower extension to the franchise, he was still determined to uphold the Charter in preference to all other measures. The phrasing was significant: and within a twelve-month he had shifted his position more or less completely toward the alliance with middle-class reformers. In April 1849 he had accepted again the parliamentary candidature for Sheffield, with the proviso that should

J.A. Roebuck (the Radical candidate) satisfy the majority on the matter of the suffrage, he – Clark – would retire. His own election address advocated votes for all men over twenty-one (those who were sane, and who were not undergoing punishment for breaking the law); the separation of Church and State; abolition of all customs, excise, stamp duties (to be replaced by a direct tax on property); complete opposition to the principles and practices of the existing Poor Law, all wars, armies and to capital punishment. Feargus O'Connor, who enthusiastically supported Clark, wrote of him at this time:

> He is a young man of very prepossessing appearance – of lively, animated, but inoffensive manners; he is one of the most eloquent men in this or any other country; he is a sound reasoner; an admirable debater; he is witty, but not sarcastic, and when he descends to sarcasm he is not illnatured. He is a teetotaller; and as to his honesty, I would trust him with untold gold [*Northern Star,* 21 Apr 1849].

Clark's election programme showed no signs of his political contacts with the Chartist left; and within a month he had retired in favour of Roebuck, despite the fact that the latter objected to both annual parliaments and the secret ballot. The Sheffield Chartist Council criticised Clark for his refusal to go forward to the poll, and Clark in his public reply admitted that he had been unwilling to stand without some chance of success. His new attitudes were made clear once again in September 1849 when, at a London meeting in support of an amnesty for the political prisoners, he asserted that the middle classes were now allies in the battle.

So far there was no public hostility between Clark and his Chartist associates, and in October 1849 he was appointed secretary to the Provisional Committee, which arranged a Chartist conference in London on 10 December. The conference drew up the constitution of the National Charter Union, and Clark was chosen, together with G.W.M. Reynolds and Christopher Doyle, to prepare an address on the relations between Chartism and Sir Joshua Walmsley's National Parliamentary and Financial Reform Association. At this juncture, however, Clark admitted that he had actually become a member of the latter body. He maintained that he had sought co-operation with the parliamentary reformers only as a means of obtaining all Six Points of the Charter, but Harney strongly objected to the fact that Clark had not obtained the sanction of the Chartist body for such co-operation.

This basic disagreement between Clark and Harney over the question of Chartist co-operation with the middle-class reformers was widely publicised during January and February 1850. Columns of the *Northern Star* were devoted to letters, in which the two men exchanged both political and personal attacks. One of Clark's letters, which appeared in the *Northern Star* of 2 February 1850, was quickly reprinted as part of a pamphlet, *Reflections upon the Past Policy and Future Prospects of the Chartist Party* which also included *A Letter condemnatory of Private Assassination, as recommended by Mr G.J. Harney.* This work received sympathetic notices from the *Nottingham Review* and the *Sheffield Independent,* and was also advertised in the *Daily News.*

Under attack from O'Connor, as well as from Clark, Harney resigned from the Provisional Committee. Clark and his O'Connorite allies also resigned, leaving G.W.M. Reynolds, as the remaining executive member, to call a Chartist conference. This conference, of 27 February 1850, witnessed the ascendancy of Harney's supporters, whose socialist leanings were now becoming increasingly defined. It may well have been at the time of Reynolds's decision to ally himself with the socialists that Clark published his other pamphlet *A Letter addressed to G.W.M. Reynolds, reviewing his Conduct as a Professed Chartist.* This pamphlet, as well as the earlier one on Harney, were striking evidence both of the political distance Clark had travelled since the beginning of 1848 and of the bitterness and spleen that was now part of the rapidly declining mass movement of Chartism.

At the beginning of April 1850 the advocates of Chartist co-operation with the middle-class reformers established the National Charter League. Clark, the founder of that body, became its secretary, with Philip M'Grath as president. The League members opposed the socialist doctrines which now predominated among their former colleagues; they did not wish to see 'vague objects concerning social rights' attached to the 'plain and simple political purpose of the Charter'. Clark met with very strong criticism from Harney, particularly in the June 1850 edition of the *Democratic Review* in an article headed 'Review of a Renegade's Revelations'. The bitter antagonism between Clark and himself was one of the factors which influenced Harney to resign the editorship of the *Northern Star*. The National Charter League continued as a small group based on London; and in an article published in the July *Democratic Review,* Howard Morton asserted that Sir Joshua Walmsley was concerned only with breaking up the Chartist movement, and that the funds for the establishment of the League came from the middle-class Parliamentary and Financial Reformers. The League was among the few bodies represented at the conference which O'Connor arranged in Manchester in January 1851. Harney described its delegation, consisting of Clark, M'Grath and Ambrose Hurst, as representing only 'a society of half-a-dozen "pure and simple" patriots, meeting at a coffee-tavern in Farringdon-Street'. Harney did, however, ask Engels to obtain for him information concerning the proceedings of the conference, including the speeches of Clark and M'Grath.

The conference also exhibited the increasing differences of opinion between Clark and O'Connor, notably around the questions of middle-class co-operation and the Land Company. Clark appears to have remained a director of the Land Company until its dissolution following an Act of Parliament in 1851. As late as March 1852, however, the *Northern Star* was still referring to Clark as a director. In this capacity he was, during June 1850 at least, receiving a salary of £2 per week. Much of the controversy between O'Connor and the directors, who also included Dixon, Doyle and M'Grath, centred upon the subject of the Land and Labour Bank. The directors disclaimed all connection with the closing of the bank and the refusal of payment to depositors; O'Connor had, they claimed, held sole responsibility for the bank since 1848. Clark now accused O'Connor of dishonesty, and attacked the whole concept that working men from the manufacturing districts should be able to make a living from the land.

The exact dates at which Clark's activities on behalf of the National Charter League and the Land Company wholly ceased are uncertain, but before they did he had already become involved in the insurance business. During its later stages the Chartist movement engendered several insurance and friendly societies. In August 1849 Clark, together with O'Connor, Doyle, Dixon and M'Grath, was named as a director of the National Freehold Benefit Building Society. In this organisation, which was intended to enable members to buy houses on mortgage, he also acted as corresponding secretary. Clark also served as a director of the National Co-operative Benefit Society at the time of its foundation in 1847, and of the Land and Building Society in 1849. In 1854 R.G. Gammage described Clark as still being resident in London, and connected with an assurance company. The name of the company was not given, but before the end of 1856 Thomas Clark had founded the National Assurance Friendly Society, and was acting as its secretary. His address at this time was 19 King's Road, Bedford Row, London. The Society was soon in financial difficulties, and Clark appealed to T.M. Wheeler (with whom, in the days of the Land Company, he had been on terms of hostility). Wheeler directed the Friend-in-Need Life and Sick Assurance Society, and arrangements were agreed by which Clark's Society was absorbed into Wheeler's.

During the last years of his involvement in Chartist affairs, Clark seems to have continued some interest in both international and Irish affairs, although the degree of his commitment is not certain. He was certainly, however, still advocating the repeal of the Union. He died suddenly on 19 March 1857 at his King's Road home at the early age of thirty-six. On 26 April G.J. Holyoake published on obituary notice in the *Reasoner* which asserted that Clark had left his widow and five young children 'not only unprovided for, but in the deepest distress'. A subscription was opened, and among the donors were Sir Joshua Walmsley, Richard Cobden, and members of the Cogers and Temple Forum discussion organisations.

Writings: *A Letter addressed to G.W.M. Reynolds, reviewing his Conduct as a Professed Chartist, and also explaining who he is and what he is, together with Copious Extracts from his most Indecent Writings; also a Few Words of Advice to his brother Electors of Finsbury* [1850] 35 pp.; *Reflections upon the Past Policy, and Future Prospects of the Chartist Party. Also, a Letter condemnatory of Private Assassination, as recommended by Mr G.J. Harney* (1850) 16 pp.; letters from Clark and his accounts of his lecture tours appear in the *Northern Star.*

Sources: (1) MS: 1841 Census, Stockport, PRO, HO 107/113; Ernest Jones, Diary 1844–7, Manchester PL Archives Department. (2) Newspapers: *Northern Star,* 1840–52; *Stockport Advertiser,* 1842–50; *Sheffield Independent,* 1847; *Democratic Rev.,* 1850 (facsimile ed. repr. 1968); *Red Republican* and *Friend of the People,* 1850–2 (repr. in two vols, with an Introduction by J. Saville, 1966); *Notes to the People,* 1851; *Reasoner,* 1857. (3) Other: S.C. on the National Land Company, *First Report* 1847–8 XIX; *Post Office London Directory* (1857); W. Stevens, *A Memoir of Thomas Martin Wheeler, founder of the Friend-in-Need Life and Sick Assurance Society, Domestic, Political and Industrial, with extracts from his letters, speeches, and writings* (1862); R.G. Gammage, *History of the Chartist Movement 1837–54* (1894; repr. with an Introduction by J. Saville, NY, 1969); P.W. Slosson, *The Decline of the Chartist Movement* (NY, 1916; repr. 1967); M. Hovell, *The Chartist Movement* (Manchester, 1918; 3rd ed., Manchester, 1966); J. West, *A History of the Chartist Movement* (1920); J. Saville, *Ernest Jones: Chartist. Selections from the Writings and Speeches of Ernest Jones with Introduction and Notes* (1952); A.R. Schoyen, *The Chartist Challenge* (1958); *Chartist Studies,* ed. A. Briggs (1959; repr. 1967); *The Harney Papers,* ed. F.G. and R.M. Black (Assen, Netherlands, 1969); A.M. Hadfield, *The Chartist Land Company* (Newton Abbot, 1970); A. Wilson, *The Chartist Movement in Scotland* (Manchester, 1970); J.T. Ward, *Chartism* (1973); C.A.N. Reid, 'The Chartist Movement in Stockport' (Hull MA, 1976); D.J.V. Jones, *Chartism and the Chartists* (1975). Obit. *Reasoner,* 28 Apr 1857.

Naomi Reid
John Saville

See also: *George Julian Harney; †George William MacArthur Reynolds.

CLEAVE, John (1795?–1850)
RADICAL REFORMER AND PUBLISHER

John Cleave was an Irishman, born about 1795. (His age was given as forty-six at the 1841 Census). Very little is known about his early life, except that he served for a period in the Navy, during which time he seems to have visited the United States. He himself stated in 1831 that he had been 'a freeman and householder in the City of London twenty-two years' [*Poor Man's Guardian*, 17 Dec 1831, 211] but this statement cannot be true in its entirety and research has only brought to light material which must still be regarded as speculative [for which see *DLB* Coll.]. By the late 1820s he was an assistant to William Carpenter, radical Dissenter and journalist who was editing the *Weekly Free Press*. This paper was a continuation of the *Trades' Newspaper*, founded in 1825, and some trade societies still had a stake in it.

Carpenter was an ardent co-operator, and the *Weekly Free Press* became the chief organ of the co-operative movement that arose in the closing years of the twenties. John Cleave also became involved. In 1829 he joined the British Association for Promoting Co-operative Knowledge (BAPCK) which had been established to co-ordinate co-operative activity in the metropolis and elsewhere. Cleave was soon elected to the committee, and remained a member until the society ended in 1831. Cleave also became leader of the Westminster Co-operative

Society which grew to be the largest in London [Prothero (1979) 242]. It was through his work in the co-operative movement that Cleave met William Lovett, Henry Hetherington and James Watson, and these four soon came to dominate the British Association, and they worked closely together in the general radical movement. It was about this time that he opened a coffee-shop in Snow Hill, Smithfield. All four, at the end of the twenties, were supporters of Henry Hunt and prominent members of the Radical Reform Association, many of whose members were Irishmen like Cleave. The four radicals also helped Hunt to set up the Metropolitan Political Union in 1830, and they were all members of its council. Cleave especially was a very fine speaker.

In the autumn of 1830 Carpenter decided to publish a series of *Political Letters*, to appear at irregular intervals and in the form of separate publications, instead of the continuous periodical which in fact they formed. This was done to avoid paying the fourpenny stamp duty on periodicals. Cleave was still working closely with Carpenter, and Cleave later claimed that the decision was a joint one. Preceded by Hetherington's *Penny Papers*, which more brazenly flouted the law, the *Political Letters* began on 9 October 1830 at 2*d* and were thus among the earliest papers to begin 'the war of the unstamped'. For several years Cleave's activity was concentrated on the 'unstamped' agitation and the National Union of the Working Classes. He joined the latter at the end of May 1831, and was first a leader of class 5 and later of class 43 (one of whose members was Robert Hartwell). Cleave was a member of the committee, a frequent speaker for the National Union – especially at the Rotunda – and as Hetherington was often away, in prison, or on the run, and as Lovett and Watson left the committee in mid-1832, Cleave was politically the most active and important of the four at this time.

At bottom Cleave was a republican revolutionary. He sometimes appeared cautious in his personal conversation and in the advice he offered, but on all the issues of the day he took a militant position. Just after the passing of the Reform Bill he stated that the Bill was not their concern; it was 'the production and the idol of the enemies of the working classes', and the 'war between labour and property had commenced' [Prothero (1979) 292]. Earlier, with Lovett, he had attended the meeting that launched the National Political Union in support of the Reform Bill, and had seconded Lovett's unsuccessful amendment for universal suffrage; and later infuriated Francis Place and J.A. Roebuck in his intransigence on the issue of universal suffrage. In March 1832 he took part in the great procession organised by the NUWC against the proclamation of a general fast (in expiation of the Cholera epidemic) and held a dinner in his house after the demonstration. In October he was in the deputation sent to Birmingham that helped set up the Midland Union of the Working Classes in opposition to Thomas Attwood's Birmingham Political Union. He then went on with Hetherington to Walsall, Northampton (where they formed a Northampton Union of the Working Classes) and Preston. During the years that followed Cleave remained active in the National Union of the Working Classes, and was so much the dominant figure that Carlile called it 'Cleave's Club'. He remained one of its most faithful members during its decline in 1834 and 1835.

During these years Cleave continued his support for Owenism and the co-operative movement although he was critical of Owen's ideas as well as his activities on a number of points. He emphasised always that it was essential to obtain political power before Owen's schemes could be put into operation, and he regarded the Labour Exchanges experiment as impracticable. He inevitably disliked Owen's attempts at political alignment with those whom Cleave regarded as conservatives or reactionaries, and he resented Owen's attacks on religion as such. His own stance was certainly anti-clerical, but he was a Baptist in the 1820s, and his wife remained very religious. On 21 January 1832, after Carpenter's release from prison, Cleave and Carpenter published another unstamped paper, *A Slap at the Church* which was mainly concerned with clerical and ecclesiastical abuses. In May this became the *Church Examiner*, the last issue of which was 1 November 1832. This was followed by the *Working Man's Friend* which Cleave edited with Watson and which began publication on 22 December 1832. As Watson was very soon imprisoned for selling the *Poor Man's Guardian* Cleave must have edited the *Working Man's Friend* almost alone. The journal reported the activities of the NUWC and campaigned for Repeal of the Union with Ireland: the latter an issue central to Cleave's politics. He was in these years in close touch with Daniel O'Connell, whom he greatly admired, and he had many Irish contacts in general. In the spring of 1833 Cleave advised a run on the banks to thwart the Irish Coercion Bill [*Poor Man's Guardian*, 23 Mar 1833]. In some respects, notably in his opposition to paper money, and to changes in the Poor Law, Cleave's views came near to those of Cobbett, and on at least one occasion (August 1835) he described himself as a follower of Cobbett. For the rest, Cleave upheld all the radical causes of his day. He took part in support of the strike of the Derby silk-weavers; in the agitation on behalf of the six Dorchester labourers; and he remained one of the central figures in the struggle for a free press. By 1834 this was his chief concern. He was tireless in his efforts to mobilise support for the movement, collect funds for the sufferers, and publicise the campaign. He was a leading member of the committee of management of the 'Victim Fund', which provided those punished for selling unstamped papers, with money and further papers to sell. The committee met at his coffee-house, and then at his home, which was on Shoe Lane near Fleet Street; the street-sellers also came there to be paid, all to the detriment of his own business. He also belonged to a Society for the Protection of Booksellers, which supported members punished for publishing illegal works. In 1834 he and Carpenter reprinted John Milton's *Speech on the Liberty of Unlicensed Printing*, and in 1836 collaborated on a short life of Milton. Both also continued their work in journalism.

In 1834 Cleave began the most successful – measured by circulation – of all the unstamped newspapers. This was the *Weekly Police Gazette*. He had helped promote Charles Penny's *People's Police Gazette* from the autumn of 1833 until its sales totalled 20,000; and then, without informing Penny, he published his own *Weekly Police Gazette* which soon drove out Penny's paper. It was a piece of sharp practice [Hollis (1970) 149–50]. Like Hetherington, Cleave was coming to concentrate on papers that provided wide news coverage, not just radical politics, and at times the weekly sale of his newspaper may have reached 30–40,000. In April 1834 Cleave was found guilty of publishing and vending an illegal newspaper, his *Police Gazette*. He was sentenced to pay a nominal fine or in default to be gaoled for three months in the City Compter. Although he claims to have chosen the latter alternative in order to dramatise the cause of a free press, an anonymous person paid his fine and he was freed. In early August 1835 his printing press and types were seized by the authorities for non-payment of an earlier judgment levied against him in the Court of Exchequer. On 5 February 1836 he was again prosecuted, this time for illegally 'carrying about' the *Gazette*. But Cleave only spent a short time in prison before his fine (of £500), and that of Hetherington, was remitted and both men were released. A powerful legal and parliamentary campaign, led by Place, Roebuck and Matthew D. Hill had been waged on behalf of the two radical publishers, and at the succeeding celebrations Hetherington and Cleave were regarded as public heroes. Like the other publishers of unstamped papers Cleave did not continue to defy the stamp duty when it was reduced to a penny in September 1836. Very soon he gave up his *Police Gazette* by merging it with Hetherington's *London Dispatch*.

After the demise of the National Union of Working Classes Cleave belonged to a succession of radical groups until he reached the eve of the Chartist years. In 1835 he belonged to Feargus O'Connor's Great Radical Association and in 1836 to the Universal Suffrage Club.

When he joined the more important London Working Men's Association in 1836 – in which he quickly became a leading figure – he reluctantly broke with O'Connell for the latter's opposition to trade unions and to factory legislation. Most Irish politicians stayed with O'Connell. Cleave went on a number of missionary tours for the LWMA, but by now he was less enthusiastic over mass agitation, and he led the opposition within the LWMA to enlarging its membership and to the use of violent and emotional language. He was elected to the General Convention of the Industrious Classes for both London and Reading, and to the London Central Committee for raising the National Rent. He was not an important member of the Chartist National Convention 1839 at which he took a consistent line, opposing violent language, the 'ulterior measures', the calling of a 'sacred month', and the move to Birmingham. Over the last he nearly resigned his seat. He was more at home collecting subscriptions for Lovett when the latter was imprisoned; and in 1840 he was treasurer of the committee to help the defence of Henry Vincent (who married his eldest daughter on 27 February 1841). In the same year (1840) he joined the Cobbett Club, a small group of ex-Chartists, and together with Hetherington, Henry Vincent and W. Hill, issued an address in favour of temperance and the formation of Chartist teetotal societies; he saw radical and moral reform as inseparable. Temperance was one of Cleave's chief beliefs, and he became a member of the East London Chartist Total Abstinence and Mutual Instruction Association. In 1841 he was still a regular Chartist speaker; he sat on several Chartist committees, and belonged to the City locality of the National Charter Association. And from 1841 to 1843 he issued the weekly *English Chartist Circular and Temperance Record*, the only Chartist periodical in London. It never, however, made a profit. He remained firm in his belief in universal suffrage, and, unlike Hetherington, would have nothing to do with Joseph Hume's household suffrage scheme.

But after 1841 he really ceased to be an active Chartist, although in that year he did sign Lovett's address in favour of a Chartist educational organisation. In the disputes that broke out over this Cleave seems to have remained popular with the main body of Chartists. He took care not to identify himself too closely with Lovett's scheme, and he continued to belong to the National Charter Association after he joined Lovett's National Association. But he was not an active member of either. In the 1840s he gradually drifted away from his former close associates, not sharing Lovett's enthusiasm for education, or Hetherington's and Watson's for anti-Christian activity. Moreover, about 1840 or 1841, he seems to have broken with his wife, Mary Ann. She had strongly supported him in his efforts for a free press; as well as the attempts to save starving boys in Smithfield. This domestic rupture appears to have alienated some of his friends; Place, for instance, felt his behaviour was abominable. Cleave acted as treasurer to the committee that arranged the London elections to Joseph Sturge's Birmingham conference in December 1842, and he favoured the O'Connorites; but though elected for the City of London, he did not take his seat. In 1842 he helped set up a Political and Scientific Institute in London, an educational body consisting of members of the National Charter Association. Thereafter his main Chartist activity was as a treasurer of this Institute, of the Victim Committee in 1842–3, and of the executive committee of the National Charter Association (he succeeded Abel Heywood). In the same year he acted as surety for O'Connor at his trial. But when O'Connor's Land Plan was launched in 1845 Cleave disapproved of it as certain to fail. He also remained faithful to his belief in repeal of the Irish Union; and in 1843 he enrolled in O'Connell's Repeal organisation at a time when the Chartists were seeking a rapprochement with the Irish movement. In 1847 he joined the Irish Democratic Federation, and later in the year he was arraigned in the *Northern Star* (6 Nov 1847) as one of O'Connor's enemies.

He had remained a publisher throughout. During the 1830s, in addition to his contributions to unstamped journalism, Cleave had published numerous cheap tracts. These included an edition in 1832 of Rowland Detrosier's celebrated *Address on the Necessity of an Extension of Moral and Political Instruction among the Working Classes*; a widely-circulated anti-clerical tract entitled *The Poor Man's Book of the Church: not by Southey* (1832); and a pirated abridged version about 1834 of William Howitt's *Popular History of Priestcraft* (1833). With Hetherington and Watson he also published the well-known birth-control tracts: Robert Dale Owen's *Moral Physiology,* and Knowlton's *Fruits of Philosophy*. In 1837 he began the penny *Cleave's London Satirist and Gazette of Variety*, later *Cleave's Penny Gazette of Variety and Amusement*. At first similar to his *Weekly Police Gazette* (1834–6), after 1841 this had much less politics and more fiction and romance. According to Thomas Cooper, Cleave made strenuous efforts to get the former's *Purgatory of Suicides* published; but more and more he left political for popular publishing. By 1845 he was pirating works by Dickens and publishing *The Penny Novelist and Library of Romance*. He was an early exponent of the popular publishing developed by Lloyd and Reynolds.

We have an interesting and quite typical comment on him by Francis Place. Cleave, wrote Place in 1831, 'was a sturdy little fellow totally devoid of fear and like Lovett ready to undergo any persecution to bear any punishment ... passionate and revengeful, and not at all scrupulous as to the use of any means of accomplishing his purpose the end of which was improving the condition of the working people. His notions were all vague, any change however brought about was in his opinion sure to be useful and this was enough to induce him to labour continuously to promote changes' [Rowe (1970) 58]. Cleave died, aged fifty-five, at 22 Stanhope Street, Clement Danes on 19 January 1850 [*Reasoner*, 23 Jan 1850]. No will has been located but he was survived by his wife and some family.

Writings: *Vindication of the Abridgement* [i.e. of *A Popular History of Priestcraft*; abr. from W. Howitt's work and published by Cleave] [1834] 8 pp. Reports of Cleave's speeches were often printed in the periodicals listed in Sources (2). He helped to edit the following publications: *Weekly Free Press and Co-operative J.* (1828–30); *Political Letters and Pamphlets* ed. W. Carpenter (1830–1); *A Slap at the Church* (1832), then *Church Examiner and Ecclesiastical Record* (1832); *Working Man's Friend, and Political Mag.* (1833). Cleave owned and published the following works and periodicals: *Cleave's Weekly Police Gazette* (1834–6); *Cleave's Picture Gallery of Grant's Comicalities* (1836); *Cleave's London Satirist and Gazette of Variety* (1837), then *Cleave's Penny Gazette of Variety and Amusement* (1837–44), then *Cleave's Gazette of Variety* (1844); *Cleave's Illustrated Metropolitan Police Act* (1839); *Cleave's New Black List* (1840); *Mirror of Corruption* (1841); *English Chartist Circular and Temperance Record* (1841–3); *Penny Novelist and Library of Romance* [1844?]. He also published a number of novels and romances; and periodicals owned by others, such as the *New Moral World* (1834–45), *Social Pioneer* (1839), *Educational Circular and Communist Apostle* [1841–2?], *Union Advocate* (1842–3), *New Age and Concordium Gazette* (1843–4), *Morning Star or Herald of Progression* (1844–7).

Sources: (1) MS: The main ms. sources are in the Place Coll. in the BL and in the Home Office papers, PRO, especially HO 64, and 40/25, 79/4. Most of these relate to his activities in the early 1830s. (2) There is much information in the following periodicals: *Weekly Free Press* (1829–30); *Mag. of Useful Knowledge* (1830); *Political Letters and Pamphlets* ed. W. Carpenter (1830–1); *Prompter* (1830–1); *Voice of the People* (1831); *Republican; or Voice of the People* (1831); *Ballot* (1831–2); *Poor Man's Guardian* (1831–5); *Weekly Dispatch* (1832); *Crisis, or the Change from Error and Misery, to Truth and Happiness* (1833); *'Destructive', and Poor Man's Conservative* (1833–4); *Man* (1833); *Working Man's Friend, and Political Mag.* (1833); *A Scourge for the Littleness of 'Great' Men* (1834–5); *Weekly True Sun* (1834–5); *Cleave's Weekly Police Gazette* (1834–6); *London Mercury* (1836); *Radical* (1836); *London Dispatch* (1836–9); *Northern Star* (1838–43); *Operative* (1838–9); *Charter* (1839); *Southern Star* (1840); *English Chartist Circular* (1841–3). (3) Other: The main sources for information on Cleave's publishing activities are: L. James, *Fiction for the Working Man* (1963); J.H. Wiener, *The War of the Unstamped: the movement to repeal the British newspaper tax, 1830–1836* (Cornell Univ. Press, 1969); idem, *A Descriptive Finding List of Unstamped British Periodicals 1830–1836* (1970); P. Hollis, *The Pauper Press: a study in working-class radicalism in the 1830s* (1970); I.J. Prothero, *Artisans and Politics in Early Nineteenth-Century London: John Gast and his Times* (Folkestone, 1979); see also: *Report of the Committee, and Proceedings at the Fourth Quarterly Meeting of the British Association for Promoting Co-operative Knowledge ... April 8, 1830* [1830] 16 pp.; *Proceedings of the Third Co-operative Congress* ... ed. W. Carpenter (1832); C.H. Timperley, *A Dictionary of Printers and Printing*... (1839); *London Radicalism: a selection from the papers of Francis Place* ed. D.J. Rowe (London Record Society, 1970); biographical information: Chamberlain's Court, Guildhall and Guildhall Library, London; Dr B.H. Harrison, Corpus Christi College, Oxford. OBIT. *Reasoner*, 23 Jan 1850.

I.J. PROTHERO
JOEL H. WIENER

See also: Richard CARLILE; †Henry HETHERINGTON; Abel HEYWOOD; William LOVETT, for Chartism to 1840; Robert OWEN; †Henry VINCENT.

COOK, Samuel (1786–1861)
CHARTIST AND RADICAL

Samuel Cook was born on 15 July 1786 in Trowbridge. He came of an old middle-class family of West Country cloth manufacturers. As a youth Cook was apprenticed to a draper at Poole, Dorset, where he met John Angell James, then also a draper's apprentice, later a Congregational minister in Birmingham. James became a lifelong friend and influenced Cook's theological views. Cook left Poole to work in London, Birmingham and Manchester. It may have been in Birmingham that he met, and in about 1810 married, Maria Jones, second daughter of George Jones, an Edgbaston builder. His wife bore him six children and died on 7 September 1827, aged thirty-nine, from the effects of her last confinement.

Cook first started business on his own account in Liverpool, in partnership with his brother Joseph. The venture was unsuccessful, and in 1818 he went bankrupt. His creditors secured his release, and he moved to Dudley, where he opened a draper's shop on 8 May 1819, at Gibraltar House, 78 High Street, a former inn at one time owned by his father-in-law. Cook subsequently made this shop a centre of Black Country radicalism, displaying in his windows a variety of proclamations and pungent commentaries on current affairs, many of which have been preserved in the remarkable poster collection in Dudley Public Library. In his business he employed travellers on weekly and fortnightly rounds in the Black Country and beyond. His affairs flourished until 1843 when he again went bankrupt. He obtained his discharge in 1844 and went into partnership with his son Samuel Quartus Cook, who succeeded as head of the firm after Samuel Cook's death in 1861. The business remains to the present day a family concern, occupying expanded premises on the site of the original shop.

For over forty years Samuel Cook was the radical conscience of middle-class Dudley, a dissident whose integrity was recognised by many who did not share his views. During May 1826 he supported a nailers' strike in Dudley and Lye and exhibited a large handwritten poster in his shop window on market day denouncing government ministers for inflicting starvation upon the people. The poster was removed and dispatched to the Home Office, and Cook was arraigned before the Dudley bench on a charge of displaying a seditious libel. He declined bail and was committed to Worcester gaol until the next Assizes. After two postponements Cook was duly tried and convicted at Worcester on 1 August 1827 and bound over to keep the peace in the sum of £100. He returned to Dudley to the acclamations of a crowd estimated at 40,000.

Cook's capacity to unite elements of middle-class radicalism with the working-class movement made him a natural leader of the local agitation for parliamentary reform. During the crisis of late 1831 he issued a series of reform posters. In April 1832, as chairman of the Dudley Political Union he delivered a speech which the Home Office considered seditious, although the local magistracy decided there was insufficient evidence on which to initiate proceedings. After the enactment of the Reform Bill, Cook and the other Dudley reformers supported the successful election campaign of Sir John Campbell, a barrister who had defended Cook at Worcester in 1827. Cook was profoundly disappointed by the failure of the Whig Government to introduce further reforms; in a poster of March 1834 he enumerated 'some of the Principles of Dudley Radicalism': his list anticipated the later Chartist demands for universal suffrage, the ballot, no property qualification and short parliaments. Nevertheless the Political Union again supported Campbell when an election was held in 1834, as a result of Campbell's appointment to the office of Attorney-General; but on this occasion without success. The seat was won by the Tory, Thomas Hawkes, a glass manufacturer, who retained it in 1835 with the support of Lord Dudley, the so-called 'Castle influence' which Cook vigorously opposed throughout his life.

A dispute arising from the 1835 election led to Samuel Cook's second legal action. At the Warwick Spring Assizes William Davis, a whitesmith, brought an action against Thomas Badger, a Dudley nailmaster and magistrate, for an alleged assault committed at Stourbridge during polling in the East Worcestershire election. The jury found for the plaintiff with £30 damages, but Badger applied to the Court of King's Bench and obtained a rule *nisi* for a new trial. Cook had clashed with Badger, a diehard Tory, on several occasions, and now proceeded to take advantage of his opponent's discomfiture by publishing a vituperative poster 'To the People of Dudley', which stigmatised the magistrate for having 'disgraced the dignified functions of his station'. Badger countered with a charge of malicious libel, on which Cook was convicted at Worcester in March 1836.

Cook's radical career entered another phase with the growth of Chartism in the late 1830s. The early leaders of the movement in Dudley were Cook and W. Smith Lyndon, a moulder. Both were arrested on 19 July 1839 after addressing a meeting outside the Founder's Tavern called to protest against the conduct of the Metropolitan police in Birmingham. Charged with 'attending a meeting of a tumultuous and alarming character', Cook was remanded on £300 bail to appear at Worcester, despite his own complaints about the bias of the magistrates. At the trial witnesses testified to Cook's seditious language: it was stated that he had supported Lyndon's threat to break the heads of the 'blue devils from London' and had advocated the abolition of the monarchy and the House of Lords. He was convicted and sentenced to six months' imprisonment.

Cook emerged from Worcester gaol in April 1840 quite unrepentant, and vociferous in his criticism of the conduct of the visiting magistrate in impounding letters he had written to his children. He quickly resumed his Chartist activities and in January 1841 became sub-treasurer of the Dudley branch of the NCA. By the summer of 1842 the branch was recruiting rapidly, 'owing to the zeal of Samuel Cook, who keeps one of the largest shops in High Street, the main thoroughfare, and who generally has his windows full of Chartist notices of meetings' [*Northern Star*, 13 Aug 1842]. Cook played a characteristically vigorous part in rallying support for the miners during the great strike of July and August 1842, and his use of window bills brought further trouble with authority. On 20 August he posted a notice published by Arthur O'Neill advertising a Chartist rally in Birmingham; he was arrested and charged with inciting the populace to tumultuous assemblage. Refusing to enter into recognizances, he was remanded to Worcester gaol until the Assizes. No available sources indicate the outcome of the prosecution.

During 1846 Cook was prominent in the organisation of branches of the Chartist Land Company in the Black Country, and in the following year he was nominated as a Chartist candidate to oppose Villiers and Thornely in the general election at Wolverhampton, although he did not go to the poll. During the mid 1850s Cook was in the forefront of attempts to revive Chartism in Dudley and the Black Country. He proposed the establishment of a South Staffordshire Chartist and Complete Suffrage Association in August 1855 and although the project came to nothing he continued to campaign throughout the following year for renewed agitation, in conjunction with any other pressure groups, for reform. At a Chartist meeting in Dudley in September 1857 he successfully moved a resolution expressing a willingness to campaign for any substantial measure of reform. Under the leadership of Samuel Cook, Simon Watts, a grocer, and Daniel Wallwork, a locksmith, radical organisation in Dudley survived the extinction of the *People's Paper* and *Cabinet Newspaper* and as late a December 1861 – only a week before his death – Cook was elected secretary of a new reform committee.

As a fervent internationalist, Cook also supported radical causes abroad. In August 1830 he published a poster and called a public meeting to celebrate the French Revolution, a gesture he repeated at the fall of Louis Philippe and the creation of the Second Republic in February 1848. He later supported Garibaldi and raised a subscription among the poor of Dudley which was forwarded to Italy and gratefully acknowledged.

Cook was a Congregationalist and regularly attended services at King Street Independent Chapel where he was a pewholder. He did not, however, profess to be a full member of the Chapel, and was not always in harmony with its administrators: he was involved in a series of acrimonious disputes with the minister, the Rev. John Raven, and other Chapel members, between 1845 and 1847, apparently over Chapel discipline and his desire to attend business meetings. Cook fought sturdily for the rights of dissenters in general, advocating the admission of nonconformists to the universities and distributing tracts in favour of Catholic Emancipation in 1829. The earliest posters in the Cook collection refer to his opposition to Easter dues in 1823 and church rates in 1827–8 and 1837, when three pairs of blankets worth £2 5*s* were seized to defray his debt of 17*s* 11*d*. The struggle against church rates was renewed in 1844, 1852 and again in 1853 when Cook seconded a motion which substituted a 1*d* rate for the 3½*d* rate demanded by the churchwardens. Denied immunity from the exactions of a Church whose tenets he did not uphold, Cook countered by demanding some right of participation in its parochial government. In 1823 and 1827 he criticised the conduct of vestry meetings and scrutinised the parish books. He returned to the theme in the 1850s, reprinting and publicising announcements of vestry meetings to encourage his fellow citizens to attend. Cook also pursued his firm belief in female equality by nominating Mrs Alice Bogle for the office of church-warden of St Thomas's Church in 1855, a position to which she was elected.

Cook's political beliefs were founded upon his religious convictions. The posters which catalogue his radical activities so excellently are shot through with biblical language and quotation. One phrase recurs: 'The Bible is the Best Political Book in the World'. Cook's emphasis upon participation in vestry meetings was symptomatic of a fundamentally populist belief that mass involvement in the decision-making processes of the community was vital to the evolution of a genuine democracy. Meetings behind closed doors or public documents unavailable for inspection, instantly aroused his suspicions. After complaints in 1853 about the behaviour of the Board of Guardians, he insisted on attending their meetings to hear their deliberations regarding a proposed new union workhouse. He was forcibly ejected by the superintendent of police, whom he later ineffectually sued for assault. In 1859–60 Cook investigated the condition of the charities of Dudley, characteristically reminding trustees of their duty to present accounts to the annual vestry meeting.

The state of the sanitation of Dudley also came under Cook's critical scrutiny. In 1826 he had mobilised opposition to proposals that a new Town Improvement Act should be obtained to grant the Town Commissioners increased powers to supply water to the town. Cook argued the case for civic economy but was also motivated by dislike of the Town Commissioners, a self-perpetuating oligarchy numbering among its members the brothers Isaac and Thomas Badger. By 1851, however, his position had apparently changed. In that year the mortality of the parish of Dudley was twenty-eight per thousand and the average age of death sixteen years seven months – the worst in England. Cook was one of the handful of people who attended the initial hearing of William Lee's public inquiry into the sanitary condition of the town. On subsequent days he diligently dogged the footsteps of the inspector and testified to the insanitary state of his own premises and the thoroughfare of High Street and King Street.

Cook related his belief in the importance of popular participation directly to the needs of the working classes by emphasising the importance of the development of industrial organisation to complement political organisation. Despite the Black Country miners' apparent repudiation of Chartist leadership after the failure of the strike of 1842, Cook and other political radicals such as Joseph Linney of Bilston and John Chance of Oldswinford continued to articulate working-class grievances. During the years 1845 to 1848, Cook published posters and organised public meetings to draw attention to the statistics of explosions and pit accidents in the South

Staffordshire mining district, where the mortality rate was higher than in any other coalfield Despite Cook's propaganda, in which he publicised pit disasters at Round's Green in November 1846 and at West Bromwich in 1848 and emphasised the importance of preventive measures, little reduction of the death toll was achieved in his lifetime.

Throughout the 1850s, Samuel Cook and Joe Linney were willing supporters of attempts to establish trade unions in the Black Country. In May 1858 they assisted in the organisation of a miners' strike in the south-east of the coalfield, urging the creation of a permanent union; and Cook later took part in arbitration procedures. When a further wages conference took place in January 1860 between the coalowners and the short-lived South Staffs. Coalminers' Association, Cook again offered his assistance; but on this occasion his presence as an intermediary was rejected by both sides, perhaps an indication of the miners' desire to dissociate themselves from latter-day Chartism as represented by Cook.

Like many of his fellow radicals, Cook came to hold the view that working-class progress was bound up with self-improvement and self-education and he became an active but highly criticial member of the Dudley Mechanics' Institute. The Institute had been established in February 1848 and extended a welcome to all working men; but its high subscription rates and domination by wealthy patrons and committee-men tended to discourage popular participation. As a member of the general purposes committee in the 1850s, Cook agitated for a democratization of the government of the Institute. In January 1857 he employed his familiar device of a broadsheet to urge the working people of Dudley to determine for themselves where a new Mechanics' Institute building should be sited. 'Remember' he wrote emphatically, 'Mechanics' Institutes were originally designed for the especial benefit of those who are usually called the *Working Classes*'. At the annual general meeting of 1858 he urged that working men should be added to the committee of the Institute to represent factories in the Dudley area. Finally, at the 1860 annual general meeting, he sought unsuccessfully to obtain the repeal of a clause in the constitution of the Institute which prohibited the discussion of matters of political or religious controversy.

Cook also sought to improve leisure activities in Dudley. As a shopkeeper he supported several campaigns from the 1820s onward for early closing and reduced working hours for shop assistants. He supported the temperance movement, but was opposed to prohibition: at three riotous United Kingdom Alliance meetings in Dudley in 1855 Cook defended the moderate use of alcohol and was acclaimed as a champion of popular culture. Another initiative came in 1854 when at his suggestion the committee of the Mechanics' Institute decided to organise an annual fete in the grounds of Dudley Castle. By June 1863 the fetes had raised some £1540 towards the financing of the new Institute building, opened in December of that year.

During the 1850s Cook and the Dudley radicals were organised both within the formal Chartist movement and in a series of *ad hoc* discussion groups, such as the Dudley Mutual Improvement Society, the Temple of Investigation, the Manhood Suffrage Association and the Working Men's Institute. These groups provided an open forum for the exchange of ideas on the most sensitive of topics: Cook led discussions on such delicate issues as suffrage reform, Bible history and the case for atheism. Besides a forum for uninhibited debate, the Dudley radical group intended to provide an acceptable social milieu for leisure, free from the vices and temptations of the pub.

Cook's support for self-help educational groups was a practical expression of his strongly-held belief in the virtues of participation, and his fierce insistence that the working classes must determine their own destiny. This was also revealed in his suspicions of the civic promotion of education. After the burgesses of Walsall had decided to establish a Free Library in June 1857 a similar proposition was raised at the annual meeting of the Dudley Mechanics' Institute in February 1858. Cook denounced the proposal as 'a matter of charity . . . because one part of the population paid for what the people could obtain for themselves'. [*Dudley and Midland Counties Express*, 13 Feb 1858]. Cook's view was overruled, but nothing came of the project of establishing a Free Library in Dudley.

Samuel Cook died suddenly at his home in Dudley on 8 December 1861, and left effects valued at under £20. His funeral at King Street Chapel was scantily attended, despite the circulation of handbills in the town urging working men to turn out to pay a last tribute to their champion.

Writings: *A Full Report of the Trial of Samuel Cook, Draper, Dudley, for an Alleged Seditious Libel, tried at Worcester, August 1, 1827, before Mr. Justice Littledale* (2nd ed., Dudley, 1827); *To All Genuine Reformers*... (Dudley, 1835) 4 pp.; *To the Magistrates of the County of Worcester*... (Dudley, 1840) 3 pp.; *Copies of Several Ancient Acts of Parliament in Reference to County and Borough Elections ... republished ... by Samuel Cook* (Dudley, 1859) 5 pp. The Samuel Cook Poster Collection in Dudley Public Library comprises some 110 handwritten and printed posters covering the period 1823–61, compiled and published by Cook. Other posters issued by Cook or referring to his activities are located in the general poster collection in Dudley Public Library.

Sources: (1) MS: Census Schedules for 1851 and 1861, Township of Dudley, District of St Thomas. (2) Newspapers: *Wolverhampton Chronicle*, 1827–61; *Berrow's Worcester J.*, 1836–56; *Charter*, 1839; *Northern Star*, 1839–48; *People's Paper*, 1853–8; *Wolverhampton Herald*, 1854; *Alliance*, 1855; *Alliance Weekly News*, 1855–8; *Reasoner,* 1855–9; *Dudley and Midland Counties Express*, 1857–8; *Dudley Weekly Times,* 1857–8; *Birmingham Daily Post*, 1859–62. (3) Other: *First Report of the Midland Mining Commission* 1843 XIII [IUP, *Mining Districts* 1 Session 1839–49]; W. Lee, *Report to the General Board of Health on a Preliminary Inquiry into the Sewerage, Drainage and Supply of Water and the Sanitary Conditions of the Inhabitants of the Parish of Dudley* ... (1852); H.H.B., *Black Diamonds, or the Gospel in a Colliery District* (1861); C.F.G. Clark, *The Curiosities of Dudley and the Black Country, from 1800 to 1860* ... (Birmingham, 1881); 'Dudley in the Nineteenth Century' in *Blocksidge's Dudley Almanack* (1892) 125–6; *1819–1897: an illustrated souvenir of F.W. Cook's drapery warehouses* ... (Dudley, 1897) [includes a portrait of Cook]; 'Working Men's Institute' in *Blocksidge's Dudley Almanack* (1899) 121–3; E. Blocksidge, (comp.), 'Particulars, concerning Dudley Castle fetes from ... 1850 up to ... 1901', in *Blocksidge's Dudley Almanack* (1902) 63–114; idem, 'History of the Dudley Mechanics' Institution, afterwards called "The Dudley Institute"' ibid. (1905) 73–105 and (1906) 45–59; *F.W. Cook Limited 1819–1919: the progress of a century* (Dudley, 1919); G. Chandler and I.C. Hannah, *Dudley as it was and as it is Today* (1949); G.J. Barnsby, 'The Working-Class Movement in the Black Country, 1815 to 1867' (Birmingham MA, 1965); idem, *The Dudley Working Class Movement 1750–1832* (Dudley, 1966) 21 pp.; idem, *The Dudley Working Class Movement 1832–1860* (Dudley, 1967) 48 pp.; idem, 'Social Conditions in the Black Country in the Nineteenth Century' (Birmingham PhD, 1969); *Cooks of Dudley 1819–1969: 150 years of service* (Dudley, 1969); V.L. Davies and H. Hyde, *Dudley and the Black Country 1760 to 1860* (Dudley, 1970); G. Barnsby, 'Chartism in the Black Country, 1850–1860' in *The Luddites and Other Essays* ed. L.M. Munby (1971) 93–114. OBIT. *Birmingham Daily Post*, 10 Dec 1861; *Worcestershire Chronicle*, 11 Dec 1861; *Staffordshire Advertiser, Wolverhampton J.* and *Worcester Herald*, 14 Dec 1861; *National Reformer*, 18 Jan 1862.

JOHN ROWLEY
ERIC TAYLOR

See also: Samuel Quartus COOK; Joseph LINNEY; †James SWEET; Daniel WALLWORK.

COOK, Samuel Quartus (1822–90)
CHARTIST

Samuel Quartus Cook was born in Dudley in 1822, the eldest surviving son of the radical draper Samuel Cook and his wife Maria. He was educated at Dudley Grammar School and then entered his father's drapery business. In 1843 Samuel Cook senior went bankrupt – his involvement in Chartist activity apparently leading to the neglect of the business – and in the following year his son became a partner. On his father's death in December 1861, S.Q. Cook took over the concern and ran it on traditional lines, restricting his trade to plain goods and relying upon the patronage of a regular clientele. In 1884, six years before his death, he sold out to his son Frederick William Cook and retired.

Cook was an active Chartist from about 1844, when he first appears as a local office-holder in the movement. In the parliamentary election of 1847 he supported the unsuccessful candidatures of his father in the Wolverhampton constituency and of Joseph Linney in Dudley (neither went to the poll), and over the next decade he assisted his father in the local organisation of the movement. He was also an enthusiastic temperance advocate and an educationalist. He took the teetotal pledge and played a leading part in re-establishing the Dudley Temperance Society in 1855. Subsequently he helped to establish the Prohibition movement in the town, and acted for many years as treasurer of the Temperance Society. Cook became first president of the Dudley Working Men's Institute, which was set up in 1859 as a radical counterpart to the middle-class Mechanics' Institute. The Working Men's Institute closed after five years. Like his father, Samuel Quartus Cook was a Congregationalist who was prominent in the affairs of King Street Chapel, Dudley.

Cook's involvement in public affairs never rivalled that of his father, however. A commemorative pamphlet on the history of the Cook firm published in 1897 noted that he had learnt caution from his father's turbulent political career, his clashes with the law and the consequent prison sentences. Cook's granddaughter, Mrs Dorothy Curtis, endorsed this but noted that there were also personal reasons for the decision. He was a diabetic and his marriage was unhappy, certainly in its later years:

> Father used to say that for the last eight years of their marriage he [grandfather] never addressed my grandmother. If he wanted to say anything to her he said it to the children, in front of her. And she dropped dead without them ever being reconciled [Interview with Mrs Dorothy Curtis, 26 Feb 1977].

Samuel Quartus Cook died in Dudley on 6 November 1890, and was buried at King Street Chapel. His wife, Eleanor Maria, had died eleven years before aged sixty-three. He was survived by one son, Frederick William, a staunch Liberal who was mayor of Dudley in 1907 and 1908. He continued and expanded the family business which still (1980) remains under the control of the Cook family. He died in 1938.

Sources: For MS and newspaper sources *see* the biography of Samuel Cook but the other main sources are: *1819–1897: an illustrated souvenir of F.W. Cook's drapery warehouses...* (Dudley, 1897); 'Working Men's Institute' in *Blocksidge's Dudley Almanack* (1899) 121–3; *F.W. Cook Limited 1819–1919: the progress of a century* (Dudley, 1919); *Cook's of Dudley 1819–1969: 150 years of service* (Dudley, 1969); personal information: Mrs D. Curtis, Wolverhampton, granddaughter. OBIT. *Dudley Herald*, 8 Nov 1890.

JOHN ROWLEY
ERIC TAYLOR

See also: Samuel COOK.

CRANE, Walter (1845–1915)
ARTIST AND SOCIALIST

Walter Crane is known both as an illustrator of books, and as an active Socialist, whose talents as artist, writer and lecturer were always at the service of the movement. He was born on 15 August 1845, the second son of the artist Thomas Crane (of an old Chester family) and his wife Maria (née Kearsley). His father was secretary and treasurer of the Liverpool Academy; but when Walter was three months old the family moved to Torquay in an effort to improve the delicate health of Thomas Crane, who was threatened with tuberculosis. Walter spent a happy childhood rambling about the countryside, going aboard the sailing ships in the harbour, and poring over the numerous illustrated books and books of reproductions in his father's library. Moreover, in his own words he 'picked up in my father's studio and under his eye a variety of artistic knowledge in an unsystematic way'. He did go to school for some time in Torquay, but the most important part of his education was due to his father. They were congenial spirits.

During the years in Devonshire, Thomas Crane's health greatly improved, and for professional reasons he thought it best to move to London, in May 1851. They lived in various houses in West London, in surroundings which were still semi-rural in comparison with today. Walter's education was carried on at home, and was chiefly in art. Although his main interest at this time was in sketching and painting animals, he had already begun to amuse himself with book illustrations and decoration. Some of his pen sketches, together with a set of pages in colour illustrating Tennyson's *Lady of Shalott*, were shown to Ruskin, who praised them, and also to W.J. Linton, one of the foremost wood engravers of the period, who liked them so much that he offered to take Walter as an apprentice without any premium and teach him to draw on wood, an art then necessary to book illustrators. So in January 1859 at the age of thirteen and a half, Walter Crane was indentured to Linton for three years.

This was indeed, as he wrote in his pocket notebook, 'One of the most important events of my life' [*Reminiscences*, 46]. A great variety of work, and of people, came to Linton's engraving shop. There Crane saw the work of many leading artists, and there his artistic career in line drawing was founded, and his social and political ideas began slowly to be formed. Linton was a Chartist, 'a true socialist at heart, with an ardent love of liberty and with much of the revolutionary feeling of '48 about him'. Although he 'never obtruded his opinions' it is impossible to believe that Crane was not influenced by this generous and enthusiastic man. Walter Crane also attended evening classes for life study and costume study at Heatherley's, the well-known art school.

In the earlier 1850s his father's health had already been failing – no doubt the move to London had been medically a mistake; he died in July 1859. A brother of Mrs Crane's, Edward Kearsley, came to the rescue of the family and set up house with them in Westbourne Park Villas. This arrangement lasted until 1861, when Edward Kearsley married, and the Cranes removed to 46 Argyle Square, near King's Cross. Later, Mrs Crane lived in Sussex House on the Upper Mall, Hammersmith, where she died in 1874.

When Walter's apprenticeship ended in January 1862 he found work of various kinds. He had drawings accepted by a number of journals, including *Punch, Fun, Once a Week, Good Words*, and the *Argosy*, a periodical started about this time by the novelist Mrs Henry Wood and her son. Crane's first experience of book illustration came very soon: he was commissioned to make sketches (to be engraved by Linton) for J.R. Wise's *The New Forest: its history and scenery* (published in December 1862); and to this end Wise took him on a six weeks' walking tour in Hampshire in the early summer of that year. Wise, a scholar and an agnostic, personally acquainted with most of the advanced thinkers of the day, introduced Crane to the ideas of Mill, Darwin, Spencer and Shelley. The result of a course of these authors was that Crane abandoned a mild inclination to ritualism and in his own words 'decided for Free Thought'. He was not yet consciously interested in political and social questions, however.

In 1863 another important event in his life took place: he was introduced to Edmund Evans, the pioneer in colour printing, whose work had already been well known for ten years or more. A collaboration began between Crane and Evans which lasted until Evans's death; and it continued with his son. It produced a very large number of brilliantly designed and beautifully printed illustrated books. Justly, the most famous were and are the series of picture books or 'toy books' for children, chiefly nursery rhymes and fairy stories. The series was begun in 1865 and continued till 1876. Crane's design and draughtsmanship are perhaps at their height in *The Fairy Ship* and *This Little Pig* (both 1870). After the series ended in 1876, Crane and Evans began a new genre with the *Baby's Opera* (1877) and the *Baby's Bouquet* (1878), books of traditional nursery rhymes and songs with their music. His work in the 1870s shows how much he had learned from Japanese colour prints, with which he had recently become acquainted. Together with his agreeable though much less brilliant illustrations for seventeen of Mrs Molesworth's stories for children, these 'toy books' made him, as the *Daily Telegraph* remarked, 'an artist inexpressibly dear to all the patrons of children's picture books' [quoted without date, *Reminiscences*, 174 n.1].

In the 1860s Crane had already begun to show his versatility, with occasional work on decorated pottery (for the Wedgwoods from 1866) and in enamelling; he was also illustrating books for adult readers. In 1867 he illustrated the third edition of a book by H. Zschokke (first edition 1852), translated by John Yeats and entitled *Labour stands on Golden Feet*. His interest in political and social affairs had been roused; and it was further stimulated by the refugees who came to London after the fall of the Paris Commune. Crane began to attend political meetings and demonstrations, and this new interest helped to inspire his work. In the later 1860s he designed his first politico-allegorical picture, 'Freedom'.

In September 1871 he married Mary Frances, the second daughter of the late Thomas Andrews, Esq., of Wynchlow Hall, Hempstead, Essex, and set out with her for a long visit to Italy. In February 1873 their first child, Beatrice, was born in Rome, and in the early summer of that year they returned to England and settled down in Florence House, Wood Lane (then a country lane), Shepherd's Bush. By this time the originality and beauty of Crane's decorative art were being discovered by several sorts of people. He continued to be asked to illustrate books: in 1878 Lewis Carroll invited him to illustrate his *Sylvie and Bruno*, an offer which Crane did not take up, not much caring for the book; he did do frontispieces for R.L. Stevenson's *An Inland Voyage* (1878) and *Travels with a Donkey in the Cevennes* (1879). But he had also become known to architects, interior decorators, to such personages as the interesting and influential George Howard, later Earl of Carlisle, and Dr William Spottiswoode, Queen's Printer, president of the Royal Society from 1878–83. Such patrons commissioned him to design wallpapers, friezes, panels, ceilings. The work of Morris's firm had become widely known among the cognoscenti, and Crane belonged in some way to the Morris line. Like Morris, he was struggling to have the importance of the arts of design and decoration realised. For this purpose the Art Workers' Guild was founded in 1884; Crane was active in the founding, and was Master from 1887 to 1889.

Although by the early 1880s Crane was already troubled about the nature of modern society, it was William Morris whose arguments and influence brought him to accept Socialism. He was greatly relieved by this step: from a pessimism uncongenial but forced upon him by the contemplation of a capitalist and industrial civilisation, he was able to develop a rational optimism under Morris's guidance – 'difficulties disappeared, and . . . I accepted the Socialist position which became a universal solvent in my mind.'

About 1884 he joined the Democratic, later the Social Democratic, Federation, and like Morris devoted much time, energy and artistic talent to the Socialist cause – lecturing, writing, designing posters, banners, cartoons, party membership cards. In the 1880s he designed covers or frontispieces for a number of Socialist periodicals and books: for Annie Besant's journal *Our*

Corner; for *To-day*, at one time edited by Hyndman; for *Time*, edited by the SDF activist Belfort Bax; for the *Practical Socialist*, and for two volumes of Socialist essays edited by the reformer Andrew Reid and called *Vox Clamantium* and *The New Party*. (The latter volume, only partly Socialist, was published in 1895).

The SDF split in late 1884, and Crane went with William Morris into the Socialist League. Crane, who was a gentle man and always concerned with Socialist unity, continued, however, to contribute to *Justice*; and he also joined the Fabian Society. Besides designing for their publications – for instance, a frontispiece for the famous *Fabian Essays* (Dec 1889) – he both lectured and took the chair for other lecturers; and when in 1886–7 the Fabians revised their 'Basis' through the executive committee, with eight co-opted members, these latter included Crane.

The political scene in the 1880s was stormy. Trade depression and high unemployment led to demonstrations, processions and meetings which alarmed the prosperous classes. Crane produced a drawing for *Justice* in 1885 which he turned into a poster for the Hyde Park meeting of February 1886; and in the next year he drew a brilliant cartoon for the *Commonweal* – 'Mrs Grundy frightened at her own Shadow'. He was present in Trafalgar Square on 'Bloody Sunday' (13 Nov 1887) when police and Life Guards charged the crowd and John Burns, Hyndman and Cunninghame Graham were arrested, Crane himself narrowly escaping from a mounted policeman. Crane designed a memorial cover for the *Death Song* which Morris wrote after the death of Alfred Linnell who had been injured in another riot a week later. The music was by Malcolm Lawson and the *Song* was sold for the benefit of Linnell's family at the funeral procession, and was sung by the marchers.

In the 1880s there were also storms in the world of art. The rebellion of younger artists against the art establishment as exemplified by the Royal Academy was being carried on by the New English Art Club, to which Crane belonged. Those artists who felt strongly about the state of the arts and the place of art in society, and who desired some recognition of the arts and crafts as being among the fine arts, founded the Arts and Crafts Exhibition Society in 1888. Crane writes of this Society that it 'arose from the ruins of a sort of secessionist movement of protest against the Royal Academy and its narrow views of art and exclusiveness. Among its members were men of very different ideas, but with these were several fully convinced and conscious Socialists, strongly imbued with Morris's ideals' [Crane (1911) 95]. The new society was an offshoot from the Art Workers' Guild and was based on the view that art, like science, needed an association for its advancement, and was intended to present its ideas to the public and to exhibit the arts of design and decoration. Its impressive first committee included Morris and William de Morgan, and Crane was the very active president (he served for the first three years, 1888–90, and again after Morris's death in 1896). The first exhibition in 1888 was very successful.

The society was first entitled the National Association for the Advancement of Art and its Application to Industry. There was an inaugural meeting addressed by Edmund Gosse, by Oscar Wilde (whose *Happy Prince* was published in that year with illustrations by Crane and Jacomb Hood); and by Crane himself, who suggested 'that we must turn our artists into craftsmen and our craftsmen into artists.' The first congress of the Association met in Liverpool in December 1888; Morris and Crane spoke on the relation of art to Socialism. Crane believed that the congress 'made way all along the line as the most practical effort to unite Art and Industry' [*Reminiscences*, 325]. But at the second congress, held in Edinburgh in December 1889, the poet and critic W.E. Henley, who was then editor of the *Scots Observer*, attacked Morris and Crane for their Socialist opinions, which for him apparently dominated the congress. After the meeting was over the two moved to Glasgow, where Crane was to lecture, with Morris in the chair, on 'The Educational Value of Art'. They met the local Socialists, including Bruce Glasier, and in their quarters at the Central Hotel they discussed Morris's scheme for starting, along with Emery Walker, the Kelmscott Press. The third and final congress was in Birmingham in December 1890.

In 1889 the Socialist leader John Burns, who was an old SDF colleague, had just been elected to the newly-formed London County Council. He asked Crane to design a Common Seal for the Council. The result was much admired – among others, by Frederic Harrison, also a councillor, and Lord Rosebery, the LCC chairman.

Crane was a fluent if not a very original writer of verse; his designs, cartoons and paintings were often accompanied by poems. In 1891 he published, in a limited edition decorated by himself, a collection of his verses entitled *Renascence*. Some of the poems are specifically political, such as the two sonnets 'On the Suppression of Free Speech at Chicago', written in June 1886, in sympathy with the Chicago anarchists, and 'Freedom in America', written in October 1887; and the sonnet 'To the Prisoners of Liberty, John Burns and R.B. Cunningham [*sic*] Graham', written after their arrest on 'Bloody Sunday'. Also in 1891, Crane had a one man show at the Fine Art Society's Bond Street galleries, and sold a number of works. On good advice, he decided to take the remainder to America in October 1891. The tour was a great success, not marred for Crane by the reaction of conservative Bostonians to his Socialist doctrines and in particular to his expressed belief that the two Chicago anarchists who had been executed were innocent. He met the Socialist Edward Bellamy, whose Utopian romance *Looking Backward* was well known in England. He sold many works, and he and his wife travelled widely in the United States, from New York and Boston to California and Florida. His collection also travelled widely. He found the younger generation enthusiastic over the new movement in English art of which he was both an exponent and a practitioner.

The Cranes were back in England by mid-August 1892. In the same year were published Crane's *Relation of Art to Education and Social Life* and his *Claims of Decorative Art*. These books were the first of a series in which Crane stated his position as artist and Socialist. They cover a period of some twenty years, from 1892 to 1911, when the series ended with *William Morris to Whistler*; and they were very influential, particularly *The Bases of Design* (1898) and *Line and Form* (1900), which were still enjoying a success as late as the 1930s. All the books went into numerous editions and reprints. They were based on lectures and articles. Many of the books express with clarity views which were essentially those of Morris (Crane was no theorist) on industrial capitalist society, the relation of art to society, the relation of the 'arts and crafts' to the 'fine arts'. In the last of these books he repeated briefly what he had long preached: 'I do not admit the justice of the distinction usually accepted between *Fine* and Decorative or Industrial Art' [Crane (1911) 249]. In *The Claims of Decorative Art* he says that art

> '. . . is in danger from a new tyranny in that unscrupulous commercialism, which is not less dangerous because less tangible, and not less despotic because it is masked under the form of political liberty' [p.12]; and later:
>
> 'Instead of sublime and noble public buildings, churches, and halls, . . . we have as a rule very dull or pretentious public offices, dull and respectable churches . . . and melancholy images of military, naval, or political idols in smoked bronze, like petrified orators for ever addressing an indifferent public, holding, as if in mockery, the dumb show of a perpetual open-air meeting under the presidency of Nelson in police-prohibited Trafalgar Square!' [pp.143–4]. And again: 'Architecture and applied art, generally speaking, are devoted to the comfort or glorification of well-to-do individuals, or to serve the ends and purposes of trade.
>
> In an epoch when personal comfort and private property seem to be the main objects of existence, at the price of the absence of both at the other end of the scale, this is not surprising, since art is bound to reflect the character of its age.
>
> Now socialism presents a new ideal to humanity. It is a religion and a moral code as well as an economic system. Its true realisation would mean again that unity of public sentiment, but in a far higher degree, and the sympathy of a common humanity freed from the domination of class and the grinding conditions of commercial competition. Such an

atmosphere could not but be favourable to art in the highest degree' [pp.79–80].

In 1896, as well as *The Decorative Illustration of Books*, Crane published a collection of cartoons originally made for *Justice*, the *Commonweal*, the *Clarion* and other Socialist publications. It was entitled *Cartoons for the Cause, 1886–1896 (A Souvenir of the International Socialist Workers and Trade Union Congress, 1896)*.

By the 1890s Crane had become involved in the business of art education. In 1893, after refusing it twice, he accepted a post with the Manchester School of Art as part-time Director of Design. He found the syllabus laid down by the Department of Science and Art 'rather cut and dried and wooden' [*Reminiscences*, 417]; but it had to be followed if the students were to take the national examinations for grants and prizes. Crane held this post for four years; but finding it increasingly difficult to combine it with his multifarious activities in London, he resigned it in 1897. He was immediately sought after by the principal of Reading University College, to become director of the Art Department there. Crane agreed, because the work involved less time and energy than he had had to spend on the Manchester appointment. In 1898, however, he was offered and accepted the prestigious post of head of the Royal College of Art in South Kensington. He accepted on condition that he should have plenty of time for his own work, and on finding this condition ignored, he resigned after a year. He served, however, as member for Design on the Council of Advice on Art set up by the Board of Education in 1899.

Crane was on the committees which arranged the British Art section of several international exhibitions, the first in Brussels in 1897. Both his work and his artistic doctrines were known and admired on the Continent, and when his collection came back from America via Montreal in 1892, he was invited to show it in some of the principal towns of Germany, Austria, Bohemia, Holland, Denmark, Sweden and Norway. It was a triumphal tour, and most of the items in the collection were bought in the course of its travels.

Even before the South African War broke out, Crane expressed his opposition to such a war and to the policy of the British Government in regard to the Boers. In his view, the 'disgraceful' Jameson Raid was 'the beginning of the long trouble which led to the South African War, with its disastrous results for England' [ibid., 462]. Some other Socialists were also against the war: Hyndman and the SDF regarded it as imperialistic and capitalist, and the ILP later followed suit. But the Fabians were split: the executive, led by Shaw, defended the war, while other members attacked it. Crane was among the eighteen members of the Society who resigned in protest at the executive's action. When the war at last ended, the *Daily News* published a cartoon by Crane showing a British and a Boer soldier, each with one arm in a sling, shaking hands under an olive branch held up by a winged figure of Peace.

In the autumn of 1900 Crane was invited to exhibit a large and representative collection of his works in Budapest and then in Vienna and several German towns. At this time preparations were being made in Turin for an extensive exhibition of decorative art, and the committee in charge asked Crane to organise the British section, with a large contribution from his own works. The Budapest collection went to Turin, and with the help of other members of the Arts and Crafts Exhibition Society, Crane assembled a representative show for the British rooms. When the exhibition opened in 1902 the Society was given a special Diploma of Honour. In January 1903 the King of Italy created Crane Commander of the Order of the Royal Crown of Italy; and in 1904 he was honoured at home by the award of the Albert Gold Medal of the Society of Arts – according to Crane, this was the first time it had been presented not to a scientist but to an artist.

The Cranes had many Indian friends and were sympathetic to the cause of Indian nationalism. They were also enthusiastic travellers. In November 1906 they set off from Marseilles for a tour of India. In the course of some three months they traversed a great part of that vast subcontinent and also spent a fortnight in exploring Ceylon. Crane's observations were published as *India Impressions* in 1907. In the preface he spoke up for the 'national aspirations' of India. He took particular pleasure in making sketches of the widely different types of native whose country it was by rights. The book abounds also in precise and evocative descriptions of Indian landscape and architecture; his sharp observation is made even sharper by the impact of strangeness, and his gentle humour is charming both in the text and in the illustrations. The consequences of the English Raj were part of what he had come to India to see and what he clearly had constantly in mind. His view of the Indian Mutiny was corrective also. He noted that British reprisals 'seem to have practically "wiped out" old Lucknow', and that in the Sikander Bagh, once a rose garden, '2000 rebels were bayoneted without mercy by the British troops. A young English officer, speaking professionally, perhaps, . . . said that Sikander Bagh gave him more satisfaction than any other memorial of the mutiny. He positively "gloated over it," and intended to go there again and "gloat"' [*India Impressions*, 189–90].

While they were in Madras the Cranes paid a visit to an old comrade, Annie Besant, who had by this time become a leading Theosophist and had settled in India at Adyar, some dozen years before. Crane had known her well in the days when she was an ardent Socialist; he found her much changed – she 'seemed to have quite removed herself into another world . . . and was now devoting her life to inculcating the principles of Theosophy and educational work among the young Hindus' [ibid., 248]. On returning to England Crane resumed his crowded life as designer, painter, illustrator, and writer – *An Artist's Reminiscences* and *India Impressions* were both published in 1907 – and honours continued to be bestowed on him. In 1906 he had been awarded a gold medal and Grand Prix for his work at the International Exhibition in Milan; in January 1912 the King of Italy conferred on him the Order of SS. Maurizio e Lazzaro.

Until fairly late in his life Crane's reputation stood higher abroad than at home. His work won awards on the Continent from 1889, when he received a silver medal from the Paris exhibition for his picture 'The Diver'; he was given a gold medal from Munich in 1895 for 'The Chariot of the Hours'. He was elected to honorary membership of the Dresden Academy and the Munich Academy, and to membership of the Beaux Arts in Paris in 1909. In 1912 the Uffizi Gallery in Florence asked him to paint a self-portrait for them – an extraordinary honour.

Information about Crane's last years is scanty. He continued to be a keen and optimistic Socialist: in a letter to the *Clarion* of 3 November 1911 he said that the formation of the British Socialist Party was 'the most important and encouraging event which had happened to the movement for a long time', adding that he felt unity on main principles to be so important as to 'reconcile membership of the Social Democratic Federation, the Socialist League and the Fabian Society at the same time' [Spencer (1975) 155]. Whether he opposed the First World War as he had opposed the Boer War is not certainly known. A clue may perhaps be found in the fact that a cartoon of his in support of the international labour movement, 'Dedicated to the Workers of the World', which had appeared in early *Year Books* of the Bradford Trades Council, was reissued in the *Year Book* for 1914 'to show the Council's anti-war attitude' [Ashraf (1972) 93]. If Crane's permission to republish had been asked, we may infer that he shared the Council's attitude; but usually Crane appears to have handed over any rights to the body – Socialist or co-operative or the like – for whom he did the work.

In December 1914 he suffered a crushing blow in the death of his wife, who was killed by a train on the South Eastern and Chatham Railway. She had been suffering from nervous debility and had been having treatment in a nursing home, Finn Farm, at Kingsford in Kent; but she was regarded as cured, and was to have left Finn Farm that day (18 December). At the inquest, the verdict was suicide whilst of unsound mind [*Kent Messenger and Ashford Examiner*, 26 Dec 1914]. Crane told a friend that this disaster left him 'only half-alive'. He died in hospital three months later, on 14 March 1915. Death saved him from what would have been a second crushing blow – his younger son Lancelot was killed in the war. Walter Crane was survived by his elder son Lionel (born in May 1876) and his daughter Beatrice (born in 1873). A third son, and another daughter, Myfanwy, died in infancy, in 1882 and 1891 respectively. Crane left unsettled property valued at £3119 gross (£2676 net).

Walter Crane had a gentle, sensitive face with well-cut features [see G.F. Watt's portrait in

Crane's *Reminiscences* (1907)]; he wore a longish moustache and a Vandyke beard. His grandson Anthony Crane describes him as 'a small, charming and unassuming man', with a 'keen and exceptional sense of humour' [Crane (1957) 107]. Shaw remarked that he never saw any trace 'of quarrelsomeness' in Crane, and Will Rothenstein said 'he had unusually broad sympathies, and . . . was free from prejudice – his spirit kept open house' [both quoted Spencer (1975) 146 and 10]. But as well as likeableness, shy manners and gentleness, Crane had a demon of energy. Few other artists except Morris worked so incessantly, and this apparently without strain or ill health. It was this energy which enabled him to translate his Socialist sympathies into the works which he gave so freely to the cause. Hyndman [(1911) 366] rated the influence of his contribution to the Socialist movement as second only to that of Morris. A recent writer regards Crane as having 'an instinct for symbol-making'; and she continues, 'In the development of the iconography of the socialist movement Crane is a keyname. His winged figures of Freedom and heroic shirt-sleeved working men and women were the prototypes of socialist imagery for many years' [Faith (1975) 1461–2].

Writings: Walter Crane's principal works and a few which are not included in Isobel Spencer's comprehensive biography of Crane (published in 1975) are listed here. He contributed to a number of journals including *Academy, Art J., Atlantic Mon., Fortn. Rev., J. of the Society of Arts, Mag. of Art, New Rev., Studio,* and *To-day.* An extensive collection of Crane's engravings and other art work is held at the Victoria and Albert Museum, London and this includes many of his well-known Socialist illustrations. His other writings include: 'The Importance of the Applied Arts, and their Relation to Common Life', *J. of the Society of Arts 35* (1887) 717–28; 'The Decoration and Illustration of Books' [Cantor Lectures], ibid. *37* (1889) 863–73, 875–82, 887–98; *Renascence: a book of verse* (1891); 'The English Revival of Decorative Art', *Fortn. Rev. 52* n.s. (Dec 1892) 810–23; *The Relation of Art to Education and Social Life* [an address], ([Leek], 1892) 25 pp.; 'Why Socialism appeals to Artists', *Atlantic Mon. 69* (Jan 1892) 110–15; 'Modern Life and the Artistic Sense', *Cosmopolitan* (NY) *13*, no.2 (June 1892) 152–6; *The Claims of Decorative Art* (1892); 'Some Impressions of America', *New Rev. 10* (Jan–July 1894) 41–54, 150–63; *Cartoons for the Cause, 1886–1896: a souvenir of the International Socialist Workers and Trade Union Congress, 1896* (1896) 40 pp.; 'William Morris', *Scribner's Mag. 22* (1897) 88–99; *The Work of Walter Crane with Notes by the Artist* [extra number of the *Art J.*], *Easter Art Annual for 1898*, 32 pp.; *The Bases of Design* (1898); *Line and Form* (1900; later eds); 'Impressions of the First International Exhibition of Modern Decorative Art in Turin', *Art J.* n.s. (1902) 227–30, 259–62; 'The Last of the Enthusiasts' [Review of *Ruskin Relics*], *Academy and Literature, 65*, 5 Dec 1903, 618–19; (with L.F. Day), *Moot Points: friendly disputes on art and industry between Walter Crane and Lewis F. Day* (1903); *Ideals in Art* (1905); *An Artist's Reminiscences* (1907; repr. Detroit, 1949); *India Impressions, with some Notes of Ceylon during a Winter Tour 1906–7* (1907); *William Morris to Whistler* (1911).

Sources: (1) MS: The main holdings of letters are at Harvard and Yale Universities, USA; for further details see I. Spencer, op. cit. 6. (2) Other: L.F. Day, 'An Artist in Design', *Mag. of Art 10* (1887) 95–100; *WWW* (1897–1916); 'A Designer of Paper Hangings. An Interview with Mr Walter Crane', *Studio 4* (1898) 76–84; A. Vallance, 'The Revival of Tempera Painting', ibid., *23* (1901) 155–65; P.G. Konody, *The Art of Walter Crane* (1902); A. Vallance, 'The Tempera Exhibition at the Carfax Gallery', *Studio 35* (1905) 289–96; H.M. Hyndman, *The Record of an Adventurous Life* (1911); idem, *Further Reminiscences* (1912); *DNB* (1912–21) [by M.H. Bell]; *Justice*, 24 Dec 1914; E.R. Pease, *The History of the Fabian Society* (1916; rev. ed., 1925, repr. 1963 with a new Introduction by M. Cole); J.B. Glasier, *William Morris and the Early Days of the Socialist Movement* (1921); E.P. Thompson, *William Morris: romantic to revolutionary* (1955; rev. ed. 1977); T. Swan, 'Prophets and Pioneers (No. 31): Walter Crane: poet, artist, author', *GMW J. 18* no. 8 (Aug 1955) 231–2; A. Crane, 'My grandfather, Walter Crane', *Yale*

Collected Letters 2 vols ed. Dan H. Laurence (1965 and 1972); S.T. Madsen, *Art Nouveau*, translated from the Norwegian by R.I. Christopherson (1967); M. Ashraf, *The Bradford Trades Council 1872–1972* (Bradford, 1972); P. Meier, *La pensée utopique de William Morris* (Paris, 1972; translated into English as *William Morris: the Marxist dreamer* (Hassocks, 1978)); G. Warren, *All Colour Book of Art Nouveau* (1972); F.B. Smith, *Radical Artisan: William James Linton 1812–97* (Manchester Univ. Press, 1973); R.K. Enger, *Walter Crane as Book Illustrator* (1975); R. Faith, 'Designs for Living' [review], *TLS*, 5 Dec 1975; I. Spencer, *Walter Crane* (1975); biographical information: Dr Malcolm Easton, formerly hon. curator, Hull Univ. Art Coll.; Miss J.D. Hamilton, Dept of Prints and Drawings, Victoria and Albert Museum, London; Mrs I. Spencer, Scottish Arts Council, Edinburgh; Professor P. Stansky, Dept of History, Stanford Univ., California; S. Tongue, archivist, London Borough of Hackney. OBIT. *Tuesday Express*, 22 Dec 1914 and *Kent Messenger and Ashford Examiner*, 26 Dec 1914 [both for Mrs Crane]; *Times*, 16 and 25 Mar 1915; *Soc. Rev. 12* (Nov–Dec 1915) 794–9.

MARGARET 'ESPINASSE

See also: †Joseph SOUTHALL.

CUFFAY, William (1788–1870)

LONDON CHARTIST

Cuffay's name was at different times spelt Cuffey, Cuffy, Coffey; but Cuffay was the spelling consistently used by the *Northern Star* during his political career in England. The spelling on the Tasmanian official records relating to his transportation from England in 1849 was Cuffey. The usual statement about his birth, taken from a profile in *Reynolds's Political Instructor* dated 13 April 1850, was that he was born in 1788 on a ship homeward bound from St Kitts, although his convict sheet stated that he was born in Chatham [Briggs (1961)6]. His grandfather was an African sold into slavery, and his father, a slave, was born on the island of St Kitts. The family came to Britain when Cuffay was a child, and he lived with his mother and his sister Juliana at Chatham. His father took a job as cook on a ship of the Navy. In his late teens Cuffay became a journeyman tailor, and he remained in the trade all his life. He was a good workman. He was three times married; his only son, according to the 1850 *Reynolds's* article, died in youth. But at his trial in 1848 the Attorney-General queried why Cuffay's son had not been called as a witness and Cuffay, in his last statement to the Court before the jury retired, said that 'he had no son, never had a son' [*Times*, 2 Oct 1848]. The Tasmanian official record of Cuffay in 1853 also listed him without children, but presumably this was on Cuffay's own statements.

It is not certain when Cuffay first became active in the working-class movement. The *Reynolds's* article, which provided many of the facts of his life in England noted that he 'disapproved of the Trades' Union movement in 1834, and was nearly the last of his society in joining the lodge'. This is presumably a reference to the Grand National Consolidated Trade Union and Cuffay's hostility did not, it must be presumed, extend to trade unionism as such. Indeed, the *Reynolds's* article goes on to say that Cuffay went on strike with his fellow members, 'thereby losing a shop where he had worked for many years', and thereafter he found it very difficult to get employment.

Cuffay joined the Chartist movement in 1839 and soon became prominent in the London leadership. In October 1839 he helped to form the Metropolitan Tailors' Charter Association, and in 1841 he was elected delegate from Westminster to the Metropolitan Delegate Council.

In 1842 with only Morgan Williams of the Chartist national executive free to act, the Metropolitan Delegate Council took it upon themselves to elect Cuffay (as president) Dron, Knight and Wheeler, together with Morgan Williams to take over the responsibilities of the executive.

During his Chartist years, Cuffay was always among the most militant of his contemporaries. In the middle 1840s he advocated interrupting Complete Suffrage meetings, and Anti-Corn Law demonstrations, and he came to be singled out by the press for his intransigence. *The Times*, for example, used to refer to the London Chartists as 'the black man and his party'. In 1844 he was on the Masters and Servants Bill Demonstration Committee, and in 1846 he was the tailors' delegate at meetings to arrange a soirée for Duncombe for his fight against the Bill. From the first he was a vigorous supporter of the Chartist Land Plan, and was delegate from London to the Manchester Conference in 1845. In the following year he was one of three metropolitan delegates to the Birmingham Land Conference, where he was made auditor to the National Land Company, a position he retained until his arrest. In the same year, 1846, he was one of the ten directors of the National Anti-Militia Association, and he was also a member of the Democratic Committee for Poland's Regeneration. In 1847 he was on the Central Registration and Election Committee, and in 1848 he was on the committee of management for a Metropolitan Democratic Hall.

1848 was the year of decision for Cuffay. He was one of three London delegates to the National Convention which opened at the Literary Institution, John Street, Fitzroy Square, on the morning of Tuesday 4 April 1848. From the first Cuffay adopted a hard-line position. He questioned G.W.M. Reynolds's standing as a Chartist, and wholly opposed giving credentials to Charles M'Carthy of the Irish Democratic Federation. A sub-committee was established to consider M'Carthy's position – Cuffay being one of its members – and on the following day the committee recommended his admission. On Thursday 6 April Cuffay seconded the resolution moved by Reynolds which opposed any further petitioning. Cuffay, as reported in the *Morning Chronicle* (7 April), considered that the programme of the executive was not up to the mark, and 'it was clear that they had shrunk from their responsibility, now that things had come to a crisis ... he had no longer any confidence in them, and he hoped the Convention would be prepared to take the responsibility out of their hands, and lead the people on themselves.' Cuffay was clearly an angry man throughout the proceedings of the Convention prior to the Kennington Common meeting; and on the 10 April itself he was opposed to O'Connor's and the platform's abandonment of the procession to Parliament. He recognised the stupidity of congregating south of the river, with the bridges under the complete control of the police and the military, and he spoke in the strongest language against O'Connor.

It is difficult to trace with precise detail Cuffay's activities during the spring and summer of this year. He was elected as one of the commissioners to further the agitation for the Charter after its rejection by Parliament, but all the evidence suggests that he was involved in a secret revolutionary committee planning some kind of uprising in London. A good deal of our information, however, comes from a fellow-member of the underground movement, Powell, an *agent provocateur*, and from another police spy, Davis. On 15 August all who were present at a meeting at the Orange Tree Tavern, Bloomsbury, were arrested. These were the 'luminaries' who, under the direction of Joseph Ritchie, were to have set London ablaze not merely to cause confusion but to act as a general signal. There were four stations from which the outbreak on 16 August was to be attempted, one being Seven Dials (under the direction of Mullins). The entire Western district of Marylebone, Paddington, Somers Town and Chelsea was to proceed to Seven Dials. On the evening of 15 August Cuffay, impatient to see his men, told his fellow conspirators: 'You know I take the Western Division' [Goodway (1979) 156]. Cuffay was arrested on 16 August at his lodgings. Presumably he could have gone underground, but according to Frost (1880) 165, 'he had refused to fly, lest it should be said that he abandoned his associates in the hour of peril.' Frost also stated in his *Recollections* (p. 162–3) that before the 15 August Cuffay had become convinced of the hopelessness of the undertaking, but that he would not, for reasons of solidarity with his comrades, withdraw on his own. As far as is known, there is no corroboration of Frost's statement. Cuffay was tried, along with Thomas Fay and William Lacey, at the Central Criminal Court towards the end of September, and judgment was pronounced on 30 September by Mr Baron Platt. Fay and Cuffay remained intransigent throughout. In his final speech before sentence was pronounced, Cuffay said:

> I say you have no right to sentence me, although the trial has lasted a long time. It has not been a fair trial – to be tried by my equals – has not been complied with. Everything has been done to raise a prejudice against me, and the press of this country, and I believe other countries too, have done all in their power to smother me with ridicule. I ask no pity – I ask no mercy.
>
> Fay, in a violent tone, and striking the front of the dock. – No more do I.
>
> Cuffay told his fellow-prisoner to be quiet, he would only increase his troubles by violence. He then proceeded – I expect to be convicted, and I didn't think anything else: but I don't want any pity. No, I pity the Government, and I pity the Attorney-General for convicting me by means of such base characters. The Attorney-General ought to be called the Spy-General, and using such men is a disgrace to the Government, but they only exist by such means . . . I am not anxious for martyrdom, but after what I have endured this week, I feel I could bear any punishment proudly, even to the scaffold. This new act of Parliament is disgraceful, and I am proud to be the first victim of it after the glorious Mitchel [*Times*, 2 Oct 1848].

Cuffay, and the others, were sentenced to transportation 'for the term of your natural lives'. He arrived in Hobart, Tasmania, in November 1849, after a voyage of 103 days. At the time of his arrival in Tasmania Cuffay's official record stated that he was aged sixty-one, four feet eleven inches tall, Church of England, married with no children, could both read and write, dark complexion, medium head, black thin hair, grey whiskers, narrow visage, high forehead, brown eyebrows, hazel eyes, broad nose, large mouth, medium chin, rather bald and his shin bones and spine deformed.

As soon as Cuffay arrived in Hobart he was immediately given ticket of leave by which he was allowed to follow his trade for wages, subject to convict regulations such as attendance at musters. T.M. Wheeler had a letter published in the *Northern Star*, 21 December 1850, reporting that the Home Office had informed Mrs Cuffay (who at the time was in Chatham workhouse) that she could not be financially assisted to join her husband until he had been granted ticket of leave. Wheeler commented that it was understood Cuffay had already been granted ticket of leave, and he urged the movement in Britain to take up the matter and press inquiries. There was, obviously, a considerable delay before permission was given, for Mrs Cuffay did not arrive in Hobart until 27 April 1853. One report speaks of a free passage; Wheeler's 1850 letter referred to half the passage that would be paid.

During the whole period of his life in Tasmania, after his free pardon on 24 February 1857, Cuffay continued to exert himself in radical causes. In this he was unusual among former Chartists [Rudé (1978) 217–18]. He especially distinguished himself in the successful agitation for the amendment of the Masters and Servants Laws in the colony (a matter that had earlier concerned him in England in 1844). He was a fluent and effective speaker, and had a considerable following among the working class, whose rights he always championed. He worked, always as a tailor, until his very last year, when in October 1869 ill health and old age forced him to enter the Brickfields Invalid Depot – the Tasmanian equivalent of the workhouse. For most of the time he was in the sick ward. After his death the local superintendent described him as 'a quiet man, and an inveterate reader' [*Mercury* [Hobart], 11 Aug 1870]. At one of his last appearances on the platform, at the meeting at the Theatre Royal, Cuffay addressed his hearers as 'fellow-slaves'. 'I'm old', he said, 'I'm poor, I'm out of work, and I'm in debt, and therefore I have cause to complain' [ibid.].

Cuffay had evoked both respect and affection from his fellow Chartists in England and T.M. Wheeler (to whom Cuffay had presented his Red Republican scarf before he left England) did all he could to keep the reputation of Cuffay alive in the movement. Apart from the Reynolds's article already noted, Wheeler had published a semi-autobiographical story 'Sunshine and Shadow' in the *Northern Star* (6 Oct and 29 Dec 1849) in which he commented at some length about his friend. Charles Kingsley's anti-Chartist and historically fraudulent *Alton Locke*, widely read in the second half of the nineteenth century, had three patronising comments on Cuffay, the last of which was also seriously misleading. Kingsley has Cuffay leaping off the platform on 10 April exclaiming that they were all 'humbugged and betrayed'; the context suggesting exactly the opposite of what later happened viz. Cuffay's move towards a revolutionary position for which he was to be transported.

The exact date of his death in July 1870 is not known, but he was buried on 2 August at Trinity burying-ground. There is much still to be discovered about Cuffay, both in London and Tasmania; and it is to be hoped that this interim biographical entry will stimulate further research into the history of a remarkable personality.

Sources: (1) MS: Home Office papers: PRO [see F.C. Mather, *Public Order in the Age of the Chartists* (Manchester, 1959) which lists the relevant records]; AOT Files: Cuffey, Chartists, CON 14/38, CON 37/5 and CB 7/13, Archives Office of Tasmania, Hobart. (2) Other: *Charter* (1839); *Northern Star*, 1841–50; *Evening Star* (1842); Contemporary London journals, Jan 1848–Feb 1849 especially *Punch*, *Illustrated London News* [in particular, 15 Apr 1848] and *Times*; *Morning Chronicle*, 5 Apr 1848 ff. [for National Assembly] and 10–11 Apr 1848 [for Kennington Common]; *Weekly Despatch*, 20 and 27 Aug 1848; *Times*, Sep–Oct 1848 [especially 'The Chartist Trials' of Cuffay, Fay and Lacey in 2 Oct issue]; 'Christopher', 'A Word in Defence of Cuffay', *Reasoner*, no. 26 n.s. 26 Dec 1849, 397–9; [T.M. Wheeler], 'Mr William Cuffay', *Reynolds's Political Instructor*, 13 Apr 1850 [includes engraving of Cuffay]; C. Kingsley, *Alton Locke* (1850, later eds.) [in Chs 33 and 34]; *People's Paper*, no. 4, 29 May 1852 [References to Chartist exiles: Cuffay, Dowling, Fay, Lacey, Smith O'Brien, Ritchie and others]; W. Stevens, *A Memoir of Thomas Martin Wheeler* . . . (1862); T. Frost, *Forty Years' Recollections: literary and political* (1880); G.J. Holyoake, *Sixty Years of an Agitator's Life* 2 vols. (1892; 3rd ed. 1893); R.G. Gammage, *History of the Chartist Movement 1837–1854* (1894; repr. with an Introduction by J. Saville, NY, 1969); E. Dolléans, *Le Chartisme* 2 vols. (Paris, 1912; rev. ed. Paris, 1949); M. Hovell, *The Chartist Movement* (Manchester, 1918); R. Groves, *But we shall rise again* (1938); G.D.H. Cole, *Chartist Portraits* (1941); A.R. Schoyen, *The Chartist Challenge* (1958); A. Briggs, 'Chartists in Tasmania: a note', *Bull. Soc. Lab. Hist.* no. *3* (autumn 1961) 4–8; I. Prothero, 'Chartism in London', *Past and Present* no. *44* (1969) 76–105; J.C. Belchem, 'Radicalism as a 'Platform' Agitation in the periods 1816–1821 and 1848–1851; with Special Reference to the Leadership of Henry Hunt and Feargus O'Connor' (Sussex DPhil., 1974); G. Rudé, *Protest and Punishment: the story of the social and political protesters transported to Australia 1788–1868* (Oxford, 1978); I.J. Prothero, *Artisans and Politics in Early Nineteenth-Century London: John Gast and his times* (Folkestone, 1979); D.Goodway, 'Chartism in London' (London PhD, 1979); biographical information: Dr D. Goodway, Leeds Univ.; Mary McRae, principal archivist, Archives Office of Tasmania, Hobart. Obit. *Mercury* [Hobart], 11 Aug 1870. The editors wish to acknowledge earlier drafts and biographical information from Mrs Dorothy Thompson, Birmingham Univ. and Dr I.J. Prothero, Manchester Univ.; and much helpful comment on the penultimate draft from Dr D. Goodway, Leeds Univ.

John Saville

*See also:** Ernest Jones;† George William MacArthur Reynolds; Thomas Martin Wheeler.

CUMMINGS, David Charles (1861–1942)
TRADE UNIONIST

David Cummings was born on 16 December 1861 in Little Thames Street in Greenwich, London, the son of George David Cummings, an engine smith, and his wife Mary Ann (née Wesborn). He was educated at Roan's School in Greenwich and at the local Board School, which he left at the age of fourteen to take up an apprenticeship in the shipbuilding trade at Rennie's yard.

Cummings soon developed an interest in trade unionism and joined the Society of Boilermakers and Iron and Steel Shipbuilders in 1880. He became a branch official and represented the Society on many occasions at the London Trades Council. For a period he served on the Trade Council's executive. Although his first political allegiance had been to the Liberal Party – he was a member of the Deptford Liberal Association – his association with union and LTC affairs led him increasingly to adopt a labour viewpoint and in 1892, responding to an appeal in the *Workman's Times*, he became a founder member of the ILP. He was an active supporter of the campaigns of Labour candidates in LCC elections but, for what he himself said were family reasons, he refused to allow his own name to go forward.

The Boilermakers' secretary was Robert Knight, elected in 1871 and not to retire until 1899. In the early 1890s the growing feeling that more democratic control should be exercised by the membership led to a vote, towards the end of 1894, that a General Council be convened to consider revision of the Society's rules. When the Council met in 1895 it had a number of controversial issues to debate, among them the proposal to replace the existing lay Executive Council by a full-time EC of seven members. Knight and the existing EC were strongly opposed to this revision but it was carried, and then put to a general ballot by the membership. Cummings played a leading role among the reformers, and the publicity within the Society he received during this episode undoubtedly helped to secure his election as district organiser for Yorkshire. This occurred just before the national ballot on the proposed rule change and although no voting results were ever published, it was clear that the proposed change had been approved.

Cummings moved to Leeds to take up his official position for the Yorkshire district, and when Knight retired in 1899 he was a candidate for the general secretaryship. There were two other candidates – F.A. Fox of South Wales and J. Conley of Scotland. In his letter of nomination Cummings stressed his considerable shop-floor experience, and his local government interests – he had become a member of the Leeds School Board in 1898. Inside the Society he favoured 'broad and democratic government', good coverage of rank and file opinion in the *Monthly Report* and the establishment of an Appeals Council that would meet every two or three years. He wanted further to see greater uniformity in piece rates; and towards the employers, like his predecessor, he stood for conciliation, on the grounds that well-organised men should not need to strike. He further argued for a greater influence of the Society upon public bodies responsible for giving contracts.

The election for the general secretaryship was a rather odd episode. The first ballot put Fox well ahead although not with the absolute majority required; and the EC decided to conduct a further ballot between Fox and Conley, the latter being the runner-up with more votes than Cummings. But before a second ballot was organised Fox withdrew, having accepted the secretaryship of an employers' organisation, the South Wales Federation of Ship-Repairers. The EC then decided to hold a ballot between Conley and Cummings in which the latter won, but only narrowly (18,389 against 17,830). Conley protested against the second ballot in principle, and further asked for a scrutiny of the votes. The membership were balloted for their opinion but voted in favour of the Cummings' election; and he took up his position on 1 January 1900. In the first month of office he wrote in the *Monthly Report*:

> It is useless for men to unite in gigantic organisations, unless we build up the character of

individual members. To make individuals better is to improve the societies of which they are members . . . Many have yet to learn that the labour question is a moral question, and that unionism is a moral force.

The Boilermakers' Society had never been enthusiastic for direct union representation in Parliament. In August 1900 the *Monthly Report* gave a fairly comprehensive coverage of the Taff Vale case, and of its implications. Cummings himself believed the main result of the case would be greater loyalty, more discretion and better discipline on the part of union membership. But as the full consequences of Taff Vale became appreciated, opinion within the Society moved steadily to a position favourable to the Labour Representation Committee. After Cummings and other members of the EC of the Boilermakers had attended an LRC meeting convened during the 1901 TUC, the EC strongly recommended affiliation to the LRC. A second poll of the membership, after a preliminary favourable result, gave a clear majority for affiliation; and in August 1902 J. Conley, J.H. Jose and John Hill were approved as sponsored candidates. Cummings declined nomination on the grounds that he had only recently assumed the general secretaryship.

Towards the end of 1902 Cummings took part in the Mosely Industrial Commission that toured industrial areas of the United States. In accordance with Boilermakers' Society custom a vote had been taken and a solid majority of 20,293 had backed his visit. Between January and June of 1903 he published in the *Monthly Report* detailed and interesting accounts of his experiences, giving his impressions of such places as Buffalo, Niagara, Cleveland and Chicago and his assessment of wages and conditions and standards of tooling in the Pittsburg and Philadelphia yards.

During the years 1902 to 1908 Cummings was a member of the Parliamentary Committee of the TUC, and was closely involved with the agitation against the Taff Vale decision. A resolution had been carried at the 1902 TUC calling for a joint committee of the Parliamentary Committee, the General Federation of Trade Unions and the LRC; but for reasons largely of mutual suspicion, it was not until February 1905 that the first joint conference was held. Out of this came a permanent co-ordinating committee, made up of three representatives from each of the three organisations, together with three joint secretaries. Cummings with D.J. Shackleton and J.J. Stevenson represented the TUC, with W.C. Steadman as their secretary [Roberts (1958) 190 ff.]. Cummings was chairman of the Parliamentary Committee of the TUC 1905/6, and in January 1906, after the election of the Liberal Government, he went on a deputation with Richard Bell and David Shackleton to the Prime Minister and the Lord Chancellor to discuss the proposed revision of trade union law. In his 1906 presidential address to the TUC Cummings referred to the significant advances made by Labour in the recent general election; and he set out a programme of social welfare, including housing, pensions and the feeding of school-children. He also called for proportional representation in national elections. In 1907 he gave evidence on behalf of the TUC Parliamentary Committee before the Departmental Committee on the Working of the Fair Wages Resolution.

Throughout his period of office as general secretary to the Boilermakers Cummings did what he could to educate his members into the realities of their times, and although a political moderate he always exhibited a marked independence of spirit in respect of contemporary issues. In September 1903 he refused to give evidence to the R.C. on Trade Disputes and Trade Combinations because there were no representatives of Labour among the Commissioners; and like so many of his trade union colleagues he vigorously condemned the introduction of indentured Chinese labourers into South Africa. When old age pensions were finally introduced in 1908, he protested at the seventy year limit and at the low level of benefits, and he drew unfavourable comparisons with the high pensions paid to statesmen and to Boer War generals.

In October 1908 he resigned from his position with the Boilermakers to become a Labour Correspondent to the Board of Trade. It was not by any means an unusual decision for a trade union official although Cummings could have expected many years more service in the movement. In addition to his position in his own union and the TUC he was on the EC of the Engineering and Shipbuilding Trades Federation and on the EC of the General Federation of Trade Unions. With his very wide experience and organising ability he did well in the Civil Service. In 1911 he became an Assistant Industrial Commissioner, and in 1916 he moved to the Ministry of Labour. He was awarded the CBE in June 1918. From 1919 to 1940 he was a permanent member of the Industrial Court, and in 1930 he was chairman of the Court of Referees. Although he naturally severed connections with the labour movement in 1908, he became active again in his retirement. He stood unsuccessfully for the LCC in March 1928 but was elected Labour member for the Bellingham ward on the Lewisham Borough Council in November 1928, serving for three years. At the time of his election he was chairman of East Lewisham Labour Party.

It is not possible to be precise concerning his political opinions. We may hazard the guess that he joined the ILP largely because he believed strongly in independent labour representation in Parliament. In general he seems to have been a typically moderate union leader of late Victorianism. He was teetotal and a long-standing member of the Ancient Order of Foresters; and in 1906 he was appointed to the Newcastle bench. Two years earlier he had written an historical survey of his own union in which he gave, apart from the descriptive story, a craftsman's attention to the technical problems of his trade.

He died at the age of eighty-one on 16 April 1942. He had married Lucy Elizabeth Watkin, and they had one son and two daughters. He left an estate of £1105.

Writings: *A Historical Survey of the Boiler Makers' and Iron and Steel Ship Builders' Society from August, 1834 to August, 1904* (Newcastle upon Tyne, 1905); Evidence before the Departmental Committee on the Working of the Fair Wages Resolution of the House of Commons of 1891, *M of E* 1908 XXXIV Cd 4423 Qs 1–188.

Sources: (1) MS: Labour Party archives: LRC. (2) Boilermakers' Society, *Monthly Reports*, 1899–1908: HQ of Amalgamated Society of Boilermakers, Shipwrights, Blacksmiths and Structural Workers, Newcastle upon Tyne; *Lewisham Borough News*, 17 Oct and 7 Nov 1928; F. Bealey and H. Pelling, *Labour and Politics 1900–1906* (1958) Ch.3; J.E. Mortimer, *History of the Boilermakers' Society* vol. *1: 1834–1906* (1973); C. Woodland (compiler), *The Taff Vale Case: a guide to the ASRS Records* ed. R. Storey (Univ. of Warwick Library Occasional Publications, no. 3: 1978) 28pp.; biographical information: A.R. Taffs, London Borough of Lewisham. Obit. *Monthly Report* [of Boilermakers' Society] (June 1942) 23; *TUC Report* (1942).

Barbara Nield
John Saville

See also: †John Hill; Robert Knight; †William (Will) Charles Steadman for The Mosely Industrial Commission (**Special Note**).

CUNNINGHAME GRAHAM, Robert Bontine (1852–1936)

SOCIALIST, SCOTTISH NATIONALIST, MP AND WRITER

Robert Bontine Cunninghame Graham was born at 5 Cadogan Place, London, on 24 May 1852. He was the eldest of the three sons of Major William Bontine of the Scots Greys, a Scottish landowner with several estates. The child was registered as Robert Bontine, with no

Cunninghame Graham following. His biographers explain that owing to the provision of an old entail the eldest son of the family had to use Bontine as his surname until his father died; then he added the names Cunninghame Graham. Robert's parents and Robert himself seem to have taken little notice of this provision: his parents used only the surname Bontine throughout their lives, while Robert was signing himself (among other versions) 'R.C. Graham' and 'Robert Graham', and was referred to as 'Mr Graham' even as a young man, years before his father died [see the letters quoted in Tschiffely (1937) 23, 56–7, 76, 102]. In later life he settled on 'R.B. Cunninghame Graham': his writings are so signed, and his letters; and Joseph Conrad and other friends used the forms Cunninghame Graham or Graham in their correspondence.

His mother was the Hon. Anne Elizabeth Fleeming, the third daughter of Admiral the Hon. Charles Elphinstone Fleeming. Her mother was Spanish, and in his youth Robert often stayed for long periods with this grandmother at Ryde, and also with her relatives in Spain. (He grew up bilingual in English and Spanish). But as a child he was brought up, along with his brothers, chiefly on his father's estates of Gartmore, by the Lake of Menteith in Perthshire, and Finlaystone in Renfrewshire. At eleven years old Robert was sent to a preparatory school and at fourteen to Harrow, where he remained for two years. On the whole he disliked both establishments. He was then sent to a private school in Brussels, where he had fencing lessons (he became a first-class fencer and at one time earned a living as a fencing master), as well as acquiring fluent French. For a short period after this his education continued under private tutors at home and in Spain.

By this time (1869) he was a fine rider, fencer and athlete generally, fearless, tough and wiry. His grandmother's reminiscences and tales of Spanish and South American history and legend had stimulated his love of adventure, and he longed to go to South America – where, moreover, he hoped he would make his fortune. (His father was heavily in debt). In November 1869, at the age of seventeen, he set out as partner of two brothers who had a ranch in Argentina, and for the next sixteen years he moved about South America, with periods in Mexico and Texas, and with not infrequent visits home and to the Continent. He started as a rancher; later he pursued various occupations which had mostly to do with horses and cattle. He had some narrow escapes from the Indians, who were constantly carrying on guerilla warfare, and for a time he was forcibly enlisted in the Argentinian revolutionary army. His chief companions were the gauchos, who lived on horseback, and he came to ride as well as they did. He acquired an intimate knowledge of horses, gauchos and ranchers, and of large tracts of South America in Argentina, Brazil, Uruguay, Paraguay and Chile. He also acquired a passion for the country, especially for the pampa or great grassland, in which he set a number of his stories.

On one of his visits to Europe, in 1878, when he was riding in Paris, his horse became restive and almost knocked over a beautiful girl, whom Robert was at once attracted to. He soon took her away to London, where they were married at the Strand Register Office on 24 October 1878. Gabrielle Marie (Gabriela), an orphan aged nineteen, was the daughter of a French merchant, Francis de la Balmondière, and a Spanish mother. She was born in Chile, but when Graham met her she was being educated at a convent in Paris under the supervision of an aunt. She was a poet and story-writer, and something of a mystic – she wrote a life of St Teresa. But she was also practical, observant and daring: she shared her husband's interests, his adventurous life, and later his Socialist views, attending his meetings, lecturing on Socialism and working with Morris's Socialist League.

The young couple soon set off for Texas; and they stayed in North America pursuing various attempts to make their fortune until 1881, when they returned to Europe, living for the next two years at Vigo in Spain and Liphook in Hampshire. In 1883 Major Bontine died, and Robert succeeded to the family estates. Gartmore in Perthshire was heavily encumbered with debt, against which Graham and his wife struggled for twenty years.

While he was in America Graham kept himself up to date with political events both on that continent and in Britain [see, for instance, his letters of 1879 quoted in Tschiffely (1937) 140–50].

After he was more or less settled in Britain he began to interest himself seriously in home politics. At first he called himself a Radical Liberal, but it was not long before he was attending Socialist meetings, where he heard – and soon met – William Morris, Bernard Shaw, H.M. Hyndman, Keir Hardie and John Burns. Presently he himself began a career as a public orator, speaking at meetings along with these and other Socialist and Labour leaders and also with the anarchists Kropotkin and Stepniak. He was a naturally excellent speaker, lucid and mordantly witty, using no notes, and yet keeping to the point. He was especially good at repartee to hecklers. He became a close friend of Keir Hardie's – whom he later called 'the only genius, probably, that the Labour Party has ever produced' [quoted Tschiffely (1937) 187].

In the general election of 1885 Graham contested the seat of North-West Lanarkshire, losing it to the Conservative candidate John Baird by 1103 votes: in the next year, however, he was elected by a majority over Baird of 332. Graham stood as a Liberal; but his programme, though some of it was accepted by moderate Liberals, was as a whole advanced. It included universal suffrage, the abolition of the House of Lords, secular education and free school meals; disestablishment of the Church of England; nationalisation of the land, mines and other industries; the eight-hour day and Home Rule for Ireland and Scotland. His speeches in the House of Commons (to which he rode on his favourite horse Pampa) were as advanced as his electoral programme. His maiden speech on 1 February 1887 was characteristic – not least because 'House kept in continuous roar for more than half an hour', according to *Vanity Fair* (5 Feb 1887): he began with a joke about losing his 'political virginity', and after upbraiding the Government for their 'evident desire . . . to do nothing at all', and referring to 'the awful chasm existing between the poor and the rich', he attacked government policies in Egypt and in Burma; the spectacle of so-called civilised people ready 'with arms of precision to shoot down naked savages' always roused his fury, as can be seen in a number of his stories and sketches.

In the middle eighties trade depression had reached its trough; there was much unemployment, and agitation by and for the unemployed. The years 1886 to 1887 saw large demonstrations in London, and the principle of assembly and free speech was being challenged and affirmed. Graham used the floor of the House of Commons to question police actions, and he was present in Trafalgar Square on 13 November 1887 when an advertised meeting had been prohibited in advance by the Metropolitan Police Commissioner. This was the 'Bloody Sunday' affair. John Burns and Graham were arrested, the latter with a head injury. At the trial, where Graham's counsel was his friend Asquith, both defendants were sentenced to six weeks' imprisonment. Ten years later Graham wrote an account of life in Pentonville gaol, in a sketch entitled 'Sursum Corda' [*Sat. Rev.*, 19 June 1897, repr. in the volume of stories and sketches *Success* (1902)]. *The Times* report included a rhetorical inquiry whether Graham ought to be – as he had been since 1884 – a deputy Lieutenant of Dunbartonshire and a JP of Dunbartonshire, Perthshire and Stirlingshire.

Graham's uncompromisingly Socialist speeches in the Commons, usually expressed with caustic wit, displeased many MPs. He spoke frequently and was a pertinacious interrupter. In the summer and autumn of 1887 he was much involved in the committee stage of the Coal Mines Regulation Bill. In his speeches he advocated the nationalisation of the mining industry and the eight-hour day for pit boys and adult miners alike. On 12 September he was suspended from the House for the first but not the last time, for refusing to withdraw a disrespectful reference to the House of Lords. For his protest inside the Commons about the Cradley Heath chain makers on 1 December 1888 he was again suspended – an incident made famous by Shaw (see the Notes to *Captain Brassbound's Conversion*). Graham also agitated effectively on their behalf outside Westminster. In later life he told Tschiffely that this was perhaps the only good thing he had achieved during the six years he was in the House of Commons. But this was too modest an estimate: 'though exactly how much he had done is difficult to assess . . . because, with someone in his solitary position, the question is one of influence and example rather than of direct political effect . . . Keir Hardie became 'Member for the Unemployed'; before him, Cunninghame Graham had been Member for the unemployed and the overworked, and was a decisive guide in Hardie's progress towards socialism.' [Watts and Davies (1979) 98–9 and note 62 p. 304]; Graham continued throughout his parliamentary career to assert vigorously the rights of working people to diminish and curb their economic and social exploitation. He once referred to the relations between labour and capital as 'under this system necessarily hostile' [*Hansard*, 22 Apr 1890]. In his last months as an MP Graham's bill for an eight hour day in all trades and occupations had its first reading, on 11 February 1892. On 8 May Conybeare, its seconder, moved the second reading; but the Government refused to find time for debating it.

Graham early defined Scottish Home Rule as 'The blessing of a national parliament, with the pleasure of knowing that the taxes were wasted in Edinburgh instead of in London' [*Notes on the District of Menteith* (1895) 19]. In spite of such sarcasms, he was a strong supporter of Home Rule for Scotland, as well as for Ireland. He and Keir Hardie were original members of the Scottish Home Rule Association founded in 1886, and he seconded the motion on Scottish Home Rule introduced into the Commons by Gavin Clark on 9 April 1889. He often spoke on Irish affairs (e.g. on 1 Feb 1887, 8 Dec 1890, 3 May and 3 Aug 1891). He was a friend and defender of Parnell, and his speech of 10 February 1892 ended with a tribute to the Irish leader: he said that death 'had deprived this House of the most remarkable man who sat in it this century'.

Support for the Irish cause brought him one of his most valued friends, Wilfrid Scawen Blunt. They had much in common: both were lovers of horses (Blunt had a famous stud), Arabian travellers, writers and anti-imperialists. They were also both landowners.

Even without his attention to parliamentary and constituency business, Graham was kept extremely busy in the late 1880s and early 90s. In 1887 he was the chief sponsor of Keir Hardie as Liberal candidate for North Ayrshire, and the next year he campaigned to have Hardie chosen for Mid-Lanark. He helped Annie Besant in the match-girls' strike, and on 25 August 1888, in Glasgow, he took the chair at the inaugural conference of the Scottish Labour Party. Graham was elected president, Conybeare and Gavin Clark vice-presidents, and Hardie secretary. The programme was Socialistic rather than Socialist; and as its representatives, Graham, Hardie and Shaw Maxwell negotiated with the Liberals for a limited electoral pact in 1889–90 [Pelling (1954) 74; Morgan (1975) 36–7]. This would have given Labour Party candidates in three Scottish constituencies; but the local Liberal Associations vetoed the proposal.

In July 1889, along with William Morris, Hardie, Aveling and Eleanor Marx-Aveling, Graham attended the Marxist Congress of the Second International in Paris. He took the chair at one of its morning sessions and was elected a member of one of its standing committees. He spoke at the first mass May Day celebrations in London on 4 May 1890 – the demonstration that provoked Engels to his enthusiastic comment – 'The grand-children of the old Chartists are entering the line of battle' [*Correspondence, 1846–1895* (1934) 469]. In 1891 Graham took part in the May Day meeting in Paris; later in the same month, at a Socialist meeting in Calais, he made two speeches so inflammatory that he was arrested and expelled from France.

Besides all this activity Graham contributed many articles, reports and letters to the press – chiefly, but not only, the Socialist and Labour press; and during the 1889 Dock Strike he and John Burns joined the editorial board of Champion's *Labour Elector*. In 1890, however, the *Elector*'s attack on Ernest Parke, editor of the radical *Star*, so disgusted them that they withdrew, as Mann and Tillett also did.

Graham's parliamentary experience ended with the general election of 1892 when, standing as a Scottish Labour Party candidate for Glasgow Camlachie, opposed by a Liberal, an Independent Liberal and a Liberal Unionist (who won), he came bottom of the poll. Several times in the next dozen years or so he was asked to stand for one constituency or another and refused on each occasion [letter to James Connolly, quoted Tschiffely (1937) 279]. But in 1918, for some reason, perhaps connected with his attitudes towards the First World War, he was willing to fight West Stirling and Clackmannan as a Liberal. Again he came bottom of the poll.

Out of Parliament in the 1890s he continued as a political journalist, commentator and propagandist. An early pamphlet was *Economic Evolution* (1891), an attack on capitalism particularised in the description of the economic and social ruin of an imagined Irish village after a textile mill was built there. It was a simple moral tale. Equally simple was another pamphlet, of 1896, reprinted from *Justice* (5 Sep 1896) entitled *The Imperial Kailyard. Being a Biting Satire on English Colonisation*. The British grab for Africa was his particular target; he stressed the degradation not only of the native Africans but of the conquerors as well. The subject was more brilliantly handled in 'Niggers', a savage satire on British imperialism included in the collection called *The Ipané* published in 1899; it had been revised from an article in the *Social-Democrat* of April 1897, where it was entitled 'Bloody Niggers'.

By the mid 1890s Graham had begun a further career, as a writer of short stories and descriptive sketches, of histories and biographies, mostly South American. 1894 saw the beginning of Frank Harris's remarkable editorship of the *Saturday Review*. His contributors included Shaw, Wells, Max Beerbohm and Arthur Symons, as well as Cunninghame Graham. According to Conrad, '*all* the fiction (it may be called) the *S.R.* publishes is furnished by C.G. alone' [Watts (1969) 66]. At the same time Graham was also commenting in the *Review* on political affairs; for example, he wrote repeatedly on the Spanish-American War, strongly defending Spain and being particularly caustic about the role of Britain; he wrote on Anglo-American and U.S.–South-American relations; on the Spilsbury expedition in Africa; and on Morocco. On the Jameson Raid and the Boer War he wrote letters and articles attacking both parties [*Sat. Rev.*, 21 Mar, 4 Apr 1896; 1 Feb, 8 Mar 1902]. The 1896 articles gave a trenchant and sarcastic analysis of the two white societies in South Africa, Boer and British.

His publications between 1896 and his death in 1936 were many, and of many kinds: seventeen collections of tales and sketches, two travel books, a guide book, ten historical and biographical works on South American subjects, and a biography of his ancestor Robert Graham. He also contributed a large number of prefaces or introductions to other people's books, both political and literary; for example, to J.L. Mahon's *A Labour Programme* (1888) to Ida Taylor's *Revolutionary Types* (1904); to M. Aflalo's *The Truth about Morocco* (1904) – Morocco was a country which Graham knew well in parts and felt strongly about – and Compton Rickett's *William Morris* (1913). Almost every one of his books includes accounts of – or telling asides on – the lives of the poor and the down-trodden; for instance, a recurrent theme is the oppression of the South American Indians by a succession of white conquerors. Almost every book also includes a forcible direct attack on some other social or economic evil.

In 1898, Graham published the account of his attempt to visit the forbidden city of Tarudant in Morocco, one of the most observant and most fascinating travel books of his time – the time, it is to be remembered, of the distinguished Arabists Doughty, Burton and Blunt. The book, *Mogreb-el-Acksa*, gives memorable detail of the primitive society of South Morocco, with its occasional incongruous acquisition of modern technological objects and with the efforts of Western capitalists to exploit it. As one would expect, Graham defended 'the relative integrity of the archaic life of the Moor' [Watts (1969) 77], which he described as 'Arcadia grafted on feudalism or feudalism steeped in Arcadia.' In Graham's own words, he 'would wish to see it [Morocco] work out its own damnation after the fashion that best pleases it' [preface to Aflalo (1904)]. Edward Garnett described the book as 'a delicious commentary on our Anglo-Saxon civilisation; a malicious and ironic comparison of British commercialised world [*sic*] with the feudal world of Morocco; a subtle, witty commentary that must rejoice all who are rejoiced by *Candide*' [*Academy*, 4 Feb 1899, 153–4]. And Shaw declared that he had stolen from the book all the setting of *Captain Brassbound's Conversion* – see his account of this and a character sketch of Graham in the Notes to that play.

By 1900 it was impossible to continue the struggle with the debt on Gartmore; the estate was sold, much to Graham's distress, and he and his wife later settled at Ardoch in Dunbartonshire. Gabrielle Graham died in 1906; she was forty-seven, and they had been married for twenty-eight years. After this, Graham took a small house in London, close to his mother's house in Chester Square, and spent much of his time with her. He was still in great demand as a political speaker, as Harry McShane, for instance, witnesses [McShane and Smith (1978) 21, 25].

On 2 August 1914 a mass demonstration for peace was held in Trafalgar Square. Among the speakers were Hyndman, Keir Hardie, Ben Tillett, George Barnes, and Graham. Once war was declared, however, all of them except Hardie supported it. [For Graham's attitude and his reasons see Watt and Davies (1979) 237–40]. Within a fortnight Graham volunteered for the Rough Rider Corps, although he was sixty-two. He was rejected, but was later put in charge of a Section of the Remount, and was appointed head of a commission sent to Uruguay in November 1914 to buy horses for the Government. In 1917 he was appointed to survey the cattle resources of Columbia [see his Report in *Three Fugitive Pieces* (1960) 19–31]. His support of the war was also manifested in other ways. In 1915 the pro-war minority of the BSP set up the Socialist National Defence Committee (a labour organisation devoted to the war effort), which held a major rally at the Queen's Hall, London in July, addressed by Tillett, Hodge, Hyndman, Roberts and Graham [see *DLB 3* (1976) 112]. In April 1916 the SNDC became the British Workers' National League, later the British Workers' League. Graham was elected a vice-president of the BWNL, and he publicly welcomed the appearance of its journal, the *British Citizen and Empire Worker*, on 25 August 1916.

In the first post-war general election of December 1918, Graham stood unsuccessfully for West Stirlingshire as an Independent Liberal. He was asked to stand again in 1921, but he refused, showing a lack of enthusiasm for the Labour Party, though he indicated that he had finished with the Liberals [Tschiffely (1937) 379, 382].

Post-war events in Ireland seem to have modified his support for Irish Home Rule. No record appears of his views of the Easter Rising of 1916; but in 1920, the year of the arrival in Ireland of the Black and Tans and the Auxiliary Division of the Royal Irish Constabulary, when in the latter part of the year violence was at its height, Graham wrote a letter on 23 November resigning from the Scottish Home Rule Association, to which he had belonged since 1886. The Association was planning a meeting at which they would attack the British Government's policy of reprisals. Graham wrote that he was 'not in sympathy with the object of the meeting'; he defended the police and army in Ireland, referred to 'the last horrible and cold-blooded murder of fourteen young men' (twelve British Army officers and two Auxiliaries were killed on 21 November), and described the killers as 'instigated . . . chiefly, and certainly paid for . . . by the band of international Jews, grouped round their fellow Jew, Mr 'de' Valera in New York.' He asserted, rather unconvincingly, that he remained 'a convinced Home Ruler . . ., so long as the British Empire is master of its own house and controls the ports, and armed forces of the Crown.' And in a postscript he added that he had 'of course, no idea of imputing complicity in murder to the Jews as a race; only to the criminal Bolshie Jews who run 'de' Valera in New York' [ibid. 380–1]. But by 1927 he had recovered his poise, and in a letter to H.W. Nevinson was able to describe both parties in Ireland as 'the two bands of scoundrels, the Gunmen and the Black and Tans (Arcades ambo).' (He was referring to Byron's '"Arcades ambo", *id est* – blackguards both', *Don Juan* IV xciii). He was already reconciled with the Scottish Home Rule Association, and in 1928 he became president of its successor, the National Party of Scotland. Earlier in the year he stood as Scottish Nationalist candidate for the Lord Rectorship of Glasgow University, and lost to the Prime Minister, Stanley Baldwin, by only 66 votes; in 1935 he stood again and was again defeated.

The 1920s brought personal blows in the deaths of three of his intimate friends, W.H. Hudson, Wilfrid Scawen Blunt, and Joseph Conrad. Blunt and Hudson died in 1922. As chairman of the Hudson Memorial Committee Graham was instrumental in getting Epstein the commission for the sculpture set up in Hyde Park in 1925, the controversial 'Rima'. He fought off a number of attacks from those who disliked either Epstein's art in general or 'Rima' in particular or both together. [Epstein gives detail of the whole affair in his autobiography (1963) 89, 107–11, 263–9]. Two years later when Lady Warwick dedicated Easton Park as a wild life sanctuary in memory of Hudson, Graham performed the ceremony.

Conrad died in 1924. He and Graham had been friends since 1897, and Conrad once said to

Arthur Symons, 'Could you conceive for a moment that I could go on existing if Cunninghame Graham were to die?' [Watts (1969) 4]. In the next year, 1925, Graham's mother, Mrs Bontine, died in her sleep at the age of ninety-seven. As a sort of pilgrimage, perhaps, late in the same year Graham went to Venezuela, where his mother was born and spent her first few years. He explored its great plains on horseback (at the age of seventy-three); and he returned there in 1926–7, this time doing some research into the archives in Caracas.

After his mother's death his chief companion was Mrs Elizabeth Dummett, whom he had met during the war. He spent summers at Ardoch, winters in travelling, chiefly in Spain and Portugal, the south of France, and North Africa. In 1934 he visited Ceylon, and in 1935 South Africa.

His failing health was beginning to be signalled, but he persisted in making a last journey to South America, in January 1936, accompanied by Mrs Dummett and her sister. He was able to visit the house where W.H. Hudson was born, but by early spring he was in bed with bronchitis, and he died in Buenos Aires on 20 March, in his eighty-fourth year. A continual stream of persons, including the President of the Republic of Argentina, filed past his body as it lay in state, and crowds surrounded his coffin as it was carried to the harbour to be transported to Scotland – he had asked to be buried beside his wife on the island of Inchmahone in the Lake of Menteith. The funeral took place on 18 April. He left a personal estate valued at £101,407. On his tombstone Graham had directed that his coat-of-arms should not appear, but instead the brand he had used for his horses when he was ranching in South America. A memorial cairn was set up at Castle Hill, Dunbartonshire, on land which he had given to the National Trust for Scotland; it was unveiled by his kinsman, the Duke of Montrose, in August 1937.

Graham's strikingly good looks were of a very unusual kind. He was tall, with a lean, wiry figure, a long patrician face, an aquiline nose, a moustache and pointed beard, and thick dark-red hair. He looked like a seventeenth century Spanish grandee – 'My outlook on most things in life has been, and is, Spanish' [quoted Bloomfield (1952) 15] – rather than a Scottish laird, still less a Socialist MP, of the nineteenth century. Some of his friends called him Don Roberto (and a new city in the Argentine was so named in his honour); he was constantly compared with a Velasquez portrait. Being picturesque in the full sense of the word, he was a very popular subject for artists, including Lavery, Rothenstein, Epstein and Strang. Perhaps the best-known portraits, reproduced in several books, are two by Lavery; one an equestrian portrait of Graham on Pampa (it is now in the Buenos Aires Museo de Bellas Artes), and the other a full-length portrait (now in Glasgow Art Gallery). He was also the subject of a number of cartoons, including one by 'Spy' in *Vanity Fair*, 25 Aug 1888 [ibid., 13].

Graham's influence on the Socialist and labour movement in the late nineteenth and twentieth century has been variously assessed. But as his latest biographers observe, a number of the important radical causes which have now partly or wholly achieved their aims were the very causes to which Graham gave constant and energetic support: 'militant trade unionism, the founding of a Labour Party, free education, the eight-hour working day, and a decent standard of living for working people; Irish Home Rule; extensive nationalisation; an end to the mystique of British Imperialism; a vigorous Scottish National Party; and social justice for women' [Watts and Davies (1979) 291].

The Avelings were in no doubt about Graham's value when they lamented, after his defeat in the general election of 1892, that the Labour MPs had lost 'something more than a head – their heart' [Tsuzuki (1967) 224].

Writings: Early bibliographies of the writings of Cunninghame Graham that have been published are almost entirely lists of his literary works. *A Bibliography of the First Editions of the Works of Robert Bontine Cunninghame Graham* (1924) was compiled by Leslie Chaundry. In 1932 H.F. West provided a check list in his biography: *A Modern Conquistador: Robert Bontine Cunninghame Graham: his life and work* and in 1938 he produced a privately printed work, *The Herbert Faulkner West Collection of R.B. Cunninghame Graham, presented in* *memory of "Don Roberto" to the Dartmouth College Library* [New Hampshire]: this lists nearly forty books, several pamphlets, thirty-four prefaces and some miscellaneous items as well as original material. In 1952 a selection of his writings appeared in P. Bloomfield's *The Essential R.B. Cunninghame Graham*. Apart from his main works, Cunninghame Graham was a prolific writer of articles, especially for the *Saturday Review*, but also for the daily as well as the periodical press. Other journals in which his writings appear include *Cont. Rev., Justice, Labour Leader, 19th C., Pall Mall Gazette, People's Press* and the *Social-Democrat*. The lacunae in the original bibliographies have been almost completely remedied by two subsequent articles: C. T. Watts, 'R.B. Cunninghame Graham (1852–1936): a list of his contributions to periodicals', *Bibliotheck 4*, no. 5 (1965) 186–99 and J. Walker, 'R.B. Cunninghame Graham and 'The Labour Elector'', ibid 7, no. 3 (1974) 72–5. In their comprehensive work, *Cunninghame Graham: a critical biography* (CUP, 1979), C. Watts and L. Davies have provided a selected bibliography by categories. The list which follows here is concerned chiefly with his political life (including *Hansard* references to all his important speeches and a few items not elsewhere noted) and is selective rather than comprehensive: such literary works as are mentioned in the text are also included. But with the bibliographic material noted above there is now available as complete a listing of his writings as may perhaps be possible. *Hansard*, 1 Feb 1887 [for maiden speech], 17 Feb, 12 May, 22 June and 12 Sep 1887; 'Has the Liberal Party a Future?', *Cont. Rev. 53* (Feb 1888) 295–300; Introduction to J.A. Mahon, *A Labour Programme* (Labour Platform Series, no. 1: 1888) 1–7; *Hansard*, 1 Dec 1888; 'An Appeal for the Chainmakers' [letter], *Pall Mall Gazette*, 5 Dec 1888; 'A Plea for the Chainmakers' in *The Nail and Chainmakers* (Labour Platform Series, no. 2: 1889) 107–10; *Hansard*, 5 Mar, 9 Apr and 8 May 1889; 'The Revolt of Labour', *Labour Elector 2*, no. 36, 7 Sep 1889; *Hansard*, 22 Apr 1890; 'The Great Demonstration: hundreds of thousands demand an Eight Hours' Bill', *People's Press*, 10 May 1890, 5–6; 'Labour Papers and Political Parties' [letter], ibid., 31 May 1890; 'People's Parliament', *People's Press*, 21 June 1890, 3; 'The Bloody City', ibid., 16 Aug 1890, 9; 'After the Congress', ibid., 13 Sep 1890, 7; 'Joined to their Idols', ibid., 22 Nov 1890, 7; "Ca Canny", ibid., 29 Nov 1890, 6–7; 'Eight Hour "Blokes" in Council', ibid., 6 Dec 1890; *Hansard*, 8 Dec 1890; 'Idealism and the Masses', *19th C. 28* (Dec 1890) 945–9; *Economic Evolution* (1891) 18 pp.; *Hansard*, 3 Aug 1891; 10 Feb 1892; 'China Dogs', *Labour Prophet 1*, no. 5 (May 1892) 33–4; *Notes on the District of Menteith* (1895); 'William Morris III. With the North-West Wind' [one of three articles, the others by G.B. Shaw and A. Symons], *Sat. Rev. 82* (July–Dec 1896) 389–90 [repr. in his book *The Ipané* (1899)]; *The Imperial Kailyard, being a Biting Satire on English Colonisation* (1896) 15 pp. [repr. by the Twentieth Century Press from *Justice*, 5 Sep 1896]; 'Bloody Niggers', *Social-Democrat 1* (Apr 1897) 104–9 [revised as 'Niggers' in *The Ipané* (1899)]; 'Sursum Corda' *Sat. Rev. 83*, 19 June 1897, 681–3 [repr. in his book *Success* (1902)]; *Mogreb-el-Acksa* [A Journey in Morocco] (1898); Introduction to M. Aflalo, *The Truth about Morocco* (1904); 'An Tighearna: a memory of Parnell', *Dana* [An Irish Magazine of Independent Thought, Dublin] *1*, no. 7 (Nov 1904) 193–9 [repr. in a selection of his works, *Thirty Tales and Sketches* by E. Garnett (1929) 186–96]; Introduction to I.A. Taylor, *Revolutionary Types* (1904); *Glasgow Herald*, 3 Nov 1906 and 28 Jan 1914 [reports of speeches by Cunninghame Graham advocating votes for women]; 'Aspects of the Social Question', *English Rev. 1* (1908–9) 165–8; 'Spain's Future is in Spain', ibid., *3* (Sep 1909) 335–42; Introduction to A. Compton Rickett, *William Morris: a study in personality* (1913); 'With the North-East Wind' [Keir Hardie's Funeral] in his book *Brought Forward* (1916) and repr. in *Thirty Tales and Sketches* (see above); 'Wilfred Scawen Blunt' *English Rev. 35* (Dec 1922) 486–92 [repr. in his book *Redeemed* (1927)]; 'A Fragment of Garibaldi' and 'Report . . . on the Cattle Resources of the Republic of Colombia', in *Three Fugitive Pieces* with a Foreword by H.F. West (Hanover, New Hampshire, 1960) 13–17 and 19–31.

Sources: (1) MS: see C. Watts and L. Davies, *Cunninghame Graham: a critical biography* (1979) 323; correspondence in Francis Johnson ILP Coll., BLPES [and on microfilm]; Labour

Party archives: LRC. (2) Other: Among the biographical works published on Cunninghame Graham the most useful, before the book by Watts and Davies in 1979, is that of his friend, A.F. Tschiffely, which appeared in 1937, the year after Graham's death: *Don Roberto: being the account of the life and works of R.B. Cunninghame Graham 1852–1936*; an abbreviated version by the same author appeared in 1955 under the title of *Tornado Cavalier*. See also: *Times*, 20 Feb 1888; *Dod* (1888); 'Strike of Matchmakers, Bryant May & Co.,' *Women's Union J.*, 16 July 1888; C.A.V. Conybeare, 'Mr. Brooke Robinson's Neglect of his Constituents: a protest', in *The Nail and Chainmakers* (Labour Platform Series, no. 2: 1889) 110–12; *Illustrated Weekly News*, 19 Oct 1889, 10; *Monthly Record of the Dock, Wharf, Riverside and General Labourers' Union* (June 1890) 2–3; W. Morris, *News from Nowhere* (1891); *Academy*, 4 Feb 1899; G. B. Shaw, *Three Plays for Puritans* [see notes to *Captain Brassbound's Conversion*] (1899); W. Crane, *An Artist's Reminiscences* (1907); *ILP Year Book* (1909) 80; H.M. Hyndman, *Further Reminiscences* (1912); *Justice*, 3 May 1913, 5; A.C. Rickett, *William Morris* (1913); *Times*, 3 Aug 1914; G. Cumberland, *Set down in Malice: a book of reminiscences* (1918); D. Lowe, *Souvenirs of Scottish Labour* (Glasgow, 1919); W.S. Blunt, *My Diaries* vol. *2: being a personal narrative of events, 1888–1914* (1920); F. Harris, *Contemporary Portraits (1915–24)* 3rd ser. (1920) 45–60; *DNB* (1931–40) [by H.M. Tomlinson]; W. Rothenstein, *Men and Memories 1872-1900* (1931); *1900-1922* (1933) and *Since Fifty . . . 1922–1938* (1939); H.F. West, *A Modern Conquistador: Robert Bontine Cunninghame Graham: his life and works* (1932); K. Marx and F. Engels, *Correspondence 1846–1895* (1934); Jessie Conrad, *Joseph Conrad and his Circle* (1935); A.F. Tschiffely, *Don Roberto* (1937) [see above for details]; S. Mavor, *Memories of People and Places* [1940] 69–82; *W.H. Hudson's Letters to R.B. Cunninghame Graham* ed. with an Introduction by R. Curle (1941); H. MacDiarmid [pseud. of C.M. Grieve], *Cunninghame Graham: a centenary study* (Glasgow, [1952]); P. Bloomfield, *The Essential R.B. Cunninghame Graham* (1952); D. Garnett, *The Golden Echo* (1954); H. Pelling, *The Origins of the Labour Party 1880–1900* (1954; rev. ed. 1965); A.F. Tschiffely, *Tornado Cavalier* (1955) [see above]; J. Epstein, *Epstein: an autobiography* (1955; rev. ed. 1963); V. Brome, *Frank Harris* (1959); J. Walker, 'Robert Cunninghame Graham', *Tribune*, 29 Apr 1966; C. Tsuzuki, *The Life of Eleanor Marx 1855–1898: a socialist tragedy* (Oxford, 1967); *Joseph Conrad's Letters to R.B. Cunninghame Graham* ed. C.T. Watts (Cambridge, 1969); 'Don Roberto's Correspondent' [review of C.T. Watts's book], *Listener*, 5 June 1969; F. MacShane, 'R.B. Cunninghame Graham', *South Atlantic Q. 68* (1969) 198–207; C. Mackenzie, *My Life and Times Octave Nine 1946–1953* (1970); *Edwardian Radicalism 1900–1914*, ed. A.J.A. Morris (1974); K.O. Morgan, *Keir Hardie: radical and socialist* (1975); Y. Kapp, *Eleanor Marx* vol. *2: The Crowded Years (1884–1898)* (1976); J. Meyers, 'The Genius of Failure: R.B. Cunninghame Graham', *London Mag.* n.s. *15* (1975–6) 54–73; H. McShane and J. Smith, *Harry McShane: no mean fighter* (1978); C. Watts and L. Davies, *Cunninghame Graham: a critical biography* (1979). Obit. *Glasgow Herald*, 21 Mar 1936; *Times*, 23 Mar 1936; *Glasgow Herald*, 24 Mar 1937 [report of a BBC broadcast by A.F. Tschiffely], 14 June, 26 and 30 Aug 1937 [for details of the memorial to Cunninghame Graham].

Margaret 'Espinasse

NOTE: The final draft of this entry was completed before the appearance of the Watts and Davies biography in 1979. A few points only have been added from this book, which remains the most important study to date. [Eds].

DAVIS, William John (1848–1934)

TRADE UNION LEADER

William John Davis was born at 263 Bradford Street, Birmingham, on 6 August 1848, the son of Thomas Charles Davis and Tharzia (née Alkins). His mother's parents were manufacturers of jewellery and electro-plate. At the time of William's birth his father was a brassfounder, although he seems to have followed other trades at various times. At all events, the family was poor, and William had no early education beyond two and a half years at a dame school. Later on, in the early 1860s, he attended a Sunday School and night classes.

When he was nine the family moved, first to Sheffield for a few months, then to Liverpool; but Thomas Davis could not find work. William helped the family finances with his wages as an errand-boy in a printing house. Within a short time they were all back in Birmingham, where in 1861 William entered the brass trade, working as a chandelier-maker and assembler for various employers including Arthur Chamberlain, brother of Joseph. He became a foreman, and also interested himself in political affairs; in 1869 he represented the Barr Street Reform Association at the second Trades Union Congress.

In 1871 the brassworkers of Birmingham began to agitate for an increase of fifteen per cent in wages, and Davis was sent by the workers in his factory (Joseph Ratcliff and Sons) to a meeting, in April of the next year, at which it was decided that a trade union should be formed. Thus the Amalgamated Society of Brassworkers was founded, and when it came to appoint a general secretary Davis was unanimously chosen. With one break when he was a factory inspector, he continued as secretary until he retired in 1921.

His immediate aim was to organise and build up his union as quickly as possible; and from the beginning of his trade union career he emphasised conciliation and arbitration in industrial relations. By July 1872 he had not only organised the brassworkers in Birmingham, but had also established branches in nearly a dozen towns; so that the Society had nearly 6000 members. Davis's industrial policy, in a period of growing prosperity, was to pick off sections of the employers one by one. He began with the cabinet branch. The Society's committee met representatives of the employers in August 1872, and after only two sessions the fifteen per cent bonus which was being asked for was conceded. In September Davis tackled the most difficult employers, those in the chandelier and gas-fittings branch of the trade. They refused the fifteen per cent bonus, but when Davis handed them notices of termination of employment from all the casters and burnishers in the trade the employers gave way. The rest was comparatively easy. By the end of the year Davis had won this bonus for all branches of the brass trade.

During his first period as secretary to the Brassworkers, from 1872 to 1882, Davis became recognised as an outstandingly able negotiator and trade union leader. He gave evidence before the R.C. on the working of the Factory and Workshops Acts in 1875, and in the same year represented his Society at the TUC; he was several times on the Standing Orders Committee of Congress. His attitude to female labour was typical of many of his generation. As early as 1874, for example, he had organised a strike at Smith and Chamberlain in protest against the employment of women in place of skilled brass workmen; and at the Leicester TUC of 1877, when Emma Paterson challenged a motion seeking to restrict the scope of women's industrial work, Davis told Congress that he wanted to exclude from certain trades 'the gentle, nay, the lovable sex – those who had to nurse and to nourish sons and daughters to conduct the world' [Davis (1910) 45]. He clashed with Mary Macarthur on the same question some thirty years later, at the Congresses of 1908 and 1909.

His general political attitudes were also typical of the trade unionists of his time. He remained all his life a Lib-Lab: insistent upon the independence of Labour within a Liberal political framework. When he was chairman of the Birmingham Labour Association in the mid-1870s, he always maintained a political distance between the Association and the Birmingham Liberal caucus. In 1875 he stood as a Labour candidate for the School Board, on a platform which included free and non-sectarian education. The local Liberals opposed him, and he lost the election, but in the following year he was returned unopposed. In 1880, this time with Liberal support, he was elected as a Labour member for the Nechells ward of the Birmingham Town Council; and he immediately became active on behalf of the low-paid Council labourers. Throughout his long career, Davis never deviated from his basic political and industrial views. He always maintained a fierce independence of spirit within the context of his mid-Victorian radicalism; and when Socialism returned to Britain in the 1880s, Davis was among its most active opponents. In the middle 1890s he attempted to establish a pressure group within the Birmingham Liberal movement with a programme on housing and unemployment capable of attracting trade unionists to the Liberal Party. The Liberal and Radical Advance group was constituted on 19 February 1894, but although there was a lively press debate around the new organisation, by the following April the established leadership had effectively re-asserted their authority.

The TUC had repeatedly urged upon successive Governments the appointment of working men as Factory Inspectors. The first to be appointed, in 1881, was John D. Prior, formerly general secretary of the Amalgamated Society of Carpenters and Joiners. In the next year Davis was offered a similar appointment, and after consulting his own union executive, and that of the Birmingham Labour Association, he accepted. This involved a move to Sheffield in 1883. He showed his usual qualities of hard work and administrative competence in his new job; but in 1889 the Brassworkers asked him, as a matter of urgency, to return to his union post. Membership had shrunk to a little over a thousand, and income to just over £2000 (as against over 5000 members and nearly £6000 income at the time of Davis's resignation in 1883). Davis returned to Birmingham and to his union in September 1889. With the combination of the man and the time, the membership of the Society soon increased and within six months had reached 8000.

Back as general secretary, Davis continued his policy of industrial conciliation. In December 1889 he made an agreement with the employers in the cabinet section of the brass trade, by which they would restore the fifteen per cent bonus, while the Society would give a written guarantee that there should be no undercutting. All employers were to pay this bonus by Michaelmas 1890. In the event, very few employers were recalcitrant: only about 1500 men had to strike, and that only for a short period, in order to get the bonus paid. At the same time Davis was involved in one of the largest strikes Birmingham had experienced, that of the brass-bedstead makers. In October 1889 their newly-founded union, the Bedstead Workmen's Association, demanded a fifteen per cent bonus, and when negotiations were protracted proposed to strike. Davis was consulted and attended a meeting on 1 December at which a very large majority of the delegates were in favour of a strike. Davis induced them to compromise, but two days later 2000 men had struck and by 4 December, 3000. The employers declared a lock-out, and blamed Davis for supporting the strikers. The mayor of Birmingham, F.C. Clayton, responded to an appeal from Davis and persuaded both sides to submit the dispute to arbitration. In January 1890 a settlement was reached under which a ten per cent bonus would be paid from the date when work was resumed. Soon after, by private negotiation between Davis and the employers' counsel, the full fifteen per cent was paid.

The 1890s were the time of the famous Birmingham 'alliances'. The plan of an alliance of employers and employees had been evolved by Richard Juggins for the nut and bolt trade in 1885. But 'alliance philosophy' became better known when it was taken up in Birmingham by an employer, E.J. Smith, and by Davis for the workers' side. In 1891 Smith founded the Bedstead Alliance which combined the principle of regulation of wages with that of an industrial cartel. Union members agreed to work only for members of the employers' association, while in return the union had a closed shop and equal representation on a wages board. Smith received firm support from Davis, and together, by 1897, they had directly or indirectly encouraged and sustained alliances in about a dozen minor Birmingham trades, covering about 500 employers and 20,000 workers [Clegg et al. (1964) 194 ff. For the economics of the Alliances see Church and Smith (1966) 635 ff.]. In brassworking, however, the employers had refused to set up an alliance. Instead, a Board of Conciliation was established in 1891. Davis's other great aim was the establishment of a minimum wage, and towards the end of the decade he achieved a partial success. The system of alliances and conciliation procedures did not, however, last very long. In August 1900 the Bedstead Alliance was dissolved, and union membership in general entered upon a decline. Earlier, in 1894, Davis had entered into discussions with David Dale, the ironmaster, on a matter always near to his heart – the need for close co-operation between masters and men. In the following year the Industrial Union of Employers and Employed was established, but it lasted only until 1896. Despite its lack of success it heralded the more impressive National Industrial Association of 1900.

After he went back to the Brassworkers in 1889 Davis also returned to the TUC, in 1890. He was elected to the Standing Orders Committee in 1893, and served on the Parliamentary Committee from 1896 to 1902, and from 1903 to 1915; he was chairman in 1898–9 and again in 1912–13. The break in 1902–3 seems to have been caused by his attitude towards the Boer War; although in 1898 he was supporting calls for peace, by 1902 he was opposed to the view that Congress should speak out against the war, opining that it should be carried through to a finish 'in the interests of the worker in South Africa' [Dalley (1914) 293]. But in 1903 he was reinstated on the Parliamentary Committee at the head of the poll. He was an influential figure on this committee and 'an unusually competent chairman' [Clegg et al. (1964) 261]. In 1913–14 he was president of Congress.

As has already been noted, Davis was a Lib-Lab, supporting progressive Liberal policies but believing in direct Labour representation; and he was first and last a trade unionist. In 1899 he chaired at Manchester the inaugural meeting and first council meeting of the GFTU, an organisation supported by both 'old' and 'new' unionists. In 1900 there was a proposal to subordinate the newly-formed LRC to the Parliamentary Committee of the TUC, and at the 2nd conference of the LRC, held in Birmingham in 1902, Davis (who was in the chair), was supported by Alexander Wilkie in an attempt to revive this proposal. He was unsuccessful. In 1904 to 1905 he was one of the leaders in persuading the TUC to vote for co-operation in political affairs between the Parliamentary Committee, the GFTU and the Labour Representation Committee [Bealey and Pelling (1958) 209]. This co-operation was designed to keep out the Socialists. Throughout his political life Davis opposed them resolutely; and he consistently tried to exclude them from labour and trade union policies. At the TUC of 1902 he had attacked 'professional men, journalists and adventurers' – that is, middle-class Socialists, with particular reference to the ILP – who tried 'to creep into the movement' [ibid., 90]; his attack was 'reminiscent of the Parliamentary Committee's anti-socialist tirades in 1894–5' [Clegg et al. (1964) 377] (See Davis's *The British Trades Union Congress 2* (1916) 95 [on nationalisation of land] for a sample of such an attack). In 1918, when the new Labour Party constitution was adopted (drawn up mainly by Webb and Henderson), Davis was still battling on. Two years earlier at the 1916 TUC a number of right-wing trade union leaders had tried, unsuccessfully, to persuade Congress to bring the Labour Party under the control of the Parliamentary Committee of the TUC. The idea of a political party which formally or virtually excluded Socialists (especially middle-class Socialists) became a serious proposition during the debates around the new constitution of the Labour Party. In the same month – January 1918 – that the first national conference met to consider the constitution, circulars were distributed to all trade unions and organisations affiliated to the Labour Party which explained the aims and purposes of the Trade Union Party movement. At the second national constitutional conference (26 Feb 1918) further leaflets were distributed to delegates; and the *British Citizen* of 11 May 1918 published the manifesto of the Trade Union Party alternative. This declaration to trade unionism concluded:

> Whatever . . . may be the views of trade unionists in regard to the War, it is beyond question that the people who will be most affected by the after-War problems are the trade unionists. If it be true that Heaven helps those who help themselves, the trade unionists must not leave

> their future, either industrially or politically, in the hands of non-unionists, middle-class Socialists, or anyone else outside the trade union ranks. We believe that a safe, a sound, and a sane policy is for the trade unionists to have their own political party under the auspices of and controlled by the Trades Union Congress, and that is why we are working for that object.

In June an 'inaugural' meeting took place in London, but at the following Derby TUC the Trade Union Party resolution was heavily defeated; largely, it may be argued, because the trade unions already had effective control with the amendments agreed to by the revised version of the new Constitution [see also Cole (1948) 48–9; McKibbin (1974) 98–106]. Davis had moved the unsuccessful resolution at the Derby TUC; and throughout this short but bitter campaign he had been a leading figure, together with J.B. Williams, of the Musicians' Union, Havelock Wilson, J.A. Seddon (chairman, British Workers' League) and James Sexton of the Liverpool dockers. It was his last political fight of any importance.

In 1906 he had been made a JP. His name had been submitted as early as 1892, but rejected apparently because of his prolonged warfare with the Stipendiary Magistrate, T.M. Colmore, against whose class-biased, vindictive and occasionally mistaken judgments Davis repeatedly and quite often successfully appealed. Davis's appointment was not made until after Colmore retired in 1905. As JP he was the watch-dog of trade union interests: in 1911 the JPs of Birmingham were about to resolve to join the Liverpool bench in asking Parliament to repeal section 2 of the Trade Disputes Act (1906) which authorised peaceful picketing; Davis made a trenchant and convincing speech, and the resolution was defeated by twenty-five to twelve. In the course of his argument Davis asserted that the composition of benches of lay magistrates was always political: the Birmingham bench had over sixty per cent of Tory members, under forty per cent of Liberals, and under two per cent of Labour men. In 1911, when Davis was put on the advisory committee for the selection of magistrates, sixteen Labour members were appointed to the bench 'in one swift swoop' [Dalley (1914) 329].

Like many trade union leaders Davis joined in the long campaign for old age pensions. Addressing a meeting of workers at Bordesley in 1891 he made public his observation that if sixty-five were to be the minimum age for a pension, comparatively few working men would live to draw it. From examining the reports of seven of the largest unions and twenty others he had discovered that only one of thirteen working men reached the age of sixty-five. This statistic was part of the criticism he was levelling at the scheme recently put forward by Joseph Chamberlain for a contributory pension, to be drawn at sixty-five. Davis's speech, taken up by the press, created something of a sensation; and for the next decade and a half he remained active in the agitation.

Davis was never an MP. Between 1880 and 1900 he declined several invitations to become a candidate; but in 1892 he consented to stand as a Gladstonian Liberal for Bordesley Division against Jesse Collings, the Liberal Unionist, who won. In 1906 he was eager to fight Joseph Chamberlain in Birmingham West, but on meeting opposition from some (a minority) of the brassworkers, he withdrew, although disappointed, rather than split the unity of his Society.

Davis's life-long policy as a trade unionist leader was to try to identify the interests of capital and labour, to establish co-operation between employers and employees. In 1901, he signed – perhaps had a share in composing – a statement of beliefs and policies issued by the GFTU. It was published in answer to a series of articles in *The Times* 'The Crisis in British Industry' (18 Nov 1901 to 16 Jan 1902) which made a savage attack on trade unionism. The Federation's reply stated the goals of unionism in a positive way, ending with the assertion that the aims of the GFTU were 'to promote industrial peace, and by all amicable means, such as conciliation, mediation, references, or, by the establishment of permanent boards, to prevent strikes or lock-outs between employers or workmen or disputes between trades or organizations. Where differences do occur, to assist in their settlement by just and equitable methods.' This reply was issued above the signatures of the GFTU officers and management committee, including Davis and Wilkie [Wright, *Eleventh Special Report* etc., (1904) 731–4; Pelling (1954) 226–7 and fn. and see special note on Ca'canny below].

Along with R.H. Best and Charles Perks, Davis visited Berlin in 1905 in order to compare the conditions of brassworkers there with conditions in Birmingham. The joint report of this visit, published in the same year, was widely reviewed in the press and quoted by social reformers.

In the First World War Davis was, inevitably, an active supporter of the Government. He was put on the Birmingham Emergency Committee as a Trades Council representative in 1914. In the course of the Trades Council's internal disputes over conscription, Davis wrote angrily that trade union money was, in fact, being used 'to put pacifists in every possible position'; and together with some other unions the brassworkers resigned from the Council [Corbett (1966) 114]. It was to be expected that Davis would oppose the movement in 1917 for a negotiated peace [Totten (1972) 24]. He assisted in recruiting and was a member of several advisory committees set up in connection with the Ministries of National Service and of Munitions. After the war he continued to serve on a number of government committees. He was made a CH in 1917.

Davis was a fluent and cogent writer and frequently contributed to the press: he wrote to the local dailies on any matter on which he thought trade union or labour views should be presented or had been misrepresented, and he wrote articles for labour and trade union journals; for five years (1892 to 1897) he acted as labour correspondent for the Birmingham area to the *Labour Gazette*. He lectured on Modern Appliances at the Birmingham Municipal Technical School; at Ruskin College on the value of trade unions to the State, and other subjects [Stead (1905) 444]. In the midst of his trade union activities he found time to write not only a two-volume history of the TUC (1910 and 1916) but also, earlier, two books on token coinage, of which he had a remarkable collection. *The Token Coinage of Warwickshire* appeared in 1895, followed in 1904 by *The Nineteenth Century Token Coinage*. Davis also designed a number of tokens and medals. Another of his intellectual interests was chess; he was a good player, vice-president in 1883 of the Birmingham Chess Club.

Davis knew most of the leading Labour and Lib-Lab politicians and trade unionists of the day. His friends included Henderson, MacDonald, Lansbury and J.H. Thomas. According to his grandson Will Horton, he spent many holidays with Thomas [Totten (1972) 13]. His son-in-law W.A. Dalley described him as having 'steel-grey piercing eyes', a 'rat-trap like mouth and firm chin'. But he qualified this rather alarming description by adding that his father-in-law was 'generous and sympathetic', with 'a warm heart'. He was a persuasive orator and an excellent reasoner and debater.

In 1921 Davis retired – unwillingly – from his union post and soon afterwards he decided that he and his daughter Mabel would go to live in France. He died at 2 Rue des Graviers, Rueilville, near Paris, on 20 October 1934, at the age of eighty-six. Davis had married in 1869 Mary Jane, daughter of Mark Thomas Cooke, an elastic-webbing manufacturer of Fazeley, Staffordshire, who had a branch and a house in Birmingham. She died in April 1914. There were six children of the marriage, three of whom were living in 1914: William John Oliver, who emigrated to Canada; Nellie, who married Albert Law; and Mabel, who after her mother's death kept house for her father both in England and, in his last years, in France.

Writings: Evidence on 11 June 1875 before R.C. on the Working of the Factory and Workshops Acts XXX 1876 [with E. Lilly] Qs 4660–711; Evidence before S.C. of House of Lords on the Sweating System XIII 1889 Qs 25233–418 [on 5 Apr 1889] and XIV pt. 1 1889 Qs 29040–107 [21 May 1889]; 'The Labour Question: will the demands of workmen check the revival of trade?', *Ironmonger*, 23 Nov 1889, 319–20; *A Short History of the Brass Trade* (1892); *The Token Coinage of Warwickshire with Descriptive and Historical Notes* (Birmingham, 1895); 'The Conditions of the Brassworkers' Settlement', *Birmingham and District Trades J.* no. 5, 11 July 1896, 1–2; *Old Warwickshire Coins, Tokens, and Metals* n.p. [1896?] 25 pp.; *History of Labour Representation and Legislative Trade Union Effort* [speech] [1901?] 10 pp.; *Industrial*

Combination, its Progress, Difficulties and Stability [address at Ruskin College, Oxford on 24 Nov 1903] (1903) 23 pp.; *A Scheme of Insurance: the insurance of the children of trade unionists* (1904) P; *The Nineteenth Century Token Coinage of Great Britain, Ireland, the Channel Islands and Isle of Man to which are added Tokens of over One Penny Value of any Period* (1904); (with R.H. Best and C. Perks), *The Brassworkers of Berlin and of Birmingham: a comparison* (Birmingham 1905; 5th ed. 1910) 54 pp.; *Lessons from Germany* [1905?] 24 pp.; Evidence on 30 Nov 1906 before Departmental Committee on [Compensation for] Industrial Diseases XXXIV 1906 Qs 2469–594; 'I remember' [on early labour leaders], *Birmingham Gazette and Express*, 17 Aug 1907; *The British Trades Union Congress: history and recollections* 2 vols. (1910 and 1916) [portrait p. 193]; *TUC Report* (1913) 55–61 [presidential address]; *Times*, 2 Sep 1913; 'Early Recollections of a Great Statesman' [Joseph Chamberlain] in *Searchlight of Greater Birmingham*, 13 Nov 1913, 19–23; Evidence to Cabinet Committee on Women in Industry XXXI 1919 [summaries of evidence p. 67]; (with A.W. Waters), *Tickets and Passes of Great Britain and Ireland struck or engraved on Metal, Ivory etc.* (privately printed, Leamington Spa, 1922); MS Reminiscences (1932) [written to H.M. Cashmore], copy in Birmingham Reference Library.

Sources: (1) MS: Labour Party archives: LRC. (2) Other: *Birmingham Faces and Places 4* (1891–2) 40–4 and *5* (1892–3) 41; E.J. Smith, *The New Trades Combination Movement* (Birmingham, 1895) 42 pp.; Departmental Committee on Conditions of Labour in the Manufacture of Brass and of Kindred Amalgams *Report* 1896 XIX; Sir W.J. Ashley, *Surveys, Historic and Economic* (1900); C.D. Wright, *Eleventh Special Report of the Commissioner of Labor. Regulation and Restriction of Output* (Washington, D.C., 1904); *Coming Men on Coming Questions Series* ed. W.T. Stead (1905) 441–4; H.W. Macrosty, *The Trust Movement in British Industry* (1907); *Edgbastonia 28*, no. 322 (Mar 1908) 49–54; W.A. Dalley, *The Life Story of W.J. Davis, J.P. The Industrial Problem. Achievements and Triumphs of Conciliation* (Birmingham, 1914); W.A. Dalley and A. Eades, *Souvenir of the Forty-eighth Annual Trade Union Congress held in Birmingham, September 1916* (Birmingham 1916); 'The New Trade Union Labour Party', *British Citizen and Empire Worker*, vol. *4*, no. 90, 11 May 1918, 222; *Birmingham Mail*, 21 May 1921; *Birmingham Post*, 23 May 1921; *Birmingham Weekly Post*, 28 May 1921; W.A.D., *An Historical Sketch of the Birmingham Trades Council 1866-1926* (Birmingham, [1927]) 37 pp.; G.C. Allen, *The Industrial Development of Birmingham and the Black Country, 1860–1927* (1929); R.D. Best, *Brass Chandelier: a biography of R.H. Best of Birmingham* (1940); G.D.H. Cole, *A History of the Labour Party from 1914* (1948; later eds.); A. Briggs, *History of Birmingham* vol. *2*: *borough and city 1865–1938* (1952); H. Pelling, *The Origins of the Labour Party* (1954; rev. ed. 1965); A. Fox, 'Industrial Relations in Nineteenth-Century Birmingham', *OEP 7* (1955) 57–70; F. Bealey and H. Pelling, *Labour and Politics 1900–1906* (1958); B.C. Roberts, *The Trades Union Congress 1868–1921* (1958); *Victoria History of the Counties of England: a history of the County of Warwick* vol. *7*: *The City of Birmingham* ed. W.B. Stephens (1964); H.A. Clegg et al., *A History of British Trade Unions since 1889* vol. *1*: *1889–1910* (Oxford, 1964); J. Corbett, *The Birmingham Trades Council 1866–1966* (1966); R.A. Church and B.M.D. Smith, 'Competition and Monopoly in the Coffin Furniture Industry, 1870–1915', *Econ. Hist. Rev. 19*, no. 3 (Dec 1966) 621–41; M. Totten, *Founded in Brass: the first hundred years of the National Society of Metal Mechanics: from chandeliers to Concorde* (Birmingham, 1972); R. McKibbin, *The Evolution of the Labour Party 1910–1924* (Oxford, 1974); R.A. Wright, 'Liberal Party Organisation and Politics in Birmingham, Coventry and Wolverhampton 1886–1914, with Particular Reference to the Development of Independent Labour Representation' (Birmingham PhD, 1977); biographical information: V.C. Jordan, Health and Safety Executive, London. Obit. *Evening Despatch* [Birmingham] and *Birmingham Mail*, 22 Oct 1934; *Birmingham Gazette* and *Birmingham Post*, 23 Oct 1934; *Ironmonger*, 3 Nov 1934, 46. The editors wish to express their gratitude to Mrs Barbara M.D. Smith, Centre for Urban and Regional Studies, Birmingham Univ. for an earlier draft of this biography and also to Mr Peter Drake, Birmingham Reference Library, for bibliographical assistance.

MARGARET 'ESPINASSE
JOHN SAVILLE

See also: †Mary MACARTHUR; †Emma Anne PATERSON; John Damrel PRIOR; and below: Ca'canny.

Ca' canny

The Oxford English Dictionary notes that 'canny' is a comparatively modern word, not found before the seventeenth century; and the examples it quotes of 'to ca' canny' – meaning to go cautiously, quietly, gently, carefully, warily – are taken from the early nineteenth century. It does not specify the industrial meaning of ca' canny, but the 1933 *Supplement* does, and gives the *Westminster Gazette* of 25 March 1896 as the first usage. According to G.D.H. Cole [*Encyclopaedia Britannica*, 1951 ed.] ca' canny in the modern industrial sense of working slowly was a workshop practice or practices undertaken in order to draw attention to a grievance, by bringing pressure upon the employer. Cole wrote that the term was first used in a dispute over wages at the Glasgow docks in 1889; the sailors and firemen were on strike in June, and the dockers came out in their support. Richard McGhee took the opportunity to enunciate the practices of ca'canny which *Seafaring* (11 Apr 1891) described as a policy based on the principle 'that, as the employers give as little wages as possible for as much work as they can get, so the workers are entitled to give, on the same principle, as little work as possible for as much wages as they can get.' Edward McHugh of the National Union of Dock Labourers, in a leaflet dated 14 February 1891, argued for ca' canny practices in the Liverpool docks, and from this time, especially on the waterfronts, the phrase became widely understood. There was, however, at least one earlier reference although again it was the dockers who provided the occasion. R.B. Cunninghame Graham, whose writings of these years deserve to be better known, had an article in the *People's Press* of 13 September 1890 describing the TUC of 1890 which had ended the previous week. His last paragraph read:

> Whilst these congressmen fretted and fumed and fought, and rose to points of order, two streets off another congress with closed doors was sitting. At it the delegates of dock labourers from Glasgow, Waterford, Belfast, Leith, Liverpool, and other places, sat in mysterious conclave, McHugh, McGhee (the fiend from Glasgow, as Liverpool shipowners called him); McKeown, and many a stalwart docker attended. No booming in the Press for them. Ca-Canny was the word, no maudlin sentiments of Christian goodwill upon their lips, and Christian hatred in the heart of their deliberations. Ca-Canny was their watchword, and the doctrines preached that if a ship should miss a tide or two, a packing case or two fall into the sea, or if Jehovah, in His carelessness, allowed a bit of iron to fall into the wheels of a machine and stop it (at a critical moment), the fault was clearly not of their contrivance. It may be, too, that the shipowners of the country have more dread of these Ca-Canny blokes than of the London crowd, who, though more known to fame, perchance may prove less dangerous.

The publication of two circulars by the International Federation of Ship, Dock and River Workers on 2 October 1896, and of an article commenting on the circulars in the *Seamen's Chronicle* of 24 October 1896 was something of a landmark in the history of this phrase, and evoked a hostile response from many sectors of public opinion. The first circular, which provided the justification for ca' canny working, concluded:

> Pay workmen the good wages and they will give you their best skill.
>
> Pay workmen an insufficient wage and you have no more right to expect the best quality and quantity of work than you have to expect to get 5 shillings for 2 shillings and 6 pence. If the employers persist in their refusal to meet the workmen's representatives in order to discuss the demands sent in, the workmen can retort by marking the ballot paper in favour of adopting "ca' canny," or the "go-easy" policy, until such time as the employers decide to meet and confer with the men's representatives. (Issued by the order of the Central Council of the International Federation of Ship, Dock, and River Workers. Bridge House, 181 Queen Victoria Street, London, E.C.)

The circular quoted above was also reprinted in 1904 in a report of the American Commissioner of Labor, Carroll D. Wright, published in 1904 following a large inquiry and entitled *Regulation and Restriction of Output* [Eleventh Special Report of the Commissioner of Labor (Washington, D.C., 1904) 725]. Part II of this volume was concerned with Britain, and it provided an important, if relatively little used, source of industrial practices in a large number of trades.

Earlier the Webbs in their *Industrial Democracy* had denied that 'deliberately regulated production' was within the competence of 'mere associations of wage-earners' [Webb (1897) 449], but contemporary opinion disagreed and continued to move steadily against the unions. Industrial practices in the 1890s were under growing criticism; the courts were handing down adverse judgments, which even before Taff Vale were beginning to threaten certain of the unions' legal rights; and the employment of 'free labour' in place of unionists was being widely welcomed. The press campaign against the unions' defensive industrial policies reached its peak with the publication in *The Times* of a series of eleven articles on 'The Crisis in British Industry' from November 1901 to January 1902. The articles were anonymous but the author, Edwin A. Pratt, collected them into a volume which he published, with an introduction, in 1904. In the first article, on 18 November 1901, Pratt stated the contemporary problem as he saw it:

> . . . the "new" unionism, with its resort to violence and intimidation, has in turn been succeeded by a "newer" unionism, which, although working along much quieter lines, is doing even more serious injury – by reason of the greater difficulty of coping with it – alike to trade, to industry, and to the individual worker.
>
> This "newer" unionism would pass among economists under the courtesy title of "restricting the output". Among trade unionists of the Socialist type, who have no regard for courtesy titles, it is better known as "Ca' canny." It got this nickname during the shipping troubles of a few years ago, and an exposition of its principles was given in an illustrated article published in the *Seamen's Chronicle* of October 24, 1896:
>
> > What (asked the article) is Ca' canny? It is a simple and handy phrase which is used to describe a new instrument or policy which may be used by the workers in place of a strike. If two Scotsmen are walking together, and one walks too quickly for the other, he says to him, "Ca' canny, mon, ca' canny," which means, "Go easy, man, go easy." [quoted Pratt (1904) 22].

The Times articles covered a large part of British industry, in all of which examples were quoted of practices which hindered or slowed down production. The correspondence columns of *The Times* were full of supporting letters, often providing new examples of malpractices, and they included a letter from William Collison of the National Free Labour Association (26 Nov 1901). There were two major replies in *The Times*: the first a letter, from Sidney and Beatrice Webb on 6 December 1901 and the second, a long statement on 20 December 1901 (also printed in Wright (1904) 731–4) from sixteen members of the management committee of the

General Federation of Trade Unions, headed by the chairman, Pete Curran of the Gasworkers and General Labourers' Union and including G.N. Barnes, of the ASE, W.J. Davis of the Amalgamated Brassworkers, and Ben Tillett of the Dockers' Union.

Chamberlain's campaign for Tariff Reform in 1903 gradually took over the correspondence columns of *The Times*, and against a background of uneven, but quite high, unemployment, the 'iniquities' of the unions became less prominently discussed in succeeding years. But the term 'ca' canny,' as well as generally unfavourable sentiments among the middle and upper classes about trade unions, remained; and restrictive practices were still quite widely commented on. D.A. Thomas, later Lord Rhondda and chairman in 1910 of the Cambrian Collieries Ltd, wrote of the background to the large scale Cambrian dispute:

> As is almost invariably the case when a new seam is being opened out in South Wales, the men were working 'ca' canny' in order to prove that the seam was a difficult one to work – in which they could only produce a small output of coal per turn – and thus influence the referees appointed to fix and arrange a list to adjudge them a better cutting price [quoted in D. Evans (1911) 8].

Union leaders have almost never accepted that 'ca' canny' was a serious problem, and only one major figure in the trade union world would seem to have expressed vigorous disapproval. This was James Mawdsley, the Conservative secretary of the Amalgamated Cotton Spinners [Wright (1904) 735]. On the other side, Havelock Wilson provided an unusual public vindication of ca' canny practice in his evidence before the Board of Trade Committee on the Mercantile Marine given on 8 May 1902 [extracts from which are printed ibid., 729–31]. In the inter-war years the term was still used, although less frequently. It was used in 1920 by W.J. Brown; C.L. Goodrich in *The Frontier of Control* (1920) – a neglected text – has some interesting comments on the subject, and the *Spectator* carried three articles in 1922, 1923 and 1925. Lloyd Dodd and Lynch in 1935 provided a summary of the theoretical justification of ca'canny which developed especially during the inter-war years as a result of large-scale unemployment. This was what the authors called the 'work-fund fallacy' i.e. that the amount of work at any one time is limited. In the most recent decades the term has tended to be superseded by other phrases. *The Dictionary of Industrial Relations* (1973) defined ca' canny:

> Go-slow methods or restrictions by workers, either in relation to some particular claim or grievance, or in order to limit output for purposes of controlling the labour market or some aspect of it. In both cases outright withdrawal of labour is avoided, but the object in the first instance is more tactical and in the second more strategic. Go-slow, slow-gear strike, lazy strike, folded arms strike, stay-in-strike, working without enthusiasm (q.v.) or in some forms work-to-rule (q.v.) are expressions used mainly to describe its tactical use. The word "ca' canny" itself is usually (but not invariably) employed to indicate strategic use, e.g. to describe a unilaterally imposed method of work sharing (q.v.) to maintain employment, limitation of output to maintain piecework prices, etc.; see restrictive practices, protective practices, craft control, quota restriction, gold bricking [p. 47].

Sources: R.B. Cunninghame Graham, 'After the Congress', *People's Press*, 13 Sep 1890, 7; idem, "Ca Canny.", ibid., 29 Nov 1890, 6–7; Anon., 'National Dockers' Union', *Seafaring*, 11 Apr 1891, 6; *Westminster Gazette*, 25 Mar 1896, 1 ['Our London Letter']; *Seamen's Chronicle*, 24 Oct 1896; S. and B. Webb, *Industrial Democracy* (1897); 'The Crisis in British Industry', *Times*, 18 and 21 Nov, 3, 14, 16, 24, 26, 27 and 30 Dec 1901 and 4 and 16 Jan 1902; these were repr. in E.A. Pratt, *Trade Unionism and British Industry* (1904) and there were letters in *The Times* almost daily on this subject including W. Collison, of the National Free Labour Association on 26 Nov and S. and B. Webb on 6 Dec which were also commented on by *The Times*'s leading article of that date; some letters were also published after the series of articles ended. P. Longmuir, 'The Possibilities of a New Trades Unionism', *Engineering Mag. 23*, no.1 (Apr 1902) 90–6; 'Chronic Laziness: a trade union cure', *Westminster Gazette*, 25 Apr 1902, 6; C.D. Wright, *Eleventh Special Report of the Commissioner of Labor, Regulation and Restriction of Output* (Washington, D.C., 1904); D.C. Cummings, *History of the United Society of Boilermakers and Iron and Steel Shipbuilders* (Newcastle upon Tyne, 1905); D. Evans, *Labour Strife in the South Wales Coalfield 1910–1911* (Cardiff, 1911); *Red Tape* (July 1920) 188 [section on ca' canny repr. in B.V. Humphreys, *Clerical Unions in the Civil Service* (1958) 127]; C.L. Goodrich, *The Frontier of Control: a study in British workshop politics* (1920; rev. edition with new foreword and additional notes by R. Hyman, 1975); S. and B. Webb, *The History of Trade Unionism* (1920 ed.); *Glasgow Herald*, 17 June 1921; Anon. 'The Madness of "Ca' Canny"', *Spec.*, 15 Apr 1922, 454–5; G.D.H. Cole, *Workshop Organisation* (Oxford, 1923); Lord Leverhulme, 'Capital and Ca' Canny', *Spec.*, 27 Oct 1923, 585–7; E.T. Good, 'The American Example. No "Ca' Canny" and No Socialism', ibid., 6 June 1925, 918–19; W.S. Bruce, 'The Field of the Slothful' Ch. 25 of *Salt and Sense* (Scottish Laymen's Library, 1926); *The Oxford English Dictionary being a Corrected Re-issue with an Introduction, Supplement and Bibliography* (Oxford, 1933); F.T. Lloyd Dodd and B.J. Lynch, *Organisation and Administration of Industry* (1935); G.D.H.C.[ole], 'Ca' canny', *Encyclopaedia Britannica 4* (1951) 507–8; *Economist*, 29 Nov 1958, 784, 16 Mar 1963, 976; *A Supplement to the Oxford English Dictionary* ed. R.W. Burchfield vol. *1* (Oxford, 1972) 410; A.I. Marsh and E.O. Evans, *The Dictionary of Industrial Relations* (1973); G. Brown, *Sabotage: a study in labour conflict* (Nottingham, 1977). The editors wish to acknowledge the information supplied by E.L. Taplin, Head of Social Studies Department, Liverpool Polytechnic.

JOHN SAVILLE

See also: David Charles CUMMINGS.

DICKENSON, Sarah (1868–1954)
TRADE UNIONIST AND SUFFRAGIST

Sarah Dickenson was born in Borsall Road, Hulme, on 28 March 1868, the second of five children of John Welsh, a native of Scotland, and his wife Jane (née Ferguson). John Welsh was an enameller and coach painter and was at the time employed as a painter of heraldic insignia by the carriage making and saddlery business of Joseph Cockshoot, in Strangeways. As a girl Sarah attended St John's Church, Salford, but later in life became an enthusiastic member of the Manchester and Salford Labour Church.

At the age of eleven she began work in a local cotton mill, Howarth's Mill in Salford, first as a tenter and later as a 'smallway weaver'; and she continued to be so employed until 1895. In August of the following year she married William Roger Dickenson, an iron enameller by trade, who had his own bicycle workshop. During the 1880s she had become strongly attracted by the efforts then being made by the Manchester and Salford Trades Council to organise women workers, and when, in February 1895, the Women's Trade Union Council (a local organisation) was formed, Sarah Welsh, as one of the few working women involved in its launching, was appointed one of the two organising secretaries. Frances Ashwell served as the other secretary until her resignation in June 1900 when she was replaced by Eva Gore Booth.

The chief objects of the Council were to stimulate union organisation among women workers and to encourage such unions as were formed to press for improved wages and working conditions. In 1896 a joint committee was set up composed of representatives from the Council, the Christian Social Union and the Manchester and Pendleton branches of the Women's Co-operative Guild to investigate and compare local conditions of pay and employment. The

Council had most success in several of the smaller manufacturing industries and in some service trades; among the early societies founded were the Society for Women employed in the Bookbinding and Printing Trades (1896) and the Manchester and Salford Association of Machine, Electrical and other Women Workers, of which Sarah Dickenson became secretary in 1899. The WTUC also gave considerable assistance to the Jewish Machinists, Tailors, and Pressers in their attempts to organise Jewish tailoresses. With Eva Gore Booth, Sarah Dickenson helped in the formation of the Ancoats Winders' Union and, in 1902, of the Association of Power Loom Weavers. A prominent local supporter of the Association was William Wilkinson, who was also a strong champion of women's suffrage and who spoke on the question at the 1904 conference of the LRC.

During these years Sarah Dickenson was closely involved, as joint secretary with a Miss Wilgar, in the activities of a local Federation of Women Workers, whose efforts in assisting women in unorganised trades were recorded in the *Annual Reports* of the WTUC from 1897 to 1904. This Federation, which appears to have had quite a small membership, offered sickness and unemployment benefits to all women workers, irrespective of trade, and tended to recruit members from industries where there was no expressed desire for trade organisation, such as fancy-box manufacturing, underclothing factories, machine works and laundries. Sarah Dickenson probably took over the secretaryship of the Federation from Miss Wilgar in 1904.

It was likely that through her friendship with Eva Gore Booth, Sarah Dickenson came to know Esther Roper, who from 1900 to 1905, was secretary of the North of England Society for Women's Suffrage. Sarah Dickenson had already become a member. Modelled very much on the lines of Mrs Fawcett's NUWSS, whose general policy it followed, the North of England Society concerned itself chiefly with addressing other progressive groups including Co-operative Guilds, ILP meetings, trade unions and Labour Churches. Sarah Dickenson took a leading part in organising such activities and spoke at many indoor and outdoor meetings on the suffrage issue. In general her commitment was to the more 'evangelical' aspect of the movement and she believed strongly in the need for the campaign to be extended among factory workers. She was closely involved in the campaign of the NESWS, from May 1900 to March 1901, to compile a petition in support of women's suffrage from women factory workers. When this petition, of almost 30,000 signatures, was presented to the Lancashire MPs at the House of Commons on 8 March 1901, Sarah Dickenson, Sarah Reddish, Selina Cooper and Annie Heaton were among the speakers.

She was a committed supporter of the attempts made by Esther Roper and Eva Gore Booth, while they were members of the Society's executive committee, to direct its interests towards the less organised sections of the labour movement. But this policy was not generally popular with the Society, which preferred to appeal to more middle-class groups; and in November 1905 a considerable section of the EC, including Esther Roper, Eva Gore Booth, Sarah Reddish, Christabel Pankhurst and Sarah Dickenson resigned in consequence. They urged members to transfer their support to a new organisation, the National Industrial and Professional Women's Suffrage Society. For a period Sarah Dickenson served on its executive committee. There was also in these years a certain movement away in sympathy on the part of WSPU members, although the break and reorganisation did not finally come about until 1910 or early 1911.

The Women's Trade Union Council was deeply divided on the issue of whether or not it should involve itself directly with the local suffrage movement. The Council had been founded at a meeting convened by prominent members of the Liberal Party, including Mrs Schwann, wife of the MP for North Manchester, W. Mather, MP for Gorton, and C.P. Scott, and it continued to depend to a large extent on their support. The setting up in September 1903 of the Lancashire and Cheshire Women Textile and Other Workers' Representation Committee led to further conflict within the WTUC on the issue. This Committee, composed in the main of women textile workers and trade union organisers and sharing a common leadership, for the most part, with the National Industrial and Professional Women's Suffrage Society, declared a firm policy of support for women's enfranchisement. In the closing paragraph of its manifesto, published in July 1904, it strongly underlined the importance to women workers of full political rights:

> Anyone who wishes to better the position of her fellow workers, and the thousands of women outside the ranks of the skilled cotton operatives, who are being overworked and underpaid, should remember that political enfranchisement must precede industrial emancipation, and that the political disabilities of women have done incalculable harm, by cheapening their labour and lowering their position in the industrial world [Leech (1971) 90].

The signatories of this manifesto, in addition to Esther Roper and Eva Gore Booth, who became joint secretaries, were Sarah Dickenson, Selina Cooper and Sarah Reddish, the last named formerly an organiser for the Women's Trade Union League and a prominent member of the Women's Co-operative Guild.

As a result of these serious disagreements within the WTUC, Sarah Dickenson and Eva Gore Booth resigned in 1904. Seven of the stronger member-unions also withdrew and a separate organisation, the Manchester and Salford Women's Trades and Labour Council, was set up with an open and clear commitment to women's suffrage and giving strong support to the Lancashire and Cheshire Women Textile and Other Workers' Representation Committee, with which it established a firm working relationship. In the general election of 1906 the WTLC and the Lancashire and Cheshire Committee supported the candidature, in the Wigan constituency, of Thorley Smith. He stood as both an ILP and equal suffrage candidate and achieved 2205 votes and second place ahead of the Liberal.

During these years Sarah Dickenson appeared on a number of platforms. In October 1905, at a large meeting in the Free Trade Hall to welcome back Annie Kenney and Christabel Pankhurst after their recent imprisonment, she was one of the principal speakers; and she seconded a resolution moved by John Harker, president of the Manchester and Salford Trades Council, which called for votes for women on the same terms as men. In May of 1906 she took part in a large deputation to the Prime Minister, Campbell Bannerman, when she spoke, following Emily Davies, on the right of women wage-earners to political enfranchisement.

Periodically she was employed as a salaried organiser for the NUWSS. Other local women employed in this work included Margaret Alderley, Ada Nield Chew, Selina Cooper and Sarah Reddish. On occasion they were 'borrowed' by the central London organisation and took part in various London trade union meetings. Sarah Dickenson also took part in several major demonstrations on behalf of women's suffrage, including the Trafalgar Square meetings in 1906, 1908 and 1910. In 1909 and early 1910 she was active in the campaign in support of A.K. Bulley in Rossendale, an Independent Labour candidate who included women's suffrage in his manifesto.

During these years Sarah Dickenson continued her close involvement with the promotion of women's trade unionism in the Manchester and Salford area. In October 1907 she was prominent in a four-day conference on Women Workers in Manchester, which was organised by the National Union of Women Workers and addressed by a number of women well known in the fields of education and trade union organisation. With Mary Macarthur, she spoke on the effects which trade unions were having on women's working conditions. Referring in particular to the progress made by the Women's Trades and Labour Council (which at that point represented nearly 4000 women workers), she stressed the need for union organisers to have technical knowledge of the trade in question so as to gain the confidence of both workers and employers. On the issue of whether men and women should belong to the same union, she tended to disagree with Mary Macarthur, saying that in her experience a union worked best when women had their own branch. She favoured the founding of separate organisations until there had been a consciousness fostered of the particular needs of women workers; after this was developed, women should join the general union of the trade. At a meeting in Manchester in October 1911, during the railway strike, Sarah Dickenson, as secretary of the WTLC, seconded a motion calling for much wider and more effective organisation of both men and women in the trade union movement.

Throughout the years of the First World War she continued to take an active part, through the WTLC, in matters touching on conditions of women's employment. Early in the war the Council protested against the fixing of the maximum wage for women at 10*s*, agreed on by the Central Committee for Women's Employment. It was felt that this would inevitably be taken as a guide-line by private employers and that it was too low a figure. This ceiling was not raised until April 1915. At that time Sarah Dickenson was one of the 180 or so delegates who were to attend the Women's International Conference on Peace at The Hague; but restrictions being placed on North Sea travel prevented the party from sailing.

On many issues the Women's Trade Union Council and the WTLC worked together amicably and successfully; and when the vote was obtained for certain sections of women in 1918 the major outstanding disagreement was resolved. Both organisations then merged into the Manchester and Salford Trades Council and became the Women's Group with Mary Quaile as its first organiser. From 1920 to 1925 Sarah Dickenson was secretary of this Group and a member of the Council's executive committee; in 1925 and 1926 she served on the Employment Exchange Committee and the Women's Housing Advisory Committee. She remained a delegate to the Council until 1930, representing the small union of the Machine, Electrical and other Women Workers. In addition to her Trades Council commitments she was an active social worker, concerned in particular with war pensioners, on whose behalf, as a member of the War Pensions Committee, she campaigned for increases in disablement pension. She was also a member of the children's sub-committee of the Council and took part in the work of the Wood Street Mission of the Ancoats Brotherhood for the poor and deprived children of the Ancoats Settlement. In 1923 she was appointed a JP, and she remained a member of the bench until 1939. She received an MBE in the New Year Honours of 1931.

A photograph of Sarah Dickenson shows a handsome and resolute face with regular features, and a good carriage. She was fond of dancing and the theatre. For most of her married life she lived at Chorlton cum Hardy and later at Burnage. After her husband's death she lived with a sister, Polly. She had no children. She died on 26 December 1954 and was cremated at Manchester Southern Cemetery. Her effects were valued at £1854.

Writings: (with M.R. Macarthur), 'The Effect upon the Condition of Working Women of Trades Unions', *Women Workers: the papers read at the conference held in Manchester on October 22nd, 23rd, 24th and 25th 1907* (1907) 84–95 [copy in London Museum].

Sources: (1) MS: Labour Party archives: AFF 2/200, GC 19/63, 21/324, 21/325, 21/326, LRC, 5/402. (2) Newspapers: *Clarion*, 30 Mar 1901, 3 Feb 1905; *Labour Leader*, 10 and 17 Feb, 7 July, 27 Oct 1905, 18 Oct 1907, 8 May and 4 Dec 1908; *Manchester Guardian*, 21 Oct 1905, 21 May 1906; *Manchester Evening News*, 1 Jan 1931. (3) Other: *Annual Reports* of the Manchester, Salford and District Women's Trade Union Council, 1895–1919, Manchester PL, Local History Library; NUWSS, *Annual Reports*, 1900–5; 'Petition of Lancashire Factory Workers', *Englishwoman's Rev*. no. *249* n.s., 15 Apr 1901, 109–12; *Reformers' Year Book* (1904); *The Case for Women's Suffrage*, ed. B. Villiers (1907); *Joint Report of Women's Suffrage Work done by the National Industrial and Professional Women's Suffrage Society, the Lancashire and Cheshire Women Textile and other Workers' Representation Committee, and the Manchester and Salford Women's Trades and Labour Council 1909–1910* (Manchester, 1911) 16 pp. [in Manchester PL, Archives Dept.]; E.S. Pankhurst, *The Suffragette: the history of the women's militant suffrage movement, 1905–1910* (NY, 1911); B. Mason, *The Story of the Women's Suffrage Movement* (1912); Manchester and Salford Trades Council, *Annual Reports, 1913–30* [in Manchester PL, Local History Library]; B. Drake, *Women in Trade Unions* [1920]; E.S. Gore Booth, *Poems of Eva Gore Booth*, with a biographical introduction by E. Roper, complete ed. (1929); S. Pankhurst, *The Suffragette Movement* (1931); L. Bather, 'A History of

Manchester and Salford Trades Council' (Manchester, PhD, 1956); D.F. Summers, 'The Labour Church and Allied Movements of the Late Nineteenth and Early Twentieth Centuries' (Edinburgh PhD, 1958); C. Pankhurst, *Unshackled: the story of how we won the vote*, ed. Lord Pethick Lawrence of Peaselake (1959); C.E. Leech, 'The Feminist Movement in Manchester' (Manchester MA, 1971); E. and R. Frow, *To Make That Future–Now!: a history of the Manchester and Salford Trades Council* (Manchester, 1976); S.M. Bryan, 'The Women's Suffrage Question in the Manchester Area 1890–1906' (Manchester MA [method 1 dissertation], 1977); J. Liddington and J. Norris, *One Hand tied behind us: the rise of the women's suffrage movement* (1978): biographical information: City Magistrates' Court, Manchester (letter of 18 Feb 1977); personal information: Miss J. Welsh and Mr D. Welsh, Manchester, niece and nephew. The editors are much indebted to Mrs Naomi Reid, Stockport, for bibliographical and other assistance with this biography.

EDMUND AND RUTH FROW
BARBARA NIELD

See also: †Ada Nield CHEW; †Mary MACARTHUR.

ELVIN, Herbert Henry (1874–1949)
TRADE UNIONIST

Herbert Elvin was born at Eckington in Derbyshire on 18 July 1874, but his early years were spent in India, where his father, Henry Elvin, was a sergeant-major with the 9th Lancers. On returning to England in 1882, or 1883 the family went to live in London. Herbert's mother (Mary Ann, née Parr) had died and his father had remarried. At the age of eight Herbert went to school until he was fourteen in Ratcliff Highway area of east London. Later, he continued his education by joining evening classes at the People's Palace, the Birkbeck Institute and the City of London College where he was a member of the Debating Society. Among the subjects he studied were geology, mathematics, English and book-keeping.

Elvin was deeply religious, a devout student of the Bible, and from the age of sixteen a lay preacher (he was a founder member of the London Baptist Lay Preachers' Association). His platform was often in the Mile End Road. On several occasions he was summonsed for obstruction, and he was once given a short prison sentence – which much to his annoyance he did not serve, since his fine was paid by a well-wisher [letter, G.H. Elvin, 1 Aug 1979]. His sternly moral evangelicalism, which also owed much to the writings of John Ruskin, was undoubtedly a strong and persistent force in his life, and seems to have largely shaped the character of his commitment to the labour movement; he was sympathetic to Christian Socialism, the broad tenets of which he supported. In London he engaged actively in social and temperance work in the East End, especially in the slums of St George's Ratcliff Highway. For many years he was on the executive committee of the Tower Hamlets Band of Hope Union, and in later life he was associated with the Industrial Christian Fellowship and the Workers' Temperance League, which he served as president, again for many years.

In 1894 Elvin joined a loosely organised group of London clerks, who had been founded under the sponsorship of the AEU in 1890; but preaching and social work remained his predominant interests, and he did not take up active trade union membership until 1905. By this time the clerks in London had joined with those in Leeds, to become the National Union of Clerks, and it was this body to which Elvin was elected honorary general secretary at the Leeds conference in 1906. For the next four years he combined the duties of this post with his full-time employment as clerk to the directors in the London office of the Sandicroft Foundry Company; but he found it increasingly difficult to continue the two jobs, although his immediate employer was not unsympathetic to organisation among clerks or to Elvin's work for them. The managing director of the Company, R.E. Commans, became, in fact, a life-long friend of the family.

With the co-operation of Mary Macarthur, Elvin had secured a London address for the Clerks at the office of the WTUL; but as the business of the union increased, including the possibilities for recruitment among shopworkers, railway clerks and others, the need for a more independent type of administration became clear. In 1908 Elvin, now the treasurer of the Federation of Shop Workers and Clerks, conducted a vigorous campaign against the sweating of office workers at the White City Exhibition, a campaign which led in July 1909 to a favourable revision of their hours of work and rates of pay but which, since one of Elvin's employers was a White City shareholder, increased his own personal problems. At the annual conference at the end of 1909 Elvin was appointed the Clerks' first full-time general secretary and he continued in this post for more than thirty years, until 1941.

The NUC was small in 1906 with a membership of about 150, but it made considerable headway in the years of the First World War, reaching a membership peak of 43,000 in 1919–20. Although this high level was not held, it can be taken as a significant achievement and a reflection of the energy and organisational skill of its executive and of Elvin in particular. Union representatives of the Clerks were extremely vulnerable from their employers, and from the outset the NUC had refused the minor safeguard of calling itself a professional association. It had joined the TUC and had affiliated to the Labour Party in 1907. Recruitment was steady among clerks in the engineering industry who were ineligible for the AEU, but mining clerks, similarly suspect by the manual section of their industry, were slower to join. The quite extensive distrust of white-collar trade unions among the established manual unions – chiefly on grounds of divided loyalties was one reason why it was a number of years before the Clerks were successful in securing a representative on the TUC's General Council. Another was the prominence of J.B. Williams of the Muscians' Union who was regarded as the most appropriate figure from the non-manual unions for membership of the Council (he served – with short breaks – from 1907 to 1925).

During the First World War Elvin was an outspoken pacifist, but he was exempted from the call-up because of his full-time union commitment, and he did not therefore have to face the decision whether or not to become a conscientious objector. He spoke frequently at anti-war meetings and quite often received rough treatment. His stand on this issue led to a certain amount of dissension within the union. There were, moreover, several strikes during these years which tested the union's organisation and unity of purpose. Notable among them was the strike over a case of victimisation which brought out the clerks of the Nobel Explosives Factory in July 1915, and which became something of a minor landmark in union relations in that the clerks had the complete support of manual sections employed there. But the strike had only partial success – one of the men victimised was not reinstated [Hughes (1953) 44]. At the end of the war when Whitley Councils were introduced, Elvin and most of the union's executive gave them their support. Elvin's personal commitment to the scheme was particularly strong; he became a member of the National Whitley Council and later chairman of the Middlesex Whitley Council for Local Government Staffs, and vice-chairman, on the employers' side, of the Middlesex Joint Industrial Council. But some of the NUC leaders hoped to see a greater measure of workers' control and policy of national ownership, and were therefore distrustful of the principles underlying joint consultation.

Foremost in this group and most vigorous in their support for the Guild Socialist basis of organisation were William Elger of the Edinburgh branch, Charles Latham, Bob Scouller and J. Henry Lloyd. Elvin, however, remained a firm opponent of the policy on the ground that it threatened to fragment the union and reduce its strength. Nevertheless, in 1920 the union was remodelled on an Industrial Guild basis, since it had been found that when it came to recruiting members that this form of organisation was more popular. In the new structure constituent guilds were given considerable freedom of action and were encouraged to co-operate closely with unions of manual workers in their respective industries. There were initial gains in membership in the chief heavy industries, but they were relatively short-lived and as membership fell through the 1920s this organisational structure continued to be severely criticised, and at a Special Delegate Meeting in 1933 a new constitution, dissolving the national guilds, was accepted [ibid. 96].

Elvin's first active political commitment was to the Liberal Party and in 1904 he tried to reorganise the Liberals in his local area – Buckhurst Hill (where he had already got a Baptist chapel built). But after the 1906 general election he resigned his secretaryship of the local Liberal organisation and joined the Labour Party. He was a member of the Epping Board of Guardians, and when he moved to Southend during the First World War he stood unsuccessfully as a Labour candidate for the borough council but he was elected to the Rochford Board of Guardians for the Southchurch ward in Southend.

From 1918, along with Fred Hughes, the NUC assistant general secretary, he was on his union's parliamentary panel. He unsuccessfully contested the Bath constituency at the 1922 general election, Watford in 1924, and Spen Valley – where he came closest to gaining the seat – against Sir John Simon in 1929 and 1931. Although the level of political interest among the mass of the NUC's membership was low (in 1929, 28 per cent paid the political levy, in 1936, 15 per cent and in 1940, 10 per cent), Elvin did introduce a degree of political discussion into its journal; and in spite of his anti-Communist views he tried to make it widely representative of political opinion within the union. He was a firm supporter of the rights of women to equality of status and pay, as he had indicated just after the First World War when giving evidence to the War Cabinet's Committee on Women in Industry which reported in 1919.

In 1925 Elvin was elected to the General Council of the TUC, where he served on the economic and non-manual workers' committees. During the General Strike, the calling-off of which he opposed, he was in control of transport licensing. In 1936 he was a member of a trade union delegation to the Soviet Union. Two years later he chaired the Congress at Blackpool. His presidential address on this occasion was characteristic and showed his political standpoint: although near the end he asserted his opposition to the Popular Front and 'the so-called United Peace Movement' as Communist traps, he gave much more prominence to a bitterly hostile summary of the Government's policy towards Abyssinia, Spain, Japan, Austria, and Germany, with a prophecy of the fate of Czechoslovakia. He described Fascism as 'Capitalist economic nudism', and while affirming the reality of the class struggle pleaded, like many more after him, for a voluntary and pacific means of securing 'a Socialist Commonwealth', by 'a change of outlook'... 'by changing society' [*TUC Report* (1938) 76–80].

In 1939 Elvin was vice-chairman of the TUC and in the same year he represented the Congress as fraternal delegate at the annual convention of the American Federation of Labor. Also in 1938 and 1939, he served as a member (replacing Ernest Bevin) of the R.C. on the Distribution of the Industrial Population. With two co-signatories he added a section to its main report, recommending that a new ministry be established combining the planning functions of the Ministry of Transport with the housing functions of the Ministry of Health. Its particular responsibilities would be to correlate new business developments and industrial location and to conduct research designed to lead to a national plan for the distribution of industry. At the 1940 TUC Elvin lost his seat on the General Council. This has been attributed to the NUC's decision at its annual conference at Leeds in that year to pass a resolution which called for 'an Immediate armistice to be followed by a socialist peace' [Hughes (1953) 114]; although Elvin did not agree, he believed that as general secretary of the union, he should move it himself at the TUC. But, with others of the same kind, it was heavily defeated and Congress affirmed 'its inflexible resolve to go on with the struggle against the aggressor powers' [*TUC Report* (1940) 371].

Apart from trade union matters, education remained one of Elvin's prime interests. For a period he was a Governor of Ruskin College. During his membership of the TUC General Council he served on the Extra-Mural Board of Cambridge University and of the British Association for Commercial and Industrial Education. He also took part in WEA courses and those organised for HM Forces, and was a member of the Council of the Working Men's

College. Throughout his life he took a keen interest in organisations which sought to promote leisure activities, in particular, athletics. In his youth he was fond of many varied kinds of sport, but in later life he tended to concentrate on golf and chess. He was a member of the National Playing Fields Association, vice-president of the International Association for Workers' Leisure, and chairman of the British Workers' Sports Association. The last named was sponsored by both the TUC and the Labour Party, and it was affiliated to the Socialist Workers' Sports International.

In 1941 Elvin was succeeded as general secretary of the NUCAW by Fred Woods. In the previous year, to Elvin's regret, the union had moved temporarily to Glasgow, and at this point the clash of opinion and of temperament between Elvin and his president, William Elger, had come to a head. In order to resolve the situation Elvin offered his resignation. His colleague Fred Hughes later made this assessment of the situation and of Elvin's reputation:

> His services to the Union had always commanded admiration and respect, but he had never enjoyed or played for the personal popularity that makes public life endurable for so many men. He was not more ambitious or egotistical than most public men, but his self-esteem was more naïve and less carefully muted than it is with most of us and, combined with a certain subtlety of mind, a Puritan outlook and rather ascetic habits, had the effect of arousing a critical spirit in many of his colleagues... He was assertive and fought for his views, sometimes hitting hard, but he never bore malice... He was diplomatic enough to work harmoniously with successive Presidents whatever their views – with two exceptions only; but those two exceptions were important ones. With Henry Lloyd and with William Elger his frequent differences of view were hard to reconcile because in both cases there was a personal incompatibility... A few years with Elger as his President, combined with the effects of years of persistent overwork and the crowning strain of the war, broke the tension of his nervous system, and the removal to Glasgow, involving, as it did, separation from his family and from all his interests in London, decided his retirement a couple of years earlier than it would have come in the normal course [Hughes (1953) 117–118].

Elvin's retirement from the NUC and the trade union world was complete, but he continued his long-standing interest in local government. For a number of years he was a Labour member of the Middlesex County Council, chairing the staffing committee and the committee responsible for drawing up the syllabus for religious teaching. He also maintained a close interest in international relations, especially those where there were possibilities for international co-operation. Between the wars, he was for many years a member of the executive of the League of Nations Union and for seven years British Labour Advisor to the ILO. For a period he was vice-president of the International Arbitration League and vice-chairman of the China Campaign Committee, and he was a keen supporter of the work of the International Association for Social Progress, the National Peace Council and the Council of Christians and Jews.

Elvin was of medium height and stockily built and generally used a walking stick because of a slight limp caused by a cricket accident as a young man. He died on 9 November 1949 at his home at Stanmore, Middlesex and was cremated at Golders Green. He was survived by his wife, Mary Jane (née Hill) whom he had married in 1899 and by three sons. Mary Elvin (known as Dolly because she was small at birth) was the daughter of the Rev. G.J. Hill of the Seamen's Christian Friend Society, who ran the Seamen's Mission in east London at the time when Elvin first became actively involved with the temperance movement there. In her younger days she was an active supporter of the women's suffrage movement, was a member of the Women's Freedom League and worked closely with Florence Underwood and Charlotte Despard. At the time of their father's death, Lionel Elvin was principal of Ruskin College, George was general secretary of the Cine-Technicians' Union and Harold was an artist. Herbert Elvin left an estate of £3471, of which £1000 was donated towards a library at Ruskin College.

Writings: *Socialism for Clerks* (Pass on Pamphlet no. 26, [1909]) 16 pp; Evidence before Cabinet Committee on Women in Industry 1919 XXXI pp. 152–3; *Election Address* (1924) [*DLB* Coll.]; *La Prolongations de la Scolarité obligatoire et ses rapports avec le travail et le chômage* (1929) 12 pp.; Foreword to TUC, *Seventy Years of Trade Unionism 1868–1938* ed. H. Tracey [1938?]; 'Address at the American Federation of Labor Convention', *American Federationist 46* (Nov 1939) 1190–3; R.C. on Distribution of the Industrial Population *Report* 1939–40 IV Cmd 6153, Section by Prof. P. Abercrombie, H.H. Elvin and Mrs Hichens, pp. 218–32.

Sources: *Clerk* (Mar 1908), (Feb 1910), (Oct 1925), (May-June 1941), (July-Aug 1951); 'The Only Way for Clerks: a word to the national union', *Socialist Standard*, 1 Aug 1908; *Labour Who's Who* (1927); W. Hannington, *Unemployed Struggles 1919–1936* (1936; repr. Wakefield, 1973); National Workers' Sports Association, *Sixth Annual Report and Accounts* (1936) 20 pp.; *TUC Report* (1938) and (1940); *WWW* (1941–50); F. Hughes, *By Hand and Brain* (1953); D. Lockwood, *The Black-coated Worker* (1958); biographical information: A.I. Marsh, St Edmund's Hall, Oxford; personal information: Dr R. Page Arnot, London; G.H. Elvin, Leigh-on-Sea, Essex, son; Lord Underhill. Obit. *Times*, 11 Nov 1949; *Clerk* (Jan-Feb 1950) [by F. Hughes]; *TUC Report* (1950).

Barbara Nield

See also: *James Henry Lloyd.

EVANS, George (1842-93)
SOCIALIST

George Evans was born in Kidderminster on 6 September 1842, the son of Calvin Evans, a carpet weaver, and his wife Jane (née Turbefield). At the age of nine he began work alongside his father, who carried him there, at 4 o'clock in the morning. They often returned home as late as 8 p.m. About a year later Calvin Evans appears to have taken the lead in an attempt to raise wages, and was apparently victimised. The family then moved to Scotland. It is not possible to reconstruct the early life of George Evans in any detail. For three years he was page boy to Alexander Thompson, of Banchory, near Aberdeen. A further twelve months were spent in the service of Brown Douglas, Lord Provost of Edinburgh, and later he became a pantry man to the Western Club of Glasgow. In his teens he worked in Liverpool as well as his native town of Kidderminster. Years later, after he had married and raised a family, he was obliged to move from Birkenhead because of his part in a strike. He was in Scotland again in 1880, at which time he was an enthusiastic supporter of Gladstone. Evans organised a penny subscription to present the Liberal leader with a tweed suit, and an address, and he headed the deputation which waited upon Gladstone at the County Hotel, Carlisle, in November 1880. Evans was then living with his wife and five children at Langholme, on the estate of the Duke of Buccleuch. Not only was the Duke an ardent Conservative, but his son and heir, Lord Dalkeith, had been the sitting member for the constituency whom Gladstone had just defeated. The Evans family were evicted and no one in the village dared help them with their 'few sticks' or offer them accommodation. Evans eventually found work in Carlisle and then removed to Salford in 1885.

Here he found employment as a home painter. Politically he was still a Liberal, but he now came into contact with William Horrocks, a former Liberal who was now one of the local leaders of the newly-formed branch of the SDF. After long discussions Evans was converted, and the South Salford branch of the SDF gained an extremely active propagandist, bill-posting at night, canvassing, selling papers, speaking in the streets. He quickly became a leading figure in the local Socialist movement. Much of his public speaking took place at Trafford Bridge, Salford, where in April 1891 he also took part in the campaign to organise the navvies working on the nearby Manchester Ship Canal. In November 1891 Evans and W.K. Hall stood as SDF candidates in the Salford School Board elections. They were bottom of the poll.

In August 1891 George Evans – at this time president of South Salford SDF branch – took part in an initial meeting to consider the formation of a Labour Party for Salford. The Salford Labour Electoral Association came into existence, with Evans its vice-president; and after the idea of a Labour parliamentary candidate had been promoted by a mixed group of Socialists the Association decided to support such a candidate at the next general election. When John Trevor founded the Labour Church in Manchester, in October 1891, Evans became one of its earliest members, served on its first executive committee and for the remaining months of his life was an active worker in its cause. In an obituary notice in the *Labour Prophet* Trevor wrote: 'I wish I could say how much I am indebted to this good man. It has been a help to me in all I have done simply to know him' [(May 1893) 36].

In 1892 the Socialist and independent Labour organisations in Manchester and Salford, already closely inter-linked, combined to hold a May Day demonstration in Alexandra Park, Manchester. Evans took the chair on the SDF platform. The enthusiasm displayed on this occasion encouraged Robert Blatchford and John Trevor to plan the establishment of an Independent Labour Party for Manchester and Salford. George Evans attended the inaugural meeting on 17 May 1892 at St James' Hall, Manchester; and in the January following he was elected its treasurer. Although he was involved with other organisations, he continued his active membership of the SDF and this was the group with which in his later years he most identified.

He was an advocate of temperance; interested in singing and cricket; and a good swimmer. On one occasion he rescued three young men whose pleasure boat had capsized at Throstle Nest Weir, near Trafford Bridge. But his health became increasingly poor. Pain in his right arm was making it difficult for him to hold a brush. He fell seriously ill in November 1892, but, after a three weeks convalescence in Southport he returned to his trade, only to fall ill again. He died, aged fifty, after a hard and active life, on 2 April 1893, leaving no provision for his wife or his family, which now included an adopted orphan child.

George Evans's funeral was not a sombre occasion, but a mass Socialist demonstration: 'a triumphal march' *Justice* described it. On 8 April a procession formed outside his home, in Ellesmere Street, Hulme, headed by the Labour Church banner and brass band, followed by members of the ILP and Labour Church, and contingents (with banners) from SDF branches all over Lancashire. Then came some of Evans's shop mates, and the officers and members of the True-as-Steel Division of the Sons of Temperance, of which he had been a member. At Evans's own request, the red flag of South Salford SDF was placed over his coffin. The band played the 'Marseillaise' most of the way to the Salford Borough Cemetery. At the Cemetery gates the crowd was about 1000 strong. The funeral service was read by the Grand Worthy Chaplain of the Sons of Temperance, and speeches were made by Fred Brocklehurst, secretary of the Labour Church, William Horrocks on behalf of the SDF and Robert Blatchford for the ILP. The 'Marseillaise' was then played for the last time over the open grave before the crowd dispersed. Both the ILP and SDF undertook to collect funds for George Evans's widow and family.

Sources: *Workman's Times*, 27 Mar 1891–4 Feb 1893; *Justice*, 7 May–19 Nov 1892; *Clarion*,11 June 1892–1 July 1893; P. Magnus, *Gladstone* (1954; rev. ed. 1963); L. Thompson, *Robert Blatchford: portrait of an Englishman* (1951). Obit. *Clarion*, 8 Apr 1893; *Justice* and *Workman's Times*, 15 Apr 1893; *Labour Prophet* (May 1893).

Naomi Reid

See also: †Robert Peel Glanville Blatchford; John Trevor

FAIRBOTHAM, Harold (1883-1968)

LABOUR ALDERMAN AND TRADE UNION OFFICIAL

Harold Fairbotham was born in Hull on 6 July 1883, the son of Fred Fairbotham, a grocer and his wife Kate (née Teanby). He attended Blundell Street School until 1896, when he began work as a messenger for the North Eastern Railway. He became successively engine cleaner and fireman but in 1907 left the railway to work for Hull Corporation as a cleaner and later turbine driver in the Hull local electricity power station. While in his job he became secretary of Hull No. 4 Branch of the Municipal Employees' Association (later the NUGMW). It was originally a small branch which grew to one of the largest in the district under his secretaryship. In 1932 he was appointed a full-time officer of the union, becoming East Coast district organiser, whch position he filled until 1948. For many years he was a member of the Joint Industrial Council for the electricity supply industry and at the time of nationalisation he was chairman of the trade union side. From 1948 until 1953 he was a part-time member of the Yorkshire Electricity Board.

He served on Hull City Council from 1933-6 for Botanic ward and from 1938, when he was elected for Alexandra ward, until his death. He was for many years secretary of the Labour group on the Council. His two main spheres of activity on the Council were the property and bridges committee, of which he became chairman in 1946 and the watch committee, of which he became chairman in 1947; he remained chairman of both until 1968. One of his favourite schemes was the establishment of a central museum for Hull, but he became especially known for his work for Hull's police force. He was a forward-looking chairman of the watch committee, responsible for pushing ahead with many schemes to modernise the city's police force, and took a great interest in the training of young policemen. He was chairman of the No. 2 district police training local authorities' committee and vice-president of Hull City Police Boys' Club. He was made a JP in 1939, an alderman in 1953 (for Paragon ward), and an honorary freeman of Hull in 1968. He was awarded the OBE in 1963.

Politically he was on the right of the Labour Party. Fairbotham was a quiet, rather staid, pipe-smoking man who retained his vitality into his eighties. He died on 27 June 1968, at the age of eighty-four. His funeral, attended by Hull's civic leaders, took place at Hull Crematorium, and about 150 policemen formed a guard of honour, with two mounted policemen flanking the cortège. He left effects valued at £2052.

Sources: *General and Muncipal Workers' J. 10*, no. 116 (Feb 1933) 46; *Hull Daily Mail*, 2 and 5 July 1968; personal information: S. Clayton, the late Ald. F. Holmes, J.W. Smith, J. Webster, all of Hull. Obit. *Hull Daily Mail*, 27 and 28 June 1968; *General and Municipal Workers J. 31*, no. 8 (Aug 1968).

Ann Holt

FORGAN, Robert (1891–1976)

LABOUR MP (LATER MOSLEYITE)

Robert Forgan was born at Montrose on 10 March 1891, the only son of the Rev. Robert Forgan DD, a minister of the Church of Scotland and Convener of the Foreign Mission Committee of the Church of Scotland. His mother was Mary Grace Forgan (née Rose). There were five other children of the marriage, all of them girls.

Although there is no documentary evidence, members of Forgan's family are sure that he was educated at Rothesay Academy before attending Aberdeen Grammar School and subsequently entering the University of Aberdeen. He graduated MA in Arts in 1911, but the records indicate that he had already registered as a medical student, and his schedule of study shows him attending medical courses from 1909 until his graduation as MB ChB in 1915. When war broke out Forgan was in the Officer Training Corps, and he served in France from May to December 1915 and again from December 1916 to October 1919, finally attaining the rank of captain in the RAMC. For over a year of this service he worked in military hospitals devoted exclusively to the treatment of VD – the 39th and 7th General Hospitals in France and hospitals in Cambridge and London. He was awarded the Military Cross in January 1916 and was mentioned in despatches in the same month.

After the war Forgan went to Cambridge University where he obtained the Diploma in Public Health in 1920 and then took a post as junior Medical Officer to the Department of Venereal Diseases of Aberdeen Royal Infirmary. In 1921 he was appointed VD executive Medical Officer to the Lanarkshire Joint Committee on Venereal Diseases. This led to his becoming secretary of the working party which took the first steps in the formation of the Medical Society for the Study of Venereal Diseases. This body was founded in 1922, and Forgan drafted the first constitution. He was a member of the Council of the Society from 1924 to 1929, was vice-president 1929 to 1930, and throughout his life remained interested in its work. His professional interest in venereal problems was also reflected in the MD thesis he submitted to Aberdeen University in 1924, on 'Smettle: some clinical and public health aspects of recurrent infectivity in syphilis'. For this thesis he was awarded an MD with distinction.

It was a combination of his wartime experiences and his encounter with conditions in Glasgow slums which turned him from an early Liberalism towards the Labour Party. He joined the ILP in 1924. Between November 1926 and November 1929 he represented the 18th (Woodside) ward on the Glasgow City Council as a Labour member. At the 1929 general election he was returned as Labour MP for Western Renfrewshire.

At Westminster Forgan was a member of the Labour Party's left-wing group, which at that time included Maxton, Fenner Brockway, Bevan, Strachey and W.J. Brown. Forgan spoke in debates on a variety of subjects, such as unemployment, housing, slum clearance, health, preventive medicine and medical research; he was particularly concerned with the Scottish experience of such matters. In general, his contributions reflected a humane and sensitive attitude, and an awareness of the links which existed between economic distress and the physical and mental health of the nation. While making such occasional contributions between 1929 and 1931 Forgan was becoming increasingly disillusioned with the failure of the second Labour Government to tackle the economic problems which he regarded as responsible for so much personal suffering; and it was in this frame of mind that he moved towards Oswald Mosley and was prepared to sign the Mosley Manifesto in February 1931. Forgan believed that government policy smacked of Cabinet autocracy and a denial of the election programme of 1929, and in his view, to accept the Mosley Manifesto would have redeemed the Labour Party. But Labour did not accept the Manifesto; and at a meeting of the Mosley group on 20 February it was decided that six Labour MPs should resign from the Labour Party – Mosley and his wife Cynthia, Forgan, John Strachey, W.J. Brown and Oliver Baldwin. Forgan and Strachey resigned on 24 February. Mosley was expelled on 10 March for 'gross disloyalty'.

The way was now open for the development of the New Party. Mosley announced its formation on 28 February 1931, but since he was taken ill almost immediately after his expulsion the main task of launching the organisation fell to Cynthia Mosley, Strachey and Forgan. The structure of the Party was never formalised, but there was a council which was responsible for policy, and Forgan sat on this. In addition, he served as New Party Whip in the Commons and contributed to its shortlived but distinguished newspaper, *Action*, edited by Harold Nicolson. Real power within the Party lay, of course, with Mosley.

For Forgan, this excursion into the political wilderness brought about his defeat in 1931 at

Western Renfrewshire, where he stood as New Party candidate. He polled only 1304 votes against the 14,419 he had gathered for Labour two years earlier. This election, in which twenty-two out of twenty-four New Party candidates finished bottom of the poll and twenty-two lost their deposits, spelt the end of the organisation. But Mosley's dynamism was not easily quelled, and his personal relationship with Forgan was such that he was to carry the latter with him on his next political odyssey. In a different setting the closeness of the two at this time was also reflected in the fact that Forgan was godfather to Michael, the third child of Oswald and Cynthia Mosley, who was born in April 1932.

It was in 1932 that Mosley founded the British Union of Fascists, and for a time Forgan was deeply involved in it. He became director of organisation and deputy leader, for which responsibilities he received salaries of £600 and £750 respectively. He also took a prominent part in a public relations campaign on behalf of the BUF. While the national campaign was gaining momentum, private functions were arranged by Forgan to enlist the support and co-operation of business and professional men. Moreover, he was one of the organisers of the January Club, which was formed on New Year's Day 1934, under the chairmanship of Sir John Squire, to discuss modern types of government, including Fascism. Forgan was also employed by the BUF in the summer of 1934 to engage in discussion with the Jewish community in an attempt to thrash out a Jewish-Fascist agreement. Such negotiations were abortive. But Forgan was not only engaged in propaganda for the BUF at home. In the autumn of 1932 he went as an emissary to Rome where he saw Mussolini, and presented him with a copy of Mosley's *Greater Britain* as part of an attempt to solicit Italian interest and support; Italian reactions to this attempt, however, were non-committal.

Such work employed Forgan until the autumn of 1934, when he resigned from the BUF. There were various reasons for his resignation. Harold Nicolson and Forgan both developed doubts, Nicolson by the spring of 1932. On 15 April he wrote to Forgan: '. . . I joined the [New] Party for two reasons. (1) Personal affection and belief in Tom [Mosley]. (2) A conviction that a serious crisis was impending and that our economic and parliamentary system must be transformed if a collapse were to be avoided. Now I feel that the New Party as such has become too much identified with Hitlerism. . . . I do not believe in fascism for England, and cannot consent to be identified with anything of the sort' [Nicolson (1966) 114].

Forgan might well have had the same two reasons for joining the New Party; and although he served Mosley until the autumn of 1934, he disagreed with the lapse from radical to conservative policies which resulted from the Mosley-Rothermere alliance of January to July 1934; and he was repelled by the increasing violence and anti-Semitism of the BUF. He probably felt less committed to the movement after the death in 1933 of Cynthia Mosley, who had never been completely convinced of the virtues of her husband's fascist views. Nicolson recorded on 11 December 1931 [ibid., 98] that she 'wants to put a notice in *The Times* to the effect that she dissociated herself from Tom's fascist tendencies. We pass it off as a joke' – a phrase which suggests that it was not intended as one.

After leaving politics Forgan practised, briefly and unsuccessfully, as a general practitioner in Golders Green. In 1935 he became medical consultant to May and Baker of Dagenham, and although he retired from full-time work in 1961, his connection with the company was maintained on a part-time basis until he was eighty. His literary ability led in 1952 to his editorship, on behalf of May and Baker, of the *Medical Bulletin*. He continued his interest in this until 1967, and his skill in medical journalism was further shown, after his retirement from May and Baker, in his work for *Medical News* and *Excerpta Medica*. He also continued his professional interest in venereal diseases: he was a regular attender at international conferences on such matters, and in 1972 he published an article on the 'History of the treatment of trichomoniasis' in the jubilee issue of the *British Journal of Venereal Diseases*.

After 1934, and his severance from the BUF, Forgan made no attempt to continue contact with his fascist colleagues, although a number did try to keep up with him. John Beckett, for instance, who had been with Forgan in the Labour Party and whom Forgan had recruited into the BUF, maintained the link, and on his release from internment he stayed for a while with the Forgans. According to Forgan it was relations of this kind which led to the rejection of his application to rejoin the Labour Party. A major influence in this decision, it was claimed, was Herbert Morrison, who was a long-standing and implacable opponent of Beckett's. But there was little political initiative from Forgan, and his support for E.R. Millington, the Common Wealth candidate who stood at Chelmsford in the 1945 elections – there was a by-election before the general election – was related to personal friendship and in no way signified a serious and active return to national politics. His chief interests were his medical work, travel, gardening (which he took very seriously).

Forgan died on 8 January 1976, at the age of eighty-four, and was cremated at Doddinghurst in Essex. Although he was a son of the manse he was not a believer, and there was no religious service. A service of thanksgiving for his life was held at the Crypt Chapel in the House of Commons on 23 February 1976.

Robert Forgan was attractive in appearance, tall and lean, with a fine head and open features. He had also an attractive personality, kindly and generous, full of vitality and gaiety; and he was a good and witty conversationalist. In his youth he was a considerable athlete, a middle-distance runner and a fine hockey player (he was once capped for Scotland). Forgan was twice married: first, on 1 August 1916, to Winifred Mary Forbes Cran of Aberdeen, by whom he had a daughter, April Katherine born in 1926; there was a divorce in 1937. His second wife was Winifred Jan Rees of Kenton, whom he married on 2 April 1938. There were three children of this marriage: Andrew, now (1978) a lecturer, born in 1944; Catherine, born in 1946; and Valerie, an occupational therapist, born in 1948. All his children survived him, as did his widow, and the two children of his widow's sister, whom he informally adopted. No will has been located and there are no private papers.

Writings: Specialist articles in medical journals.

Sources: M.D. Allardyce, *Roll of Service in the Great War* (Aberdeen, 1921); *Daily Herald,* 5 July 1929; *Hansard* (1929–31); *Dod* (1931); *Action* (1931); *Manchester Guardian*, 25 Feb 1931; *Fascist Week* (1934) *passim; Blackshirt, Spec.* and *Times*, 2 Oct 1934; *Manchester Guardian*, 12 Oct 1934; J. Jones, *Unfinished Journey* (1937); W.J. Brown, *So Far . . .* (1943); C. Cross, *The Fascists in Britain* (1961); H. Nicolson, *Diaries and Letters 1930–1939* ed. N. Nicolson (1966); R.J. Benewick, *Political Violence and Public Order* (1969; rev. as *The Fascist Movement in Britain* (1972); *WW* (1972); R. Skidelsky, *Oswald Mosley* (1975); biographical information: R. Dell, principal archivist, Strathclyde Regional Council; the late T.A.K. Elliott, CMG; personal information: P.L. Dickinson, grandson, London; Dr Robert Forgan (correspondence); Dr N. Wattie, Glasgow. Obit. *Times*, 16 Jan 1976; *British Medical J.* and *Lancet*, 24 Jan 1976; *British J. of Venereal Diseases 52* (1976).

Barbara Hill
Colin Holmes

See also: John [William] Warburton Beckett;† Cynthia Blanche, Lady Mosley.

GAMMAGE, Robert George (1820/1–88)

CHARTIST AND RADICAL REFORMER

Gammage was born of working-class parents at Northampton in 1820 or 1821. The first date is the more likely. He published his reminiscences, up to the year 1843, in the *Newcastle Weekly Chronicle* at irregular intervals between 24 November 1883 and 10 January 1885; and it is from these articles that most of the details of his early life are taken. His father died when he was eleven years old, Gammage having begun work a year earlier at one of the local inns, but he then became apprenticed as a trimmer to a coach builder, although no formal articles were signed. His family background was Tory. 'My grandfather', he wrote, 'was of the sternest Tory cast, and so was my uncle. I was thus brought up in a very hot-bed of Toryism' [*Newcastle Weekly Chronicle*, 29 Mar 1884]. It was the shop floor discussions that began to alter his views, and he became a reader of the unstamped press. Tom Paine and Robert Emmet were his heroes, and he seems to have engaged in radical activity in his later teens, almost certainly not later than the age of seventeen. He was particularly impressed with a large meeting on 1 August 1838 addressed by Henry Vincent.

Gammage left Northampton on 6 February 1840. He was by now a time-served craftsman. He went to London where he visited Henry Hetherington's shop, and heard a speech by Thomas Wakley, the Radical MP for Finsbury. Eventually, since work was difficult to find, he obtained employment in Sherborne, Dorset, but after an eight months stay, he went on the tramp once again. He met G.J. Harney in Sheffield, Robert Lowery in Aberdeen, the Rev. Archibald Browning in Tillicoultry; and he first heard Feargus O'Connor and P.M. M'Douall speak in his native town of Northampton. From his own recollections, Gammage would appear at this time to have been a very committed Chartist, a capable organiser, and a good speaker. For the rest of the 1840s he remained a competent middle-rank propagandist, never achieving national status. It was only after 1850, when the Chartist movement was fast losing its mass appeal, that Gammage appeared as a national figure, being elected to the EC of the National Association in May 1852. Almost immediately he went on speaking tours as a Chartist missionary. He was invited to stand for Exeter in the general election of 1852, but the plan fell through. He did, however, go to the hustings at Cheltenham where according to his own account in his *History of the Chartist Movement*, he spoke to 10,000 people. In June 1853 he joined up with Ernest Jones, and together they spoke at towns and villages in the industrial North and the Midlands; and it was on this tour that they both pronounced orations at the funeral of Benjamin Rushton, the veteran West Riding Radical (*People's Paper* 2 July 1853). Gammage was soon, however, to break with Jones. In November 1853 Jones began to discuss the idea of a Parliament of Labour, initially in support of the great strike of Preston workers; but as the weeks passed the idea became elaborated into a national scheme for the support of strikes and lock-outs and for the establishment of national co-operative enterprises on the land and in industry. Gammage, much opposed to these later suggestions, which he thought wholly impractical, withdrew from the project, and his name did not appear as a sponsor or as a delegate to the meetings of the Labour Parliament which opened on 6 March 1854 [Saville (1952) 54]. Gammage was now allied with Bronterre O'Brien, and the relationship with Jones ended in a confusion of accusations, political and financial. By the middle of May 1854 Gammage had removed to Newcastle upon Tyne, and he was to remain in the North-East until his death.

He must have begun writing his *History of the Chartist Movement* soon after he settled in Newcastle, with the political bitterness of the previous months still upon him. He was to admit thirty years later that he would have done better to have waited a few more years [*Newcastle Weekly Chronicle*, 7 Apr 1883]. The *History* was issued in seven parts, with different coloured title and end pages. The first two parts were published in the later months of 1854, the other five parts in 1855, and the bound volume in November 1855. The size of the imprint is not known, but it was little noticed at the time, and this first edition is rarely found in public or private collections. Gammage later stated that he was in serious financial difficulties at the time he was writing his *History*, and it is not known what he did for a living when he first went to Newcastle. Later, *Ward's North of England Directory* for 1857-8 lists him as an insurance agent living in Sunderland. His brother Thomas was also listed in the *Directory* as an accountant, and he too later became an insurance agent. The two brothers were living at the same address at this time. In 1864 Gammage qualified as a medical doctor at Newcastle Infirmary. He first acted as assistant to a Dr Heath in Newcastle and then returned to Sunderland to enjoy 'a modest practice'.

Gammage entered local politics almost as soon as he arrived in Newcastle in the middle 1850s. It was a politically lively town, with the young Joseph Cowen already making contact with European nationalists and revolutionaries, and G.J. Harney was editing the monthly *Northern Tribune*. Its first issue appeared in January 1854. Gammage seems to have become a member of Newcastle Foreign Affairs Committee in November 1854, and his name also appeared as a member of the Newcastle upon Tyne Committee for Watching the War in March 1855. When Joseph Cowen formed the Northern Reform Union in 1858 [for which see Muris (1953)] Gammage appeared in the local press as one of its spokesmen in Sunderland and the villages around. He seems always to have remained a Radical. His brother was secretary of a Garibaldi Committee in the early 1860s, and Gammage himself was ready to organise a Sunderland meeting at the time of Garibaldi's short visit to England in 1864. But it was for his political work in the Reform agitation that Gammage was most remembered in the North-East region. He shared platforms in 1866 and 1867 with Edmond Beales and Ernest Jones; and in April 1867 both he and his brother were delegates from Sunderland at a representative conference of the Northern Reform Union.

The local press seems to be silent on Gammage's political activities in the 1870s – if there were any – and it is only in the early 1880s that he appears again in print. There developed an interesting correspondence in the *Chronicle* in the spring of 1883 on the Chartist movement, to which Gammage contributed, and it was this exchange which led to the publication of his reminiscences, beginning with the issue of 24 November 1883.

He retired from medical practice in 1887, and then went to live in his home town of Northampton. According to the obituary notice of his death, he fell from a tram on Tuesday, 3 January 1888, and he died the following Saturday, 7 January, aged sixty-seven, leaving a widow and a mother, and personal estate valued at £365.

Gammage was a typical radical of the Chartist years, one who followed Bronterre O'Brien in his social thinking rather than the Jones of the post-1850 period. His intellectual position was clearly stated in a published lecture originally delivered at Newtown, Montgomeryshire in October 1852 [for which see J. Saville's Introduction to the 1969 reprint of the 1894 edition of Gammage's *History* 8 ff. and for the text of the lecture, 439–65]. The 1894 edition of Gammage's *History of the Chartist Movement* has been widely used and quoted, although collation of the texts of the two editions of 1854 and 1894 shows some important changes; and this fact has often been overlooked by historians. It is not known who undertook the revision and re-writing for the 1894 edition but the compiler of the index was a Sunderland solicitor, Thomas Marshall, who must have been a young man in the town in Gammage's last years. Between the texts of 1854 and 1894 there were no changes of substance for the first 414 pages of the 1854 edition (which ran to 450 pages), but from the last fifty pages or so of the first edition a number of fairly important passages were omitted in 1894; much relating to the internal quarrels within the Chartist movement after 1852, including the removal of a good deal of Gammage's critical comments on Ernest Jones. It is likely that W.E. Adams was involved in the discussions which took place about the revised work, and Adams was undoubtedly very favourably disposed towards Jones, and at the least wary of Gammage's criticism of him. The other changes which affected the text as a whole were verbal and stylistic including a re-arrangement of the chapters; and although there were many of these alterations, the original meaning seems to have been faithfully adhered to. The 1894 edition also included sixteen illustrations of the main Chartist leaders and it was given an index. Analysis of the textual changes is discussed in more detail in Saville's introduction to the 1969 reprint, upon which this present entry is based.

Writings: *The Social Oppression of the Working Classes: its causes and cure* [a lecture] [1852] repr. in Gammage's *The History of the Chartist Movement, from its Commencement down to the*

Present Time (1854–5; 2nd ed. Newcastle, 1894; repr. with an Introduction by J. Saville, 1969); *Beershops: England's felon manufactories* [one of the essays of the Anti-Beer Shop Association] 3rd ed. [1864] 14 pp.; Gammage's reminiscences were published in the *Newcastle Weekly Chronicle*, 24 Nov 1883, 5 and 12 Jan, 23 Feb, 29 Mar, 3, 24, 31 May, 21 June, 5 July, 16 Aug, 13 and 27 Sep, 8 Nov, 13 Dec 1884 and 10 Jan 1885.

Sources: *Newcastle Weekly Chronicle* (esp. Oct 1883-Nov 1885); J. Saville, *Ernest Jones: Chartist* (1952); C. Muris, 'The Northern Reform Union 1858–1862' (Durham [King's College, Newcastle] MA, 1953); J. Saville, 'R.G. Gammage and the Chartist Movement', Introduction to Gammage's *History* (see writings) 5–66; see also the standard texts on the Chartist movement; biographical information: Central Library, Sunderland. Obit. *Sunderland Daily Echo*, 9 Jan 1888; *Newcastle Weekly Chronicle*, 14 and 21 Jan 1888; *North-Country Lore and Legend* (Mar 1888) 139.

John Saville

See also: †Joseph Cowen; William Lovett, for Chartism to 1840.

GLYDE, Charles Augustus (1869-1923)
SOCIALIST

'Charlie' Glyde, as he was always known in adult life, was born on 29 December 1869 in Leeds, the son of C.A. Glyde, a licensed hawker, and his wife Jane (née Lodge). Charlie later described his father as a radical in politics; and when, in later years, he became well-read in the Chartist movement, he used to recall with pride that his family were related to the Rev. Jonathan Glyde, the Bradford nonconformist minister who had done much to help the woolcombers in the 1840s. The actual relationship, however, has not been substantiated.

Glyde left school at an early age, and never learnt a trade. In 1887 the family went to Bolton where his father had obtained work, and it was there that Charlie Glyde became a Socialist. He was already, however, a member of the Salvation Army and it was the Army that gave him his first experience of public speaking. His own account of how he became a Socialist is worth reprinting:

> On August 19th, 1887, I was walking around the centre of the town of Bolton, a stranger, wondering how I should spend the evening, when I saw a man stood on a chair vehemently haranguing a crowd. I drew near out of curiosity to hear what he had to say.
>
> His name was Young Walkden and he was denouncing the callousness of the Poor Law system. I listened to him with great attention, my mind was in the stage of entering the threshold of citizenship. I was about to form my life's opinions. He not only threw brickbats (figuratively speaking) at the Poor Law system, but he threw paving stones at it. I found myself endorsing every word that he said . . . At the end of the meeting I enquired the name of the Society under whose auspices the meeting was being held, and I was informed the Bolton Branch of the Social Democratic Federation. The following week I enrolled as a member and I threw myself into the movement heart and soul [*Bradford Socialist Vanguard* (Oct 1917)].

Glyde was soon to come under the influence of one of the oustanding Socialist agitators and propagandists: Tom Mann. Mann had visited Bolton during the engineers' strike in the town in the latter part of 1887, and he spent most of 1888 there, having been 'set up' as a newsagent and tobacconist to finance his work for the Socialist movement. Charlie Glyde was his devoted disciple, attending the Marxist economics classes that Mann organised and in later years describing himself as Mann's 'towel carrier, bottle holder and sponger down'. His reminiscences of Mann in Bolton are a valuable record of a provincial Socialist movement in its early days. Although in later years his memberhip of the Salvation Army lapsed, Charlie Glyde always remained a Christian.

Glyde moved to Bradford in May 1890 and during his first winter in the town was a witness to the Manningham Mills strike (Dec 1890–Apr 1891) which had such a crucial influence upon Labour politics in the West Riding. Glyde joined the Bradford Labour Union, established within a month of the strike's collapse, and in the same year, 1891, he also joined the Bradford Fabian Society.

In the autumn of 1892 he made his first election speech on behalf of E.R. Hartley who stood in the municipal elections as a Fabian Society candidate for the Bradford Moor ward. This began a close political friendship. Although Hartley was defeated in 1892 he was to contest the seat on three further occasions, until returned for the Manningham ward in 1895, and each time Glyde was his principal lieutenant, acting either as election agent or chairman.

During the 1890s Glyde worked zealously for the independent Labour movement. He had a succession of jobs, mainly as a small shopkeeper, which enabled him to sustain his work for the cause. In 1895 he was running a fish and chip shop. At various times he was in business as a tailor's agent and draper (trading as the 'Merrie England Supply Stores'), an insurance agent and the proprietor of a sweet shop. In 1900 when the Bradford ILP was in financial difficulties he became its unpaid secretary and it was in this capacity that in the same year he attended his first national ILP conference as a Bradford delegate with F.W. Jowett.

In 1901 the members of the Dudley Hill and Tong Socialist Club invited Glyde to fight the Tong ward for the ILP. Although he lost at his first attempt he was to win the seat in 1904, beating the Liberal by seven votes. Soon after his election he joined with his fellow labour councillors, led by Jowett, in a vigorous campaign against the decision of the Bradford Liberals not to allow the municipality to feed school children. Outside the council chamber Glyde was one of the leaders of the Bradford unemployed, gaining notoriety by his aggressive speeches and flamboyant style. Together with Hartley he led a march of the unemployed on the Bradford workhouse in the autumn of 1904, a move designed to 'swamp the workhouse' with applicants for relief. The most spectacular event he organised was the Bradford 'land-grab' in July 1905, when a group of unemployed men occupied a vacant site owned by the Midland Railway Company in Girlington. The 'colonists' attempted to grow vegetables for sale; but the onset of bad weather in the autumn forced the men to abandon their attempt at a land colony. Nonetheless the 'land-grab' did succeed in highlighting the plight of the Bradford unemployed, and the ground itself became a centre for meetings and demonstrations. Glyde became a member of the Corporation's Distress Committee, formed to provide work and relief for the unemployed, where he frequently clashed with middle-class philanthropists and members of the Board of Guardians. He was elected to the City Council in 1904, and he also became a member of the North Bierley Board of Guardians, representing Tong. Here he advocated Socialist remedies for the treatment of the poor, arguing for a liberal out-relief policy and more lenient treatment of the workhouse inmates. He particularly campaigned for a land colony to be established by the Guardians to provide work for the able-bodied unemployed.

It was as a propagandist that Glyde made his outstanding contribution to the Bradford Socialist movement. In 1901 he published the first of his 'Pamphlets for the People' entitled *Liberal and Tory Hypocrisy in the Nineteenth Century*. He was to publish eight in all, with each pamphlet going through many editions, *Liberal and Tory Hypocrisy* reaching twenty-three. The pamphlets reflected his main interests: old age pensions, the poor law and the history of the workers' movement, particularly during the Chartist period. The pamphlets were written in a highly individual style, colourful, witty and irreverent. Glyde used every opportunity to sell them, taking copies to all the many public meetings he attended; and he claimed by the end of his life that he had sold over a million copies.

In the early years of the century he had been president of the Tong Socialist Society, a non-sectarian body which welcomed all varieties of Socialism among it members, and like his friend E.R. Hartley, Glyde for a long time belonged to both the ILP and the SDF. Before he was elected to the Council in 1904 he had already started a paper: the *Tong Pioneer of Social Reform*, edited by 'Peter Plainspeech'; and in 1908 this became the monthly *Bradford Socialist Vanguard* which continued, under Glyde's editorship, until 1920.

In 1907 Glyde was appointed secretary of the Bradford branch of National Union of Gasworkers and General Labourers. He was especially active in representing the interests of those members employed by the City Council and used his position as a councillor to contrast the salaries paid to council officials with the low wages of council workmen. He joined the Bradford Trades Council in 1907 and the following year became vice-president. In 1910 he resigned this position when the Trades Council sent a telegram of condolence to the widow of Edward VII. Glyde, as a staunch republican, opposed this:

> He looked upon the humblest scavenger or surfacemen with the same respect as he looked upon the members of the Royal Family, and as they did not pass votes of condolence with such members of the community he did not see why it was necessary, on the part of a working class organization such as the Trades Council, to pass such a vote as was proposed [*Bradford Daily Telegraph*, 27 May 1910].

It is worth noting that he was shouted down at this meeting.

In 1913 when the Leeds Corporation workers went on strike Glyde did his utmost to support them and the Bradford branch donated £100 to the strike fund. On one occasion he was summonsed by the Leeds magistrates for selling the *Vanguard* at a Sunday meeting held in support of the strike. He was a member of his union's executive committee for the Bradford and Leeds District and from 1912 to 1917 was a member of the general council of the NUGW. In 1918 the Bradford branch, which had grown from 200 members to 2300 while Glyde had been secretary, split into two with Glyde remaining the secretary of the Corporation branch.

His Socialist journalism made him unpopular with both city officials and elected council members, including some of the Labour group. Glyde was always happy, for example, to provide readers of the *Vanguard* with details of the spending habits of certain councillors when on visits and deputations: the cost of their meals and hotels. In the April 1911 issue of the *Bradford Socialist Vanguard* he criticised the conduct of the Bradford Tramways manager and the latter took the matter to court, with Glyde maintaining that the manager had been encouraged to do so by his political opponents in an attempt to gag him. The local Magistrates' Court found Glyde guilty of libel, fining him and his printer £500 in total. The money was raised by supporters and the paper was able to continue.

When the war came in 1914 Glyde opposed it, declaring that it was contrary to all the principles of Christian brotherhood and Socialist internationalism. He was especially vituperative towards those in the labour movement – trade unionists and politicians – who co-operated with the Government's war effort. He campaigned for those on war relief and took up many individual cases with the authorities. In 1916 the *Vanguard* published allegations about the treatment afforded a soldier's widow by the Army and once more Glyde was prosecuted, this time under the Defence of the Realm Act for publishing material 'likely to interfere with the success of His Majesty's Forces and with making false statements'. He was fined £20 and costs, a payment of £35.10*s*.

His intense political activity began to tell upon his health. Although he suffered from a heart condition he refused to cut down on his work. By 1920, however, he was forced by ill health to retire from his posts of councillor, guardian and union secretary and to stop publication of the *Vanguard*. He now found time to write articles on the history of the labour movement for the *Labour Pioneer*, edited by his old friend, Ben Turner. These exhibited his considerable knowledge of working-class history, and it was his understanding of the struggles of the past that provided much of the emotional energy for his many years of Socialist agitation and propaganda. F.W. Jowett, in an obituary notice of Glyde, after emphasising his basic class consciousness continued:

> The elemental truths, which Glyde preached by tongue and pen, were made all the more vividly real to him by reading of a somewhat unusual kind. He read everything he could discover about Ernest Jones, the Chartist, Richard Oastler and the Reverend Wm. Bull, Vicar of Bierley. Glyde's unceasing attack and denunciation of the poor law system with its "bastille", its degrading test work and enquiries, and its paltry doles (half in money and half in kind), was no more severe than Oastler and the Vicar of Bierley had launched at mass meetings of Bradford workers, when the system was just established in its worst form nearly ninety years ago [*Bottom Dog* (Sep–Oct 1923)].

Just before his death, in the belief that his health had improved, Glyde established a new paper, the *Bottom Dog*. Only one issue was published before he died on 21 August 1923. The second issue was produced as a memorial tribute.

His funeral was organised by the Dudley Hill and Tong Socialist Club. The service was held at Holme Lane Chapel, and he was buried at Tong Cemetery. The large procession which accompanied the mourners was composed of representatves of all the Bradford labour and Socialist organisations, but the majority were the ordinary men and women of Tong who came to honour the man who had devoted his life to their cause. Glyde had always been a maverick; he was not always sensible in his judgments, and deafness for many years was a serious handicap. But he was, as the *New Leader* said in its obituary notice, 'wonderfully successful in giving the breath of life to the abstract theories of Socialism, and presenting them to the common people in such a manner that they could be discussed and felt.'

Glyde married Lizzie Mould in 1893. He met her through the Salvation Army and while she seems to have played little part in public, she was throughout their married life a source of great strength and comfort. There were no children of the marriage. Glyde left an estate of £971 (gross).

Writings: Glyde's principal writings were his 'Pamphlets for the People'. Most of these were either reprinted or republished a number of times: *Liberal and Tory Hypocrisy during the Nineteenth Century* (Bradford, 1901) 32 pp., *Britain's Disgrace – an Urgent Plea for Old Age Pensions* (Bradford, 1903) 32 pp., *The Misfortune of being a Workingman* (Keighley, n.d) 24 pp., *Liberalism, Toryism, a People's Party: which will save the workers?* (London, [1903?]) 20 pp., *A Peep behind the Scenes on a Board of Guardians – the Brutality of the Poor Law System* (Keighley, [1905?]) 32 pp., *Spurious Patriotism: a grateful country will never forget you* (Keighley, 1915) 20 pp. [republished as *A Grateful Country will never forget you* (Keighley, 1915) 20 pp.], *If Christ applied for Parish Relief: the doom of the Poor Law* (Bradford 1918) 16 pp., *The Centenary of the Massacre of British Workers, Peterloo, Manchester, Monday, Aug 16th 1819* (Bradford, 1919) 25 pp. Glyde also wrote most of the articles in the *Tong Pioneer of Social Reform*, 1903–8, and its successor the *Bradford Socialist Vanguard*, 1908–20, in which he published his reminiscences under the title of '32 Years' Recollections of the Labour Movement', Sep 1917–May 1918, Jan, Feb and Apr 1920. These related particularly to local personalities but he also wrote a series of articles which were published in the *Labour Pioneer* [later *Yorkshire Factory Times and Workers' Weekly Record*], 18 Aug 1921 – 6 July 1922 with the title of '30 Years' Recollections of the Socialist and Labour Movement'. These contained detailed reports of the early history of the movement including the Manningham Mills strike. Glyde's last publication was the *Bottom Dog* in 1923.

Sources: (1) MS: Correspondence from a cousin, Miss Muriel Lavington Glyde, Wellington, NZ, 14 Oct 1915, 16 May 1922 [copies in *DLB* Coll.]. (2) Other: *Memoirs and Remains of the* *late Rev. Jonathan Glyde, pastor of Horton Lane Chapel, Bradford*, ed. G.W. Conder (1858); T. Mann, *Memoirs* (1923, repr. 1967); F. Brockway, *Socialism over Sixty Years* (1946); A.L. Brown, *Our Golden Jubilee: a history of the Dudley Hill and Tong Socialist Club* (Bradford, 1950) 20 pp.; D. Torr, *Tom Mann and his Times* (1956); W. Hustwick, 'Chartists influenced this Bradford Labour Speaker', *Telegraph and Argus* [Bradford], 18 June 1960; J.F.C. Harrison, *Learning and Living, 1790–1960: a study in the history of the English adult education movement* (1961); K.D. Brown, *Labour and Unemployment 1900–1914* (Newton Abbot, 1971); J.E. Williams, 'The Leeds Corporation Strike in 1913', in *Essays in Labour History* vol. 2, ed. A. Briggs and J. Saville (1971) 70–95; J.C. Halsall, 'Jonathan Glyde', *Forster Bull.* (Bradford, May 1972) 25–7; R. Wharton, *The Girlington 'Klondike'* (Bradford, 1978) 16 pp.; personal information: Mrs S. Mitchell, Bradford; Mrs C. Tempest, Bradford, niece. Obit. *Bradford Daily Telegraph, Yorkshire Evening News, Yorkshire Observer*, 22 Aug 1923; *Yorkshire Factory Times*, 23 Aug 1923; *Bradford Pioneer*, 24 Aug 1923; *New Leader*, *4*, no. 9, 31 Aug 1923; *Bottom Dog*, no. 2 (Sep–Oct 1923); *TUC Report* (1923).

Michael Cahill

See also: †Edward Robertshaw Hartley; *Frederick William Jowett, for Independent Labour Party 1893–1914.

GRAHAM, Robert Bontine Cunninghame
see **CUNNINGHAME GRAHAM, Robert Bontine**

GRAY, John (1799–1883)
EARLY ENGLISH SOCIALIST AND CURRENCY REFORMER

Gray's own statements place his date of birth in or near 1799 and claim an education, between the ages of nine and fourteen, at Repton School, Derbyshire. Corroborative evidence for his early years is lacking, and the admittedly incomplete register of Old Reptonians contains no mention of Gray. By his own account, he entered a London manufacturing and wholesale house at the age of fourteen. Imbued with ideas for the improvement of mankind, he wrote a treatise on the means of reforming the social system; a friend recommended him to consign the manuscript to the kitchen fire. However, his elder brother, James, encouraged the continuation of his inquiries and suggested that he should acquaint himself with the opinions of Robert Owen. Some of these he heard in August 1817 at the London Tavern debates which Owen used as a platform. In August 1823 he wrote to Owen to tell him that 'the same ideas were in some instances expressed almost in the same words by you, as I had written twelve months before.' He went on to ask permission to forward in more detail his ideas. Owen's response is unknown, but later Gray was to insist that he had developed his views independently, and that they were significantly different from those of Owen.

In January 1825 Gray brought out *A Lecture on Human Happiness*, the first and most significant work he published. On this small book largely rests Gray's reputation as a pioneer of English Socialist thought. It consisted mostly of an analysis of society based upon the statistical tables in Patrick Colquhoun's *Treatise on the Wealth, Power and Resources of the British Empire* (1814) (although owing nothing to Colquhoun's social conservatism). Gray divided the population into useful and useless classes to demonstrate his view that about one third of the total were useless members of society who, by exploiting the labour of others, nevertheless enjoyed four-fifths of the wealth produced. He emphasised the injustice of a system that not only refused to recognise labour as the foundation of property but also denied the productive classes the fruits of their efforts. Apart from a discussion of Owen's views in his introduction, the only other reformer named was Abram Combe. In an appendix to Gray's pamphlet were the articles of agreement recommended by the London Co-operative Society for the formation of co-operative communities, and this, together with the remarks about Owen, identified Gray with Owenism, especially in America. His lecture was republished in Philadelphia in 1826 by members of the short-lived Valley Forge community and his ideas enjoyed a brief popularity among American utopians. In England, William Lovett was to acknowledge Gray's influence and place him in the company of Owen, William Thompson and Minter Morgan as authors of inspirational writings [Beer (1919) *1*, 184]. When H.S. Foxwell came to write his Introduction to Anton Menger's *The Right to the Whole Produce of Labour* (1899 and 1970) he described Gray's *Lecture* as 'perhaps the most striking and effective socialist manifesto of the time.'

The *Lecture on Human Happiness* was to be the first of a series, and at the end of it Gray referred to a future lecture in which he would explain his alternative arrangements for society – plans 'altogether different' from those proposed by Owen – but the failure of his publisher brought the project to an end. Gray, however, attracted by Combe's scheme for a co-operative community at Orbiston, had travelled to Scotland to give assistance. On his arrival, the weaknesses of the venture became apparent to him and he wrote *A Word of Advice to the Orbistonians* to explain his objections. Essentially, his view was that Combe's efforts, though selfless, were premature; greater preparation should have been made before opening the community and the members chosen should have been more like-minded.

Gray then turned to business and started in 1825 the *Edinburgh and Leith Advertiser*, a paper devoted to advertisements and given away until problems arose with the restrictions on unstamped newspapers. With his brother, James, he formed the firm of J. and J. Gray and converted the paper into a regular newspaper, but it soon failed. Soon after, he established the *Edinburgh, Leith, Glasgow and North British Commercial and Literary Advertiser*, another advertising paper also distributed free, which proved successful. Its title was later changed to the *North British Advertiser*, but its short editorials were on business matters and avowedly non-political. In their commercial activities, the Grays appear to have been technically innovative and astute in building up their enterprise [Timperley (1839) 857n].

In 1830 Gray issued a printed address proposing the conversion of the premises of the Edinburgh Portable Gas Light Company into a 'Printers' Hall' which would allow the use of modern machinery and house several firms of printers. This particular scheme, with its distant echo of the co-operative principle, appears to have been a failure and resulted in a spell of imprisonment for debt. This is stated in a remarkable pamphlet written by James Gray defending himself against John's attacks. According to this work, John issued a pamphlet in June 1831 – *The Case of John Gray,* no copy of which appears to survive – attacking his business partner and brother. In his reply, James questioned John's sanity and alleged that he had been bankrupt in London and left behind him a load of debt.

The quarrel seems to have been resolved by arbitration and the drafting of a new partnership agreement. The firm of J. and J. Gray prospered with the *North British Advertiser* as its most lucrative interest. At its peak in 1845 some 19,000 copies were said to have been distributed in parts of Scotland and northern England each week; in Edinburgh alone a team of sixty delivered a copy to every house with an annual rental of £12 and over. Gradually the *North British Advertiser* was eclipsed by the *Scotsman*, and on 25 July 1874 it was merged into the *Ladies' Own Journal*, a weekly which J. and J. Gray had founded in 1844 [Scott (1892) 37]. During the 1830s Gray also issued a directory of Edinburgh containing a miscellany of civic information. When in 1834 he was denied access to the Post Office lists he characteristically published as a supplement the correspondence between himself and the unhelpful official. In one of these letters Gray claimed that in the previous seven years the *North British Advertiser* had paid the Government £30,000 in stamp duties.

Gray still wished to persuade the world of his proposals for reform. Though he continued to look for fundamental changes within society, he began to emphasise the question of exchange (the basis of production and distribution) and the need for reform of the commercial system. On 18 June 1831 he wrote to Owen that he had retained some of the ideas of his *Lecture* – 'that rather virulent production' – in a book, *The Social System*, which, when he could afford it, he hoped to publish. He regretted that the London Co-operative Society was pursuing the 'phantoms of theology', and his own work paid no attention to religion, being 'purely commercial'. As early as 1827 he had privately printed a pamphlet on the means of preventing bank-note forgeries, and he reprinted it in *The Social System*, which he succeeded in bringing out in 1831. In this substantial book Gray returned to some of the views of the *Lecture on Human Happiness*, but his main concern had become a reform of the existing system of exchange. Showing some familiarity with the writings of Adam Smith, James Mill, McCulloch and Malthus (whose population theory he rejected), Gray proposed a system of commerce based on a visionary scheme of national warehouses to be administered by a beneficent chamber of commerce. The problem of production, he appeared to assume, was not great; distribution through equitable exchange was the central issue.

In an autobiographical appendix to *The Social System* he criticised Owen for paying insufficient attention to monetary questions, and in April 1832 he declined an invitation to attend the third Co-operative Congress, though offering the participants his 'most cordial approbation of your general object; and of the means you are using to attain it' [Carpenter (1832) 124]. During the congress, Owen read extracts from his *Report to the County of Lanark*, published in 1820, to show that Gray had been anticipated in his views: in reply, William Thompson and William Pare both made points in support of Gray. In September 1832 Gray again declined an invitation to the fourth Co-operative Congress, held at Liverpool, though in his letter, part of which was printed in the proceedings, he claimed he would have attended if he had been given sufficient notice.

Although *The Social System* was of some interest to reformers – Pare described it as 'masterly' – it added little to Gray's reputation and his ideas continued to evolve. By the 1840s the currency question had come to dominate his writings. He brought out a scheme for a 'Standard Bank' in 1842, under the title *An Efficient Remedy for the Distress of Nations*. A certain crankiness became more evident in this work: reviews of the *Social System* were reprinted with his comments, and he devoted a whole chapter to controverting an article (by T. Perronet Thompson) in the *Westminster Review* that had linked him with St Simonism. He also commented, for the most part unfavourably, on the six points of the People's Charter. On his old premise that 'the foundation of all property is labour', he opposed universal suffrage because it would allow those who had not laboured for property to regulate those who had. The proposal for the secret ballot was, Gray wrote, 'un-English, mean, pitiful, despicable'. It was a book without influence, but this did not deter its author from producing another volume in 1848. In the form of eight *Lectures on the Nature and Use of Money*, Gray again developed his programme which he attempted to force on an indifferent public opinion by large-scale free distribution. He sent a copy to every MP, forty peers, a variety of newspapers and periodicals and a number of individuals, including Prince Albert, Carlyle, Dickens, and Ernest Jones. As well as giving away 1200 copies of his book, Gray resorted to offering a hundred guineas to whoever could refute its contents. He had issued a similar challenge to *The Times* in the previous year, again without obtaining the publicity he wanted. In an appendix to the *Lectures* he stated that many years ago he had given his attention to schemes for 'co-operative communities, hives for wingless bees, and the like' and had satisfied himself of 'the injustice, impracticability, and, in a word, futility, of all such combinations' [Gray (1848) 281–2]. Ironically, it was only when he had been associated with these early ideas that Gray had the influence he later craved. However, he had apparently not lost all contacts with the Owenites of the 1820s, for he printed in the *Lectures* a letter of March 1848 from William Pare, in which Pare encouraged him to serve France by giving the new government a reformed monetary system. Gray sent an outline of his scheme to the head of the provisional government, and received no reply. In April 1853 he sent Gladstone, then the Chancellor of the Exchequer, a printed letter on the question of newspaper duties. This gave numerous details of his publishing activities, but contained nothing of wider political interest.

Why he gave up his propaganda for currency reform is unknown. Perhaps public indifference defeated him. He had reached an intellectually isolated position. He was estranged from political radicalism, and also far outside the economic orthodoxy of his day. Such response as he had stimulated was unsympathetic; J.S. Mill, for example, in the second (1849) edition of his *Principles* referred in a footnote to the *Lectures on the Nature and Use of Money* as a work pervaded by transparent fallacy. But Mill was uncomprehending or ignorant of the early writings in particular, for Gray was one of the first political economists to develop a theory of labour exploitation and to enunciate, however incompletely, a theory of capitalist crisis. In a *Contribution to the Critique of Political Economy* (1859), Marx acknowledged that Gray had, in *The Social System*, been the first to set forth systematically the theory that labour-time directly measured money; but he added that by developing his theories in terms of bourgeois reform he had become tangled up in 'flagrant absurdities' [Marx (1971 ed.) 85]. Otherwise Gray was hardly noticed. He fell into obscurity in his own lifetime, and G.J. Holyoake writing in 1875 regarded him as a figure of the past:

> He was a well-meaning, disinterested writer . . . His books never sold, nor could they be given away; and there is still a stock at two places in London where they can be had now for asking, and those who apply are looked upon with favour [Holyoake (1875) 367–8].

When rediscovered by historians such as Foxwell and Lowenthal, Gray was classified somewhat misleadingly as a 'Ricardian Socialist'. The revival of Socialism in England at the end of the nineteenth century led to the study of its origins, and pioneer writers like Max Beer and G.D.H. Cole surmised that Gray had died around 1850. In fact, as Janet Kimball showed in a published doctoral dissertation, Gray lived until 1883. Little is known about the last thirty years of his life, but it may be assumed that he continued to make a good living from his publishing interests.

His private life, too, is shadowy, though he was apparently twice married. A monument in St Cuthbert's Parish Churchyard, Edinburgh, records the death of Caroline Mordaunt, his first wife on 30 January 1831, and mentions a second wife, Jane Renny. She and a married daughter survived him. It has been established also that he sold an estate near Edinburgh in 1866, having moved to Church Road in the Upper Norwood district of London. It was there that he died on 26 April 1883, aged eighty-four. Apart from a formal announcement of his death in the *North British Daily Mail* (28 Apr 1883), the *North British Advertiser* and the *South London Press* (5 May), no obituary notices have been located. He left a personal estate of £14,831 in his will.

Writings: *A Lecture on Human Happiness* . . . (1825; repr. 1931; German ed. with Introduction by G. Adler, Leipzig, 1907); *A Word of Advice to the Orbistonians on the Principles which ought to regulate their Present Proceedings. 29 June, 1826* ([Edinburgh?], 1826) P.; *An Address to the Printers of Edinburgh* . . . (Edinburgh, [1830]) 40 pp.; *The Case of John Gray* ([Edinburgh, 1831?]) P.; *The Social System: a treatise on the principle of exchange* (Edinburgh, 1831; repr. Clifton, NJ, 1973); *An Efficient Remedy for the Distress of Nations* (Edinburgh, 1842); *The Currency Question: a rejected letter to the editor of "The Times" . . . challenge to "The Times" to discuss the subject for the sum of five hundred guineas* (Edinburgh, 1847) 23 pp.; *Lectures on the Nature and Use of Money: delivered before the members of the "Edinburgh Philosophical Institution" during the months of February and March, 1848* (Edinburgh, 1848); *Edinburgh Monetary Reform Pamphlet, No. 1: committee of enquiry into the validity of the monetary principle advocated in Gray's lectures* . . . (Edinburgh, 1849).

Sources: (1) MS: Owen Correspondence, Co-operative Union Ltd, Manchester; Add. MSS, Gladstone Papers, CCCXC 44,675, BL. (2) Other: James Gray, *Reply to "The Case of John*

Gray" (Edinburgh, 1831) 23 pp.; *Proceedings of the Third Co-operative Congress*... ed. W. Carpenter (1832); *Proceedings of the Fourth Co-operative Congress*... ed. W. Pare (Manchester, 1832) 44 pp.; *Gray's Annual Directory*... (Edinburgh, 1832–8); C.H. Timperley, *A Dictionary of Printers and Printing with the Progress of Literature Ancient and Modern*... (1839); G.J. Holyoake, *The History of Co-operation in England: its literature and its advocates 1: 1812-1844* (1875); W. Norrie, *Edinburgh Newspapers Past and Present* (Earlston, 1891) 48 pp.; J.W. Scott, 'A Bibliography of Edinburgh Periodical Literature', *Scottish Notes and Queries* 6, no. 3 (Aug 1892) 35–7; A. Menger, *The Right to the Whole Produce of Labour* (English trans. 1899, with an Introduction by H.S. Foxwell; repr. NY, 1970); E. Lowenthal, *The Ricardian Socialists* (NY, 1911); M. Beer, *History of British Socialism* 2 vols (1919); *Monumental Inscriptions in St Cuthbert's Churchyard, Edinburgh* ed. J.B. Paul (Scottish Record Society, Edinburgh, 1919); A. Gray, *The Socialist Tradition: Moses to Lenin* (1947 ed.); J. Kimball, *The Economic Doctrines of John Gray – 1799–1883* (Washington, 1948); A.E. Bestor, *Backwoods Utopias: the sectarian and Owenite phases of communitarian Socialism in America: 1663–1829* (Philadelphia, 1950; 2nd ed. rev. and enlarged, Philadelphia, 1970); G.D.H. Cole, *Socialist Thought: the forerunners, 1789–1850* (1953); M. Blaug, *Ricardian Economics: a historical study* (New Haven, 1958); J.F.C. Harrison, *Robert Owen and the Owenites in Britain and America* (1969); K. Marx, *A Contribution to the Critique of Political Economy* (English trans. 1971, with an Introduction by M. Dobb); R.G. Garnett, *Co-operation and the Owenite Socialist Communities in Britain, 1825–45* (Manchester, 1972); biographical information: W.B. Downing, Repton School; R.P. Sturges, Loughborough Univ.; N. Thompson, Dept of Economic History, Univ. College of Swansea.

DAVID E. MARTIN

See also: †Abram COMBE; Robert OWEN; †William PARE.

GROSER, St John Beverley (John) (1890–1966)

CHRISTIAN SOCIALIST

John, as he was habitually called, was born on 23 June 1890 at Beverley, a cattle station in West Australia. He was the youngest son of missionary parents: his father, Thomas Eaton Groser, had worked among the North American Indians, and his mother, Phoebe Wainwright, in Labrador. John's education during the first fifteen years of his life consisted more in learning the outdoor life of the station hands than in academic study. So when his father took him to England along with his two elder brothers in 1905, he had to spend three years at school (Ellesmere College in Shropshire, a Woodard foundation, High Anglican) before going on to be prepared for ordination at Mirfield (the Community of the Resurrection); he also had a year at Leeds University. His love of Britain and his acceptance of her imperial role were reinforced by the charm of upper-class life in a traditional style, as he enjoyed it in holidays spent with two devout ladies on their Hertfordshire estate. 'I just took Imperialism for granted', he wrote forty years later [*People and Politics* 30]. In spite of socialistic teaching at Mirfield, he seems to have been unaware of the obverse of the imperial mission. But this defect was remedied when in 1914 he became curate of a dockside parish in Newcastle upon Tyne. Here he also discovered that most of the wealthy and powerful had no desire to alter the condition of the poor except by charitable works. This became especially clear to the young curate when he tried to interest local industrialists in a scheme for apprenticeships. The police, too, warned him 'to be careful', and his bishop rebuked him for concerning himself with the physical and economic condition of his parishioners instead of concentrating on saving their souls.

The First World War was an even more disturbing experience. Groser served in France as an army chaplain for three years from 1915. He believed that if he had not been invalided home with wounds in 1918 (he was then awarded the Military Cross), he would again have been in trouble with his superiors; for he was openly admitting a growing want of faith in the Allied cause and was beginning to take the view that the war was caused by capitalism. After an unsatisfactory year with the Church of England Men's Society, he accepted the curacy of St Winnow in Cornwall. On leave in December 1917 he had married Mary, the daughter of the priest of that parish, Father Marc Antony Bucknall. He spent two years in Cornwall, studying Socialist literature and endeavouring to settle his position in regard to the social and economic structure of Britain. His brother-in-law Jack Bucknall, who was assistant to Conrad Noel at Thaxted, introduced the Grosers to Noel and to the Catholic Crusade. The Crusade was broadly Marxist, condemning the capitalist system and the clergy who accepted it.

Groser was much influenced by Noel's personality and ideals (though not blindly: of one of his Crusade leaflets he remarked, 'a bit unbalanced, but still pretty splendid, don't you think?' [Brill (1971) 14]). Groser's theology was not original; it was based on the thought of Maurice, Gore, Stewart Headlam, William Temple, and Noel. What was individual was the ardour with which he preached and practised the 'total interdependence between theology and politics' – or Socialism. By the early 1920s he was a convinced Socialist, and in 1922 he was happy to accept the invitation of C.G. Langdon to assist him at St Michael's, Poplar, where Jack Bucknall was already curate. Groser arrived there shortly after Lansbury and the other Poplar Guardians had come out of prison. He was, of course, entirely on their side, and Lansbury and he became lifelong friends.

The two curates organised open-air meetings, where Groser presented Jesus as a rebel against the rich and powerful and against Imperialism. He spoke on behalf of workers on strike or locked out; he spoke at mass demonstrations in Hyde Park and Trafalgar Square, advocating Home Rule for Ireland and for India, and he was much in demand as a speaker on behalf of Labour candidates for Parliament. He was a thoroughly 'political' priest, and a popular leader, relied on for support and advice. Langdon, however, did not approve of some of his curates' activities; there was continuing friction, and in August 1924 he gave them notice of dismissal. Groser then conducted a spirited correspondence with the Bishop of London, Winnington-Ingram, who had given Langdon 'leave to sack us' – although according to Groser the vicar had 'no right' to do this – and had forthwith departed for a month's holiday on the inaccessible island of Mull (the Bishop of Stepney had also gone out of town for a month). Groser writes of Winnington-Ingram's 'injustice', and asks whether he wants to 'drive us from the Church of England into schism'; he adds that he and Bucknall have strong support in the parish [letter quoted in Brill op.cit., 41-2].

In the event, Langdon moved to St Matthew's, City Road, and in the spring of 1925 his place was taken by Kenneth Ashcroft, like his curates an Anglo-Catholic and a Labour sympathiser; but later there was to be considerable friction between Ashcroft and his curates. During the events of 1925–6 which led up to the General Strike and during the strike itself, Groser conducted a vigorous campaign on the side of the workers. He was clear that there was to be 'a major attack on their standard of life' and that the first target of this attack was to be, as so often before, the miners [*Politics and Persons*, 40]. He was speaking on their behalf in early 1926, and during the General Strike itself he shared platforms with Labour leaders and trade unionists, and also advised the local strike committee. At the end of the strike he was injured, along with others, when the police made a baton charge on a peaceable crowd of workers outside Poplar Town Hall; several men were arrested, but were discharged by the magistrate the next day, largely as a result of Groser's evidence.

In consequence of all this political activity his licence was withdrawn. He resigned his curacy in 1927. During the next year the Bishops of London and Stepney struggled to find 'the right niche' for him, although some of Groser's parishioners doubted their zeal in the business [Brill, 53]. He took various temporary jobs, and his wife and children went for a time to live with her father in Cornwall. In September 1928 Groser agreed to become curate-in-charge of Christ Church, Watney Street, Stepney, a church which was scheduled for closure and demolition. For a year he worked at reconstructing a congregation and organising the sort of religious and social activities he had carried on in Poplar. He was so successful that in 1929 he was offered the living.

The parish was as much of a challenge as St Michael's. The workers' homes were for the most part over-crowded, insanitary and dilapidated. Vandalism and theft were commonplace – and the church buildings and the parish hall were not exempt, a fact which distressed Groser and apparently surprised him.

He continued to shoot an occasional arrow at his Bishops: in February 1929 the Suffragan Bishop of Stepney refused his request that church halls should be used for the lodging and feeding of hunger marchers; on the whole, Groser won that fight. In June 1931 his target was his old antagonist, Winnington-Ingram, the Bishop of London, who had made a statement at the London diocesan conference about the unemployed. Groser wrote 'to protest as emphatically as possible against your statement'; and in relation to the report of the Government's Economy Committee, the May Report, he wrote, 'that you as Bishop of this Diocese should go out of your way publicly to call upon your clergy to "back it up" is beyond endurance. You say that it is the duty of the Church to keep up the Soul of the Nation and yet you ask that my parishioners, who are unemployed through no fault of their own, should be driven below subsistence level. Is this to restore their independence? The Soul of a Nation is shown in its regard for its poorer members. May our Lord Jesus Christ, the Lover of the Poor, help you to see Him in them. I remain, yours obediently in Christ, St John B. Groser' [Brill, 52]. Groser was never afraid of strong words, or of goading his superiors, in a righteous cause.

In the Whitechapel and St George's by-election of December 1930 Noel requested Catholic Crusade support for the Communist candidate Harry Pollitt, but the London group of Catholic Crusaders, most of whom worshipped at Watney Street, decided to back the Labour Party candidate James Hall (who was elected). A number of the group resigned from the Crusade (in some people's view this was the beginning of its demise), and Groser and his Watney Street group signified a general reconsideration of their attitude towards the Soviet Union and the CPGB. After he had left the Catholic Crusade Groser became active in the old Christian Socialist League, and under his leadership a strong and influential branch was established at Christ Church, Watney Street. Among its members were Anglicans, Nonconformists, Quakers and Roman Catholics. An offshoot of this branch was the Christian Arts Left which helped to develop new ideas for posters and banners for the general Labour movement. The branch was for the most part in abeyance during the Second World War, but it had a revival after 1945, when for a time Groser was its chairman.

In 1932–3 the group carried out the Christ Church campaign for Socialism. They were already giving practical support to the Hunger Marchers, support which they continued during the 1930s, and they were active in advising and organising against Mosley's Blackshirts.

In the course of the 1930s Groser was active politically in a number of causes, including Indian freedom, the Spanish Republican Government and the Basque refugee children; but one iniquity of capitalism almost obsessed him: the Means Test. In an article in the *Daily Herald* [20 Mar 1934] he gave detail of the finances of some families in his parish suffering under the test, and in the same year he preached in St Paul's Cathedral a passionate sermon against it. Apart from the physical hardship, the chief evil he saw was the breaking of the spirit of the victims, which he regarded as one of the aims of the ruling class (if not an admitted one), since they feared a revolt of the workers. As he said to a huge street audience, 'They [the authorities] don't want you to feel that you are persons with the right to make real decisions for yourselves. They want you to feel that you have no will of your own, for they are afraid of what will happen if you begin to act as persons' [*Politics and Persons*, 63]. In 1932 he was nominated by the Labour Party as a co-opted member of the local committee which adjudicated on applications for poor relief. For two years he fought hard against the Conservative majority's policy towards applicants, a policy which he regarded as punitive and also arbitrary. In 1934 Labour gained control of the LCC, and Groser was elected chairman of the local public assistance committee, a post in which he was not, however, wholly successful.

Groser was responsible for starting in 1938 a scheme of free legal advice for tenants, which operated from his vicarage. By 1939 this service had developed into the Stepney Tenants' Defence League, with Groser as president. He wrote of it in 1949: 'It was over housing that we fought some of our fiercest battles between 1937 and 1939 . . . I sometimes think that, if the war had not come when it did, that revolt would have been the prelude to the overthrow of the Government. The Means Test had already done much to destroy family life, but this growing menace bid fair to destroy home life altogether. For a working man to lose his house is to lose everything' [*Politics and Persons*, 70]. When a group of tenants resisted eviction in June 1939, and six were arrested, the Mayor and the Bishop of Stepney, Rabbi Brodie and Groser persuaded the landlord to negotiate; this was only one of a series of similar mediations. Groser worked in close co-operation with local Communists in the Stepney Tenants' Defence League. In his autobiography he wrote warmly of their contribution: 'I cannot praise too highly the work which Tubby Rosen and Michael Shapiro, two Communists, put into it till the war came and then we found ourselves in different camps . . .' [ibid., 71]. It was the Communist Party's change of line in the early weeks of the war that started the breach between them. Groser felt increasingly that the CP were using the Tenants' League for their own political purposes, and he formally resigned in February 1940 [Brill (1971) 104].

The Munich agreement of 1938 horrified Groser. With others he prepared and the Christian Socialist League sent out, a manifesto which condemned Chamberlain's policy and the failure of the Church authorities to give a lead against it. In a private letter of February 1939 Groser was even angrier: 'I accuse Mr Chamberlain, I accuse Lord Halifax. I accuse the Archbishop of Canterbury [Lang]: that is specific, heathen, Christian laymen, dignitaries of the Church, etc. of consistently furthering a policy which is contrary to Christian principles: . . . [as for] those who are in control of our national destinies . . . I believe they are idolatrous and blasphemous and that even people like the Archbishop of York [Temple] are failing us in this critical situation . . . We are not even given the chance of deciding what we shall do by the leaders of the State, and the leaders of the Church equate their decisions with the will of God' [quoted Brill, 188-9]. It was this view of British governmental actions which led Groser to say of the Russo-German pact, 'We believed that the Russians only signed that agreement when they had been persuaded by our past diplomacy and our present vacillation that Great Britain and France were willing to turn Hitler eastwards again as they had done at Munich' [*Politics and Persons*, 77].

Of Communism in general Groser could not finally approve, although he worked with individual CP members on various occasions. In chapter 5 of *Politics and Persons*, headed 'The Appeal of Communism', he set out the arguments for and against, introduced by the proposition that 'Modern Communism must be approached sympathetically . . . It is not easy to find in modern history a parallel to the readiness for self-sacrifice and devotion to a cause shown by members of the Communist Party'. Earlier in the book he had pointed to 'the deep gulf between them [Communists] and the mass of the British working class, who have never been able to accept their doctrine that the end justifies the means' [p. 77]. Communism is, moreover, incompatible with Christian belief. Groser put his trust preferably in British Labour politics, 'that peculiar democratic Christian tradition which is the better way and the hope of the world' [p. 163].

In the first period of air raids on London, September 1940 to May 1941, Groser was indefatigable in pressing for large-scale evacuation and for the provision of more than short-term accommodation for the homeless in rest centres. He also organised food and recreation for the people using the air raid shelters in his parish: 'it was said that he was the real government of Stepney' [*TLS*, 6 Aug 1971]. In April 1941 his Church and vicarage were both seriously damaged by bombs, as was the Church of St George's-in-the-East. Groser was looking after this parish in the absence of its incumbent, and he moved into its rectory, which was hardly damaged.

In 1945 he invited four Brothers of the Society of St Francis to live in his parish and help the coloured residents. Six years later he helped to found the Stepney Coloured People's Association and was its president from 1951 to 1954.

1945 was a year in which he was more concerned than ever with housing. He was the founder, and an active member of the Stepney Reconstruction Group, and a member also, succeeding Archbishop Cyril Garbett, of the Government's Central Housing Advisory Committee. He also served on a number of religious bodies: in 1942 he was associated with Archbishop William Temple in the Religion and Life Movement, and with Alfred Blunt, Bishop of Bradford, in the Council of Clergy and Ministers for Common Ownership; from 1943 to 1945 he served on the Church Assembly's Commission which published the report *Towards the Conversion of England*. In 1947 he spent two months in Germany supporting the work of Christian Reconstruction in Europe (later Christian Aid). He held the posts of Rural Dean of Stepney (1945 to 1956) and honorary chaplain to the Bishop of London. These were changed days for the turbulent priest. From a rebel against authority, with confidence in the working classes and hope for the future, he became something of a *laudator temporis acti*.

In *Politics and Persons*, published in 1949, he lamented the decay of Christian belief and of morals. 'I believe,' he wrote, 'that deep down there is still something sound in the common people of Britain. It is not too late to arrest the process of decay which is destructive of all social life . . . the lack of faith in one another, the subterfuges, the lies, the low standards of morals, the black markets, the bad and shoddy work, the slackening on the job . . .' [p. 172]. This change within him was perhaps also symbolised by his accepting the headship of St Katharine in Ratcliffe. This twelfth century royal foundation in East London, demolished in 1825 to build St Katharine's Dock, had carried on in a subdued manner some religious, charitable and educational functions on a site in Regent's Park – this until 1913–14, when these functions ceased and the buildings were sold for secular uses. St Katharine's however, then returned to the East End in the new shape of a maternity and child welfare clinic set up in Poplar under royal patronage. This was taken over by the local authority under the National Health Service Act of 1946; but influential people had become interested in the idea of establishing St Katharine's as a religious community and a centre for training men and women in social work, promoting educational and cultural activities, evangelising in the East End, and helping the aged. The centre was to serve Stepney and Poplar, so St James's, Ratcliffe, seemed to be an appropriate site. Groser was appointed Warden in 1948, and immediately started work.

St Katharine's soon became a centre for conferences, courses, lectures, retreats. Staff and accommodation were provided for the Stepney Old People's Welfare Association, of which Groser became chairman, a post he held for the rest of his life. He was also chairman for life of the Stepney Old People's Housing Association, which built flatlets specially designed for the elderly.

One of Groser's ambitions was to involve the clergy with industrial workers – as early as 1930 he had asked the Bishop of London to train priests for work in factories. Nothing was done until in 1961 a scheme was drawn up for deacons and ordinands to have a year's training under Groser in industrial problems. Groser concentrated his attention on organising research and study: yearly courses were arranged for newly-ordained clergy and theological students; they were addressed by active trade unionists and by Labour MPs. There were annual courses for sixth-formers from public schools, and a WEA centre was established. Activities at St Katharine's increased every year, and Groser started or took part in most of them. In 1960 he was, furthermore, involved with the Board for Social Responsibility of the Church Assembly, whose chairman was Sir John Wolfenden.

In September 1958 he became ill with a threatened thrombosis and spent some weeks in hospital. He retired from St Katharine's in 1962, and after visiting their son Tony in New Zealand he and his wife lived at Walnut Tree Cottage, Watlington, Oxfordshire, where he gardened and played golf, took services, and not infrequently preached or lectured in various places or went to London for meetings of the bodies on which he still sat. He died on 19 March 1966, and left effects valued at £999. His funeral was at Watlington Parish Church on 25 March 1966 and he was buried in the churchyard there.

John Groser was a man of extraordinary vitality and energy, and remarkable gifts. His excellent physical co-ordination made him enjoy performing manual work of the most varied kinds, skilled and unskilled, from weaving (he wove vestments and altar cloths for more than one of his churches), carpentering (making hen-houses, for example), and painting, to clearing gutters. It also made him an outstanding games player and athlete – soccer, rugger, cricket, fives, running – he excelled at them all, and at indoor games too, including chess, billiards, bridge and shove ha'penny.

He was a striking figure, with his fine physique, his upright carriage, graceful movements, and strongly marked features – the face of a bishop or archbishop. (It is no surprise to learn that he was chosen by the director Hoellinger to play the part of Becket in the film of Eliot's *Murder in the Cathedral*.) But Groser's wishes did not incline towards such dignities. In spite of the position of prestige he reached in the post-war years, he remained the Socialist priest.

His impact on his time was notable: he was a strong stimulus to Socialist thought and activity in the Church of England; and if he is forgotten today, it is probably because he exerted so personal an influence. He was an inspiration to followers and audiences. It might be a congregation attending his celebration of the mass – in which, we are told, he was totally rapt, oblivious of the external world. Or it might be as speaker, agitator, activist that he carried his audience with him; or as participator in discussion. In all these roles it seems that Groser needed to play the leading rather than a secondary part. He needed, furthermore, to feel that he was in the right. These needs were perhaps in part the cause of his difficulties in the 1920s. In the thirties some of the young people who belonged to his church and youth groups showed a degree of ambivalence towards him, and some of the colleagues who admired him were not blind to his faults. Kenneth Brill writes of 'his terrible need to win, to have his own way and to be appreciated by those whose opinion he valued. He found it hard to listen for long to an opposing argument; he was not good at delegation; his curates, lieutenants and deputies had a rough time and he notably failed to find and train a successor to carry on his work at St Katharine's' [Brill, 94]. This is an assessment which not all who knew him well would accept. The strain of the war years had taken a great deal out of him both physically and mentally – hence, as many of his friends thought, and as he himself was prepared to admit in his last years, the 'mistake' of St Katharine's. But there were a number of matters he felt not completely at home with in the 1950s. When, for example, following the Khrushchev secret speech in 1956, the basis of division between the Socialist Christian League and other bodies crumbled, and permitted a merger under Tom Driberg's chairmanship into the Christian Socialist movement in 1960, Groser was soon unhappy with both the influence of Donald Soper and the Movement's insistence on close ties with the Labour Party, and he resigned. He always believed that organised Christian Socialism should be independent of party dogma; and it was his own cragginess and independence of spirit that was his outstanding characteristic. His part in the Labour movement was that of prophet and teacher. He was a marvellous propagandist, was capable of extraordinary empathy with ordinary people, and caught the imagination of the Cockney masses he served. His name among the speakers was sufficient to fill any hall in the East End, but as he once said 'the workers would do anything for me except go to Church' [letter from J.T. Desormeaux, 20 Nov 1979].

Mary Groser shared her husband's beliefs and interests and made his activities possible by her devoted support. She was self-effacing in public, but her good judgment and her gentle friendliness were admired by all who knew the family. She was a musician, organist both at Christ Church and at St Katharine's. But her place was mostly in the home, which was constantly overflowing with visitors and colleagues, for whom she catered and to whom she listened, sympathising, advising and helping. She had also the job of mediating between this perpetual inflow of people and the home life of her children. The eldest, Michael, born in October 1918, was educated at the Mercers' School in Holborn (to which he got a scholarship) and Leeds University, where he took a first in English. When the Second World War broke out he left Mirfield, where he was training for the priesthood, and became a coal miner. Afterwards he took up stone carving, and professional church singing. He married Eileen Harris in 1951 and they have four children. The second child, Peggy, born in January 1920, died in her seventh year. Antony, born in March 1921, was debarred by poor eyesight from military service in the Second World War. He became an actor, appearing in London and Stratford, and he and his wife Joanna were for several years in the 1950s leading members of the Perth Repertory Company. In 1958 they emigrated to New Zealand, where Antony became a Director of Broadcasting and Television. They have a married daughter, and a son, Timothy, who entered the Diplomatic Service. The youngest Groser, Gillian, born in March 1929, is a musician, like her mother. She was educated at St Paul's School for Girls and the Guildhall School of Music and Drama, and then held several teaching posts. In 1958 she married David Platt, in 1971 the vicar of St Katherine's, North Hammersmith, now (1979) of All Saints, Woodham, Woking, Surrey; they have four children. After her husband's death Mary Groser lived with the Platts until her death in 1970.

Writings: *Politics and Persons*, with a foreword by R.H. Tawney (1949).

Sources: (1) MS: some correspondence in Conrad Noel Coll., MRC. (2) Other: P. Piratin, *Our Flag stays Red* (1948); R. Woodfield, *Catholicism: Humanist and democratic* (1954); R. Groves, *Conrad Noel and the Thaxted Movement* (1967); *For Christ and the People*, ed. M.B. Reckitt (1968); *John Groser: East London priest* ed. K. Brill (1971); personal information: T. Carthy, Thaxted; Rev. Canon E. Charles, Hitchin; J.T. Desormeaux, Harlow; Norah Neal, London; S.P. Piratin, London; Rev. and Mrs D. Platt, Woking, son-in-law and daughter. OBIT. *Times*, 26 Mar 1966.

KENNETH BRILL
MARGARET 'ESPINASSE

See also: †Conrad le Despenser Roden NOEL.

HAMPSON, Walter ('Casey') (1866?–1932)
SOCIALIST PROPAGANDIST AND MUSICIAN

Some of the information that follows comes from a series of autobiographical sketches by Hampson entitled 'Reminiscences of "Casey"' which appeared in the ILP weekly *Forward* from 28 March to 31 October 1931 (except 24 October). In the early years of the twentieth century, when signing letters to the local press he used the pen name 'Casey'; 'The name stuck to me', he wrote, 'so I finally adopted it.'

According to his own account, Walter Hampson was born in 1864 in Coombe Hospital, Dublin, and his mother's maiden name was Cahill. There are two entries in the Dublin register which could record his birth, but which differ in some detail; both give the year as 1866. His mother belonged to a family of fishermen, and when Walter was a small boy she sold fish in Dublin, tramping the streets with a fishbasket on her head. Walter's father spent his childhood as a sweep's climbing boy; in adult life he was 'a kind of jack of all trades', and something of a nomad. In Dublin Walter first attended the Christian Brothers' school, and when he and his father settled in Stockport, Cheshire, he went first to a Catholic school – from which he ran away because of the brutality of the master – and then to a nonconformist school. William

Hampson soon began training his son in his own childhood trade of climbing boy. The horrors of this occupation Walter described in faithful detail. When he was still only eight years old he began to work with his father. He rose between 3 and 4 a.m., climbed chimneys until 8 a.m., and after a hurried breakfast went to school.

He learnt to play the violin, and had a few lessons from an elderly teacher; after several months of practising he began his musical career by accompanying marionettes. His chief desire in his early teens was to escape from chimney sweeping, and he ran away from home seven times. He spent one year in Canada but returned to England in response to appeals from his mother and sister. In 1885 he found employment at Whittingham Asylum near Preston; and it seems that it was here he became aware of his lack of education, and began reading. Besides some major Greek and Latin authors, he read Dickens, Thackeray, Carlyle, Darwin and Huxley. He married in 1886, in Stockport, and his wife, Frances Emily, returned with him to the asylum as an attendant. They left Whittingham before the birth of their first child, a daughter, in September 1887, and for several years Hampson lived in Stockport, where he resumed his dual role of violinist and chimney sweep.

But he was determined to take up the serious study of the violin. After being appointed leader of the Stockport Theatre Royal Orchestra he became a pupil of Leon Veerman, formerly of the Hallé Orchestra, with whom he studied for over five years. He was now fully occupied, taking lessons and practising, rehearsing and playing in the theatre. His wages, initially 18*s* a week, never rose above 23*s*, but some married men in similar positions were getting only 7*s* a week; the need for a trade union was apparent. In 1893 the Musicians' Union was formed in Manchester by J.B. Williams. In his 'Reminiscences' Hampson says that 'my old friend Harrison and I formed the first branch of the Musicians' Union in Stockport, and I was unanimously elected President.' Hampson played in other orchestras in the North, and he also began taking private pupils. He published his own illustrated violin tutor *Hampson's Violin School*, and his longing for a Stradivarius was finally satisfied in the 1920s when the Countess of Warwick gave him one from the Warwick Collection.

It is not possible to date Hampson's definite conversion to Socialism, but it may have been during the period when he was teaching at the Xavierian Brothers' school in Manchester. He was greatly influenced by Keir Hardie and was fascinated by the writings of Robert Blatchford. The utopias of Bacon, More, Morris, Bellamy and Robert Owen as well as the writings of the Fabians, Marx and Achille Loria helped to clarify his thinking. He joined the ILP probably before 1900; and after the turn of the century he was closely linked with the Socialist movement.

Hampson's political views and his membership of the Musicians' Union and the ILP often caused him to be victimised. At the Theatre Royal, Manchester, the orchestra agreed not to take part in an extra rehearsal, but only Hampson adhered to the agreement; he was dismissed. In those days the Union could not generally afford strike or victimisation pay. Hampson found work at a Variety Palace in Salford, but he was again dismissed when the conductor saw him give someone a copy of Hyndman's *Unrest in India*. Undaunted, while he was later playing at the Albert Hall, Southport, he spoke in public and delivered leaflets attacking local landowners. On one occasion, when Lloyd George was addressing a gathering in the Albert Hall, he assisted a group of suffragettes to disrupt the meeting. The militants were led by Mrs Baines and Patricia Woodcock 'and an Amazonian Greek goddess' who floored a policeman attempting her arrest. Hampson managed, however, to retain his orchestral post until the time of the Manchester North-West by-election in April 1908, when Dan Irving of the SDP stood against W. Joynson-Hicks and Winston Churchill. Hampson, a friend of Irving's, paraded the streets of Manchester as a sandwich man with boards bearing the slogan 'Fiddle and I speak for Socialism'. He was dismissed from the orchestra as a result.

In 1905 Lord Stanley, the Postmaster-General, in his official reply to the postmen's plea for an increase in their average weekly wage of £1, spoke of 'this continual bloodsucking on the part of public servants.' Hampson was spurred by this letter to defend the workers in a pamphlet entitled *Who are the Bloodsuckers? With a list of the Principal Ones*. In the form of a conversation in dialect between 'Casey' and 'Philbin' it examined the ownership of land, annual rental, and the manner in which landed families, including the Stanleys, had acquired their property. The pamphlet was reprinted in the *Postal Workers' Journal*; and when Lord Stanley was defending his Westhoughton seat at the 1906 general election, postal workers came from many parts of the country to work for his defeat. (He lost the seat to the LRC candidate, W. Tyson Wilson.) By 1905 Hampson had evolved his own brand of Socialist instruction – propaganda with and through music. The *Clarion* announced on 22 September that 'the Stockport fiddler and humorist' was about to take the road in October with a small group of musicians, giving concerts and 'Socialist lantern lectures'. Casey's distinctive form of propaganda soon became popular at Socialist meetings all over the country. 'Everything he said or played was effective material for Socialist propaganda' [Paton (1935) 300].

Hampson was a fluent writer and contributed many articles to Labour papers. Some of his earliest appeared in the *Stockport Herald*, a monthly Labour news-sheet edited by Fred Plant and distributed by local activists. Unfortunately only one sheet from one issue survives – No. 41, July 1907 – and this makes no mention of Hampson. In 1907, however, he became a regular contributor to the *Labour Leader*. Some of his articles were again in the form of dialect conversations between 'Casey' and 'Philbin' on varied themes, for example 'Philosophy' or 'Curran Topics'. He also wrote some short stories for the paper. Many of his pieces were a mixture of travel description, reminiscences of his youth, and musical topics. For these *Labour Leader* articles he was at first paid 5*s* a week, rising to £1 by the 1920s. In the summer of 1908 he was asked to write occasional articles for the *Sunday Chronicle*; he sent in four, but found them so drastically cut that he wrote no more. The *Chronicle* later offered to take twenty-seven articles a year, at six times the amount he was paid by the *Labour Leader*, but apparently he declined.

Until 1913 Casey was usually provided with an accompanist by the organisation which made the booking, an arrangement which was not very satisfactory. In the spring of that year he began to travel with his own accompanist, Dolly Pickard, then a girl of fourteen. It is not certain who she was or how she came to be his accompanist; but Casey did have a musician friend W. Pickard, who wrote some of the melodies for *Hampson's Violin School*, and Dolly may have been his daughter. During this itinerant phase of Casey's life his wife and children lived in Stockport. According to Mrs Muriel Nicol, a friend of the family, several of the children were musical.

Hampson's conception of Socialism did not recognise party divisions, and he avoided involvement in the internal controversies of the ILP. In 1907 he canvassed and delivered leaflets for Victor Grayson in the Colne Valley by-election, and in November 1910 announced that he had played on platforms for Hardie, Shaw, Snowden, Hyndman, Tillett, Will Gee and Robert Blatchford; 'for fiddle and I are at the service of every *Socialist* organisation.'

The Burston School Strike of April 1914 won Hampson's active support: he played at the school during that month and he wrote a pamphlet on the strike, the proceeds of which were to go to the strike funds; he also devoted some of his articles in the *Labour Leader* to the continuing struggle. His concern was not only for Tom and Annie Higdon, who had been evicted from their school as a result of their support for the agricultural labourers, but also for the village families threatened with eviction from their homes because their children had come out on strike in support of the Higdons. In February 1916 a London Trade Unionists' Committee was instrumental in arranging for the Higdons, with some of the school children and their parents, to visit London and attend four large meetings. Hampson and Dolly were in London for the visit, and played at a meeting on 22 February chaired by Dr Alfred Salter, in Bermondsey Town Hall.

Like many of his ILP colleagues Hampson opposed the First World War. He was too old for conscription. One of his sons had at first been a conscientious objector; having refused military service, he received a certificate of exemption in April 1916 and at once attested. Another son was also a conscientious objector; in May 1916 he had just been released from Chester Castle, 'and he hops it to the hills'; so 'we've now a soldier and an outlaw in our group' [*Labour Leader*, 11 May 1916]. From November 1914 he and some other musicians regularly played, without fee, to wounded soldiers in hospital; and once, at the request of Havelock Wilson, he played to members of the National Sailors' and Firemen's Union interned as enemy aliens. After the war, Hampson continued to play, write and speak in the cause of peace; *Forward* for 7 November 1931 printed '"The Conchy": an Armistice Day play' by 'Casey'.

Hampson had already paid several visits to Belfast when in 1917 he received an invitation from the Socialist Party of Ireland to speak and play in Dublin. Upon their arrival in November of that year, Casey and Dolly were taken by a Party member to visit James Connolly's widow. Hampson's sympathies were all with Connolly; his article in the *Labour Leader* for 19 December 1918, 'A Chapter of Irish History', called Connolly the first Socialist martyr in Irish history. In June 1918 Casey and Dolly were invited to play at the Mansion House, Dublin, in a Connolly birthday concert organised to raise funds for a Connolly Memorial Labour College. Both this concert and another in Waterford were 'proclaimed' – banned from being held in the districts concerned; both were successfully transferred to trade union premises.

In the *Labour Leader* Hampson not only recorded the events of the tour but also provided more general articles on aspects of the Irish economy. His experiences in Ireland led him to be increasingly critical of the progress of Socialism in England. In May 1921, examining the situation 'Through Irish Eyes', he reproached the English for their lack of revolutionary spirit and expressed his sympathy with Sinn Fein.

Hampson continued his wandering Bohemian life until the late 1920s, when he suffered a complete breakdown. For some three years he was obliged to live in retirement at Stockport, his last home being in London Road, Hazel Grove. He died on 12 July 1932 and was buried at Norbury Parish Church, Stockport. In spite of his doubts about Roman Catholicism and his burial in an Anglican churchyard, the notice of his death in the *Stockport Express* records that he was 'Fortified by Rites of Holy Mother Church'. He was survived by his widow, to whom he left his effects valued at £234, and a grown-up family. There had been nine children in all. Mrs Hampson died on 12 September 1937, aged seventy-two and was buried in the same grave as her husband. His autobiographical reminiscences are worth attention. The obituary notice in *Forward* included the words that follow:

> Many an audience of working folk listened to "Casey and his Fiddle" who would never have gone inside a celebrity concert. And he always gave them of his best, spending hours rehearsing for his concerts with as much care as if he were going to perform before the King and Queen at the Albert Hall.
>
> A lovable, whimsical, elfish character with a streak of genius, a kindly, generous, happy-go-lucky personality that one met in all sorts of strange places to whom Socialism was not merely a matter of every-day politics but a striving towards the beautiful that was expressed in the philosophy of William Morris and Bruce Glasier.
>
> "Casey" did more than his share in the way of Socialist propaganda and agitation. In his way he was unique [16 July 1932, 16].

Writings: *Mr James Watts' Collection of Violins* (Stockport, [n.d.]) 14 pp. [privately published]; *Hampson's Violin School* (Stockport, 1901); *Who are the Bloodsuckers? With a List of the Principal Ones* (1905; repr. Stockport, Clarion Club, 1907) 16 pp.; *A Wandering Minstrel I: vagrom sketches by 'Casey'* [Walter Hampson] with a preface by E. Wharrier-Soulsby (NLP, [1912?]); *The Burston School Strike* (NLP, 1915) 20 pp.; *Casey's Mixture. No Lloyd George Tax on it* [privately printed, 19–?] 16 pp. [copy in Evans Coll., Sheffield City Library and on microfilm in Brynmor Jones Library, Hull Univ.]; Contributions by 'Casey' appear weekly in the *Labour Leader*, 1907–22; His serialised autobiography, 'Reminiscences of "Casey"', was published weekly in *Forward*, 28 Mar–31 Oct (24 Oct excepted) 1931, and in the issue for 7 Nov 1931 there is a play by him entitled '"The Conchy": an Armistice Day play'.

Sources: Slater's, *Royal National Commercial Directory of Cheshire* (1890); idem, *Royal National Commercial Directory of Stockport, Heaton Norris and District* (1891) and (1893); Kelly's, *Directory of Cheshire* (1896), (1902), (1906); *Stockport Labour J.* (Sep 1898); Wood's, *Directory of Stockport* (1899); *Stockport Directory* (1902), (1905), (1907); *Clarion*, 8 and 22 Sep, 17 Nov 1905, 15 Jan 1909; *Labour Leader*, 12 Jan 1906–31 Aug 1922; Stockport Labour Church, *Our Winter Work: being a syllabus of the lectures and other work arranged by the Stockport Labour Church for the winter session, September 1908 to April 1909* (Stockport, [1908?]) 47 pp.; idem, *Syllabus, September 27–December 27 1914* ([Stockport?], 1914) 4 pp.; *New Leader*, 29 Dec 1922; *What is Socialism?: a symposium*, ed. D. Griffiths (1924) 38 [includes Casey's definitions of Socialism]; J. Paton, *Proletarian Pilgrimage* (1935); F. Brockway, *Inside the Left* (1942; 2nd imp. 1947); D.F. Summers, 'The Labour Church and Allied Movements of the Late Nineteenth and Early Twentieth Centuries' (Edinburgh PhD, 1958) App. 2, p. 720; B. Edwards, *The Burston School Strike* (1974); F. Brockway, *Towards Tomorrow* (1977); personal information: Lord Brockway; Mrs Muriel Nicol, Welwyn Garden City. OBIT. *Stockport Express*, 14 July 1932; *Stockport Advertiser*, 15 and 22 July 1932; *Forward* [Glasgow], 16 July 1932; *Stockport Express, Annual* (1933) 119.

NAOMI REID

HEMM, William Peck (1820–89)

CHARTIST AND CO-OPERATOR

William Hemm was born in Nottingham in 1820. By trade a mechanic, he became an active Chartist in the mid-1840s. In August 1847 he seconded Feargus O'Connor's nomination as Chartist candidate for the Nottingham constituency, and he assisted in the organisation of O'Connor's successful campaign. When the Nottingham Chartist movement split, after the events of April 1848, Hemm followed the line of the moderate wing in trying to secure union with middle-class radicals in pursuit of an extension of the suffrage. This so-called 'People's League' did not long survive its inception in June 1848. Hemm remained sympathetic to Chartism and was one of the nominees of Charles Spurgeon, a lawyer who stood unsuccessfully as a Chartist candidate for Nottingham in July 1852, polling 631 votes.

Shortly after this date Hemm left his birthplace and worked as an engineer for several years in Manchester. From there he moved to Derby, where he entered the employment of the Midland Railway Company. He also joined the Derby Co-operative Society, which had been formed in 1850 by members of the local branch of the Society of Carpenters and Joiners, but which only began to expand from 1860, when other workers were admitted. In 1863 Hemm was elected to the committee of the Derby Society. In later years, wrote the *Co-operative News*, 'He was fond of relating how the committee had to personally prepare and serve out the provisions and groceries to the members in the evening after working hours, his own duty being to weigh up and sell flour' [31 Aug 1889].

About 1868 William Hemm returned to Nottingham, where he continued to work as an engineer; he was a member of the ASE until the late 1880s. But his main interest was in the co-operative movement. He soon became involved in the organisation of the Lenton and Nottingham Co-operative Society, which had been established in May 1863 on the initiative of Benjamin Walker and Thomas Bayley, Liberal industrialists and leaders of the Lenton Temperance Society. Hemm was elected to the committee of management of the Society on 5 January 1869, and he remained a committee member for the next twenty years, holding the positions of auditor and treasurer at various times. He also helped to spread the idea of co-operation further afield, and assisted in the establishment of several of the local societies, notably those at Mansfield and Long Eaton. His enthusiasm made him a popular choice as Nottingham delegate to the Midland Section of the Co-operative Central Board in December 1877. He became chairman of the Midland Section in 1884, and when he retired from this office in June 1889 he was presented with a framed photograph of the members of the Section. On a number of occasions Hemm stood as a candidate for the Board of the Co-operative Wholesale Society. He was finally elected in 1888, and was a Board member at the time of his death.

In addition to his work as a co-operator, William Hemm was active in the social and political life of Nottingham. He was identified with the radical fringe of the Nottingham Liberal Association in the 1870s, a group whose leaders – James Sweet, David W. Heath and William H. Mott – had, like Hemm, been prominent Chartists in earlier years. Education was the main focus of Hemm's interests. He was nominated for the first Nottingham School Board election in 1870, but withdrew before the poll. In November 1873, however, he stood as one of a group of 'unsectarian' candidates – actually anti-Anglican – and was elected, securing fourth place among thirteen candidates, with 8439 votes. He retired from the School Board after one term, in 1876.

William Hemm was an ardent Primitive Methodist. His two elder sisters were early members of the Canaan Street Primitive Methodist Church, Nottingham, in the 1830s, and through their influence he was induced to attend meetings and join the society. He became a Sunday school teacher there about 1836, and later held the positions of assistant Sunday school superintendent and class leader. He was best known, however, as leader of the chapel choir, a position he held for many years. He was also a strict teetotaller and active temperance advocate.

William Hemm died at his home, 57 Healey Street, Nottingham, on 21 August 1889, after a short illness. He was buried on 24 August at the General Cemetery, the service being conducted by the Rev. T. Randall of the Canaan Street Circuit, and attended by a large number of local co-operative dignitaries. He was survived by a widow and children.

Sources: *Northern Star*, 1847–50; *Nottingham Rev.*, 1847–52; *Nottingham Daily Express*, 1873; *Reports* of Annual Co-operative Congresses, 1878–90; J.F. Sutton [rev. by H. Field], *The Date-Book of Remarkable and Memorable Events connected with Nottingham ... 1750–1879* (Nottingham, 1880); *Guide to the 16th Annual Co-operative Congress of 1884, and to the Borough of Derby* (Derby, 1884); G.J. Holyoake and A. Scotton, *The Jubilee History of the Derby Co-operative Provident Society Limited 1850–1900* (Manchester, 1900); W.J. Douse, *The Simple Story of the Fifty Years' Sturdy Progress for Human Betterment by the Nottingham Co-operative Society Limited 1863–1913* (Nottingham, 1913) 32 pp.; F.W. Leeman, *The History of the Nottingham Co-operative Society Limited, 1863–1944* (Nottingham, 1944); idem, *Co-operation in Nottingham* (Nottingham, 1963); R.A. Church, *Economic and Social Change in a Midland Town: Victorian Nottingham 1815–1900* (1966). Obit. *Nottingham Daily Express*, 23 and 26 Aug 1889; *Nottingham Evening Post*, 23 Aug 1889; *Nottingham Daily Guardian*, 24 Aug 1889; *Co-op. News*, 24 and 31 Aug 1889; *Primitive Methodist*, 19 Sep 1889.

John Rowley

See also: †Jonathan Barber; †Thomas Bayley; *William John Douse; †David William Heath; William Henry Mott; †James Sweet; †Benjamin Walker.

HENSHALL, Henry (Harry) (1865–1946)
SOCIALIST AND JOURNALIST

Harry Henshall was born on 17 July 1865 at 21 Brunswick Street, Heaton Norris, Stockport. He was the son of James Henshall, a cotton power loom weaver and his wife Ann (née Allcock). His first school was a two-roomed cottage in Prison Street, Newbridge Lane, kept by an old man named Aaron Collier. The floor was covered with sand, and the furniture comprised two small forms, and two trestle tables running across the room. They began study 'when the looms began to clack across the street', and ended when the mill engine slowed down. The pupils, 'about a dozen little urchins', each paid 2*d* per week, and were disciplined by means of a long cane. Collier kept no register, and was in the habit of indulging in frequent drinks from a cupboard.

At the age of ten Henshall started work as a half-timer in a cotton mill and attended half-time at the National School in Wellington Road. Shortly afterwards he became a tenter for his mother, who ran four looms at Thornely's mill in Newbridge Lane. He was also encouraged to read by his parents who were determined to do the best they could for him. At the age of twelve he began his first full-time job but his life's career commenced when he was indentured to a master printer, J.N. Davenport, whose premises were on Union Road. This establishment was what was then known in the trade as a 'cock robin' shop: i.e. an office in which only one man was employed. Bored by his ten-hour days of setting type and performing other tasks which he found tedious, Henshall tried to enlist as a drummer boy in Salford before he was fifteen. His effort failed, but he was given 2*d*, together with some bread and cheese, to help him on his tramp back to Stockport. Before another year had elapsed, Henshall walked to Liverpool, pawning his overcoat *en route* to get a night's lodging. He wanted at this stage to be a cabin boy or 'powder monkey', but above all he wanted to travel.

In spite of these lapses, Henshall completed his seven-year apprenticeship as a compositor. He was married on 30 April 1887 at the Unitarian Church, Blackley, Manchester to Letitia Apted, of Oak Bank, Harpurhey. Once he had a wife and growing family, Henshall was anxious to advance his career and he moved to London, working in a printing house in Bouverie Street. It was the year of the great London Dock strike, and Henshall became acquainted with the leaders of the strike. This seems to have led him into the Radical and Socialist movement. He may have joined the SDF, but this is not certain. What influenced him more at this time was secularism, and he got to know both Charles Bradlaugh and Annie Besant and worked actively on their behalf. This was an interesting intellectual development since in Stockport he had attended the Unitarian Sunday School and Chapel in St Petersgate, and in London, when he first arrived, he had attended the Metropolitan Tabernacle.

Exactly why Henshall left London to return to Manchester is not known. This was in 1890 or 1891, and he found himself unemployed. Employment came only after weeks of tramping round the printing offices. It was now that he became an active Socialist, largely through the personal and literary influence of Robert Blatchford, and the writings of Edward Bellamy (*Looking Backward*) and William Morris (*News from Nowhere*). He later attempted Marx's *Capital*, much of which, however, he was unable to understand; 'but three chapters on rent, interest and profit appealed to me so much that I published them in book form for a shilling' [*Stockport Express*, 2 Apr 1936].

Henshall soon became active in the labour movement in Manchester. He attended the debates at the County Forum, a café in Market Street, and joined the local Fabian Society, which had been founded in November 1890, and in which Blatchford played a leading role. The Manchester Fabians encouraged the formation of a Labour Electoral Association in north Manchester in September 1891, and Henshall became the Association's first treasurer. The Manchester Fabian Society and North Manchester Labour Electoral Association were among several local organisations having for their aim independent Labour representation in Parliament. When the Lib-Lab dominated Manchester and Salford Trades Council failed to take the initiative in organising a May Day demonstration in 1892, these bodies collaborated to plan a demonstration, and elected a committee to carry out the arrangements. Three joint secretaries were appointed: J.F. Quinn, of the Tailors' Society, Trades Council and SDF; George Rogerson, of the Gasworkers' and General Labourers' Union, and president of Salford Labour Electoral Association; and Henshall, Fabian and LEA activist and a member of the Manchester Typographical Association. Their efforts proved successful: a march from Stevenson Square culminated in a mass meeting at Alexandra Park. From six platforms, whose chairmen included Robert Blatchford, John Trevor and George Evans, resolutions were adopted calling for a legal eight hour day, adult suffrage, shorter parliaments, payment of MPs, nationalisation of the land and means of production, and the foundation of an Independent Labour Party. The enthusiasm generated by this meeting prompted the formation of Manchester and Salford Independent Labour Party at St James's Hall on 17 May.

The newly-founded ILP, in conjunction with the North Manchester Fabians, planned to run Alfred Settle as a candidate for Harpurhey ward in the November municipal elections. Henshall spoke in support of the candidate at a meeting held to introduce Settle to his constituents in August 1892. He also took part in a demonstration at Hyde which led to the formation there of an ILP branch, dedicated, like the Manchester branch, to the 'Fourth Clause'. At the same time Henshall continued his membership of the North Manchester Fabian Society, being elected its corresponding secretary in December 1892.

His greatest contribution to the movement, however, was in the establishment and day to day running of the Manchester Labour Press Society. This came about through the initiative of the North Manchester Fabians who established the Society towards the end of 1892, and issued a prospectus and share application forms. The immediate response was poor, but after about three weeks £10 worth of shares had been subscribed, and the Society was launched. Henshall at the time was out on strike, drawing special 'victimised' pay of 35*s* a week from his trade society. This he gave up to start a printing office with the first £10, and to act as 'compositor, warehouseman, manager and general staff'. For the next five weeks or so he received neither strike pay nor wages.

The Manchester Labour Press Society Ltd started its operations in a small back bedroom, over a provision shop in Harpurhey rented for some eighteen pence per week. Equipment comprised a few ounces of type and a small platen machine. Life for Henshall and his colleagues was not easy; when printing the first edition of a pamphlet – Russell Smart's *The Independent Labour Party: its programme and policy* – they spent four nights out of bed, taking turns at treadling the machine, and between turns lying on the floor in all directions to sleep. On the Saturday they had no money to pay the boy's wages, let alone Henshall's; but Henshall set out with a bundle of pamphlets under his arm to walk to a demonstration in Rochdale, in the hope of raising money for wages.

Once the trade unions started to take out shares and place their orders, the Manchester Labour Press began to flourish. It moved to larger premises at 59 Tib Street, and also became the proprietor of the *Workman's Times*. That paper produced an illustrated front page article on the Press (3 Mar 1894) in the course of which 'Autolycus' (Joseph Burgess) described the manager:

> Harry Henshall is a big man in a little compass. Not much over five feet in height, and slim in proportion, his spare frame is crowned with a longish head and beardless face, out of which his honest laughing eyes flash a hearty welcome to every visitor. Henshall is perennially enthusiastic. Gifted with a sanguine nature, he sees unbounded possibilities in every new enterprise, and with a dogged perseverance sets to work to realise them.

Once the Labour Press was firmly established, Henshall was able to spare time for other political activities. In February 1893 he attended a conference of Fabian Societies of Lancashire and Cheshire, held at North Manchester Fabian Institute. Already serving as secretary of the

North Manchester Society, he was elected to the same office in the county organisation. At the municipal elections in November 1894 he stood as ILP candidate for Miles Platting ward. With 607 votes, he was defeated by a Conservative, but managed to push a Liberal opponent into third place. At the general election of 1895 Henshall supported Dr Pankhurst in Gorton, and the next year took part in the ILP's campaign for the right of free speech in Boggart Hole Clough. He spoke at a meeting of over 2000 people in the Clough on 24 May 1896, and together with John Harker, the Rev. Conrad Noel and Joseph Nuttall had his name taken by the police. In June he was obliged to appear at Manchester Police Court, to answer two summonses, and was subsequently fined forty shillings with costs. It is doubtful whether he ever paid; but he did not, as his obituary [*Stockport Express*, 26 Dec 1946] asserts, go to gaol.

In 1898, after the right of free speech in the Clough had been firmly established, Hensall turned his attention to trade unionism. On 28 March the *Clarion* reported a proposal to start a branch of the Workers' Union in Manchester. Intending members, together with those willing to assist in its formation, were asked to contact Henshall at the Labour Press now established in premises in Miller Street. Henshall then convened a preliminary meeting on 26 April at Lee's York Restaurant and in October of the same year he was re-elected to the executive committee of his own union, the Typographical Association.

Apart from the Labour Press, Henshall's work for the ILP was concerned chiefly with propaganda. In 1896 he compiled what became a well-known publication, the *ILP Song Book*, which began with Edward Carpenter's 'England Arise' followed by Socialist lyrics set to popular tunes. In March 1900 the *Labour Leader* announced that anyone wanting to assist the Stop-the-War propaganda should contact Henshall at the Labour Press. But a new direction to his political life came when the Labour Press Society announced it had gone into voluntary liquidation. On 11 June 1901 it showed a net deficit of £2080. None of the firm's records has survived, and it is not possible to reconstruct its internal history from other sources; but it is likely that part at least of its problems was due to the growing tendency of labour organisations to undertake their own printing and publishing.

Henshall had left the Labour Press (and Manchester) before it went into liquidation, but why, and exactly when is not known. *Clarion* of 24 November 1901 carried a notice to the effect that he was prepared to undertake printing and publishing at the Kelmscott Printeries, St Anne's-on-the-Sea, Lancashire. Less than a month later, in December 1901, he was declared bankrupt. He continued to live in St Anne's, and in May 1903 was advertising his services as a lecturer. But his future career was mostly in journalism, and at various times down to 1914 he worked for the *Lytham Times*, the *Daily Star* [Blackburn], the *Accrington Express*, the *Manchester Evening Chronicle*, the *Sunday Chronicle* (for which he acted as 'Special Commissioner'), and *Tribune*, a Liberal daily, edited at the time by J.L. Hammond. Henshall later claimed to have organised and controlled the first Labour Press Agency in England, but no details are available. He was one of the first reporters on the *Daily Dispatch*, which began publication in Manchester in February 1900, and was later appointed its lobby correspondent in the House of Commons. It was at this time that he became friendly with Victor Grayson, and it was Henshall who was responsible for Grayson publishing in the *Daily Dispatch*.

Henshall played some part in the formation of the National Union of Journalists, established in Manchester in 1907, and he continued to be politically active on the left. In 1908 for example he published a sixteen-page pamphlet: *The Unemployed Stream: dam it. Or it may be your turn next* in which he tried to emulate the style of Blatchford's *Merrie England*.

Henshall lived in various towns in Lancashire and Cheshire in these years. In the summer of 1909 he spoke at over a dozen open-air meetings for the ILP branch at Stockport, where he was now living. But on 19 November 1909 the *Labour Leader* carried a notice that he had been expelled from the Stockport ILP 'for using his position as a journalist to injure the interests of the Party through the Capitalist Press.' A fortnight later Albert Wilks, secretary of Stockport ILP asserted that Henshall had been expelled for writing a letter to the *Cheshire Evening Echo* of 20 October, which was detrimental to the interests of the Party. The letter in question, which was actually published in the *Cheshire Daily Echo* under the heading 'To your Tents, O Toilers. "Whose Dog art thou?"' was true to the tradition of 'Manchester Fourth Clause Socialism'. Henshall's basic objection was to the Parliamentary Labour Party's support for the Liberal Government and its failure to champion the cause of the unemployed. The actual incident which led to his outburst was G.N. Barnes's speech at Scarborough on the previous Sunday, in which the vice-chairman of the Labour Party had stated that Socialists should vote for the Liberal Party, which was pledged to carry through the Budget. In Stockport, a double-member constituency, this would mean that Socialists were being asked to vote for G.J. Wardle and Sir James Duckworth, the latter an opponent of the 'Right to Work' Bill. Wardle, Fred Jowett and Charles Duncan were all due to speak at a demonstration in Stockport's Central Hall that night, and Henshall concluded his letter: 'I ask them to say straight out, in the name of our glorious leaders, Marx, Engels, Hyndman and Blatchford, whose dogs we must be. To your tents, O toilers!' Henshall's expulsion almost split Stockport ILP, and correspondence concerning the affair in the *Cheshire Daily Echo* also brought to public notice the extent of the opposition within the local party to G.J. Wardle.

This expulsion from the ILP was to mark the end of Henshall's Socialist career. He was already a member of the Tariff Reform League; he now became one of its organisers and his shift to conservative positions and attitudes was becoming marked. When war broke out in August 1914 Henshall became chief recruiting officer for Stockport, and he later obtained a commission in the 9th battalion of the Cheshire Volunteer Regiment, composed of men too old for military service. In the late summer of 1917 he assisted the ultra-Conservative Sir Henry Page Croft to organise a National Party, and Henshall became its secretary for Yorkshire.

When the war ended Henshall had a variety of employments. He opened a Stockport School of Shorthand in 1918; later worked full-time for the Chamber of Trade; acted as an honorary propagandist for the Manchester University Extension Fund, and confirmed his political position by joining the Great Moor Conservative Club, of which he later became president.

In August 1929 Henshall, now apparently in semi-retirement, began a weekly column in the *Stockport Express* under the pseudonym 'The Idler'. His articles were a popular mixture of personal reminiscences, local gossip and commentaries on current events. The notes last appeared in the issue which bore his obituary, that of 26 Dec 1946. Immediately after the Second World War, Henshall expressed opinions which appeared sympathetic towards the Labour Party. He received several letters asking him to join the Party, but he declined with the remark, 'I can do good work in different directions without having to start pioneer work all over again' [*Stockport Express*, 1 Mar 1945].

In 1937 Henshall celebrated his Golden Wedding. He had at this time five sons, four grandsons, five granddaughters, and one great-granddaughter. Three of the sons were well known in commercial life in Stockport. His wife Letitia Henshall had then just recovered from a long illness, occasioned by a fall. She died in the early 1940s and on 10 July 1946, at the age of eighty-one, Henshall married Jane Hazeldine. Harry Henshall died at his home in Buxton Road, Great Moor, Stockport, on 19 Dec 1946, and his funeral took place at Stockport Crematorium two days later. His effects amounted to £533, probate being granted in March 1947 to his sons Russell Henshall, a radio engineer, and Frank Henshall, a bank cashier.

Writings: Compiler of *The ILP Song Book* (Manchester, [1896?]) 32 pp.; 'Co-operation and Socialism', *ILP News* (May 1898) 2–3; 'Trades Unionism and Socialism', ibid. (July 1898) 2–3; *The Unemployed Stream: dam it. Or it may be your turn next. An Open Letter to Bill Green* (Oldham, [1909?]) 16 pp. As a professional journalist (c. 1901–14) Henshall contributed at various times to the *Accrington Express, Daily Dispatch, Daily Star* [Blackburn], *Evening Chronicle, Lytham Times, Sunday Chronicle* [as 'Special Commissioner'] and *Tribune*. From August 1929 until his death in Dec 1946 he wrote a regular weekly column as 'The Idler' in the *Stockport Express*.

Sources: (1) MS: 1871 Census, Heaton Norris [Stockport], PRO: R.G. 10/298–300; Stockport Chamber of Trade, Minute Book I, 2 Dec 1919–28 Aug 1924, Stockport Public Library, Archives Coll. (2) Other: *Workman's Times*, 14 Nov 1891; 9 Apr, 21 May, 20 Aug and 24 Dec 1892; 4 Feb, 13 May and 1 June 1893; 3 Mar 1894; *Clarion*, 2 Apr, 15 Oct and 17 Dec 1892; 11, 18, Feb, and 10 June 1893; 27 Oct and 10 Nov 1894; 9 Mar 1895; 27 June and 23 Dec 1896, 26 Mar, 23 Apr, 21 May and 24 Dec 1898; 24 Nov 1900; 29 May 1903; 11 Dec 1908; *Labour Prophet*, May 1892; *Labour Leader*, 12 May, 27 Oct and 10 Nov 1894; 30 May, 13 June, 11 July and 29 Aug 1896; 24 Apr 1897; 17 Mar 1900; 26 Mar, 19 Nov and 3 Dec 1909; H.C. Rowe, *The Boggart Hole Contest* (Manchester, 1896) 18 pp.; I.L.P., *Report of the 5th Annual Conference* . . . (1897); *Labour Annual* (1897) 82; ibid. (1898) 39; *Reformers' Year Book* (1901) 148; *London Gazette*, 14 June and 6 Dec 1901; 10 Jan and 19 Aug 1902; Stockport Labour Church, *Our Winter Work: being a syllabus and other work arranged by the Stockport Labour Church for the Session September 5, 1909, to April 24, 1910.* ([Stockport], 1909) 48 pp. *Cheshire Daily Echo*, 20, 21 Oct and 1, 10, 11, 19, 22 Nov 1909; *Stockport Express, Annuals*, 1922–4, 1932; *Stockport Express*, 6 May 1937; A. Crookenden, *History of the Cheshire Regiment in the Great War* (Chester, [1939?]); M.J. Harkin, 'Notes on the Labour Press' and E. and R. Frow, 'The Manchester Labour Press Society Ltd: a comment', in *Bull. Soc. Lab. Hist.* no. *28* (spring 1974) 22–5, 27–8. Obit. *Stockport Express*, 26 Dec 1946; *Stockport Advertiser*, 27 Dec 1946.

Naomi Reid

See also: Frederick Brocklehurst for **Special Note** on Boggart Hole Clough and Free Speech; †George James Wardle.

HEYWOOD, Abel (1810–93)

CHARTIST, RADICAL AND BOOKSELLER

Abel Heywood was born at Prestwich, near Manchester in February 1810. He was the youngest son of the second marriage of John Heywood, a putter-out for weavers. The father died in 1812, and the widow, with four children, then moved to Manchester. There Abel obtained a rudimentary education at the Anglican Bennett Street School, which he later supplemented by evening classes at the Mechanics' Institute. When he was nine years old he began working in a warehouse in High Street at a weekly wage of 1*s* and 6*d*. He was still in the same employment at the age of twenty, but sometime in the middle of 1831 he set up business in Oldham Street. It was a penny news room for which he obtained the Manchester agency for the *Poor Man's Guardian*. This was the beginning of a remarkable career in bookselling and publishing. On 6 January 1832 he moved to larger premises at 28 Oldham Street, and steadily increased the number of his agencies. The shop and news room were open from 8 a.m. to 8 p.m. and for one penny all the political and periodical publications of the day could be read. Heywood also contracted agencies to the suburbs and smaller towns around Manchester within a twenty-mile radius, and he also supplied quite large numbers of street sellers.

Two months after the move to new premises Heywood was prosecuted for selling the *Poor Man's Guardian*, an unstamped paper. The case for the defence was that the *Guardian* was not a newspaper within the meaning of the Act (an argument that was to be upheld in June 1834 when Lord Lyndhurst in the Court of Exchequer suggested to the jury at Henry Hetherington's trial that the *Guardian* was too puny to be described as a newspaper). But Heywood in 1832 was fined £5 and £3 costs on each information, making a total of £48. He refused to pay the fine and was imprisoned for four calendar months in the New Bailey gaol. None of his memorials to the Secretary of State asking for the annulment of his sentence was successful. During his imprisonment the shop and news room were kept open by his mother and family. In 1834 he was again prosecuted for selling the *Guardian*, and fined £18 which on this occasion he paid. He was twice fined in 1836 for refusing to pay stamp duty on almanacs.

Heywood has an honoured place in the history of the agitation for a free press. One of his agents for a time was the Macclesfield hatter, Joseph Swann, a former shop assistant of Richard Carlile, with a remarkable career of struggle for working-class rights [Thompson (1963) 731–2]. Heywood himself was also centrally involved in local politics. He was a lively supporter of the Short Time Movement, was respected by most of the radical politicians of the decade and was active in the early development of Chartism in Manchester. He was also engaged in local municipal politics at a time when most radicals often stood aside from such involvement. In 1836 Heywood was elected a Commissioner of Police, and he played an active part in the proceedings which led to the incorporation of the borough of Manchester in 1838, under the Municipal Corporations Act of three years earlier. Incorporation meant taking over the responsibilities of the 180 Commissioners of Police, whose powers were largely those of an ordinary town council. Heywood was initially a Commissioner of Police for paving and sewerage. In 1843 he was elected to represent the Collegiate ward and ten years later he became an alderman. For the rest of his life he remained at the centre of Manchester politics.

Before, however, his municipal career really got underway, he was deeply implicated in what can only be described, for a Radical of Heywood's reputation, as a distinctly ambiguous political relationship with the established order. In April 1840 he had again been prosecuted, this time for selling blasphemous literature, to wit, Haslam's *Letters to the Clergy of all Denominations*. The trial took place in May 1840 and at the request of the Crown Heywood pleaded guilty to the indictment. He then presented an affidavit in extenuation, in which he stated that as soon as he learned that certain papers were deemed improper, he gave orders that their sale should be stopped. The counsel for the prosecution accepted the accuracy of the affidavit and stated that he was instructed by representatives of the Government not to press for judgment, but to consent to Heywood's discharge on his entering into recognizances for good behaviour. It was further revealed by the Home Secretary (Marquess of Normanby) in the House of Lords that Sir Charles Shaw, the commissioner of police at Manchester had urged the Government to take the course they did on the grounds that Heywood had rendered 'great assistance in preserving the peace last winter' [*Hansard*, 3rd ser. vol. *55* (1840) 1231: for the full debate, *ibid.*, 1224–36]. Correspondence in the PRO rounds out the story. In answer to an inquiry from the Home Office, Sir Charles Shaw confirmed that when he arrived in Manchester he made the acquaintance of Abel Heywood

> . . . one of the most influential men among the Chartists . . . I found that though his opinions were 'Chartist', that he was a decided enemy to 'Physical Force' . . . and I discovered that at all *Private Chartist Meetings* he argued against 'Physical Force'. Finding that his speeches *there* were in accordance with his words to *me*, I thought I might have confidence in him, and I told him that I depended on him not allowing any outbreak to take place without giving me sufficient warning. He promised to give me notice. At great personal risk and the chance of losing his business as a 'Chartist Bookseller' he gave me private information of a Rising which was to take place at Bolton during the night of 22nd and 23rd January [1840] . . . I instantly made arrangements with Colonel Wemyss in command of the Troops here, who ordered a Squadron of Cavalry to march on Bolton, while I myself proceeded there . . .
>
> I consider that the information given to me by Abel Heywood prevented much serious damage being done, and that the threatened outbreak was prevented by that information. I understand that Abel Heywood has very peculiar notions on religious subjects. From many enquiries which I have made and from what I myself have seen, no one can prove anything against him as a man in business, as a Father or Husband, in short that I think him a respectable man. However his being able to give me such correct information proves that he must be a man of influence among the Chartists and I believe he does not pretend to deny

that he belongs to a Sect called 'Socialists' [HO 44/35: Charles Shaw to S.M. Phillips, 20 May 1840].

To return briefly to Heywood's trial. There was much indignation in Manchester at his prosecution, and some of his friends brought similar charges of the sale of blasphemous literature against four other booksellers in the town, including the publisher of the *Manchester Courier*, the organ of the Conservative Party. The blasphemous publication in question was the works of Shelley, including Queen Mab. The Grand Jury returned a true bill, but because of Heywood's position, only a nominal judgment was recorded.

Heywood's standing in the Chartist movement was unchanged after the statements in the House of Lords' debate, and apparently no one troubled to take further the one incriminating sentence. On the 17 August 1840 Heywood proposed the toast to the *Northern Star* at a great celebration in the Hall of Science to welcome Peter M'Douall and John Collins on their release from gaol [D. Thompson (1971) 139–74, esp. 173–4]; and in 1841 he was elected treasurer of the National Charter Association, and sat for a time on the executive committee.

Most of the remainder of his long life was associated with Manchester politics. He made without difficulty the transition from Chartist radical to radical Liberal, and in his case there was very little ground to traverse to reach the politics of reformism after 1850. The translation of the Owen Hall of Science at Campfield, in which Heywood had taken an active interest, to become the Manchester Free Library in 1852 may be taken as a symbol of the changes that were taking place. Heywood was twice Lord Mayor of Manchester; the first time in 1862–3, during the cotton famine, and then again in 1876–7. It was during this second term of office that the new Town Hall was opened. Heywood had been chairman of the committee in charge of the project, and when Queen Victoria refused an invitation to be present at the opening ceremony – widely believed to be a matter of political prejudice against Heywood – he himself was invited to open the building. The occasion was a massive demonstration of the Manchester trade unionists [Frow (1977) 6–7].

His political ideas after the mid-century were typical of the moderate radicalism of the mid-Victorian period. In 1859, with W.P. Roberts as his agent, he stood as a Radical Liberal candidate for Manchester but was unsuccessful, the two official Liberals being elected. Heywood denied, at one of the meetings of this election campaign, 'that he came forward on Chartist principles. He was an advocate of the rights of the great body, and if those known as Chartists supported the same principles, well and good. He did not wish to be the representative of any party, but of all classes. He had been charged with introducing discord into the borough, but this was untrue' [*Manchester Guardian*, 27 Apr 1859, p. 3]. Heywood stood again, as an advanced Liberal, in 1865, but was again unsuccessful. He did not further contest parliamentary elections.

His business career was remarkably successful. In addition to the very large publishing and bookselling concerns, he started in 1847, with his brother John, a successful wallpaper and paper-staining business; and everything he touched in the world of commerce seemed to prosper. In evidence to the 1851 S.C. on Newspaper Stamps he claimed that he handled ten per cent of the whole national issue of popular publications (His complete evidence to the Committee, Qs 2474 ff., is of the greatest interest to the literary as well as the social historian).

He received much recognition from his fellow Mancunians of his many services to the city and he was made a Freeman in November 1891. He died on 19 August 1893, at Bowdon, aged eighty-three. He left an estate valued at £27,306. He was twice married: his first wife, formerly a Miss Shelmerdine, died in 1887 and left £10,000 to Owen's College for the instruction of women and girls; his second wife was Mrs Thomas Goodsby, the widow of Alderman Goodsby, a former mayor of Manchester. There were two sons, G.W. Heywood, a county court judge in Manchester and Abel Heywood who conducted the publishing business.

Writings: For details of the radical periodicals published by Abel Heywood see *The Warwick*

Guide to British Labour Periodicals 1790–1970: a check list, compiled by R. Harrison, G.B. Woolven and R. Duncan (Hassocks, 1977), and texts on the unstamped press and Chartism. In the second half of the nineteenth century his firm published *inter alia* lists of MPs [*House of Commons* (1881), (1885), (1886), (1895)], tourist guides, and a Temperance Directory, details of which are listed in the catalogues of the BL and Library of Congress. Only a few of Heywood's own writings have been located but his evidence before the S.C. on Newspaper Stamps 1851 XVII Qs 2474–613 is of prime importance to historians of this period; *Reasons why a Drawback should be allowed on Stocks of Paper Hangings provided a Repeal of the Paper Duty takes place on 1st July 1860* n.d. 2 pp.; *Letter to the Mayor, Aldermen and Councillors of the City of Manchester, on the Manchester Gasworks* (1861) 12 pp.

Sources: (1) MS: Correspondence relating to Abel Heywood's prosecution, 7 Apr, 19, 20 May and 2 Aug 1840, HO/43/59 and HO/44/35, PRO. (2) Other: *Poor Man's Guardian*, 31 Dec 1831; *Manchester and Salford Advertiser*, 5 Jan 1839; *Hansard* [Lords], 4 Aug 1840; *Manchester Guardian*, 22, 27 Apr and 2 May 1859; 'The Conservatives and Mr Abel Heywood', ibid., 17 July 1865; W.E.A. Axon, *The Mayor of Manchester and his Slanderers* (Manchester, 1877) 15 pp.; *Manchester Guardian*, 17 Sep 1877; W.E.A. Axon, *The Annals of Manchester* (Manchester, 1886); *Manchester Faces and Places*, *1*, no.8, 10 May 1890, 121–4; W.A. Shaw, *Manchester Old and New*, *1* [1896?]; A. Heywood jr, 'English Almanacks during the First Third of the Century' in *Three Papers on English Printed Almanacks* (privately published, 1904) 31 pp.; T. Swindells, *Manchester Streets and Manchester Men* 2nd ser. (Manchester, 1907); *Boase 5* (1912); G.B. Heywood, *Abel Heywood, Abel Heywood and Son, Abel Heywood and Son Ltd, 1832–1932* (Manchester, 1932) 16 pp.; S.D. Simon, *A Century of City Government: Manchester 1838–1938* (1938); A. Redford, *A History of Local Government in Manchester* (1940); R.D. Altick, *The English Common Reader* (Chicago, 1957); J.T. Ward, *The Factory Movement 1830–1855* (1962); A. Briggs, 'Manchester: a symbol of a new age in Victorian cities' in *Victorian Cities* ed. A. Briggs (1963; later eds.) 88–138; E.P. Thompson, *The Making of the English Working Class* (1963; rev. ed. 1968); J.H. Wiener, *The War of the Unstamped: the movement to repeal the British Newspaper Tax, 1830–1836* (Cornell Univ. Press, 1969); P. Hollis, *The Pauper Press: a study in working-class radicalism of the 1830s* (1970); *The Early Chartists*, ed. D. Thompson (1971); D.S. Gadian, 'A Comparative Study of Popular Movements in the N.W. Industrial Towns, 1830–50' (Lancaster PhD, 1976); E. and R. Frow, *Trade Unions and the Opening of Manchester Town Hall, 1877* (Manchester, 1977) 15 pp.; biographical information: T.K. Campbell, archivist, Bolton Metropolitan Borough; Professor W.H. Chaloner, Manchester Univ.; A.G. Rose, Manchester. OBIT. *Manchester Guardian* and *Times*, 21 Aug 1893; *Illustrated London News*, 26 Aug 1893; *British Printer 6*, no. 35 (1893) 324.

EDMUND AND RUTH FROW

See also: Richard CARLILE; William LOVETT, for Chartism to 1840; *John WEST.

HUMPHREYS, George Hubert (1878-1967)

BIRMINGHAM BUSINESSMAN AND FABIAN SOCIALIST

Hubert Humphreys was born on 14 July 1878 in Handsworth, the son of George Humphrey Humphreys, a blacksmith working from a smithy in Constitution Hill close to the centre of Birmingham, and his wife Emily (née Baker). Hubert Humphreys was educated at Vicarage Road and Lozells Road Board Schools and then at King Edward's School, Aston. Leaving school at fourteen, he went to work in his father's smithy. He spent nine years there; but his overriding interest was in the theatre, and in 1902 he became a professional actor, a career which he followed for three years, but had to give up in 1905. He appeared in numerous melodramas, as well as playing a Stratford season with the Benson Company, and left the theatre only because Alfred Wareing, the producer and impressario, could not afford to pay him £5 a week. He then became a commercial traveller, until in 1912 he founded his own business, the Midland Fan Company, manufacturing ventilating and spraying plant in Aston Road, Birmingham. The business remained his livelihood for the fifty-five years till his death.

Humphreys was a convinced Socialist from his youth. His father was one of the first members of the ILP in Birmingham, but it was Robert Blatchford who captured his imagination. He had read the first issue of the *Clarion* when he was only thirteen, and he subsequently became an enthusiastic member of the Clarion Cycling Club. During his twenties he joined a number of Socialist organisations in Birmingham, including the Labour Church, the Socialist Centre and the ILP Federation; but his constant travelling limited his involvement. He did become chairman of the Birmingham ILP Federation in 1912, but resigned within a year, as a result of what he termed 'MacDonald's domineering'.

While he built up his own business active politics took second place, and up to 1930 the theoretical discussions of the Fabian Society were the principal focus of his Socialism. He became president of the Birmingham Fabian Society. He was a regular participant in the Summer Schools, during practically the whole of their existence, and was director of the School several times from 1930 onwards. He was a member of the Fabian executive, almost continuously from 1925 to 1941. But from that time he played little part in the Society, for he was not a thinker or a policy-maker. He was also a member of the 1917 Club. Through these activities Humphreys became friendly with the Webbs, Shaw and Wells. His friendship with Shaw was lifelong; Shaw became a mentor both in politics and the theatre, so much so that Humphreys could in 1927 describe his recreations as 'upholding the faith on Fabian lines by pushing forward Shavian and up-to-date dramas.' In the 1920s Humphreys was closely associated with the People's Theatre movement in Birmingham, and he gave frequent public readings of Shaw's works.

By 1930 Humphreys had decided he 'did not care enough for money to make a successful businessman in the orthodox sense'; and he began to involve himself more in local politics. He was elected to the Birmingham Labour Party executive as a Fabian Society representative in 1931. In July 1934 he was adopted as prospective parliamentary candidate for Ladywood, one of the six Birmingham seats captured by Labour in 1929. He fought the seat at the 1935 general election on a pacifist platform. In his election address Humphreys distanced himself from party policy and declared that the fight was 'against war and its horrors and the universal starvation of the workers afterwards.' Humphreys' campaign made little impact on the Ladywood electors; the popular Tory Geoffrey Lloyd was returned with a 11,254 majority, Humphreys polling nearly 2000 fewer votes than the Labour candidate in 1931.

In 1936 Humphreys was elected president of the Birmingham Borough Labour Party. He inherited a Party still very much shaped by the apostasy of Oswald Mosley, who had been its leading light. The Party was unrepresented in Parliament, and was in a small minority on the city council. His three years as president saw little improvement in the position. Foreign affairs, especially the Spanish Civil War, dominated the Party's considerations to the detriment of municipal policy and Party organisation and efficiency. Humphreys himself visited Spain early in 1938 as a member of a delegation of provincial Labour leaders and witnessed the results of the aerial bombardments of Barcelona. Spain challenged both his pacifism and his leadership of the local Party. He came to modify his pacifist views, but along with the Birmingham Labour movement he also became involved in the United Front and Popular Front controversies. These had the effect of dividing the Borough Party from the Trades Council and further weakening Labour's morale in the city. Eventually, to the accompaniment of criticism from both wings of the movement, Humphreys was defeated in the 1939 election for president. He had found particularly wounding the criticism by such trade union leaders as Walter Lewis of the 'Fabian intellectual domination' of the Borough Party [*Town Crier*, 24 Feb 1939].

Humphreys had been elected a city councillor for Northfield in 1937 and following his years as Borough Party president his civic work increasingly occupied him. In 1942 he was appointed a magistrate. Throughout the Second World War he fought hard on the council for better civilian protection and social conditions. The wartime activities of Humphreys and his colleagues transformed Labour's image in Birmingham and paid electoral dividends in 1945. By then Humphreys had abandoned his parliamentary ambitions.He was elected an alderman in 1945, and when Labour at last gained control of the council in 1946 he became chairman of the water committee, and was Lord Mayor in 1949. In 1949 to 1950 he took part in a research group to study the reports of Divisional Labour Parties and draw up Speakers' Notes. He was a vice-president of the Borough Party for several years and acted as a father-figure to a younger generation of Birmingham Labour politicians, most notably to Denis Howell. He retired from the council in 1958. He was made an honorary member just before his death.

Humphreys was always regarded as an unorthodox figure in the Birmingham Labour movement. He had joined the ASE while working for his father, but later, as the owner of a small business, he was not closely identified with the trade union movement. He delighted in membership of both the Fabian Society and the Rotary Club. Even in dress he was unconventional. As Lord Mayor he attended official functions in a lounge suit, yet he was rarely seen without a bow tie. He was an inveterate attender of meetings – whether council committees, Fabian Summer Schools, Clarion Easter meets or Labour Party conferences. It was, in fact, at the Scarborough Labour Party conference, which he was attending against his doctor's orders, that he died on 4 October 1967.

Humphreys was an atheist and was cremated at Yardley Crematorium. He had married twice, having two sons by his first marriage and a step-daughter from the second. One son, Kenneth, a Clarion cyclist, was killed in a road accident on Christmas Day 1927 at the age of eighteen. The other son Bernard and his son Kenneth inherited and still (1978) run the Midland Fan Company. Humphreys' second wife, the former Gertrude Greenwood, whom he married in 1927, had been an active suffragette and was for some years secretary of the Birmingham Fabian Society. Humphreys left an estate valued at £31,658, one fifth willed to the Fabian Society 'for the purposes of Socialist propaganda'.

Sources: (1) MS: Hubert Humphreys' correspondence files 1947–67, Social Sciences Dept, Birmingham Reference Library. (2) Other: *Labour Who's Who* (1927); *Town Crier*, 20 July 1934, 24 Feb and 14 Apr 1939 and 27 Nov 1948; *Northfield Labour Messenger Election Special*, Oct 1937; *Sunday Mercury*, 18 Jan 1948; *Birmingham Gazette*, 2 Feb 1949; *Birmingham Post Year Book* (1958–9) 802; R.P. Hastings, 'The Labour Movement in Birmingham 1927–1945' (Birmingham MA, 1959); *WWW* (1961–70); P.D. Drake, 'Labour and Spain: British Labour's response to the Spanish Civil War with particular reference to the Labour movement in Birmingham' (Birmingham MLitt., 1978); personal information: the late Dame Margaret Cole, London; Kenneth Humphreys, Birmingham. Obit. *Birmingham Mail* and *Birmingham Post*, 26 Mar 1952 [for Mrs G. Humphreys]; *Birmingham Mail*, 4 Oct 1967; *Birmingham Post*, 5 Oct 1967.

Peter Drake

See also: †Walter Samuel Lewis.

KENDALL, George (1811-86)

CHARTIST AND TRADE UNION LEADER

George Kendall was born in the village of Hoton-on-the-Hill, near Loughborough, in 1811, being baptised in the village church on 26 July 1811; he was the son of George and Sarah Kendal as the surname was spelt in the parish register. Little is known of his childhood, except that he was sent out to work at the age of five, probably in the local hosiery industry. In the early 1830s he moved to Sutton-in-Ashfield, an industrial village approximately fifteen miles north of Nottingham, and married. Two children were born to George and his wife (also called Sarah), Elizabeth and George (born in 1834 and 1836 respectively).

Kendall obtained employment in the Sutton hosiery industry as a framework knitter, producing stockings and socks on a hand frame. In the industrial villages of North Nottinghamshire, most knitters were employed by middlemen or 'bag hosiers,' who rented out frames and provided raw materials for their workers in the villages, and then sold the finished product to hosiers in Nottingham. During the 1840s, the framework knitting industry was economically depressed with low wages made worse by work-spreading and the practice of paying in truck.

Kendall explained the working of the truck system in his evidence to the Commission on the Condition of the Framework Knitters of 1845:

> At that time, on the average, I earned 12*s* a-week after I had paid my frame-rent, and in the whole of that time, within a week or two of two years, all the money that I received of my employer, was 16*s* 6*d*; and 10*s* 6*d* of that I had of him to pay interest of the pawn tickets, where I had pledged things for necessities for my wife and family, when I could get no money, in order to buy things he did not sell – in cases of sickness. It makes me unmanned when I think of these things. When Saturday night came, I had to turn out with a certain quantity of meat and candles, or tobacco, or ale, or whatever I had drawn as wages, to dispose of at a serious loss. I used to take a can of ale to the barber to get shaved with, and a can of ale to the sweep to sweep my chimney. I was in good receipt of wages, and, in company with my neighbours, I used to take in a newspaper, and I was obliged to take a pound of candles at 7*d*, and leave it for the newspaper, the price of which was 4½*d*, I used to take my beef at 7*d* a pound, and sell it to the coal woman that I had my coals of for 5*d*; and any bit of sugar, or tea, or anything of that kind that my employer did not sell, I used to get from the grocer living at the bottom of the yard by swapping soap and starch.

In the same evidence Kendall noted that his wife was very ill- 'in the worst stage of consumption... Starvation and destitution have brought it on... The employers of this town have no more compassion for the workmen, than the lion has for the lamb' [Q.3414].

Such grinding poverty encouraged massive participation by hosiery workers in radical politics, particularly from 1841. The main leaders of the Chartist movement in Sutton – John Simmons, John Alvey, and George Kendall were all framework knitters. Kendall and several neighbours subscribed to the *Northern Star*, paying the price (4½*d*) with seven pennyworth of candles. In the autumn of 1841, Kendall was a Sutton delegate to several Chartist meetings in the East Midlands, and when O'Connor made a triumphal visit to Sutton in July 1842, Kendall was one of the speakers at a mass meeting. During the following spring, G.J. Harney and R.G. Gammage both visited Sutton, and Kendall presided over meetings at the Royal Forester, a radical public house whose landlord, James Turner, was a relative of the William Turner who had been hanged for his part in the Pentrich Rising of 1817.

During 1844 to 1845 the radicals of Sutton turned their attention to industrial grievances. An anti-truck association was established, with Kendall acting as secretary, and a vigorous campaign against truck paying masters was organised, twenty prosecutions being initiated in a month. This checked the abuse for a time, but the truck system proved too pervasive to be extirpated by such means, and Kendall, who was concerned with over seventy prosecutions, was blacklisted for his activities. The report of the 1845 Commission constituted a striking indictment of industrial relations in the hosiery industry, but did little to alter working conditions. In July 1846 a collection in Sutton for John Frost realised only £1 1*s* 6*d*. Kendall forwarded the sum to the *Northern Star* with a covering note, 'it would have been more, but we poor fellows at Sutton are in a very deplorable situation' [*Northern Star*, 4 July 1846].

Economic conditions in the hosiery trade gradually improved, however, from about 1849. Knitters using the traditional hand frames were beginning to face competition from steam-powered factory production, but the new technology spread only slowly, and hand knitters continued to hold their own in many areas. As markets broadened, wages steadily improved, although hand-frame workers always earned less than factory workers, and had to work longer hours to compensate for lower productivity. Kendall remarried in the 1850s; his second wife, Mary Ann, was eighteen years his junior. Two children were born to this second marriage: Eliza (1859) and William (1861).

After the economic crisis of 1857, prosperity reached new levels in the years 1858–61, and this was reflected in renewed union organisation and militancy. A wide-hand framework knitters' trade society was re-established in Sutton, and Kendall became its secretary. During the single year 1860 there were three hosiery strikes in Nottinghamshire, the most damaging being an eleven week stoppage of the Sutton men in support of a wages increase. Representatives of the employers, middlemen and workers involved in the dispute met at the Commercial Exchange, Nottingham, in September 1860, and after three days of discussion achieved a settlement on 27 September which pioneered an experiment in industrial relations. The conference agreed to the establishment from December of a Board of Arbitration consisting of eighteen members, nine on the employers' side and nine on the workers'. An employers' representative acted as chairman, but had no casting vote, contentious issues being settled by what was termed 'a long jaw'. The Arbitration Board met every three months, and provision was made for a Standing Committee of Inquiry to deal with disputes as they arose. The worker delegates to the Board were elected by membership vote within the various branches of the hosiery industry. George Kendall was elected at the outset and remained an influential member of the Board throughout its active existence. A.J. Mundella, who provided the inspiration for the scheme was the Board's first chairman.

The avowed aim of the Hosiery Board of Arbitration was to achieve improvements in working conditions and general prosperity within the industry through co-operation and conciliation rather than competition and conflict. The workers' representatives on the Board opposed strike action, except when the pressure of the most influential Nottingham hosiers failed to bring a recalcitrant manufacturer into line. Workers in the industry derived some benefits from this policy, as Kendall recognised in his testimony before the 1871 Commission on the Truck System. The amount of frame rent by knitters was significantly reduced, and uniform wage and price lists were introduced by 1867. Truck was totally eradicated from Nottingham, although one or two masters there continued to pay wages in public houses, but it persisted in the North of the county.

The Board of Arbitration recognised the right of hosiery workers to organise themselves in trade unions. In 1865 Kendall and James Saxton, then vice-president of the Board, held meetings at Kegworth and Heanor to persuade workers to join trade societies. In June of the following year the local unions in Nottinghamshire, Leicestershire and Derbyshire became federated in the United Framework Knitters' Society, under Kendall's leadership. Reliance on the Board of Arbitration, however, tended to militate against really strong union organisation; subscriptions to the union were as low as 1*s* per year in 1866.

The essential weakness of the employees' position in relying on Board decisions was exposed in the 1870s. In the spring of 1870 hand-frame knitters in Nottingham, Carlton, Hucknall and Sutton were threatened with wage cuts so that their employers could meet competition from increasingly efficient factory production. After deadlock on the Board of Arbitration a prominent Nottingham lace manufacturer, W.G. Ward, was called upon to arbitrate; he negotiated a compromise which still involved wage reductions. The Nottingham and Ruddington knitters wanted strike action, but Kendall successfully opposed this, arguing the weakness of their position, especially in relation to financial reserves. But it was now becoming difficult to reconcile the interests of the prosperous power-frame knitters with those of the hand knitters, and in 1871 the Nottingham machine operatives left the United Framework Knitters' Society and formed a separate organisation, the first of a number of secessions. The Board of Arbitration became increasingly ineffective from 1872 until its demise in 1884. Earlier in 1875 Kendall, who remained secretary of the White Branch Framework Knitters' Society in Sutton, tried unsuccessfully to establish a separate Board for the town's decaying wrought-hose manufacture.

He was also much involved in quite another field of activity during the 1870s. In 1870 he and T.B. Adin, a nonconformist tradesman, agitated for the establishment of a School Board in Sutton-in-Ashfield. Kendall was elected to the first Board in April 1871, when its members were predominantly Anglican and Tory, but in 1874 there was a nonconformist-Liberal majority, and Kendall was elected chairman; he served a second term in office from 1877 to 1879. During Kendall's eight years on the School Board great efforts were made to extend the availability of education at places for the working-class children of the area. The Board tried to keep children at school until the age of eleven, and school fees were waived for poor families; but it became politically necessary both to condone frequent absenteeism and to allow half-time employment from the age of nine. By 1880 a vigorous school building programme had given Sutton a comparatively high level of educational provision compared with nearby towns of similar size.

The labour force in hand-frame knitting diminished in the 1870s as steam-powered machines in factories supplanted the domestic industry. After a period of illness during the winter of 1877–8, Kendall resigned his chairmanship of the Sutton School Board, in April 1879, in order to take up salaried employment in the service of the Board as caretaker of the recently-erected Hardwick Street Schools. He held this post for seven years, while apparently continuing to act as an adviser to local hosiery workers.

George Kendall died of cancer at his home, 21 Union Street, Sutton-in-Ashfield, on 14 October 1886. He was buried in St Mary's churchyard on 16 October, the funeral being conducted by the Rev. F.T. Marsh and attended by numerous friends. He was survived by his second wife, Mary Ann. No will has been located.

Sources: (1) MS: Parish registers, Hoton-on-the-Hill, Leicestershire RO, and Sutton-in-Ashfield, Nottinghamshire RO; Census schedules of Township of Sutton-in-Ashfield, 1841–71; Minutes of the Sutton-in-Ashfield School Board 1871–92, Nottinghamshire RO; Webb Trade Union Coll. vol. 39, The Hosiery and Lace Trades, BLPES. (2) Other: *Nottingham Rev.*, 1839-70; *Northern Star*, 1841–6; R.C. on the Condition of the Framework Knitters, *Report* 1845 XV [evidence of Kendall Qs 3399–414]; R.C. on Trade Unions, *Tenth Report* 1867 XXXIX; W. Felkin, *A History of the Machine Wrought Hosiery and Lace Manufactures* (1867); E. Renals, 'On Arbitration in the Hosiery Trades of the Midland Counties', *JRSS 30* (1867) 548–56; Commission on the Truck System 1871 XXXVI [evidence of Kendall Qs 40631–827]; *Nottingham Daily Express*, 1871–5; H. Crompton, *Industrial Conciliation* (1876); R.C. on Factory and Workshops Acts, *Report* 1876 XXIX, *M of E* 1876 XXX; J.S. Jeans, *Conciliation and Arbitration in Labour Disputes* (1894); S. & B. Webb, *Industrial Democracy* (1920 ed.); W.H. G. Armytage, 'A.J. Mundella and the Hosiery Industry', *Econ. Hist. Rev. 18* (1948) 91–9; E.H. Phelps Brown, *The Growth of British Industrial Relations: a study from the standpoint of 1906–1914* (1959); D.M. Smith, 'The British Hosiery Industry at the Middle of the Nineteenth Century', *Trans. of the Institute of British Geographers* (June 1963) 125–42; R.A. Church, 'Technological Change and the Hosiery Board of Conciliation and Arbitration', *Yorkshire Bull. of Economic and Social Research 15*, no. 1. (May 1963) 52–60; idem, *Economic and Social Change in a Midland Town: Victorian Nottingham 1815–1900* (1966); E.P. Thompson, *The Making of the English Working Class* (1963; rev. ed. 1968); J. Neal, *The Pentrich Revolution* (Pentrich, 1966 ed. [repr. of c. 1894 ed.]); R. Gurnham, *A History of the Trade Union Movement in the Hosiery and Knitwear Industry 1776–1976* (Leicester, 1976).

Obit. *Midland and North Notts. Advertiser and Nottinghamshire Free Press*, 22 Oct 1886.

John Rowley

KESSACK, James O'Connor (1879–1916)
SOCIALIST AND TRADE UNION OFFICIAL

James O'Connor Kessack was born in Aberdeen on 19 October 1879. He was the second son of James O'Connor Kessack, a baker, and Isabella (née Davidson), the daughter of a farmer. When the boy was three years old the family moved to Huntly, where his father opened a baker's business of his own. It proved to be a disastrous failure, and from that time the family experienced extreme poverty. Unable to find work in Huntly, the father moved to Inverurie in 1892, but remained unemployed. James worked as a drover, fetching cattle from distant farms to the butchers; and for some time the family (there were now nine children) subsisted on his meagre wages, supplemented by poaching. When James's father finally found permanent work, his wife fell ill, and died within a fortnight. By then James was taking on any job to supplement the family income: he became a navvy for a time, and then a stoker. Eventually he drifted to Glasgow in search of work. Shortly after he had settled there his father died, and James took upon himself the role of providing for the orphaned family. The children were all brought to Glasgow where, on intermittent earnings, he managed to establish a home for them and was known to be living at 16 Russell Place, Kelvinhaugh Street, in 1907.

Although Kessack's early life had been one of grinding poverty, the family was deeply religious and he was a regular church member. As such he had little sympathy with Socialist views expressed at open air meetings. But doubts began to grow in his mind, and his conversion to Socialism followed the by-election at Lanarkshire North-East in September 1901 when Robert Smillie was the defeated ILP candidate. So struck was Kessack by Smillie that he began to read Socialist literature, especially the *Clarion,* and to attend meetings.

It was Councillor Sam MacDonald of Clydebank ILP who first noticed Kessack's ability. Kessack was listening to an anti-Socialist speaker at an outdoor meeting and spoke up heatedly in defence of the Socialist cause. MacDonald, who was in the audience, was so much impressed that he invited Kessack to speak at the Clydebank branch of the ILP. With some diffidence he accepted. Before long he was a member of the Glasgow City branch of the ILP. For a time he belonged to the Socialist Labour Party (SLP) and the Industrial Workers of the World ('the Wobblies') and he helped to establish a club in Glasgow for the propagation of industrial unionism called 'Advocates of Industrial Unionism'. But the doctrinal wranglings within the SLP and the IWW at local level led him to resign from both. In 1907 the SLP in committee had passed a resolution forbidding members to speak on the platforms of any other oganisation unless it had adopted Industrial Union attitudes. Kessack was not prepared to accept this view and a speech he made at a meeting of the Dressmakers' Union led to his resignation. He explained his position in the Glasgow *Forward* of 2 February 1907.

By that time he was well known in left-wing circles in Glasgow: he was frequently invited to speak at branches of the ILP in the city and the surrounding rural districts, and increasingly his activities were reported in the Socialist *Forward*; but pressure of work ultimately broke his health. He developed a serious throat infection in 1908, and on medical advice was sent to Arizona for some months to recover, the ILP financing him through a public appeal. When he returned he continued his political activities, and in 1909 was adopted as Labour candidate for the Camlachie division of Glasgow. In both elections of 1910 the seat was won by the Unionist H.J. Mackinder, Kessack coming in third place, below the Liberal candidate.

After his second defeat Kessack abandoned any interest in becoming an MP. His belief in Socialism remained unimpaired, but he had no stomach for the practices of election campaigns.

In any case by then his work in the trade union movement was proving to be a more absorbing and satisfying outlet for his eloquence and administrative skills.

In 1909, at the age of thirty, he was appointed organiser for the National Union of Dock Labourers (NUDL), a post he held with growing distinction and authority until he enlisted in the Army shortly after the outbreak of the First World War. The NUDL had been formed in Glasgow in 1889 but rapid recruitment on Merseyside, followed by a major strike there in 1890, led to the transference of the central office to Liverpool in 1891. Glasgow became Branch No.1, but, beset by internal squabbling and recrimination, the branch never prospered, and relationships between the Liverpool leadership and the Glasgow branch officials were stormy. Nevertheless, the union policy was to establish and maintain strong branches in both Scotland and Ireland. James Larkin was appointed organiser in 1906, but in December 1908 he was expelled from the union. By then the NUDL was in a relatively weak position. Strikes in Liverpoool in 1905 and Belfast in 1906 had drained the union of funds, and the clash between Larkin and James Sexton (the general secretary) had created some wider dissension. Larkin had not neglected the Scottish branches, but his chief interest had been increasingly to organise the Irish workers, and his expulsion from the union led to the loss of most of the Irish branches to Larkin's newly formed Irish Transport and General Workers' Union. This made Scotland all the more important to the NUDL.

The exact circumstances surrounding Kessack's appointment as organiser are unknown. The NUDL executive report for 1909 merely recorded that he had been appointed on a temporary basis. It is plausible to suggest that if the Scottish branches needed reviving and the Glasgow branch, in particular, required further reorganisation, it was advantageous to have a Scotsman as organiser. Although there is no record that Kessack had ever worked at the docks, he had made his mark in Labour political circles in Glasgow as a good speaker and administrator, and as a man of integrity. Moreover, Sexton must have reflected that Kessack knew nothing of Liverpool and was hardly likely to challenge him as Larkin had done.

Within twelve months Kessack had shown himself to be able and diligent. Nevertheless, in spite of persistent efforts in Glasgow the branch finally collapsed, and when the Scottish Union of Dock Labourers was founded in 1911, most of the west coast ports were organised by the new union. Kessack's organising skills were more successful among the ports of the east coast of Scotland. Many of these ports had long established branches of the NUDL, but their fortunes had fluctuated considerably. Kessack set about reviving and reorganising these branches with a considerable measure of success, especially at Leith, which became the largest Scottish branch of the union, although smaller than the Mersey and Humber districts.

But his most conspicuous achievement was in the Humber ports of Hull and Goole. After the disastrous strike of 1893 in Hull, trade union organisation among waterfront workers along the Humber remained at a low ebb for over a decade. Before 1902, however, a branch of the NUDL was established at Goole. The Dock, Wharf, Riverside and General Labourers' Union maintained a small branch in Hull, but it was not until a branch of the NUDL was established there, probably in 1911, that trade union organisation began to revive on a significant scale. Kessack was a frequent visitor to the Humber ports and played a prominent role in the disputes that took place in 1911. By 1912 four branches of the union had been established in Hull and a district office had been formed, making the Humber district the second largest concentration of members of the NUDL after the Mersey district.

By this time Kessack's authority and standing within the union were considerable. His administrative and oratorical skills had materially assisted the expansion and stability of union branches in eastern Scotland and the Humber, and he had managed to retain a handful of Irish ports despite the competition from Larkin's Irish Transport Workers' Union. By the outbreak of the First World War George Milligan (in Liverpool) and Kessack had emerged as the major assistants to James Sexton, the general secretary.

Kessack's progress as a trade union official came to an end when he enlisted in the Army as a private in the Scottish Horse in November 1914. He was commissioned as a second lieutenant on 13 July 1915 and attached to the 25th Battalion of the Middlesex Regiment. He was promoted to captain on 1 March 1916 and posted to the 17th Battalion during the Somme battles which started in July 1916. He was killed in action, aged thirty-six years, on 13 November 1916, at the Battle of the Ancre. He left a widow, Margaret C. Kessack, and two children, all resident in Glasgow. His estate was valued at £246.

Kessack was clearly a man of considerable abilities. He was a committed Socialist who believed strongly in the importance of trade union organisation among waterfront workers, and he was notable for his honesty and integrity. He supported the development of the National Transport Workers' Federation, becoming secretary of the East Coast of Scotland District Committee; and he was anxious to secure an amalgamation of dockers' unions to create a single national organisation. Had it not been for his untimely death there is little doubt that he would have played an important role in the creation and development of the TGWU in the inter-war period.

Writings: 'The Drink Problem', *Forward,* 15 Dec 1906; 'The Wanderings of a Socialist Soul: O'Connor Kessack and the IWW,' [letter] ibid., 2 Feb 1907; 'How I became a Socialist', ibid., 20 July 1907; 'Socialism in the Far North' [account of lecture tour in the Orkney and Shetland Isles], ibid., 10 Aug 1907; 'Why I support the Budget', ibid., 30 Oct 1909; 'The Evils of Casual Labour', *Humberside Transport Workers' Gazette and Monthly Record,* no. 10 (Oct 1912); 'Scab Labour', ibid., no. 11 (Nov 1912); 'A Great Transport Federation', ibid., no. 15 (Mar 1913) 2–3.

Sources: NUDL, *Reports of the executive committee,* 1902–21, TGWU, London; T.J., 'The Woman Question and Mr O'Connor Kessack', *Forward,* 2 Feb 1907; idem, 'Camlachie's next M.P.! The Life History of James O'Connor Kessack'; ibid.; 4 Dec 1909; *Eastern Morning News,* 28, 30 June, 1, 3, 4, July 1911; *Humberside Transport Workers' Gazette and Monthly Record,* Jan 1912–June 1913; NTWF, *Report of 7th Annual General Council Meeting* (1917); R. Brown, *Waterfront Organisation in Hull, 1870–1900* (Hull, 1972); K. Brooker, *The Hull Strikes of 1911* (E. Yorks, Local History Series, no. 35: 1979) 46 pp.; biographical information: D.B. Nash, Dept of Printed Books, Imperial War Museum, London; Scottish Record Office. OBIT. *Eastern Morning News,* 22 Nov 1916.

ERIC TAPLIN

See also: †George Jardine MILLIGAN; *James SEXTON

KNIGHT, Robert (1833–1911)

TRADE UNION LEADER

Robert Knight was born on 5 September 1833 at Lifton in Devon where his father was a self-employed engineer and general smith. Robert left the village school at the age of twelve and began work with his father. Like so many young mechanics of his time, in his later teens and early twenties he went on the tramp round Britain, and then in 1857 started work in the Royal Steam Factory, Keyham, Devonport (a section of the docks), where he continued to be employed for the next fourteen years. In December 1857 he joined the Society of Boilermakers and Iron Shipbuilders, and soon became involved in union activities. He was to serve as president and later secretary of the Devonport lodge, and he became widely known throughout the West of England as a powerful and articulate advocate of trade unionism in general and of the Boilermakers in particular.

In 1871, when the Devonport lodge put Knight forward for the position of general secretary they especially referred to his vigorous support of the Boilermakers against the Shipwrights during the technological changes and craft demarcation disputes of the 1860s. In this first period of his union career, Knight also played a part in the local co-operative movement and was an energetic member and officer of the Ancient Order of Foresters. He was a Sunday school teacher for the Congregational Church and a teetotaller.

In March 1871 Knight was elected, by a national ballot, from among eight candidates, to succeed John Allen as general secretary of the Boilermakers. There had recently been a revision of rules which began to put the Society on a more efficient working basis; but Knight was to carry through further and more far-reaching administrative changes which made the Boilermakers one of the most effectively organised unions in the country. When Knight took office there were 7000 members in ninety-four branches, with a total of £9000 in the funds. At the end of a decade membership had increased to 22,965 in 177 branches, and the assets to £50,277; and just before his retirement in 1899 the number in the union was 40,776, in 258 branches, and funds were £175,516. These figures in part, of course, reflected the rapid growth of British shipbuilding, but they were also the result of the rapidly growing influence that the Boilermakers enjoyed in these years. Moreover, there was no other union that had the same degree of power and control over general working conditions. The Boilermakers were subject to the usual cyclical ups and downs of the economy, and unemployment in some years – the middle eighties for instance – was very high; but given work, the Boilermakers then collectively exercised greater power over their workplace than almost any other sizeable group of workers (for this, see the highly informative evidence given by Knight to the R.C. on Labour in 1892).

Wage levels, too, were higher than in most skilled trades. On Tyneside, at the time when Knight gave his evidence to the R.C. on Labour, the weekly rate for platers was 38*s*; for riveters 32 to 33*s*; for angle-iron smiths, 38*s* to £2; for holders-up 28 to 30*s*; and for caulkers 32 to 33*s* [Qs 21045–051]. Most areas elsewhere had rates that were somewhat lower. It was not only in the matter of wages that the Boilermakers had achieved more impressive results than most skilled unionists, for they also controlled vigorously the number of apprentices – one apprentice to five journeymen; they largely controlled the supply of skilled labour in that employers normally made application for labour to branch secretaries; the whole industry was unionised, and it was virtually impossible for a non-Society man to obtain employment. There was an unbridgeable gulf between Society men and their labourers, and Knight himself exhibited at its most emphatic all the craft pride and obstinacy of the aristocracy of Victorian working men. His evidence in 1892 was a classic statement of craft attitudes:

> 20801. There are certain divergencies of interest between the members of your Union and the members of the Tyneside Labour Union? – There ought not to be if we could only get the labourers to keep their places; that is the difficult point of the dispute.
> 20802. You mean there is insubordination? – I mean the plater is the mechanic, and as a matter of course the helper ought to be subservient and do as the mechanic tells him.
> 20803. The plater stands, to some extent, in the position of the employer of the helper? – To some extent, although our people do not want to pay them.
> 20804. Then there is a cleavage of interests as between the skilled workman and the employer, and there is a corresponding cleavage of interests as between the unskilled and the skilled workmen? – Yes.
> 20805. You would not allow, I understand, a Tyneside labourer, however skilful he might be, to become a member of your Union if he had not served a certain number of years apprenticeship? – We have never had a case where they have applied, and I have never found a man who was sufficiently skilful to come within our rules.
> 20806. Applications have been made, but they have invariably been rejected upon the grounds you mention, have they? – No, we have never had such a thing.
> 20807. You would not allow them to do your work? – We think everyone should do their own work. We believe in the old adage of the shoemaker sticking to his last.

20808. Yes, but if you carry that principle very far you would separate the working classes into cast-iron divisions, and it would be impossible for a man to pass over from the class to which he belonged to another class. Do you think that would be desirable? – I do not think it would be desirable for a man of one class to go to another class; and, in fact, for the interest of the man, I do not think it would be desirable.

20809. You think it would be desirable to maintain such an arrangement as would keep a working man in the class to which he originally belonged all his life? – Do you mean that we should be agreeable for a labourer to come and do a mechanic's work?

20810. Provided he was able to do it? – But we have never found that to be so.

20811. But if he was able to do it, would you object to that man on the ground that he had not served an apprenticeship? – We should object to receive him as a member of our Society unless he had served his time at the trade; certainly we should [*M. of E.* Group A vol. III, 18 May 1892].

The union was highly centralised, and in the crucial matters of the right to strike, and the award of strike pay, the executive council 'have full control of the Society's money, and in no case can one penny be spent in disputes without the dispute is first sanctioned by them' [R.C. on Labour Q. 20683]. On the average in the 1880s just under four per cent of income was spent on disputes [ibid. Q. 20750]. As well as having an industry relatively free from strikes, the shipbuilding employers could also rely on the union to insist on their boilermakers completing satisfactorily their contract; and there were examples, which Knight approved, of the Society's reimbursing an employer for work either not completed or not satisfactorily completed and exacting the money from the workmen themselves.

In their *Industrial Democracy* (1897) the Webbs characterised Robert Knight as an autocrat. 'Mr Knight's unquestioned superiority in Trade Union statesmanship', they wrote, 'together with the invariable support of the executive committee, have enabled him to construct, out of the nominally independent district delegates, a virtual cabinet . . . In effect the general secretary and his informal cabinet were, until the change of 1895, absolutely supreme' [Webb (1897) 30–1].

During the early 1890s there developed within the Society a demand for greater internal democracy in policy making. The existing rules stipulated that a membership vote should be taken every five years to decide whether a General Council should be convened to revise the rules of the Society. When such a ballot was taken towards the end of 1894, members voted 14,048 to 2237 in favour of a General Council; and it met in the following year. The most controversial new proposal to be made was the replacement of the lay Executive Council – who were normally drawn from the areas geographically close to head office in Newcastle by a full-time Executive Council of seven members. The existing lay Council as well as Robert Knight were bitterly opposed to the new proposals, and a vigorous attack was made in the Monthly Report for August 1895. D.C. Cummings of London – who later succeeded Knight as general secretary – was a leading figure among the reformers. The new rules proposed by the General Council Board had to be submitted to a ballot vote of the members, and although no voting figures were ever published in the Monthly Report, the proposed changes had been approved by the membership and the new salaried Executive Council assumed office in January 1897. Despite Knight's opposition to the changes proposed by the General Council he was re-elected unopposed in 1896. He had served twenty-five years. In the following year a donation of £600 was made to Knight; the money being subscribed by both union members and employers [Mortimer (1973) 130].

The characterisation of Knight as more or less a dictator of policy has been followed by Clegg, Fox and Thompson, who refer to his 'autocratic rule' [(1964) 150] by Fraser [(1974) 33] and also by the official historian of the Society [Mortimer (1973) 8]. It is a view which has been challenged by Clarke (1974); and what is now needed is a further inquiry into the matter. Knight was an extremely successful organiser, to the great benefit of his members, and success of the kind he achieved greatly discouraged the acceptance of criticism from any quarter. His monthly and annual reports in the official journal provided extraordinarily detailed information about funds and benefits. 'They became', Mortimer has written, 'a model for the trade union movement'. Moreover, as both Mortimer and Clarke emphasise, a notable feature of the Boilermakers' history has always been the crucial importance of bargaining at the workplace, over which a general secretary or head office had little control. The union also quite frequently resorted to a ballot of the whole membership, sometimes over matters that now appear trivial. Thus, whether or not the first Tyne delegate, Peter Jones, should be paid removal expenses, was decided by a national ballot; and in 1894 a membership vote agreed by a narrow margin to raise the wages of the twenty-year old clerical assistant at head office, as well as to the appointment of an office boy. And all officials, of course, were subject to periodic elections. We may conclude that the general question of the nature and character of union democracy in Knight's long term of office is worth further analysis, and this in spite of the admitted strength of Knight's personality which by itself must have been discouraging to would-be critics.

The biography of Robert Knight, as with so many union officials, is inextricably intertwined with the history of his own union; but he also played a part in the wider movement. He served on the Parliamentary Committee of the TUC from 1875–83 and again from 1896–1901. Apart from the R.C. on Labour he gave evidence before other committees and commissions, notably the S.C. on Employers' Liability (1877) and the R.C. on Depression of Trade and Industry (1886). Soon after he became general secretary, at a time when the head office was in Liverpool, he actively supported Plimsoll's campaign against the over-loading of ships. Knight's most persistent advocacy was for various kinds of union federation in order to strengthen their bargaining position. In 1875 he made his first attempts to achieve a federation of the engineering trades; and in 1890, largely as a result of his efforts, the Federation of Engineering and Shipbuilding Trades came into existence. The new organisation was, in part, intended to act as a counterweight to the employers' Shipbuilding Federation, which had been formed in the previous year, but the union federation was seriously weakened by the refusal of the ASE to join. Knight also urged a more general federation of unions in order to strengthen the position of the Parliamentary Committee in national affairs. At the 1879 Congress he introduced a proposal that the TUC should reorganise itself as a federation, but although his resolution passed by a majority of two votes, nothing was done. It was not until 1897, following the engineers' lock-out, that the TUC set up a committee to inquire into the problems of federation. Knight was its chairman, and the committee reported to the 1898 Congress, at which it was agreed that the Parliamentary Committee should convene a special conference not later than January 1899. Thus was born the General Federation of Trade Unions.

In his political and social attitudes Knight was a conservative Lib-Lab trade unionist. He was willing on occasion to criticise the workings of capitalism, as he did in his annual report for 1886, on the grounds that it produced unemployment and distributed wealth unequally; but much more important for his general style of work was his belief that 'it is to the interest of both [sc. employers and workers] to pull together as far as it is possible to do it' [R.C. on Labour, Q. 20949]. But like all his union colleagues, careful of the well-being of his members, Knight was also aware that these interests would at times diverge. His general faith in the viability of the industrial system, and in the need for capital and labour to harmonise their differences, led him to persuade the Boilermakers' Society to invest £10,000 in Armstrong's Elswick Works at Newcastle, where many of his members were employed; and to invest further in railway shares. Inevitably he was anti-Socialist in the 1890s; and almost inevitably too, he declined the offer to join the new Labour Department of the Board of Trade in 1893, at a salary of £400 per annum. Again, like almost all the craft union leaders of his day he was in favour of an increased working-class representation in the House of Commons. As early as 1871 he was appointed by his executive as the Society's delegate to the Labour Representation League. Later on, he approved of the idea of raising a TUC fund to assist independent Labour candidates and was one of the group (including James Macdonald, Burns, Clynes and Havelock Wilson) which pressed for and achieved this end in 1893.

Knight retired in January 1899, and the Society voted by a narrow margin to continue with his services as consulting secretary at a salary of £3 10*s* a week. The next year this position was abolished, but Knight continued to draw his salary as a retirement pension. He was by now approaching the age of seventy. He gave some support in his retirement to the National Industrial Association, formed in 1900 as an alliance of trade unions and employers; and he continued for a time with his public services. He had been a JP since 1892; he was for many years a governor of the Newcastle Royal Infirmary, and of Armstrong College; and he was a member of the management committee of the Barrasford Sanitorium. He had been a member of the Ancient Order of Foresters for fifty years; and he was an active worker for the cause of temperance, which he was always ready to urge upon his members.

He died from pneumonia on 17 September 1911 at his home in Jesmond, Newcastle. His funeral took place at St Andrew's Cemetery, after a service at St James's Congregational Church, of which Knight had been a life deacon. He was survived by his second wife (his first had died in 1879), two sons, Robert Clifton Knight, an assistant manager, and Stanley Christie Knight, a ship's draughtsman, and by a daughter then living in India. He left effects to the value of £9078.

Writings: Evidence to S.C. on Employers' Liability 1877 X Qs 2073–88; *The Practical Boilermaker and Iron Shipbuilder and Mastmaker* (Cardiff, 1880, later eds.); Evidence to R.C. on Depression of Trade and Industry 1886 XXIII Qs 14733–979 and to R.C. on Labour 1893–4 XXXII Group A vol. III Qs 20676–21154; and House of Lords Committee on Betting 1902 V [pp. 175–82].

Sources: *Bee-Hive,* 27 Sep 1873; Boilermakers' Society, *Annual Reports,* 1874–86, 1896–9, 1901, 1911; S. and B. Webb, *The History of Trade Unionism* (1894, later eds.); idem, *Industrial Democracy* (1897, later eds.); *Labour Leader,* 21 Jan 1899; D.C. Cummings, *A Historical Survey of the Boiler Makers' and Iron and Steel Ship Builders' Society* (Newcastle, 1905); F. Williams, *Magnificent Journey* (1954); B.C. Roberts, *The Trades Union Congress 1868–1921* (1958); H.A. Clegg et al., *A History of British Trade Unions since 1889 1: 1889–1910* (Oxford, 1964); J.F. Clarke, 'Labour Relations in Engineering and Shipbuilding on the North East Coast in the Second Half of the Nineteenth Century' (Newcastle MA, 1966); J.E. Mortimer, *History of the Boilermakers' Society* vol. *1: 1834–1906* (1973); J.F. Clarke, 'History of the Boilermakers' Society' [Review], *North East Group for the Study of Labour History Bulletin 8* (Oct 1974) 54–65; W.H. Fraser, *Trade Unions and Society* (1974); J.F. Clarke, 'Workers in Tyneside Shipyards', in *Essays in Tyneside Labour History,* ed. N. McCord (Newcastle upon Tyne Polytechnic, 1977) 109–13; biographical information: J.E. Mortimer, London. Obit. *Newcastle Daily J.* [portrait], 18 Sep 1911; *Times,* 19 Sep 1911; *Newcastle Weekly Chronicle,* 23 Sep 1911; Boilermakers' Society, *Monthly Report* (Oct 1911); *TUC Report* (1912).

Barbara Nield
John Saville

See also: David Charles Cummings; †Alexander Wilkie.

LEWINGTON, William James (1862–1933)

DOCKYARD TRADE UNIONIST, CO-OPERATOR AND LABOUR COUNCILLOR

William James Lewington was born in the Rotherhithe area of London on 20 August 1862, the only son and youngest child of William Redgate Lewington, a blacksmith's labourer, and his wife Ann Elizabeth (née Hunt). His father died while he was an infant, and his mother supported the family by practising and retailing as a herbalist. Lewington preserved a good deal of her herbalist lore and would make herb teas and medicines for his own family in later years. This background probably gave him the original impetus toward his temperance creed, which in turn propelled him into public life.

As a youth Lewington at first worked as a general labourer and saved enough money to open a small business in the Medway towns in Kent. The business did not prosper, however, and he found himself before long with a home in Gillingham and a family to maintain, but no income. In 1888, therefore, he entered the Royal Dockyard at Chatham as an ordinary labourer, where after six months his literacy and shop-keeping experience led to a post as storehouseman. This work entailed the sorting, custody and checking of goods in the storehouse. The Admiralty habitually drew storehousemen from the pool of unskilled labour in the Dockyard; but the men had to be literate and reliable. Lewington was both. At this time he was working for 16*s* a week, although classed as a 'skilled labourer' (a category similar to a 'semi-skilled' workman). In this period he drew some public attention to himself by a newspaper correspondence in which he defended the temperance movement against the position of the Anglican Church in Rochester.

The generally low rates of pay for labourers in the Government dockyards at this time was felt the more strongly when the dock labourers improved their own position by the strike of 1889. Lewington wrote to the local press on this issue, and was approached by labour organisers from the South Side Labour Protection League, then organising among workmen at Woolwich Arsenal, a workplace with which Chatham Dockyard had close traditional connections. With the help of Harry Quelch and others Lewington formed the Dockyard Labourers' Protection League, with about three hundred members each from Chatham and Sheerness Dockyards, as an affiliate of the SSLPL. This new organisation conducted a vigorous public campaign in 1890, enlisting at first the sympathies of local MPs, councillors, clergymen and other influential people. In the course of the campaign the tactical policy afterwards employed by the dockyard men in general up to 1914 was first elaborated; namely, waiving of the strike weapon in favour of detailed formal petitions to the Admiralty through the dockyard officers, coupled with direct appeals to the House of Commons through MPs for the dockyard constituencies. The campaign was successful in raising wages for labourers in 1891, and the policy was used to gain general improvements in wages and conditions throughout the period. The Government did not oppose political activity by employees so long as it was carried on outside the dockyard; inside, it was strictly forbidden – although the Liberal Government of 1892 took a more permissive attitude towards the formation of trade unions in the yards.

Dockyard labourers' organisations formed by the Dockers' Union at Portsmouth, Plymouth and Pembroke Dockyards federated with Lewington's Labourers' Protection League in the middle of 1890 to form the Federal Council of Government Employees. Of this body Lewington became secretary and remained so until 1899, when on his retirement from the post he was presented with a purse of sovereigns as the 'father and mother of the organisation'. The policy of the Council, besides the general advance of wages, was to secure recognition as dockyard tradesmen for certain occupational groups of 'skilled labourers' – riveters, drillers, iron-caulkers and others.

In June 1892, Lewington gave evidence before the R.C. on Labour on behalf of the labourers employed in HM Dockyards. He pointed out a number of abuses in the system (e.g. the employment of 'boy' labourers on youth wages up to the age of twenty-one), which were afterwards rectified. In 1894 the Admiralty was challenged on its refusal to allow its dockyard employees to sit on District Councils, and with the help of the Chatham Liberal Party was induced to change its policy in this respect.

Apart from his work as a dockyard organiser Lewington was also active in the trade union movement outside the dockyard, in the ILP and in the Eight-Hour League of Kent, and in 1890 he organised the first May Day demonstration in Chatham in support of the eight hour day. He was the first secretary of the Medway District Trades and Labour Council, formed in 1890; was a founder-member of the Gillingham Labour Party in November 1891, and in July 1893 was elected president of the Kentish ILP at its foundation meeting in Dover. In his trade union work he was assisted from 1897 by his successor, James Ireland, a joiner and a Rochester City councillor. It is not certain when Lewington actually became a Socialist, but it could not have been later than 1890–1.

Lewington was associated with the Rochester Co-operative Society in an interesting venture, the Medway Barge, Yacht and Boat-Building and Repairing Co-operative Society, set up in 1892, with Lewington as secretary and Rochester councillor R. Powell, a shipwright, as president. Joseph Black, a pioneer of working men's education in Rochester, also joined in this effort to create a producers' co-operative out of the special skills of the Medway towns. It had some initial success: it launched its first barge in 1894, and by 1897 had built four, and had six to eight barges employed in trade between the Thames and Medway Co-operative Societies. It later foundered for lack of capital.

Local government was also a field in which Lewington left his mark. In 1893 he led an agitation for the foundation of a School Board in Gillingham, a dockyard residential town experiencing a rapid increase of population in the era of the naval arms race. When the School Board was secured by Government decree, he served on it from 1893 to 1903, during which period it built three schools to house 3000 children.

From 1896 to 1898 Lewington was a member of the Gillingham District Council, standing on the co-operative movement ticket. In 1898 he failed to obtain re-election; but he presided over the formation of a Civic Union to press for the incorporation of the town as a borough and to agitate for the institution of municipal schemes for the supply of water, electricity and electric tramways. He also called for a public pier and dock to cheapen consumer goods, and for parks, public swimming baths and other amenities. From 1902 to 1904 he was again a member of Gillingham District Council. In 1904 he resigned his seat on being posted in September to service in Hong Kong Dockyard. This was promotion. But some felt that his removal was a way of dealing with him as a political nuisance, especially as it came just before a wholesale reduction, for technical reasons, of the number employed at Chatham yard. He spent the years 1905 to 1910 in Hong Kong, and was not therefore present at the general election of 1906 when John Jenkins, the Cardiff shipwright, was elected Labour MP for Chatham (in which constituency Gillingham lay).

In December 1910, back in Gillingham, he wrote letters in support of the Labour campaigns of that year, but did not take an active part in the election. From 1913 to 1920 he was stationed in Gibraltar, and on the basis of his experience there drew up a memorial to the Admiralty which was published in 1925 as *Impeachment. Gilbraltar as a Fortress. A Sham! A Delusion! A Snare!* This was a plea for the evacuation of Gibraltar on military grounds (in view of the new air warfare); but it also laid great stress on the national aspirations of the people of the surrounding countries, and emphasised the right of all people to be free from both foreign and domestic oppression. He included a series of letters to his family in Gillingham describing his rambles in the Spanish mountains in peace-time. After his retirement he went to live in Hassocks, Sussex in 1925; there he organised the Hassocks Labour Party and took an energetic part in its development.

Lewington had a large family, of four sons and two daughters for whom he is said to have cooked the Sunday dinner and made bread. His wife, who suffered from arthritis, did not share his public life, although her personal contribution was publicly acknowledged. His eldest daughter, Nancy, a teacher, who used to accompany him to various functions, married a business man in Hong Kong, and remained there. The second daughter, Amy, emigrated to Canada. The eldest son was apprenticed in the dockyard and was best known in the town for his sporting activities, especially as a football referee. Another son was also employed by the Admiralty, the third emigrated to Australia, and the fourth owned a newsagent's business in Maidstone. At the age of twenty-nine Lewington was reported as being 'a good-looking fair-faced youngish man with abundant dark hair' [*Chatham Observer*, 5 Sep 1891]. He was said by his daughter-in-law to have been full of fun, but temperamental, up and down like a cork. He died in Hassocks on 26 January 1933. He left effects valued at £498.

Writings: 'True Basis of Trades Unionism' [letter], *Monthly Record of the Dock, Wharf, Riverside and General Labourers' Union*, no. 4 (July 1890) 4–5; Evidence before the R.C. on Labour 1893–4 XXXII Group A vol. III Qs 23996–24132; *Impeachment. Gibraltar as a Fortress. A Sham! A Delusion! A Snare!* [1925].

Sources: (1) MS: Illuminated Address to J.J. Lewington from Chatham Dockyard Labourers' League, 23 June 1891 [copy in *DLB* coll.]. (2) Newspapers: *Rochester and Chatham News* and *Rochester and Chatham Observer*, 1860–1910; *Rochester and Chatham Times*, 1889–92; *Chatham Standard*, 30 Nov 1910. (3) Other: *Report by Mr Forwood on Memorials presented to the Lords Commissioners of the Admiralty by the Workmen employed in H.M. Dockyards and Victualling Yards at Home, together with Minutes of Evidence and Appendices* (1890) 127–30 [copy in Naval History Library, Ministry of Defence Ref. Da 053]; [Interview with Lewington], *Workman's Times*, 17 Feb 1894; C.S. Leeds, *Chats about Gillingham* (Gillingham, 1906); J. Fox, *Education in Gillingham 1893–1974* (Local History Series, no. 9: Gillingham PL, 1974) 35pp.; M. Waters, 'The Social History of the Chatham Dockyard Workforce, 1860–1906' (Essex PhD, 1979); personal information: Mrs S. M. Lewington, daughter-in-law, Gillingham. OBIT. *Brighton Gazette and Southern Weekly News*, 4 Feb 1933.

MAVIS WATERS

See also: †John Hogan JENKINS.

LINNEY, Joseph (1808–87)

CHARTIST AND TRADE UNIONIST

Joseph Linney was born in Macclesfield in 1808. Little is known of his early life; sources state that he was 'brought up to the silk trade' and 'connected with a branch of the cotton trade'. In an election address delivered at Dudley in 1847, he himself said that he began work in a factory at four and a half and had been employed for many years as a power-loom weaver. During another speech of 1866 he stated that he had been 'mixed up with political affairs ever since he was a boy' [*Wolverhampton Chronicle*, 27 June 1866]. His wife, Mary, came from Blackburn. By 1839 the Linneys had moved to Manchester, where Joseph became a well-known Chartist leader and opened a radical bookshop. He was one of the local leaders arrested in the tense days prior to the National Holiday of August 1839.

Late in 1841 Linney visited Stafford and Birmingham as a Chartist lecturer. His success was such that in May 1842 he was engaged by the Bilston Charter Association to lecture on a peripatetic basis within a circuit of three miles around Bilston. The Bilston Association was the most rapidly expanding of the local Chartist groups, with a reputed 1000 members in April 1842, and Linney was apparently appointed to assist Henry Candy, who had been lecturing and disseminating propaganda in the area since June 1841. Linney was soon working diligently in Bilston and further afield; he was one of the Black Country leaders who initiated a vigorous mission to the Shropshire coalfield, culminating in a mass rally on the Wrekin on Whit Tuesday. Linney was particularly successful in popularising the Chartist cause among the South Staffs. colliers in 1842, establishing new Chartist cells in the mining communities of Prince's End,

Sodom, and Ettingshall Lane.

The underlying discontents which found expression in the strike which paralysed the Black Country coalfield for six weeks in July and August 1842 were primarily economic in origin, the miners being concerned with grievances about pay, drinking usages and the truck system. The Chartist leaders, however, notably Linney and Sam Cook of Dudley, made tremendous efforts to unite the industrial militancy with the growth of working-class political consciousness. They succeeded in giving the strike a cohesive organisation and a sense of purpose, so that a succession of mass meetings at West Bromwich, Brockmoor, Wednesbury, Dudley and Bilston passed off without violence. As it became clear that such violent incidents as occurred were spontaneous rather than premeditated, the authorities became more confident and began to break up meetings and arrest leaders. A warrant was issued for Linney's arrest on 27 August, after he had spoken at a meeting at Brockmoor, when the Riot Act was read and troops dispersed the crowd. Linney avoided capture for four days, but on 31 August he was recognised and arrested in Wolverhampton, and committed to trial at Stafford. He was tried at the Special Commission of Assize at Stafford in October 1842, and was sentenced to two consecutive terms of imprisonment: fifteen months for using seditious language and six months for attending an illegal meeting. He served eighteen months of his sentence in Millbank Penitentiary, followed by three months in Stafford Gaol, where Arthur O'Neill and Thomas Cooper were fellow prisoners.

Linney was released in June 1844, and returned to Bilston to an ecstatic reception. He was elected to the committee of the Bilston Charter Association; and appointed manager of a Chartist Day School (according to a report in the *Northern Star* of 12 October 1844). By July 1845, however, Linney had become landlord of the White Horse Inn in Bilston High Street. This seems somewhat paradoxical, as he had signed Henry Vincent's Teetotal Chartist pledge in 1841, and was to describe himself in 1855 as a teetotaller of long standing. Probably he remained an abstainer, but saw the public house as an ideal organisational base, and as a ready source of income which freed him from the tyranny of an employer.

During the years 1845 to 1851 Linney was deeply involved in all aspects of Black Country Chartist activity. From November 1845 the White Horse became a centre for local Land Company activity, and Linney attended the second Land Company conference at Lowbands in August 1847, when he urged the directors of the company to appoint schoolmasters for the education of the communities, and to insure the properties. He later attended the third Land Company conference, in October 1848.

In July 1847 Linney was nominated Chartist candidate for the borough of Dudley, in opposition to the Tory John Benbow. An election handbill listed sixteen specific policies, which embraced the points of the Charter and a series of other reforms, including the repeal of the new Poor Law, the Navigation Acts and the Game Laws; the abolition of capital punishment, disestablishment of the Church of England, support for voluntary education, and the introduction of a comprehensive system of direct taxation. At the hustings Linney won on a show of hands, but when Benbow demanded a poll he was obliged to retire, lacking the finances to fight an election.

Linney attended the national Chartist conventions of July 1846 and April 1848 as a south Staffordshire delegate. In a fiercely militant speech at the 1848 convention, he declared that the people of the Black Country would endorse any policy for action recommended by the convention. He was appointed Chartist missionary to the Midlands, and during the re-organisation of the movement which took place during the summer of 1848, he became a Midland counties commissioner.

The 1850s saw a marked diversification in the range of Linney's radical activity. His involvement in Chartism diminished, although he persevered in his promotion of the Land Company, and assisted in its final winding up. On the industrial front, he was a prominent working-class leader of the campaign against the truck system of wage payment which started in Darlaston and Walsall in January 1850 and spread throughout the Black Country during the next few months. After a series of public meetings addressed by Linney and sympathetic local tradesmen, anti-truck societies were establishing in Walsall, Wolverhampton, Dudley and Tipton. According to W.H. Duignan, a radical Walsall solicitor who acted for the societies, some 600 prosecutions were initiated against truck-paying masters during 1850, producing some 250 convictions. By the later stages of the campaign, the local press were reporting Linney's activities with respect, and in two subsequent anti-truck publications of 1856 and 1861, he was quoted as a leading authority on the subject.

In 1851 Linney obtained two part-time posts in local government, as inspector of nuisances and market keeper in Bilston. He carried out his duties with typical pertinacity, becoming something of a scourge of purveyors of bad meat and other adulterated food.

In the late 1850s Linney relinquished the licence of the White Horse and set up in business as a pork butcher at 162 Oxford Street. He did not entirely dissociate himself from mining unionism, addressing meetings during the bitter strike of July–November 1864 against a wage reduction of 6*d* per day. By 1864, however, the Black Country miners were led by a new generation of leaders, and Linney turned his attention to the renewed working-class agitation for the franchise. He was a leading member of the Wolverhampton Working Men's Liberal Association, formed in May 1865 and later affiliated to the Reform League, which popularised the cause and tried to exert pressure on recalcitrant middle-class Liberals in the town. Linney spoke on the eighth platform of a 'monster Reform demonstration' held at Brookfields, Birmingham in April 1867.

After 1867 Linney disappeared from public life, and nothing is known of his next eighteen years, except that he continued to live in Bilston and later Wolverhampton. Some clue to his circumstances may be derived from a speech he made at a reform meeting in June 1866, when he stated that domestic affliction had compelled him to move from a £16 to an £8 house. This suggests that the death of his wife Mary had compelled him to give up his butcher's business.

Linney was found in Wolverhampton workhouse in 1885 by his old comrade-in-arms, Arthur O'Neill, who visited him and provided him with small creature comforts for two years, assisted by W.H. Duignan, the Walsall solicitor who had been associated with Linney in the anti-truck agitation of the 1850s. Linney had apparently re-married, and a son of sixteen and several smaller children were dependent upon him. He died in Wolverhampton workhouse on 19 June 1887, and was buried in Bilston Cemetery at the sole expense of Arthur O'Neill, who conducted the funeral service in company with another old Chartist, Thomas Cooper.

Sources: (1) MS: Census Schedules for 1851, Township of Bilston, District of St Luke, and for 1861, Township of Bilston, District of St Mary. (2) Other: 'To the electors and non-electors of the borough of Dudley' (poster 760, Dudley PL); *Charter*, 1839; *Northern Star*, 1839–52; *Wolverhampton Chronicle*, 1842–67; 'The Staffordshire Collieries and the Truck System' [letter 24] in a series of letters entitled 'Labour and the Poor – the Manufacturing Districts', *Morning Chronicle*, 7 Jan 1850; *Report of the Commissioner appointed to inquire into the State of the Population in the Mining Districts* 1851 XXIII, 1852 XXI; *People's Charter*, 1852–8; D. Bailey, *The Truck System: a book for masters and workmen* (1859) 24 pp.; H.H.B., *Black Diamonds: or, the gospel in a colliery district* (1861); T. Cooper, *The Life of Thomas Cooper* (1872; repr. with an Introduction by J. Saville, Leicester, 1971); W.H. Duignan, 'A Forgotten Patriot', *Walsall Observer*, 16 Apr 1887; R.G. Gammage, *History of the Chartist Movement 1837–1854* (1894 ed.; repr. with an Introduction by J. Saville, NY, 1969); F.W. Hackwood, 'Wednesbury Notes and Queries', vol. *3* [c. 1900] p. 381 [album of press cuttings, Wednesbury PL]; D. Read, 'Chartism in Manchester' in *Chartist Studies* ed. A. Briggs (1959); G.J. Barnsby, 'The Working-Class Movement in the Black Country, 1815 to 1867' (Birmingham MA, 1965); idem, 'Social Conditions in the Black Country in the Nineteenth-Century' (Birmingham PhD, 1969); idem, 'Chartism in the Black Country 1850–1860' in *The Luddites and Other Essays* ed. L.M. Munby (1971) 93–114; E. Taylor, 'The Working-Class Movement in the Black Country,

1863–1914' (Keele PhD, 1974); G.J. Barnsby, *The Working Class Movement in the Black Country 1750–1867* (Wolverhampton, 1977). OBIT. *Wolverhampton Chronicle*, 29 June 1887.

JOHN ROWLEY

See also: Samuel COOK; Arthur George O'NIELL.

LISTER, David Cook (1888–1961)
TRADE UNIONIST AND LABOUR ALDERMAN

David Cook Lister was born on 29 September 1888, in Hull, the son of George Lister, a general labourer and his wife Harriet (née Bradbury). After an elementary education he worked as a flour miller, was active in his union, and became district secretary of the National Union of Millers in Hull in 1921; when this union amalgamated with the Transport and General Workers' Union in 1922 he was appointed secretary of the general workers' group which included the flour and oil millers. In January 1943 he succeeded G.E. Farmery as area secretary of the union and remained in this position until September 1953, when he retired. He served on the Joint Industrial Councils of the seed crushing and flour milling industries and was at one time chairman of the flour millers' National Technical Education Committee.

He became a member of Hull City Council in 1927 and was at this time a member of the ILP but gradually his political attitudes shifted towards the right. He was a member of many council committees and was especially interested in education, serving on the education committee from 1929 until his death. He was chairman from 1935 to 1939 and from 1946 to 1961. In 1964, three years after his death, the first of Hull's purpose-built comprehensive schools was named after him. He became an alderman in 1945 and was three times offered the Lord Mayoralty but declined because his wife was too shy to undertake the social duties of the Lady Mayoress.

He was appointed a JP in 1936 and also served on the Juvenile Court Bench until he retired in 1953. He was a representative of the Council on the governors of the Marist College, Hull, from 1936 and of Hymers College, Hull, from 1946 until his death. Lister was also interested in higher education and was council representative on Leeds University Court from 1942 until 1946 when he became its representative on both Court and Council. His contribution to Hull University was recognised in 1957 with the award of an honorary MA. He had been local education authority representative on its Court from 1930–5 and on its Council from 1954–61. He was also a trustee of the Charterhouse, Hull, from 1933 to 1961.

David Lister was a man of medium height and colouring, slim with a rather thin, serious face. He was always quietly spoken, but when among friends was a good talker and quite humorous. He was a deeply religious man, a member of the Church of England who became diocesan lay reader attached to the Church of St Saviour, Hull, the Church in which he had been choirboy, choirman, scout, server, Sunday school teacher, Parochial Church Council member and reader. He is remembered as a good, down-to-earth preacher whose deep conviction showed in his sermons. His religious beliefs underlay his political attitudes and the strength he drew from them enabled this very shy man to have a public life. He was not a person easy to get to know, but all who came into contact with him agreed on his honesty and integrity.

He died on 25 July 1961 at the age of seventy-two, after a long illness. The funeral service took place at Holy Trinity Church, Hull, attended by many representatives of the civic and trade union life of the city, and the coffin was carried by six headmasters from Hull schools. He was cremated. His wife, Edith, survived him but there were no children of the marriage. He left effects worth £4881.

Sources: *Labour Who's Who* (1927); *Hull Daily Mail*, 1 Feb 1945, 29 July 1961 and 9 Sep 1961;

personal information: H. Bindoff, Hornsea. Obit. *Hull Daily Mail*, 25 July 1961; *T & G W Record* (Sep 1961).

Ann Holt

LITTLEWOOD, France (1863–1941)
ILP ACTIVIST AND LABOUR COUNCILLOR

France Littlewood was born on 5 August 1863 at Smithy Place, Honley, near Huddersfield. He was the eldest son of Zeruiah Littlewood (née France) and Thomas Littlewood, who was in business as a master wool dyer at Woodroyd Mills, Honley. France received his early education at Honley National School, and then from the age of ten at Almondbury Grammar School, Huddersfield, where he was a boarder.

His formal schooling ended at the age of fourteen when he joined his father in the mill to train as a master dyer. In September 1882 France Littlewood married Fanny Morton at Moorbottom Congregational Church, Honley. He lived first at West Wood End, then for more than forty years (1890 to 1931) at Grove House, and finally at Crosland Moor, Huddersfield. In January 1892 Thomas Littlewood died, leaving an estate of £10,492. The mill was then mortgaged to secure annuities for the beneficiaries, including France. The three sons continued their father's business, first at Woodroyd Mills, and then, from 1892, at Grove Mills, Honley. But Thomas had unfortunately overestimated his wealth, and the terms of the complicated will could not be realised. One result of this was that in 1900 the Littlewood brothers were forced into bankruptcy, with liabilities of £10,122 and assets of £1058. In 1902, however, they set up the new firm of Littlewoods Ltd, bleachers, shrinkers and finishers of cloth.

Politics began to interest Littlewood when he was in his twenties, and he became a member of the Liberal Association. In August 1890 he was co-opted on to the Honley Local Board on the death of the sitting councillor; he was elected to the Board in April 1891, and in August was made chairman. By November he had left the Liberals and joined the Colne Valley Labour Union; but he remained on the Local Board until in the first elections for the newly established Honley Urban District Council in December 1894, he successfully contested the East ward as an ILP candidate. He lost his seat, however, at the 1896 elections, and for the next eleven years he took no part in local government, concentrating his energy on the ILP.

Characteristically, on joining the Independent Labour movement he worked unceasingly for his new cause. He was the key figure in the formation of the Honley Labour Club in 1891, and was a stalwart in the Club's fight for survival in the difficult years at the end of the nineteenth century. He was elected vice-president of the Colne Valley Labour Union in May 1892, and he remained either an officer – holding almost every office – or on the executive, for most of the first twenty-five years of the Union's existence. In December 1893 he was appointed treasurer of Tom Mann's Parliamentary Election Fund. When the Yorkshire Federation of the ILP was formed in 1894, Littlewood was elected treasurer. He was a supporter of Victor Grayson and was one of the principal workers in the famous by-election triumph of 1907. In 1908 and 1909 he was president of the Colne Valley Socialist League, as the local constituency party was then named. But Grayson's behaviour, especially his attacks on Keir Hardie, upset Littlewood; in the general election of 1910 he felt unable to support Grayson in an official capacity, refused an invitation to chair the election committee and resigned as president of the CVSL in protest against Grayson's candidature [*Huddersfield Examiner*, 1 Jan 1910]. Before long, however, he resumed active work for the constituency party, of which he was secretary in 1914 and 1915.

His energies, however, were not restricted to local politics. Early in the ILP's existence he was appointed an auditor to the national Party, along with Fred Jowett. In December 1894 he presented the NAC with a plan enabling the Party to benefit from the sale of cloth. He supplied the committee with samples of cloth which he suggested they should circulate to branches, inviting orders on which the ILP would draw the profits. Although this scheme was rejected, the NAC was nevertheless intent on using Littlewood's financial and organising abilities, and in

1895 he was invited to join the Party election sub-committee. In the same year he was one of the eight guarantors for £200 with the Halifax Joint Stock Banking Company in respect of any ILP liabilities; the other guarantors included T.D. Benson (a Clitheroe estate agent who later became ILP treasurer), Keir Hardie, John Lister, R.M. Pankhurst and Arthur Priestman (a Bradford business man). Three years later France Littlewood was one of the guarantors for £400.

On the retirement of John Lister as ILP treasurer in 1896 Littlewood was elected as his successor, an office he held until 1901 when he resigned it. He was always generous towards the Party, as Keir Hardie apparently acknowledged in 1900 during a discussion of the financial difficulties facing the ILP. He concluded that 'nothing much could be done . . . beyond asking Littlewood to meet accounts from his own purse: "He happens to be in a position to do so."' [Thompson (1971) 119]. In view of Littlewood's imminent bankruptcy, his ability to pay had obviously been overestimated.

After his bankruptcy Littlewood withdrew from the national Labour scene, but resumed his activity in local government. In 1907 he won a seat on the Honley Urban District Council which he held until he stood down in 1913. Also in 1907, he was elected to the Huddersfield Board of Guardians, on which he served until it was disbanded in 1930. The work of the Guardians caught his imagination and interest, and he increasingly devoted his energies to it. From 1918 to 1926 he was chairman of the Board, and he won considerable approval for his sympathetic handling of the distress experienced during the General Strike of 1926. Another of his particular concerns was the Board's policy for children in care, and he was responsible for several progressive reforms in this field.

Many of the ILP leaders were guests at Grove House, including MacDonald, Snowden, Tom Mann, Keir Hardie (one of the Littlewood daughters has recalled the opprobrium she had to face at the local school when the children heard that Hardie was to stay with her family) and the Pankhursts, for Littlewood was a strong advocate of women's suffrage. Another guest was the former general secretary of the ILP, John Penny, who stayed at Grove House with his family for several months, at a time when he was in financial difficulties, probably in 1903 (Penny was secretary of the ILP from 1898 to 1903 when he resigned for personal reasons).

Littlewood finally severed his connection with the ILP at the same time as Philip Snowden, in January 1928; he explained his action thus:

> The founders of the ILP had to face the fact that the workingman could vote only Liberal or Tory. As that in itself was not a thing to be commended from our point of view, we decided to form an Independent Labour Party. But before that Party came into existence there were in many parts of the country, little groups, such as the Colne Valley Labour Union, whose aim it was to focus attention on the need for independent Labour representations. The object – a Labour Party separate from the other two parties – having been attained, the special mission of the ILP would appear to have ended [*Huddersfield Examiner*, 7 Jan 1928].

Littlewood remained in the Labour Party, however, at least for a while; but he seems to have lost interest in politics before the Labour crisis of 1931.

Littlewood had the reputation of being a model employer, a pioneer in the field of industrial relations: he operated a guaranteed five-day week, insisted that all his workers should be members of a trade union, paid wages in excess of the negotiated rate, and paid all of his employees' insurance costs in return for good time-keeping. In one respect he was an employer of the old type: he spent his working time in the mill, and so was accessible to his workers. He was active in the British Research Association for the Woollen and Worsted Industries (WIRA), a member of its research control committee in 1922 and of its council from 1922 until he resigned on his retirement from business in 1936.

Littlewood was of big build and strong physique, and in his young days was well known for his all-round sporting abilities. He played full-back for Honley RUFC and was a member of the

Honley Cricket Club. He was a keen cyclist and made many cycling tours, sometimes with his daughters. He was, moreover, a first class chess player, who won a national postal chess championship; and an accomplished musician. From his boyhood he delighted in music; on the receipt of his first week's wages, at the age of fourteen, he walked the three miles from Honley to Huddersfield in order to buy a musical score. He was a viola player in the Huddersfield Choral Society's orchestra from 1892 to 1924, and in the Huddersfield Philharmonic Orchestra. He formed the Woodroyd Handbell Ringers, who practised on his mill premises; and he was the conductor of Honley Silver Band. For many years he was a member of the Huddersfield Glee and Madrigal Society, of which he was president in 1929; but he resigned from the society when a nominee whom he supported for the position of conductor was rejected on account of 'the fellow being a Socialist'.

During the First World War Littlewood was a sergeant in the 2nd Volunteer Battalion of the Duke of Wellington's (West Riding) Regiment. He was active in the co-operative movement and was chairman of the Honley Society in the early 1890s. He always refused to become a magistrate, maintaining that he was not prepared to sit in judgment on his fellow-men. Religion meant little to him, but he was very familiar with the Authorised Version of the Bible, which he regarded as a treasure-house of stories told in superb prose.

Littlewood's health was already failing in the 1930s. He died on 22 January 1941, aged seventy-seven. The interment took place at Honley Parish Church Burial Ground on 24 January and was preceded by a service at Honley Congregational Church. He was survived by his wife and five daughters – a sixth had died in childhood. No will has been located. Two of his daughters were associated with the family firm: Mary Elsa as a director and Edna in catering and social work. Two others, Gertrude and Margaret trained at the Royal College of Music and the fifth, Jessie was a Froebel teacher.

Sources: (1) MS: Colne Valley LP minutes, The Polytechnic Library, Huddersfield [now available on microfilm]; Honley Labour Club minutes, 1892–99 [in private hands but also microfilmed]; Honley Local Board minutes, Huddersfield PL.; ILP, NAC minutes, BLPES; ILP, Finance Committee, Guarantee for Overdraft, 1895 [copy in *DLB* Coll.]. (2) Other: *Yorkshire Factory Times*, 4 Dec 1891, 13 Apr 1894, 17 Aug 1900, 1 Mar 1901; *Worker*, 30 Mar 1907, 9 Apr 1910; *Huddersfield Examiner*, 1 Jan 1910, 8 Mar 1913, 7 Jan 1928; L. Thompson, *The Enthusiasts* (1971); H.J. O'H. Drake, 'John Lister of Shibden Hall (1847–1933) (First Treasurer of the Independent Labour Party); a portrait of an individual in late Victorian provincial society' (Bradford, PhD, 1973); D.G. Clark, 'The Origins and Development of the Labour Party in the Colne Valley 1891–1907' (Sheffield PhD, 1978); biographical information: G.A. Feather, WIRA, Leeds; personal information: Edna and Albert Mosley, daughter and son-in-law, Honley. OBIT. *Holmfirth Express* and *Huddersfield Examiner*, 25 Jan 1941.

DAVID CLARK

See also: *Albert Victor GRAYSON.

LOVETT, William (1800–77)

CHARTIST AND RADICAL REFORMER

Lovett was born on 8 May 1800 in Newlyn near Penzance. His father, captain of a small trading vessel, was drowned before his birth. He was reared by his mother, Kezia Green, an aunt, and his grandmother. It was a strict Methodist household. Although he learned to read, write and do simple arithmetic, Lovett regarded his education as rudimentary, and all his life he sought to repair the deficiency by painstaking self-education. He was apprenticed to a harsh and drunken master-ropemaker, but finding no employment on completing his articles he migrated to London by sea in 1821. After near starvation and a prolonged struggle to gain acceptance in the trade he became a cabinet-maker and was eventually president of the Cabinet-Makers' Society. On 3 June 1826 he married a lady's maid from Kent. Judging by the regular letters Lovett wrote to his wife while he was in Warwick gaol in 1839–40, and by his comments at the end of his autobiography, it was a happy marriage; and he was an affectionate father to his daughter Mary (another daughter died in infancy).

Lovett's first contact with radical ideas occurred when in 1825 or later he joined a mutual improvement club called 'The Liberals', most of whose members were Deists in religion and Republicans in politics. His claim in his autobiography that he also joined the London Mechanics' Institute is not supported by its membership register; but it is probable that he frequented the coffee house at which Richard Carlile, Gale Jones and other radicals were leading speakers. Lovett, however, first achieved some prominence when he was active as a member of the committee of London artisans which successfully promoted the Friendly Societies Act of 1829.

By this time he had become deeply interested in Owenite co-operation. At Christmas 1829 he took over from James Watson, absent in his native Yorkshire on a missionary tour, the post of storekeeper of the London Co-operative Trading Association at its premises at 19 Greville Street, Hatton Garden. The store's purpose was to supply goods to the growing number of co-operative societies in London and to generate funds for founding a co-operative community. Lovett was 'sanguine that these associations formed the first step towards the social independence of the labouring classes'. Hence when the London Association hived off its propaganda efforts by forming the British Association for Promoting Co-operative Knowledge (BAPCK) Lovett willingly became its secretary following the resignation of George Skene. In this capacity he was eminently successful in carrying on an extensive correspondence with an increasing number of co-operative societies up and down the country. By October 1830 the BAPCK was in contact with 400 to 500 societies in what had become a considerable national movement capable of mounting a series of half-yearly national congresses.

But Lovett did not become a life-long co-operator. Owen's authoritarianism, the withering of the co-operative societies, the failure of community building, and probably the urgings of Francis Place, the populariser of political economy, played their part in Lovett's rejection of Owenism by 1836. The fundamental reason, however, was that Lovett's own success in self help and the residual Methodism which shaped his character as a sober, honest, self-reliant, clean-living man predisposed him to have a profound respect for individual effort at self-advancement, the ideology on which the capitalist system of his day was built. Certainly his 'feelings for his fellow workmen were intense', as Place put it, and he never lost sight of their contribution to the development of Victorian Britain nor of the evils of that society, which he regarded as condemning millions to poverty and lack of rights while exalting the aristocratic few to power and wealth. He also rejected some of the nostrums of political economy; and to Place's disgust, throughout the thirties he resorted to slogans from the anti-capitalist writers of the twenties which maintained that the working classes as the producers of wealth had first claim on its enjoyment. But Lovett lacked the intellectual power of Bronterre O'Brien to fashion for himself a coherent alternative to the current views on political economy, so that eventually he came to accept rather than reject the economic system of his day.

Moreover, unlike the pure Owenites, Lovett also saw no conflict between political radicalism and Owenism. While he was secretary to BAPCK the two were linked together in novel fashion by public meetings simultaneously commending universal suffrage and co-operation. He also joined the Radical Reform Association (RRA) with its programme of universal suffrage, annual parliaments and the ballot. In its stormy affairs Lovett was at his most militant. The July 1830 revolution in France and the enormous political excitement in November of that year stirred him to the depths. His speeches at the RRA's weekly meetings at the Rotunda became so vehement that the experienced police spy, Abel Hall, singled him out as 'a dangerous man' who was urging the political unions to arm themselves and declaring that he for one was ready to fight against the plundering aristocracy. Lovett's militancy was evident also in the quarrels which led to the collapse of the RRA in December 1830. He strongly opposed Hunt's attempt to purge it of supporters of Richard Carlile and the veteran revolutionary Gale Jones and to prevent it from displaying the provocative tricolour at its meetings.

By this time Lovett was also deeply committed to the working-class campaign for the abolition of the newspaper stamp duty. He was not a journalist – although he wrote on occasion for the unstamped press – nor did he publish or edit an unstamped paper, as his close friends Hetherington, Watson and Cleave did. His contribution was organising support for them. It was Lovett who first suggested the Victim Fund and served as its secretary. In its heyday from 1831 to 1833 more cash was contributed to it than to any other contemporary working-class cause in London, and it played a crucial role in succouring the street sellers of the unstamped whom the authorities in unprecedented fashion arrested and imprisoned in their hundreds. Throughout the unstamped campaign Lovett also acted as lieutenant to one of its protagonists, Hetherington, standing in for him to oversee his periodicals while he was on provincial tour or in prison. Eventually Hetherington probably made over his expensive printing press to Lovett in order to thwart the authorities.

On occasion Lovett also acted independently, as in 1831 when he refused to serve in the militia or to find a substitute, taking a principled stand on the grounds of 'no vote, no musket', and suffering in consequence a forced sale of his goods to the amount of £30. This experience, which gave him lasting prestige, led him to join the National Union of the Working Classes (NUWC) from which he had hitherto held aloof. He became a class leader and central committee member in an organisation which had absorbed all the ultra-radical groups in London, developed contacts with working-class unions in the provinces, especially in Lancashire, formed branches in the capital, and was by now holding successful public meetings.

In October 1831 when the House of Lords rejected the Reform Bill political London erupted. There was tremendous excitement and an unprecedented spate of public meetings. Lovett clearly shared the NUWC's hopes that the crisis would end in the achievement of full radical reform. He was much in the limelight when in an unusually powerful speech he moved an amendment in favour of universal suffrage at the inaugural mass meeting in Lincoln's Inn Fields of the Place-inspired National Political Union (NPU) which sought to unite middle- and working-class reformers behind the Whig bill. But Lovett's seconder, John Cleave, was howled down, with Lovett retorting savagely that all the middle class wanted was to make the working classes 'tools of their purposes'. Lovett's supporters were sufficiently numerous to elect him one of the few NUWC members of the NPU's original council although Place soon saw to it that he was rejected at the new elections in January 1832. Furthermore it was Lovett and James Watson who drew up the declaration of principles which the NUWC sought to have endorsed by a mass meeting of London's working classes on 7 November 1831 outside White Conduit House – a meeting which the Government prohibited in spite of protest from a delegation including Lovett that their intentions were entirely peaceable. The declaration itself, while rebutting widespread allegations that the NUWC intended to destroy property, uncompromisingly proclaimed its commitment to the three classical ultra-radical demands of the vote, the ballot and annual parliaments, as well as its particular hobby horse of no property qualifications for parliamentary candidates. Following the Government ban Lovett was again heard urging working people to arm in self defence. He was furious with authority for prohibiting a working-class meeting while allowing meetings of the middle class. He also angrily attacked the authorities for arresting Nathan Broadhurst and his Lancashire friends, initially on the major charge of treason, for their agitation against the sentences passed on the Bristol rioters.

However, there were limits to his militancy. He did not favour, as some of the NUWC did, persisting with the White Conduit meeting in defiance of the Government. The declaration he drew up was designed to sidetrack more radical ideas, especially those of Benbow, who particularly excited Lovett's disapproval by the violence of his language in rejoicing over the Bristol riots, and by disparaging Owenism, in which Lovett still had faith. He was entirely hostile to any secret proceedings by the NUWC as proposed by some of its Lancashire allies. Nor did he favour calling a National Convention or Benbow's Grand National Holiday. Although he regarded the Whig Reform Bill as quite inadequate, and in the crisis of May 1832 would again be heard saying the NUWC would have to arm if it was to get equal rights, his opposition to the Government measure came later and was less consistently vehement than that of Hetherington. Nevertheless he took a leading part in the NUWC's most successful public demonstration, its protest in March 1832 against the Government-approved Fast Day prescribed to avert cholera. For his leadership of the march, which rallied 20–25,000 participants and provoked massive police action to discourage it, Lovett, along with Benbow and Watson, was arrested and charged with making a riot, but scored a triumph in being acquitted.

However, Lovett was disgusted by the NUWC's endorsement of Benbow's alleged double dealing over the expenses of their trial. He could not stomach or successfully challenge Benbow's current ascendancy in the NUWC and therefore resigned from its central committee in June 1832. Nor did he sympathise with Lee, Petrie and others who displaced Benbow; he specifically disapproved of their plans for a National Convention in the spring of 1833, leading to the Cold Bath Fields affray, which he believed himself lucky to have escaped, in view of attempts by a police spy to lure him there. He was on the sidelines during the NUWC's campaign against the Whigs' Irish legislation and the agitation which led to the Grand National Consolidated Trades Union. Lovett joined the union and vainly tried to persuade it to make the vote its first priority, but only found common ground with it when taking part on 21 April 1834 in the great procession of protest against the sentences on the Tolpuddle labourers.

The mid-thirties was a period of withdrawal for him, and while politics were quiet he characteristically turned to education. Between 1834 and 1836 he ran a coffee shop, with rooms for a library, newspaper-reading and 'conversation', where he gathered friends in a society known as the Social Reformers. This was the model for launching the much more celebrated London Working Men's Association (LWMA) which was the most important organisation of working men in the capital between 1836 and 1838.

Lovett was its secretary and a key figure in its policy making. His part in launching the Association stemmed from his continued involvement in the 'unstamped' struggle and the friendly connections he formed for the first time with Francis Place and his ally Dr J.R. Black of Kentucky. These two, anxious to indoctrinate working men with ideas of 'correct' political economy, won the confidence of the suspicious Lovett by setting to work a renewed agitation for total repeal of the newspaper stamp duty. Lovett became a member of a committee of artisans formed by Black as part of the agitation. This spawned a group for collecting subscriptions to pay off the fines imposed on the unstamped publishers Hetherington and Cleave. Lovett was one of the two secretaries of this group. He also became a member of a further group, inspired by Black, although wholly working class in composition, the Association of Working Men to Procure a Cheap and Honest Press. This was established in April 1836 specifically to campaign against the Government's Newspaper Bill with its harsh penalty clauses designed to kill the unstamped. The Bill passed – a major defeat for working-class activists like Lovett – but the Association did not disband. With Black's encouragement Lovett and his circle converted it into the LWMA.

In the Address and Objects of the new Association which Lovett drafted, he envisaged it as a select body of the sober, moral and intelligent among the working classes, who would reject pot-house ranting and instead by study and discussion examine great political and social issues and learn to take the lead themselves rather than to rely on some great 'idol of a lord, M.P. or esquire'. The aim was to unite similarly-minded people up and down the country, so that by the pressure of their reasoned opinion everyone would achieve 'their equal political and social rights and the well being and improvement of the working classes would be promoted without commotion or violence'. In the context of 1836 the only specific object was to remove 'the cruel law' of the Newspaper Duties Act to permit 'free circulation of thought'.

Early meetings of the LWMA were held in Lovett's house; he kept its minutes and handled its correspondence and played a major role in composing its Addresses, some of which were remarkable as early expressions of the international character of the class struggle. The LWMA began in the manner Lovett had envisaged as an élite body committed to the tactics of an informed pressure group. Members were admitted only after careful scrutiny and in small numbers. Throughout its existence only 291 would be admitted as full members, the great majority from the most prestigious trades. A library was formed and regular lectures, discussions or readings were instituted. Sub-committees studied particular questions, one publishing a famous report late in 1836 entitled *The Rotten House of Commons*. From the beginning the support of supposedly sympathetic Radical MPs was sought, Lovett being one of a sub-committee appointed for this purpose in August 1836. Honorary members were accepted from a wide spectrum of radicals ranging from Place and Black to Owen and Feargus O'Connor.

Eventually, having drawn up a petition embodying the famous six points, the LWMA began to expand its role early in 1837 by holding its first public meeting to endorse this. Lovett and his colleagues then had meetings with Radical MPs in May and June 1837, to persuade them to accept the six points and to sponsor a parliamentary bill embodying them. This led to the selection of six Radical MPs and six LWMA members, including Lovett, who were to draft the bill. In fact they failed to do so, and ultimately Place, stimulated by Lovett, cast the six points into the precise and complex form and detail of a bill which when printed and published in May 1838 became known as the People's Charter. No one person can be called its author: Place contributed the indispensable legal and drafting expertise, Lovett was chiefly responsible for launching the body which originated it; but its basic six points represented the summation of a radical tradition which stretched back to the days of John Wilkes, if not beyond them. Lovett himself ever afterwards, with pardonable pride, regarded the Charter proprietorially.

By the time the Charter was published the LWMA was being increasingly overshadowed. Initially its importance lay in its success in reviving London radicalism by recruiting men such as Hetherington, Cleave and Gast, who were prominent in their own right in the capital. Then in 1837, through Lovett's efforts as secretary, and through public meetings and propaganda, but above all by the dispatch of its missionaries, it had contacted and encouraged the activities of 135 to 150 provincial working men's associations. Now, however, in 1837 to 1838 in the Midlands, the industrial North and Scotland, there was common activity in the campaigns in support of the convicted officers of the Glasgow cotton spinners' association, the Birmingham National Petition, and Feargus O'Connor's successful launching of the *Northern Star* and the Great Northern Union.

The LWMA responded with divergent results. The Glasgow Society of Trades sought its help in petitioning Parliament for an investigation of the cotton spinners' case. Lovett was convinced that injustice had been done: the most serious charges had not been proven, the jury had convicted on the lesser charges only by a majority and the sentence of transportation was exceptionally harsh. Consequently he established a joint LWMA-London Trades' Combination Committee to publicise the case, and as its secretary wrote an Address staunchly defending trade unions against press attack. He also sought the help of Radical MPs to forward the Glasgow petition, but in so doing committed a tactical error which exposed him to furious attack from O'Connor, who had also vigorously championed the spinners. For although Lovett realised the possible danger to trade unions of a general inquiry into their affairs by a Commons' Select Committee he agreed to this proposal of Daniel O'Connell's as a price for his support of the Glasgow petition. But the inquiry misfired as far as the unions were concerned, and O'Connor and Harney heaped obloquy on the LWMA as betrayers of the working class. A smarting Lovett retorted furiously, denouncing O'Connor as 'the great I AM of politics' for his claim, not wholly without substance, that it was he rather than Lovett who had rekindled

London radicalism. Some of Lovett's anger probably sprang from an uncomfortable awareness that the LWMA had taken a false step which enabled O'Connor to strengthen his position in the provinces substantially. Thenceforward, with differences in temperament and outlook playing their roles, Lovett regarded O'Connor with undisguised hostility and O'Connor sided with those like Bronterre O'Brien and Harney who had fallen foul of Lovett's circle. Such was O'Connor's popularity in 1838 to 1839 that the LWMA was bound to be overshadowed.

It was saved from eclipse by co-operation with the revived Birmingham Political Union (BPU) which in the autumn of 1837 to Lovett's delight abandoned household suffrage for universal suffrage. A delegate from the LWMA was sent to applaud the BPU's stand and pledge co-operation. This action had no immediate result. But when a delegation from a rather apathetic Birmingham had a vastly encouraging reception for its Petition from Scottish radicals in Glasgow in May 1838 and when a similar welcome was given to the People's Charter, presented by two of the LWMA's honorary members, delicate negotiations began which resulted in the LWMA's acceptance of the BPU's Petition as the first Petition for the Charter and the BPU's adoption of the LWMA's Charter. It was no doubt a proud moment for Lovett when a huge meeting in Birmingham on 6 August 1838 – the first Chartist meeting – formally adopted the Charter and the National Petition as twin symbols of a single movement and proceeded to choose delegates to represent Birmingham in a National Convention designed to present both to Parliament. A month later the LWMA organised a meeting at Palace Yard, Westminster, to elect London's delegates, of whom Lovett was one; members of the rival London Democratic Association (LDA) were carefully excluded.

This was the high point of the LWMA's success. Lovett's plea for a 'moral and peaceful agitation' was increasingly rejected by those attracted to O'Connor's tactic of intimidation – 'peacefully if we can, forcibly if we must'. The LWMA struggled in vain. Its missionaries were very active in the months before the Convention met, but to Lovett's chagrin most towns chose delegates for the Convention who followed O'Connor's lead, including Norwich, which rejected Lovett's close colleague John Cleave. Lovett and Hartwell established the *Charter* as a counter to the *Northern Star* and as offical newspaper of the Convention; but rivals – selling at a lower price – denounced them as sham radicals or tried to pre-empt their moral force stance. Lovett bravely crossed swords with O'Connor himself on 20 December 1838 at the Hall of Science, Commercial Road: among boos and groans he condemned violent language, criticised J.R. Stephens, whom O'Connor stoutly defended, repudiated wholesale denunciation of 'all classes', and declared point blank that 'if there was to be any arming he was not one of them'. All the evidence, however, shows that Londoners were either apathetic – Petition signatures and 'Rent' contributions were not impressive – or more inclined to follow O'Connor than Lovett. Indeed, on the eve of the Convention he had to beat off a move within the LWMA itself from close colleagues who deplored his breach with O'Connor and wished to make the LWMA more of a popular than an élitist body.

Lovett was chosen secretary of the Convention at its first meeting on 4 February 1839. He worked extremely hard, not missing one of the sixty-seven meetings held up to his arrest on 6 July. He drew up the Convention's procedural rules, was responsible for the elaborate questionnaire dispatched to local Chartist bodies inquiring into social and political conditions in the provinces, and received and replied to the numerous letters addressed to it. He accepted no salary, since he thought that to do so would preclude him from taking part in debate as a delegate for London. He sided with the majority, and probably this involved much sacrifice 'for the sake of Union and the cause', as he claimed many years later. He supported disciplining those who appeared to seek violent confrontation with government, but he resisted attempts to restrict the Convention to moral force tactics and accepted O'Connor's strategy of intimidating the authorities by seeking to persuade them that the country would be ungovernable unless the Charter became law. He fully supported the Convention's call for the ulterior measures of withdrawal of savings, exclusive dealing, arming and the sacred month or the general strike.

Lovett was arrested in Birmingham on 6 July 1839 on a charge of seditious libel. He had drawn up and had signed as secretary resolutions unanimously accepted by the Convention then meeting in that city; resolutions which vigorously protested against the action by 'a bloody and unconstitutional force' of Metropolitan police in breaking up a Chartist meeting in Birmingham's Bull Ring. The police, it was noted, had acted on the orders of middle-class magistrates who themselves had been prominent in similar meetings sponsored by the BPU. John Collins, who had taken Lovett's manuscript resolutions to the printer for turning into a placard, shared his fate. Lovett was tried at Warwick Assizes on 6 August and conducted his own defence against the prosecution case that the magistrates had only done their duty by suppressing a threatened riot. In Lovett's view the meeting had been entirely peaceable, the authorities were the aggressors, and the right of public meeting had been overthrown. The jury, some of whom Lovett always maintained had been heard to say 'down with Chartists' as they came into court, took but a few minutes to find him guilty and Mr Justice Littledale passed sentence of one year in gaol.

This year in gaol was a severe ordeal for a sensitive, hypochondriacal and far from robust man; but whether he was ill-used is open to question. He claimed that he was, and through his political contacts demanded that he should not be treated as an ordinary prisoner, although that was normal routine for the political offender. There is evidence that he was in fact allowed some indulgences – a more palatable diet, a fire in his cell and a table and two chairs for writing. Certainly he suffered debilitating bouts of illness; on his release all remarked that by contrast with his fellow prisoner Collins he seemed a shattered man. Nevertheless it was in Warwick gaol that Lovett with Collins's help managed to write his most extended publication to date, *Chartism, a New Organization of the People*, which appeared in the autumn of 1840. In it Lovett put the Chartist case and drew up a constitution for a new organisation to embrace all Chartists and to be called the National Association. Its purpose would be the creation of an enlightened opinion in favour of the Charter and through the improvement of the people especially by education. He concluded with an extended essay enthusiastically setting out his ideals and plans for education. Although much influenced by Robert Owen, Lovett anticipated later educational thought in his emphasis on the self-activity of the child, and his insistence that subject to democratic control, government had a duty to provide the means for educating the whole nation. In the book he described in considerable and loving detail the wide range of institutions through which this should be done. When politics turned sour for him Lovett would find solace in working as a teacher. Education was an alternative strategy to achieve his unchanging aim of 'Promoting the Political and Social Improvement of the People', to cite the rest of the title of the National Association.

Politics soon did turn sour. Since the prison authorities carefully censored his reading matter and closely supervised visits, Lovett probably did not know that while he was drawing up his own proposal the Chartists had already established in July 1840 a national organisation, the National Charter Association (NCA). Once out of prison, after spending some time in Cornwall to recover his health, Lovett attempted to launch his own National Association. He denied he was trying to supplant the NCA, but it was, not surprisingly, viewed in this light by O'Connor and denounced as 'the new move' in the *Northern Star* in March 1841. Lovett now found himself accused of conspiring with O'Connor's *bête noire* O'Connell and with middle-class radicals, notably Hume and Roebuck, in order to split the Chartists, destroy the NCA and substitute household for universal suffrage. O'Connor, derisively branding Lovett's new move as 'Knowledge Chartism', argued that it was destructive of the movement as it implied that 'a standard of learning was a necessary qualification to entitle a man to his political rights.'

Much but not all of this was unjust. Lovett had entered into no conspiracy and O'Connor's jeers at Knowledge Chartism ignored the evidence that many Chartists were just as enthusiastic for self-education as Lovett. But Lovett's sincerity in denying he sought to supplant the NCA is debatable. He refused to join it, believing that initially at least it was so constituted as to be an illegal organisation. In this he was correct, since the NCA amended its rules with Place's help to bring it within the law. But even when this was done, Lovett still refused to join, and in 1843 and 1846 refused invitations to become its secretary. At bottom there was a radical difference between him and the NCA activists over strategy. Lovett believed that the wild talk, secret plotting and sporadic violence in the movement while he was in gaol, for which unfairly, he held O'Connor chiefly responsible, had done the cause enormous harm; and he concluded that the only way forward was by an alliance of 'the virtuous exceptions' among the middle class and 'the reflecting part of his own class'. In 1841 this was anathema to NCA activists. The *Northern Star* was full of repudiation of co-operation with the middle class.

Denunciation of 'the new move' as traitorous, and a clear-cut demand from the uncrowned King of the Chartists that they should stand up and be counted as followers of either O'Connor or Lovett was almost fatal to Lovett's career as an influential Chartist. He did go ahead with his National Association, the first and only branch being founded in London in September 1841. The great bulk of London Chartists, however, were members of the NCA localities, often based on trade membership, and Lovett's National Association gathered only a relatively small number of ex-LWMA members, some from the defunct LDA and some talented newcomers such as J.H. Parry. Increasingly it developed into a tolerably successful educational institution, much aided by subscriptions from middle-class sympathisers. Lovett was justifiably proud of what it achieved, but the National Association was clearly divorced from the main Chartist body. The Association drew up its own Remonstrance to the Commons in favour of the Charter instead of backing the NCA's 1842 Petition, and issued an appeal to the middle classes to rescue the Chartist cause from 'the bad men' of the NCA.

An opportunity to attempt the strategy of class co-operation occurred early in 1842 when Joseph Sturge and his supporters in the Anti-Corn Law League, who believed repeal impossible without further parliamentary reform, sought Chartist co-operation to campaign for an undefined 'complete suffrage'. While welcoming the idea of co-operation, Lovett's National Association was clear that its basis must be the People's Charter; the NA minutes of 19 February 1842 declared that this could not be given up, since 'with its aid the working class had done what they had never done before, created a party of their own.' Throughout his dealing with Sturge in 1842 – indeed until his dying day – Lovett did not shift from this position. As a leading delegate at the first Birmingham Conference of the middle and working classes in April 1842 which launched the national Complete Suffrage Union (CSU), he was content that the Conference should accept the six points of the Charter even if this meant agreeing that a second conference should consider the Charter and consider in addition other similar documents embodying those points. At this stage the future of an alliance of middle- and working-class radicals depended on what support both Sturge and Lovett could arouse, and whether a further conference could reconcile middle-class distaste for the Charter with working-class conviction that it alone embodied their legitimate aspirations.

On both counts the months between April and the second Birmingham Conference in December 1842 were a profound disappointment to Lovett. Fleetingly, after the 1842 Petition had been rejected in the Commons, and O'Connor had reversed his previous hostility to the CSU, it seemed as if the way might be opened for anti-O'Connorite Chartists like Lovett to be reconciled with the main body, and an alliance with middle-class radicals cemented. The widespread strikes of the summer of 1842 killed that possibility. O'Connor believed that in arresting him rather than Cobden the Government was making him a scapegoat for strikes encouraged by Anti-Corn Law Leaguers; he reverted to his previous hostility to Leaguers active in the CSU and sought to ruin its second conference by packing it with his own supporters. For Lovett there was a further blow when the conference met. The middle-class radicals introduced their own 'bill of rights' and insisted that it should form the basis of discussion of 'complete suffrage'. Lovett was surprised and angry at what he regarded as an unworthy trick, maintaining, probably with justice, that although he was a member of the council of the CSU he had not been consulted. His reaction was to insist that the Charter must be the basis for discussion and O'Connor was only too delighted to second his proposition and see the middle-class delegates troop out to meet on their own after being defeated by a two to one majority. Lovett did not follow them as a few Chartist delegates such as Vincent did, nor did he respond to O'Connor's fulsome praise for his stand, and offer of reconciliation. Lovett knew perfectly well that O'Connor was no friend of the ideals which had prompted him to enter the CSU.

From then on Lovett was on the fringes of the Chartist movement. In 1844 he was active in stirring up protests, which culminated in a parliamentary storm, over the action of the Home Secretary, Sir James Graham, in having Mazzini's post opened, as a favour to the Austrian Government; the agitation over this was a landmark in arousing public interest in the issue of Italian unity. During the same year he joined the Democratic Friends of All Nations and wrote its launching Address, in which he asserted that for the first time, if only temporarily, Chartists of all shades of opinion joined with continental exiles 'to answer the union of Kings with the fraternization of democracy'. But his educational work at the National Hall increasingly absorbed his energies and gradually separated him even from some of his long-standing friends. Hetherington and Watson did not agree with his policy of refusing to allow the National Hall to be used for controversial purposes such as Owenite meetings or Sermons on freethought, or other causes to which Lovett was not sympathetic. Eventually in 1846 they quarrelled with him over his opposition to the appointment of 'the avowed atheist' G.J. Holyoake as a teacher in the day school attached to the National Hall. The result was that when the Chartist cause revived in 1847 to 1848 the anti-O'Connorite Chartists were divided. Lovett tried to unite middle- and working-class radicals in the People's League whose main policies were the Charter, reduced government spending, and progressive direct taxation on property. Hetherington and Watson supported Thomas Cooper's People's Charter Union.

The People's League, attacked by O'Connor and Ernest Jones and failing to attract Cobden and Hume, was unsuccessful; after recruiting a few hundred members it was wound up in September 1849. The League did bring Lovett into closer contact with radical Dissenters such as Edward Miall, and contributed to the increasingly liberal-radical stance of his later years. During these years he toiled away as a teacher at various schools, and wrote text books on geology, astronomy and physiology; he was in demand as a 'representative working man' to give evidence before parliamentary inquiries; and he supported numerous 'good causes' of a liberal radical kind, particularly temperance, international peace, the abolition of slavery, land tenure reform, the repeal of the game laws, better public housing and more parks. In 1856 he testified to his long-standing commitment to political rights for women by publishing a poem, *Women's Mission*, written fourteen years earlier. Reduced to poverty in old age, he was looked after by old friends such as the barrister Sergeant J.H. Parry, and occupied himself with making models of celebrated public buildings and writing his autobiography, published in 1876.

It is worth recalling Place's description of Lovett in his earlier days (although either the original or the transcription seems to have gone somewhat astray towards the end of the first sentence quoted):

> Lovett was a journeyman cabinet maker, a man of a melancholy temperament, soured with the perplexities of the world, he was however an honest hearted man, possessed of great courage and persevering in his conduct, in his usual demeanour he was mild and kind, and entertained kindly feelings towards every one whom he did not sincerely believe was the intentional enemy of the working people, but when either by circumstances or his own morbid associations he felt the sense he was apt to indulge of the evils and wrongs of mankind he was vehement in the extreme. He was half an owenite half a Hodgskinite a thorough beleiver [*sic*] that accumulation of property in the hands of individuals was *the* cause of *all* the evils which existed. He believed that in endeavouring to procure the adoption of his resolution he was promoting the good of his own class [Rowe (1970) 58].

Lovett died at 137 Euston Road, London, on 8 August 1877. The funeral was conducted by Moncure Conway, minister of South Place Chapel, and burial was at the Highgate Cemetery.

Lovett left effects valued at under £450. It is not certain whether his wife survived him, but she was still living when Lovett published his autobiography, only a year or so before he died. His daughter Mary married a compositor who later set up a tobacconist's shop. She was first a teacher and then, in the 1870s, went on the stage. She had one daughter, Kezia, born in 1857.

Writings: (with F. Place), *The People's Charter and National Petition* (Kilmarnock, 1839) 24 pp.; (with J. Collins), *Chartism: a new organization of the people, embracing a plan for the education and improvement of the people, politically and socially; addressed to the working-classes of the United Kingdom, and more especially to the advocates of the rights and liberties of the whole people as set forth in the "people's charter". Written in Warwick gaol* (1840; 2nd ed. 1841; repr. with an Introduction by Asa Briggs, Leicester Univ. Press, 1969); *To the Political and Social Reformers of the United Kingdom* [an address] (1841) 4 pp.; *A Letter to Daniel O'Connell, Esq., M.P. in reply to the Calumnies he put forth in the Corn Exchange, August 8th, in answer to the Address of the National Association to the People of Ireland* (1843) 8 pp.; *Letter from Mr Lovett to Messrs. Donaldson and Mason; containing his Reasons for refusing to be nominated Secretary of the National Charter Association* [1843] 4 pp.; *Enrolment of the Militia for Immediate Service!!* [1846] 2 pp.; *A Proposal for the Consideration of the Friends of Progress* [1847] 8 pp.; *Justice safer than Expediency: an appeal to the middle classes on the question of the suffrage* (1848) 8 pp.; *The Peace Principle, the Great Agent of Social and Political Progress* (1849) 16 pp.; *Elementary Anatomy and Physiology, for Schools and Private Instruction; with Lessons on Diet, Intoxicating Drinks, Tobacco, and Disease* (1851; 2nd ed. 1853); *Social and Political Morality* (1853); *Woman's Mission* [poem] (1856) 21 pp.; *Proposals for establishing a Cheap, Just and Efficient Mode of electing Members of Parliament, and for securing the Just and Equal Representation of the Whole People* (1869) 8 pp.; *Life and Struggles of William Lovett in his pursuit of Bread, Knowledge, and Freedom* (1876; repr. in 2 vols. with an Introduction by R.H. Tawney, 1920; another ed. minus the last three chapters, 1967).

Lovett's name appeared on Addresses by bodies whom he served as secretary. It is not known whether he was solely responsible for their composition but it is probable that he was at least part author of the following:

(a) **LWMA**
An Address to the People of Canada; with their Reply [1837?] 8 pp.; *The Rotten House of Commons, being an Exposition of the Present State of the Franchise, and an Appeal to the Nation on the Course to be pursued in the approaching Crisis* . . . [1837?] 20 pp.; *The Queen and her Ministers* [correspondence] [1837] 1 page; *Address . . . to the Radical Reformers of Great Britain on the Forthcoming Elections* [1837] 8 pp.; *Address and Rules . . . for benefiting politically, socially, and morally, the useful classes* [1837?] 8 pp.; *An Address . . . to the People of England, in reply to the Objections of the Press* [1838] 8 pp.; *The Working Men's Association, to the Working Classes of Europe, and especially to the Polish People* [1838?] 8 pp.; *An Address . . . to the Working Classes on the Subject of National Education* [1838?] 8 pp.; *The People's Charter; being the Outline of an Act to provide for the Just Representation of the People of Great Britain in the Commons' House of Parliament: embracing the principles of universal suffrage, no property qualification, annual parliaments, equal representation, payment of members and vote by ballot* (1838; 3rd ed. rev. 1838).
(b) **National Association for promoting the Political and Social Improvement of the People.**
An Humble Apology for Peace . . . [1844] 8 pp.; *Address . . . to the Working Classes of France on the Subject of War* [1844] 8 pp.; *An Address to the Chartists of the United Kingdom . . . on the Conduct of some Chartists* (1845) 8 pp.; *An Address . . . to the Working Classes of the U.K. on the Subject of the Militia* (1846) 8 pp.; *An Address . . . to the Working Classes of America, on the War Spirit . . . between the Two Countries* (1846) 8 pp.; *An Address to the French People* [In reference to the re-establishment of Republicanism in France] [1848] 1 page.

(c) **Other organisations.**
An Address from the London Trades' Combination Committee appointed to watch the Parliamentary Inquiry into Combinations, to the Working Classes (1838) 8 pp.; *"All Men are Brethren": an address to the Friends of Humanity and Justice among all nations by the Democratic Friends of all Nations* (1845) 8 pp.; *The People's League: to the people of London and its vicinity* [1848] 12 pp.

Speeches and articles by Lovett and information about him can be found in:

(i) Reports of Trials
A Correct Report of the Trial of Messrs. Benbow, Lovett and Watson, as Leaders of the Farce Day Procession [1832] 40 pp.; *The Trial of W. Lovett, Journeyman Cabinet-Maker, for a Seditious Libel, before Mr Justice Littledale, at the Assizes at Warwick, on Tuesday, the 6th August, 1839* 2nd ed. [1839] 20 pp.; *The Eloquent and Patriotic Defence of William Lovett as delivered by him during his trial at Warwick . . . 6 August 1839* (Birmingham, 1839).

(ii) The Periodical Press
The three periodicals with which Lovett was most closely associated were the *Charter*, 1839–40; the *National Association Gazette*, 1842; and *Howitt's Journal of Literature and Popular Progress*, 1847–51, for which he acted as publisher for a time. Details of his views and activities can be found in a wide range of newspapers and journals particularly those published by Henry Hetherington, James Watson, John Cleave and William Carpenter in the thirties, the Chartist press (listed in J.F.C. Harrison and D. Thompson, *Bibliography of the Chartist Movement, 1837–1976* (Hassocks, 1978) 99–113); and the Owenite press of the early thirties (listed in J.F.C. Harrison, *Robert Owen and the Owenites in Britain and America* (1969) 347–54). In later life Lovett occasionally contributed to the *Alliance News, Bee-Hive* and the *Transactions of the National Association for the Promotion of Social Science.*

Sources: (1) **MS:** The materials for a full biography of Lovett are scattered in many collections. Among the most important are the two volumes of the Lovett Coll. in Birmingham Central Reference Library which also contains the minute books of the General Committee and the General Council of the Complete Suffrage Union; Add MSS 34245 A and B, the papers of the 1839 Convention, Add MSS 37773–6, the minute books of the LWMA and the National Association, the Place papers, newspaper coll. and the papers of John Bright, all in the BL; HO records, PRO. (2) **Contemporary printed sources:** (i) Lovett's imprisonment: *A Copy of Report of the Visiting Magistrates of Warwick Gaol, on the Allegations in the Petition of Messrs. Lovett and Collins; and also the Evidence on which the Report was founded* 1839 XXXVIII; *Hansard,* 3rd ser. *49,* 2 Aug 1839, cols. 1188-91; *Correspondence relating to the Treatment of William Lovett and John Collins, Prisoners in Warwick Gaol* 1840 XXXVIII; *A Letter to Mr William Lovett, sometime resident in Warwick Gaol* (1841) 31 pp.; (ii) Lovett's National Association: *National Association Gazette*, 1842; *Address of the National Association of the United Kingdom for promoting the Political and Social Improvement of the People, setting forth their Objects* [1841?]; *First Annual Report of the National Association . . .* (1842); *First Balance Sheet of the National Association* [1843?]; *Plan, Rules and Regulations of the . . . Association* [1841] 21 pp.; (iii) For Lovett's part in the Complete Suffrage Union see: *Minutes of the Proceedings of the Conference of Representatives of the Middle and Working Classes of Great Britain, held first at the Waterloo Rooms, and afterwards at the Town Hall, Birmingham; April 5th 1842 and the Three Following Days* (Birmingham, 1842); *Nonconformist*, 6, 13 Apr and 31 Dec 1842; *British Statesman*, 9, 16, Apr 1842, 7 Jan 1843; *Northern Star*, 9, 16 Apr, 31 Dec 1842. (3) **Other:** No detailed biography of Lovett exists. There are brief studies by L.B. Hammond (Fabian pamphlet, no. 199: 1922 24 pp.); G.D.H. Cole, *Chartist Portraits* (1941) Ch. 1; J.J. Beckerlegge, *William Lovett of Newlyn* (Penzance, 1948) 19 pp.; Introduction by A. Briggs to the reprint of Lovett's *Chartism* in 1969; and D. Large in *Pressure from without* ed. P. Hollis (1974) Ch. 5. Documents with considerable references to Lovett have been published in G. Howell, *A History of the Working Men's Association from 1836 to 1850* (1900; ed. from the ms. and with an Introduction by D.J. Rowe, Newcastle upon Tyne, [1972]); G.D.H. Cole and A.W. Filson, *British Working Class Movements: select documents, 1789–1875* (1951); *London Radicalism: a selection from the papers of Francis Place* ed. D.J. Rowe (London Record Society, 1970); D. Thompson, *The Early Chartists* (1971); and P. Hollis, *Class and Conflict in Nineteenth-Century England, 1815–1850* (1973). See also: *DNB 12* [by J.A. Hamilton]; F.F. Rosenblatt, *The Chartist Movement in its Social and Economic Aspects* (NY, 1916; repr. London, 1967); M. Hovell, *The Chartist Movement* (Manchester, 1918; 2nd ed. 1925); J. West, *A History of the Chartist Movement* (1920; repr. NY, 1968); T. Rothstein, *From Chartism to Labourism* (1929); R. Groves, *But we shall rise again: a narrative history of Chartism* (1938); A.R. Schoyen, *The Chartist Challenge: a portrait of George Julian Harney* (1958); *Chartist Studies* ed. A. Briggs (1959); B. Simon, *Studies in the History of Education, 1780–1870* (1960); D. Read and E. Glasgow, *Feargus O'Connor: Irishman and Chartist* (1961); J. Hamburger, *James Mill and the Art of Revolution* (New Haven, Conn., 1963); E.P. Thompson, *The Making of the English Working Class* (1963; rev. ed. 1968); F. Boase, *Modern English Biography 2* (1965); D.J. Rowe, 'The London Working Men's Association and the "People's Charter"', *Past and Present*, no. 36 (Apr 1967) 73–86; idem, 'Chartism and the Spitalfields Silk-Weavers', *Econ. Hist. Rev.* 2nd ser. *20*, no. 3 (Dec 1967) 482–93; idem and I.J. Prothero, 'The London Working Men's Association and the "People's Charter"', *Past and Present*, no. 38 (Dec 1967) 169–73; D.J. Rowe, 'The Failure of London Chartism', *Hist. J. 11*, no. 3 (1968) 472–87; J.F.C. Harrison, *Robert Owen and the Owenites in Britain and America* (1969); I. Prothero, 'Chartism in London', *Past and Present*, no. 44 (Aug 1969) 76–105; D.J. Rowe, 'The Chartist Convention and the Regions', *Econ. Hist. Rev.* 2nd ser. *22*, no. 1 (Apr 1969) 58–74; J.H. Wiener, *The War of the Unstamped* (Cornell Univ. Press, 1969); P. Hollis, *The Pauper Press: a study in working-class radicalism of the 1830s* (1970); D.J. Rowe, 'Class and Political Radicalism in London, 1831-2', *Hist. J. 13*, no. 1 (1970) 31-47; F. B. Smith, 'British Post Office Espionage, 1844', *Hist. Studies 14*, no. 54 (Apr 1970) 189-203; F.A. D'Arcy, 'The Artisans of Dublin and Daniel O'Connell, 1830–1847: an unquiet liaison', *Irish Hist. Studies 17* (Sep 1970) 221–43; A. Plummer, *Bronterre* (1971); I.J. Prothero, 'London Chartism and the Trades', *Econ. Hist. Rev.* 2nd ser. *24*, no. 2 (May 1971) 202–19; R.G. Garnett, *Co-operation and the Owenite Socialist Communities* (Manchester, 1972); T.M. Parssinen, 'Association, Convention and Anti-Parliament in British Radical Politics, 1771–1848', *Engl. Hist. Rev. 88* (July 1973) 504–33; F.B. Smith, *Radical Artisan: W.J. Linton, 1812–1897* (Manchester, 1973); J.T. Ward, *Chartism* (1973); D.J.V. Jones, *Chartism and the Chartists* (1975); K. Judge, 'Early Chartist Organisation and the Convention of 1839', *Int. Rev. Social Hist. 22*, pt 3 (1975) 370–97; W.H. Fraser, 'The Glasgow Cotton Spinners, 1837' in *Scottish Themes* ed. J. Butt and J.T. Ward (Edinburgh, 1976) 80–97; T.R. Tholfsen, *Working Class Radicalism in Mid-Victorian England* (1976); D.J. Rowe, 'London Radicalism in the Era of the Reform Bill', in *London in the Age of Reform* ed. J. Stevenson (Oxford, 1977) 149–76; T.M. Kemnitz, 'The Chartist Convention of 1839', *Albion 10*, no. 2 (summer 1978) 152–70; D.J. Moss, 'A Study in Failure: Thomas Attwood, M.P. for Birmingham 1832–39', *Hist. J. 21*, no. 3 (1978) 545–70; I.J. Prothero, *Artisans and Politics in Early Nineteenth Century London* (Folkestone, 1979). OBIT. *Times*, 10 Aug 1877; *Examiner*, 17 Aug 1877.

DAVID LARGE

See also: William BENBOW; Richard CARLILE; John CLEAVE; †Henry HETHERINGTON; †Robert LOWERY; †Henry VINCENT; and below: Chartism to 1840.

Chartism to 1840

The bibliography which follows relates to the principal ms. sources, Chartist periodicals, non-Chartist newspapers and other writings of the early years of the movement. In addition there are special sections of memoirs of contemporaries and anthologies. Readers are directed to the following sources for additional references: F.C. Mather, *Public Order in the Age of the Chartists* (Manchester, 1959, repr. 1966); A. Wilson, *The Chartist Movement in Scotland* (Manchester & NY, 1970); J.A. Epstein, 'Feargus O'Connor and the English Working-Class Radical Movement, 1832–1841: a study in national Chartist leadership' (Birmingham PhD, 1977); J.F.C. Harrison and D. Thompson's Chartist *Bibliography*, op. cit.; *A Catalogue of some Labour Records in Scotland and some Scots Records outside Scotland* ed. I. MacDougall (Edinburgh, 1978); D.J. Goodway, 'Chartism in London' (London PhD, 1979). It should be noted (i) that annual bibliographies of all sections of the labour movement are published in the *Bulletin* of the Society for the Study of Labour History; (ii) the *Economic History Review* publishes detailed annual lists of all material relating to British economic and social history; (iii) completed theses are to be found in the ASLIB *Index to Theses* (1950 to date) and the *Lists* published annually by the Institute of Historical Research; current historical research is also listed by the IHR. Only those theses completed since 1975 are included below.

(1) **MS:** The principal ms. sources for the study of Chartism in the years to 1840 are: BL, especially the Place Coll. which includes the LWMA minute books; PRO, for the Home Office and other departmental papers, in particular those relating to interviews with prisoners (HO 20/10), disturbances (HO 40 and 41) and Metropolitan Police records HO 61/21–5, HO 65/13, MEPO 1/32 and 34, 2/26 and 59, and 7/6; Birmingham PL (Lovett Coll.); Newport PL (for 1839 Rising). For further details see: Epstein (1977) 545–6, Harrison and Thompson (1978) 5–26 and Goodway (1979) 348–52.

(2) **Theses** (completed since 1975; for earlier years see Harrison and Thompson, op.cit., 141–7): C.A.N. Reid, 'The Chartist Movement in Stockport' (Hull MA, 1976); C.S. Bebb, 'The Origin of Chartism in Dundee' (St Andrews BPhil, 1977); J.A. Epstein (1977) and D.J. Goodway (1979) [see above].

(3) **Chartist periodicals** (published in London except where indicated): *Advocate and Merthyr Free Press*, Merthyr Tydfil, July 1840–Apr 1841; *Ayrshire Examiner*, Kilmarnock, July 1838–Nov 1839; *Brighton Patriot and South of England Free Press*, Brighton, 5 July 1836–13 Aug 1839 (continued as *Southern Star and London and Brighton Patriot*, Brighton, 19 Jan–12 July 1840); *Bronterre's National Reformer*... 7 Jan–18 Mar 1837; *Champion*, 18 Sep 1836–26 Apr 1840; *Charter*, 27 Jan 1839–15 Mar 1840 (incorp. with *Statesman and Weekly True Sun*, 22 Mar 1840); *Chartist*, 2 Feb–7 July 1839; *Chartist Circular*, 28 Sep 1839–9 July 1842; *Dundee Chronicle*, Dundee, 1834–42; *Edinburgh Monthly Democrat and Total Abstinence Advocate*, Edinburgh, 7 July–1 Oct 1838 then *True Scotsman*, 20 Oct 1838–June/July 1843; *Hetherington's Twopenny Dispatch and People's Police Register*, 1834–6; *London Democrat*, 13 Apr–8 June 1839; *London Dispatch and People's Political and Social Reformer*, 17 Sep 1836 – 6 Oct 1839; *London Mercury*, 18 Sep 1836–17 Sep 1837; *Monthly Liberator*, Glasgow, June 1838–Apr 1839; *National: a Library for the People*, 5 Jan–June 1839 [repr. NY, 1968]; *New Liberator*, Newcastle upon Tyne, 21 Oct 1837–26 Apr 1840 (continued as *Northern Liberator and Champion*, 26 Apr–19 Dec 1840); *Northern Star and Leeds General Advertiser*, Leeds, 18 Nov 1837–23 Nov 1844 (continued under other titles to 1852); *Odd Fellow*, 1839–42; *Operative*, 4 Nov 1838–30 June 1839 (continued as *Operative and London Dispatch*, then merged with *Champion*, Oct 1839); *Perth Chronicle*, Perth, 1836–42; *Poor Man's Guardian*, 9 July 1831–26 Dec 1835; *Regenerator,* Manchester, Oct 1839 [continued as *Chartist Circular*, 1840]; *Scots Times*, Glasgow, 1825–41; *Scottish Patriot*, Glasgow, 6 July 1839–Dec 1841; *Scottish Radical*, Glasgow, Dec 1840–Feb ? 1841; *Scottish Vindicator*, Paisley, 1839; *Stephens' Monthly*

Magazine of Useful Information for the People, Manchester, Jan–Oct 1840; *Udgorn Cymru* [The Triumph of Wales], Merthyr Tydfil, March 1840–Oct 1842; *Western Star*, Bath, 3 Oct–5 Dec 1840; *Western Vindicator*, Bristol, 23 Feb–30 Nov 1839, n.s. 7 Dec 1839–Jan 1841 [cont. as *National Vindicator and Liberator of the West and Wales*].

(4) **Other contemporary periodicals:** *Aberdeen Herald; Annual Register* (especially 1839); *Birmingham J.; Bolton Free Press; Cambrian*, Swansea; *Cleave's London Satirist and Gazette of Variety*, 14 Oct–9 Dec 1837, then *Cleave's Penny Gazette of Variety*, 16 Dec 1837–20 Jan 1844; *Cork Advertiser; Evangelical Reformer and Young Man's Guide*, 30 Dec 1837–30 May 1840; *Examiner; Freeman's J.*, Dublin, 1839–42; *Glasgow Chronicle; Glasgow Herald; Glasgow Saturday Post; Halifax Guardian; Leeds Mercury; Leeds Times; Manchester Guardian; Manchester and Salford Advertiser; Merthyr Guardian; Monmouthshire Merlin*, Newport; *New Moral World. . . ; Nottingham Rev.; Penny Satirist*, 1837–45; *Plain Speakers; or Politics for the People*, 2 and 9 Dec 1827; *Political Mirror*, 1837; *Scotsman*, Edinburgh; *Scotch Reformers' Gazette*, Glasgow, 1837–54; *Sheffield Iris* [pro-Chartist until 1839]; *Silurian, or South Wales General Advertiser*, Brecon, 6 Jan 1838–29 Dec 1855; *Southern Reporter*, Cork; *Struggle*, 1840; *Weavers' J.*, Glasgow, 1835–7; *Weekly True Sun*, 10 Feb 1833–29 Dec 1839 [cont. as *Statesman*]. Note: The *DLB* Coll. has a volume of press-cuttings collected by George Hines (1839–1914) [see *DLB 1* (1972) 174-6]. These include accounts of the Chartist movement published mainly between 1880 and 1890 and mostly taken from the *Newcastle Daily* and *Weekly Chronicle*, the *Leeds Mercury* and *Workman's Times*.

(5) **Contemporary works:** The contemporary literature was extensive. It comprised addresses, broadsides, printed letters to Chartist leaders and to the middle and working classes, reports of committees on riots, sermons, and some books and pamphlets [see especially Harrison and Thompson (1978) 29–99]. Included among these works were memoirs and biographies, of which the principal items are listed below together with some later edited versions of contemporary autobiographic material, not already included in Lovett above: *Particulars of the Trial of Mr John Frost for High Treason . . . with an Account of his Life etc.* [1839?; later eds.]; S. Bamford, *Passages in the Life of a Radical*, and *Early Days* (Middleton, 1839–41; later eds. and facsimile repr. ed. W.H. Chaloner, 1967); A. Somerville, *The Autobiography of a Working Man* (1848; later eds.); *The Life and Character of Henry Hetherington* . . . ed. G.J. Holyoake (1849) 16 pp.; R.G. Gammage, *The History of the Chartist Movement, from its Commencement down to the Present Time* (1854–5; 2nd ed. 1894, repr. with an Introduction by J. Saville, NY, 1969); J. Turner, *Recollections* (Glasgow, 1854); James Burn [The "beggar boy"], *An Autobiography* (1855; later eds. and ed. with an Introduction by D. Vincent, 1978) [see also *DLB* Chartist press cuttings]; [R. Lowery], 'Passages in the Life of a Temperance Lecturer connected with the Public Movements of the Working Classes for the last Twenty Years' [autobiography], *Weekly Record of the Temperance Movement*, 15 Apr 1856–30 May 1857, ed. with an Introduction by B. Harrison and P. Hollis as *Robert Lowery: Radical and Chartist* (1979); W. Napier, *The Life and Opinion of General Sir C.J. Napier* 4 vols. (1857); W. Stevens, *A Memoir of Thomas Martin Wheeler*. . . (1862); H. Richard, *Memoirs of Joseph Sturge* (1864); [J.D. Burn], *A Glimpse at the Social Condition of the Working Classes during the Early Part of the Present Century* . . . [1868]; T. Cooper, *The Life of Thomas Cooper* (1872; repr. with an Introduction by J. Saville, Leicester, 1971); 'Mr Urquhart's letters on the "International": his connexion with the Chartist conspiracy in England', *Diplomatic Rev. 20*, no. 1 (Jan 1872) 21–3 and 'Chartism: a historical retrospect', ibid., *21*, no. 3 (July 1873) 209–31; H. Cockburn, *Journal of Henry Cockburn: being a continuation of the Memorials of his Time, 1831–1854* ed. T. Cleghorn (Edinburgh, 1874; later eds.); W. Lovett, *Life and Struggles* . . . (1876) (*see* writings above for details); E. Edwards, *Personal Recollections of Birmingham and Birmingham Men* [repr. from *Birmingham Daily Mail* with . . . additions] (Birmingham, 1877); C. Mackay, *Forty Years' Recollections of Life, Literature and Public Affairs: from 1830 to 1870*

2 vols. (1877); W. Dorling, *Henry Vincent: a biographical sketch with a preface by Mrs Vincent* (1879); T. Frost, *Forty Years' Recollections: literary and political* (1880); W.J. Linton, *James Watson: a memoir* (Manchester, 1880; repr. in *Literacy and Society*, ed. V.E. Neuburg (1971)); F. Peel, *The Risings of the Luddites, Chartists and Plug-Drawers* (Brighouse, 1880; 3rd ed. 1895 repr. with Introduction by E.P. Thompson, 1968); C.H. McCarthy, *Chartist Recollections* (Bradford, 1883); B. Brierley, *Home Memories, and Recollections of Life* (1886); 'The Late Mr John Mitchell, one of the First and Ablest of the Chartist Leaders in Aberdeen'; *Aberdeen People's J.*, 19, 26 Feb, 5 Mar 1887; B. Wilson, *The Struggles of an Old Chartist: what he knows and the part he has taken in various movements* (Halifax, 1887); G.J. Holyoake, *Sixty Years of an Agitator's Life* 2 vols. (1893); Rev. H. Solly, *These Eighty Years* 2 vols. (1893); H. Vizetelly, *Glances back through Seventy Years: autobiographical and other reminiscences* 2 vols. (1893); W.J. Linton, *Memories* (1895); G. Howell, *A History of the Working Men's Association from 1836 to 1850* (1900; ed. from the ms. and with an Introduction by D.J. Rowe, Newcastle upon Tyne, [1972]); W.E. Adams, *Memoirs of a Social Atom* (1903; repr. with an Introduction by J. Saville, NY, 1968); W.H. Chadwick, *Pages from a Life of Strife: being some recollections of William Henry Chadwick, the last of the Manchester Chartists* ed. T. Palmer Newbold (1910); Lord Broughton [J.C. Hobhouse], *Recollections of a Long Life* 6 vols. ed. Lady Dorchester (1909–11); C.C.F. Greville, *The Greville Memoirs 1814–1860* ed. L. Strachey and R. Fulford (1938); *The Autobiography of Francis Place (1771–1854)* ed. M. Thale (Cambridge, 1972); *Testaments of Radicalism: memoirs of working-class politicians 1790–1885*, ed. and introduced by D. Vincent (1977) [Thomas Hardy, James Watson, Thomas Dunning, John James Bezer and Benjamin Wilson].

(6) **Anthologies:** *From Cobbett to the Chartists, 1815–48: extracts from contemporary sources* ed. M. Morris (1948; repr. 1951); G.D.H. Cole, and A.W. Filson, *British Working Class Movements: select documents 1789–1875* (1951, repr. 1965); *An Anthology of Chartist Literature* ed. Y.V. Kovalev (Moscow, 1956); D. Thompson, *The Early Chartists* (1971); *Class and Conflict in Nineteenth-Century England 1815–1850* ed. P. Hollis (1973).

MABEN, William (1849–1901)

SOCIALIST COUNCILLOR

William Maben was born on 30 June 1849 at Coatbridge, Lanarkshire, the son of William Maben, a mason, and Cecilia (née Waddel). He was baptised on 29 July at Gartsherrie, in the parish of Old Monkland, Lanark. Apart from the fact that he began work at the age of twelve, nothing is known of Maben's early life. When he removed to Manchester, in 1870 or 1871 he was a builder and contractor by trade.

Maben became a zealous advocate of the temperance cause in Manchester. He also became active in the Manchester Radical Association, and in January 1884 was elected to its executive committee. This Association was initially composed of the Liberal-Radical supporters of Dr Richard Marsden Pankhurst, who defied the local Liberal Association by contesting the 1883 Manchester by-election as an Independent. However, the Radical Association soon drew into its ranks advocates of the most advanced political movements of the day, including supporters of the International Working Men's Association, republicanism and the National Secular Society. Among its members were some of the future founders of the local branches of the SDF and the ILP. It therefore seems likely that it was through his contact with the Manchester Radical Association that Maben was eventually drawn into the Socialist movement.

From the early 1890s he was prominent in Manchester politics. Municipal affairs were always his chief interest and one of his closest associates, S. Norbury Williams, had been elected Citizen's Auditor under the aegis of the ILP. In September 1894 Maben was appointed election agent for Richard Anderson, who contested a by-election in St George's ward, Manchester, on behalf of the ILP. Anderson was defeated, and in 1896 Maben himself stood as SDF candidate for the ward. Maben's move from the ILP to the SDF is not particularly surprising in the light of local political events. In October 1894 St George's ward ILP refused to accept the set of rules for election candidates drawn up by the party's Manchester and Salford executive. As a result the executive suspended the branch from the district party, and referred the matter to the National Administrative Council which in December declared the branch dissolved and abolished. The members, however, refused to disband their organisation, and in March 1895 resolved to become a branch of the SDF.

Maben lost the 1896 municipal election by only a narrow margin: he emerged second in a three-cornered fight, obtaining 1191 votes against the 1208 of the retiring Conservative councillor. Bottom of the poll was an Independent candidate with only 203 votes. It appears that the SDF was unable to maintain a branch in the Hulme district after the beginning of 1897, and in the following November, Maben, although still a member of that party, contested St George's ward as the candidate of Hulme Socialist Society. In a straight fight, he defeated the sitting Conservative member by 1798 votes to 1575.

Once a member of Manchester City Council, Maben came to be 'regarded by Socialists as their ablest practical advocate, and by the exploiters and oppressors as their most determined and dangerous foe' [*Justice*, 12 Jan 1901]. The question of housing took up much of his attention. He wished to see municipal houses erected at low rents (a shilling per room per week) before, not after, the slums were demolished; and he was against the lodging houses favoured by Manchester Corporation. He also argued the case for building artisans' dwellings in the suburbs, and providing cheap workmen's trams and trains for their occupants. He was much impressed by the well-equipped municipal washhouses in Glasgow, and advocated their provision in Manchester. Such and indeed all municipal building work should, he believed, be carried out by a direct works department, rather than by private contractors. But before agitating for this extension of municipal enterprise, he sought the removal of incompetent officials. Maben's exposure of irregularities within the cleansing department resulted in the forced resignation of the department's indoor superintendent.

With the aid of Norbury Williams, Maben prevented a costly and inefficient sewerage scheme from being rushed through the council. He also exposed the abuses and swindles connected with the culverting of Manchester. The *Clarion* later recalled 'his heroic effort from Hulme to Miles Platting, where he personally lifted every man-hole till he found the source of the poisonous gas that had destroyed poor men's lives' [*Clarion*, 12 Jan 1901]. Among his other notable achievements as a councillor were his campaign against the smoke nuisance, and his exposure of the insanitary and overcrowded conditions in Hulme, together with his successful efforts to improve the conditions of Corporation labourers.

Much of Maben's contribution to the work of the council was dependent upon his knowledge of the building trade. Although he gave up his own business, he subsequently acted as a consulting engineer and specialist in the building trade. By the turn of the century, however, he was suffering from bronchitis and in spite of several months spent in the South of France, his health continued to fail. He retained his council seat without opposition in the November 1900 municipal elections, but subsequently appears to have been able to attend only one council meeting before being confined to bed. He died on 3 January 1901 at his home in Great Jackson Street, Hulme, leaving a widow and family. No will has been traced. His funeral, at Manchester Southern Cemetery on 7 January, was attended by the Lord Mayor of Manchester and a deputation from the Corporation. There were also representatives of Manchester and Salford SDF; Hulme, Moss Side and Manchester Socialist, Liberal and Radical Associations; and the Bands of Hope but . . .

> more touching was the presence of some two to three hundred poor people, who had come some four to five miles on this bitterly cold day to testify their love and respect for, as one of

them said, 'One who was a poor man like ourselves, and who worked for the like of us' [*Justice*, 12 Jan 1901].

Sources: (1) MS: Parish Register, Old Monkland, Lanark. (2) Other: *National Reformer*, 1883–5; *Manchester Examiner and Times*, 26 Jan 1884; *Labour Leader*, 1894–1901; *Clarion*, 1896–8, 1901; *Justice*, 1896–1901; *Labour Annual* (1898) 134; City of Manchester, *Proceedings of the Council, 1900–1901* (Manchester, 1902); E.S. Pankhurst, *The Suffragette Movement* (1931). Obit. *City News* and *Manchester Evening News*, 3 Jan 1901; *Manchester Guardian*, 4 Jan 1901; *Clarion, Justice* and *Labour Leader*, 12 Jan 1901.

Naomi Reid

MacDONALD, Margaret Ethel Gladstone (1870–1911)
SOCIALIST AND FEMINIST

Margaret Ethel Gladstone was born on 20 July 1870 at 17 Pembridge Square, London, the only daughter of John Hall Gladstone, FRS, and his wife, Margaret Thompson King, daughter of a Presbyterian minister and a niece of Lord Kelvin. Her mother died shortly after her birth and she was brought up with a number of half-sisters from her father's first marriage. Her father, a distant relative of W.E. Gladstone, was a well-known professor of chemistry at the Royal Institution, an ardent Liberal, and an active supporter of social and religious work. He was a member of the London School Board for twenty-one years and one of the founders of the Young Men's Christian Association. Margaret attended Doreck College for Girls in Bayswater, the Women's Department at King's College, and later studied political economy under Mrs Henry Fawcett at King's College. As a child and young woman she travelled extensively in Scotland and Europe with her family. There are reminiscences of her youth in a small book by Isabella Holmes, one of her older half-sisters (1938). Her attraction to evangelicalism, at the age of seventeen, led her to place great importance on religious education and Christian charity. She taught a weekly class for servant girls at the Nassau Senior Training Home, and in 1889 she began teaching Sunday school classes for boys at Latymer Road Mission and St Mary Abbots, Kensington, followed soon after by work in the boys' clubs of St Mary Abbots. She became manager for several Board Schools and in addition, in 1893, secretary of the Hoxton and Haggerston Nursing Association. About this time she became a visitor for the Charity Organisation Society in Hoxton.

Margaret Gladstone's evangelicalism and the Liberal family environment in which she lived were, in her case, intellectual and emotional brakes upon the development of more radical political attitudes. Her Sunday school teaching had brought her into contact with working-class poverty, and at this time she was much influenced by the writings of F.D. Maurice and Charles Kingsley. The shift to a more defined, and Socialist, position took place fairly slowly. In 1890, the year when she became a member of the British Association for the Advancement of Science, she read Edward Bellamy's *Looking Backward*. She heard, and was impressed by, Ben Tillett at the 1891 Unitarian Congress; and in 1893 found *Fabian Essays in Socialism* had given her 'rather clear and more hopeful views about Socialism and the way to carry out better the love of the brotherhood and sisterhood . . .' [MacDonald (1912) 92–3]. Two women helped to inspire her: Amie Hicks and Mrs F.C. Hogg; and by 1895 she was acknowledging herself to be a Socialist. In that year she first met Ramsay MacDonald. In April 1896 she joined the ILP, and in the following November she was married. The MacDonalds set up house at 3 Lincoln's Inn Fields. From its inception their partnership met with approval from the labour movement. Long Eaton Trades Council resolved: 'That this meeting of the Workingmen of Long Eaton congratulates Mrs J.R. MacDonald in having won the esteem of Comrade J.R. MacDonald which in due time matured into love and it further resolves that she is one in a thousand' [quoted Marquand (1977) 49].

For the next decade and a half, until her death in 1911, Margaret MacDonald was involved in most of the social issues that contemporaries identified as problems of working-class women. She had joined the Women's Industrial Council in 1894, and immediately became secretary of its legal and statistical committee, and a member of its investigations and education committees. In the middle nineties she organised a Women's Industrial Council inquiry into thirty-five home industries in London. The results were published in 1897, with supplementary studies in 1906 and 1908; and the scandals of sweated home work became a central preoccupation, not only of hers, but of many contemporary radicals, Socialists and feminists. In 1897 Margaret MacDonald visited the United States, where she made a special study of the Massachusetts laws regulating home working, and she came to the conclusion that one immediate requirement was the establishment of a system of licensing and inspection of the dwelling places of the home workers. The growing agitation against sweating, in the home and elsewhere, led to the 1906 Select Committee on Home Work to which Margaret MacDonald gave evidence. Both she and her husband had become opposed to the much debated solution of Wages Boards, and in the autumn of 1906 Margaret MacDonald had spent two months in Australia and New Zealand, inquiring into the practice of Wages Boards and conciliation procedures. She returned convinced that Wages Boards did not offer a practicable model for Britain. It would not be possible, she argued, to establish a wage that would be substantially better than an improved form of sweating, and the low levels of wages actually fixed by the first Wages Board in Britain confirmed her views [MacDonald (1912) 156 ff.].

Her industrial interests always ranged widely. When unemployment became a national issue in the early years of the century, Margaret MacDonald involved herself in the agitation. She was a persistent critic of the Board of Trade unemployment schemes of 1904, and of the Unemployed Workmen Act of 1905, both of which she regarded as ineffective and unfair. She made numerous proposals to alleviate distress among women, and repeatedly claimed that the Central Unemployed Body, the local Distress Committees and the borough councils did not give women their proportional share of public unemployment assistance.

Using the Women's Industrial Council's organisation, she helped to produce a series of studies on women workers. One volume, *Women in the Printing Trades*, edited by her husband, was published in 1904. It was through her efforts that the Central Unemployed Body for London appointed a special Women's Work Committee, of which Ramsay MacDonald was chairman, and which established municipal workrooms for unemployed women in the clothing trades in Camberwell, St Pancras and Poplar. To publicise the unemployment crisis among women she assisted in the organisation of a march of unemployed women in Whitehall on 6 November 1905, a deputation from whom was received by Balfour; and in 1907 she initiated, through the Women's Industrial Council, a national conference on unemployment of women dependent on their own earnings. It was held at the Guildhall on 15 October, and was attended by 500 delegates from trade unions, local government and the women's movement. She addressed the conference on the legal prohibition of overtime and deprecated the excessive hours worked for limited periods followed by lengthy unemployment [WIC, *Report* (1907) 32–4]. In the same year Margaret MacDonald provided the R.C. on Poor Laws with a memorandum on unemployment among women, and she appeared in person before the Commission. She wrote part of *Wage-earning Mothers* [1911?] and a further investigation, on married women in industry, had been more or less completed before she left the Council in 1910; but it was not published until 1915, when it was edited by Clementina Black.

She was a member of the National Union of Women Workers, chairman of its industrial committee and secretary of its legislation committee. Through the NUWW she worked on numerous issues of importance to women including housing, leadless glaze, the registration of midwives and nurses, courts for children, police-court matrons, women probation officers, medical inspection and feeding of school children, restaurants for women workers, women's enfranchisement, the early closing of shops, and the hours of florists. She gave frequent lectures on these subjects and wrote most of the industrial section of the *Englishwoman's Year Book* from 1899 to 1909. Her last working days were spent obtaining better terms for women under the National Insurance Act of 1911, urging Lloyd George to include non-working wives and married homeworkers, on a voluntary basis, in the Act, and to expand medical services for women. It was also through the NUWW that she carried on a crusade to abolish the employment of women as barmaids, a campaign which brought her considerable and adverse publicity. In 1903 letters were published in *The Times* on this controversy and in 1905 the NUWW's Joint Committee on the Employment of Barmaids published a pamphlet, *Women as Barmaids* which revealed the impact of that trade on the character of girls. In January 1908 Margaret MacDonald presided over a conference on the employment of barmaids which urged the Government to amend its Licensing Bill to prevent girls from entering the trade.

Margaret MacDonald was also a pioneer in the movement for industrial education for women and girls. She criticised the London County Council Technical Education Board for its lack of concern for the education of women. Allied with Grace Oakeshott and the Women's Industrial Council, she persuaded the Board to appoint a committee on education for women, of which her husband was first chairman, and which, in turn, established the first trade school for girls, at the Borough Polytechnic, in October 1904. By 1908 there were over 400 girls attending classes at six locations in London. She argued that technical education would enable English women to compete with the trained French women who dominated sectors of the high class clothing trades (she went to Paris to study the women's trade schools there) and would, as well, enable women to improve their wages and combat casual labour and unemployment. In 1907 and again in 1908 she organised a national conference on the industrial training of women and girls, bringing together a large number of women to discuss ways of providing more and better education for working women and girls. Following the 1907 conference, she led a WIC deputation to urge the LCC to establish a children's nurses' training school for working-class girls; the school (the Nursery Training School) was eventually established on a private basis in Hackney in August 1911.

Marriage to Ramsay MacDonald inevitably brought her into increasing contact with the political side of the labour movement. Their flat in Lincoln's Inn Fields became a centre of political activity, with a constant stream of visitors from Europe as well as the movement at home. Both Margaret and Ramsay were opposed to the Boer War, and they were part of the important minority which resigned from the Fabian Society over this question [Cole (1961) 100]. Although Margaret MacDonald was a member of the National Union of Women's Suffrage Societies she was never in accord either with the social conservatism of Mrs Fawcett or with the militancy that developed after 1906. In particular she was incensed by the general refusal to support legislation for the industrial rights of women workers. Her own political energies in the last years of her life were centred upon the Women's Labour League. The Railway Women's Guild had passed a resolution in June 1905 in favour of a political organisation of women in the labour movement. Mrs Fenton Macpherson, secretary of the Guild, called a preliminary meeting which was held in Margaret MacDonald's flat, and the first public meeting of the WLL was held on 9 April 1906. The first conference, over which she presided, was convened at Leicester on 21 June. Mary Middleton was elected honorary secretary. Margaret MacDonald wrote in April 1909 for the *Women's Labour Day Souvenir:*

> ... We do not want to organise ourselves separately from the men, but we have found that the best way to co-operate effectively with them is to educate ourselves, to teach ourselves to discuss and understand and take responsibility in our own meetings, and thus to increase our knowledge and at the same time our power to do right.
>
> We are affiliated nationally to the Labour Party, and our local Leagues work with the local Labour Councils. We have about half a hundred branches now, from Brechin in the North to Portsmouth in the South, from Belfast in the West to Hull in the East; and the

> Railway Women's Guild is also affiliated to us. We have occasional great gatherings, witness our recent Annual Conference at Portsmouth, where Miss Margaret Bondfield presided over an assembly of women from all parts of the United Kingdom. The activities of our members are as varied as are their districts. Our subscription is low, usually one penny a month, to let the poorest join, but the real contribution of the members is in time and thought and work.
>
> We glory in the name 'Labour'. To us it means that every able-bodied woman shall do useful work for the community, whether as housewife or as worker for wages; that she shall have the training and the opportunity to give the best service of which she is capable, with hand and eye and brain, and that in return she shall have a share of leisure, of beauty, of comfort . . .
>
> . . . by political methods we believe that we can win freedom, economic and spiritual, for ourselves and for the generation that is growing up around us. To this we consecrate ourselves by our membership of the League, and we work through that for the young strong giant of the future – the Labour Party [quoted MacDonald (1912) 215–17].

She was an internationalist. When the MacDonalds visited India, Margaret wrote the two chapters on women in her husband's book *The Awakening of India* (1910). She took an enthusiastic part in international Socialist congresses and the International Congress of Socialist Women. One of the last acts of her life was to arrange for the English publication of the autobiography of her German working-class friend, Adelheid Popp [*The Autobiography of a Working Woman* (1913)].

Margaret MacDonald died at her home on 8 September 1911 at the age of forty-one following blood poisoning due to an internal ulcer. Apart from the personal bereavements she had suffered – a son, David, had died on 3 February 1910 and her friend Mary Middleton only five months before her own death – it is apparent that problems connected with her women's work had also affected her. Among the tributes was one which recalled that she 'found herself obliged to sever her connection with the Women's Industrial Council, after months of controversy which caused this peace-loving woman acute distress' [WLL (1912) 6]. Services were conducted on 12 September at her home and at Golders Green Crematorium. Two services were held for her at Leicester and her ashes were buried in the beautiful churchyard at Spynie, near Lossiemouth. Three memorials were created: her name was linked with a baby clinic in North Kensington already being planned in memory of Mary Middleton; a new ward in the Leicester Children's Hospital; and a statue in Lincoln's Inn Fields, which was unveiled on 19 December 1914. From her youth she was interested in poetry, and shortly before her death she published a book of her poems *The Poet's Calendar* (1911), dedicated to her sister. She had five surviving children: Alister (b. 1898), Malcolm (b. 1901), Ishbel (b. 1903), Joan (b. 1908) and Sheila (b. 1910). She left effects valued at £271, but this must not obscure the much more important fact that her private income, after her marriage, was about £460 a year, and there was a trust fund which eventually amounted to more than £25,000. His marriage brought Ramsay MacDonald a degree of economic security he had never known earlier, and which was, indeed, unusual in his own generation of labour leaders. These matters are discussed in Marquand (1977) p. 50 ff.

Margaret MacDonald's death was an emotional blow from which her husband never recovered. As his biographer wrote:

> Marriage meant even more to MacDonald than it does to most men . . . Though Margaret was a downright and strong-minded woman, determined to speak the truth as she saw it and unwilling to stifle her opinions for the sake of a quiet life, she had an inner serenity that he lacked, and while she lived his earlier prickliness was less obtrusive. Above all, she gave him, for the first time in his life, a secure emotional anchorage [ibid., 50].

Writings: (with others), *Home Industries of Women in London* (WIC, 1897, other reports, 1906 and 1908); 'Regulation of Home-work in Foreign Countries', *WIN* (Sep 1897) 3–7; 'Industrial Section', *Englishwoman's Year Book*, 1899–1909; Introduction to *Women in Industrial Life* (International Congress of Women, 1899); 'Labour Legislation for Women' *Report* of the British Association for the Advancement of Science, Section F (1900) 850–1; 'Working Women in Stuttgart', *WIN* (Sep 1900) 191–2; 'The Housing Problem' in *Women Workers: papers read at conference in Brighton 23–26 Oct 1900* [1900] 145–51; *Labour Laws for Women: their reason and their results* (ILP, City Branch pamphlets no. 2: 1900) 24 pp.; 'Factory Inspector's Report, 1900 and 1901', *WIN* (Dec 1901) 278–81 and ibid. (June 1902) 314–16; (with others), 'On the Economic Effect of Legislation regulating Women's Labour' [Committee appointed to investigate this subject], *Reports* of the British Association (1902) 286–313 and (1903) 315–64; 'Unemployed Women', *WIN* (Mar 1905) 272–8; (with others), *Women as Barmaids* with a Preface by the Lord Bishop of Southwark [E.S. Talbot] (1905) 58 pp.; (with J.R. MacDonald), 'Sweated Home-Industries', *Independent Rev. 10*, no. 35 (Aug 1906) 150–64; 'Some Recent Investigations in Home work' *Reports* of the British Association, Section F (1906) 653 and ibid. Section L p. 778 [title only] 'The Education of Wage-earners of School Age'; 'Conditions of Home Work in the United Kingdom' in *Reports* of British Association for Labour Legislation (British Institute of Social Service, 1906) 9–36; 'A Legal Minimum Wage: the case against it', *Labour Leader*, 17, 31 May, 7 June 1907; Evidence before S.C. on Home Work 1907 VI Qs 4296–606; 'Report on Enquiry into Conditions of Work in Laundries', *WIN* (June 1907) 629–42; 'Day Trade Schools for Girls', *Report* of British Association, Section L (1907) 725–6; 'Sweated Industries and Wages Boards', *Econ. J. 18* (Mar 1908) 140–5; 'The Women's Labour League' in *Women Workers: souvenir of Women's Labour Day, Saturday July 17th 1909* (WTUL and WLL, [Manchester, 1909?]) 14–17; Evidence before the R.C. on the Poor Laws and Relief of Distress 1910 XLVIII Qs 82466–763; 'The Women of India', Chs 9 and 10 of Part 2 of J.R. MacDonald, *The Awakening of India* (1910) 75–96; *The Poet's Calendar and Other Verses* (1911); (with others), *Wage-earning Mothers* [1911]; (with others), *Married Women's Work, being the Report of an Inquiry undertaken by the Women's Industrial Council*, ed. C. Black (1915).

Sources: (1) MS: Margaret MacDonald Papers, BLPES. (2) Newspapers and journals: *Labour Leader*, 10 June 1899, 15 Feb 1907; *Times*, 7 and 18 Feb 1903, 7 Nov 1905, 16 Oct 1907, 16 Dec 1908, 17 June, 5 July 1911 and 21 Dec 1914; *WIN*, Mar, Sep and Dec 1908, July and Oct 1909, Apr and July 1910. (3) Other: WIC, *Annual Reports*, 1895–1910; J.R. MacDonald, *What I saw in South Africa, September and October 1902* [1902]; *Women in the Printing Trades: a sociological study*, ed. J.R. MacDonald (1904); National Conference on the Unemployment of Women dependent on their own Earnings, *Report* (1907) 39 pp.; *What has already been done* [WIC, 1910?] 4 pp.; 'The Insurance Bill: Mr Lloyd George and the Case of Women', *Times*, 17 June 1911; R.C. on Divorce and Matrimonial Causes, evidence of Mrs Ruth Homan, 9 Nov 1910, *M of E* 1912–13 XX; J.R. MacDonald, *Margaret Ethel MacDonald*, (privately printed memoir, Letchworth, 1911); idem, *Margaret Ethel MacDonald* (1912; later eds); J. Rowntree, *Social Service: its place in the Society of Friends* (1913); L. Herbert, *Mrs Ramsay MacDonald* (1924); *DNB* (1931–40) [for J.R. MacDonald by Lord Elton]; I.M. Holmes, *The Girlhood of Mrs Ramsay MacDonald* (1938) 16 pp.; H.P. Adams, *Women in Council* [on NCW] (1945); D. Marquand, *Ramsay MacDonald* (1977); personal information: Dr Joan M. Mackinnon, Leeds, daughter. Obit. *Times*, 9, 12 and 18 Sep 1911; *WIN* (Oct 1911); NUWW, *Annual Report* (1910–11); J.B. Glasier, 'Margaret MacDonald: in memoriam', *Soc. Rev. 8* (1911–12) 154–5; *Margaret Ethel MacDonald* [obituary notices] (WLL, 1912) 22 pp.

JOHN SAVILLE
JAMES A. SCHMIECHEN

See also: †Amelia (Amie) Jane HICKS; *Mary MIDDLETON; †James Ramsay MACDONALD.

MANN, Jean (1889–1964)
LABOUR MP

Jean Mann was born at 22 Calder Street, Govan, on 2 July 1889, the daughter of William Stewart, an iron moulder, and Annie (née Morrison). She was registered as Janet, but later preferred the name of Jean. She was educated at Kinning Park School and Bellahouston Academy, trained and worked as an accountant, and in her public career became recognised as an authority on finance and statistics.

In 1907 she married William Lawrence Mann. They worked and lived in Rothesay after the First World War, and it was there that Jean Mann made her first entry into political life, when she joined the local branch of the ILP (of which her husband was chairman) and became branch secretary. In this step she was much influenced, she writes, by *Forward* [Mann (1962) 117]. She also became a member of the speakers' panel of the ILP and, at some time, of the ILP Scottish Council.

In 1923 and 1924 she stood, unsuccessfully, for the Rothesay Town Council. She was a friend of Rosslyn Mitchell, the Glasgow solicitor who as Labour candidate defeated Asquith for Paisley in 1924. And in 1929 she was agent for Craigie Aitchison (Lord Advocate 1929–33, Lord Justice Clerk 1933–41) in his unsuccessful general election fight for Glasgow Central.

By this time the Manns had apparently moved to Glasgow, and in 1931 Mrs Mann was elected to Glasgow Corporation as Labour member for Provan ward. In the general election of the same year she stood as ILP candidate for West Renfrewshire, in opposition to Robert Forgan. But she shared in the landslide defeat of Labour; and she was again unsuccessful when she contested the same seat in the 1935 election.

She served on Glasgow Corporation until 1938, becoming a Bailie in 1934 and in 1937–8 Senior Bailie and hence chairman of the magistrates' committee. Her special interest was housing. She was convener of the housing committee from 1935 to 1938, organising secretary of the Town and Country Planning Association for Scotland, and a member of the Housing Advisory Council of the Secretary of State for Scotland. She also edited the *Scots Town and County Councillor*.

Jean Mann won the constituency of Coatbridge for Labour in 1945. She sat for Coatbridge until 1950, and was member for Coatbridge and Airdrie from 1950 to 1959. After the 1945 election a S.C. of the House of Commons reported that her election and that of John Forman for the Springburn division of Glasgow were invalid, since at the time of their election they were members of a tribunal under the 1945 Emergency Laws Act [Rent of Furnished Houses Control (Scotland) section], and thus 'held office of profit under the Crown'. The Committee were satisfied, however, that Mrs Mann and Mr Forman incurred disqualification by inadvertence, and they recommended an Indemnity Bill, which was rapidly passed through both Houses and received the Royal Assent [*Times*, 23 Mar 1964].

In Parliament Jean Mann continued her work for housing. She was a member of the PLP groups on Housing and Town Planning, Health and Social Insurance. She spoke most frequently on the first of these subjects. But she had already been dubbed and called herself, 'the housewives' MP', and as such she concerned herself with a variety of what may be regarded as the interests of housewives, such as prices of food and clothing. She also concerned herself with widows' pensions, pointing out the gross anomalies in their allocation, and along with Horace King she presented the Minister with a petition on the subject. In her book *Woman in Parliament* (1962) she wrote of the period 1945 to 1950 as the happiest of her parliamentary life: 'There was a Labour government and the women M.P.'s, with one exception [Lady Tweedsmuir] were all Labour women. . . . We had all met each other before, at propaganda meetings and conferences. So that first day in the [women members'] room on the terrace was a great, happy reunion' [p. 11].

In her next parliamentary period (1950–9), Jean Mann was on the NEC of the Labour Party. She served from 1953 to 1958 and for some time was on one of its policy sub-committees, that on housing. Herself somewhat to the right in the LP by this time, she was necessarily involved in the internecine warfare of those years, the continuing anti-Left and anti-Communist crusades. She gives a fairly full account of all this in the book cited above. For one figure of the Left, however, Aneurin Bevan, she shows admiration: she describes him as misrepresented, his statements distorted or ignored [p. 111]. In 1955, however, she was regarded (rightly or wrongly) as 'a reliable and implacable anti-Bevanite' [Hunter (1959) 109]; yet in the NEC altercation over the question of Bevan's expulsion from the Party it was Jean Mann who saved him: 'I was glad that my vote turned the scale in his favour', she wrote in 1962. This apparent volte-face astounded many Party members. Jean Mann herself gave two different accounts of her motives – see her own book p. 112 and Hunter, 110 and fn. 1 [For the whole dispute see NEC minutes vol. 116, 309–12; Hunter (1959) 94–111; Jackson (1968) 128–31; Foot (1973) 464–76; Donoughue and Jones (1973) 533–4]. Jean Mann was convinced that much of the trouble of the 1950s would have been avoided if Bevan had been appointed Foreign Secretary in 1951, as in her view he ought to have been [Mann (1962) 95]. She has sharp criticisms to make of most of the other left-wing figures, including Barbara Castle, Judith Hart, Ian Mikardo, Harold Wilson (then on the Party's Left); and of Palme Dutt and Communists in general. She gives a detailed account in chapter eleven of the famous dinner given by the Labour Party to Bulganin and Khruschev in 1956.

In 1958 Jean Mann resigned from the NEC after 'a first-class row' over the method chosen for the appointment of a Party organiser for Scotland [ibid., 115; *Scotsman*, 23 Mar 1964]. In her public life Jean Mann's attention was concentrated on internal and domestic affairs. But she was three times chosen as a delegate – the only woman delegate – to conferences in Switzerland, in 1949, 1952 and 1955. In 1952 the delegation was to the Inter-Parliamentary Union, and she was invited to speak by the Conservative leader of the delegation. On all three occasions she was asked by the Swiss women to help them in their struggle for the franchise. She did not contest her parliamentary seat at the 1959 general election, and subsequently lived in Gourock, where she had been elected to the Borough Council in 1958. Jean Mann was made a Police Judge (Scotland) in 1961. She was an honorary life member of the Royal Society for the Prevention of Accidents (one of her children died in a fire at her house), and vice-president of the Haemophilia Society. She continued to play a part in local politics, as a representative of the Second ward of the Gourock council, until her death.

When in 1963 she visited the U.S.A., where one of her sons was a medical practitioner, she was received by Eleanor Roosevelt. This honour was no doubt in recognition of her long service to a number of women's causes. On this trip she also visited Canada where she was received by Prime Minister Diefenbaker.

She died, after an illness of some months, in Larkhall Hospital, Greenock, on 21 March 1964, aged seventy-four. Her husband had died in 1958, but she was survived by three sons and two daughters. Two sons and one daughter were doctors. The funeral was at Gourock Cemetery on 23 March. She left a personal estate in England and Scotland valued at £2200.

Jean Mann was not appointed to any parliamentary post during her fifteen years in the Commons; she remained a backbencher. She did not rise higher in the Labour Party than her membership of the NEC, and she never held office in the PLP. But if she was not a figure of first-rate importance, she was an able, practical and dogged worker, an enthusiastic and clear-headed advocate of the causes she espoused. Her autobiographical *Woman in Parliament*, however, although briskly written, is superficial and unreliable.

Her physique and appearance did not seem especially conducive to forwarding a public career: she was small and slight; her features were clear-cut and her expression lively, but her looks were not striking. Her voice was not powerful; yet she was a good and popular speaker, who could hold an audience with the clarity and force of her argument, often assisted by pleasantries of a not very subtle kind. She frequently appeared on BBC 'Brains Trusts'.

Writings: editor of *The Scots Town and County Councillor* and of *Replanning Scotland: expert* *evidence on pre-war conditions in Scotland and post-war speeches delivered at Planning Conference, Largs, 1941* (Glasgow, [1942?]); *Woman in Parliament* (1962).

Sources: (1) MS: Labour Party NEC Minutes vol. 116, 309–12 [meeting of 23 Mar 1955], LP archives. (2) Other: *Coatbridge Express*, 13, 20, 27 June and 4 July 1945, 18 Jan, 1, 8, 15, 22 Feb and 1 Mar 1950; *Times House of Commons* (1945), (1950), (1951); C. Bunker, *Who's Who in Parliament* (1946); *Dod* (1946) and (1958); *Hansard* (1946), (1948), (1959); F. Illingworth, *British Parliament* (1948); *Daily Express*, 17, 24 Mar 1955; L. Hunter, *The Road to Brighton Pier* (1959) [esp. Ch. 11 'The Guile of Mrs Mann']; *WWW* (1961–70); P. Brookes, *Women at Westminster* (1967); R.J. Jackson, *Rebels and Whips* (1968); L. Manning, *A Life for Education* (1970); H. Macmillan, *Riding the Storm 1956–1959* (1971); B. Donoughue and G.W. Jones, *Herbert Morrison: portrait of a politician* (1973); M. Foot, *Aneurin Bevan* vol. *2* (1973); P.N. Norton, *Dissension in the House of Commons* (1975); biographical information: R. Dell, Principal Archivist, Strathclyde Regional Council, Glasgow; the late Anthony Elliott, CMG; R. Gillespie, Mitchell Library, Glasgow; personal information: Mrs M. Auld, East Kilbride; Dame Jean Roberts, DBE; Councillor W.L. Taylor, and Dr N. Wattie, all of Glasgow. OBIT. *Greenock Telegraph*, 21 Mar 1964; *Guardian*, *Scotsman* and *Times*, 23 Mar 1964; *Buteman and Rothesay Express*, 27 Mar 1964; *LP Report* (1964).

MARGARET 'ESPINASSE

MARTIN, Emma (1812–51)

SOCIALIST, FREE THINKER AND WOMEN'S RIGHTS ADVOCATE

Born in Bristol early in 1812, Emma was the fourth child of William Bullock, a Bristol cooper, and Hannah Jones, who came from prosperous yeoman stock. Her father died shortly after her birth, and her mother remarried, to John Gwyn, in June 1813. Emma was brought up in a conventionally religious home, but when seventeen she was attracted to the Particular Baptists, whom she joined about a year later. By the age of eighteen she was conducting her own Ladies' Seminary in Montague Street, Bristol, and shortly afterwards, on 15 February 1831, she was married at Twyning (Gloucestershire) to Isaac Luther Martin, the son of a brick and tile manufacturer from Bristol. In 1832, the trade directories record Mrs Martin as keeping a Ladies' Boarding School in Hillgrove Street with her elder sister, Louisa, while Isaac was running a grocery business in Bath Street – this was possibly Emma's property, as her mother's family had had a tea-dealing business in the city. Their first child, Elizabeth Howe, was born at Almondsbury in 1832 or 1833 and baptised into the Church of England on 20 January 1834. She was their only child to be so baptised, which suggested later religious differences between Emma and her husband. A second daughter, Louisa Georgina, followed in 1834, and a third, Emma, was born at Bedminster on the outskirts of Bristol in 1836 or 1837. Meanwhile, in 1835, Mrs Martin had begun editing a periodical entitled the *Bristol Literary Magazine*, and Isaac had returned to his family trade of brick and tile manufacture. Emma Martin also continued with her Ladies' Boarding School, now run in Bedminster, and in 1838 she delivered her first recorded public lecture, in Bristol, on the subject of education.

As far as can be determined, her religious views were still Christian when early in 1839 she heard the Owenite missionary, Alexander Campbell, lecture in Bristol. After the lecture she challenged his attack on the Scriptures, and on 5 and 6 March they debated the issue in the Merchant Taylors' Hall. Preparing for this debate, she began to rethink her views on the Bible, and gradually over the next few months she moved towards freethought, regarding the God of the Old Testament as morally unworthy, and Christianity as unphilosophical and unoriginal. She later recalled that her faith had also been unsettled by the pettiness of the Christian fellowship she encountered.

Her career as a lecturer gathered pace during 1839, her main topics initially being educational or feminist matters. She attended, as a visitor, the Owenite Congress which met in Birmingham in May, and which evidently regarded her as an opponent of Socialism. Nevertheless, the young Birmingham Owenite, G.J. Holyoake, noted in his diary that he went to hear her lecture on 'Woman'. A year later the Congress was able to hail her conversion and report that she was 'now engaged in advocating Socialism in London with much success.'

This transformation in her opinions and her removal to London from Bristol appear to have signalled the break-up of her marriage. Isaac Martin seems to have dissipated much of her property since their marriage, and it is possible that the deterioration in the relationship accounts for the growing militancy of her feminist views in the days before married women's property was protected by law. This feminism, coupled with her interest in education, would certainly explain her attraction to Owenism. Her three daughters followed her to London, where she set up house for them. She still maintained some contact with her own family, her half sister, Elizabeth Gwyn, occasionally looking after the children when their mother was on a lecture tour.

During 1840 and 1841 Emma Martin became one of the most prominent and successful of lecturers in the Owenite Halls of Science and Social Institutions, both in London and in the provinces. Her early lectures, delivered to the A1 branch at the John Street Institution were on Physiology, the Condition of Woman, and Socialism: three topics closely linked in her mind. In these early lectures she attributed the position of women to defective education, particularly with respect to a knowledge of Anatomy, Physiology and Medicine. She also attacked the lack of political rights for women (which, in true Owenite style, she believed must follow upon, not precede, a better education), and she condemned the marriage system which made woman a mere article of merchandise. She was doubtless recalling her own experience; but she later argued the full Owenite thesis that women's inferior status derived in the first instance from the existence of private property and the 'competitive system', through which all human relations, and above all marriage, became reduced to market relationships. The single family structure, the Owenites argued, perpetuated private property and encouraged competitive attitudes, thereby ensuring the subordination of women. Education was crucial as the key strategy for social transformation; the errors of the Old World would dissolve in the light of truth; and the New World would remedy the depraved and ignorant condition of women.

These views remained the basis of her message throughout her lecturing career, though, in common with such Owenites as Charles Southwell and G.J. Holyoake, much emphasis was placed upon the need to attack the tenets of orthodox religion. She had become a convinced atheist, and her experiences and those of her friends in the Owenite movement brought her to their conclusion that the religious battle would first have to be won before the Socialism of the New Moral World could be established. Late in 1840 she held a discussion in London with the Rev. W. Carpenter, the result of which was that a large part of his congregation transferred its Sunday 'worship' to the Owenite John Street Institution. In February 1841 she encountered the slanderous opposition of the Rev. J. Fox of Oldham, which seems to have stimulated her to lecture more often against religion. In March she was overwhelmingly successful in Newcastle with lectures on the 'Trinity', the 'Creation and Deluge', the 'Soul', and – her favourite topic – 'Marriage considered as a Civil Contract'. On this latter theme she was an orthodox follower of Owen, arguing the case he had put in his Lectures on Marriage (1835, and subsequent eds.) for simpler divorce and an end to the legalised prostitution of women in marriage, and condemning the family as a socially disuniting and corrupting institution.

When blasphemy prosecutions were brought against the 'infidel' Owenite missionaries, Southwell, Holyoake and Thomas Paterson, Mrs Martin doubled her efforts in their cause. She was active in the Anti-persecution Union, founded in 1842 after the imprisonment of Southwell. In 1844 she issued a series of 'Weekly Addresses to the Inhabitants of London'; in March of the same year she was fined £3 for taking a crowd of 3000 to church with her in the

Glasgow Gorbals after promising to criticise the minister's sermon in the service; and in October she lectured in defiance of the magistrates of Hull after the mayor had banned her lecture on 'The Crimes and Follies of Christian Missions'. In the same year she filled Leicester market place after the Assembly Rooms had been closed to her, and Holyoake had vain hopes of refurbishing the Blackfriars Rotunda – the scene of Richard Carlile's and Eliza Sharples's former triumphs – as a Philosophical Institute for her. Early in 1845 she spent two nights in Arbroath Gaol after arranging to discuss Christianity with the Christian Chartist, Robert Lowery; and again in Dundee rooms were closed to her in an effort to silence her propaganda.

This Scottish tour of 1845, however, was to be her last extended mission, for by June she was physically and financially exhausted. She decided to settle permanently in London. When she recovered she took a course in midwifery and the diseases of women and children at the Royal Adelaide Lying-in Hospital in Great Queen Street, and became fully qualified as an *accoucheur*. She then began practising at 100 Long Acre, offering both private consultations, and a weekly free surgery for the poor. She also gave a series of lectures on the Physiology of Woman to help her sex to understand themselves better. In common with many of her kind she was hostile to the male dominance of the medical profession and a strong advocate of female midwives. She also turned herself into an agency for the supply of nurses, both wet and dry, and after moving to larger premises off Burton Crescent in 1847, she was able to advertise 'Apartments for Invalid Ladies. Warm and Cold Baths.'

All this proved to be a severe strain on her finances. She applied to the Royal Maternity Charity, but in spite of her impeccable qualification she was refused when she was identified as 'Mrs Martin, the Social Lecturer'. Through her friend, Holyoake, she appealed in his *Reasoner* (23 Feb 1848) for patrons and help towards the costs of a 'Young Mother's Guide', which was announced as to be published in October 1848, but seems never to have appeared; and in August she published *A Miniature Treatise on Some of the Most Common Female Complaints*. She also went into the surgical garments business, advertising her 'Patent Cholera Prevention Belt, approved by the Board of Health' in October 1848, and 'Martin's Elastic Boddice [*sic*]' in 1850. The 1851 Census return lists her as a midwife and her daughters as elastic bandage makers. In addition to this business activity and medical work, she was also running a French class in 1848, and was still active in freethinking and Owenite circles. The periodicals continued to record her occasional lectures in the provinces, though apparently rumours of her death-bed repentances were being circulated by religious groups in Scotland [Holyoake (1851) 8]. At Robert Owen's birthday celebration in 1848 she and the other great feminist, Frances Wright, each gave an address; and when Henry Hetherington died of the cholera in 1849 she was the only medical person he would allow near him.

In mid 1845, about the time of her illness, she began living with Joshua Hopkins, an engineer ten years older than herself, who made a new home for her and her three daughters. A fourth girl, Manon Roland (named after Madame Roland), was born early in 1847. This second union at last brought some domestic stability to her life, but in October 1851, at the early age of thirty-nine, she died of tuberculosis at her home on Finchley Common. She was buried in Highgate Cemetery in a grave subsequently occupied also by G. J. Holyoake's son, Max, and his wife, Ellen, who was one of Mrs Martin's closest friends during her later years. The funeral oration was delivered by Holyoake.

Emma Martin was widely regarded in her day as second only to Frances Wright as a pioneering popular advocate of Women's Rights, and was later to be ranked with Harriet Law and Annie Besant as among those who broke through into the male-dominated world of radical social agitation. She was described by Holyoake as the most womanly of all the public advocates of Women's Rights – a possible reference to the notorious dowdiness of Frances Wright in her later years – but she was opposed to the frivolities of female fashions in clothing. As a courageous and effective public speaker, she championed educational and social reform under Owen's influence, her prime concerns always being feminism and freethought, though she deserves also to be remembered for her application of the former in female medicine.

Writings: *A Funeral Sermon, occasioned by the Death of Richard Carlile, preached at the Hall of Science, City Road, London, by Emma Martin, on Sunday Evening, the 26th of February, 1843* [1843?] 24 pp.; *God's Gifts and Men's Duties, being the Substance of a Lecture delivered by Emma Martin, at the Hall of Science, Manchester, Oct. 9, 1843, in reply to Two Sermons, preached by the Rev. J. W. Massie, in the Chapel Street Chapel, Salford, Oct. 1, 1843, to which is added, An Address to the Minister, Members, and Congregation of that Chapel; and a letter acknowledging the Receipt of "The Sinner's Friend", which had been presented to her by that Gentleman* n.d. 3rd ed. 20 pp.; *Weekly Addresses to the Inhabitants of London* [n.d. although no. 4 'To the Christians of the Metropolis' was published in the *Movement*, 13 Jan 1844, where it was stated to have been published in December 1843]; *Baptism, a Pagan Rite; or a Mythological Essay, proving the Existence of this Ceremony in the most Remote Ages, with an Exposition of the Materials used in its Celebration, being Earth, Water, Fire, Air, Blood, &c., and the Subjects of its Administration in Various Times being not only Adults and Infants, but also Gods, Religious Symbols, Buildings, Bells* (1844) 16 pp.; *The Missionary Jubilee Panic, and the Hypocrite's Prayer, addressed to the Supporters of Christian Missions* (1844) 24 pp.; Translator of *The Maxims of Francis Guicciardini, with Parallel Passages from the Works of Machiavelli, Lord Bacon, Pascal, Rochefoucauld, Montesquieu, Mr Burke, Prince Talleyrand, M. Guizot and Others* (1845) and *Frederic and the Falcon: done into English Verse* [from Boccaccio's *Decameron*] (1847) 16 pp.; *A Miniature Treatise on Some of the Most Common Female Complaints* [1848?]; *The Punishment of Death: a lecture delivered by Mrs Martin at the Hall of Science, Manchester, November 23rd, 1849* n.d., 16 pp.; *Prayer,* n.d., 8 pp.; *The Bible no Revelation, or the Inadequacy of Language to convey a Message from God to Man* n.d. 28 pp.; *The Exiles of Piedmont* [a novel] n.d., n.p.; *First Conversation on the Being of God* n.d., 8 pp.; *Second Conversation on the Being of God* n.d., 8 pp.; *A Few Reasons for renouncing Christianity and professing and disseminating Infidel Opinions* n.d., 16 pp.; *Religion superseded, or the Moral Code of Nature sufficient for the Guidance of Man* n.d. 16 pp.; [A Young Mother's Guide was announced in *Reasoner*, 16 Aug 1848, but there is no evidence of publication].

Sources: Mrs Martin's weekly activities are recorded in the periodicals of Socialism and Freethought, notably the *New Moral World* (1839–45), the *London Social Reformer* (1840), the *Movement* (1843–5) and the *Reasoner* (from 1846). Details of her early life are taken from Bristol parish registers and trade directories. *A Few Reasons for renouncing Christianity* contains autobiographical passages. Later freethought sources are derived from the obituary and add nothing to it. See also: R. Owen, *Lectures on the Marriages of the Priesthood of the Old Immoral World* (Leeds, 1835; later eds.); E. Royle, *Victorian Infidels* (1974); J. Saville, 'Robert Owen on the Family and the Marriage System of the Old Immoral World' in *Rebels and their Causes* ed. M. Cornforth (1978) 107–21; biographical information: Barbara Taylor, London. OBIT. *Reasoner 11*, no. 23, 22 Oct 1851 [repr. as G.J. Holyoake, *The Last Days of Mrs Emma Martin* (1851) 8 pp.; copy in *DBL* Coll.]

GRACE G. COWIE
EDWARD ROYLE

See also: †Annie BESANT; †George Jacob HOLYOAKE; †Harriet LAW.

MOTT, William Henry (1812–82)
CHARTIST AND RADICAL

William Henry Mott was born in Birmingham in 1812, one of seven children of Alexander Mott, a prosperous currier and leather cutter, of Edgbaston Street. He received his formal education at King Edward's School, Birmingham. After working for some time in his father's business, Mott moved to Nottingham. The precise date at which he settled in the town is unknown; he first appears in *Pigot's Directory* of 1841, which lists him as a currier working in Carlton Street. Three years later he moved to premises at 36½ Goose Gate, which he occupied for some thirty years.

Mott emerged as a Nottingham Chartist leader in the autumn of 1842. He was a member of the Peacock Inn, Nottingham, Chartist locality and attended the Complete Suffrage Union conference in Birmingham in December as one of the town's two Chartist delegates. During the next years Mott became one of the most respected and influential Chartists in the area. Probably because of his status as a skilled artisan and tradesman, he frequently acted as treasurer to the working-class movement, like his friend and neighbour in Goose Gate, the radical bookseller James Sweet: at various times Mott held the funds of the Nottingham Charter Association, the Land Company branch and the Victims' and Dependents' Fund. He also assisted Sweet and William Hemm in the organisation of Feargus O'Connor's successful election campaign in August 1847. Mott nominated O'Connor at the hustings.

When the Nottingham Chartist movement split, after the rejection of the National Petition in April 1848, Mott joined Sweet and Hemm in urging unity with middle-class radicals in pursuit of suffrage reform, in opposition to the more militant group led by the framework-knitter Jonathan Barber. At two meetings in April and June, Sweet and Mott pressed the adoption of a reform programme based on the points of the Charter. Lord Rancliffe and the middle-class reformers were not prepared to accept anything more specific than a commitment to a general extension of the suffrage, however, and the so-called 'People's League' foundered almost as soon as it had been launched.

During the early 1850s Mott continued to work for the Chartist cause; he was an enthusiastic supporter of Ernest Jones's 'Labour Parliament' of 1854, one of the directors of which was a local man, George Harrison of Calverton. As mass backing for Chartism fell away, however, his attention was concentrated on local affairs. He had had experience of parochial administration as a member of the St Mary's Board of Highways in the 1840s, and in 1858 he was elected a Poor Law Guardian for St Mary's, a position he held until 1871. Mott became a prominent member of the left-wing Liberal group led by councillors Sweet and Heath, a persistent thorn in the side of the Whig clique who controlled the municipal politics of Nottingham in the 1860s and 70s. Although he never held a council seat, his support was valuable; he was 'undoubtedly a power in the town, as he was looked up to by many working men as a political adviser and guide' [*Nottingham Daily Express*, 6 Sep 1882]. The extent of the political expertise and influence of the radical cadre was indicated by their part in engineering the electoral successes of the Radical Tory Sir Robert Clifton at a by-election for Nottingham in 1861, and of Clifton and Samuel Morley in 1865, though both were subsequently unseated after petition.

In the early 1870s Mott became afflicted by paralysis, and gradually withdrew from political life, and in 1878 from business affairs. He died at his home, 1 Corporation Oaks, Nottingham, on 4 September 1882, and was buried in the General Cemetery on 7 September. His wife Elizabeth had died some years earlier, but he was survived by two sons; William Alfred Mott, who carried on the leather business in Goose Gate, and George Robert Mott, city rate collector. His estate was valued at £52.

Sources: (1) MS: Census schedule for 1871, Nottingham, St Ann's sub-district. (2) Other: *Pigot's Directory of Nottingham* (1829) and (1841); *Northern Star*, 1842–52; *Nottingham Rev.*,

1842–65; *People's Paper*, 1853–8; Morris & Co.'s, *Commercial Directory of Nottingham ... 1877* (1877); C.N. Wright, *Commercial and General Directory ... of Nottinghamshire*... 9th ed. (1879); R.G. Gammage, *History of the Chartist Movement 1837–1854* (1894; repr. with an Introduction by J. Saville, NY, 1969); M. Hovell, *The Chartist Movement* (Manchester, 1918); C. Holmes, 'Chartism in Nottingham 1837–1861' (Nottingham Univ. BA Dissertation, 1960); R.A. Church, *Economic and Social Change in a Midland Town: Victorian Nottingham, 1815–1900* (1966). OBIT. *Nottingham Daily Express*, 6 and 8 Sep 1882; *Nottingham Daily Guardian*, 7 Sep 1882.

JOHN ROWLEY

See also: †Jonathan BARBER; †David William HEATH; William Peck HEMM; †James SWEET.

O'NEILL, Arthur George (1819–96)

CHRISTIAN CHARTIST AND RADICAL

Arthur O'Neill was born at Chelmsford, Essex in September 1819, the son of Arthur O'Neill, a coachmaker, and his wife, Ann. His father, who died three months before Arthur's birth, was an Irish Protestant who had fled to England after being proscribed. His mother was an Essex woman who claimed descent from John Rogers, the Deritend martyr. While O'Neill was still a child his mother married an army quartermaster sergeant named Cooper, and as a boy he was commonly known by his step-father's surname. Sergeant Cooper served with the 73rd Regiment in the Mediterranean for several years and O'Neill was educated at the barrack school and the University in Malta, and at the college in Corfu. He was 'of a studious turn of mind, and fond of botany' and his step-father decided he should become an army surgeon [*Handsworth Chronicle*, 16 May 1896]. Accordingly he acted as dresser and compounder for the 73rd Regiment for two years and in 1835 returned to Britain to study medicine at Glasgow University.

Shortly after entering the University, O'Neill 'came under strong religious influences, which changed the whole current of his life' [*Handsworth Herald and North Birmingham News*, 16 May 1896]. He abandoned his medical studies to train for the ministry and in February 1837 signed the teetotal pledge. In 1838 he was caught up in the excitement generated by the rise of Chartism and the heady atmosphere of that time remained a vivid memory for the rest of his life. Almost fifty years afterwards he gave this account of the impact which Chartism had on him:

> I was brought among the Chartists through sympathy for the Canadians, awakened by the speeches of Arthur Roebuck. One of the four essays required from me as a student in the logic class at Glasgow College was written in the form of a political oration against the Government, who had sent my regiment (the 73rd) to suppress the revolt. I was at once compromised amongst the students and in the eyes of the professor. I used to read with horror of the ruthless, murderous deeds of officers and soldiers known to me personally, and this made me a peace man and a Chartist through nearly half a century [*Birmingham Post*, 24 Nov 1885].

He attended the great rally on Glasgow Green on 21 May 1838, at which the national petition and the Charter were presented together for the first time. At the Scottish Chartist Convention in August 1839 O'Neill was elected a member of the Universal Suffrage Central Committee for Scotland. He had left the University by this time and was earning a precarious living by lecturing to working men's associations and scientific institutions. He combined this with propaganda work for the Suffrage Committee and quickly became well known throughout western and central Scotland as an excellent speaker on a wide range of subjects. On the introduction of Chartist Sabbath services in the autumn of 1839 O'Neill proved an inspiring lay preacher, attracting great crowds wherever he spoke, and when the Lanarkshire Universal Suffrage Association was formed in January 1840 he was appointed its first full-time paid missionary.

O'Neill's work for the Lanarkshire Association involved preaching to Chartist congregations on Sundays and building up organisation during the week. Outside the larger towns he encountered widespread apathy among working men and strong opposition from the churches and employers of labour, but sheer perseverance 'enabled him to raise a crop of small branches' [Briggs (1959) 275]. His dedication earned him the respect of all sections of the Scottish movement and in June 1840 he was appointed a delegate to the demonstration being arranged in Birmingham to welcome William Lovett and John Collins on their release from Warwick gaol. In his speech at the demonstration, on 27 July 1840, O'Neill emphasised the need for unity and advised the Birmingham Chartists 'to go on steadily, avoiding all useless squabbles with the middle class' [*Birmingham J.*, 1 Aug 1840]. His sincerity made a profound impression and he was appointed secretary of the delegate conference held on the day after the demonstration to consider the scheme of national organisation submitted from the Chartist assembly in Manchester on 20 July. The conference resolved to support the formation of a National Charter Association and O'Neill agreed to return to Scotland to direct the work of organisation there.

When O'Neill returned to Scotland he found there were widespread doubts about the legality of the National Charter Association and despite his personal prestige he could muster little support for it. His proposal for another national petition also brought no response but he remained in Scotland throughout the autumn, lecturing on metaphysics, and temperance as well as Chartism. Then towards the end of the year he accepted an invitation from John Collins to return to Birmingham to give a series of lectures and sermons at the opening of a Chartist Church. On arriving in Birmingham O'Neill was offered the position of district lecturer by the Midland Chartist Association. He declined this offer but agreed to stay as pastor of the Chartist Church, which was a converted house in Newhall Street.

The Birmingham Chartist Church was opened on Sunday 27 December 1840. O'Neill, who preached the inaugural sermons, had firmly-developed views on the nature of Christianity and the ways in which Christian worship should be organised. He believed in a universal church, and was insistent that the true church must not remain aside from daily affairs but 'must enter into the struggles of the people and guide them.' Within a month of the opening of the Chartist Church he was setting forth the obligations of its members:

> The characteristics of members of a real Church was on the first day of the week to worship at their altar, and on the next to go out and mingle with the masses, on the third to stand at the bar of judgement, and on the fourth, perhaps, to be in a dungeon. This was the case in the primitive Church and so it should be now [*Birmingham J.*, 23 Jan 1841].

The Chartist Church did achieve a simple common creed acceptable to its members – centred on the Atonement – and the emphasis in its services and in its pastoral work was upon simplicity, brotherly love and the practice of good works. There were regular tea-meetings at the Church, a sick club, Sunday schools, and a political association to study the works of Cartwright and Paine, Cobbett and Hunt. The Church rejected the hierarchy of both the Anglican and the Catholic churches, and although O'Neill was the most prominent of the preachers at the Chartist Church, there were ten appointed pastors in all. 'Whosoever will be the chief among you, let him be your servant', *Matthew*, XX, 27 was their precept.

The Chartist Church was a political association, and in its ideology as well as in its political practice it reflected the strengths as well as the tensions and contradictions of the Birmingham radical movement. O'Neill had always emphasised the importance of the middle-class connection, but it was not, in his early years, the offer of a blank cheque. In a letter to the 'Working Men of England', published before he took up residence in Birmingham he emphasised that 'you need a wider spread of political information . . . and a junction with the middle classes.' But elsewhere in the same article he quoted Henry Hunt's advice in respect of the middle-class alliance: 'We are profiting by the once-scorned lessons of the noble Hunt . . . In our ignorance we heeded not the warnings of that great man. We united with the middle-classes for the attainment of a half-measure of reform. We erred, and are now suffering the punishment that nature inflicts on those who break her laws of social practice' [*Birmingham J.*, 15 Aug 1840]. A more extended statement came in 1842 when the Chartist Church published a tract entitled *The Question: what good will the Charter do?* Much of the language of the pamphlet is that of traditional radicalism, reminiscent of the twenties' and thirties' attacks on 'Old Corruption', but the new industrial society was also centrally challenged: with a swingeing criticism of the middle-class failure to fulfil the promises of the 1832 Reform Act; a bitter denunciation of the New Poor Law; an insistence upon the inhumanity of the new factory system; and a glowing, almost millennial, description of the new order which would follow the enactment of the Charter. It was undoubtedly O'Neill who played the major part in determining the political attitudes and activity of the Church. He was not in favour of physical force, and he always leaned, even in his most radical phases, towards the middle-class alliance. But his political stance in the summer of 1842 illustrated the problems and difficulties of a Christian political activist. The great strike movement was approaching its climax, and the Christian Chartists called a public meeting for 22 August to consider 'the present awful state of the country'. O'Neill issued a placard:

> Men of Birmingham. The crisis has now arrived. Britain and Ireland are aroused. The nation's voice declares, in the loudest tones, the noble struggle must now be made. The days of tyranny are numbered. Shall Birmingham, once the pole star of liberty, now slumber? No! Awake! Arise! Stand forward in the Nation's moral battle, and declare that our Country shall now be free.

On 20 August two men belonging to the Chartist Church were arrested for displaying the placard. The magistrates banned the meeting, but O'Neill persisted, and led his supporters to the appointed place, where they found their way blocked by police. At this point Joseph Sturge intervened and persuaded the Christian Chartists to disperse peacefully. Four days later, on Friday 26 August, O'Neill was arrested after addressing a crowd of striking miners at Cradley. He was taken to Dudley under armed guard and brought before the magistrates late at night to minimise the risk of public disorder at his arrest, charged with having attended an illegal meeting. He was committed for trial at Stafford Assize and held in close confinement over the weekend. When he was transferred to Stafford gaol on Monday 29 August his carriage was escorted from Dudley to Wolverhampton station by a troop of cavalry. The bail offered by two Birmingham town councillors was refused 'because the sureties were of the same political opinion as the prisoner' and he was held in prison until the Special Assize in October.

At the Special Assize he was discharged on bail because the indictment of conspiracy and sedition 'was in no way part or parcel of the original charge' [*Birmingham J.*, 15 Oct 1842] and he was not finally brought to trial until August 1843. The Chartist movement to which he returned in October 1842 had been divided between two main groupings almost since the Chartist Church was established. Feargus O'Connor had made a major criticism of Christian Chartism in an all-embracing attack upon the various groupings that were using the name of Chartism. His well-known letter 'Church Chartism, Teetotal Chartism, Knowledge Chartism, and Household Suffrage Chartism' published in the *Northern Star*, 3 April 1841 was a critique of all these movements as diversionary, and as undermining the basic unity of the national movement and he later specifically opposed the Birmingham Chartist Church on particular as well as general grounds. He thought it ill-advised to establish a church that excluded Irish

Roman Catholics for example; and O'Connor's attitudes were vigorously supported by George White, the leader of the NCA in Birmingham. There was hostility, often bitter, between the local branch of the NCA and the Chartist Church, and sectarianism was not limited to one side. The leaders of the Chartist Church would not allow its members to join the NCA, while from within the NCA, apart from their fervent support for O'Connor, it was probably the many aspects of the Irish question that were the causes of most friction. There were occasions when the two groups came together – the joint petitioning for the release of Frost, Williams and Jones being an example – and the common opposition to the Anti-Corn Law League was another; and it must always be emphasised that the simplistic division of physical force and moral force advocacy and advocates is no longer tenable. The lines dividing individuals and groups were often crossed. Nevertheless, the basic opposition of the Christian Chartists to physical force, and the predilection of O'Neill himself for a working agreement with middle-class radicals such as Joseph Sturge did undoubtedly provide a division within Birmingham Chartism that was not finally resolved until the following decade. The history of the Complete Suffrage movement in 1842 afforded an illustration of the ways in which the conflicts were worked out. Joseph Sturge and his journal, the *Nonconformist* were often congratulating the Christian Chartists, but the latter *were* Chartists, and it was the Complete Suffrage movement's reluctance to accept the Charter that maintained a serious obstacle to a closer alliance. When O'Neill returned to Birmingham after his release on bail, he was elected one of six delegates to the second December conference of the Complete Suffrage Union. When Sturge and his supporters withdrew, after the vote to endorse the Charter, O'Neill remained with the Chartist majority, but the experience served to confirm his fears about the Chartist leadership. In January 1843 he attended a meeting of the council of the Complete Suffrage Union, at which a plan to strengthen its organisation was accepted.

In March 1843 O'Neill again appeared before Stafford Assize but his case was further delayed by being removed into the Queen's Bench Division. He was finally brought to trial in August 1843, almost a year after being arrested, charged with having uttered seditious language tending to bring the laws and government of the country into contempt. He conducted his own defence, concluding with an address to the jury which lasted more than seven hours, but was found guilty and sentenced to one year's imprisonment without hard labour. His companions in Stafford gaol included his fellow Chartists Joseph Linney, John Richards and Thomas Cooper.

On his release from prison O'Neill briefly resumed his pastorate at the Newhall Street Church. He declared 'that he was still a Chartist' [*Birmingham J.*, 20 Dec 1845], but in the Birmingham context this no longer implied a commitment to the national movement led by O'Connor. The pattern of 'harmonious co-operation' between classes established by the Political Union was now beginning to revive and this absorbed both Christian Chartism and the Complete Suffrage movement. The last official act of the Complete Suffrage Union was carried out in December 1845 and the Chartist Church was dissolved in the following year. O'Neill then became minister at Zion Baptist Chapel, which was situated just below the site of the Chartist Church in Newhall Street, and served there for almost forty years.

The change in O'Neill's attitude was confirmed in 1848, when Chartism revived in Birmingham as elsewhere. Together with other former Christian Chartists he joined middle-class Radicals in forming a Reform League in the town, which supported Joseph Hume's campaign for 'the Little Charter'. The Reform League proved short-lived but the alliance between Birmingham artisans and middle-class Radicals endured. When the Birmingham branch of the National Reform League was formed towards the end of 1865 the local Liberal Association combined with it to make the reform agitation in the town particularly impressive. O'Neill took a leading part in the agitation and was among the principal speakers at the two great demonstrations which were held at Brookfields in August 1866 and April 1867. He also spoke at many reform rallies in the Black Country, and helped to establish branches of the League in this area.

He had by now come to lay particular emphasis on the need to consolidate political advance by establishing social organisation among the working class. He encouraged the formation of retail associations and savings banks, and during the 1860s and 1870s he acted as counsellor to the early unions of ironworkers and miners in the Black Country. In turn he hoped that the experience of organising their own social institutions would engender among working men a sense of sobriety and responsibility.

O'Neill also held strong views on international affairs. He believed that it was Britain's duty, as the foremost imperial nation, to act against moral evil anywhere in the world and sought to foster this attitude by personal example. During the 1840s he had been active in the affairs of the short-lived Anti-Slavery League and played a prominent part in the periodic agitations against opium trafficking. In June 1843, while awaiting trial, he attended the first general peace convention, held in London, and subsequently became a leading figure in the Society for the Promotion of Permanent and Universal Peace. He represented the Peace Society at international conferences in many of the principal cities of Europe until he was well into his seventies, becoming widely known as an advocate of using arbitration to settle international disputes. He also acted as secretary of the Midland Arbitration Union for a number of years.

In later life O'Neill identified strongly with the Gladstonian Liberal Party and its cry of 'Peace, Retrenchment and Reform', but he always placed principle above party allegiance. Thus he 'dissociated himself' from the Birmingham Liberal Association because he was 'out of harmony' with its policy of excluding Bible teaching from the Board Schools created by the 1870 Education Act, and he strongly opposed Gladstone's coercive legislation on Ireland.

O'Neill's attitude on matters of conscience, together with his moderation and personal courage, earned him the respect of most sections of the community and though he never held any civic office in Birmingham he was honoured at public gatherings on two occasions. On 23 November 1885, at the Town Hall, he was presented with an illuminated address and his portrait, commissioned by friends from Jonathan Pratt, was given to the Corporation for exhibition in the Birmingham Gallery of Portraits. On 12 August 1891 a meeting was held in the Council Chamber to mark his fifty years of political and philanthropic work in Birmingham. On this occasion he was presented with another address and an album containing photographs of those who had been associated with him in this work. The fiftieth anniversary of his ministry in Birmingham was commemorated at a Christmas tea meeting at Zion Baptist Chapel in December 1890, when he was presented with a purse of money.

O'Neill died on 14 May 1896 at his home in Hall Road, Handsworth and was buried in the churchyard of Handsworth Old Church four days later, following a service in Zion Baptist Chapel. On the day before the funeral, Sunday 17 May, special services to celebrate his life and work were held at the chapel. O'Neill's wife predeceased him by sixteen years and he was survived by a son and two daughters and left an estate valued at £2721. At the time of O'Neill's death his son, Arthur Rogers O'Neill, was postmaster at Villa Cross Post Office, Handsworth.

Sources: (1) MS: National Suffrage Union Minute Book 1842–3 and National Complete Suffrage Union Minute Book, Committee for General Purposes nos. 1 and 2, Birmingham Central Library; Home Office papers, HO 40 and HO 45, PRO. (2) Newspapers: *Scottish Patriot*, 1839–41 *passim*; *True Scotsman*, 1839–41 *passim*; *Birmingham J.*, 1840–50 *passim*; *Northern Star*, 1840–50 *passim*; *Staffordshire Advertiser*, 1842–3 *passim*; *Wolverhampton Chronicle*, 1842–3 *passim*; *National Association Gazette*, 1842 *passim*; *Glasgow Saturday Post*, 1843 *passim*; *Glasgow Argus*, 1845 *passim*; *Manchester Guardian*, 29 Apr 1846; *Aris's Birmingham Gazette*, 8 May, 5 and 12 June 1848; *People*, Oct 1857; *Birmingham Daily Post*, 11 and 23 Feb, 9 and 20 Mar, 24 Nov 1885, 13 Aug 1891; *Birmingham Daily Mail*, 24 Nov 1885, 9 Dec 1890; *Handsworth Herald*, 9 Aug 1890, 3 Jan 1891. (3) Theses: H.J.R. Bennett, 'Social Aspects of the Chartist Movement' (Birmingham MA, 1927); H.G. Smith, 'The Reform Movement in Birmingham 1830–1848' (London PhD, 1930); R.A. Jones, 'Knowledge Chartism' (Birmingham MA, 1938); L.C. Wright, 'Scottish Chartism and its Economic

Background' (Edinburgh PhD, 1951); A. Wilson, 'The Chartist Movement in Scotland' (Oxford DPhil., 1951); A.D. Bell, 'The Reform League, from its Origins to the Passing into Law of the Reform Act of 1867' (Oxford DPhil., 1961); K. Geering, 'George White, a Nineteenth-Century Workers' Leader and the Kirkdale Phenomenon' (Sussex MA, 1973); J. Ryan, 'Religion and Radical Politics in Birmingham 1830–1850' (Birmingham MLitt., 1979). (4) Other: *The Question: what good will the Charter do? Answered by the Birmingham Christian Chartist Church* (Birmingham [1842?]) 4 pp.; *Report of the Proceedings at the Conference of Delegates of the Middle and Working Classes at Birmingham April 5, 1842* (Birmingham, 1842); 4 pp.; *Report of the Proceedings at the Conference of Delegates of the Middle and Working Classes at Birmingham April 5, 1842* (Birmingham, 1842); *The Brummagem Heroes* (Birmingham, [1843?]) 16 pp.; *The Proceedings of the First General Peace Convention, held in London ... 1843 ... with the Papers laid before the Convention* (1843); Midland Mining Commission, *First Report*, S. Staffordshire 1843 XIII; *National Complete Suffrage Union Tracts* (1843–4); *Report of the Proceedings of the Fourth General Peace Congress, held in the Exeter Hall, London on the 22, 23, 24 July, 1851* (1851) P; *International Arbitration: the public conference in Birmingham . . . December 11 1872* (1872) 2 pp.; T. Cooper, *The Life of Thomas Cooper* (1872; repr. with an Introduction by J. Saville, Leicester, 1971); J.A. Langford, *Modern Birmingham and its Institutions* 2 vols. (Birmingham 1873–7); H. Solly, *James Woodford: carpenter and Chartist* [a novel] 2 vols. (1881); T. Woollaston, *Police Experiences and Reminiscences of Official Life* (West Bromwich, 1884) P; T. Cooper, *Thoughts at Forescore, and Earlier* (1885); *Proceedings of the Universal Peace Congress, held in Westminster Town Hall, London from 14 to 19 July 1890* (1890) P; *Troisième Congrès international de la paix, Rome, Novembre, 1891* (Rome, 1892) P; H. Solly, *These Eighty Years* 2 vols. (1893); L. Appleton, *Memoirs of Henry Richard, the Apostle of Peace* (1889); *Bulletin officiel du sixième congrès international de la paix tenu à Anvers (Belgique) du 24 aôut au 1 septembre 1894* (Antwerp, 1895) P; R.G. Gammage, *History of the Chartist Movement* (1894; repr. with an Introduction by J. Saville, NY, 1969); H.U. Faulkner, *Chartism and the Churches* (NY, 1916; repr. NY, 1968); M. Hovell, *The Chartist Movement* (Manchester, 1918; later eds.); S. Hobhouse, *Joseph Sturge: his life and work* (1919); *Boase 6* (1921); S. Maccoby, *English Radicalism 1832–1852* (1935); C. Gill, *History of Birmingham* vol. *1: manor and borough to 1865* (1952); A. Briggs, *History of Birmingham* vol. *2: borough and city 1865–1938* (1952); T.R. Tholfsen, 'The Artisan and the Culture of Early Victorian Birmingham', *Univ. of Birmingham Hist. J. 4*, no. 2 (1954) 146–66; idem, 'The Chartist Crisis in Birmingham', *Int. Rev. Social Hist. 3* pt 3 (1958) 461–80; idem, 'The Origins of the Birmingham Caucus', *Hist. J. 2*, no. 2 (1959) 161–84; idem, 'The Transition to Democracy in Victorian England', *Int. Rev. Social Hist. 6*, pt 2 (1961) 226–48; *Chartist Studies* ed. A. Briggs (1959); Victoria County History, *Warwick 7* (1964); J.T. Ward, *Chartism* (1973); P. Hollis, *Pressure from Without in Early Victorian England* (1974); T.R. Tholfsen, *Working Class Radicalism in Mid-Victorian England* (1976). OBIT. *Birmingham Mail*, 14 May 1896; *Birmingham Post*, 15 May 1896; *Birmingham Weekly Post, Handsworth Chronicle, Handsworth Herald and North Birmingham News*, 16 May 1896; *Temperance Record*, 21 May 1896; *Illustrated London News*, 23 May 1896; *Baptist Handbook* (1897). The editors wish to acknowledge assistance from Mrs Dorothy Thompson, Birmingham Univ.

JOHN ROWLEY
JOHN SAVILLE
ERIC TAYLOR

See also: William LOVETT, for Chartism to 1840.

ORAGE, [James] Alfred Richard (1873–1934)
JOURNALIST AND GUILD SOCIALIST

Orage was born on 22 January 1873 at Dacre Banks, near Pateley Bridge, Yorkshire. His father, William Stevenson Orage, an unsuccessful Huntingdonshire farmer, had squandered his inheritance in gambling and drink and had taken to schoolteaching. The family moved to Dacre in 1872, two years before William died, aged forty-two. William's wife, Sarah Ann McQuire (d. 1893) was of Irish extraction. She bore him four children, Florence, William, Edith and the youngest christened James Alfred. On William's death the family moved back to live with Sarah's mother at Fenstanton, Hunts, where Alfred attended the non-denominational school. Here he acquired the name of 'Dickie' and preferred thereafter to be known as Alfred Richard Orage. As if further to distance himself from his rustic origins, Alfred chose the spelling and pronunciation 'Orage' instead of the local form of the surname, 'Orridge'. He was encouraged by his schoolmaster George Hicks and helped financially by the local squire's grandson Howard Coote, who paid Sarah a small weekly allowance to maintain Alfred at school, where he became a pupil teacher in 1887. He was a studious boy, eager to learn, even taking the trouble of tramping to Cambridge Art School for drawing classes. Two years later he won a scholarship to Culham College, an Anglican teachers' training centre near Abingdon. There he edited the college magazine and qualified as an elementary teacher in 1893, when he secured a post with the Leeds School Board at Chapel Allerton, with a salary of £80 a year.

He heard Tom Mann speak, at Sheffield, and this apparently turned him towards Socialism. He joined the newly established ILP in Leeds, and became a proficient platform speaker; he met many of the local Socialists, including Tom Maguire, Joseph Clayton and Albert Marles. It was Marles who published Orage's first essays, in a collection called *Hypnotic Leeds*, in 1894. In August 1895 Orage began to contribute to the *Labour Leader* for 5*s* an article, and continued to do so until July 1897. An insatiable appetite for books and ideas led him to join the Theosophical Society in 1896, and for a time he became an active member of the Society for Psychical Research. He helped to start the Leeds Theosophical Society, and later to form a Plato study group at which he first met A.J. Penty, in 1900. These interests were good guides to the nature of Orage's Socialism, as was his *Labour Leader* column. There he could be found enthusing over Whitman, John Davidson, William Morris, and, especially, Edward Carpenter. Although he did discuss various fringe works on economics and money, and warned that 'Carpenter without Marx is useless' [*Labour Leader*, 20 Feb 1897], the strong idealist, not to say mystical bent of Orage's mind was already apparent.

In 1900 he met Holbrook Jackson, who lent him a copy of Nietzsche's *Thus Spake Zarathustra*. Orage succumbed to its spell immediately, and his two books on Nietzsche, published in 1906 and 1907 marked him as one of the philosopher's most lucid exponents in England. Nietzsche's doctrines and style blended well with those of Orage's early mentor Plato, as well as providing a withering moral criticism of bourgeois society which related closely to the ideas Orage had already absorbed from Ruskin and Blake. The concept of a new morality for new men had some affinity with Theosophy, but he had become critical of the Theosophists, and eventually broke with them in 1907. His own educational experience and temperament disposed him to a view of education as a process of self-discovery under tutorial guidance. This conviction probably helped him later to his success as an editor, but more immediately it may have decided him to leave schoolteaching in 1905. Only a year after his arrival in Leeds he had made some caustic criticisms of the system as he found it. Ridden with examinations and inspectors, hostile to originality and naturalness, he wrote in *Hypnotic Leeds* 'our system makes permanent excellence impossible' [Marles (1894) 46]. The true ideal as Orage conceived it was 'to fit a child for self-education . . . the aim should always be to lead and not to drive.' This was perhaps the secret behind his success with the *New Age*, and the rationale behind his ceaseless and unfinished journey of intellectual inquiry.

His friendship with Holbrook Jackson had led in 1902 to the formation of the Leeds Art

Club, which seems to have been a centre for radical culture; but it proved insufficient to keep Orage in Leeds. Always a charmer, he was able to persuade a Theosophist banker, Lewis Wallace, and a Pudsey coal merchant, Joseph Smith, to finance his move to London, where in 1905 he went at first to live with Penty in Hammersmith. His marriage to Jean Walker in 1896 had not been successful, and in London she left him for Holbrook Jackson, while Orage himself went to live in Chancery Lane with the brilliant young South African, Beatrice Hastings, whom he had met at the Theosophical Society and who was to help him so substantially on the *New Age* before 1914.

The *New Age*, once edited by Joseph Clayton, was then an ailing radical weekly run by the Rev. Harold Rylett. Orage and Jackson purchased it in 1907 with the help of £500 each from Bernard Shaw and Lewis Wallace. After a year Jackson left the business because Orage would pay no attention to the need for advertisement revenue. Indeed, it was only with substantial and regular subsidies from Wallace, Joseph Smith and from other wealthy men, and even from friends and colleagues like Beatrice Hastings, that the paper was carried on at all. Few contributors received any payment, and from 1913 the *New Age* contained no advertisements. In 1908 a limited company was formed which provided Orage with more capital, but this was wound up in debt in 1917. Circulation rose to a peak of 23,500 in 1908 [*New Age*, 7 Jan 1909], when Victor Grayson was assocated with the journal and it was selling at a penny, but fell to less than 5000 in 1914 at threepence, and to less than 2000 in 1921 at sixpence.

For all its financial problems the *New Age* was one of the most important cultural, and for a time political weeklies in early twentieth-century England. Hosts of young writers and artists who were later to make substantial reputations for themselves were given their first or major chance there. They included Ivor Brown, Will Dyson, T.E. Hulme, Katherine Mansfield, Edwin Muir, Ruth Pitter, Ezra Pound, Llewellyn Powys, and Herbert Read. Beatrice Hastings, J.M. Kennedy, C.H. Norman, Cecil Chesterton, A.E. Randall, Huntley Carter and Arnold Bennett were early regulars, joined by Ramiro de Maeztu and Muir during the war. And, in addition, the paper was the cradle of Guild Socialism.

In helping to give it a start Shaw had probably envisaged something rather different – more Fabian, since Orage and Jackson had been the main movers of the Fabian Arts Group in the same year as they took over the *New Age*. The Group, however, proved to be a cave formed against Shaw and the 'old gang' in an attempt to revive the Socialist side of the arts and crafts movement. Orage's wife had become an embroideress with William Morris's firm, and Orage and Jackson were attempting to further the concept of self-governing craftsmen as against the dominant voice of trade union collectivism. Orage, already 'Anti-Fabian (*sotto voce*)' [Carpenter (1922) 85, quoting Orage], joined the unsuccessful revolt against the Fabian executive later in the year, and from that time the *New Age* waged an increasingly bitter war on the Fabians, and also on the Parliamentary Labour Party. The *New Age* was 'out for revolution'. It found in Victor Grayson 'the most significant force in British politics' [*New Age*, 7 Jan 1909] and Orage made him political editor from October 1908 until February 1909 when he left to join the *Clarion*. Although it temporarily became a platform for Grayson, there was always a wide range of differing and conflicting opinions in the paper. For example, while Teresa Billington-Greig wrote regularly in favour of the women's suffrage movement, Beatrice Hastings, Belfort Bax and eventually Orage himself wrote shrill criticism of it, although in the 1890s Orage had not been unfavourable. Again, Cecil Chesterton, who also wrote some of the 'Notes of the Week', argued for a new Socialist party, but he does not appear to have had the support of Orage, who had yet to become a close collaborator with another separatist, S.G. Hobson [*New Age*, 29 Apr 1909]. Chesterton, however, together with Hilaire Belloc, whose *Servile State* first appeared in the *New Age* in 1910, did give the paper a marked anti-Statist character, and thus prepared the way for Guild Socialism.

Orage's early rejection of the idea of a Socialist party had been followed by disillusion with the Parliamentary Labour Party, and his championship of Grayson. By 1910 he had virtually come round to a form of syndicalism, arguing that the trade unions should stick to their industrial last and leave politics alone. This flirtation with syndicalism was not inspired by French doctrines (as Orage later pointed out [Matthews (1979) 153–4]), and it did not lead him and the *New Age* to advocate giving the unions complete control over their respective industries, an arrangement which would only work against the interest of society as a whole. Thus there was preserved a role for the 'state' and the 'nation' and the *New Age* became the first popular platform for Guild Socialism, although Orage preferred the term 'National Guilds'.

Orage's interest in Guilds went back to his association with A.J. Penty, with whom he had discussed the matter at length before 1906 when Penty's *Restoration of the Gild System* was published. The idea was rescued from its mediaevalist and arts and crafts context by S.G. Hobson, who with Orage's help set it out in a modernised and secularised form in the *New Age* during 1912 and 1913. Both Penty and Hobson protested that Orage had either taken or been given too much credit for the idea, but Orage made no public claim beyond that of collaboration, and the omission of Hobson's name from the first edition of *National Guilds* (1914) may have been due to a genuine misunderstanding. Certainly Orage made no attempt to control or claim personal credit for the numerous other writings which had first appeared in his paper. In a later bitter but brilliant attack on Orage, Beatrice Hastings claimed otherwise, but in this respect her criticism seems unfounded [Hastings (1936)]. In any case, the technical side of *National Guilds*, the role of the unions, the mechanics of the transition, the hierarchy of the groups, and the place of the state – on which subjects it differed sharply from the syndicalists – all these were almost certainly Hobson's work, for Orage's interests were more theoretical. He had read much economic literature, but his chief concern was not with the mechanics of either capitalism or Socialism. As he put it in 1907, 'Socialism as a means to the intensification of man is even more necessary than Socialism as a means to the abolition of economic poverty' [*New Age*, 2 May 1907] and in a series of articles entitled 'Towards Socialism' published in the same year he looked towards 'the ladder of becoming' up which men would be led by great individuals who would educate democracy. The primary aim of the 'Guild Idea' was to destroy the 'wages-system' and thus eliminate exploitation, enhance the value of labour, and elevate the status of the worker; all these events, as Hobson later admitted, would depend upon 'a change of heart' [Hobson (1917) 165]. This was what so appealed to Orage, who, like all the Guild Socialists, denied the charge of utopianism whilst insisting on the need for vision.

When the guild movement began to pick up momentum, and was joined by other renegade Fabians, notably G.D.H. Cole, Maurice Reckitt and William Mellor, more positive steps were proposed to unite the proletariat and 'the salariat' as it was termed during the war. But Orage was reluctant to become a man of action. He declined to join the National Guilds League in 1915 and drifted further away from the centre of the movement as the war continued. His dislike of the term 'Guild Socialism', and his preference for the intellectual as against the practical were not inconsistent with the guild idea, but as the emphasis came to be placed increasingly on the unions Orage, always critical of the unions' leadership, was pessimistic about the ability of the rank and file to break out of the system.

He was also having doubts about the adequacy of the Guildsmen's economic analysis. His *Alphabet of Economics* (1917), a collection of *New Age* articles, showed little deviation from the economics to be found in S.G. Hobson, or in Bechhofer and Reckitt's *The Meaning of National Guilds* (1918), with its Marxist theory of property and value. He had never been schooled in economics, and he wrote later that 'every "crank" on the subject was eagerly welcome to my time and consideration' [*Commonweal* (NY), 17 Feb 1926]. The *New Age* had, indeed, carried much 'funny money' theory, and Orage was particularly impressed with Arthur Kitson, with whom he continued to be associated in the 1930s. When in 1919 his old friend Holbrook Jackson introduced him to the engineer Major C.H. Douglas, Orage was ready with a sympathetic ear. Douglas argued – far from lucidly, as even Orage admitted – that there existed a radical flaw in the economic system, a flaw which led to a chronic deficiency in purchasing power. It arose not because the wages system deprived the workers of their just reward, as the Guild Socialists argued, or out of the maldistribution of income and wealth as in

J. A. Hobson's analysis, but out of accounting practice which resulted in industry being permanently and increasingly in debt to finance. As the theory of 'social credit' was developed, two parts of the remedy were emphasised. First, there had to be a mechanism for producing a 'just price', and not a price overloaded with the costs of interest charges. Second, there would be a method of increasing spending power, a 'national dividend' paid to all citizens as of right and not as a reward for work. The radical implications of this analysis attracted Orage and some other National Guildsmen, and the *New Age* was quickly made an organ of the 'new economics'. It presented a non-revolutionary and reformist way to the new society which the Guildsmen had predicted. But while in 1918 the *New Age* was recommending the lessons of the Soviets to its readers, a year later it had firmly turned its back on 'Bolshevism'.

In order to understand the attraction the social credit idea had for Orage, it is important to recognise the continuing moral concern of the Social Crediters, their concern for the quality of life, for the status of the worker, and for a new departure towards a world of abundance in which both the servile and the workers' states would give way to the 'leisure state'. It is true that Orage allowed himself to be imprisoned in the narrow doctrines of Douglasism, and, it seems, was captivated by Douglas himself, but the Social Credit movement was wider than either of them; many of the old Guildsmen who joined it, like Reckitt, had a largely religious basis for their Socialism, and the links between them, the Christian Socialists, the Distributivists and other Catholic reformers of the time were very close. Orage, as his friend Ezra Pound put it, 'was a moralist and thence an economist' [*Criterion* (Apr 1935)], and it was as moralist that the continuity of his efforts is most apparent. For economic wisdom he called not upon Mill and rarely even on Marx, but upon Ruskin and Blake; and later he was much impressed by Veblen. But his 'bizarre lack of judgement' [Muir (1974) 31–2], led him to throw in his lot with Douglas, and it was to the propagation of Douglas's ideas that he devoted most of his energy between 1919 and 1922. Publicity was given to a scheme for the mining industry published in Douglas's *Credit-Power and Democracy* (1920) with a commentary by Orage; but the plan found little response in the labour movement. It rejected nationalisation and depended upon a producers' bank and government subsidies to coal-owners to keep prices down. The Scottish Labour Party asked the Scottish miners to examine the scheme, but they turned it over to a sub-committee of the Labour Party. Dismayed by the composition of this committee, which included Cole, Tawney and J.A. Hobson, Douglas and Orage refused to give evidence. Working without their assistance the committee produced in 1922 a very cool interim report; and no final report was issued. The characteristic Douglas line was lost in competition with other, related, analyses, particularly Mosley and Strachey's Birmingham Proposals of 1925 and the ILP Living Wage Policy of 1926. The TUC never debated Social Credit. The *Clarion*, had shown some interest, but while Blatchford supported the substitution of dividends for wages, he rejected the Douglas 'theorem' and the man himself. Some rank and file support appeared in the Plebs League, but not among its leaders; and on the Communist side, while C.M. Grieve ('Hugh MacDiarmid') was a notable recruit, William Mellor was a more important political opponent.

When Orage was ill with appendicitis at the end of 1919, Douglas took over the 'Notes of the Week' in the *New Age*, but unsuccessfully; and during Orage's continued absence in January 1920 no 'Notes' were published. He was by this time leaning heavily once more to his mystical side. He was making the *New Age* the leading vehicle for the lay discussion of psychoanalysis in general, and he recognised the impact which war hysteria might have upon western civilisation. A Second Coming was in the air [*New Age*, 1 Jan 1920]. Orage was steeped in the occult tradition. Beatrice Hastings claimed that when she went to live with him in 1907, she had found 'a collection of works on sorcery' in his room and he had reputedly wanted to publish the entire 200,000 lines of the *Mahabharata* in the pre-war *New Age*. In 1919, the year of his meeting Douglas, Orage and Bechhofer had arranged for the Russian mystic P.D. Ouspensky to come to London. Orage had met him briefly before the war, and now fell under his influence in a group which enjoyed the financial patronage of Lady Rothermere and included the editor of the *New Statesman*, Clifford Sharp, and a former editor of the *Daily Herald*, Rowland Kenney.

Another important mystical influence on Orage at this time was the Serbian D. Mitrinovic. Orage got him to write in the *New Age* a regular (and impenetrable) mystic commentary on world affairs under the name 'M.M. Cosmoi'. It was through these occult connections that Orage became interested in and eventually dominated by G.I. Gurdjieff, to whose 'school' at Fontainebleau he went in the autumn of 1922.

The disciplines were harsh, but Orage survived a year there, and for the next nine years spent most of his time in the United States teaching Gurdjieff's doctrines. He made a considerable impact on his American contacts, and built up an enthusiastic personal following.In 1927 he married an American, Jessie Dwight, who was to give him in his fifty-fifth year his first child, Richard, and in 1934 a daughter, Ann, to whom Hugh MacDiarmid wrote a 'Genethliacon' which he published in his *Stony Limits*. In 1930 Orage visited England and made contact with the Chandos Group, which had been formed in 1926 by a variety of Social Crediters, Distributivists and Christian Socialists. They welcomed him back, but declined to allow him to return to the *New Age* (then under their control), which many of them, like Reckitt, considered he had irresponsibly deserted in 1922. He decided, therefore, to launch a new paper with the financial help of an American (who so far has not been identified) and of Michael Arlen, and with £1000 of his own money.

The *New English Weekly* (1932–8) was no new *New Age*. The cultural articles were fewer, although some new writers, Dylan Thomas for instance, were given their chance. The journal was devoted to a Social Credit crusade, although dependent on no one section of the movement. Orage was made a member of the Social Credit Council of Representatives in 1934. To the basic principles of Social Credit were added a new emphasis on autarky and a vision of a world in which international trade would no longer be important. At first Mussolini's corporatism was looked upon with favour, but in spite of continued support for the dictator among Social Crediters Orage turned against him, and after 1933 against Nazism too. Communism and Fascism, Orage reiterated, were mere varieties of the one evil, 'Planning'. There had always been a danger within the Social Credit movement that an enthusiasm for a 'functional society' and hostility to the mechanical centralism of Capitalism and of Communism, both of which were for many Crediters indissolubly linked with international Jewry, would lead to something which approached, or which indeed was, Fascism. De Maeztu, Pound and Penty all became Fascists, but Orage did not. Although he had published Pound, Wyndham Lewis, Marinetti, T.E. Hulme and others hostile to bourgeois-cum-liberal values, he had usually been cautious and often critical of them, following instead the path of what he termed 'brilliant common sense'.

He had broken with Gurdjieff before leaving America; but he remained with the occult movement, and a short time before his death he was joint director with Mitrinovic of *New Europe*, a short-lived organ of what might be termed the Adlerian wing of the Social Credit movement.

On 5 November 1934 Orage made his first and only radio broadcast, in the series on 'Poverty in Plenty'. He was evidently exhausted, and died at his Hampstead home in the early hours of the next morning, survived by his wife and two children. He was buried in Hampstead parish churchyard under a stone bearing the Gurdjieff enneagram, carved by Eric Gill, who had twenty-six years previously designed the title piece for the *New Age*, Orage's true monument.

He had been from the first dominated by a desire for understanding, and had switched many times from theory to theory, from guru to guru in its pursuit. He had come to Socialism through the activist Tom Mann, but it was the intellectual legacy of Morris, Ruskin, Blake and Carpenter which determined the paths he would take. It is doubtful whether he contributed any original idea or concept to Socialism, but as midwife of Guild Socialism and as editor of the fecund *New Age* he was invaluable to the movement. He never produced a sustained piece of work. His writing was usually dialectical or aphoristic in form; it often consisted of reprints from his weekly journalism, and it lacked rigour and coherence. His search for the universal, 'elementary', 'fundamental' and 'simple' explanation – which he referred to in *Political and*

Economic Writings (1936) – led him far from the mainstream of modern British Socialism, but his career was an important illustration of one complex strand within the intellectual history of Socialism in Britain.

Writings: 'A Study in Mud' and 'Quixotic Energy', in *Hypnotic Leeds*, ed. A.T. Marles (Leeds, 1894) 17–20 and 43–7; *Friedrich Nietzsche, the Dionysian Spirit of the Age* (1906); *Nietzsche in Outline and Aphorism* (1907); *Consciousness, Animal, Human and Superhuman* (1907); Editor of [S.G. Hobson], *National Guilds: an inquiry into the wage system and the way out* (1914, 3rd ed. 1919); *An Alphabet of Economics* (1917); Introductory essay to S.G. Hobson, *Guild Principles in War and Peace* (1917); *An Englishman talks it out with an Irishman* (1918) 31 pp.; Draft scheme for the mining industry and a commentary in C.H. Douglas, *Credit-Power and Democracy* (1920; rev. ed. 1934); *Readers and Writers 1917–1921* (1922); *The Art of Reading* (NY, [1930]); Editor of *Psychological Exercises* (NY, 1930); *On Love* (1932) 24 pp.; Editor of *Politicians and the Public Service* (1934); *Social Credit and the Fear of Leisure* (1935) 32 pp. [The first of these (pp. 3–12) was a BBC talk broadcast in the series 'Poverty in Plenty', 5 Nov 1934; the second (pp. 13–32) an address to the Leisure Society]; 'Social Credit' in *The Burden of Plenty*, ed. G. Hutton (1935) 62–72; *Selected Essays and Critical Writings*, ed. H. Read and D. Saurat (1935); *Political and Economic Writings*, arranged by M. Butchart et al. (1936); *The Active Mind: adventures in awareness* (1954); *Essays and Aphorisms* (1954) 55 pp.; Translator of G. I. Gurdjieff, *Meetings with Remarkable Men* [from the Russian] (1963); *Orage as Critic*, ed. W. Martin (1974).

Most of Orage's work was journalism which appeared chiefly as follows: 'Bookish Causerie' and other articles, *Labour Leader* (Aug 1895–July 1897); *Forward* [Leeds] 1896–8; *Monthly Rev.* and *Theosophical Rev.*, 1902–7; 'Politics for Craftsmen', *Cont. Rev. 91* (1907) 782–94; 'Notes of the Week', 'Unedited Opinions', 'Readers and Writers', 'Tales for Men only' and 'Towards Socialism' in the *New Age*, although the first three bylines were not invariably Orage; 'An Editor's Progress', *Commonweal* [NY], 10, 17 and 24 Feb and 3 Mar 1926, repr. in the *New Age 38* (1926) 235–6, 246–7, 258, 271–2, 283–4 and 295–6); 'Notes of the Week' and 'Readers and Writers' in *New English Weekly* (1932–8); occasional pieces in *Atlantic Monthly* [Boston], *Commonweal* [NY], *Little Review* [Chicago], and the *New Republic* [NY].

Sources: (1) MS: A.J. Penty Coll. on microfilm, Brynmor Jones Library, Hull Univ.; H.G. Wells papers, Univ. of Illinois; Peter Neagöe papers, Syracuse Univ. Library. (2) Theses: E.E. McCarthy, 'A History of the Social Credit Movement' (Leeds MA, 1947); J.A. Hall, 'The Crisis of the Edwardian Intelligentsia 1900–1920' (London PhD, 1976). (3) Other: H. Jackson, *Bernard Shaw* (1907); C.E. Bechhofer and M.B. Reckitt, *The Meaning of National Guilds* (1918); G. Cumberland, *Set down in Malice: a book of reminiscences* (1918); 'Orage and National Guilds' in F.J. Gould, *Labour's Unrest and Labour's Future* (Apr 1919) 6–16; *Guildsman*, 1920–1; N. Carpenter, *Guild Socialism; an historical and critical analysis* (1922); Labour Party, *Labour and Social Credit* (1922) 16 pp.; *WWW* (1929–40); Hugh MacDiarmid, *Stony Limits and other Poems* (1934); W.R. Hiskett, *Social Credits or Socialism* (1935); B. Hastings, *The Old "New Age": Orage – and others* (1936) 42 pp.; P. Mairet, *A.R. Orage: a memoir* (1936, 2nd ed. with 'Reintroduction' NY, 1966); S.G. Hobson, *Pilgrim to the Left* (1938); W. Hiskett and J.A. Franklin, *Searchlight on Social Credit* (1939); R. Kenney, *Westering: an autobiography* (1939); M.B. Reckitt, *As it happened* (1941); E.J. Kiernan, *Arthur J. Penty: his contribution to social thought* (Washington, 1941); *DNB* (1931–40) [by H.B. Grimsditch]; C.D. King, *The Oragean Version* (NY [1951]); *The Letters of Ezra Pound, 1907–1941*, ed. D.D. Paige (1951); E. Muir, *An Autobiography* (1954); P.P. Selver, *Orage and the New Age Circle* (1959); C.S. Nott, *Teachings of Gurdjieff* (1961); Hugh MacDiarmid, *The Company I've kept* (1966); S.T. Glass, *The Responsible Society: the ideas of the English Guild Socialists* (1966); W. Martin, *The New Age under Orage: chapters in English cultural history* (Manchester 1967); C.S. Nott, *Journey through this World* (1969); D.S. Thatcher, *Nietzsche in*

England, 1880–1914 (Toronto, 1970); S. Hynes, *Edwardian Occasions* (1972); J.L. Finlay, *Social Credit: the English origins* (1972); T. Gibbons, *Rooms in the Darwin Hotel: studies in English literary criticism and ideas, 1880–1920* (Nedlands, S.A., 1973); *Selected Letters of Edwin Muir*, ed. P.H. Butter (1974); R. Groves, *The Strange Case of Victor Grayson* (1975); J. Webb, *The Occult Establishment* (La Salle, Illinois, 1976); J.P. Carswell, *Lives and Letters: A.R. Orage, Beatrice Hastings . . . 1906–1957* (1978); *Letters of Sidney and Beatrice Webb, 1912–1947*, ed. N. MacKenzie (1978); F. Matthews, 'The Ladder of Becoming: A.R. Orage, A.J. Penty and the Origins of Guild Socialism in England', in *Ideology and the Labour Movement*, eds. D.E. Martin and D. Rubinstein (1979) 147–66; S. Pierson, *British Socialists: the journey from fantasy to politics* (Harvard Univ. Press, 1979); J. Webb, *The Harmonious Circle* (NY, 1979). OBIT. *Times*, 7 Nov 1934; *Hampstead and St John's Wood Advertiser*, 8 Nov 1934; *New Statesman and Nation*, 10 Nov 1934; *New English Weekly*, 15 Nov 1934; *Life and Letters 11* (1934) 273–9; *Criterion* (Jan 1935) 260–4 [by T.S. Eliot] and (Apr 1935) 391–407 [by E. Pound; repr. in E. Pound, *Selected Prose 1909-1965* ed. W. Cookson (1973)].

ALAN J. LEE

See also: *Samuel George HOBSON; †Malcolm SPARKES, for Guild Socialism.

OWEN, Robert (1771–1858)

SOCIALIST, CO-OPERATOR AND EDUCATIONIST

Owen was born in Newtown, Montgomeryshire, on 14 May 1771, the son of Robert Owen, saddler, ironmonger and postmaster in the town. His mother's family (Williams) were 'respectable farmers' in the neighbourhood, and Robert was the youngest but one of seven children, two of whom died young. In his fifth year he attended a local school kept by a Mr Thickness, and from the age of seven served as his assistant. He left school at the age of nine to work in a local drapery and grocery store. According to his autobiography, which is the only source of information for Owen's early life, he apparently had a happy and relatively uneventful childhood. He read widely – novels, histories, biographies – as he was able to borrow books from a clergyman, a physician and a lawyer of the town. During school holidays he visited his farming relatives. At the age of eight and nine he was, he later wrote, 'religiously inclined'; and was helped in this direction by three maiden ladies who were Methodists and friends of the family. However, the conflicting views of different denominations of Christians and the competing claims of other religions later created doubts in his mind, which led him to abandon his early faith.

Owen left home at ten and was apprenticed to James M'Guffog, a draper in Stamford, Lincs. There he learned how to conduct a high-class business, and in his spare time continued his reading from M'Guffog's 'well-selected library'. In spite of pressing offers to stay in Stamford, Owen decided to seek wider experience on the expiration of his apprenticeship; and in his fifteenth year went to London as an assistant in the haberdashery house of Flint and Palmer on the Borough side of old London Bridge. His salary was £25 a year, plus board and lodging on the premises. The business was of a lower class than M'Guffog's and the hours were long and the work exhausting. Owen therefore soon looked for a move; and in his seventeenth year took a position with John Satterfield, a draper of 5 St Ann's Square, Manchester, who paid him £40 a year together with 'board, lodging and washing in his house'. During the course of his work at Satterfield's, Owen met John Jones, a mechanic who supplied the shop with wire bonnet frames, and who was interested in making spinning mules if he could find the necessary capital. Owen agreed to enter into partnership with him, borrowed £100 from his elder brother William in London and in 1790 (or early in 1791) left Satterfield's to become a manufacturer. Owen and

Jones soon had forty men at work making spinning mules, with Jones supervising the production and Owen (who as yet knew nothing about the new machinery) directing the business side of the venture. But after a few months Jones found a partner with more capital, and Owen was bought out, agreeing to take as his share of the business six mules, a reel and a making-up machine. He then rented a factory ('as such places were beginning to be called') in Ancoats Lane, hired three men, and began cotton spinning on three mules – all that he ever received of his share. In the following year he claimed that he was making a profit of £300 per annum. Owen was now launched on his career as a successful cotton spinner, at the very heart of the cotton manufacturing area and at the crucial period of its rapid expansion. As he noted, 'about this period cotton spinning was so profitable that it began to engage the attention of many parties with capitals' [Owen (1857) *1*, 26]. Among these was Peter Drinkwater, who in 1792 advertised for a manager of his large Piccadilly cotton mill in Manchester. In a well-known passage [ibid. 27–8], Owen described how he applied for and won the job, although he was only twenty. (Owen's account of these events in his *Life* is not entirely accurate: see Chaloner (1954) 92–4). His management was so successful that he was soon offered a partnership in the business. But when Drinkwater withdrew the offer Owen indignantly resigned; and shortly afterwards entered into a partnership with Jonathan Scarth and Richard Percival Moulson of Manchester, 'two young men, inexperienced in the business, although they had capital' [Owen (1857) *1*, 42]. This partnership began the building of new cotton mills at Chorlton on land purchased from Samuel Marsland; but before they were completed Owen formed the Chorlton Twist Company in 1796, in partnership with Borradaile and Atkinson (merchants and hat manufacturers of London and Salford) and Barton of Manchester under his own management.

During his residence in Manchester (1787–9) Owen developed not only his entrepreneurial talents but also his intellectual and social interests. He made friends at Manchester Academy (a Unitarian college), and through this circle of liberal, Dissenting intellectuals (which included Dr Thomas Barnes and John Dalton) he gravitated towards the Manchester Literary and Philosophical Society, of which he was elected a member in November 1793. He read four papers to the Society; and it is possible that Owen's interest in social questions was first aroused by his acquaintance with the president and founder of the Society, Dr Thomas Percival, FRS, who was active in factory and public health reform. Acquaintance with prosperous Manchester merchants and professional men made Owen acutely aware of his shyness, social ignorance and general gaucherie; and he welcomed the opportunity of the 'Lit and Phil' to remedy the educational and social deficiencies of his upbringing.

Owen lived at various addresses during his bachelor days in Manchester. In 1794 he was a lodger at 8 Brazen-nose Street; and while there entered into a partnership with a fellow-lodger, Robert Fulton, to share in the profits of Fulton's engineering inventions. Owen later moved to lodgings in Chorlton Hall; and then purchased half of a large house, Greenheys, where he lived until he left Manchester. In the course of his duties as managing director of the Chorlton Twist Company, Owen visited Glasgow where he was introduced to Ann Caroline Dale, daughter of David Dale, a wealthy cotton spinner and philanthropist of New Lanark. Owen and Caroline were married on 30 September 1799; and Owen and his partners bought the New Lanark mills and village from Dale. During the autumn of 1799 Owen and his bride lived at Greenheys; but in January 1800 they returned to New Lanark, where Owen assumed the management of the mills.

The period of Owen's life from 1800 to 1824 was in many ways his most splendid. A vigorous young man at the height of his powers, he was sole manager and dominant partner of one of the very largest cotton spinning establishments in Britain. In these years he made New Lanark a model factory, acquired a large fortune, and raised his family. Owen's career was one of the big success stories of the early industrial revolution. Because of the failure of his later attempts at community building, doubts have sometimes been cast on Owen's capacities as a business man [Podmore (1906) *2*, 642–4]. But recent research confirms his financial shrewdness, profit-making capacities and management skills [Butt (1971) 168–214].

Owen found that labour relations and management at New Lanark were poor: workers were drunken and irregular in their habits, theft was widespread, and managers were slack. The work force included 400–500 pauper apprentices, aged between five and ten years.Owen quickly set about changing all this, despite opposition from the workers. Factory discipline was tightened, productivity increased, and paupers replaced gradually by free child labour of at least ten years of age. Believing that behaviour would in the long run be determined by environment, Owen steadily introduced changes in the village to promote 'sobriety and correct conduct'. He destroyed the private retail shops (which encouraged the sale of spirits and buying on credit) by a company store which sold food, fuel and clothing at low prices and yet made sufficient profit to finance schools. A contributory sickness and superannuation fund was maintained, and free medical services and a savings bank were available. He enforced a system of fines for drunkenness, and insisted that tenants should keep their homes and roadways clean. An elaborate system of educational and recreational institutions was established and gardens and allotments were laid out. In 1806 an American embargo on the export of cotton brought the mills to a standstill, but for four months Owen paid full wages to his work people while they were unemployed. This, perhaps more than anything else, reconciled the inhabitants of New Lanark to Owen's drastic paternalism. He did not pay high wages and the mills were extremely profitable for their owners. This combination of high profitability with enlightened philanthropy created the image of New Lanark as a model factory. It became one of the most visited places in Europe, and Owen's talent for publicity was nowhere more evident than in the conducted tours round the village and mills. Owen complained later that his schemes of benevolent improvement were frustrated by his partners, and in 1809 or 1810 the original partnership (the New Lanark Twist Company) was dissolved, and he chose new partners whom he thought would be more sympathetic. But in 1812–13 the search for another set of partners was begun, and a third partnership, which included Jeremy Bentham and William Allen, was formed.

Of all the institutions at New Lanark, none attracted more encomiums than the schools. Owen had a great love of children and his infinite patience and good temper made him a beloved figure to them everywhere. His desire to extend and remodel the original schools, which had been started by David Dale, was frustrated by his partners until 1809. But by 1812 the New Institution was built, and in 1816 he opened the more ambitious Institution for the Formation of Character. This last served a threefold purpose: as an infant school, a day school, and a centre for adult education and recreation. The pedagogical techniques and assumptions were quite revolutionary and, apparently, original to Owen himself. The building was constructed according to the fashionable Lancasterian plan, but the monitorial system was not used; and in fact the schools were far removed, both in purpose and method, from the contemporary instruction-factories of Bell and Lancaster – though Owen had earlier supported their efforts and in 1812 took the chair at a public dinner in Glasgow given in honour of Lancaster. Owen decided that small children should not 'be annoyed with books', but were to be taught by 'sensible signs' and 'familiar conversation'. The interests of child-nature were utilised in teaching basic subjects, and play (and the playground) was treated as an educative agency. Dancing, singing and 'military exercises' were part of the daily curriculum, and the need for variety and flexibility in teaching methods was enjoined on all teachers. No 'artificial' rewards or punishments were permitted, and kindness was observed in precept and practice.

Owen's philanthropic endeavours were extended beyond New Lanark to factory reform in general. In January 1815 he addressed a meeting of cotton manufacturers in Glasgow, at which he condemned import duties on raw cotton and then went on to demand reform of the conditions of child labour in mills. Later in the year he expanded his views in a pamphlet, *Observations on the Effect of the Manufacturing System*. He proposed legislation to prohibit the employment of children in mills under the age of ten or for more than six hours per day until they were twelve; educational tests before admitting children to the mills; and a twelve-hour working day, inclusive of one and a half hours for meals. To promote his campaign Owen went to London and visited the Chancellor of the Exchequer, Nicholas Vansittart, who (according to Owen) gave him some encouragement. But the main support came from the Tory, Viscount Lascelles, and from Sir Robert Peel who introduced a bill in the Commons in June 1815. Peel's bill was deferred, but in April 1816 a Select Committee of Inquiry, under Peel's chairmanship, was set up. Owen gave evidence before the Committee, and in preparation toured the factory districts to collect material for his case. No action was taken on the evidence collected by the 1816 Committee, and in February 1818 Peel introduced another bill. Owen supported the campaign with a pamphlet addressed to Lord Liverpool, *On the Employment of Children in Manufactories*. After a further committee of investigation had been established by the Lords, the Act was finally passed in July 1819. It provided that children should not be employed under the age of nine, and that those under sixteen should not work more than twelve hours a day, exclusive of meal times, nor at night. The Act applied only to cotton mills, and there was no provision for education or inspection. Owen quite rightly regarded the Act as wholly inadequate: it had, he said, 'finally spoilt' his original proposal of 1815.

Owen's reputation as a benevolent philanthropist was further enhanced by his writings. In 1812 he published an anonymous pamphlet, *A Statement regarding the New Lanark Establishment*, and in the same year he wrote his first 'Essay on the Principle of the Formation of Human Character', published early in 1813 under the title, *A New View of Society*. A second Essay was published at the end of 1813; and a third and fourth, after circulating privately, were published in July 1816 (and referred to as the second edition, i.e. of the complete work). The *New View* was Owen's best-known work. It consisted of a theory of character formation ('the character of man is formed for and not by him'); an account of the reforms at New Lanark; and a plea for a system of national education, a programme of public works for the unemployed, and reform of the Poor Laws. In the summer of 1816 Owen spoke at a public meeting in London convened by several public figures who were concerned at the widespread distress following the ending of the Napoleonic Wars. He elaborated his remarks in the *Report to the Committee of the Association for the Relief of the Manufacturing and Labouring Poor* [1817], which was then referred in March 1817 to Sturges–Bourne's Select Committee of the House of Commons on the Poor Laws. The *Report* diagnosed the cause of unemployment as a combination of the effects of peace and the spread of machinery; and the proposed remedy was the creation of self-supporting communities of about 1200 persons, with accommodation arranged in a parallelogram of buildings, and provision for all the educational and social needs of the inhabitants. Here, in the form of an improved method of relieving the unemployed, was the first presentation of Owen's famous Plan. Not surprisingly, the Plan found little favour with the economy-minded Select Committee. Owen therefore turned elsewhere for support, and throughout 1817 carried on a large-scale publicity campaign, using press, pamphlets and public meetings to great effect. However, as the propaganda expanded so also did the range of his expectations. By September 1817 Owen was using millennial language and equating his plan with the emancipation of mankind: the Villages of Unity and Mutual Co-operation were now to include all classes, not just paupers. Owen's publicity drive attracted criticism of, as well as support for his ideas, and through the necessity of defining his position more fully he was led to a mature formulation of his ideas in the *Report to the County of Lanark* (1821). The details of the villages of co-operation were as in his earlier proposals, but they were now embedded in a theory of co-operative socialism and prophetic utterance. Owen's Plan, which had begun as a method of unemployment relief, emerged as a scheme for the thorough reorganisation of society. He was questioned on this at length when he gave evidence before the Select Committee on Employment of the Poor in Ireland in June 1823.

The philanthropic mould of his thinking at this period is indicated by the title of the first Owenite organisation, the British and Foreign Philanthropic Society for the Permanent Relief of the Labouring Classes, founded in 1822 to promote Owen's community schemes. But already his views were sufficiently unorthodox to arouse alarm in conservative minds. The political economists condemned his plans as impracticable and wrong in principle. In the summer of 1817, during his great propaganda campaign, Owen had denounced all existing religions as false and superstitious and he later considered this to be the turning point in his career. These attacks on religion brought immediate hostility from the conservative groups in society; and at the same time his benevolent paternalism alienated popular radicals like Cobbett, Hone and Wooler.

By 1821 Owen's theory of utopian socialism was virtually complete (though the term 'socialist' was not used by his followers until 1827). Three elements gave Owenism its distinctive characteristics as a philosophy of social reform. First, was a concern for community, which Owen felt was essential for satisfactory human relationships in any society. The absence of such community he diagnosed as the chief ill of British society, and in his efforts to restore harmony he became a socialist and was led to condemn all institutions which 'individualised' man. In practice, this meant the founding of communities, in which (ultimately, if not immediately) property would be held in common. Society would be radically transformed by these experimental communities, and communitarianism was advocated as a practical method of social reform, alternative to other methods such as revolution or parliamentary legislation. The peaceful nature of desirable social change was fundamental to all Owen's thinking: communitarianism, he argued, offered a way to social betterment that was both radical and non-violent.

Second, Owen's socialism contained a critique of capitalism and an alternative theory of co-operative economics. Despite some elements of backward-looking agrarianism and paternalism, Owen did not turn his back on industrialisation nor become what Marx and Engels called a feudal socialist. On the contrary, Owen believed that the material abundance produced by the new forms of industry made possible, for the first time in human history, the necessary basis for the good environment which would be productive of happy human beings. Capitalism stood condemned, he argued, because in the midst of potential plenty it produced only poverty for a majority of the people. In the *Report to the County of Lanark* he adopted a version of the labour theory of value; and after 1825 he expressed belief in the need for social equality.

Third, Owen claimed that he had discovered the laws of a science of society. His moralistic terminology and inability to refine his original 'principles', today obscure some of his meaning – and the matter was made worse by his polemicism and tendency to exaggerate. But in his calmer writings he provided some of the beginnings of behavioural science. Owen's sociology and social psychology were incomplete and inconsistent. Nevertheless in certain areas – notably the role of institutions, the concept of ideology, social change and the sociology of education – Owenism came near to justifying its claim to be a social science in the modern sense.

In the summer and autumn of 1818 Owen toured in Europe, under the guidance of Charles Pictet, a Swiss diplomatist and savant, who introduced him to distinguished people in Paris and Geneva. Owen visited experimental schools in Switzerland, including the establishment of Philipp Emanuel von Fellenberg at Hofwyl. He was sufficiently impressed with this to send his two elder sons, Robert Dale and William, to be educated there in the following year, and his two younger sons, David Dale and Richard, attended later. At Frankfurt, Owen wrote *Two Memorials on Behalf of the Working Classes* (1818), addressed to the Governments of Europe and America and to the Allied Powers assembled at the Congress of Aix-la-Chapelle. There he attempted to lobby leading statesmen and rulers, including the Tsar of Russia, in support of his new ideas; and persuaded Lord Castlereagh to distribute copies of his *Memorial* to members of the Congress. The following year (1819) Owen stood as parliamentary candidate for the combined boroughs of Lanark, Selkirk, Peebles and Linlithgow at a by-election, but was unsuccessful; and he repeated this failure when he stood again at the general election in 1820.

Until 1824 Owen was endeavouring, unsuccessfully, to start an experimental community by gaining support from wealthy philanthropists and members of the aristocracy. But in the summer of that year he decided to go to America and found a community himself. He was already knowledgeable about American communitarians, including the Shakers and Rappites, and when he heard that the Rappites wished to sell their property at Harmony, Indiana, he determined to investigate the possibilities. Owen arrived in New York in November 1824, and this first visit to the United States (until July 1825) was one long triumphal tour. Everywhere he went he was listened to with respect, and in Washington he gained the ear of the President and leading members of the Government. In February and March, 1825, he gave two discourses in the Hall of Representatives. He bought New Harmony from the Rappites in April 1825. The purchase price of the town was $125,000 and Owen's additional expenditures brought the total to about $200,000, which accounted for the bulk of his fortune. He thus acquired 20,000 acres of land and a complete village with houses, churches, dormitories and workshops. All was ready for immediate occupation as a community, and as the Rappites moved out some nine hundred new-comers moved in, answering Owen's public invitation to 'the industrious and well disposed of all nations'. Community life was begun in May, but Owen was away from New Harmony during the critical early months, and his second son, William, was left in charge. Owen returned in January 1826 and set about reorganising the community; but practical difficulties soon led to separatist tendencies, and the Harmonists divided themselves into several communities. Owen made an unsuccessful attempt to reorganise the whole community in the spring of 1827 and then left New Harmony for a year. He returned briefly in April–June 1828 and thereafter New Harmony lapsed into individualism. As an experiment in Owenite communitarianism New Harmony virtually came to an end with Owen's departure in June 1827. While in America Owen lost no opportunity of travelling widely and lecturing on his plans. In April 1829 he debated publicly with the Rev. Alexander Campbell in Cincinnati on the evidences of Christianity – the forerunner of many such debates by Owenites in the 1830s and 1840s. After the failure of New Harmony, Owen had proposed a community experiment on an even larger scale, namely the colonisation of Texas, then a province of the Mexican Republic. He visited Mexico early in 1829 to promote his scheme, but nothing came of it.

The American or communitarian phase of Owen's career lasted only five years (1824–9) but was crucial for him in several ways. It marked the end of his long association with the world of business, for he never went back to New Lanark. It established his reputation as a radical social reformer and attracted disciples in two continents. He sank practically the whole of his fortune in New Harmony and transferred his family (though not his wife) to America, where they became citizens.

On his return to England in 1829 Owen lived in London but was no longer able to enjoy the large income he had formally had. During his absence in America some of his philanthropic followers, led by Archibald James Hamilton and Abram Combe, founded a community at Orbiston, near Motherwell, which lasted from 1825 to 1827. Owen was not involved in this venture, though he visited it briefly on his trip from America in 1827. At the same time his social schemes were also attracting support among working men who were anxious to adapt them to their needs. They founded co-operative stores of retail trading, but Owen was not greatly interested. When, however, some of the co-operative societies extended themselves into labour exchange bazaars, he became involved. Early in 1830 he took the Burton Street Chapel, London, and delivered a series of Sunday morning lectures, published as *Lectures on an Entire New State of Society*. These showed a marked radical progression in his social thinking, for he now came out quite unequivocally against private property, commercialism and inequality in general. His solution to social problems was still basically communitarian, but during the next few months his approach was modified by his contacts with working-men co-operators. He started the Institution of the Industrious Classes in December 1831, intended to promote weekly lectures, a school and allotments; but these objectives faded into the background after he launched the National Equitable Labour Exchange as an off-shoot of the Institution in September 1832. The Exchange was located in a large building in Grays Inn Road and operated as a depot where working-men producers exchanged their products by means of labour notes representing hours of labour time. For some months the Exchange did a brisk business, but in May 1833 Owen had to find a new home for it (in Charlotte Street, Fitzroy

Square), and it was wound up in the early summer of 1834. The main users of the Exchange were members of the metropolitan trades societies, organised in the United Trades Association, and through them Owen became aware of the potentialities of his new audience. For a brief period he put himself at the head of the whole working-class movement.

Throughout 1833 trade unions in all parts of the country announced their support for co-operative producers' associations. Owen toured the kingdom, lecturing and attending union meetings at which he tirelessly repeated his prophetic plans for fundamental social change, and by the summer of 1833 he was the acknowledged national leader of the trade union movement. Support was particularly strong in four main areas: London, Birmingham, Yorkshire and Lancashire, and the Staffordshire Potteries. In November 1833 he joined with John Doherty and John Fielden in launching the Society for Promoting National Regeneration, which demanded an eight-hour day in the factories as a prelude to the extinction of capitalist society. Owen gave full vent to his millenarian convictions that the crisis was at hand and the old immoral world was about to be swept away. To effect this he proposed a national organisation, 'for the purpose of emancipating the industrious and useful classes.' Early in 1834 this body emerged as the Grand National Consolidated Trades Union. Within a few weeks the Union was reported to have a million members, and the alarm which it aroused among the Government and employers soon provoked conflict. Strikes and lock-outs occurred in many parts of the country, and the Union inherited the protracted Derby turn-out, which had begun in November 1833. Then came the sudden set-back with the sentencing of the Tolpuddle Martyrs in March 1834. The GNCTU campaigned vigorously on this issue, and Owen led a huge demonstration in Copenhagen Fields, London on 21 April. Efforts to support members on strike or locked-out proved to be far beyond the Union's means, and under pressure from the employers the individual unions collapsed or left the GNCTU. By the summer of 1834 discord arose within the top councils of the Union, and Owen parted company with his two lieutenants, James Morrison and J.E. (Shepherd) Smith. The *Crisis*, which Owen had started inAugust 1832, and which had been edited by Smith since September 1833, was closed down in August; and Owen called a meeting of delegates in London which resolved that the Union should be renamed the British and Foreign Consolidated Association of Industry, Humanity and Knowledge. Owen was elected Grand Master, and his leadership of the trade union movement was now ended. Nevertheless, Owenism as distinct from the views of Owen himself, was now widely diffused, and formed an important element in the thinking of working-class leaders and social reformers. A series of co-operative congresses, at which Owen presided or took a leading part, had been held from May 1831 to April 1835, and provided a focus for his followers in the co-operative movement, labour exchanges and trade unions.

Owen's social thinking in the autumn of 1834 now reverted to the positions he had held in 1829. He founded a new journal, the *New Moral World*, under the editorship of George Alexander Fleming and he occupied himself for the next few years in a ceaseless round of lecturing, writing and organising. The British and Foreign Association was reorganised in May 1835 as the Association of All Classes of All Nations. At the Manchester Congress in May 1837 a Missionary and Tract Society was set up and also the National Community Friendly Society, to promote the foundation of communities. In May 1839 the AACAN and the NCFS were amalgamated to form the Universal Community Society of Rational Religionists, which from May 1842 was known simply as the Rational Society. A Home Colonisation Society was established in 1841 to raise funds for communities, and a Central Board served as the executive committee of the UCSRR. Annual congresses were held, continuing the tradition established by the earlier series of co-operative congresses of 1831 to 1835. Essentially the Owenites were now a sect, and their institutions were organised accordingly. Owen himself was referred to as the Social Father.

He continued to develop his social and psychological propositions, which appeared in their final form as the *Book of the New Moral World* (1836–44). But his views aroused increasing antagonism, particularly when he criticised such fundamental institutions of Victorian society as religion, marriage and the family. Basically Owen was a deist; and he dismissed all organised religions, including Christianity, as 'so many geographical insanities.' [R.D. Owen (1874) 166]. He was scurrilously attacked, among many others by John Brindley, a Birmingham preacher; and in January 1840 Henry Phillpotts, the Bishop of Exeter, raised the matter of the socialists in the House of Lords. In the summer of 1839 Owen had been presented at Court, and the Tory bishop used the incident to embarrass the Whigs as well as to attack 'infidelism'. Owen in the 1830s was criticising the family as the main bastion of private property and the guardian of all those qualities of individualism and self-interest to which he was opposed. He regarded the family as a fundamentally divisive force, much more so than class; and he refused to regard class divisions as primary. Moreover, the family was an organ of tyranny, by which the wife was subjected to, and in fact made the property of her husband. Community, argued Owen, provided an alternative to the institution of the family. He denounced the institution of Christian marriage in his *Lectures on the Marriages of the Priesthood* (1835). Unfortunately his more reasoned and sensible views on marriage, divorce and sexual relationships were obscured by his desire to blame the clergy. In consequence a torrent of hysterical abuse was heaped on Owen and his followers. Owen had favoured artificial birth control, and his name had been linked with Francis Place and Richard Carlile on the 'diabolical handbills' controversy of 1823. But he subsequently denied that he had been so involved, and his exact role in the birth control movement is somewhat obscure [Himes (1928) 627–40]. His followers, including his son Robert Dale, however, were open advocates of contraception; and inevitably some of the outcry against the 'horrible abominations' of Owenism included Owen himself.

From October 1839 the main body of Owenites focused their attention on a new communitarian venture at Queenwood, East Tytherley, in Hampshire. Owen was nominated as governor, but resigned on the grounds that the members were not yet prepared, either with funds or experience, for community life; and his attitude towards the community remained ambivalent throughout its six years of existence. He served as governor in 1841–2 and again in 1843–4, but did not concern himself with its day-to-day running. In August 1841 he laid the foundation stone of Harmony Hall, Queenwood's elaborate community building designed by Joseph Hanson. Owen's plans for the community were impossibly ambitious, and in 1844 a group of working-class Owenites revolted against his extravagant policies and took over control. They were unable to extricate the community from its financial plight, and in the summer of 1845 most of the residents left. For a short period in 1844 Owen lived at Rosehill, one of the farms which the community had acquired; but he was not actively involved in the winding up of Harmony Hall.

In August 1844 he returned to America, where he remained until the summer of 1847, with the exception of a few weeks in June–July 1845 and April–May 1846 when he was back in England. In the United States he stayed with his sons at New Harmony, visited socialist communities, gave lectures, interviewed prominent persons, and summoned a World's Convention of his followers in New York in October 1845. While in America Owen was briefed by his son, Robert Dale, who was then a United States congressman, with proposals for settling the Oregon boundary dispute between Britain and the United States. Owen returned to England in April 1846 and approached Robert Peel and Lord Aberdeen about the matter. The dispute was settled, and Owen cherished the belief that his efforts had helped. He went back to America in May, and returned to England in the summer of 1847. He was nominated as parliamentary candidate for Marylebone and he contested this seat at the general election of July 1847 as a Chartist candidate, proposed by Lloyd Jones. There were five candidates in all; and at the declaration of the poll Owen received one vote out of 15,050 votes cast. In 1852 he offered himself as candidate for Oldham but was apparently not accepted. The French revolution of 1848 had excited Owen by its apparent possibilities for the realisation of some of his plans, and in March 1848 he went to Paris, remaining there until August. He enjoyed being lionised, and talked with Louis Blanc, Lamartine, Étienne Cabet and other prominent citizens, urging on them the advantages of his system. He addressed the Comité du Travail, issued proclamations, prepared translations of his earlier works, and wrote new pamphlets: Paris was subjected to an intensive propaganda campaign.

Although Owen never tired of reissuing his earlier works and repeating his familiar dogmas, there is a developmental element discernible in his later writings (contrary to the opinion of most of his biographers that his views, once formulated remained unchanged from about 1820 for the rest of his life). During his last decade he issued *The Revolution in the Mind and Practice of the Human Race* (1849) and *The New Existence of Man upon the Earth* (1854–5). *The New Moral World* came to an end in 1845, and his need for a journal was met by *Robert Owen's Journal* (1850–2), the *Rational Quarterly Review* (1853) and the *Millennial Gazette* (1856–8). Owen's last work, his autobiography, was published in 1857, and stands apart from his other writing. The volume was to some extent a compilation of earlier autobiographical fragments, and it has a freshness and charm not found in most of his other works.

In his last years Owen became a spiritualist. After meeting Mrs Hayden, an American medium who was visiting London in 1853, he became convinced of the existence of a future state of life, and subsequently had seances with mediums. However, his new experiences did not shake his belief in the correctness of his plans for the new moral world. Owen's spiritualism was a practical device for ushering in the millennium.

Owen was active to the very end of his life. His final effort was an attempt to address the annual meeting of the newly-formed National Association for the Promotion of Social Science at Liverpool in October 1858. He was unable to go on with his speech, and on 17 November he died at the Bear's Head Hotel in Newtown, his birthplace. Owen was buried, in accordance with his wishes, in the old churchyard, Newtown, in a grave next to his parents. The funeral was attended by his son, Robert Dale, and several of his devoted followers from London. A monument in the form of an obelisk with a bronze medallion of Owen was erected, by public subscription, in Kensal Green Cemetery, London in 1879. This stands alongside the Reformers' Monument, a memorial to men and women associated with nineteenth-century reform movements which was erected by Joseph W. Corfield, of South Place Institute, London, in 1885. In 1902 Owen's grave was restored by the co-operative movement, when ornamental railings and a bronze bas-relief were added. The Robert Owen Memorial Park near the centre of Newtown was completed in 1958, with a statue of Owen and a bronze relief; and the Robert Owen Museum and a plaque on the site of his birthplace were provided by the Co-operative Union. He was also commemorated in the GPO Social Reformers stamp series in May 1976.

In his last years Owen's administrative affairs were looked after by James Rigby, an old Owenite and former social missionary. Henry Travis and William Pare were his joint literary executors but no will has been located. Shortly after his marriage Owen went to live at Braxfield House, New Lanark, and it was there that his family was raised. From 1829 he resided in London, but had no fixed home. In the 1840s he stayed at Cox's Hotel, Jermyn Street; and from 1853 he lived at Park Farm, Sevenoaks. Owen had eight children. The first-born son died in infancy. The other four sons went to New Harmony and settled in America. Robert Dale, the eldest, became a member of the Indiana State Legislature in 1835, congressman in the United States House of Representatives in 1843, and U.S. minister at Naples in 1852. The second son, William, died at New Harmony in 1842. David Dale, the third son, won a considerable reputation as a pioneer geologist; and Richard, the youngest, served as a colonel in the Civil War and was a founder and president of Purdue University. Owen's eldest daughter, Anne, died in 1830; his wife in 1831; and his youngest daughter, Mary, in 1832. The surviving daughter, Jane, then went to New Harmony, where she later married Robert Fauntleroy.

The many-sidedness of Owen's life and thought precludes any concise evaluation of his influence and achievement, and reference on specific points must be made to the extensive bibliography. However, his personal qualities seem to be beyond dispute. He was the kindest, gentlest and most patient of men; he was 'a man without guile' and 'without malice' [Podmore (1906) 637]; and he was also autocratic, self-complacent and limited in his intellectual conceptions. In a rare tribute Engels, in *Anti-Dühring*, described Owen as 'a man of almost sublimely child-like simplicity of character and at the same time a born leader of men' and he went on to declare 'all social movements, all real advance made in England in the interests of the working class were associated with Owen's name' [also quoted Morton (1962) 183–4].

Writings: The most comprehensive source for the writings of Robert Owen is J.F.C. Harrison, *Robert Owen and the Owenites in Britain and America* (1969) 266–77. Only those works to which reference has been made in the above biographical entry are included below and, unless otherwise specified, it is the date of the first edition which is cited: *A Statement regarding the New Lanark Establishment* (Edinburgh, 1812) 23 pp.; *A New View of Society: or, essays on the principle of the formation of human character* (1813–14, complete ed., 1816); *Observations on the Effect of the Manufacturing System: with hints for the improvement of those parts of it which are most injurious to health and morals* (1815) 18 pp. [3rd ed. privately printed, without author's name and date]... *To which are added two Letters on the Employment of Children in Manufactories, and a Letter on the Union of Churches and Schools* (1818) 44 pp.; *On the Employment of Children in Manufactories* (This is a reprint of the letter in Owen's 3rd ed. ibid., New Lanark [1818]); Evidence before S.C. on State of Children employed in the Manufactories of the United Kingdom 1816 III *M of E* pp. 36–40, 66, 86–95, 113, and before S.C. on Education of Lower Orders of the Metropolis 1816 IV *M of E* pp. 238–42; *Report to the Committee of the Association for the Relief of the Manufacturing and Labouring Poor* ... [1817] 24 pp.; *Two Memorials on Behalf of the Working Classes* ... (Lanark, 1818) 27 pp.; *Report to the County of Lanark, of a Plan for relieving Public Distress, and removing Discontent* (Glasgow, 1821); Evidence before S.C. on Employment of the Poor in Ireland 1823 VI *M of E* pp. 70–103, 156–8; *Lectures on an Entire New State of Society* ... [1830?]; Founder of the *Crisis* (1832–4) and *New Moral World* (1834–45); *Lectures on the Marriages of the Priesthood of the Old Immoral World, delivered in the Year 1835, before the Passing of the New Marriage Act* (Leeds, 1835); *The Book of the New Moral World, containing the Rational System of Society* pt *1* (1836), pts *2* and *3* (1842), pts *4* to *7* (1844); *The Revolution in the Mind and Practice of the Human Race* (1849); *Robert Owen's Journal* (1850–2) *succeeded by Robert Owen's Rational Q. Rev. and J.* (Feb–Nov 1853); *The New Existence of Man upon the Earth* nos. 1–5 (1854), nos. 6–8 (1855); *Robert Owen's Millennial Gazette* (1856–8); *Life of Robert Owen: written by himself with selections from his writings and correspondence* vol. *1* (1857), vol. *1A* (1858) [a supplementary appendix to vol. *1*] (repr. NY, 1967).

Sources: The most important collections of Owenite materials (ms. and printed) are the libraries of the Co-operative Union, Manchester, and the International Institute of Social History, Amsterdam; smaller groups of letters by and to Owen are in the BL and Goldsmiths' Library, London. For further details see Harrison op. cit., R.G. Garnett, *Co-operation and the Owenite Socialist Communities in Britain 1825–45* (Manchester, 1972), *Robert Owen: checklist of books, pamphlets, press-cuttings and mss. in the library of the Co-operative Union Ltd* (Manchester, Jan 1975), and *A Catalogue of Some Labour Records in Scotland and Some Scots Records outside Scotland* ed. I. MacDougall (Edinburgh, 1978) 498–504. See also (1) below for ms. sources additional to those listed in Harrison op. cit.: (1) **MS:** Letters from Robert Owen to Thomas Allsop and his wife Anna [c. 1832-53?] in John Burns papers, vol. 64, Add. MSS, 46,344, BL; Letters from Owen to Boulton and Watt, Birmingham PL [B. & W. Coll., 1793, 1795]; Papers about Owen, 1830–58, National Library of Wales; Invoices made out by Owen, 1793, Oldknow MSS, John Rylands Library, Manchester; Letter on Corn Law of 1815, Owen to Lord Sidmouth, 16 Mar 1815, Sidmouth–Addington Correspondence, Devon Record Office, Exeter [repr. in *Bull. Soc. Lab. Hist.* no. *28* (spring 1974) 13–15]; the Journal of the New Lanark Company from the date of its re-formation on 14 January 1814 to December 1816 is on microfilm: copies at Brynmor Jones Library, Hull Univ. (microtext 3168) and Univ. Archives, Glasgow. This account book, of approx. 300 pages, sets out in detail the firm's financial transactions for these years. It should be noted that so far nothing from the ms. has been published. (2) **Theses** (not included in above sources): F. Fraser, 'Robert Owen and Christian Socialism' (Edinburgh PhD, 1927); E. Lloyd, 'Robert Owen and Social Legislation' (Wales MA, 1932); W. C. Eisel, 'The Social Views of Robert Owen: their source and their influence on the social reform movement since his time' (Durham MLitt., 1935); F.L.P. Knight, 'Owenite Socialism in the Period 1817–1840' (Manchester MA, 1965); D.A. Turner, 'The Educational Influence of Robert Owen in England with Particular Reference to the Infant Schools directly developed from the New Lanark Pattern between 1819–1839' (London MPhil., 1969); D.S. Gadian, 'A Comparative Study of Popular Movements in the N.W. Industrial Towns, 1830–50' (Lancaster PhD, 1976). (3) **Other:** The writings listed below supplement the published sources cited by Harrison in his 1969 study of Owen and include also works mentioned in the above biographical entry. [R. Torrens], 'Mr Owen's Plan for relieving the National Distress', *Edin. Rev. 32* (Oct 1819) 453–77 [based partly on Torrens's speech at London Tavern on 26 July 1819 published in *Scotsman*, 21 Aug 1819]; 'Memoir of Robert Owen', *New Moral World 9*, 2 Jan 1841; 'Biographical Sketch of Robert Owen', ibid., *6* 3rd ser., 5 July 1845; R.D. Owen, *Threading my Way: twenty-seven years of autobiography* (1874); L. Jones, *Life, Times and Labours of Robert Owen* ed. W.C. Jones 2 vols, (1889–90); M.K.E. Blake, *Hearts Haven* [a novel on the New Harmony Community] (Indianapolis [1900]); F. Podmore, *Robert Owen: a biography* (1906; repr. 1923 and 1969); A. Macalister, *James Macartney* (1908); H.P. Bonner, *Penalties upon Opinion* (1912; 3rd ed. 1934, repr. 1943); J. Hodge, 'Owenism in Scotland', *Soc. Rev. 15* (1918) 274–80; J. McCabe, *A Biographical Dictionary of Modern Rationalists* (1920); N.E. Himes, 'The Place of John Stuart Mill and of Robert Owen in the History of English Neo-Malthusianism', *QJE 42* (Aug 1928) 627–40; A. Gjöres, *Robert Owen och hans tid* (Kooperativa Forbundet, Stockholm, 1932; rev. and enlarged ed. 1971) [in Swedish]; S. Gotô, *Robert Owen, 1771–1858: a new bibliographical study* (Osaka Univ. of Commerce, 1934); A.E. Bestor Jr, *Backwoods Utopias: the sectarian origins and the Owenite phase of Communitarian Socialism in America, 1663–1829* (Philadelphia, 1950; 2nd ed. rev. and enlarged, Philadelphia, 1970); W.H. Chaloner, 'Robert Owen, Peter Drinkwater and the Early Factory System in Manchester, 1788–1800', *Bull. of the John Rylands Library 37* (Manchester, 1954–5) 78–102; J. Salt, 'The Sheffield Hall of Science', *Vocational Aspect 12*, no. 25 (autumn 1960) 133–8; B. Thomas, 'Robert Owen of Newtown (1771–1858)', *Trans. of the Honourable Society of Cymmrodorion* (1960) 18–35; A.L. Morton, *The Life and Ideas of Robert Owen* (1962); W.H. Oliver, 'The Consolidated Trades' Union of 1834', *Econ. Hist. Rev.* 2nd ser. *17*, no. 1 (1964) 77–95; P. Fryer, *The Birth Controllers* (1965); J. Gans, 'Un essai de coopération intégrale au début du XIXe siècle', *Revue des études coopératives* 44th year, no. 143 (1966) 45–57; W.H. Oliver, 'Tolpuddle Martyrs and Trade Union Oaths', *Labour History* [Australia] no. 10 (May 1966) 5–12; W.E. Wilson, 'Robert Owen: gentle revolutionist', *Colorado Q. 15*, no. 1 (summer 1966) 29–39; E. Pride, 'Work Study and Robert Owen', *Trans. of the Honourable Society of Cymmrodorion* pt 1 (1967) 92–9; W.A.C. Stewart and W.P. McCann, *The Educational Innovators, 1750–1880* (1967); A.C. Grant, 'New Light on an Old View', *J. of the History of Ideas 29* (Apr–June 1968) 293–301; J. Salt, 'Local Manifestations of the Urquhartite Movement', *Int. Rev. Social Hist. 13*, pt 3 (1968) 350–65; S. Gotô, 'The Family Tree of Robert Owen', *Rev. of Economics and Political Science 37*, nos. 5–6 (Meiji Univ. Press, Oct 1969) 515–46 [repr. in pamphlet form, 32 pp.]; M.F. Neufeld, 'Realms of Thought and Organised Labor in the Age of Jackson', *Labor History 10*, no. 1 (winter 1969) 5–43; A.J. Robertson, 'Robert Owen and the Campbell Debt, 1810–22', *Business History 11*, no. 1 (Jan 1969) 23–6; Robert Owen Bi-Centenary Association, *Bulletin* nos. 1 and 2 (1970) and 3 (1972); E.V. Jones, *Robert Owen* (Newtown, 1970) 8 pp.; *Robert Owen: prince of cotton spinners* ed. J. Butt (Newton Abbot, 1971); M. Cole, J. Butt, W.P. Watkins and J.F.C. Harrison, *Robert Owen: industrialist, reformer, visionary, 1771–1858* [four essays] (Robert Owen Bi-Centenary Association, 1971) 32 pp.; Co-operative College, *Robert Owen and his Relevance to our Times: addresses contributed during the Robert Owen Bi-*

centenary Summer School, July 17th to 23rd-1971 (Co-op. College Papers, no. 14: Sep 1971) [essays by W.H.G. Armytage, J. Butt, S. Pollard, B.J. Rose, H. Scanlon, and H. Silver]; J. Butt, I. Donnachie and J.R. Hume, *Robert Owen of New Lanark (1771–1858)* (Open Univ. in Scotland, 1971) [repr. from *Industrial Archaelogy 8,* no. 2 (May 1971) 186–93]; *Robert Owen: prophet of the poor* ed. S. Pollard and J. Salt (1971); J. Salt, 'Isaac Ironside, 1808–1870: the motivation of a radical educationist', *British J. of Educational Studies 19*, no. 2 (1971) 183–201; S. Shipley, *Club Life and Socialism in Mid-Victorian London* (Ruskin College History Workshop Pamphlets, no. 5: Oxford, 1971); M. Lane, *Frances Wright and the "Great Experiment*" (Manchester Univ. Press, 1972) 50 pp.; Burgh of Motherwell and Wishaw Public Libraries, *The Orbiston Community, 1825-1828* (Motherwell, 1972) 14 pp.; *Robert Owen's American Legacy: Proceedings of the Robert Owen Bicentennial Conference . . . 1971* (Indiana Historical Society, Indianapolis, 1972); J. Butt, 'Robert Owen of New Lanark: his critique of British society', in *The Victorians and Social Protest: a symposium*, ed. J. Butt and I.F. Clarke (Newton Abbot, 1973) 13–32 and 218–20; R.L. Muncy, *Sex and Marriage in Utopian Communities: 19th Century America* (Indiana Univ. Press, Bloomington, 1973); C.Ó. Gráda, 'The Owenite Community at Ralahine, County Clare, 1831–33: a reassessment', *Irish Economic and Social History 1* (1974) 38–48; R. Faherty, 'The Memoir of Thomas Martin Wheeler, Owenite and Chartist', *Bull. Soc. Lab. Hist.* no. 30 (spring 1975) 11–13; R.G. Kirby and A.E. Musson, *The Voice of the People: John Doherty, 1798–1854, trade unionist, radical and factory reformer* (Manchester, 1975); R.O. Roberts, 'The Garn-lwyd Owenite Community', *Carmarthenshire Historian 12* (1975) 85–6; H. Dippel, 'Robert Owen' in *Enzyklopädie: Die Grossen der Weltgeschichte 7* (Zurich, 1976) 304–17; A. McLaren, *Birth Control in Nineteenth-Century England* (1978); G. Malmgreen, *Neither Bread nor Roses: Utopian Feminists and the English Working Class, 1800–1850* (Brighton, 1978) 44 pp.; J. Saville, 'Robert Owen on the Family and the Marriage System of the Old ImmoralWorld', in *Rebels and their Causes: essays in honour of A.L. Morton* ed. M. Cornforth (1978) 107-21; B. Taylor, 'The Woman-Power: religious heresy and feminism in early English Socialism' in *Tearing the Veil: essays on femininity* ed. S. Lipshitz (1978) 119–44; A.J. Cooke, 'Robert Owen and the Stanley Mills, 1802–1811', *Business History 21*, no. 1 (Jan 1979) 107–11; E. Royle, 'Robert Owen 1771–1858', in *Biographical Dictionary of Modern British Radicals 1: 1770–1830* ed. J.O. Baylen and N.J. Gossman (Hassocks and NJ, 1979) 353–8. Obit. *Times*, 19 Nov 1858.

J.F.C. Harrison

Note. A *See also* reference is not included for Robert Owen since he influenced so many individuals, in his own lifetime, and after his death. Readers should refer to the categories Owen and/or Owenism and associated titles in the subject indexes of successive volumes of the *DLB*.

PILLING, Richard (1799–1874)
CHARTIST

Richard Pilling was born on 15 December 1799, the son of a handloom weaver. The available sources of information differ slightly over the exact place of his birth. The 1861 Census has Sharple, near Bolton, while the 1871 Census simply states Bolton; his obituary (*Ashton Reporter*, 5 Dec 1874) gives both Bolton and Shepley. At all events he seems to have lived in the Bolton area until about 1832. Pilling began work in his father's trade at the age of about ten, and later claimed that in his first week earned 16*s*. It was certainly a time of extraordinary prosperity for the weavers that was, of course, soon to end. Pilling was probably married in the early 1820s, his eldest son, William, being born about 1824. His wife, Elizabeth, was a native of

Little Bolton.

On 16 August 1819 Pilling set out to attend the meeting at St Peter's Fields, Manchester, but apparently he was informed *en route* that a disturbance had occurred, and so he avoided actual involvement in the Peterloo massacre. Nothing seems to be known about his political activities during the 1820s. He did, however, take part in the agitation for the 1832 Reform Bill. In 1832 or 1833 Pilling removed to Stockport and began work in a weaving factory. It was not that he had any real desire to become a power-loom weaver – he spoke of 'the factory, which I detested to the bottom of my heart' [[O'Connor] (1843) 249] but the 6*s* 6*d* which he managed to earn in his last week at the handloom was far from sufficient to support a wife and – by this time – three children. Once in the mill which he detested, Pilling soon joined the Weavers' Association, and became involved in the Ten Hours Movement.

From 1834 to 1835 Pilling was a member of Stockport's Ten Hours Committee. In December 1836 spinners in Preston were dismissed for belonging to a trade union. Pilling took part in a meeting, called by a united committee of the different trades in Stockport, which expressed its support for the Preston spinners, and arranged to collect subscriptions for them. During 1838 he campaigned on behalf of the five Glasgow cotton spinners who had been sentenced to seven years' transportation as a result of strike activities. When, in May 1838, working-class ratepayers in Stockport protested against the Corporation's refusal to accept the decision of two public meetings concerning the local gas works, Pilling was again associated with the political activists, many of whom subsequently became Chartists.

By December 1838 Pilling had become a member of the Chartist Working Men's Association, and thereafter his political activities centred in that organisation. During the spring of 1839 he took part in meetings at the Stanley Arms and on Newbridge Lane. Although he chose his words carefully, he undoubtedly adhered to a militant position. Parliament rejected the National Petition for the Charter on 12 July, and on 20 July at a meeting in Greek Street, Pilling recommended a run on the banks, and all the other 'ulterior measures' of the Chartist Convention. The Stockport Chartists began to acquire arms, but on the night of 30–31 July came the arrests of James Mitchell, Charles Davies, James Burton, George Wareham, John Wright and Isaac Armitage, the last named with his sons Isaac and Erasmus. On the following morning David Roberts, secretary of the Manchester Political Union, Timothy Higgins of Ashton, and a man known as Dakin or Deegan (who was subsequently discovered to be John Nichols of Newtown, Montgomeryshire), were also taken into custody. The examination of the prisoners began at Stockport Court House on Thursday, 1 August, and on the next morning the magistrates directed that James Leah and Richard Pilling should also be taken into custody. Pilling, who was in court at the time, was immediately arrested and placed in the dock, charged with sedition, conspiracy and attending unlawful meetings. He was at the time described as being the former secretary of the Chartists' Association. Like most of his fellow-prisoners, Pilling was required to find bail of £400, and two sureties of £200 each. Not surprisingly, such sums were not forthcoming, and the prisoners were committed to Chester Assizes for trial. The Chartist trials at Chester, which began on 12 August 1839, resulted in prison sentences for Mitchell and Davies, together with Higgins, George Thompson (a Birmingham gun maker), John Bradley of Hyde, the Rev. J.R. Stephens, and Peter Murray M'Douall. Pilling and the other Stockport Chartists traversed – that is, they denied all the material allegations, and they were released on bail, their trial being postponed until the next assizes.

Undeterred by the conditions of his bail, Pilling resumed his political activities in Stockport. He took part in the municipal election campaign against the Whigs (who had been responsible for the arrests), arguing that if the Chartists 'could not find good honest Radicals, they should fold their arms and let the Tories beat them.' When Chartists collecting for the prisoners were intimidated by the police, Pilling went with John Fisher Linney to present an address to the borough Bench. By way of reply to their complaint the Police Superintendent informed them that the collection was illegal. Pilling also assisted in the Chartist take-over of an Anti-Corn

Law meeting held in Stockport on 6 January 1840; and the following month he addressed a meeting convened to memorialise the Queen in favour of a free pardon for Frost, Williams and Jones, the transported Newport Chartists.

Pilling appeared again at Chester Assizes in April 1840, being joined in the dock by his fellow Stockport Chartists, and by the veteran reformer William Benbow, who subsequently received eighteen months' imprisonment for a seditious speech delivered at Stockport on 9 June 1839. More fortunate, Pilling was discharged, and returned home to join in the campaign demanding the immediate dismissal of the Queen's ministers and their replacement by men favourable to universal suffrage.

In April 1840 some 4000 Stockport power-loom weavers were threatened with a massive reduction in wages of 2*d* in every shilling. They organised a large open-air meeting on 29 April, at which Pilling was one of the principal speakers. He urged the weavers to resist the reduction: otherwise they would be brought down to the condition of the handloom weavers, then earning only 5*s* a week after twelve-hour days. Pilling became one of the leaders of the ensuing strike. He later recalled that the strike, which involved 6000 power-loom weavers, lasted eight weeks. As a result of these activities, all the Stockport manufacturers refused to employ Pilling or his children.

In search of work, the family moved to Ashton-under-Lyne, where at the time of the 1841 Census they were living in Fleet Street. Pilling was now employed as a cotton check weaver, while his wife Elizabeth apparently had no occupation outside the home. His other sons, William (17) and James (15), were cotton print weavers, while the eldest daughter Mary (11) was a silk throwster. Richard Pilling had four younger children to support: Rachael (9), Elizabeth (6), Thomas (4), and Richard (1). On his arrival in Ashton Pilling had again become identified with the short time movement. Local employers attempted to secure the continuance of the eleven hour working day, which was then customary, and endeavoured to persuade the women in their employment to sign documents in support ot this; Pilling and Joseph Leach addressed a meeting of women in Stockport on this matter. During 1841 Pilling himself suffered wage reductions; and at Easter 1842, his son James, who was suffering from tuberculosis, was obliged to leave his work. The family now had an income of about 16*s* per week, of which about 3*s* were needed for rent. They were reduced to a diet of potatoes and salt. When Pilling went to a 'gentleman's' house in Ashton, to ask for a bottle of wine for his ailing son, he was refused on the ground that he was a Chartist. James Pilling died that summer, and the people of Ashton collected £4 towards his burial.

In the summer of 1842, notice of a further reduction in wages was given by a Stalybridge firm, Jeremiah and John Lees, and this example was quickly followed by their competitors in that town, and in Ashton. A protest meeting of operatives was held on 26 July in Ashton, at which Pilling used 'strong language' against the employers. At a further meeting on 29 July at Stalybridge, Pilling made a proposal in support of a fair day's wage which, he maintained, could not be obtained until the Charter was made the law of the land; and he was always at this time trying to relate the operatives' economic demands to the wider political issues that the Charter represented. What the operatives were aiming at was the withdrawal of the notices of reductions. During July and August a group of about twenty men were meeting to compile a list of their demands. With Pilling as their chairman, they drew up a placard headed 'Behold the Reckoning Day is nigh', which advertised the 26 July meeting, and they were probably also responsible for a further placard, entitled 'The Voice of the People is the Voice of God.' This demanded the 1840 wage rates, as well as a ten hour day, and called upon shopkeepers and manufacturers to support the operatives. In spite of all these efforts, one firm, William Bayley and Brothers, implemented a 25 per cent wage reduction on 5 August. Upon refusing to accept these terms, their workers were dismissed. This began the strike movement in the cotton district, soon to be known as the 'Plug Plot'.

Although the strike had been triggered off by a wage reduction, the evidence available suggests that Pilling at least wished to extend it as a means of political pressure upon the

Government. On Saturday 6 August he set off to Oldham, both to raise support for a meeting planned at Mottram Moor on the following day, and to advise the Oldham operatives to turn out. After this advice had met with some opposition, he sent some of his 'lads' to the town on the following Monday, 8 August. They proceeded to rake out fires in the mill boilers, and knock out plugs. Pilling had arranged for two men to come from Oldham to Ashton on 10 August, to let him know whether or not they were to strike. And also on Monday, 8 August, a meeting at the Haigh, Stalybridge, divided into groups and proceeded to fetch out the hands from all the mills in the town. They were assisted by reinforcements from Ashton and elsewhere. The strikers then formed a procession, which turned out factories in Dukinfield, Ashton, and Hurst. That afternoon the strikers re-assembled for a meeting in Hyde. Upon Pilling's proposal, the body then divided into two groups, the people of Ashton setting off to Oldham, and those of Stalybridge to Hyde. Pilling led the party which turned out mills in Oldham, mainly in the southern part of the town. Two of the strikers were arrested, and some of the Oldham police injured, before the party returned to Ashton. On the following day the Ashton and Stalybridge strikers held their own meetings before setting off to Manchester; Pilling was in the forefront of the Ashton contingent. He was appointed chairman at the ensuing mass meeting, in Granby Row Fields.

Much of the impetus for extending the strike came from Pilling. The Oldham mills actually resumed work on the Tuesday, but the operatives were then persuaded to join the strike by agitators from Ashton, who addressed a meeting that evening. When his emissaries arrived from Oldham on 10 August, Pilling apparently threatened that if the town did not turn out quietly, his 'lads' would break some of their heads. At the mass meeting held at Ashton Market Ground on the same day, six delegates were appointed to travel around parts of Lancashire and Yorkshire, in the cause of the strike; Pilling and Thomas Storer went to Manchester, Bolton, Blackburn, Clitheroe, Padiham and Burnley. At Bolton, on the evening of 10 August, he again threatened forcible measures by the people of Ashton if the operatives should fail to join the strike. He returned home on Sunday afternoon, 14 August, to find that his son James had died some twenty minutes before his arrival.

On 10 August the strikers had also proceeded to turn out mills in Stockport, but Pilling himself was doubtful about the extent of support for the strike within that town. Moreover the Stockport operatives, having been turned out, generally demonstrated more interest in the limited wages question than in the Charter. Pilling attended a meeting in the town on Monday, 15 August, at which he announced:

> I do not know whether it would be safe for me to own it or not; but I may avow that I have the honour to be the father of this movement, and the sole cause of your being ladies and gentlemen at the present time; for the masters of Ashton had thought proper to offer a reduction of 25 per cent upon their wages. I then caused the bellman to go round and call the meeting, swearing by the God of heaven that, if the reduction took place, we would annihilate the system, and cause the day of reckoning.

In the course of this speech, Pilling who claimed to have been to all parts of South Lancashire: Burnley, Chorley, Bolton, Preston, Colne, Padiham, Clitheroe, Todmorden and Blackburn, was obviously concerned with the problem of morale and solidarity among the Stockport strikers; but in spite of his desire to extend the strike, Pilling did not approve of the attack on Stockport Workhouse.

The Stockport magistrates, meeting on the afternoon of 17 August, considered arresting Pilling, but finally decided that it was not advisable at that time. So he remained free to serve as one of the delegates from the manufacturing districts, who began meeting in Manchester on 20 August, to draw up a list of demands to submit to the manufacturers. Basically these were the January 1840 wage rates, and a ten hour day. Pilling was also delegated to see the first mayor of Manchester, Sir Thomas Potter, a progressive Whig, and ask him to mediate between the strikers and their employers; but Potter was reluctant to become involved. Pilling also attempted, unsuccessfully, to negotiate with two Stockport manufacturers, in order to persuade them to employ men, as well as women, in their mills.

In spite of the activities of Pilling and his fellow-delegates, a gradual drift back to work began throughout the district of the strike. The local authorities began arresting leading Chartists; and on Monday, 12 September, when Pilling was addressing strikers in Charlestown Meeting Room, Ashton, the building was surrounded by two troops of infantry and a troop of dragoons, and he himself was arrested, on a warrant issued several weeks before. When he appeared for examination before the local magistrates, Charles Hindley, MP for the town, made one of his rare appearances on the Bench, and advocated bail, which was granted. Pilling was immediately employed by a master cotton spinner, Mr Platt. Both men were members of the Anti-Corn Law League, and this sign of personal or political sympathy was one of the incidents which were interpreted by some contemporaries as a sign of League complicity in the strike. The Chartists, inevitably however, bore the brunt of the reprisals. After an appearance at a Special Commission in Lancaster, Pilling stood trial, together with Feargus O'Connor and fifty-seven other Chartists, at the Lancaster Spring Assizes in March 1843. The charges included sedition, conspiracy, tumult and riot. Pilling made a moving and powerful speech in his own defence, which concentrated primarily upon the sufferings inflicted upon his own family as a result of successive wage reductions [*Trial of Feargus O'Connor*, 248 ff.]; and he was subsequently acquitted. It is worth noting that in summing up his defence, Pilling insisted that 'Whatever it may have been with others it has been a wage question with me. And I do say that if Mr O'Connor has made it a chartist question, he has done wonders to make it extend through England, Ireland, and Scotland. But it was always a wage question, and ten hours bill with me' [ibid. 254–5].

He soon resumed trade union activities. In August 1843 spinners employed by James Buckley in Ashton turned out as a result of wage reductions. Pilling took the chair at strike meetings, and was one of the delegates who drew up a list of prices, and decided upon a general turn-out, if Buckley should fail to withdraw the cuts. After about a fortnight, however, several of the manufacturers agreed to give the list prices, and a possible repetition of the 'Plug Plot' was avoided. In the following November, Ashton weavers and card room hands turned out for an extra 1¼*d* per cut (this being the amount taken from them at the last reduction). Pilling addressed their meeting at Charlestown on 8 November. The strike continued until early December, when the list prices were finally conceded. Among the weavers who returned to work was Pilling's eldest son, William, who had himself played a part in the 'Plug Plot' meetings in Ashton. On the following day William was dismissed, solely on the ground that he was Richard's son. The *Northern Star* (9 Dec 1843) suggested that its Chartist readers should subscribe a few pounds, either for shares in a co-operative provision store, which William could then manage, or as a loan to set him up in a business; there is, however, no evidence that any such scheme materialised. Richard Pilling also took part in the Ashton power-loom weavers' agitation for a wage increase in November 1844. When, in September 1847, manufacturers in Mossley and Stalybridge proposed 10 per cent wage reductions, most of their spinners came out on strike. Again Pilling addressed a strike meeting in Ashton, and at the beginning of October he went over to Stockport to attend a meeting of operatives, which expressed its support for the strike. Pilling also took an interest in municipal affairs, being involved in the agitation for the incorporation of Ashton, which was accomplished in September 1847.

Although the mid-forties witnessed a general lull in Chartist activity, Richard Pilling maintained his active membership of the movement in Ashton. In April 1844 he was a delegate to the National Convention, which met in the Carpenters' Hall, Manchester. Here he moved that a petition against the Masters and Servants Bill should be sent to Thomas Slingsby Duncombe, MP, for presentation to the Commons; and he also recommended that Chartists should take part in all local affairs, thereby proving their power by placing their friends in elected offices. At the Convention which was hastily called to meet in the Carpenters' Hall,

Manchester on 22 December, Pilling again represented Ashton. When the delegates met for supper at the Mosley Arms Hotel, Feargus O'Connor proposed a toast to the 'plug drawers of 1842', and called 'upon Mr Pilling, the father of the movement, to speak for his children'. Pilling replied 'in his usual style of simple but effective eloquence' [*Northern Star*, 7 Dec 1845]. In August 1846, when the Convention met in Leeds, Pilling, again the Ashton delegate, supported the plan to present another petition to Parliament for the return to England of Frost, Williams and Jones. His Chartist activities also extended to the National Land Company: in September 1847 he addressed a Land Company meeting at Hyde, which was attended by deputations from Dukinfield, Ashton and Stalybridge.

The spring of 1848 witnessed not only an upsurge of Chartist activity, but also a movement towards rapprochement with the Irish Repealers. On 19 March the Chartists and Repealers combined to hold a camp meeting at Oldham Edge. Pilling, described as 'the veteran Chartist', was called to the chair, 'to the no small delight of the meeting', and proceeded to express his support for the recent revolution in France. In April, after Parliament's rejection of the third petition, a further Chartist camp meeting was held at Hurst Green, near Ashton. Pilling, again in the chair, denounced the 'Gagging Bill' (the Crown and Government Security Bill), then being considered by Parliament and which was passed on 13 April. On 1 May the Chartist National Assembly met to reorganise the movement. 'Father Pilling' was nominated for the executive, and was elected as one of the twenty Commissioners, whose task it was to carry into practical operation the instructions of the executive. Pilling's Chartist activities continued into the summer of 1848. On 10 July he was on the platform of Charlestown Meeting House when M'Douall arrived to address the meeting. As a result of his activities in Ashton that day, M'Douall was subsequently tried at the South Lancashire Assizes. During the summer, the Ashton Chartists began to acquire arms. Summing up the situation, the *Manchester Guardian* claimed (23 August) that there had existed in the town for some months a body of English Chartists, known as the National Guard; another body of Irish, both Confederates and Repealers; and a third body, of colliers. All were said to be quite distinct, but under the control of one secret committee. On the night of 14 August an Ashton policeman, James Bright, was shot in Bentinck Street. The police immediately arrested some eighteen people, most of whom merely happened to be out in the streets, and then proceeded to round up the local Chartist leaders. Pilling himself had left Ashton on the afternoon before Bright was shot, with the intention of going to America. John Sykes, 'a semi-police officer and rate collector', subsequently testified that he had accompanied him as far as Manchester, and it does appear that Pilling was not involved in the actual shooting. It seems obvious, however, that he had expected arrest as a consequence of his Chartist activities. The extent and details of his possible, perhaps certain, involvement in the underground activities of the Ashton Chartists remain unknown.

On 11 October 1848 Pilling landed in New York, where he remained for six days, but failed to find work. Then, hearing that weavers were required at Stuyvesant Falls, in Columbia County, he sailed up the Hudson and got a job weaving on four looms. In a letter to his wife and children (dated 12 November and published in the *Northern Star* on 16 December 1848) he noted a greater degree of egalitarianism in American society, but he was not by any means optimistic about its future. Trade was bad, and there were thousands of unemployed immigrants, many of whom wished to return home. Without the protection of an act to limit the working day, work for twelve hours in winter and thirteen in summer was common, while manufacturers kept truck shops, in which they made 50 per cent profits. In his letter, Pilling asked his wife and children what they intended to do about coming to America, as he wished to make preparations. Whether some, or any, of the family did in fact join him is uncertain, and no further information concerning Pilling's life in America has been discovered.

Pilling returned to Ashton in 1850; the *Ashton Reporter* of 5 December 1874 dated his homecoming as '24 years since, last Ashton Wakes.' It also commented that 'since that time he has never been employed in any of the factories in the district, and has had to eke out a living the best way he could.' At the time of the 1861 Census Pilling, again resident in Fleet Street (no. 199), was working as a grocer, and four of his unmarried children were living at home and employed in the textile industry. Thomas, now aged twenty-three was a silk throwster, while Rachel [*sic*] (28), Richard (20) and James (16) were all cotton weavers. It should be added that James was the youngest of the family and apparently named after the son who had died at the time of the 'Plug Plot'. By 1871 Pilling had removed to 211 Fleet Street, and was now described as a tea dealer. Only James, still unmarried and employed as a cotton warper, remained at home with his ageing parents.

Politically, Richard Pilling appears to have remained a Chartist until the final demise of the movement. When Ernest Jones addressed a Chartist revival meeting at the Temperance Hall, Ashton, in October 1858, Pilling presided. He denounced recent attempts to undermine Chartism, and declared confidence in its executive; but like many other local Chartists, he was now demonstrating or beginning to demonstrate, Liberal sympathies. The *Ashton Reporter* (5 Dec 1874) stated that 'ever since his return from America he has exerted himself strenuously at election times in the Liberal interest. Throughout his life he was a sincere and consistent Radical in politics.' Pilling attended town council meetings in Ashton, and at the 1860 municipal elections nominated a retiring Liberal councillor, Joseph Smethurst, who shared Pilling's desire to extend the franchise. In 1866 to 1867 Pilling was again active in the campaign for parliamentary reform, attending meetings of both the Ashton branch of the National Reform Union and the Ashton auxiliary of the Reform League. At a meeting organised by the latter body, in January 1867, Ernest Jones delivered the principal speech, in support of manhood suffrage, and Pilling seconded his resolution. Pilling's political activities continued almost to his death. The *Ashton Reporter* (5 Dec 1874) remarked:

> At the last municipal election in Ashton he delivered a characteristic speech, full of hard hits and humorous sallies. It is feared by some of his friends that the excitement of the election was too much for his enfeebled frame, and that it has had the effect of hastening his departure from our midst.

Pilling's youngest son, James, died on 25 January 1873, aged only twenty-nine. Richard and William were both living in America when their father died on 29 November 1874, leaving no will. The *Ashton Reporter* (5 Dec 1874) commented in its obituary notice, that 'If ever there was a time in his life that Mr Pilling looked back to with pleasure, it was 1842 and the part he played in the events of that year.'

Sources: (1) MS: Report accompanying letter from Henry Coppock to Lord John Russell, PRO: HO 40/41 Stockport, 16 May 1839; 1841 Census: HO 107 532 F1–37 for Ashton-under-Lyne; Mr Sadler's minutes [n.d. Aug 1842?] and minutes of meeting of Stockport magistrates, 17 Aug 1842, in Stockport Chartist papers, Stockport PL; Letter from Col. Martin to Gen. Arbuthnot, 24 Sep 1842, PRO: HO 45; 1861 Census and 1871 Census: RG 9/2980 and RG 10/4069 for Ashton-under-Lyne at PRO. (2) Other: *Stockport Advertiser*, 1835–48, 8 Oct 1858; *North Cheshire Reformer*, 1838–9; *Northern Star*, 1838–48; [Anon.], *A Report of a Trial of Chartists (The Majority Inhabitants of Stockport) for Conspiracy and Sedition, including that of the Rev. J. R. Stephens, of Ashton* (Stockport, [1839?]); *Stockport Chronicle*, 1840–2; *Manchester Guardian*, 13–27 Aug 1842, 16–30 Aug 1848; [F. O'Connor], *The Trial of Feargus O'Connor Esq.*, (*Barrister-at-Law*) *and Fifty-eight Others at Lancaster on a Charge of Sedition, Conspiracy, Tumult, and Riot* (1843; repr. NY, 1970); *Ashton Reporter*, 31 Mar and 27 Oct 1860, 27 Jan and 24 Mar 1866, 26 Jan and 25 May 1867, 1 Feb 1873; *Reports of State Trials 1839–43* n.s. vol. *4* ed. J. E. P. Wallis (1892) 1097, 1108; R. G. Gammage, *History of the Chartist Movement 1837–1854* (1894; repr. with an Introduction by J. Saville, NY, 1969); T. E. Ashworth, *An Account of the Todmorden Poor Law Riots of November 1838, and the Plug Plot of August 1842* (Todmorden, 1901) 25 pp.; M. Hovell, *The Chartist Movement* (Manchester,

1918); M. Beer, *A History of British Socialism* (1919); C. Smith, 'Stockport in the Age of Reform 1822–1870' [unpublished typescript in Stockport Public Library, 1938]; *From Cobbett to the Chartists*, ed. M. Morris (1948); P. M. Giles, 'The Economic and Social Development of Stockport 1815–1836' (Manchester MA, 1950); A. G. Rose, 'The Plug Riots of 1842 in Lancashire and Cheshire', in *Trans of the Lancashire and Cheshire Antiquarian Society 67* (1957) 75–112; W. M. Bowman, *England in Ashton-under-Lyne* (Altrincham, 1960); J. T. Ward, *The Factory Movement 1830–1855* (1962); E. P. Thompson, *The Making of the English Working Class* (1963; rev. ed. 1968); *The Luddites and Other Essays*, ed. L. M. Munby (1971); J. T. Ward, *Chartism* (1973); N. Kirk, 'Class and Fragmentation: some aspects of working-class life in South-East Lancashire and North-East Cheshire, 1850–1870' (Pittsburgh PhD, 1974) [Note: The quotations on p. 13 of this thesis are wrongly attributed to Pilling. They will be found in Feargus O'Connor's Introduction to *The Trial of Feargus O'Connor and Fifty-Eight Others at Lancaster on a Charge of Sedition, Conspiracy, Tumult and Riot* (1843; repr. NY, 1970)]; C. A. N. Reid,' The Chartist Movement in Stockport' (Hull MA, 1976); T. D. W. Reid and N. Reid, 'The 1842 "Plug Plot" in Stockport', *Int. Rev. Social Hist. 24*, pt 1 (1979) 55–79; biographical information: Bolton Local Studies Library; Tameside Local History Library; N. Kirk, Manchester Polytechnic.

NAOMI REID

See also: William BENBOW.

POTTER, George (1832–93)
TRADE UNIONIST AND JOURNALIST

George Potter, born in Kenilworth in 1832, was the son of Edmund William Potter, a carpenter employed at Stoneleigh Abbey, and his wife Anne. He learnt the rudiments of reading and writing at a dame school, and then passed on to a small endowed school in the neighbourhood, known as Aldridge's Charity. Since his father had a family of seven children to bring up on his wages of 3*s* a day, young Potter left school 'before his studies had progressed very far', becoming a ploughboy, and then 'errand-boy to a neighbouring gentleman'. At the age of sixteen he turned to his father's trade, and was apprenticed to a master joiner and cabinet-maker in Coventry. His apprenticeship lasted four years, after which he worked for brief spells as a journeyman carpenter in Rugby and in Coventry before leaving for London in 1853 – in the hope, as he put it himself, that he might 'improve his condition'. During the next six years, he was employed as a carpenter by several well-known London firms. In 1857, he married the daughter of a Warwick shoemaker, and settled in Pimlico, a district in which he was to live for nearly thirty years.

In later years, Potter claimed that he had been 'a workman that needed not to be ashamed.' After he became a public figure, he was more than once accused of having left his trade because he was unskilled and inefficient; and in 1867 *Blackwood's Edinburgh Magazine*, in what purported to be a circumstantial account of his early career, described him as 'utterly worthless . . . whatever branch of his trade they sent him' [Gleig (1867) 125–6]. When Potter started legal proceedings, *Blackwood's*, together with eight other journals that had copied the story, published an unqualified apology [ibid., 260], the *Standard* adding that he had always 'received the highest rate of wages as a skilled and experienced workman' [10 Jan 1867].

Soon after his arrival in London, Potter joined a small local union, the Progressive Society of Carpenters and Joiners, which had its headquarters at the Rose and Crown in Tottenham Court Road. He soon became established as a leading member. The Society had a tradition of fairly rapid rotation of offices, and between 1854 and 1858 Potter held office as corresponding secretary, then financial secretary, and finally chairman. It was during the period of his chairmanship, and apparently at his suggestion, that the Progressive called a meeting that led to the revival of the nine-hours movement – first among carpenters, and then as a joint effort by the London building trades. This sparked off a dispute that was to become a turning-point in labour history – the London builders' strike and lock-out of 1859–60. Potter became secretary to the Building Trades Conference; and as organiser and chief spokesman, he played his part admirably. By February 1860, when the employers' Document was withdrawn (though without the granting of the nine hours) the workmen had won at least a partial victory; and Potter had achieved a national reputation. He was helped by his appearance and his restrained style of oratory, which contrasted sharply with the popular image of a labour agitator. (*Reynolds's* reporter described him as 'a pale, thin, intellectual-looking young man'; and supporting speakers regularly worked up to a climax with 'I ask the meeting – does Mr Potter look like a demagogue?'). For some years to come, he has widely regarded by the general public as the acknowledged leader of the whole trade union movement. As late as 1864, even Gladstone described him as 'the far-famed secretary of the trades' unions' [*Hansard*, 7 Mar 1864].

There can be no doubt that this gave Potter an exaggerated confidence in his own powers of leadership – even though he played a far less effective part in the ensuing and much more confused dispute over the introduction of payment by the hour. His experiences during this time, especially his contacts with the press, also led him to make the most important decision of his career. By the summer of 1861 he had decided to launch a national trade-union newspaper; and by October he had established the Trades Newspaper Co., Ltd, with himself as manager, and seven of his friends from the building trades as the first board of directors. On 19 October 1861 appeared the first issue of the *Bee-Hive*, published at 2*d* weekly. The paper was to run under this title until the end of 1876, and then for two more years as the *Industrial Review*; and during these years, the history of the *Bee-Hive*, and Potter's career in the labour movement, were inextricably interwoven. The paper made a promising start, under the editorship of George Troup, a professional journalist, with the assistance as sub-editor of the old Chartist, Robert Hartwell. The newly-formed London Trades Council, after deciding that it was 'inadvisable to assist any private speculation of this kind', changed their minds, and adopted the *Bee-Hive* as their organ. But the paper soon ran into debt; by 1863 Troup's pro-Southern view of the American Civil War (a view which Potter at that time supported) had resulted in his dismissal by a more representative board of directors, and his replacement by Hartwell; and in 1864 came the first clear signs of conflict with Robert Applegarth, when the *Bee-Hive* supported strikes which Applegarth believed should have been abandoned or settled. This, of course, merged into Potter's quarrel with the Junta, which spanned the middle years of the 1860s, and became the real turning-point in Potter's career.

It was in 1864 that the five men who have come to be known as the Junta began to work together, mainly through the London Trades Council. The traditional view of these men as a closely-knit group does need to be partly modified. Daniel Guile, for example, more or less consistently supported Potter until the interests of his union brought him into the Conference of Amalgamated Trades in 1867; and it was not until the formation of that organisation that they really worked as a team. Even then, there were still minor disagreements between them. Nevertheless, from 1864 they were increasingly brought together by a belief in common policies, based on the need to achieve full recognition of the unions – by employers, by the public and by the law. This did not really mean industrial pacifism; but it did imply a more cautious trade policy, and a disciplined union membership. Since Potter believed that any group of men who decided to strike knew the rights and wrongs of their own case, without reference to distant officials or national executives, he naturally seemed to these leaders of amalgamated Societies to be threatening to undo their work. Led by Applegarth, they came to attack him as 'a manufacturer of strikes', and (more plausibly) as a man in an essentially irresponsible position, holding no office in the trade union movement, but still, through the *Bee-Hive* and meetings notified in its columns, claiming a position of leadership.

Some aspects of the coming struggle were foreshadowed in March 1864, when Potter called a meeting to protest against the proposed Annuities Bill, and the leaders of the LTC regarded this as usurping their authority. Odger, Applegarth and Coulson went on a deputation from the LTC 'to disabuse the mind of the Chancellor of the Exchequer as to there being any organised opposition to the principles of the bill by the trade societies.' Then came the Birmingham building trades disputes of May and December to January, with Potter and Applegarth ranged on opposite sides. Once Applegarth's antagonism had been thoroughly aroused, the stage was set for the full-scale trial of strength that followed. This came over the North Staffordshire puddlers' strike in the early months of 1865. A series of rival meetings (called on the one hand by the LTC, on the other by Potter through the *Bee-Hive*) included some wild scenes, and much angry denunciation. At one of these meetings, Odger launched a number of charges against Potter, which were eventually arranged under nine heads, and formally investigated by a committee composed of Edmond Beales (chairman), Godfrey Lushington, Frederic Harrison and Thomas Hughes. The charges ranged from personal dishonesty, through maladministration in the *Bee-Hive* office, to support for the South in the American Civil War, and Potter's 'mischievous and untruthful conduct' over the North Staffordshire strike. Many of these charges had at least an element of truth in them. But Odger's evidence was poorly presented, and Beales was already practising the role of peacemaker which he was to adopt as president of the Reform League. When the verdict was finally published, most of the charges were left as 'not proven' and Potter escaped with some fairly mild censure of his activities during the puddlers' strike [*Bee-Hive*, 24 June 1865]. However, the annual meeting of the LTC in August decided (as Hartwell put it) to 'excommunicate' the *Bee-Hive*, which till then had still ranked as its official organ; and Potter lost the seat on the Council which he had held since 1863.

Potter retaliated by establishing the new London Working Men's Association, in February 1866. Potter became president, Hartwell secretary, and the *Bee-Hive* was adopted as the Association's organ – although this relationship might just as well have been seen in reverse, since the LWMA's function was really to give the *Bee-Hive*'s policies the backing of a permanent organisation. Since the quarrel had already moved into the political field, these policies covered broader issues than those involved in antagonism to the Trades Council. Potter had previously shown little interest in purely political questions; but in February 1865 he had called the meeting that brought the various London Reform associations into one body – the Reform League. However, the League soon became dominated by his opponents, and Potter served only as an ordinary member of the Executive Council; he lost his seat in 1866. So the LWMA became a rival body to both LTC and Reform League – even though their policies were frequently identical.

This situation continued until 1868, when Potter began to come to terms with the Junta. During this time, with Hartwell's loyal support, he used the *Bee-Hive* and his standing in the trade union movement to build up opposition to them – appealing especially to the smaller London unions, and those provincial unions that also resented the Junta's exclusiveness. In March 1866 he was presented with an illuminated address and a purse of 300 sovereigns, subscribed by 'trade unionists and Reformers' from all parts of the country. Just a year later, he made his last real bid for trade union leadership, when he presided over the St Martin's Hall conference called by the LWMA to consider the Hornby *v* Close decision and the defence of trade unions before the recently-appointed Royal Commission. Although the meeting was boycotted by the LTC and the amalgamated societies, most of the provincial leaders were present; and they criticised the Junta rather than the LWMA for this division of forces.

The establishment of the Commission had been announced in the Queen's Speech of 5 February 1867. Spencer Walpole, the Home Secretary, had originally intended to appoint nine commissioners on the criterion of judicial impartiality, but it was the Potter–led delegation of 8 February which argued for the inclusion of either workingmen or 'gentlemen . . . well known to the working classes as possessing a practical knowledge of the working of Trades Unions, and in whom they might feel confidence' [*Times*, 9 Feb 1967]; and Frederic Harrison was appointed. Further, the LWMA, or rather the St Martin's Hall Conference Committee, did as much as the Conference of Amalgamated Trades to secure the attendance of trade union representatives before the Commission, although the St Martin's Hall Committee's own nominee, Thomas Connolly, was excluded for remarks he had made in public about the Commission. But it was the Conference of Amalgamated Trades, and Applegarth in particular, which came out of the hearings of the Commission with enhanced reputations. Potter himself was unimpressive, generalising rather feebly, failing to establish any importance for the LWMA, and finding himself questioned mainly on the affairs of the small and uninfluential Progressive Society of Carpenters. Meanwhile, Applegarth's triumph before the Commission, the supporting evidence from other amalgamated society secretaries, and the far more business-like activities of their Conference of Amalgamated Trades, swung opinion in their favour. At the Manchester TUC of June 1868, their policies were endorsed with a vote of confidence moved by John Kane of the Ironworkers. Since the *Bee-Hive* was again running into serious financial difficulties (after an upswing in 1865 to 1866) Potter found his position becoming increasingly untenable.

Already, in 1867, there had been signs that he was trying to tone down his reputation as an extremist. He had become associated with the radical manufacturer Samuel Morley, and in February 1867 he helped Morley to organise a meeting of trade unionists to consider 'The Working Classes and Religious Institutions'. During the later stages of the reform agitation, the LWMA took the initiative in bringing trade unions as organisations into the movement, and Potter was active as a speaker on LWMA, Reform League and even National Reform Union platforms; but he showed himself somewhat readier than Hartwell to compromise on the reform issue, telling meetings that he would be satisfied with household suffrage and a lodger franchise, even without the ballot. Similarly, when the LWMA, after the Act was passed, moved on to its agitation for the 'direct representation of Labour', it was Hartwell who stressed the need for 'independent' representation, while Potter was more anxious to assure middle-class sympathisers that working men MPs would 'represent all classes of the electors – not those of one particular interest.'

These developments helped to prepare the way for the opening of a new phase in the *Bee-Hive*'s history. In June 1868, Daniel Pratt, a radical and nonconformist publisher, and a friend of Samuel Morley's, saved the paper from bankruptcy by buying up sufficient of the unsold shares to make him controlling shareholder – on condition that every attempt should be made to heal the rift with the Junta. The one tangible result in 1868 (besides the toning down of *Bee-Hive* comments) was a jointly-convened meeting to discuss the Junta's proposed Trade Union Bill. In fact, the new policy was difficult to implement while Hartwell remained editor. But at the general election of November 1868, Hartwell, true to his principles, attempted to stand for Stoke on Trent as 'independent working men's candidate'. Potter ostentatiously withheld his support, preferring to assist Pratt in his candidature 'in the Liberal interest' at Lymington. The resulting quarrel ended the working partnership between Potter and Hartwell, and Hartwell resigned from the editorship at the end of December. Thereafter, the LWMA meetings were allowed to lapse; Potter himself edited the *Bee-Hive*, still more cautiously, during 1869; and he, and some of his supporters, were co-opted as members of the Conference of Amalgamated Trades. Throughout that year he also contributed a regular column to the Edinburgh radical weekly paper, the *Reformer*, which stressed two of his constant preoccupations (national organisation and shorter hours) when he warmly supported the Edinburgh Trades Council campaign for a national conference on the shorter hours movement [*Reformer*, 27 May 1869; Minutes of Edinburgh Trades Council, 19 Jan 1869 ff., see MacDougall (1968)].

In August 1869 Potter helped to establish the 'united front' Labour Representation League, which forthwith adopted the *Bee-Hive* as its organ. Potter's old opponents, still to some extent distrusting him, then manoeuvred the Rev. Henry Solly into the editorial chair, with Potter as his assistant – although appearances were preserved by the announcement of a joint editorship. This was the first time that Potter had been forced to accept a clearly subordinate position in the day-to-day running of the paper. But Solly's 'informing and elevating' journalism satisfied few of the London trade union leaders; and when he gave up the editorship at the end of 1870, Potter again became sole editor.

From then on, chastened by his experiences, and recognising the failure of his earlier policies, Potter constantly used his influence on behalf of 'amalgamated principles' and against sectional movements. He was given a free hand by Daniel Pratt, who by this time had become personal proprietor of the *Bee-Hive*; and on Pratt's death in 1873 Potter became editor-proprietor – a position which he held until the last issue of the *Industrial Review* in 1878. Now that he was working in some degree of harmony with the leading trade union officials, he was also able to come back into a position of some prominence within the labour movement. He was elected president of the TUC when it met in London in March 1871 (the first Congress that had the Junta's whole-hearted support), and for the following year was chairman of its Parliamentary Committee. Throughout the labour laws campaign, from 1871 to 1875, the *Bee-Hive* was the recognised organ of the Parliamentary Committee; and Potter did much useful work in publicising their views. In the same way, he loyally supported the policies of the Labour Representation League, with their increasing stress on independent working-class political activity, which culminated in their thirteen candidatures at the 1874 general election, and then their retreat into Lib-Lab attitudes. Potter was one of their candidates in 1874, standing at Peterborough; but he ended in fourth place out of six candidates, being beaten by two Liberals and a Conservative.

His other main concerns during the 1870s were his secretaryship of the National Emigration League from 1870; membership – along with Howell, Guile and Applegarth – of the Working Men's Committee for promoting the separation of Church and State (a Samuel Morley organisation); vigorous support for the agricultural labourers, both NALU and the local unions in the eastern counties, in 1872 to 1873; and his work on the London School Board. He stood for Westminster at the first School Board election in 1870, but was unsuccessful. What was widely noted, however, was that now for the first time he publicly stressed the fact that he was a Congregationalist. (Samuel Morley and Daniel Pratt were also Congregationalists; and in fact Pratt came forward at one of Potter's meetings to refute suggestions of a 'sudden conversion'). He stood again in 1873, and this time was elected, holding his seat until 1882. During these years he continued to press for nonconformist educational policies, and he moved the enquiry into the use of educational endowments which was then carried out by the Board. This work, and the responsibility of running what had at last become his own paper, made him less active as a public speaker and committee man. (In 1874 and 1875, he refused nomination for the Parliamentary Committee, on the grounds of 'pressure of work'.) He continued to support all unions under attack, became, in his own words, 'a good Gladstonian Liberal', and managed against all odds to keep the *Bee-Hive* (and then the *Industrial Review*) in circulation until the end of 1878. When the economic depression eventually forced the paper to close down, Potter became bankrupt – with debts of £2000 and assets of £670.

Having compounded with his creditors, Potter was soon back in business as a publisher, operating from the same office in Fetter Lane. He published a number of cheap novelettes, political pamphlets, brief lives of Gladstone and Lord Salisbury, and a monthly illustrated *Record of Eminent Men*. Some of these were written by Potter himself; but few copies appear to have survived. He was not associated with any of the new movements, or new working-class newspapers, which came into existence during the eighties and early nineties. Nor did he show any leanings towards the Radical wing of the Liberal party; and his pamphlets and letters to the press, while showing still a wide variety of interests, proclaimed a consistently Lib-Lab approach. His most important public appearance was his final attempt to become an MP, when he stood for Preston in 1886 as an official Liberal candidate. 'Next to being a Gladstonian', he told the electors, 'he was one of the people'; and he stressed his long connection with the trade union movement, while adding that 'employers need not be afraid of him.' But he made little impression, both seats falling to the Conservatives, while Potter came in fourth. After the death of his wife, also in 1886, he moved to Clapham, where a married daughter kept house for him. It was there that he died, on 3 June 1893. He left property worth some £520.

It is now generally recognised that the Webbs, writing under Applegarth's influence, dismissed Potter too contemptuously. All the same, he had many weaknesses; and these were clearly exposed through the circumstances of his defeat by the Junta. There seems no doubt that, in the conditions of the 1860s, it was their policy that best served the interests of the unions. Potter, who had no clearly defined alternative policy of his own, and whose position in the labour movement depended so much on the fortunes of the *Bee-Hive*, could only come round to accepting their views. Nevertheless, he did have the support of some influential leaders, even in London – including Thomas Dunning throughout the quarrel, and Daniel Guile until he joined the Conference of Amalgamated Trades in 1867 – and he was always in favour of establishing some permanent organisation at national level. On this aspect of policy, it was the Junta who came to accept Potter's view. This was demonstrated in 1871, when, attending the TUC in force, they supported Potter's election as president. Thereafter, although the Junta soon began to break up, Potter was back in the main stream of trade union affairs. He played a useful part in the campaigns of the 1870s – especially the labour laws campaign and the movement in support of the agricultural labourers. He was also the first really effective working-class member of the London School Board.

His political record was less impressive. Until at any rate the later years of his life, he was always, as an American interviewer noted in 1871, 'a trade unionist rather than a politician.' But his early support for Troup's pro-Southern views, although probably no more than acquiescence in the policies of his chosen editor in a field in which at that time he had little interest, helped to build up antagonism against him; and purely political affairs, especially after 1865, could never be pushed far into the background. Here again, Potter had no coherent social or political philosophy as a basis for his actions; and even before he announced himself 'a good Gladstonian Liberal', he had shown that he was, in fact, a natural Lib-Lab. He normally stood well to the right of Odger, or even Applegarth. He was never a member of the International, or any of the republican groups, and he soon turned away from the Land and Labour League in order to support the Land Tenure Reform Association. Since he had never really seen anything incompatible between middle-class Liberalism and working-class interests, the moderate Liberalism of his later years was a natural development.

As an orator, Potter could expound a given policy with force and clarity, often winning passionate support from his audience. This tended to conceal the fact that the policies he advocated had almost always been worked out by other men. As a writer, he was less effective, and his style too often became turgid and clumsy in any sustained argument. His best writing, in fact, appeared in the *Contemporary Review* in 1870 to 1871, when during the Solly *régime* at the *Bee-Hive* he had more leisure to polish his work. However, he did evolve a style that was adequate for the purposes of weekly journalism; and he became quite a competent editor, having the sense to realise that he could not, like Hartwell, impose his own personality on the *Bee-Hive*, and concentrating on making the paper largely an 'open forum' of controversial signed articles. But the most important aspect of his work for the *Bee-Hive*, whether as manager, editor, or editor-proprietor, was the sustained effort that kept the paper in existence for more than seventeen years. This, in the last resort, should be seen as his main service to the labour movement.

Writings: (with others), *Nine Hours Movement: builders' lock-out* (1859) 8 pp.; 'A Reply to Mr Charles Buxton on Trades' Unions' [letter], *Morning Advertiser*, 21 Nov 1859 [repr. as a pamphlet of 12 pp.]; (with others), *The Strike and Lock-Out in the Building Trades being a Brief Statement of the Facts in Relation thereto together with a Vindication of the Proceedings of the Conference of the Nine Hours' Movement* (Jan 1860) 16 pp.; 'The Case of the London Operative Builders', *Weekly Wages* (Aug 1861) [copy in Manchester PL]; *The Labour Question: an address to capitalists, and employers of the building trades being a few reasons on* *behalf of a reduction of the hours of labour* (1861) 16 pp.; *An Address to the Miners of North Staffordshire upon the Necessity of Combination delivered at the Great Demonstration, Hanley, June 9, 1862* [1862?] 15 pp.; 'The Trade Societies of England from the Workman's Point of View', *Cont. Rev. 14* (June 1870) 404–28; 'Strikes and Lock-Outs from the Workman's Point of View', ibid. *15* (Aug 1870) 32–54; 'Conciliation and Arbitration', ibid. (Nov 1870) 543–66; 'The Future of Capital and Labour', ibid. *17* (Apr–July 1871) 525–39 [This was in reply to an article in the same volume by S. Fothergill (pp. 107–26) commenting on Potter's earlier article on this subject]; 'The First Point of the New Charter: improved dwellings for the people', ibid. *18* (Nov 1871) 547–65; *Republicanism in England* [four letters repr. from *Nonconformist* (1871) in Howell Coll.] 22 pp.; 'Reform of the House of Lords', *Bee-Hive*, 23 Dec 1871, 5; 'The Church of England and the People', *Fortn. Rev. 17* (Feb 1872) 176–90; 'On the Advantages of attending Religious Services', *Bee-Hive*, 26 Oct 1872, 6; *Dr Kenealy and the Public* (1875) 8 pp. [two articles repr. from the *Bee-Hive*, 20 and 27 Nov 1875 explaining the cause and results of his legal proceedings against Dr Kenealy for libel and conspiracy]; 'Working Men and the Eastern Question', *Cont. Rev. 28* (Oct 1876) 851–65; *The London School Board and its Critics: extravagance versus economy and duty* (1876) 14 pp.; *The Conservative Working Man and the Liberal Working Man* (1876) 13 pp. and *History of the Tory Party* (1876) 28 pp. both of which were re-issued by National Reform Union (1877); *Household Suffrage in Counties* (Tracts for the People, n.d.) 24 pp.; 'The Labourers and the Vote', *19th C. 3* (Jan 1878) 53–70; *The State-Church and Disestablishment* (Tracts for the People, n.d.) 23 pp.; 'The Workman's View of 'Fair Trade'', *19th C. 10* (Sep 1881) 430–47 [repr. for Cobden Club (1881) copy in Manchester PL] 15 pp.; *The Channel Tunnel and International Progress* [1882?] 24 pp.; 'Imperial Emigration', *Nat. Rev. 1*, no. 2 (Apr 1883) 193–207; *The Canadian Emigrant, being a Complete Guide to the Various Provinces of Canada* (1884) 16 pp.; *Liberalism v Toryism, or how Working Men should vote* (1885) 16 pp.; *The Peers and the Franchise* [1885?] 23 pp.; *Home Rule: the truth about Ireland* [1886?] 16 pp.; *The Silver Question: England, India and America* [1887?] 8 pp.; *The London School Board and the Coming Election* (1888) 8 pp.; *The People's Edition of the Life of the Right Honourable the Marquess of Salisbury* (1888); *Notable Events in the Life of His Royal Highness the Prince of Wales* (1889); Potter wrote a weekly column entitled 'The Labour Question' in the Edinburgh *Reformer*, Jan-Dec 1869 and editorials in the *Bee-Hive* in 1869 and 1871–6 and in its successor the *Industrial Review*, 1877–8. He also edited *The Monthly Record of Eminent Men* 4 vols. (1890–1).

Sources: (1) MS: Howell Coll., Bishopsgate Institute, London which also includes a number of Potter's printed pamphlets, some of which he published himself; London Trades Council minute books, TUC Library, London which also has some relevant printed material in its Burns Coll.; Solly and Webb Colls., BLPES. (2) Other: *The Strike: trade rules, conduct of the masters, etc.* (1859) 11 pp.; Building Trades Conference, *Balance Sheet of the Late Strike and Lock-Out in the London Building Trades from July 24th 1859 to May 1st 1860* (1860); NAPSS Committee, *Trades' Societies and Strikes* (1860; repr. NY, 1968); London Operative Bricklayers' Society, *Report and Balance Sheet of the Dispute relating to the Attempt to introduce a System of Hiring and Paying by the Hour* (Nov 1861) 16 pp.; *Hansard*, 7 Mar 1864; London Trades Council, *Mr Potter and the London Trades' Council* [1865] 8 pp.; *Report of the Trades Conference held at St Martin's Hall on March 5, 6, 7, & 8, 1867* [1867?] 32 pp.; *Report of St Martin's Hall United Kingdom Trades' Conference Committeee on the Trades' Union Inquiry Commission till 7th August 1867* [1867] 20 pp.; *Standard*, 10 Jan 1867; [G.R. Gleig], 'Who are the Reformers, and what do they want?' *Blackw. Edin. Mag. 101* (Jan 1867) 115–32 and ibid. (Feb 1867) 260 [Editorial note]; biographical sketch of Potter in *Bee-Hive*, 2 Aug 1873 [portrait] [repr. in slightly altered form in *Labour Portrait Gallery 1* (1873)]; *Times*, 25 June 1886; *DNB 16* [by C.G. Boase]; H. Solly, *These Eighty Years* (1893); S. and B. Webb, *The History of Trade Unionism* (1894, later eds.); *Co-operators' Year Book* (1905) 88; W.J. Davis, *The British Trades Union Congress: history and recollections* (1910); R. Postgate, *The Builders' History*

(1923); *Plebs 15* (Feb 1923) 81-2; F.E. Gillespie, *Labor and Politics in England, 1850–1867* (Duke Univ. Press, 1927); *TUC Souvenir* (1928); G.D.H. Cole, 'Some Notes on British Trade Unionism in the Third Quarter of the Nineteenth Century', *Int. Rev. for Social Hist. 2* (1937) 1–27; idem, *British Working Class Politics 1832–1914* (1941); idem, *A Short History of the British Working–Class Movement, 1789–1947* (1948); G. Tate, *London Trades Council, 1860–1950: a history* (1950); A.E. Musson, *The Congress of 1868: the origins and establishment of the Trades Union Congress* (1955); S. Coltham, 'George Potter and the *Bee-Hive* Newspaper' (Oxford DPhil., 1956); B.C. Roberts, *The Trades Union Congress 1868–1921* (1958); S. Coltham, 'The *Bee-Hive* Newspaper: its origin and early struggles', in *Essays in Labour History*, ed. A. Briggs and J. Saville (1960) 174–204; idem, 'George Potter, the Junta, and the *Bee-Hive', Int. Rev. Social Hist. 9*, pt 3 (1964) 391–432 and *10*, pt 1 (1965) 23–65; H. Collins and C. Abramsky, *Karl Marx and the British Labour Movement: years of the First International* (1965); *Boase 2* (1965); *The Minutes of Edinburgh Trades Council 1859–1873*, ed. for Scottish History Society by I. MacDougall (1968); S. Coltham, 'English Working-Class Newspapers in 1867', in *Victorian Studies 13*, no. 2 (1969) 159–80; F.M. Leventhal, *Respectable Radical: George Howell and Victorian Working Class Politics* (1971); W.H. Fraser, *Trade Unions and Society: the struggle for acceptance 1850–1880* (1974); D. Kynaston, *King Labour: the British working class 1850–1914* (1976). The editors wish to acknowledge comments received from Dr W.H. Fraser, Univ. of Strathclyde; Alan Jones, Univ. of East Anglia; Professor F.M. Leventhal, Univ. of Boston, U.S.A. OBIT. *Times*, 5 June 1893.

STEPHEN COLTHAM

See also: †William ALLAN; †Robert APPLEGARTH.

PRIOR, John Damrel (1840–1923)

TRADE UNION LEADER

Prior's birth certificate shows that he was born at Bradford, Devonshire, on 27 July 1840 and given the names John Dameral, although later in life this second name (that of his mother before marriage) became Damrel. He was the eldest son of Jacob Hunt Prior, a nonconformist minister, and his wife, Mary. His parents wanted him to become a teacher and ensured that he received a good education; but instead he chose to become apprenticed in 1854 as a carpenter and joiner in Plymouth. On completing his apprenticeship there, he joined the local lodge of the Manchester Unity Order of Odd Fellows, and became the holder of various offices, including that of secretary.

In 1862 Prior was one of the founding organisers of a local trade society which in the next year was incorporated as a branch of the London-based Amalgamated Society of Carpenters and Joiners. Two years later, during a three-weeks' dispute over demands for improved working conditions in the Plymouth and Devonport area, he served as a member of the lock-out committee, and in the following year, 1865, as the secretary of the strike committee during a similar confrontation with the employers.

In Plymouth Prior took an active part in the formation of a branch of the Reform League and was its representative at the St Martin's Hall Conference of 1867. In the same year he was selected by the Society of Arts as one of the artisan members of the group which visited the International Exhibition in Paris. His reputation as a trade union leader was steadily growing, and as a result of his contribution to the strike effort in the Devonport area, he was appointed to the General Council of the ASCJ. Shortly afterwards he moved to London in search of work and was largely responsible for the establishment of a branch of the Society in Islington. Moreover, by reason of his living in London, Prior was now qualified for membership of the

Society's executive council. In London he also became associated with Lloyd Jones, the secretary of the Labour Representation League and he seems to have remained a member of its business committee until about 1873. But, during this period Prior was moved to Manchester.

In June 1871 following the resignation of Robert Applegarth Prior was elected general secretary of the ASCJ. It was a time of growing tension and conflict within the Society. Applegarth had always been a public figure since he entered trade union affairs, and in September 1870 he had been appointed to serve on the R.C. which was to inquire into the workings of the Contagious Diseases Acts. There was already a growing opposition to Applegarth in the London area – in which W.R. Cremer played, and was to continue to play, a leading part; and this latest public appointment brought the intrigue into the open. Resolutions of opposition were sent to the EC asking that the general secretary should resign from the R.C., with counter-resolutions from the provinces. A new EC elected in April 1871 – which now included Cremer – took the London branches' part against Applegarth, and he soon resigned his union office, giving two months notice as the rule book demanded. In this interim period, however, Applegarth organised a counter-attack. He wrote to every member of the General Council (who were elected by the provincial members) and arranged a meeting with the new EC on 18 May 1871. On the day appointed, the EC refused admission to the members of the General Council, and the rupture within the Society began. The story is told in most detail in Higenbottam (1939) Ch. VII. The General Council arranged elections for a new general secretary, and J.D. Prior came head of the list; the Society moved to Manchester in June 1871 leaving the London branches still calling themselves the Amalgamated Society; and after a series of court cases and finally a trade union arbitration award, the Manchester group retained the title of the Amalgamated Society of Carpenters and Joiners and filed under that name with the Registrar of Friendly Societies. The London group were allowed to register as the London Amalgamated Society of Carpenters and Joiners, but their membership then quite rapidly declined. In all this Prior naturally played a central part. He was cautious as well as efficient, and he kept his new EC on a steady keel during all the difficult times they came through. He also won the respect of the wider trade union movement. The arbitration group whose ruling finally gave the positive decision to Prior's Amalgamated Society was composed of a powerful group of contemporary unionists: John Kane, Daniel Guile, George Odger, Robert Austin, and William Hicking.

The building trades had remained prosperous throughout the middle years of the seventies, and the downturn in building activity, in most areas, did not occur until 1877–8. In midsummer 1877, at a time when trade was still good, the Manchester lodges of the General Union of Carpenters and Joiners put in a claim for a wage increase. The strike which followed lasted fifty-three weeks, and by the time it was over the finances of the General Union were exhausted. It was an unqualified defeat, and Prior then invited the General Union to consider amalgamation. The invitation was refused, and the Amalgamated Society forthwith began war upon them. Postgate describes the ruthless tactics which were used. 'We used Prussian methods on them' one old official remarked to Postgate when the latter was collecting material for his *Builders' History*. 'No doubt', Postgate wrote, 'some decline [in the General Union] would have occurred in any case, but the extreme disorganisation and demoralisation was due to Prior's deliberate attack. Perhaps fifty per cent of the General Union membership was annexed by the Amalgamated: five-sixths of the rest abandoned trade union membership altogether. In 1883, when a new secretary, William Matkin, was appointed, there were only 1750 members. The Amalgamated had then nearly 23,000 members. It had begun the crisis with 16,000, the General Union with 11,000' [ibid., 309].

When Prior moved to Manchester in the early seventies, he very soon made contact with the labour movement in Lancashire. In particular he became an active supporter of the co-operative movement, and he gave all his union printing to the newly-established North of England Co-operative Printing Society. He later became one of its directors. He was also for a time president of the Manchester-based Association of Trade Union Officials, the chief object of which, according to W.J. Davis, was 'to protect an official who was unjustly dealt with by the members of his society in consequence of his using his influence to prevent strikes when a large minority was clamouring for extreme action' [Davis (1910) 89]. This body was also known as the 'Peculiar People', doubtless because it was both elect and convivial – and each year there were a number of 'annual' social gatherings [and for a further description, see Webb (1894) 310].

Towards the end of 1874 he co-operated with John Kane of the Amalgamated Iron Workers and Robert Knight of the Boilermakers and Iron Shipbuilders in drawing up a proposal for a federation of the iron and building trades [ASCJ, *Monthly Report* (Jan 1875) 15]. The idea behind this was the provision of greater financial resources during strikes but the proposal came to nothing. Prior represented the ASCJ at the TUC in the 1870s, being elected as a member of the Parliamentary Committee from 1875 to 1880. On the death of John Kane in March 1876 he became chairman (1876–9) of the Parliamentary Committee and he presided over the Newcastle Congress of that year.

Little is known definitely of Prior's political views. At a public meeting of March 1875 in support of the locked-out Welsh miners he moved from the platform a resolution of sympathy; and he appears to have been a member of the Manchester Relief Committee which was set up and which sent money to South Wales. But this was a trade union interest. Fraser [(1974) 166] includes Prior among the union leaders he calls 'the true Lib-Labs', and Prior was one of the members at the TUC of 1879 who justified the imperial role of Britain in Africa and supported British enterprise there.

During his ten years as general secretary of the ASCJ, Prior was responsible for the creation of a stable central organisation and for the establishment of a set of rules to replace a situation where vague unwritten conventions prevailed. He had little false modesty about his achievements, and a few sentences from a long letter to the EC, written on the eve of his resignation, give the flavour of his leadership:

> I think that the members of the General Council who have from time to time visited this office will be able to satisfy their constituents that the business done here has been transacted in a painstaking, orderly, and methodical manner. When I first took office I was removed into a strange town, without books or documents, with a council quite inexperienced in their duties, and I had to create the machinery necessary for efficiently and promptly supplying the requirements of our branches . . . Our society was then divided by party faction. We became involved in expensive law suits, the results of which it was hard to determine. Our organisation at that time needed a dictator, rather than a deliberative assembly . . . and I am free to confess that on more than one occasion I have been compelled to take immediate action, and have reported to the council when the emergency had been met and the danger averted. The necessity for such action on the part of the general secretary has long passed away, and I confidently believe that with ordinary prudence, the recurrence of such difficulties as those with which we then contended is rendered impossible, and my successor will be exempt from responsibilities which have cost me many an anxious hour [ASCJ, *Monthly Report* (Mar 1881) 41–3].

Prior was a strong supporter of the TUC's recommendation that the factory inspectorate should include some working tradesmen. This principle was partly accepted by the Home Secretary, Harcourt, in January 1881, when he agreed to appoint one working-class representative on an experimental basis. In the first instance the post was offered to Henry Broadhurst, but he declined it, proposing instead his colleague Prior, who was officially appointed as a junior inspector on 21 March 1881. Within the trade union movement there was widespread gratification at what was seen as a concession to its requests. There was some criticism, from George Howell for example, who also wanted the post, and from others, who pointed out that Prior had not taken the usual qualifying examinations. In the Commons

Harcourt explained the circumstances that had led to an Order in Council being invoked to dispense with an examination. Among the subjects were languages, and mathematics, and candidates were required to be under thirty years of age; requirements which in almost all cases would inevitably debar 'artisans' [*Hansard*, 21 Feb 1881].

Prior (who was succeeded both in general secretaryship of the ASCJ and in the inspectorate by James Murchie) served as a junior inspector in the Birmingham no. 1 district until November 1885. He was then promoted to second class inspector and transferred to the Huddersfield area, where he remained for the rest of his career, being made a first class inspector in November 1898 and retiring in July 1905.

Prior's face was full of character, with a broad forehead, well-set eyes, a largish nose and mouth – the mouth partially hidden by a moustache and a rather scanty beard; his expression was confident and determined. Prior died at his home, 25 Claremont Grove, Didsbury, Manchester, on 4 February 1923 and was cremated at Manchester Crematorium. He was survived by his wife, Eliza Ann Prior, to whom he left an estate of £775.

Sources: *TUC Report* (1871–81); *Bee-Hive*, 11 Oct 1873; ASCJ, *Monthly Report* (Jan 1875); *Hansard*, 21 Feb 1881; ASCJ, *Monthly Report* (Mar 1881); S. and B. Webb, *The History of Trade Unionism* (1894, later eds.); H. Broadhurst, *Henry Broadhurst, M.P. The Story of his Life from a Stonemason's Bench to the Treasury Bench* (1901); F. Chandler, *Amalgamated Society of Carpenters and Joiners: history of the Society 1860–1910* (Manchester, 1910); W.J. Davis, *The British Trades Union Congress: history and recollections* vol. *1* (1910); R.W. Postgate, *The Builders' History* (1923); S. Higenbottam, *Our Society's History* (Manchester, 1939); T.J. Connelly, *The Woodworkers 1860–1960* (1960); V.L. Allen, *The Sociology of Industrial Relations* (1971); F.M. Leventhal, *Respectable Radical: George Howell and Victorian working class politics* (1971); W.H. Fraser, *Trade Unions and Society: the struggle for acceptance 1850–1880* (1974); biographical information: V.C. Jordan, Health and Safety Executive, London; Ms J. Druker, Warwick Univ. OBIT. ASW, *Report* (Mar 1923).

DAVID E. MARTIN
BARBARA NIELD

See also: †Robert APPLEGARTH; †John KANE; Robert KNIGHT

ROWLANDS, James (1851–1920)
WORKING-CLASS LIBERAL MP

James Rowlands was born on 1 October 1851 at East Finsbury, North London. He was the son of William Bull Rowlands, and his wife Matilda (née Franch) and in his youth was apprenticed to a watch-case maker. He studied further at the Working Men's College, in Great Ormond Street, and at the School of Mines. Early in his adult life he showed considerable powers of oratory, and in 1876 he spoke at an Exeter Hall Meeting called to discuss the Turkish atrocities in Bulgaria; this campaign brought him in touch with certain of the more radical members of the Liberal Party leadership, including John Bright and Passmore Edwards. Rowlands began to work politically for the Liberal Party in London. Throughout the 1880s and 1890s he was involved in most of the advanced radical campaigns of the day, such as those for municipal reform in London, an improved workmen's train service, open space and land reform. He became secretary of the Leasehold Enfranchisement Society, a position he continued to hold for many years when the Society merged with the Free Land League and became known as the Land Law Reform Association. In 1893 he helped to promote the Gas Consumers' Protection League, and he became a co-opted member of the London School Board (1901–4). He always spoke of himself as an advocate of the rights of labour, and certainly was active on behalf of post-office employees and mail-cart drivers; and he supported the agitation for better conditions in government arsenals and dockyards. He also took an active part in the cause of international arbitration, and in 1877 was on the Council of the Workmen's Peace Association.

He unsuccessfully contested East Finsbury in the general election of 1885, but won the seat in the following year, standing as a Radical and Home Ruler, and held it until he was defeated in the 1895 election. In the general election of 1906 he stood under Liberal Party auspices for the constituency of North-West Kent or Dartford. The constituency had been established in 1885 and had been represented continuously by the Conservative Chief Whip in the previous Parliaments, Sir William Hart Dyke, although the election majorities had fluctuated and were never large. The social composition of the area was mixed and 'just less than predominantly working class' [Pelling (1967) 71]. Rowlands was often described in the local press as the Liberal and Labour candidate, and from his election speeches it was clear that he set himself out to win the working-class vote. He was introduced at one meeting as 'one of the veterans of the Labour movement' [*Express*, 5 Jan 1906]. Rowlands spoke to many specifically working-class audiences, and he always stressed his vigorous support for trade unionism and the repeal of the Taff Vale decision. Asked whether he would support the Labour Party 'as against the Liberal Party, Mr Rowlands replied he would support the Labour Party on every rational thing brought forward, and he did not think there would be much difference between them.' For the rest, Rowlands's programme showed the usual radical emphasis upon free trade, taxation of ground values, a national system of small holdings, prohibition of further importation of Chinese labour into South Africa, abolition of the veto of the House of Lords and shorter Parliaments. He asked for greater efficiency and preparedness in the armed forces at the same time as he was advocating the establishment of a court of international arbitration for the settlement of all disputes. What is omitted from his programme is any reference to Old Age Pensions, and it does not seem to have been an issue in this constituency during the election.

In Parliament Rowlands was a frequent speaker and actively concerned with a number of radical issues. His contributions were well-informed, practical and incisively expressed. He was an interesting transitional figure within both the labour movement and the Liberal Party. Some commentators regarded him as a labour representative and in a number of lists of the new House of Commons drawn up after the election he was classified in this way; even the official *Liberal Year Book* (1907–10) described him as a 'Labour Member'. He clearly won considerable working-class support (his majority was 2804), but both the ILP and the SDF in Erith – the most radical part of the constituency – refused to back him. He continued to be active in a wide range of Radical-Liberal organisations; he was honorary secretary of the Land Law Reform Association in 1905, and in 1906 he was on the central executive of the Municipal Reform League.

Rowlands lost the seat at the January election of 1910, but regained it in the second general election of that year, and was re-elected in 1918, as a Coalition Liberal, with a large majority over the Labour candidate. He died on 1 March 1920. In his earlier days at least he had been an avowed free thinker [*Islington Gazette*, 21 June 1885]. He had married Kate Boyden in 1879, and she died in 1905; there was at least one daughter of the marriage. Rowlands was cremated at Golders Green and his ashes interred in the family grave at Finchley Cemetery. He left an estate valued at £4636.

Writings: *Address on Land-Tenure Reform* (Political Committee of the National Liberal Club [1906]) 16 pp.

Sources: *Times*, 25 June 1886; *Hansard*, 30 Aug 1888 [maiden speech], (1890–5), (1906–19) *passim*; *Dod* (1888), (1909), and (1919); *Chronicle and District Times* [Dartford], 2, 9, 16 and 23 Jan 1906; *Express* [Dartford], 5, 12 and 19 Jan 1906; *Liberal Year Book for 1907* (1907); *Pall Mall Gazette 'extra'* (Jan 1911); *WWW* (1916–28); H. Pelling, *Social Geography of British*

Elections 1885–1910 (1967); T. Lloyd, 'Lib-Labs and "Unforgiveable Electoral Generosity"', *Bull. of the Institute of Historical Research, 48,* no. 118 (Nov 1975) 255–9; biographical information: the late T.A.K. Elliott, CMG. OBIT. *Islington Daily Gazette* and *Times*, 2 Mar 1920; *Islington Daily Gazette*, 3 Mar 1920; *Holloway Press* and *Times*, 5 Mar 1920.

JOHN SAVILLE

ROWLINSON, Ernest George (1882–1941)
LABOUR ALDERMAN

Rowlinson was born in a small Cambridgeshire village, Great Shelford, on 15 March 1882, the son of a labourer, John Rowlinson, and his wife Susanna (née Ryder). He was brought up a Baptist, and had only the minimum of education. He left Cambridgeshire in his early 'teens, looking for better employment prospects and he obtained work on the railways in Chesterfield, earning sixteen shillings a week for long hours of work. He joined the ILP and quickly became an active member of the Amalgamated Society of Railway Servants; on moving to Sheffield, he became leader of the Midland Station platform branch. He was a tough fighter for better pay and conditions and during the 1911 railway strike was a prominent and vigorous member of the 'vigilante' committee. When the strike failed he was victimised.

He retained membership of the ASRS (later the NUR) for life but never again worked on the railways. Soon after the strike he obtained a job as an agent for the Co-operative Insurance Society, employment which quite commonly offered security and independence to union and political militants who could find no other work. He had joined the Sheffield Trades and Labour Council in 1911, as a delegate of the ASRS; and in the following year he became vice-president of the Council and in 1913, president. The Council had sunk to a very low ebb by 1912, weakened by the split with the Lib-Lab Federated Trades Council in 1908, and by repeated electoral failures. Rowlinson did much to revive confidence. He was a very hard worker, an excellent organiser, a skilful, often humorous speaker and in general had the capacities of a natural leader able to inspire devotion and loyalty. There is no doubt he was responsible for a new sense of purpose in the affairs of the Council, and in 1913 the three years of electoral defeat ended with a victory in Attercliffe ward. When the First World War broke out, Rowlinson volunteered for a Scottish Highland Regiment. He was twice wounded, and gassed, and never afterwards recovered full health.

From 1919 the number of Labour members on the Sheffield City Council began to increase steadily. Rowlinson himself was elected for the Crookesmoor ward in 1921, having failed the previous year, but he was defeated in 1924, and once again re-elected in 1925. In 1922 he had become chairman of the Labour Group on the Council. This meant that he was now the leader of both the united Trades and Labour Council and the City Council group. In November 1926 the Labour Party achieved a majority in the local city elections. Rowlinson gave up his presidency of the Trades Council in order to concentrate on City Council work; and it was his leadership which turned a 'rather raw, large party into one which became a model and an inspiration to struggling Labour parties all over the country' [Marshall (1947) 7]. In its first few years of office, the Labour administration undertook major projects in the fields of education, public health, blind welfare and housing, built a new Central Library and Art Gallery and a new City Hall, established a municipal printing works and direct labour for municipal projects. Rowlinson was not only chairman of two committees and member of six others, but also kept up-to-date with the details of the work of all the other committees, and ensured through successful diplomacy that the Labour group never entered a Council meeting divided on a major issue.

Rowlinson's own major interest was education. He was chairman of the education committee and 11,000 new primary and 5800 new secondary school places were provided during his first six years of office. Recognised as a 'great municipal administrator' by Whitehall [*Sheffield Daily Telegraph*, 6 Jan 1941] he was invited to serve on the consultative committee of the Board of Education in 1936. He was president of the Association of Education Committees in 1934 and in 1937 chairman of the education committee of the Association of Municipal Corporations. He was appointed to the Ray Committee reviewing local expenditure, and to the Advisory Council on Housing in 1932. In 1938 he was a member of a national advisory committee dealing with the administration of the 1909 Cinematograph Act. In February 1940 he was appointed one of twelve trustees of the Nuffield Hospitals Trust.

Rowlinson became a magistrate in 1924, an alderman in 1929 and served as Lord Mayor in 1937–8. Typically, he invited 300 schoolchildren to the Church Service on Lord Mayor's Sunday. He was asked to stand for Parliament several times but refused, saying that things 'moved too slowly' in Parliament and that he could achieve more if he remained at the local level. In political matters, in the years after the First World War he was always a moderate.

Rowlinson was twice married, and had two daughters, Minnie and Eileen, who both became teachers in Sheffield. His second wife, Kathleen was also a teacher. In 1926 they moved from their home in Hillsborough to the new suburb of Beauchief. Rowlinson died at the age of fifty-eight on 4 January 1941 and his funeral was held at Upper Chapel, Sheffield. He left £1945. In tribute to him, Sheffield's new technical school was named 'Rowlinson School'. More than anyone else, Rowlinson laid the foundation of the almost unbroken tenure of office by the Labour Party on Sheffield City Council from 1926 until the present day (1980).

Sources: *Sheffield Guardian*, 27 June 1913; Sheffield Trades and Labour Council, *Annual Report,* nos. 10–11 (1913–15); Sheffield Federated Trades and Labour Council, *Annual Report*, nos. 1–7 (1920–7); *Sheffield Co-operator* (Dec 1926); Sheffield City Council Labour Group, *Six Years of Labour Rule in Sheffield, 1926–32* (Sheffield, 1932) 33 pp.; 'Next Year's Lord Mayor and Lady Mayoress', *Park and Heeley Gazette* (Oct 1937) 7; F. Marshall, 'Speech on Ernest George Rowlinson', *Edward Carpenter Memorial Service* (Sheffield, 1947) 7–8; J. Mendelson et al., *The Sheffield Trades and Labour Council 1858 to 1958* (Sheffield, [1958?]); H. Mathers, 'Sheffield Municipal Politics 1893–1926. Parties, Personallties and the Rise of Labour' (Sheffield PhD, 1979); personal information: J. Curtis, S. Davison and Dr J.W. Sterland, Sheffield; Mrs E.G. Rowlinson, Sheffield, widow. OBIT. *Sheffield Daily Telegraph and Independent*, 6 Jan 1941; P. Sharp, 'An Appreciation', *Education*, 17 Jan 1941; Sheffield City Library News Cuttings, *22* (Jan 1941) 2.

HELEN MATHERS

See also: †Joseph POINTER.

SAKLATVALA, Shapurji Dorabji (1874–1936)

INDIAN NATIONALIST AND BRITISH COMMUNIST MP

Shapurji Saklatvala (Sak) was born on 28 March 1874 in the State of Bombay, British India. Both his parents were Parsees and belonged to the Zoroastrian faith. His father, Dorabji, was manager of a cotton mill; his mother, formerly Jerbai Tata, whose brother Jamsetji Nasarwanji Tata established the famous firm of Tata Industries, originally largely based on textiles, later extending to iron and steel. The young Saklatvala was brought up in what was virtually a joint family of the Tatas and the Saklatvalas, within which there were, however, considerable family tensions. J.N. Tata, who died in 1904 remained always a fervent nationalist, but his sons were more inclined to Anglophilia. Saklatvala as a young man supported his uncle.

Saklatvala was educated at St Xavier's School in Bombay, and later attended St Xavier's College, where he was deeply influenced by the Jesuit fathers. After joining his uncle's firm in 1897 he spent three years in the jungle areas of Bihar and Orissa prospecting for coal, iron and limestone and it was these explorations that greatly promoted the development of the Tata Iron and Steel Works. He contracted disease in the jungle, was for some time confined to a wheelchair, and in October 1905 came to Britain to receive medical treatment. There was also the possibility that his removal from Bombay was at least in part the result of increasing tensions between himself and the Tata sons who now controlled the family firm. In London Saklatvala became personal assistant to his cousin, Sir Ratan J. Tata, who was a confirmed Anglophile and who at this time lived at York House, Twickenham. Saklatvala also joined Tata's London office as manager of the cotton mills department; and he made an unsuccessful foray, as a Liberal candidate, into a local government election.

Saklatvala had already developed a social conscience when he first arrived in England. He had undertaken welfare work in the slums and plague hospitals of Bombay during the 1890s, and he was deeply shocked on his arrival in London to discover that a Christian country practised so little charity towards its own poor and unprivileged. He steadily moved towards the Left in politics. He joined the Workers' Union in 1910 (and the National Union of Clerks in 1916); and in 1910 also he took what must have been for him the decisive step in his political career by becoming a member, and very soon an active member, of the Central London branch of the ILP. He quickly became prominent as a spokesman for left-wing causes with inevitably an emphasis upon the relation between the British labour movement and the forces of Indian nationalism. During the war years, his political adherence to a left Socialist analysis became stronger, and like many others he was enormously influenced by the Russian revolutions of 1917 and more particularly by the success of Lenin and the Bolsheviks. He became prominent within the section of the ILP which accepted a Marxist approach, and after the formation of the Communist International he was one of the group which agitated strongly for ILP affiliation. Other well-known colleagues were C.H. Norman, Emile Burns, J.T. Walton Newbold, E.H. Brown, Helen Crawfurd and R. Palme Dutt. Saklatvala tried unsuccessfully to win election to the NAC of the ILP in 1919 and 1920, and at the Glasgow national conference in April 1920 he and his political friends formed themselves into a left-wing committee for agitation. They ran for about a year a fortnightly paper, the *International*; but when their motion for affiliation to the CI was defeated by 521 votes to 97 at the March 1921 Conference, Saklatvala was one of the 'couple of hundred' [Dowse (1966) 57] who left the ILP to join the British Communist Party. He became a member of the Central London branch.

In the general election of October 1922 Saklatvala contested John Burns's old seat of Battersea North. After much debate and discussion he was given the support of the Battersea Trades and Labour Council and the Labour Party, and was endorsed by the NEC of the Labour Party. The agreement was that Saklatvala should run as a Labour candidate and pledge himself publicly to support the Labour Party's constitution and policy. This he did. His election address was unusually lengthy; in it Saklatvala wrote with emphasis: 'If elected, I pledge myself to the fullest extent to support the well-known programme of the Labour Party'; and he made only an oblique reference to his membership of the Communist Party. His penultimate paragraph began: 'In spite of desperate and ludicrous efforts on the part of Liberals and Tories alike to split the Working Class Movement into hostile fragments, THE LABOUR PARTY IS TODAY THE ONLY PARTY IN GREAT BRITAIN THAT STANDS SOLIDLY TOGETHER. The scare-cry of "Communist", which is sure to be raised by eleventh-hour leaflets, will fortunately not frighten the Electors of North Battersea . . .'. Those were the years when the Communist Party was making strenuous efforts to obtain affiliation to the Labour Party [Klugmann (1968) 166 ff.] and Saklatvala's statements in this 1922 election, and his general attitude towards the Labour Party, were not inconsistent in fundamentals with Communist Party policy. One of his most active supporters in the election campaign was Mrs Charlotte Despard. In all, in this election, there were six Communist candidates, four standing as Labour: but apart from Saklatvala only Walton Newbold at Motherwell was successful. Saklatvala obtained a clear majority of 2000 votes, but in the November 1923 general election he lost his seat by a narrow margin. Between the 1923 election and that of October 1924 which brought the first minority Labour Government to an end, the Labour Conference of early October 1924 – which Saklatvala attended as a delegate from St Pancras Labour Party – had banned Communists standing as Labour candidates and had excluded individual Communists from Labour Party membership. Saklatvala was, therefore, forced to contest North Battersea as a Communist in 1924, and with the overwhelming support of the North Battersea LP, he secured a narrow majority over his Liberal opponent. It was a significant victory in the 'Zinoviev Letter' election.

During both his periods in the House of Commons Saklatvala worked closely with the left-wing Scottish ILP members. He made it his particular responsibility to emphasise the inseparable nature of the workers' struggle in different parts of the Empire, and inevitably was most concerned with the problems of workers and peasants in the colonial countries, above all in India. There were two organisations in Britain which provided connections between India and the British labour movement. One was Annie Besant's Indian Home Rule League, which she had founded in 1916 to encourage constitutional reform. In the closing years of the First World War the League was able to arouse a certain amount of support for its aims among ILP branches and trades councils in Yorkshire and South Wales and in some of the larger industrial towns [Gupta (1972) 72–3]. Saklatvala was a member of the League, and it was he who formed the Workers' Welfare League in 1916, originally to work among Indian seamen in London, although it soon broadened its aims to take in matters affecting working conditions of all occupational groups of Indians. When the All-India Trade Union Congress (AITUC) was established in 1921, the Workers' Welfare League became its agent in Britain. Among leading members of the League in its early years, apart from Saklatvala himself, were Arthur Pugh (until at least 1924), J. Potter-Wilson and George Lansbury. By the mid-1920s Saklatvala had identified the Workers' League with the Communist and non-Communist Left, and with the political rupture of the 1926 General Strike the League began to be viewed with increasing hostility by both the Labour leadership and the General Council of the TUC.

Saklatvala's political career was always turbulent. After he joined the Communist Party he took a full part in the many political and industrial disputes of the period; his home was searched in October 1921; in 1925, when he was appointed a member of the British delegation to the Inter-Parliamentary Union Congress in Washington, his visa was revoked by F.B. Kellogg, the American Secretary of State, and the affair received wide coverage in the press; on the first day of the General Strike, 4 May 1926, he was arrested and charged with sedition for a speech made in Hyde Park on May Day, urging the Army not to fire on the people. On refusing to be bound over, Saklatvala was sentenced to two months' imprisonment, which he served in Wormwood Scrubs. During the time of his arrest and trial Saklatvala's home and those of several other well-known Communist Party members had been raided [Morris (1976) 380]. After his release Saklatvala was very active in addressing meetings on behalf of the locked-out miners.

Saklatvala went to India three times after he settled in England: once in 1912–13 with his family, and then on a second occasion by himself in 1913–14; on his third visit he had some trouble in obtaining permission to enter the country but finally arrived in Bombay on 14 January 1927. He had an enthusiastic reception from most sections of Indian nationalist opinion, and he addressed himself especially to the need for trade union and peasant organisation. He attended the conference of the AITUC as a fraternal delegate; received an official welcome from several large municipal corporations – the decision to give this always being challenged; and spoke on many platforms to huge audiences. He made a vigorous appeal for communal unity in the struggle for an independent India, and he urged the Left to work within the Congress Party. Before he left India, he published an Open Letter to Gandhi in which the latter's policies were severely criticised. Gandhi replied in an article published in the

Bombay Daily Mail on 17 March 1927, and there was a further exchange of letters. The whole correspondence was published at the time as a pamphlet in Britain, and has been republished in P. Saha's brief biography of Saklatvala (1970).

After a visit of about three months, Saklatvala returned to Britain and India was deleted from the list of countries for which his passport was valid. He had earlier been refused entry to Egypt when *en route* for India. When the Labour Party returned to office in 1929, Wedgwood Benn, Secretary of State for India, and Arthur Henderson, Foreign Secretary, continued to deny him the right of entry into India. He was to find the same sort of difficulties elsewhere when he was refused admission into Belgium in January 1929 on his way to attend a meeting of the League Against Imperialism.

The origins of the League went back to a foundation meeting of the 'League Against Colonial Oppression' held in Berlin on 10 February 1926. At this meeting Willi Münzenberg, one of the great organising personalities of the international Communist movement, elaborated proposals for a large-scale anti-colonial conference. This was duly held in Brussels in February 1927 when the organisation became the League Against Imperialism. George Lansbury was elected chairman but he resigned after two months and James Maxton ultimately took his place. Willi Münzenberg became one of the two international secretaries – and the dynamic force behind the organisation – and among the members of the executive committee were Jawaharlal Nehru, Saklatvala, and Diego Rivera of Mexico. Reginald Bridgeman, the former British Foreign Office diplomat, became secretary of the British section. The League Against Imperialism was the object of immense vilification by most of the world's press. Two months after its foundation, the Indian Government prohibited all its literature; and the Dutch Government took stringent action against its representatives in Indonesia. In January 1929 James Maxton, Saklatvala, Reginald Bridgeman, A.J. Cook and Alex Gossip were on their way to a meeting of the League in Cologne. They arrived in Ostend, where Cook and Gossip were allowed to proceed, but the other three were arrested by the Belgian police and sent back to Britain. The political divisions on the left in Britain were now worsening. Saklatvala had already begun to be highly critical of the Labour Party some time before the Communist International developed its own hard line towards reformism. In a letter dated 7 October 1925 from Saklatvala to the Political Bureau, he had argued that since the Labour Party had now turned itself into a Liberal reformist group, the Communist Party should accept that it was the only anti-capitalist party and should seek trade-union affiliations. These suggestions were not accepted at the time, but the general argument foreshadowed some of the discussions on the 'new line' in 1928–9. When the 'Class against Class' debate developed after the Ninth Plenum of ECCI (February 1928) and the Sixth World Congress of the Communist International in the summer of 1928, Saklatvala was to be found with R.P. Dutt and Harry Pollitt demanding a major change of policy. Eventually this was achieved at the 11th Congress at Leeds in late November and early December 1929. Before that, Saklatvala had defended his parliamentary seat in the general election of 1929 and was easily defeated by the Labour candidate who polled twice as many votes. Saklatvala stood again in the following year in a by-election in Shettleston, Glasgow, but came bottom of the poll. In 1931 he returned to Battersea, but secured only half the number of votes he received in 1929; the Conservative was returned with a substantial majority.

During the last years of his life Saklatvala continued to speak at meetings all over the country. As with most agitators at this time, unemployment was the main issue. In 1934, with Reg Bishop, his close personal friend and secretary, he visited the Soviet Union for the third time and was greatly impressed by the changes among the non-Russian peoples in Central Asia and Trans Caucasia. In 1935 he was actively engaged in the election campaigns of Harry Pollitt in the Rhondda and Willie Gallacher in West Fife; and he continued addressing meetings until within two weeks of his death.

Saklatvala was employed by Tata Ltd until the autumn of 1925. Then the publicity which his ideas were receiving in the press, and the refusal of his American visa, led to the severance of his connection with the family firm. He had always refused to hold any stock and his status was that of a salaried executive. He wrote a civilised letter of resignation, on 16 September 1925, which ended with the paragraph: 'In this step I assure you of the inseparable good will on my part towards all the members of the firm, and I am sure of the continuance of the same on their part.' At the time of his resignation arrangements were made with a London financier, Richard Tilden-Smith, who had business connections with Tata, for a sum of £500 to be paid annually to Saklatvala for the education of his children. This sum was the subject of a successful action brought by Saklatvala against Tilden-Smith for non-payment in July 1928.

He had married on 14 August 1907 Sarah (Sehri) Elizabeth Marsh, the daughter of Henry Marsh of Tansley in Derbyshire. After leaving the village school at thirteen, she had gone into domestic service and later became a junior waitress at Smedley's Hydro – at which Saklatvala received medical treatment soon after his arrival in England. They were married in Moorside Church, Oldham, and there were three sons and two daughters of the marriage, all of whom were initiated into the Zoroastrian faith in 1927. One reason for this ceremony was the existence of a family trust under the terms of which the children might have been disinherited had they not been accepted into the faith. As it happened, there was an unforeseen birth of a nearer heir, but at the time Saklatvala was censured by the Communist Party for his action. In a comment to the *Daily News* [6 Aug 1927] he accepted the criticism as proper, but suggested that this was a domestic decision which had no relevance to his political position.

Saklatvala remained a Communist Party member until the end of his life, with his principles and personal commitment unchanged. He was a small, lean man with a cultivated manner and immense vitality and energy. He had an excellent and versatile command of English and was a fluent and eloquent speaker, given to lively gesticulation. Hymie Fagan wrote of him: 'He was a marvellous speaker, the only one I knew who at Sunday morning meetings in Regents Park would go on speaking after the pubs had opened. On one occasion he kept the crowd until 1.30 p.m. It was unheard of!' Saklatvala's recreation was chess, and he was also keenly interested in art, of which he had some considerable knowledge. It is possible, as Page Arnot suggested in an interview [28 Oct 1977] that the Party leadership – including himself – never fully appreciated Saklatvala and that they had somewhat underrated him; for his political commitment was total. He was not very sophisticated theoretically but he was extremely quick-witted and very practically oriented. Certainly, Arnot continued, in general Saklatvala accepted party discipline, but where his own views or interests were concerned he could be 'single-minded' on occasion.

Shapurji Saklatvala died of a heart attack at his home in Highgate on 16 January 1936. He was cremated at Golders Green on 20 January, with Harry Pollitt speaking the funeral oration on behalf of the executive committee of the Communist International and the central committee of the CPGB. Saklatvala's ashes were buried with Parsee rites at Brookwood Cemetery, Surrey. No will has been located. He was survived by his wife and family. Dorab, the eldest son, became a doctor. Candida, the elder daughter, joined one of the Inns of Court and simultaneously took a degree in psychology at the University of Reading. Beram, the second son, joined the family firm of Tata Ltd after Saklatvala's death, and he himself died in 1976. He was also a poet and author who had published some seventeen books, partly under his own name and partly under the name of Henry Marsh (his maternal grandfather). Kaikoo, the third son, became an engineer, and Sehri, the younger daughter, after a career on the stage joined the staff of India House in 1947.

Writings: *The Empire Labour* [1919] 21 pp.; 'India in the Labour World', *Lab. Mon. 1* (Nov 1921) 440–51; *Election Address* (1922) [4 pp.]; 'India and Britain', *Lab. Mon. 9* (June 1927) 361–4; (with M.K. Gandhi), *Is India different?: the class struggle in India: correspondence on the Indian Labour movement and modern conditions* (CPGB, 1927) 35 pp.; *Socialism and "Labourism": a speech in the House of Commons* (CPGB, [1928]) 15 pp.; 'The Simon Commission', *Communist 3*, no. 3 (Mar 1928) 128–32; *With the Communist Party in Parliament*

[Speech] [1928?] 12 pp.; 'Who is this Gandhi?', *Lab. Mon. 12* (July 1930) 413–17; 'The Indian Round Table Conference', ibid. (Dec 1930) 720–4 and *13* (Feb 1931) 86–92; 'Gandhi and the Pacifist Variety of Imperialism', *Anti-Imperialist Rev. 2,* no. 1 (Nov–Dec 1932) 32–8; 'The Indian Struggle', *Indian Front 2,* no. 9 (Mar 1935) 3–5.

Sources: (1) MS: New Scotland Yard Special Branch, 'Reports on Revolutionary Organisations in the U.K.' [typescript] in MacDonald papers, ref. 30/69/1/220, PRO. There are a number of references to Saklatvala in Foreign Office correspondence: see the Kraus/Thomson *Index to General Correspondence of the Foreign Office* (1969) for the years 1925–31, 1933 and 1935 [None of this material has been checked for the above biography. Eds]. (2) Other: *Communist,* 1920–3, 1927–8; *Times* [of India], 18 Nov 1922; *Daily Herald*, 24 Nov 1922; *New York Times*, 7 Dec 1922; *Hansard* (1922–9); Labour Party, *Annual Reports* (1922–6, 1930); S.V. Bracher, *The Herald Book of Labour Members* (1923); *Daily Herald*, 19 Apr 1923; *Dod* (1923), (1925) and (1929); *Labour Who's Who* (1924); *Times,* 7 Sep 1925; L. Hore-Belisha, 'The Amazing Saklatvala', *Daily Express*, 9 Sep 1925; *Evening Chronicle* [Manchester], 17 Sep 1925; *Morning Post,* 18 Sep 1925; *Daily Telegraph*, 21 Sep 1925; *Manchester Guardian*, 22 Mar 1926; *Times*, 5 May 1926; R. Page Arnot, *The General Strike May 1926; its origin and history* (1926; repr. 1967); '"Comrade Sak"', *Near East and India 31*, 17 Feb 1927, 184; *Sunday Worker*, 1 May 1927; *Morning Post*, 5 Aug 1927; *Daily News*, 6 Aug 1927; *Times*, 5 Sep 1927; *Manchester Guardian*, 11 Oct 1927; *Morning Post* and *Times*, 13 July 1928; *Times*, 14 July 1928; 'Report on the Development of the League Against Imperialism', *Anti-Imperialist Rev. 1*, no. 1 (July 1928) 83–96; *Morning Post*, 18 Sep 1928; *Manchester Guardian*, 10 Dec 1928; *Times*, 15 and 21 Jan 1929; *Daily Herald* and *Manchester Guardian*, 20 Nov 1929; *WWW* (1929–40); *DNB* (1931–40) [by J.S. Middleton]; W.H. Crook, *The General Strike* (Univ. of N. Carolina, Chapel Hill, 1931); *Kelly* (1932); *Manchester Guardian*, 11 July 1932; T. Bell, *The British Communist Party* (1937); J.T. Murphy, *New Horizons* (1941); A.F. Brockway, *Inside the Left* (1942); G.D.H. Cole, *A History of the Labour Party from 1914* (1949); T.A. Jackson, *Solo Trumpet* (1953); H. Pelling, *The British Communist Party* (1958); N. Wood, *Communism and British Intellectuals* (1959); G.D. Overstreet and M. Windmiller, *Communism in India* (California Univ. Press and Cambridge, 1960); R.E. Dowse, *Left in the Centre* (1966); L.J. Macfarlane, *The British Communist Party: its origin and development until 1929* (1966); J. Klugmann, *History of the Communist Party of Great Britain* 2 vols (1968–9); W. Kendall, *The Revolutionary Movement in Britain 1900–21* (1969); P. Saha, *Shapurji Saklatvala: a short biography* (New Delhi, 1970); J.P. Haithcox, *Communism and Nationalism in India* (Princeton, NJ, 1971); C. Farman, *The General Strike* (1972); P.S. Gupta, 'British Labour and the Indian Left 1919–1939' in *Socialism in India* ed. B.R. Nanda (Delhi, 1972); idem, *Imperialism and the British Labour Movement* (1975); R. McKibbin, *The Evolution of the Labour Party 1910–1924* (Oxford, 1974); M. Woodhouse and B. Pearce, *Essays on the History of Communism in Britain* (1975); J. Mahon, *Harry Pollitt: a biography* (1976); M. Morris, *The General Strike* (1976); A.J. Mackenzie, 'British Marxists and the Empire: anti-imperialist theory and practice, 1920–1945' (London PhD, 1978); biographical information: the late T.A.K. Elliott, CMG; Councillor J.A. Goldring, Battersea; Mrs M. Kentfield, Marx Memorial Library, London; personal information: Dr R. Page Arnot (interview with John Saville, 28 Oct 1977), B. Pearce, H. Fagan, Miss Sehri and the late B. Sh. Saklatvala, daughter and son, all of London. Obit: *Daily Herald, Daily Telegraph, Manchester Guardian, News Chronicle* and *Times*, 17 Jan 1936; *Daily Worker*, 18 Jan 1936; *Lab. Mon.* (Feb 1936); B. Bradley, 'Comrade Shapurji Saklatvala', *Indian Front 3,* no. 3 (Feb 1936); W. Gallacher, 'Shapurji Saklatvala 1874–1936', *Lab. Mon.* (Jan 1937) 51–3.

Barbara Nield
John Saville

See also: *Reginald Francis Orlando Bridgeman; *Rajani Palme Dutt; *James Maxton.

SHORROCKS, Peter (1834–86)
TRADE UNIONIST

Peter Shorrocks was born in Manchester on 8 April 1834. He was the third son in the family of eight children of James Nelson Shorrocks, a journeyman tailor, who had been active in movements within his trade for regulation of piece-work prices after the transition from a day-work system. Peter Shorrocks received most of his early education at home from his mother, though he was also an irregular attender at a local Lancasterian school. For three years from the age of eleven he was a pupil at the Oldham Blue Coat School at a time when there was considerable Chartist activity in the area. After leaving school he began work in a tailor's workshop and was soon involved in the beginnings of a movement for some form of workshop organisation, a movement which led to the nucleus of a trade society being formed in 1853.

On becoming a journeyman tailor, Shorrocks travelled for a time, and then returned to Manchester, where in 1860 he joined the Manchester Society of Journeyman Tailors and three years later became its secretary. The Society at this period was low both in membership and funds and could make no sickness, old age or death provision for its members; in addition it faced very strong animosity from employers. After a period of unsuccessful negotiations early in 1865 over a new price list for piece-work, a strike followed in April, after which some of the workmen's demands were satisfied.

Later in 1865, no doubt encouraged by this modest advance, the Manchester Tailors' Society took the lead in a move to amalgamate with other trade societies, and on 12 March 1866 a conference of seventy delegates, representing more than sixty societies, took place in the Manchester Mechanics' Institute. The outcome of the six-day conference was the formation of the Amalgamated Society of Journeyman Tailors, of which Shorrocks was unanimously elected secretary. The London and Irish societies, however, remained outside this merger and united to form the London Operative Tailors' Association. In January 1867 at a joint meeting in Manchester both unions agreed to act together 'for practical purposes'; their strength of purpose was considerably tested later in the year, during a lock-out in Manchester in the course of which Shorrocks was summonsed for conspiracy under the Combination of Workmen Act of 1859, but was subsequently acquitted.

In Manchester, where he was known to have advanced Radical views, Peter Shorrocks played a prominent part in the foundation of the Manchester and Salford Trades Council. Following a demonstration of the Reform League in September 1866, several representatives from a variety of trades had formed themselves into a provisional committee with the intention of founding an association of organised trades. At a meeting which followed in November the Trades Council was inaugurated and Shorrocks was elected to its executive committee. In 1868 the Manchester and Salford Trades Council issued an invitation to trade societies to establish an annual congress; and on 2 June 1868 the first Trades Union Congress assembled at the Mechanics' Institute in Manchester. W.H. Wood, the secretary of the Trades Council, was elected president and Shorrocks acted as secretary. He also read a paper on the law of conspiracy, intimidation and picketing. Shorrocks later circulated the account of the Manchester Congress and at the same time added a statement regarding the forthcoming general election (in the autumn of 1868). This urged trade unionists to put up 'men of your own class' as candidates. At the second TUC he introduced the main subject of the week: the report of the Royal Commission on Trade Unions and the possible legislation which would follow. He argued, rather sweepingly, that the only legislation the trade union movement required was the total abolition of all laws affecting combinations: a view which George Howell, following a line of policy advocated by Frederic Harrison, rejected, on the ground that such a policy would leave the unions at the mercy of the courts. Congress decided in 1869 to appoint a committee to prepare a public statement of the TUC resolutions and Shorrocks was among its members

[Musson (1955) 43]. He represented the Tailors' Society again at the 1871 TUC and served on its Parliamentary Committee in 1873; from 1877–79 and again in 1881 he was a member of the TUC Standing Orders Committee. He was vice-president of the 1880 Dublin Congress but after 1881 his official participation in TUC activities ceased – which may account for the lack of any obituary notice in Davis's history of the TUC.

During the 1860s Shorrocks had been drawn into contact with the International Working Men's Association, as a result of his relationship with the London Society of Tailors, who were themselves affiliated to the Association. In February 1868 he wrote to its general council offering his services in persuading unions in the Manchester area to subscribe; and at the annual meeting of the Trades Council in October 1870 he secured the adoption of a resolution supporting its work. In the autumn of the following year a branch was established in Manchester. Shorrocks seems to have continued support for the aims of the IWMA: in November 1872 he chaired the meeting of the Manchester Federal Council of the Association, upon which he sat as a delegate from the Salford branch. The IWMA in Manchester was, however, shortlived and the branch in Salford became a Republican Club, Shorrocks continuing to be involved with its activities.

It is, however, difficult to chart precisely the evolution of Shorrocks's political views. His radicalism does appear to have been of a relatively moderate kind within the labourist tradition. In May 1868, for example, he had proposed in the Trades Council that the local Chamber of Commerce should be approached with the suggestion that two bodies should form a court of arbitration and conciliation [Fraser (1974) 109–10]; and later he appears to have supported the 'new social movement' which involved political contacts with Tories (ibid., 160–4). In his last years he moved further towards what may be described as a traditional Lib-Lab position.

In 1877, on the resignation of W.H. Wood, Shorrocks was elected secretary of the Manchester Trades Council, and he continued in this office until 1883, when he resigned, probably on account of ill health. He was succeeded by G.D. Kelley of the Lithographic Printers. During his term as secretary, Shorrocks gave his wholehearted support to the idea of an alliance being formed of trades councils and societies. He envisaged such a federation providing a permanent centre of communication, which would both safeguard advances already made by unions and strengthen the hand of organised labour in its relations with employers. In April 1879 he organised a conference on the subject, which was attended by delegates from seventeen trades councils but little progress appears to have been made. Shorrocks told the Birmingham Trades Council that what he wanted was that

> . . . an alliance of trades councils be formed for the purpose of securing to trades councils a permanent centre of communication with a ready means of rendering mutual advice and assistance in times of difficulty or distress for the purpose and furtherance of the great interests of trade societies and for the elevation of the members of trades councils and societies in alliance [BTC minutes, 12 Apr 1879].

Nothing seems to have come of this, but in 1881 he was involved in further efforts to form a federation of Manchester trade societies. On this occasion a joint letter from the Trades Council and the Manchester and District Association of Trade Union Officials was addressed to the 'Trade Societies of Manchester, Salford and District' appealing for support for a centre of communication in every industrial district whereby information 'on subjects of special interest to our associations' may be disseminated [*Labour Standard,* 25 June 1881].

This Association of Trade Union Officials (sometimes described as Trades' Union Officials) was an interesting organisation with which Shorrocks was connected and which has been little noticed by modern historians. The annual meeting of the Manchester Association for 1882 was reported in the *Labour Standard* of 9 December from which it would seem that the Association at times actively recommended individuals for union positions (in this case the Engineers), although when challenged in subsequent correspondence about their activities, the Association's secretary, R. Spencer, denied any interference with the free action of ASE members in the selection of an officer [ibid., 16 and 23 Dec 1882]. The Webbs, in the 1894 edition of their *History of Trade Unionism* wrote that the Manchester Association of Trade Union Officials

> ... grew out of a joint committee formed to assist the South Wales miners in their strike of 1875. The frequent meetings, half serious, half social, of this grandly named association, known to the initiated as "the Peculiar People", served for many years as opportunities for important consultations on Trade Union policy between the leaders of the numerous societies having offices in Manchester. The society still continues, and both the writers of this work have the honour of being among its Vice-Presidents [p. 310 n.l. It should be noted that this comment is reprinted in the 1911 ed. but not in the last (1920) ed. of the *History;* see also Davis (1910) 89].

Until the end of his life Shorrocks remained secretary of the Amalgamated Society of Tailors and in his twenty years of office was responsible for establishing the principles and organisation on which the Society developed. In 1877 he was instrumental in setting up within the Society a committee of inquiry into the ways by which it was possible to transmit diseases, through clothes produced under sweated conditions. He took an active part in the committee's investigations in the south Lancashire area and was a member of the deputation which set out some of the worst abuses before the Home Secretary. At a conference held in Manchester in February he read a paper on the subject, in which he put a forceful case for the abolition of sweating in the tailoring trade and pointed clearly to the need for a much greater measure of and higher general standards of government inspection. 'Sweating', as a descriptive term for certain types of economic exploitation, seems to have disappeared in the middle decades of the century (after having been used in the 1840s) and Shorrocks's use of the term as well as his inquiry in 1877 foreshadowed the widespread discussions and investigations of the nature and character of 'sweating' in the decade which followed [Saville (1968) 24 n. 50].

Shorrocks died on 9 January at his home in Grosvenor Street, Chorlton, Manchester, at the age of fifty-one. The obituary in the *Cotton Factory Times,* 15 January 1886, said that 'in his latter years his abilities were somewhat clouded by unfortunate circumstances' but no details were given. His wife, Elizabeth, whom he had married in 1858 had predeceased him. She was the daughter of Robert McKenzie, with whom Shorrocks had been employed in the workshop as a youth, although it is not known in what capacity. They had a family of six children, of whom one son, James, became a compositor, and a daughter married Terence Flynn, who was secretary of the Amalgamated Tailors in 1905.

Shorrocks was buried in Southern Cemetery Manchester, on 14 January and his funeral was attended by many union representatives. He left a personal estate of £50.

Writings: *How Contagion and Infection are spread, through the Sweating System in the Tailoring Trade: being a report of a conference of trade unionists of South Lancashire ... held on February 24th, 1877* (Manchester, 1877) 28 pp.

Sources: (1) MS: TUC, Report (1869). (2) Other: *Bee-Hive,* 30 Aug 1873; *Labour Standard,* 25 June 1881 and 9, 16 and 23 Dec 1882; S. and B. Webb, *History of Trade Unionism* (1894; later eds.); W.J. Davis, *The British Trade Union Congress: history and recollections 1* (1910); A.E. Musson, *The Congress of 1868* (1955) 48 pp.; B.C. Roberts, *The Trades Union Congress 1868–1921* (1958); M. Stewart and L. Hunter, *The Needle is threaded* (1964); J. Saville, Introduction to reprint of *Industrial Remuneration Conference* [1885]: *the Report of Proceedings and Papers*

(NY, 1968) 5–44; W.H. Fraser, *Trade Unions and Society* (1974); E. and R. Frow, *To make that Future – Now!* (Manchester, 1976); biographical information: E. and R. Frow, Manchester; Dr W.H. Fraser, Strathclyde Univ. OBIT. *Cotton Factory Times,* 15 Jan 1886; *Manchester City News,* 16 and 23 Jan 1886.

BARBARA NIELD
JOHN SAVILLE

SUTHERLAND, Mary Elizabeth (1895–1972)
LABOUR PARTY ORGANISER

Mary Elizabeth Sutherland was born on 30 November 1895. She was the second child and only daughter of Alexander Sutherland, farm-worker, and later crofter at Nether Anguston, Peterculter, a village on the north bank of the river Dee eight miles from Aberdeen. But Mary was born at Burnhead, Banchory Ternan, a few miles further up the river Dee; possibly this was the home of her maternal grandparents. Her mother was Jessie (née Henderson). Mary had two brothers. Alexander, born in 1894, graduated from Aberdeen University, and after serving in the First World War and being invalided home, joined the staff of the Liberal daily paper the *Aberdeen Free Press,* where he was sub-editor from 1916 to 1920. In 1921 he became assistant editor of the *Scottish Farmer,* and finally editor, a post he held until his death in 1951. The youngest of the family, James, who was also invalided home from the forces, became a successful farmer on Donside.

After attending the local school Mary won a bursary to the Girls' High School in Aberdeen. During her last years at school her mother was very ill with pulmonary tuberculosis – she died in 1911 – and Mary had to combine schooling with at least some of the nursing and housekeeping for the family. She travelled between Peterculter and Aberdeen every day, and continued to do so for a time at least after she went up to the University of Aberdeen, with a bursary, in 1913. At first she expected to take only an ordinary degree (that is, without honours), but she was recommended for another bursary which enabled her to take an honours course in history. She graduated in June 1917. During the next session she qualified as a teacher at the Aberdeen Training College. It was here that her special ability first appeared: in the account she gave almost twenty years later, she 'helped to organise the teachers in training and pressed for a minimum salary' [*Clarion,* 6 June 1934].

After a year of teaching at the Girls' High School she was from 1919 to 1920 assistant secretary to the Departmental Committee on Women in Agriculture in Scotland, and from February 1920 to November 1922 organiser for the Scottish Farm Servants' Union, founded in 1913 and led by Joseph Duncan. This was a suitable beginning for Mary's professional career: her father had been a farm-worker and was a Radical, her parish minister preached Socialist sermons and while still at school she 'found she was a Socialist' [ibid.]. During her years with the Farm Servants she travelled widely over Scotland, paying special attention to the unionising of women workers in agriculture. In 1922 her official travels extended to Europe, when she went as a delegate to the International Federation of Landworkers, which was meeting in Vienna. She also found time in those years to become vice-chairman of the Stirling Trades and Labour Council (1921–2).

The editorship of her union's journal, the *Scottish Farm Servant,* no doubt helped her to get her next job, that of sub-editor (Jan 1923 to Jan 1924) on the Glasgow ILP weekly, *Forward.* But she seems to have decided that she preferred organisational work to journalism, even Socialist journalism, and in 1924 she was appointed to the post of Labour Party women's organiser for Scotland, a position she held until 1932 when she became the national Labour Party's Chief Woman Officer, succeeding Dr Marion Phillips. In this capacity it was her business to advise and encourage women's sections of local Labour parties, to address meetings up and down the country, to arrange a number of annual conferences, and to edit the monthly journal *Labour Woman,* a publication which did a good deal to enlighten and educate novices in the women's sections. Moreover, she served on a number of important committees. Throughout her career as Chief Woman Officer she was secretary to the Standing Joint Committee of Industrial Women's Organisations (from 1941 the National Joint Committee of Working Women's Organisations). This body, set up in 1916, comprised representatives from the trade unions, the Co-operative Women's Guild and the Labour Party. During Mary Sutherland's secretaryship the members included such distinguished Labour women as Eleanor Barton (chairman 1934), Anne Loughlin (chairman 1935), Jennie Adamson, Susan Lawrence, Grace Colman and Dorothy Elliott. Its functions included presenting a 'policy document' (for which as secretary Mary Sutherland was largely responsible) to the annual conference of Labour women, and advising the NEC of the Labour Party on matters affecting women workers, such as factory act regulations, family allowances and social services policy. In the 1930s the Committee led a successful campaign for free school milk and for the extension of free school meals.

In foreign affairs the Committee was at this time concerned with India: it supported the Indian leaders' protest against the political imprisonments, and published a pamphlet on the Indian women's franchise.

From 1934 to 1938, on behalf of the Committee and the International Council of Social-Democratic Women, Mary Sutherland conducted a campaign – in which her own sympathies were firmly engaged – to obtain from the Soviet authorities the recall from banishment of a veteran Russian Socialist, Eva Broido, who had been tried and sentenced as a dissident in 1928. The effort to have her freed was unsuccessful; Broido is believed to have died in 1941. The whole affair, including the part played by Ivan Maisky, then Soviet ambassador to Britain, so angered Mary Sutherland that in 1937 she refused (as James Griffiths also refused) to attend a dinner given for Maisky by the Anglo-Russian Parliamentary Committee. She sent a copy of her letter of refusal to Eva Broido's daughter, Vera, who lived in London and with whom Mary Sutherland had been in close touch.

In the 1930s Mary Sutherland opposed with energy the views and activities of 'the extreme Left' in the Labour Party – the Socialist League, the United Front and all the other manifestations of what she condemned as Communism or crypto-Communism. In 1936 she wrote an agitated letter to the Labour Party's general secretary, Jim Middleton, reporting an account she had been given by a Labour Party member of a Socialist League meeting in Swansea at which J.T. Murphy had made a 'disloyal' speech attacking trade union leaders and Labour Party reformists; the sort of speech which constituted 'a subtle undermining of the faith of our people in the Party, the Trade Union movement and the "Herald"' [letter, 5 Mar 1936]. In 1937 she was urging members to back the Party's expulsion of the Socialist League, and trying to discourage Labour Party members, especially among the women's sections, from supporting the United Front.

In March 1941 Bevin as Minister of Labour established the Women's Consultative Committee to the Minister, to advise on matters affecting women workers during the war. The membership included representatives of women MPs from the three main parties, of women from trade unions, the Services, the BBC, and from important voluntary organisations such as the Red Cross and the WVS. Also included were the Chief Women Officers of the Labour and Conservative Parties. It was a heterogeneous body, but according to Dorothy Jones (née Elliott) it was remarkably successful [letter, 2 Apr 1979].

During the Second World War Mary Sutherland became closely involved, along with William Gillies, secretary of the International Department at Transport House, in a Labour anti-German group. In October 1941 Gillies prepared a document entitled 'German Social Democracy: notes on its foreign policy.' Its general argument was that no German, not even a Social Democrat, could ever again be entrusted with power; and in these notes, and subsequently, Gillies and those who agreed with him were in general sympathy with Vansittart's *Black Record* (1941). The notes by Gillies were the beginning of a bitter struggle inside the war-time Labour Party over the problem of Germany in the post-war world. Among the prominent personalities supporting Gillies were George Dallas, A.J. Dobbs and James Walker; and by 1942 the Fight for Freedom group had been established to carry the anti-German argument to the widest possible audience [Burridge (1976) Ch. 5]. Mary Sutherland was never a prominent figure in this campaign, but because of her official position she must have been a powerful ally.

In 1946 the Labour Government set up the National Institute of Houseworkers, which continued in being until the 1970s; in 1963 the name was changed to the National Institute for Housecraft. Its function was to raise the status of domestic employment by training women who would become domestic workers in institutions such as hospitals, and 'Home Helps' under local health authorities. Dorothy Elliott was chairman of the Institute from 1946 to 1962, and Mary Sutherland was on the Board of Directors from 1946 to 1966. The report for 1966–7 pays tribute to her zeal, and the chairman has noted her 'passionate belief in the status of Domestic Workers'. Mary was also secretary (1964–5) and a trustee of the Houseworker Trust.

At some time she was a member of the Fabian Women's Group, which was one of the women's organisations presenting evidence to the R.C. on Equal Pay (1945–6); according to Dame Margaret Cole, Mary Sutherland 'took [an] active part' in the Group [*Times,* 20 Oct 1972]. After the war her political position in the Labour Party continued to be somewhat to the right of centre. She would have nothing to do with what she regarded as the Communist-dominated CND at the end of the 1950s, and she warmly supported British entry into the EEC.

She served for many years on a number of international bodies. She represented the British Labour women's movement on the Women's Committee of the Labour and Socialist International from 1932 to 1939. After the war she was British representative, from 1947 to 1952, on the UN Commission on the Status of Women; she stressed the importance of the Commission in the *Bulletin* for August 1955 and April 1962 of the International Council of Social-Democratic Women, a Council of which she was a member from 1955, and to whose *Bulletin* she contributed a number of articles from 1955 to 1964. In 1959 she was unanimously elected chairman of the Council.

She was especially interested in the position of women in the Scandinavian countries. In the summer of 1960 she attended the Congress of the Swedish Social Democratic Women's League (founded in 1920), 'to bring them the greetings of the National Executive and our Women's Sections', and she reported the Congress in the *Labour Woman* for September. Her international interests were reinforced by the friendships she made among women Socialist leaders from other countries, to whom she enjoyed offering hospitality when they visited Britain. She delighted in travelling and holidays abroad. All these experiences and interests combined to make her known both during and after the Second World War for her active aid and personal service to refugees of various nationalities.

In 1949 Mary Sutherland was awarded the CBE. In December 1960 she retired. At the Labour Party conference of the preceding October Bessie Braddock was called on to pay a tribute to her. It is worthy of note that Mary Sutherland had left the conference before the membership was asked to show its appreciation of her work. Bessie Braddock's speech was somewhat equivocal, in that it included both the information that the women's section was to be reconstructed (it should be said that this had also been done when her predecessor, Marion Phillips, retired) and the assertion that 'in the midst of all the debates and discussions and disagreements that we have, this Party will never forget to pay its respects and its compliments for the excellent work that they [the women officers] do throughout the movement. That is why I have been asked to move this message of thanks . . .'. After her retirement Mary Sutherland continued in a voluntary capacity to assist women's movements. In addition to her directorship on the National Institute for Housecraft until 1966 she was a member of the Women's Consultative Committee of the Ministry of Labour until 1965.

During her working years in London Mary Sutherland lived first in Highgate, then in West Kensington, and then, till she retired, in Collingwood House, Dolphin Square. After her retirement she took a flat in central London. According to a colleague her flats were always decorated in dark colours – and she herself habitually wore brown. It is clear from personal information and from photographs that Mary Sutherland was decidedly handsome. She had thick dark wavy hair, large well-set eyes and regular features; though not graceful but rather solidly built, she had a good carriage. She always read a great deal and over a wide range, from diplomatic history to Jane Austen, whom she greatly admired.

Mary Sutherland was a highly competent administrator and organiser. Mary Agnes Hamilton described her as 'one of the quite first-rate women I have known', who as Chief Woman Officer 'does an A1 job' [Hamilton (1944) 190–1]. And Dorothy Elliott, her colleague for many years, has described her professional qualities as follows:

> Mary would have been the perfect Permanent Secretary to a great government department . . . [she] was a perfect committee member – she had the patience to listen to long discussions and then often at a moment of impasse would come in with a quiet solution which was generally acceptable – a very important gift which gave her great status! She was indeed much loved and respected [letter of 2 Apr 1979].

Opinion about Mary Sutherland, however, was mixed, and there seems no doubt that she was a person of sharply contrasting dispositions. A close colleague, who worked with her for many years, wrote a frank appraisal:

> Mary was an excellent chief as far as I was concerned. She never interfered, she never complained of one's work . . . she stood by one but she was moody to a serious degree – one always had to wait to see what would be the state of her mind and her attitude the next day. I had holidays with her year after year and always knew in advance that there'd be some days almost a nightmare but there would be days that would be delightful. She was extremely sympathetic about any problems in one's job and understood the sort of life that we [political organisers] had to lead . . . She wrote extremely well – her written word was more effective than her speech because she had an impediment when addressing an audience tho' people who knew her earlier than I did say she hadn't it when working with the Scottish Farm Workers Union – I think in total those were happier days for her than her many years in Transport House where I think she became quite a "loner" . . . [letter, 8 Nov 1979].

Mary Sutherland loved London and would have liked to remain there, but she suffered a stroke, followed by a traffic accident, and these disablements seem to have led her to return to south-west Scotland, where relatives would be near, particularly her brother Alexander's widow, to whom Mary was much attached. She spent her last years in East Kilbride at 63 Dunlop Towers, Telford Road. She occasionally took part in local Labour functions, but her public life was ended. She had a second stroke, and died on 19 October 1972 at Hairmyres Hospital in East Kilbride. She died intestate. Her books were divided, the more elementary ones going to a local secondary school and the rest to Strathclyde University; but her papers were all destroyed by her nephew, Alexander's son. Whether she had asked for this to be done is not known.

Writings: 'Rebel born: Mary Sutherland tells how I began', *Clarion,* 16 June 1934; (with D.M. Elliott, NUGMW), 'The Factories Bill', *Labour Woman* (Dec 1936) 184; 'Malnutrition and Underfeeding', ibid. 185; Evidence with Women's Group of the Fabian Society to R.C. on Equal Pay 1945–6 XI *M of E* (non-parl.) App. XIX of vol. *4*; 'The Labour Party Organisation of Women', *Bull. of Int. Council of Social-Democratic Women* (BICSDW) *1*, no. 1 (Jan 1955) 3–6; 'British Labour Women's Jubilee', ibid. *2,* no. 3 (Mar 1956) 19–23; 'British Labour Women's Conference', ibid. *4,* no. 6 (June 1958) 34–5; 'Swedish Women in Conference',

Labour Woman 48, no. 9 (Sep 1960) 109, 113; 'United Nations Commission on the Status of Women', *BICSDW 7,* no. 5 (May 1961) 33–6; 'Living Memorial to a British Woman Leader, Mary Macarthur, 1880–1921', ibid. *8,* no. 4 (Apr 1962) 24–5; 'An International Report on Day Nurseries', ibid. no. 5 (May 1962) 30–2; 'Mary Saran', ibid. *10,* no. 2 (Feb 1964) 9–11. She edited *Labour Woman* from 1932 to 1960. See also references to her correspondence in Sources below.

Sources: (1) MS: Correspondence relating to Eva Broido, 1935–8, Mrs Vera Broido-Cohn, London [copies in *DLB* Coll.] and Labour Party archives; see also William Gillies papers, 1933–5 [WG/IND/223 and 275 (re Indian Women's franchise)], Socialist League papers 1937 [SL/35/21–2], Women Organisers' reports, 1936–7 [WORG/37] and NEC reports 1960–1 (re National Labour Women's Advisory Committee), Labour Party archives, London. (2) Newspapers: *Daily Herald,* 1932–49 *passim* [copies in *DLB* Coll.]; *Glasgow Evening News,* 30 Apr 1938; *Times,* 21 Oct 1940 and 'Sense and Sensibility' [on Mary Sutherland], *Times,* 12 May 1958; *Manchester Guardian,* 22 Sept 1941; *Reynolds News,* 25 July 1943 and 21 Sep 1947. (3) Other: M.A. Hamilton, *Remembering my Good Friends* (1944); V. Markham and F. Hancock, *Report on Post-War Organisation of Private Domestic Employment* Cmd 6650 (1944–5) 21 pp.; *TUC Report* (1947), (1949), (1951), (1953), (1957) [re National Institute of Houseworkers]; 'Women in the Under-developed Countries' [debate] *BICSDW 1,* nos. 7–8 (Aug 1955) 56–8; 'Mary Sutherland. The New Chairman', ibid. *5,* nos. 7–8 (July–Aug 1959) 55–6; *LP Report* (1960); 'New British Labour Woman Officer', *BICSDW 7,* no. 1 (Jan 1961) 6; 'Mary Sutherland', *Labour Woman, 49,* no. 1 (Jan 1961) 12–13; *Annual Reports* of the Institute of Houseworkers [later for Housecraft], 1962–3, 1963–4, 1964–5, 1966–7; A.I. Marsh and E.O. Evans, *Dictionary of Industrial Relations* (1973); biographical information: Dr N. Wattie, Glasgow; personal information: Mrs M. Auld, East Kilbride, Glasgow; Rt. Hon. Lady Bacon PC; Mrs Vera Broido-Cohn, London; Mrs K. Cope, London; Mrs M.H. Gibb OBE, Cambo, Morpeth; Mrs Dorothy M. Jones (née Elliott) CBE, Hereford; Ian Mikardo MP; Mrs Lucy Middleton, London; John Parker MP; Mrs M. Sutherland, Bearsden, Glasgow, sister-in-law. OBIT. *Times,* 23 and 26 Oct 1972; *Labour Weekly,* 23 Feb 1973; *LP Report* (1973).

MARGARET 'ESPINASSE

See also: †Marion PHILLIPS.

TREVOR, John (1855–1930)
FOUNDER OF THE LABOUR CHURCH

John Trevor was born on 7 October 1855 in Liverpool, the son of Frederick Francis Trevor, a linen draper, and his wife, Harriet, daughter of John Cripps of Wisbech. Both his parents died while he was young, and Trevor was brought up at Wisbech by his maternal grandmother, her husband and her unmarried daughter. The family were Johnsonian (Calvinistic) Baptists and Trevor became an earnest, dogmatic Christian. 'My earliest clear recollections', he wrote in his autobiography, 'are associated with the fear of Hell' [Trevor (1897) 4]. The rigours of his sect marked Trevor for life, and his search for an acceptable faith, which led him through Unitarianism to the Labour Church, may be understood in large measure as a reaction against the religious fundamentalism of his childhood associated with the sexual repression of his youth. He grew up, again in his own words, 'a nervous, lonely and unsociable child' [ibid., 12].

In 1871 he was articled to a Norwich architect; he 'worked, studied and brooded alone' [*Labour Annual* (1895) 188] for six years until ill health forced him to take an Australian voyage. In 1878 he went to the United States, where he spent a short period at Meadville (Pa)

Theological School to prepare for the Unitarian ministry. On his return to England, he studied for a short time at Manchester New College in London, but he was soon discouraged by preaching, and returned to architecture, married, and then in July 1884 retired to the country for three years, to Ballingdon in Essex, where he found 'his religion – a full, rich, free, obedient, harmonious life' [ibid., 188]. At Ballingdon he became involved in attempts to re-establish the Agricultural Labourers' Union and to unionise the mat-weavers of Glemsford. Subsequently in Manchester, Trevor was again involved in the organisation of mat-makers. After a second period of study at Manchester New College, from 1887 to 1888, he became assistant minister to Philip Wicksteed, in November 1888, at the Unitarian Chapel in Little Portland Street, London, where he remained until June 1890.

Wicksteed's own formative intellectual influences – Comte, W.S. Jevons, Henry George and the modernist Dutch theologian, Abraham Kuenen – had not made him a Socialist, but he shared with many of his intellectual contemporaries a profound concern with social and economic problems; and his advanced Liberalism was expressed in sympathetic humanist terms. He was a major influence on Trevor. C.H. Herford, Wicksteed's biographer, wrote that he recognised in Trevor a man 'who, otherwise frail and ineffectual, possessed something of poetic and prophetic power' [Herford (1931) 99]; and it was this appreciation that led Wicksteed to invite Trevor to join him in London and there Trevor was involved with the organisation of young people's clubs and influenced by Stanton Coit, from whom he learned the principles of club management. On Trevor's admission, it was on Wicksteed's "broad shoulders" that the Labour Church rested during Trevor's connection with it, and Wicksteed's affection for and belief in Trevor persisted into their old age. Trevor moved to Manchester in the summer of 1890, to take up the ministry of Upper Brook Street Chapel, and a year later in April 1891 heard Ben Tillett and Wicksteed at a national conference of Unitarian Churches deliver vigorous criticisms of the alienation of religion and the Churches from working-class life.

Trevor had already become aware of the ways in which current religious activity repelled many working people and entrenched anti-clericalism among them; and he was now moved to establish in Manchester the first Labour Church. He failed to win financial or other support from his own Unitarian congregation, but secured it from Wicksteed and others; and on 4 October 1891 the first service of the Labour Church was held in Chorlton Town Hall, Manchester. The meeting place was well filled; and after opening music from a string orchestra and a prayer from Trevor, there was a reading of James Russell Lowell's poem, 'On the Capture of Fugitive Slaves'. A Unitarian minister read the fifth chapter of Isaiah, the choir sang 'England Arise' and Trevor gave a sermon. He spoke of the need for bringing 'religion into the struggle', attacked the absence of support from the traditional churches, and concluded that what was required was 'a religious movement of their own outside the churches, which should allow them to live a righteous and godly life, and yet secure the freedom for which they lived' [*Workman's Times*, 9 Oct 1891].

On the second Sunday of the new Labour Church, Robert Blatchford spoke to a congregation that overflowed the hall; and support for the new type of organisation spread rapidly through the industrial North. Trevor and his own close associates were not, at first, involved in any proselytising. Indeed the main characteristics of the Labour Church movement were its spontaneity, its reflection of local conditions and the absence of any strong centralised direction. In January 1892 Trevor founded the monthly *Labour Prophet* (which became the quarterly *Labour Church Record* in 1898), and there were annual conferences from 1893. The connection between the spread of the ILP and the establishment of Labour Churches was close without being exclusive, and while the heaviest concentration of Churches was in the industrial centres in Lancashire and Yorkshire, the movement spread to Birmingham and the Midlands, South Wales, parts of Scotland, and to isolated centres elsewhere.

Trevor was not by temperament suited to the role of a national organiser, and his frequent illnesses and partial or complete withdrawals from public activity meant that local initiatives could and did flourish independently of developments elsewhere. His energies went most consistently into the *Labour Prophet* until his resignation in 1896, when he was succeeded for a time as editor by Reginald Beckett. Trevor also became chairman of the Labour Church Pioneers and the Labour Church Union, founded in 1893, which included among its activities fund raising for the movement. At its greatest extent, some twenty-five Labour Churches were members, nearly all in Yorkshire and Lancashire [Pelling (1954) 135].

Trevor's own understanding of the Labour Church's aims and purposes were stated in the five rather vague principles which were adopted at the establishment of the Labour Church Union in 1893. The labour movement was always to him a religious movement, and class bias was specifically denied. What the principles did was to add a vaguely defined spiritual dimension to the idea of the emancipation of labour, and they provided a sufficiently broad statement to allow the Labour Churches to offer a wide variety of reforming and reformist tendencies in their pulpits. At times there seemed to Trevor a danger that the spiritual side of the labour movement would be ignored. He felt this particularly about the connection of the Labour Churches with the ILP. In 1895 he attacked the Party – which he had helped to form – for 'failing to recognize the forces making for progress in other spheres of life, jealous and suspicious of any extension of their own principles where they touch man's deeper needs and higher aspirations.' 'All this', he added, 'I have been watching with perplexity and sorrow during the past twelve months . . .' [*Labour Prophet*, Feb 1895, quoted Pierson (1960) 472]. He accepted the Socialist objective of collective ownership of the means of production, but the essence of Socialism was the 'growing yearning of man toward man' [*The Labour Church in England* (1896)].

Trevor's views were in conflict with those of Fred Brocklehurst, another leading figure in the Labour Church movement, who was for a time secretary of the Labour Church Union. Brocklehurst took a much more secular approach to the aims and objectives of the movement, and argued strongly for what Trevor described as 'political supremacy'. Trevor's hope that the Labour Church would generate a new and lasting religious idealism was not to be fulfilled, and after 1900 – some commentators put it earlier – the movement entered upon a quite rapid decline. Much later his son, Stanley S. Trevor, wrote to D.F. Summers: 'My father once told me he lost interest in the Labour Church largely because it tended to become merely a Sunday meeting of Trade Unionists and so lost its religious character' [Summers (1958) 52]. Between 1891 and 1910 about 120 Labour Churches can be identified in the issues of the *Clarion* and *Labour Leader* [Pierson (1960) 478, n. 27]; but only one or two Churches survived the First World War. (It may be remarked that the upsurge of Socialism and the ILP after the 1906 election produced the foundation of nearly twenty new Labour Churches, but these were more secular and political than religious in outlook).

Trevor continued his formal association with the Labour Church movement into the early years of the new century. He and his family lived at Horsted Keynes in Ashdown Forest, Sussex, from 1897 until 1909. Here he had a smallholding and a studio, and organised annual religious summer schools. In 1902 he moved for a short time to Clerkenwell, East London, where he occupied a large flat, capable of holding several dozen at a meeting; and he issued a prospectus in November 1902 announcing the formation of the Labour Church Settlement and of his intention of making the Settlement a centre of social and intellectual life for the Labour Church movement. In 1909 he went to live in Hampstead, where one of his close friends was John Russell, principal of the pioneer co-educational King Alfred School. At this time Trevor was earning a somewhat precarious livelihood, working for some years as a professional photographer. He had a growing preoccupation with sexual questions and this appears to have caused a section of his family some embarrassment. The most explicit statement was *The One Life*, published in November 1909, but his appeal for the establishment of a new autonomous group, the 'Oasis', met with little success and does not seem to have emerged in any institutional form.

Trevor never wholly severed links with the Unitarian Church, and as late as 1922 to 1923 he was a 'supply' minister at Newbury, Berkshire. His last decade was one of increasing loneliness; and the year before his death in 1930 he wrote to a dismissed minister that he was 'completely in despair' of Unitarianism, as he was of all churches. They were 'all dependent on the capitalist class for their maintenance', with the obvious and inevitable result that 'God is working outside the churches' [letter to Rev. L.B. Short, 29 Jan 1929].

Trevor died on 7 January 1930 and was buried in Highgate Cemetery. No will has been located. He was married twice: first in 1881 to Eliza, his first cousin; they had four sons, only two of whom survived to adult life and she died in late 1894. His second marriage three months later was to Annie Jones Higham, who had nursed his wife through her illness and cared for the children. She died in 1919, having had two daughters. One of Trevor's sons, Hugh, emigrated to New Zealand, where, through the introduction of Harry Atkinson, founder in 1896, (inspired by Trevor), of the Socialist Church in New Zealand, he met and married a daughter of the Rev. James Hoare, founder of Our Father's Church. Although inclined towards the left, Hugh Trevor was not, according to his family, associated with Labour Church groups. A.J. Waldegrave visited John Trevor in his last years:

> Trevor at 73 had the same child-like simplicity he had at 40. In appearance he had a 'weak mouth', a sort of tiny twist in his mouth which was particularly obvious when he dispensed with his beard. He had a charming personality; he carried his attitude of 'aloofness from leadership' to an extreme. He was no orator, though he had a charming voice, resonant and pleasant. His manner was modest and frank [Summers (1958) 50].

Writings: 'Religion as Esprit de Corps', *Time 19* n.s. 8 (1888) 429–39; editor of *The Labour Church Hymnbook* (1892) and of the *Labour Prophet*, 1892–6; *God in the Labour Movement* (Labour Church Tracts, no. 1: 1892) 16 pp.; *An Independent Labour Party* (Labour Church Tracts, no. 2:1892) 16 pp.; *Theology and the Slums* (Labour Church Tracts, n.s. no. 1: 1894, repr. as Labour Prophet Tracts, no. 1: 1895) 14 pp.; *Man's Cry for God* (Labour Church Tracts n.s. no. 2: 1894) 11 pp.; 'The Labor Church: religion of the labor movement', *Forum 18* (1894–5) 597–601; *From Ethics to Religion* (Labour Prophet Tracts, no. 2: [1895?]) 16 pp.;*Our First Principle* (Labour Prophet Tracts, no. 3: [1895?]) 15 pp.; *The Labour Church in England* (Labour Prophet Tracts, no. 4: 1896) [16 pp.] [translated into Dutch and German]; *My Quest for God* (1897; 2nd ed. Horsted Keynes, 1908); *The One Life: a free occasional paper* no. 1. (Horsted Keynes, Nov. 1909) 36 pp. Trevor also edited the first and only issue of *Prophet* [a monthly magazine of personal and social life] (Mar 1894) which was intended to replace *Labour Prophet.*

Sources: (1) MS : Working papers of the late Rev. G.W. Brassington towards a life of Trevor, including two long letters from him: MRC, Warwick Univ. Library Ref: MSS 143; see also Trevor's own books: *My Quest for God* and *The One Life* and C. Cook, *Sources in British Political History 1* (1975) 126–7. (2) Other: *Labour Prophet*, 1892–5, succeeded by *Labour Prophet and Labour Church Record*, Manchester, 1895–8, then *Labour Church Record* (Horsted Keynes, 1899–1901); S.G. Hobson, *Possibilities of the Labour Church* (1893) 15 pp.; P.H. Wicksteed, *What does the Labour Church stand for?* (Labour Prophet Tracts, 2nd ser. no. 1.: [1895?]) 14 pp.; *Labour Annual* (1895) 188, 191; A. Woollerton, *The Labour Movement in Manchester and Salford* (Manchester ILP Branch pamphlet no. 1: 1907); C.H. Herford, *Philip Henry Wicksteed: his life and work* (1931); L. Thompson, *Robert Blatchford: portrait of an Englishman* (1951); H. Pelling, *The Origins of the Labour Party 1880–1900* (1954, 2nd ed. 1965); K.S. Inglis, 'The Labour Church Movement', *Int. Rev. Social Hist. 3* (1958) 445–60, with note by H. Pelling, ibid. *4* (1959) 111–12 and reply 112–13; D.F. Summers, 'The Labour Church and Allied Movements of the Late Nineteenth and Early Twentieth Centuries' (Edinburgh PhD, 1958); H. Roth, 'The Labour Churches and New Zealand', *Int. Rev. Social Hist. 4* (1959) 361–6; S. Pierson, 'John Trevor and the Labour Church Movement in England,

1891–1900', *Church History 29* (1960) 463–78; K.S.Inglis, *Churches and the Working Classes in Victorian England* (1963); S. Pierson, *Marxism and the Origins of British Socialism* (Cornell Univ. Press, 1973); S. Yeo, 'A New Life: the religion of Socialism in Britain, 1883–1896', *History Workshop*, issue *4* (autumn 1977) 5–56.

JOHN SAVILLE
RICHARD STOREY

See also: Frederick BROCKLEHURST;* Stanton COIT.

TUCKWELL, Gertrude Mary (1861–1951)
TRADE UNIONIST AND CAMPAIGNER FOR WOMEN'S RIGHTS

Gertrude Mary Tuckwell was born in Oxford on 25 April 1861. She was the second daughter of the Rev. William Tuckwell and his wife Rosa (née Strong). William Tuckwell was the Master of New College School and a chaplain of New College until 1864. He was a celebrated Oxford personality, a fairly well-known writer, a Christian Socialist, and an advocate of tax and land reform; he was so appalled by the condition of agricultural labourers that he parcelled out the land he owned into smallholdings which he then let at £1 per acre with security of tenure. Gertrude Tuckwell recalled that her father would plead with his congregations to support 'the abolition of poverty, destitution and the Utopia that should be' [MS Reminiscences, 36]. He dedicated his autobiography, *Reminiscences of a Radical Parson* (1905) to Gertrude. From an early age therefore, Gertrude Tuckwell was exposed to an atmosphere of Christian radicalism; but an even more informative intellectual influence came from her maternal aunt, who later became Lady Dilke and was in those years married to Mark Pattison, the Rector of Lincoln College.

It was while Gertrude Tuckwell was staying with Mrs Pattison in 1878 that she met two active members of the Women's Trade Union League (WTUL), Edith Simcox and Alice Westlake, both of whom urged her to become a teacher. She went, therefore, as a boarder to a pupil teachers' training college in Liverpool. The city was a revelation to her; nothing could have provided a greater contrast with her comfortable life at Oxford or the parsonages in which she had been brought up. For the first time she came into direct contact with poverty and the slums. In 1882 she left Liverpool and went to Bishop Otter's College at Chichester, where she finished with a first class qualification two years later. From 1884 to 1890 or 1892 she taught in an elementary school under the London School Board, in Park Walk, Chelsea. She was paid a salary of £85 p.a., and lived modestly first in two rooms in Oakley Street and then in Tite Street, sharing her flat at some period with May Abraham. Gertrude Tuckwell was a progressive teacher, critical of the prevailing rigidity of discipline in overcrowded classes of up to seventy, and tried to compensate for the inadequacies of school life by inviting her pupils to tea at her home. It is clear from her writings at the time that she was aware of the deficiencies of formal teaching techniques in conditions such as were common among poor and slum children, who were often exhausted and undernourished, and obliged to help their families by earning a living as well as attending school; and it was this personal knowledge that led her to oppose all forms of half-time child labour. It was from these contacts with working-class children that Gertrude Tuckwell acquired some of the insight and sympathy shown in the investigation of children in State and voluntary institutions which she undertook either towards the end of her teaching career, or else soon after her resignation, which was partly precipitated by ill health. Her first book, *The State and its Children* (1894), bore the unmistakable mark of personal research and involvement in the lives of the unfortunate victims she described. Her criticism of reformatories, workhouses, asylums and hospitals demonstrated vividly her concern for the poor, whom she regarded as stunted and defenceless objects of neglect and abuse. She was somewhat less critical of voluntary bodies and their systems of child care. Her main plea was for a prohibition of half-time employment and a restoration of children to their parental homes. Unlike many of her contemporaries, she advocated, though as a last resort, State intervention and supervision of children in the absence of adequate parental care.

With her retirement from teaching Gertrude Tuckwell began to be involved in trade union and political work. At the outset she devoted herself to campaigning for an improvement in the condition of women workers through protective labour legislation and trade union organisation. Though firmly in favour of women's suffrage, based on adult suffrage reform [*Fortn. Rev.* (1906) 546], she preferred to work with Lady Dilke, Mary Macarthur, Margaret Bondfield and other leaders in the WTUL, and later the National Anti-Sweating League, the Women's Industrial Council and the Labour Party. She had been on the WTUL committee since 1891, and she became secretary to Lady Dilke in 1892 (in succession to May Abraham, who left to become the first woman factory inspector); she also became honorary secretary of the WTUL and editor of its journal, the *Women's Trade Union Review*, a post she held until 1905. She was especially active in the League's campaign for the protection of women workers from injuries sustained at work, particularly from lead poisoning and sulphuric necrosis, or 'phossy jaw'. From 1892 to 1895 she personally investigated the pottery industry areas, and the white lead mills of Newcastle-under-Lyme, which latter she described as 'death traps' [Tuckwell (1895) 5]. The 1895 Factory Act made notification of industrial poisoning compulsory and prohibited the employment of women in the worst of the dangerous trades; but it was not until 1897 that it became illegal to employ women in the manufacture and storage of white lead. Lead poisoning, however, continued to be endemic in the manufacture of pottery because of its use as an ingredient in the glaze. Gertrude Tuckwell therefore devoted herself to publicising leadless glaze pottery – encouraging shops to stock such ware, organising exhibitions of it and disseminating information on its use abroad. At the same time, through the medium of the League which ran a special Potteries Fund, she campaigned for the inclusion of industrial poisoning into workmen's compensation legislation.

The Factory and Workshop Act of 1901 prescribed the use of low solubility glazes containing no more than the 5 per cent standard, and prohibited the employment of women and young persons in other lead processes. Nevertheless, cases of poisoning continued to occur in large numbers. Her expertise in the field was acknowledged by her appointment in 1908 to the Departmental Committee on the Dangers attendant on the Use of Lead. The Committee's Report did not recommend outright prohibition of the use of lead in pottery glazes, in spite of overwhelming evidence that leadless glazes were equally effective; and Gertrude Tuckwell therefore registered her protest by issuing a dissenting Memorandum. She called upon the Home Office to compile a list of goods in which the use of lead would be prohibited and to ban the importation of articles containing lead glaze: as had been done in the case of those containing yellow phosphorus. Through their sympathisers and allies in Parliament, Gertrude Tuckwell and the League did not cease to press for industrial health legislation and for compensation to victims of industrial injury. Long-term phosphorus poisoning sometimes became evident only after many years' work in the industry, and it was one of Gertrude Tuckwell's aims to bring up such cases in Parliament, as she did for example through Will Crooks in 1904 [*Hansard*, 8 June 1904].

Gertrude Tuckwell also took up the struggle for protective legislation in the international arena. She joined the International Association for Labour Legislation in 1897 and went on to its executive committee in 1906. In 1904, at the instigation of Dr Stephen Bauer, the Association's secretary, she founded the British Section, with Sidney Webb as its Chairman and Arthur Henderson as honorary treasurer. Mary Macarthur, Constance Smith, Margaret MacDonald and Adelaide Anderson were among its active members. In 1910 Miss Tuckwell attended the international meeting at Lugano, where she presented a paper on lead poisoning, and she also intervened successfully against a resolution which attempted to keep women out of compositors' work on the ground of possible lead poisoning. She remained on the British Delegation list of the Association until 1920, although she did not attend every annual meeting.

Throughout the years of her campaign against what she called 'commercial manslaughter', when her chief aim was legislation to improve the conditions of women workers, she also compaigned against truck – a Departmental Committee of Inquiry into the Truck Acts was set up in 1906 and finished its work in 1908 – and she agitated for better workshop conditions, hours and pay. She warmly supported the fight for a minimum wage which began with Sir Charles Dilke's unsuccessful Wages Bill in 1897 and which gathered momentum during the next decade.

Gertrude Tuckwell had maintained her connection with the Christian Socialist tradition of her family through her collaboration with the Christian Social Union. In the 1890s she was a frequent speaker at the Union's meetings, and in 1898 became secretary of the Christian Social Union Research Committee, which had from 1896 onwards become a useful source of information by initiating inquiries into low-paid women's trades such as laundry work, food manufacture, fish curing, brush making and tea packing. When the Committee's chairman, Canon (later Bishop) Charles Gore resigned in 1911, Gertrude Tuckwell resigned also 'out of loyalty' but not on an issue of policy, and she handed over her work for the Committee to her close friend Constance Smith [MS Reminiscences, 186]. She also appeared on other Church platforms in order to forward the various demands of working women: she spoke on these themes at the Pan-Anglican Congress of 1908 and again at the Church Congress of 1911.

The agitation against sweating had been developing from the later 1880s; and in the early years of the century after 1900 the campaign reached national proportions. Gertrude Tuckwell, along with Mary Macarthur was deeply involved. Throughout the campaign Tuckwell's conception of sweating was imaginatively broad. In addition to the obvious and much discussed areas of sweating, she urged legislators to concern themselves with all workshop manufacture as well as the less publicised occupations such as office work, where girl clerks were being paid a wage of 10*s* per week [*Worker's Handbook* (1908) 24]. The Sweated Trades Exhibition of 1906 sponsored by the *Daily News* and mounted at the Queen's Hall, showed actual work being done in authentic conditions. It was a spectacular success and subsequently toured the provinces. Gertrude Tuckwell took part in the formation of the National Anti-Sweating League and in arranging the Guildhall Conference on the Minimum Wage in 1907. This conference brought together civil servants, trade unionists, Socialists and representatives from Australia and New Zealand. In 1907, as the recognised authorities on women's employment, Gertrude Tuckwell and Mary Macarthur appeared before the S.C. on Home Work. The years of agitation and the increased Labour group in a Liberal Parliament finally yielded results, and in 1909 the first Trade Boards Act was passed.

Ever since the time in 1891 when she first joined the WTUL Gertrude Tuckwell had done a great deal of public speaking in the cause of women and women's trade unionism, and was regarded as 'one of the most famous women speakers in England' [Norman (1951) 123]. Tuckwell believed in women's trade unionism not only as a means of improving working conditions but also because it assisted in raising women's consciousness. As she wrote in 1902: 'A girl can be turned from the average limited dolly person to a thinking citizen and this marvel can be worked by Trade Unionism' [*Postal Clerk's Herald* (Sep 1902) 1]. She travelled up and down the country to address meetings and organise union branches. Her audiences were mixed: the Women's Liberal Associations, branches of the ILP, the Student Christian Movement, the Christian Social Union, the National Union of Women Workers, and women's trade societies. Some of these women's trade unions were tiny; but none was too small for her encouragement. The National Union of Dressmakers' and Milliners' Assistants whose total receipts in 1906 were £5 12*s* 2*d* recorded her presence at their AGM [Tuckwell papers, 504]. In 1899 she had appeared before the S.C. on the Aged Deserving Poor, where she testified that women workers earned far too little to be able to contribute to pension funds, or friendly societies. It was typical of her diligence in these matters that before presenting herself to the

Committee she prepared her evidence by obtaining information from women co-operators about insurance and friendly society benefits.

Gertrude Tuckwell became president of the WTUL in 1905, succeeding Lady Dilke, with Mary Macarthur continuing as secretary. In 1908 she also became the president of the National Federation of Women Workers (NFWW) which had been founded in 1906, under the aegis of the WTUL, by Mary Macarthur who was its general secretary from 1908 to 1921; its object was to organise women workers who were not being admitted to other unions. Gertrude Tuckwell remained active in both organisations until 1918, when she announced her retirement. She withdrew effectively from both organisations when on 1 January 1921 the WTUL was merged with the NFWW, which in turn formally merged with the Women Workers' Section of the NUGMW on the same date.

From about 1908 Gertrude Tuckwell began to be treated as the elder and respected pioneer of womens' unionism, and was accorded a deference sometimes denied to her younger friend and collaborator, Mary Macarthur. W.J. Davis, a bitter opponent of women's employment in brass manufacture, complained in 1908 about Mary Macarthur's uncompromising pressure for women to be accepted in the Brassworkers' Union. 'I feel sure', he wrote, 'that Miss Tuckwell and the Lady Organisers do not share the view expressed by Miss Macarthur' [Tuckwell papers, letter to Miss Smythe, 17 Sep 1908]; and Tuckwell herself recalled how differently Lloyd George had treated Mary Macarthur and herself [MS Reminiscences, 234]. In 1911 she suffered a personal loss from which she found it hard to recover, by the death of her uncle by marriage, Sir Charles Dilke. She became ill, and went to Egypt to recuperate. She cherished his memory and that of his wife (who had died in 1904). Dilke had designated her as his literary executor. So she undertook the task of writing her uncle's biography and vindicating his memory. She shouldered most of the responsibility, for her co-author Stephen Gwynn MP neglected the work for a good deal of the time. It was in the same spirit of dedication that she tried to clear Dilke's name of the scandal that had ruined his political career; but in the course of this undertaking she unfortunately destroyed many of his papers for fear that they contained incriminating material. She deposited the remainder in the British Museum in 1939.

For some time after the First World War Gertrude Tuckwell continued to appear on WTUL and NFWW platforms and was still a recognised representative of women's industrial interests. In 1918, together with Mary Macarthur, she was appointed to the Labour Advisory Panel of the Engineering Trades Committee which had been set up by the Ministry of Reconstruction to investigate the state of the engineering industry in the post-war period, and the possibilities it held for women's employment. She was also a member of several other advisory panels appointed by the Ministry of Reconstruction, and from 1920 to 1922 she was a member of the Central Committee on Women's Training and Employment. From 1905 to 1923 she was a member of the Advisory Committee to the Ministry of Health.

Gertrude Tuckwell emerged from the war an ardent supporter of equal pay for women as the only system which could guarantee levels for men, and for women fair returns for work done. In common with other women in the Labour Party she was one of the first at the time to support the endowment of motherhood, and the payments to widows and invalids which were being demanded in the minority report of the War Cabinet Committee on Women in Industry; she was also in favour of children's allowances: a measure being vigorously advocated by Eleanor Rathbone. At a later date, however, Gertrude Tuckwell modified her views on the subject of children's allowances; she came to regard them as a possible threat to workers' wage levels, and on being asked her opinion on the subject she replied: 'I have never been clear that family allowances would not adversely affect the raising of wages ... In any case I should not be prepared to advocate any proposal which had not the agreed support of the workers whom it would affect' [Rice (1939) 207].

The post-war period of Gertrude Tuckwell's life was marked by new and different public activities and by a revival of the practical, social and Christian concerns of her early years. She had throughout remained a member of the Church of England, and it was said about her that 'she always wanted the Church to lead the way in caring for God's family' [Norman (1951) 124]. It was partly in a Christian spirit, therefore, that she turned her energies after the war to the magistracy, probation, women's health and maternity services. In 1920 she was appointed JP for St Pancras and thus became one of the first women magistrates in England, and at the same time was chosen as a Labour member, together with Beatrice Webb, of the Lord Chancellor's [Birkenhead] advisory committee for the selection of women justices [MS Reminiscences, Ch. 20, a-c and *Hansard*, 26 Apr 1920]. She retired from the bench in 1931. She was always active in the Magistrates' Association, which was founded in 1920, and in 1921 was elected to its Council, a position she held until June 1940. She was also a member of the Association's Treatment of Offenders Committee and the Poor Persons' Defence Committee, through which she campaigned for the extension of legal aid. At the same time she channelled her lifelong concern for children and juveniles into probation work, and became deeply committed to extending its reforming functions 'which if properly developed will do away with crime' [Tuckwell (July 1933) 244]. She saw crime as taking its origin from poverty and deprivation [see article in the *Magistrate* (Jan 1928)] and she became interested in the possible correlation between the physiology of delinquents and their crimes, and in the biological basis of the delinquent personality. In 1927 she became president of the National Association of Probation Officers, vice-president of the National Association of Probation Officers, vice-president in 1930, and was its chairman from 1933 to 1941.

Her comfortable social standing and material circumstances, as well as her reputation, gave her opportunities to mingle with people of influence. During this period her house at 13 Chester Terrace became an informal meeting place for her friends in the world of social reform and in the Establishment, both Labour and Conservative. This easy access to the world of power also meant that she could count on a receptive audience when she decided to start a project. For example, it was during her presidency (1922 to 1929) of the Women Sanitary Inspectors' and Health Visitors' Association that, together with her friend May Tennant, she launched in 1928 the Maternal Mortality Conference; and until 1937 she remained active in the effort to reduce maternal mortality. Her concern for women's health was intensified by her participation in the R.C. on National Health Insurance of 1926. She dissented from the Commission's recommendations and signed the minority report, which criticised a strict adherence to the contributory principle and to insurance schemes linked to approved societies. The minority report also recommended the provision of medical care for children and the extension of benefit to women of child-bearing age. She campaigned in person for better maternity services and a higher sickness benefit. Her work was facilitated by her personal friendship with Dame Janet Campbell and Sir George Newman [MS ibid., Ch. 28]. She was also a member of a Committee of Enquiry on the Liberty of Trade Unions and Professional Associations under the auspices of the International Association for Social Progress. A report of the British section of this was published in June 1936.

Throughout her active years in the labour movement Gertrude Tuckwell formed close personal links, and sometimes shared households, with many women colleagues, among them May Abraham (who married H.J. Tennant in 1896), Mona Wilson, Constance Smith, and towards the end of her life, her last companion, Jennet Lush. After the death of her close friend, Mary Macarthur, with whom she had worked for twenty-one years, she became chairman of the Mary Macarthur memorial which was set up to provide scholarships to women who worked in the trade union and labour movement. She was also a member of the committee which ran the Mary Macarthur Home for Working Women at Ongar, Essex.

Gertrude Tuckwell was a sociable woman, who could establish easy relations with politicians of all parties. She was described by one of her associates as having a 'distinguished appearance, being rather imperious in manner, and having about her an air of plumes, lace and elegant clothes' [Norman (1951) 123]. Gertrude Tuckwell was made a CH in 1930. For the last twenty years of her life she made her home at Little Woodlands. Wormley, Godalming, Surrey. She died on 5 August 1951 aged ninety at the Royal Surrey Hospital, survived by her brother Henry

Maurice and by her companion Jennet Lush. She left an estate of £12,685 to be shared between them, apart from a few bequests including the last portrait (1908) of Sir Charles Dilke by William Strang to the National Portrait Gallery and a smaller portrait of him by the same artist to the Historical and Ethnological Museum in Athens, to commemorate Sir Charles's attachment to Greece.

Writings: (1) MS: Reminiscences and correspondence etc., Tuckwell papers, TUC Library, London. (2) Other: *The State and its Children* (1894); *The Jeopardy of a Department!* (WTUL, [c.1895]) 7 pp.; *Women's Work and Factory Legislation: the amending act of 1895* [paper read before the Fabian Society] (1895) 18 pp.; 'Competition among Manual Workers' in *Official Report of the Conference held at Manchester on 27–30 Oct 1896* (NUWW, 1896) 103–12; 'Commercial Manslaughter' [lead-poisoning], *19th C. 44* (July–Aug 1898) 253–8; Evidence before S.C. on the Aged Deserving Poor, *M of E* 1899 VIII Qs 1755–1953; 'A Seventeen Hours Working Day', *Fortn. Rev. 71* o.s. 65 n.s. (May 1899) 783–8; 'The Government Factory Bill of 1900', ibid., *73* o.s. *67* n.s. (June 1900) 972–9; 'The More Obvious Defects in our Factory Code' in *The Case for the Factory Acts*, ed. B. Webb (1901) 124–68; 'What a Trade Union can do' [addressed to the young ladies in Post Office employment], *Postal Clerk's Herald 5*, no. 49 (Sep 1902) 1–2; 'The Industrial Position of Women', *Ind. Rev. 3*, no. 11 (Aug 1904) 365–76; 'Women's Opportunity', *Fortn. Rev.* n.s. *79* (Jan–June 1906) 546–56 [repr. as a pamphlet, WTUL [1907?] 12 pp.]; 'A Minimum Wage', *Ind. Rev. 11* no. 39 (Dec 1906) 297–304; Evidence before the S.C. on Home Work, *M. of E.* 1907 VI Qs 2331–689; 'The Radical Parson – Rev. W. Tuckwell', *Goodwill 14*, no. 2 (Feb 1907) 30–2; (with C. Smith), *The Worker's Handbook* (1908); 'Women's Trade Unions and "Sweated Industries"', *Socialist Annual* (1907) 63–6; 'Regulation of Women's Work' in *Women in Industry from Seven Points of View*, ed. D.J. Shackleton (1908) 2–23; *Sweating* (1908) 7 pp.; *The Factory Laws relating to Women* (Christian Social Union leaflet no. 17: 1908) 4 pp.; *Lead Poisoning in China and Earthenware Manufacture* (WTUL, [1910]) 8 pp.; Departmental Committee on the Dangers attendant on the Use of Lead and the Danger or Injury to Health arising from Dust and other Causes, *Report* 1910 XXIX, [Memorandum by Miss Tuckwell, 245–6]; (with others), *Industrial Work and Industrial Laws* ed. for the Industrial Law Committee by Mrs H.J. Tennant (1910) 42 pp.; 'Women's Liberal Federation', by Miss Tuckwell, 245–6]; 'Women Liberal Federation', *Monthly News* 5, 1 Mar 1914; (with S. Gwynn), *The Life of the Rt. Hon. Sir Charles W. Dilke Bart M.P.* 2 vols. (1917); 'Equal Pay for Equal Work', *Fortn. Rev. 105* (Jan 1919) 63–76; 'The Human Interest in Industry', ibid., *106* (July 1919) 91–103; 'Women's Employment' in *Labour Women on International Legislation* (Labour Party, [1919]) 5–10; 'Women in Industry', *19th C. 87* (Feb 1920) 331–43; (with others), 'Tributes to a Great Woman: Mary Macarthur, trade unionist and lover of freedom', *Labour Woman* 9, no. 2 (Feb 1921) 22–6; 'The Story of the Trade Boards Acts', *Cont. Rev. 120* (July–Dec 1921) 600–6; 'Health Visitors', *Trans JRSI 42*, no. 5 (1921–2) 298–301 [presidential address by Miss Tuckwell at Folkestone conference]; 'Trade Boards at the Cross Roads', *Labour Mag. 1*, no. 2 (June 1922) 81–3 [comments on the Report of the Cave Committee]; 'A Popular Whip' [Willie McArthur], *Cont. Rev. 124* (Dec 1923) 773–6; (with S.L. Gwynn), *A Short Life of the Rt. Hon. Sir Charles Dilke* (1925); 'National Health and the Royal Commission', *Cont. Rev. 129* (June 1926) 750–5; 'National Health Insurance from the Labour Point of View', *Labour Mag. 5*, no. 4 (Aug 1926) 159–61; 'Maternal Mortality', *COPEC News 4* (Jan 1928) 9; 'Towards Justice' [from an address given before the Magistrates' Association in Oct 1927], *Magistrate 1* (Jan 1928) 215; 'The Need for Women Officers' [address], *Probation 1*, no. 1 (July 1929) 6–7; 'Looking Backwards: fifty years of social reform', *Listener*, 3, no. 58, 19 Feb 1930, 323–4; 'The Need for a Probation Library', *Probation 1*, no. 7 (Apr 1931) 97–8; *Constance Smith*: *a short memoir* with a Preface by Bishop Gore (1931) 48 pp.; 'On Probation': the door through which thousands of boys and girls escape from disaster', *John Bull*, *51*, no. 1347, 9 Apr 1932, 8–9; 'That Mother needn't die', ibid., *52*, no. 1379, 19 Nov 1932, 21; 'The Clarke Hall Fellowship', *Probation 1*, no. 14 (Jan 1933) 209–

10; 'Retrospect and Prospect', ibid. *1*, no. 16 (July 1933) 244 and 248; 'The New Women's Crime and how to deal with it', *John Bull 56*, no.1464, 7 July 1934, 9; 'Who made that Carnival Hat? Sweating still goes on' [Interview between Irene Clephane and Gertrude Tuckwell about the passing of the first Trade Boards Act in 1909], *Reynolds's Illustrated News*, no. 4, 398, 16 Dec 1934, 10; 'Our Zenith: have we reached it?', *Probation 2,* no. 1 (July 1935) 3–4 [chairman's address to 23rd Annual Conference of Probation Officers]; 'The Factories Bill', *Labour 4*, no. 7 (Mar 1937) 171; (with others), *Report on Nutrition* (British Association for Labour Legislation, 1938); Foreword to M. Miller, *Labour in the U.S.S.R.* (British Association for Labour Legislation, 1942).

Sources: (1) MS: see Writings above; Christian Social Union papers [including *Handbooks* (1911–13) and *Lists* (1895–1914)] and Pattison correspondence (1879–83) Add.MSS 44886, all at BL; further correspondence, Lady Dilke to Gertrude Tuckwell (1868–88) MS Pattison 139, Bodleian Library, Oxford. (2) Other: *Woman's Signal*, 13 Sept 1894; Women's Industrial Council, *Annual Reports* (1902–15); *Hansard*, 8 June 1904, cols. 1065–6; 'Chats with Women Workers', *Hearth and Home 30*, no. 780, 26 Apr 1906, 1144; 'Miss Tuckwell', *Woman Worker 1*, no. 1 (Sep 1907) 7; *Report of the Inquiry into the Wages of Women and Girls in the Following Trades: fruit preserving, pickle making, confectionery, tea packing, coffee and cocoa packing, biscuit making* (CSU, 1913) 12 pp.; Anon. 'The Story of Sir Charles Dilke: two peeps into Miss Tuckwell's great book', *Woman Worker* n.s. no. 23 (Nov 1917) 3; B. Drake, *Women in Trade Unions* [1920]; *Hansard*, 26 Apr 1920; R.C. on National Health Insurance, *Report* 1926 XIV [Gertrude Tuckwell was one of the signatories of the Minority Report]; J.R. Johnston, 'Gertrude Tuckwell', *Millgate* (June 1931) 551–6; M.J. Symons, 'Gertrude Tuckwell', *Labour Mag*. (July 1931) 99–100; G. Crosse, *Charles Gore: a biographical sketch* (1932); W. Citrine et al., 'How Women played their Part' [Discussion] in *Seventy Years of Trade Unionism 1868–1938* [TUC, 1938] 65–79 *passim*; M. Spring Rice, *Working Class Wives: their health and conditions* (Women's Health Enquiry Committee, 1939); M.A. Hamilton, *Women at Work: a brief introduction to trade unionism for women* (1941); M. Bondfield, *A Life's Work* [1949]; *WWW* (1951–60); *Women in the Trade Union Movement* (TUC, 1955) ; S. Lewenhak, *Women and Trade Unions: an outline history of women in the British trade union movement* (1977); *Women in the Labour Movement: the British experience* ed. L. Middleton (1977); J. Morris, 'The Gertrude Tuckwell Collection', *History Workshop* issue 5 (spring 1978) 155–62; N.C. Soldon, *Women in British Trade Unions 1874–1976* (Dublin, 1978); Sir T. Skyrme, *The Changing Image of the Magistracy* (1979). OBIT. *Times,* 6 Aug 1951; *Labour Woman 39*, no. 8 (Sep 1951); H.E. Norman, 'Gertrude Tuckwell: a memoir', *Probation* (Sep–Oct 1951) 123–4; *Magistrate* (Oct 1951); *TUC Report* (1952).

MARION KOZAK

See also: †Margaret Grace BONDFIELD; †Emily (Emilia) Francis STRONG, Lady DILKE; †Arthur HENDERSON; †Mary MACARTHUR.

WALLWORK, Daniel (1824–1909)
CHARTIST AND SECULARIST

Daniel Wallwork was born in the village of Littleborough, Lancashire, on 5 December 1824, the son of Howarth Wallwork, fulling miller, and his wife Ann Wallwork (née Whitworth). One of a large family, he received an elementary education at the village school, later supplemented by attendance at a night school, and went to work in a factory at the age of twelve.

Wallwork became interested in social and political issues in his youth. He attended Sunday school, and became a Sunday school teacher and church member. He was influenced by the spread of the temperance movement in Lancashire in the 1830s; as an old man he was fond of recalling the drunkenness of industrial towns, and the battle between the champions of moderation and of total abstinence. In 1841 he signed the teetotal pledge, and shortly afterwards he became secretary of the Perseverance tent of the Independent Order of Rechabites at Heywood, a position he held for a number of years.

Wallwork was also involved in the factory reform movement in the 1840s, and became an agent for the *Ten Hours' Advocate*. When the fact became known to his employer, an opportunity was taken to discharge him. He subsequently worked in a number of industrial towns in Lancashire and Yorkshire, until in 1848 he moved to Dudley, where he lived for fifteen years.

Soon after Wallwork's arrival in Dudley he was befriended by a Mr Truman, a locksmith and sheet metal worker, and a local temperance enthusiast, who offered to teach the young man his trade. On 7 January 1851 Wallwork married Fanny Truman, daughter of Joseph Truman (presumably Wallwork's master and benefactor). The couple set up house in Flood Street, Dudley. Their marriage was childless.

During the 1850s, Dudley was a centre of radicalism and dissent, with the most militant Chartist movement in the Black Country, led by the radical draper Sam Cook. Wallwork was a prominent local activist throughout the decade, particularly in the later years. In May 1857 Ernest Jones proposed a national conference of reformers, at which Chartists and middle-class radicals would meet to evolve a programme for comprehensive suffrage reform. The scheme provided the impetus for a minor Chartist revival in the Black Country, and after a series of district meetings Wallwork was elected in August to be regional delegate to the conference. When this took place in March 1858, Wallwork played an active part, vehemently urging that Jones should constitute a one-man executive for the movement. The proposal was adopted after a debate. Wallwork also acted as secretary of the Dudley district Charter Association during 1857–8. When Sam Cook died in 1861, Wallwork wrote his obituary for the local press.

Chartism was only one aspect of the radical sub-culture of Dudley. The class-conscious working men of the town were also keenly interested in education and self-improvement. Cook and Wallwork were both committee members of the Dudley Mechanics' Institute during the years 1857–60, and Wallwork was a founder of a literary and debating class formed as a subsidiary of the Institute by younger members in 1855. The Mechanics' Institute, however, was controlled by a middle-class élite who were highly sensitive to the discussion of certain issues. One clause in its constitution stated that 'No political questions, or religious controversies shall at any time be introduced, and all publications of an immoral or irreligious tendency shall be totally excluded' [quoted in a letter published in the *Dudley Weekly Times*, 24 Oct 1857]. Unable to obtain the repeal of this obnoxious rule, the Dudley radicals established a series of *ad hoc* rival educational organisations: the Dudley Mutual Improvement Society (*fl.* 1851–4), the Temple of Investigation, the Manhood Suffrage Association and the Working Men's Institute (*fl.* 1859–64).

Wallwork took part in the affairs of each of these bodies, but his views on religion often provoked controversy. By 1853 he had thrown off the religious convictions of his youth, and had become a belligerent and outspoken atheist. In 1856 he became a Black Country correspondent for G.J. Holyoake's journal, the *Reasoner*, and organised an informal secularist discussion group in Dudley. Appearing at Worcester Assizes the following year as a witness in a case of theft, Wallwork denied the truth of the Bible and exercised his right to affirm instead of testifying on oath. When, in March 1859, the Dudley secularists helped to establish the Working Men's Institute in a former Methodist New Connexion schoolroom in New Mill Street, Samuel Quartus Cook – the son of the Chartist leader – became president, and Wallwork acted as secretary and librarian. During the summer and autumn of 1860, however, the Working Men's Institute was convulsed by a series of disputes. There was trouble over financial irregularities; over the introduction of 'infidel productions' into the reading room and the committee's policy of opening the reading room on Sundays; and with the institution's sponsorship of a series of public lectures in Dudley by the well-known secularist Joseph Barker. The situation was resolved in October 1860 when Wallwork resigned his position; he and some sympathisers then severed all further connections with the Institute.

Wallwork continued to propagate secularism in the Black Country, particularly in the Oldbury area, where a secularist group bought the local temperance hall as a meeting place in 1861. In August of that year an apparently short-lived Midlands Secular Union was established, based on Oldbury with Wallwork acting as secretary and chief propagandist. His secularist beliefs also estranged Wallwork from the Dudley Temperance Society. He had joined the Society in 1853 when it was revived after several years' abeyance, and he became secretary in 1855, when he also helped to establish an auxiliary of the United Kingdom Alliance in the town. The temperance cause flourished, and by 1860 there were four distinct societies in Dudley. In February 1861, however, an editorial in the *National Reformer* commented caustically on the omission of Wallwork from the speakers' panel of the Dudley Temperance Society: 'the sole reason . . . was owing to his theological opinions.' He was also blackballed by a co-operative society formed in Dudley in November 1861, on account, it was said, of his conduct as a member of the temperance society and Working Men's Institute.

In the spring of 1863, Daniel Wallwork emigrated to New South Wales. He apparently decided to leave Dudley because of the economic depression in the town in the early 1860s. His choice of destination was influenced by an earlier emigrant. In March 1858, George Bewick, inspector of the permanent way of the Oxford, Worcester and Wolverhampton Railway, and a committee member of the Dudley Temperance Society, emigrated to Newcastle, New South Wales, having obtained a similar post in the service of the New South Wales Government Railways. The two men kept in contact, and when Wallwork arrived in Australia in autumn 1863 he proceeded straight to Newcastle. The day after his arrival he was taken on as a labourer on the Hexham branch of the Newcastle to Maitland line. He subsequently obtained a post as a machinist in the locomotive yards at Newcastle.

Wallwork worked for the NSW Government Railways until his retirement in 1892. During 1870 and 1871 he co-ordinated a successful campaign among railway workers in Newcastle and Sydney to secure an eight hour day, culminating in a mass rally in the Sydney Temperance Hall. 'It is claimed', his obituary says, 'that he was the originator of the eight-hour system in New South Wales' [*Newcastle Morning Herald*, 14 Oct 1909]. On several occasions he negotiated with the Government on behalf of Newcastle railway workers over entitlement to paid holidays and superannuation payments. His workmates presented him with a watch and gold chain and a purse of sovereigns in recognition of his efforts on their behalf.

Wallwork also continued his social and political activities in Australia. He became secretary of a secular society which had been set up in Newcastle in 1862, operated a lending library, and held debates with local Methodist revivalists. For some years he sent reports of meetings to the *National Reformer*. He opposed a campaign in favour of Sunday observance in Newcastle in April 1866. He was a prolific writer in the correspondence columns of the *Newcastle Morning Telegraph*, particularly on the subject of temperance, and was a member of the Newcastle lodge of the Sons of Temperance for forty years.

After the death of his first wife, the date of which is not known, Daniel Wallwork married again at Honeysuckle Point, New South Wales, in February 1871. His second wife, Emily Goodsir, was a widow born in Reading, England. She gave birth to their only child, Ernest, in December 1872 at their home in Blane Street (later Hunter Street West), Newcastle. She died in April 1883. Wallwork revisited England in 1893 and again in 1900 and on one of these visits he married his third wife, a Miss Horrocks.

In 1897 Daniel Wallwork moved from Newcastle to the suburb of Carrington, one mile to the north across the Hunter river. During his residence there he supported the establishment of a school of arts and other public works; and he played cricket for a local team, although he was now in his seventies. He suffered a stroke in July 1909, and died at his home in Young Street, Carrington, on 12 October 1909. He was survived by his wife and son.

Sources: (1) MS: Register of Marriages, St Thomas, Dudley, 1851; Census Schedules for 1851 and 1861, Township of Dudley, District of St Thomas; Register of Marriages in New South Wales, 1871; Register of Births in New South Wales, 1872. (2) Newspapers: *Wolverhampton Chronicle*, 1850–62; *People's Paper*, 1852–8; *Berrow's Worcester J.*, 1855–61; *Wolverhampton J.*, 1855; *Reasoner*, 1856–9; *Dudley and Midland Counties Express*, 1857–8; *Dudley Weekly Times*, 1857–8; *Birmingham Daily Post*, 1859–62; *Reasoner Gazette*, 1860; *National Reformer*, 1861–7; *Newcastle Chronicle* [NSW], 1865–6; *Newcastle Morning Telegraph* [NSW], 1866–7; *Newcastle Morning Herald* [NSW], 1883. (3) Other: Samuel Cook Poster Coll., Dudley PL for: 'At a Public Meeting held in the Lancasterian School Room . . . 10 September 1857' (Poster 302) and 'Mutual Improvement Society, Five Ways Dudley . . .' (Poster 644); *Knagg's Newcastle Almanac*, 1879–97, *passim*; C.F.G. Clark, *The Curiosities of Dudley and the Black Country, from 1800 to 1860 . . .* (Birmingham, 1881); 'Working Men's Institute' in *Blocksidge's Dudley Almanac* (1899) 121–3; E. Blocksidge, 'History of the Dudley Mechanics' Institution, afterwards called "The Dudley Institute"' ibid. (1905) 73–105 and (1906) 45–59; *The Federal Directory of Newcastle and District for 1909*; A. McLagen, *History of Newcastle District Trade Unions* vol. *1: To 1918* (NSW, 1955); G.J. Barnsby, 'The Working-Class Movement in the Black Country, 1815 to 1867' (Birmingham MA, 1965); idem, *The Dudley Working-Class Movement 1832–1860* (Dudley, 1967) 48 pp.; idem, 'Chartism in the Black Country, 1850–1860' in *The Luddites and Other Essays* ed. L.M. Munby (1971) 93–114; E. Royle, *Victorian Infidels* (Manchester, 1974); personal information: Frank Wallwork, Kogarth, NSW, grandson; Miss Jennifer Affleck, Pymble, NSW, great-granddaughter. Obit. *Newcastle Morning Herald* [NSW], 14 Oct 1909.

John Rowley

See also: Samuel Cook; Samuel Quartus Cook; Joseph Linney; Arthur George O'Neill.

WATSON, William Foster (1881–1943)

ENGINEERING SHOP STEWARD

William, or 'Billie' Watson as he was commonly called, was born at 56 Hardinge Street, east London, on 19 August 1881, the son of William John Watson, a lithographic printer, and his wife Elizabeth Catherine (née Hill). Billie Watson started part-time work at the age of ten in a local oil chandlers and began full-time employment two years later. He worked for a year or so as a clerk, and then moved to the Bell Punch and Printing Company, Tabernacle Street, Finsbury. So began his career as an 'itinerant mechanic' – the title he gave to his autobiography – for he moved constantly from one London workshop to another. His parents could not afford the premium for an apprenticeship, but over the years he learnt the trade of turning. By the time he was twenty-one he had persuaded one management to pay him the craftsman's rate, and he was then admitted into the Tower Hamlets branch of the Amalgamated Society of Engineers, on 24 May 1902. Within a few years he began to take an active interest in trade unionism, and when a lock-out was instituted on 1 January 1907 by the management of Speedwell's, where he was working, he was elected to the position of secretary of the local strike committee. The strike lasted for three months, and was unsuccessful; but as a result of his experiences, Watson began to move towards Socialist ideas.

By 1910 he had transferred his union membership to the Chiswick branch, and it was in this year that he began to work for the amalgamation of all unions in the engineering industry. Late in 1910 a provisional committee was established and from then on Watson was to be the outstanding personality in London in the amalgamation movement. He must have been influenced by the ideas of Tom Mann, but there is no evidence of any contact between them before September 1912; and as far as can be discovered, there is no record of Watson's attending a syndicalist meeting during 1910–11.

At first the amalgamation movement was made up of a small group of enthusiasts in the London area; and progress was slow. Watson had two letters published in the ASE *Journal* in June and November 1911, and by the latter date a pamphlet (*A Plea for the Amalgamation of Existing Trade Unions*) setting out the general views of the movement, was on sale. In March of the following year Watson unsuccessfully contested the position of ASE executive council-man for the No. 7 Division. He used his election address to state the case for amalgamation, and he also advocated what he described as 'Socialism of a revolutionary type', acknowledging his membership of the British Socialist Party. At this same period he also stood in the local municipal elections as a Socialist.

During 1912 a series of meetings took place between the leaders of the amalgamation movement and the Industrial Syndicalist Education League; and on 25 September a meeting of rank-and-file engineering workers in the London district formed the Engineering and Shipbuilding Amalgamation Committee with Watson as secretary and Dave Armstrong as his assistant. On 9 and 10 November 1912 a joint conference between the Amalgamation Committee and the Syndicalist League took place at the Holborn Hall, London. Both Tom Mann and Watson were prominent speakers. Watson's pamphlet, published in 1913, *One Union for Metal, Shipbuilding and Engineering Workers* was widely circulated, and the amalgamation movement continued to grow up to the outbreak of war in August 1914. The organisation by this time had changed its name to Metal, Engineering and Shipbuilding Amalgamation Committee (MESAC), but the movement virtually collapsed in the early months of war. Watson himself went to work at Woolwich Arsenal, and always played an active role in local industrial struggles. Following a rejected wage claim inside the Arsenal, the shop stewards set up a Trade Union Rights Committee which called a London conference in 1915. A London Workers' Committee was established, with Watson as president and F. Knight as secretary; and towards the end of 1915 the amalgamation committee began to revive. In November 1915 Watson joined Tom Mann and E.L. Pratt in producing a monthly paper, the *Trade Unionist*.

The first national conference of the amalgamation movement was held on 5 and 6 August 1916, with seventy delegates present; and a second conference, with 124 delegates, was convened in Leeds on 10 and 11 November 1916. At the third conference, on 3 March 1917, Watson pressed strongly for action to form a new united union, but he was opposed by the leaders of the shop stewards' movement, one of whom, J.T. Murphy, wrote an open letter to the conference. 'Remember', Murphy wrote, 'it is not only the amalgamation of unions you require, but the amalgamation of the workers in the workshop' [*Solidarity*, Mar 1917, 2]. The clash of views was resolved by the adoption of a compromise resolution.

The large scale strikes of engineering workers during May 1917 found Watson among the leaders of the shop stewards. He was present at the conference of 15 May at the Fellowship Hall, Walworth, and was one of those who signed the letter to the Minister of Munitions (Christopher Addison) asking him to receive a deputation – to which he agreed. The conference also decided to send Watson and Dave Ramsay to Glasgow in order to persuade the Clyde workers to join the strike. Their visit was unsuccessful. Ten of the strike leaders were arrested, including Watson; but following the intervention of the ASE executive it was agreed that a statement would be signed calling off the strike and Watson and the others were released on their own recognisances [see George Peet, *DLB 5* (1979) 171].

The failure of the executives of the major engineering unions to respond to the pressures for an all-inclusive union led to increasing demands from within the amalgamation movement for the establishment of a new union. In August 1917 the fourth conference resolved, on Watson's initiative, to take a workshop ballot; but the national shop stewards were opposed to Watson's 'dual unionism' [for which see Hinton (1973) Ch. 11], and were unenthusiastic over the ballot, with the result that relatively few completed papers were returned. At the fifth conference, held in Newcastle in October 1917, a motion to merge the amalgamation committee with the shop stewards' and workers' committees was carried by 78 votes to 24. It was, in fact, a defeat for Watson's line of 'dual unionism' [ibid., 283 ff.], although he seems to have accepted the situation. From early in 1918 he began a close association with Sylvia Pankhurst, contributing regular articles on industrial questions to the *Workers' Dreadnought*. He was very much in support of strike action to end the war, and vigorously criticised the national administrative council of the shop stewards' movement for their refusal to call the workers out. He wrote in the *Dreadnought* (6 Apr 1918): 'Had the leaders possessed a little more courage and imagination we should have developed a movement which would have compelled the powers that be to open up negotiations and declare an armistice.' The issue was fully debated a week later, on 13 and 14 April, at the shop stewards' conference in Manchester, where J.T. Murphy and George Peet successfully argued that Watson's policy was unrealistic; and they shifted the emphasis to workshop organisation and away from political initiatives. Hinton [p. 268] called this 'the bankruptcy of the shop stewards' movement.' The final wartime conference was held in Birmingham on 7 and 8 September 1918. It was attended by about fifty delegates from twenty-three localities, and although the conference voted by thirty-three to thirteen in favour of a resolution requesting the British Government to withdraw Allied troops from Russia, the majority continued to be opposed to any active political commitment against the war. The rank-and-file movement was to decline sharply after the war ended in spite of the high level of industrial militancy during 1918.

In 1918 Watson (who was again elected to the shop stewards' NAC in September) was playing an active part in the 'Hands off Russia' movement. He was chairman of a national conference convened by the London Workers' Committee (a body of which he was president) held at the Memorial Hall in Farringdon Street, London, on 18 January 1918. Watson also helped to circulate Lenin's *Appeal to the Toiling Masses of France, Britain, America, Italy and Japan* of 1 August 1918, and on 8 February 1919 he was one of the speakers at a 'Hands off Russia' meeting in the Albert Hall, for which he was arrested under the Defence of the Realm Act. He was charged with using words which could be interpreted as a call to take up arms, and on 22 March 1919 he was sentenced to six months' imprisonment. He appealed and was released on bail, but his sentence was confirmed in July. He was freed on 5 December 1919. There had been an agitation in London for his release and for financial support for his family: Harry Pollitt was among the speakers at a meeting called in Trafalgar Square, on 24 August 1919, organised by the East London Workers' Committee.

It was during Watson's period in prison that his connections with the police became known; and it was this which effectively ended Watson's career among industrial militants. Four days after his release from prison he met an investigating committee set up by the West and East London Workers' Committees. The members of this committee were Jack Tanner (chairman), T. Kime (secretary), W. Fordyce, J. Hunt, T.F. Knight and David Ramsay. Watson made a full statement of his case, but the committee rejected his explanation, finding that he had been in the pay of, and working with, Scotland Yard from the middle of 1918. At the Rank and File Convention held in London on 10 to 12 March 1920, Watson was elected to the Standing Orders Committee and to a special committee set up by the Convention to assist the South Wales miners in their propaganda for workers' control. Apparently there was no immediate questioning of his election to these bodies; but at a crowded third session on 12 March Jack Tanner moved that Watson was 'not a fit and proper person to sit on any committee appointed by the Convention' [*Watson's Reply* (1920) 81 and 83]. Watson was allowed twenty minutes to reply, but the vote (twenty-five to three) was overwhelmingly against him. In June 1920, at his own expense, he published his apologia: *Watson's Reply: a complete answer to the charges of espionage levelled against W.F. Watson, and an exposure of the espionage system*. He had never denied contact with the CID, the delivery of reports to them, or the payment of £3 a week. His defence was that he entered into the business in order to mislead the CID with inaccurate or uselessly generalised reports, and that he had informed a number of his comrades of his actions. He was unable to produce any copies of his reports and working-class opinion was pretty solidly against him, although there was a minority prepared to accept the view that he had shown extreme foolishness rather than straight betrayal. The matter was raised in the Commons on several occasions; by Robert Young, Labour MP for Newton, Lancashire, and general secretary of the ASE from 1913–19, and by J.H. Thomas [*Hansard*, 12 and 24 July and 12 August 1919 and *Watson's Reply* (1920) 38–42].

Watson lived on for another twenty years. He wrote a letter to the *Workers' Weekly* (7 Dec 1923) saying that he was still a fighter on behalf of the working class; and in 1926 he represented the Southwark Trades Council at the annual conference of the Labour Party. During the depression of the early 1920s he was unemployed for over three years and then found work at his trade. But he suffered from bronchitis, and during the thirties was unable to work as an engineer, although he had a short spell in this job in the early months of the Second World War. Towards the end of his life, in 1941, Watson was nominated for membership of the AEU executive council. He was ruled against on the ground that he had not worked at his trade for twelve months before his nomination; but in the Chancery Division he won an injunction to restrain the union from proceeding with the ballot without including his name on the paper, and he was awarded 40*s* damages and costs. His action was much resented, since the delays incurred meant that the No. 7 Division of the AEU (which included London) was without a representative on the executive council for over two years.

In 1935, Watson published his autobiography, *Machines and Men*. It is a well written book which is almost wholly concerned with his workshop experiences, and for the account of these it deserves to be better known. But there is practically nothing about his career as an industrial militant. At the end of the book he reprinted an article of his published in the *Quarterly Review* (Oct 1933), entitled 'The Machine and its Purpose'; and he wrote other works of a technical-economic kind, including one in the Hogarth Press series of 'Day to Day Pamphlets': *The Worker and Wage Incentives* (1934).

Watson was a widely read man, capable and energetic in practical affairs, and in his militant days an important personality in rank-and-file movements. He died in hospital at Aylesbury on 23 November 1943. No will has been located.

Writings: 'Class Unions' [letter], *ASE* n.s. 7, no.78 (June 1911) 45–6; 'Provisional Committee for Amalgamating Existing Trade Unions' [letter], ibid. no.83 (Nov 1911) 46–7; *One Union for Metal, Engineering and Shipbuilding Workers* (1913) 16 pp.; *Report of the Rank and File Conference on Amalgamation* (1916) 31 pp.; *Trade Union Amalgamation: difficulties and how to overcome them* (1917) 8 pp.; *Fusion of Forces: report of the fifth national Rank and File Conference held in Newcastle upon Tyne* (1917) 24 pp.; *Should the Workers increase Output?: a reply to the paper ["The Gate to more"] read by J.T. Brownlie at the Ruskin College Conference held in the Memorial Hall, London on January 17th, 1920* (1920) 19 pp.; *Jim Foster's Philosophy: no. 1 the screw gauge and the bolt* [1920?] P; *Watson's Reply: a complete answer to the charges of espionage levelled against W.F. Watson, and an exposure of the espionage system* (June 1920); *The Workers' Council: being an explanation of the aims and objectives of workers' councils* (1922) 8 pp.; *Bedaux and Other Bonus Systems explained* (1932) 32 pp.; 'The Machine and its Purpose', *Q.Rev.* (Oct 1933) 306–19; *The Worker and Wage Incentives: the Bedaux and other systems* (Day to Day Pamphlet no. 20: 1934) 46 pp.; *Machines and Men: an autobiography of an itinerant mechanic* (1935); *Tips for Turners: a . . . workshop manual for mechanics* (Tips Series no. 1: [1936]); (with W. Pitt), *Turning and Screw-Cutting: containing all the features of 'Tips for Turners' and the New Turners' Handbook* revised and enlarged (Aston Clinton, [1941]). With Tom Mann and E.L. Pratt, Watson edited the *Trade Unionist*, 1915–16 and the *Masses*, Feb–Aug 1919.

Sources: *ASE J.*, 1911–15; J.T. Murphy, *Preparing for Power* (1934); *Watson* v. *AEU* judgment, 13 May 1941; B. Pribićević, *The Shop Stewards' Movement and Workers' Control 1910–1922* (Oxford, 1959); J. Hinton, *The First Shop Stewards' Movement* (1973). Obit. *AEU J.* (Dec 1943).

Edmund and Ruth Frow
John Saville

See also: †George Peet.

WHEELER, Thomas Martin (1811–62)
OWENITE AND CHARTIST

Wheeler was born on St Martin's day, 23 November 1811, at the King's Arms, Walworth, where his father, Joseph Wheeler, by trade a wheelwright, carried on the business of a licensed victualler. Joseph Wheeler was an adherent of the school of Major Cartwright and the radicals of the early nineteenth century. When Thomas Wheeler was seven, he was sent to an academy at Walton-le-Dale, near Preston. Later he came back to London and attended a school at Stoke Newington until he was fourteen. Two of his later novels describe his schooldays: Walton-le-Dale in *Glimmerings in the Dark, an Old Man's Tale* and Stoke Newington in *Sunshine and Shadow, a Tale of the Nineteenth Century*.

His first job after leaving school was an apprenticeship with an uncle at Banbury in the woolcombing and haberdashery business. But the unpleasantness of his aunt encouraged him to walk the ninety miles back to London, and he was then apprenticed to a baker in Reading. He stayed long enough to learn the trade although he did not complete his apprenticeship, and then journeyed over southern England, finally settling down at Henley-on-Thames. About the age of twenty-four he married a young widow – Ann Alldeer – and shortly after went on an extended tour of the industrial North and the Midlands, returning to the South to work once more as a baker.

It is not clear from the biographical accounts of Wheeler when or why he became an Owenite. He was working as a gardener in the late 1830s in Kensington, having moved out of baking because of night-work and the long hours involved. In 1839 he was persuaded by Owenite friends to establish a school, and he took 2 King Street, Kensington for that purpose. He described the activities of the school in the *New Moral World* (16 Nov 1839) and it would appear to have been a combination of ordinary day school and evening institute. Every Sunday evening there was a lecture on the principles of Socialism, and Wheeler enrolled himself as a member of the Universal Society of Rational Religionists. It seems, however, to have become increasingly influenced by the politics of Chartism; a growing conflict between Owenite Socialists and Chartists discouraged the scholastic side of the institution, and numbers declined sharply. Had Wheeler not been appointed London correspondent of the *Northern Star* in 1840, the school would have had to close down.

His journalistic work for the *Northern Star* was the beginning of a close involvement with the Chartist movement. He became a well-known Chartist lecturer in the metropolis, represented Kensington in 1840 in the National Charter Association, and in the following year was elected a member of the executive committee. On Christmas Eve, 1841, Wheeler and his wife were in a railway accident that nearly cost them their lives; but both eventually recovered, although Wheeler's injuries permanently affected his health. By the time he returned to active political life the anti-Corn Law agitation was well under way, and Wheeler became one of the most vehement and vociferous critics of the middle-class movement for repeal. The intensity of his opposition was related to his argument for protection and a back-to-the-land movement; and in a few years he was to become the leading exponent, after O'Connor, of the Chartist Land Plan.

In the meantime he continued active for the six points of the Charter. He was taking a hard line towards government opposition to the Chartist movement. In September 1842, in his capacity as secretary to the Metropolitan Delegates, he issued an 'Address' to the Trades which contrasted the peaceful disposition of the workers with the treatment they had met with from the Government. When O'Connor and a number of other leaders were arrested on the last day of September, Wheeler took over the general secretaryship of the NCA in place of J. Campbell. A meeting of the Metropolitan Delegate Council appointed Wheeler, Cuffay, Dron and Knight to form an executive committee in the absence of those arrested. Wheeler went to the Birmingham conference of the Complete Suffrage Union at the end of December 1842 as a delegate from Marylebone; but he resigned his office as secretary of the Metropolitan Delegates in February 1843, although he continued to be active in many parts of the movement: he was, for instance, secretary of a relief committee for Peter M'Douall's family, and he was auditor of the national Political Victims' Defence Fund – of which John Cleave was the treasurer. At the NCA Conference in Birmingham, 5–8 September 1843, Wheeler was elected general secretary of the movement, a position which meant he had to resign as correspondent to the *Northern Star*. This was the conference which first discussed the land question, and from it a Land Fund was established. The Land Plan proper, however, was not to get under way for a further two years, although from the middle of 1843 the columns of the *Northern Star* were increasingly filled with discussions of what could be done with a four-acre holding. In the same year Feargus O'Connor published his book *On the Management of Small Farms* a work for which, according to Wheeler's biographer [Stevens (1862) 25] the materials were principally collected by Wheeler. O'Connor and Wheeler certainly visited together the model farm of a Mr Linton at Selby, Yorkshire, and inquired closely into the spade husbandry used there. Although the detailed discussion of the economic and social advantages of small farm cultivation continued in the Chartist press throughout 1844, it was not until a national conference in late April 1845 that the Land Plan was formally adopted. Wheeler was elected to the secretaryship, and for the next two years his life was entirely absorbed in the propagation and practical application of the Plan. The original directors were O'Connor, Philip M'Grath, Christopher Doyle and Thomas Clark, with W.P. Roberts as treasurer, and James Knight and William Cuffay as auditors. When in August 1846 O'Connor established the Land Bank, in premises adjacent to the High Holborn office of the Land Company, Wheeler took up the position of chief clerk to the Bank, in addition to his duties for the Company.

For reasons probably connected with internal dissension and in particular with the hostility of Thomas Clark towards him, Wheeler resigned from the secretaryship of the Land Company in July 1847 and retired to a two-acre allotment at O'Connorville. Philip M'Grath took his place. Wheeler was still a director of the Land Company, but from that position he also withdrew a few months later, in October 1847, thus ending all official involvement in the scheme. There was no doubt, however, of his continued and enthusiastic support for the Land Plan, and for the general politics of the Chartist movement. He was active in defence of the reputation of Frost, Williams and Jones, transported for their part in the South Wales disturbances; he defended himself and the Plan against the attacks of Thomas Cooper at the Leeds conference of early August 1846; he was a member of the Fraternal Democrats and supported the Democratic Committee for the Regeneration of Poland; and he was active in the spring months of 1848, both in the National Convention (before 10 April 1848) and in the National Assembly. But he took no part in the more militant phase of the movement in the summer of 1848, and his retirement at this time to his home in O'Connorville was the end of his career as a working-class politician of any importance. Wheeler did not, however, turn his back on politics, as his later career showed, and had the Chartist movement not gone into rapid decline he would no doubt have once more been a significant figure. He was always, it should be noted, ready to succour the victims of political oppression, and he never failed to help his former colleagues.

When he moved out of political life in the early summer of 1848, to work his allotment, he also began to write fiction. His first novel, *Sunshine and Shadow*, was published in instalments in the *Northern Star*, beginning in March 1849 and continuing for some nine months. At O'Connorville Wheeler lived with his wife and daughter. His only brother, George, with whom he had a close relationship, also had an allotment on the estate, and their parents at this time lived with George. Local vestry affairs at Rickmansworth also occupied some of their time.

By the beginning of 1850 Wheeler was looking round for further activity of an intellectual – political nature. He began writing an occasional letter to the *Northern Star*, and on 13 April published a useful and very sympathetic account of the life of William Cuffay in *Reynolds's Political Instructor*. About August 1850 he became once again a correspondent for the *Northern Star*; and he always came, when necessary, to the political support of O'Connor. Wheeler was a delegate to the Chartist Convention of 31 March 1851. This in its agreed programme represented the high peak of Socialist influence in the Chartist movement [repr. in Saville (1952) App. III], although Wheeler himself had certainly not changed from the radicalism of his earlier days. When the Land Company's affairs went into chancery, a meeting of the London shareholders on 12 April 1851 decided to try to save some part of the estates from private buyers. Wheeler was one of the committee who established a National Loan Society [Stevens (1862) 56 ff.]. It was a scheme that was impracticable, and within a year it was wound up. Wheeler now became secretary of the shareholders of the *People's Paper*, but soon broke with Jones over the latter's management of the finances of the paper; and from this incident he began to move towards self-help institutions. He was for a short time connected with the 'British Industry Association' – a working-class life assurance society – but it was his reorganisation of the Friend-in-Need Life and Sick Assurance Society at the end of 1853 that brought him the occupations in which he was to work full time until his death. He became manager and secretary, with his brother George as provincial manager and John Shaw in charge of the London branches. The Society was highly successful, and it had a number of former Chartists among its employees. At the beginning of 1857 it took over the ailing National Assurance Friendly Society, established by the same Thomas Clark who had shown so much hostility to Wheeler in the mid-1840s and who died a few months later, on 19 March 1857.

Wheeler's concern with political affairs never died away. Soon after O'Connor's death he published a brief laudatory memoir of the Chartist leader; he continued to give evidence as required before the Commissioner engaged in winding up the National Land Company, and in 1858 he was one of a group of London Chartists who founded the National Political Union in opposition to what they considered to be the temporising policies of Ernest Jones [Saville (1952) 69 ff.]. But when Jones later asked Wheeler to stand surety for a loan of £50 to enable the *People's Paper* to continue, Wheeler agreed; and he was imprisoned for a short time for the unpaid debt.

Wheeler was 'about five feet four inches in height, with a small and sinewy, but well-formed frame. He had quick, observant eyes, and a restless agitation of the right leg was perceptible when talking; his right shoulder drooped a little from the effects of the accident' [Stevens (1862) 96–7]. He was a well-read man, and his great success as lecturer and public speaker sprang from his wide range of information together with the clarity and vigour of his oral style. Moreover, his personal letters to friends and relatives could be admirably direct and colloquial. But in his writings for the public – novels, short stories and poetry – he tended, as his biographer remarks, to favour 'the ornate school of literature' [ibid, 93]. He enjoyed field sports and cricket, had many friends, of whom J.B. Leno was one of the closest, and would seem to have been a man of generous sympathies. He died, at the age of fifty, at his London home, on 16 February 1862, leaving a wife and married daughter. He was buried in Highgate Cemetery. No will has been located.

Writings: 'Notes of a Journey from O'Connorville to the Chartist Estates of Minster Lovel [*sic*],

Snig's End, Moate and Redmarley', *Northern Star*, 5 and 12 Feb 1848 [identical title in second article except for the deletion of Redmarley and the inclusion of Lowbands]; 'Walks and Wanderings around O'Connorville', ibid., 1 Apr 1848; 'Sunshine and Shadow: a tale of the nineteenth century', 31 Mar 1849–5 Jan 1850 (Chs 1–37); 'William Cuffay', *Reynolds's Political Instructor*, 13 Apr 1850; (with others), *Truth versus Falsehood* (1852) 4 pp.; 'The National Land Company to the Shareholders' [letter], *People's Paper*, 13 Nov 1852, p.3; 'A Brief Memoir of the late Mr. Feargus O'Connor MP' in W. Jones, *A Funeral Oration delivered over the Grave of Mr. Feargus O'Connor* (1855) 6–8; (with others), *National Union*, May–Dec 1858; *The Lost Money found!: a reply to a lecture delivered by the Rev. Charles J. Williams*... [on the Friend-in-Need Life Assurance Society] (1861) 20 pp.; *Glimmerings in the Dark: an old man's tale* [story] [date and place of publication not located].

Sources: (1) MS: Correspondence, leaflets, etc., Columbia Univ., USA; Place papers, set 56, BL. (2) Other: *New Moral World*, 1839; *Northern Star*, 1838–52 *passim*; *British Statesman*, 1842; *Evening Star*, 1842; F. O'Connor, *A Practical Work on the Management of Small Farms* 3rd ed. (Manchester, 1846); *People's Paper*, 1852–8; *Reynolds's Weekly Newspaper*, 1850–62, esp. 1858–9; *London News*, 1858; *Libel exposed ... Ernest Jones v. G.W.M. Reynolds...* (1859) 8 pp.; W. Stevens, *A Memoir of Thomas Martin Wheeler: founder of the Friend-in-Need Life and Sick Assurance Society*... (1862); R.G. Gammage, *History of the Chartist Movement 1837–1854* (1894 ed; repr. with an Introduction by J. Saville, 1969); J. West, *A History of the Chartist Movement* (1920); J. Saville, *Ernest Jones: Chartist* (1952); A.M. Hadfield, *The Chartist Land Company* (Newton Abbot, 1970); P.J. Keating, *The Working Classes in Victorian Fiction* (1971); J.T. Ward, *Chartism* (1973); R. Faherty, 'The Memoir of Thomas Martin Wheeler, Owenite and Chartist', *Bull. Soc. Lab. Hist.* no. *30* (spring 1975) 11–13. OBIT. *Daily News* 18 Feb 1862; *Morning Star*, and *Orr's Kentish J.*, 22 Feb 1862; *Reynolds's Newspaper*, and *Weekly Times*, 23 Feb 1862; *Friend-in-Need J. 2* n.s. no.3 (Mar 1862) 33–6. The editors wish to acknowledge earlier drafts of this biography from Mrs Dorothy Thompson, Birmingham Univ. and Dr. I.J. Prothero, Manchester Univ.

JOHN SAVILLE

See also: Thomas CLARK; William CUFFAY; William LOVETT, for Chartism to 1840.

WILLIAMS, John (Jack) Edward (1854?–1917)

SOCIALIST

'Jack' Williams was born in Holloway, North London about 1854 but it has not been possible to locate a birth registration in official records. His early life was one of poverty and deprivation and as he later wrote: 'my childhood's experience made me feel more bitter against the present system, and more earnest in my efforts towards changing it' [*Justice*, 21 July 1894]. On the day that Williams was born his father, a shoemaker by trade, died of wounds received during the Crimean War, and in 1861 his mother died, of cancer, in a workhouse infirmary. Consequently, at the age of seven Williams entered the Strand Union workhouse at Edmonton, and was later in the Westminster and Hornsey workhouses. The only break from workhouse life was provided by an aunt and uncle who took him into their home until the aunt died. From these relatives Williams derived a passionate belief in Irish nationalism, particularly in the contemporary Fenian movement, a belief which was reinforced by reading Irish nationalist newspapers such as the *Nation* and the *Flag of Ireland*. In 1867 he walked from London to witness the public execution of the Manchester Martyrs. He had run away from the workhouse when he was ten (returning his workhouse clothes by post with a letter of thanks and a hope expressed of never again being in need of their hospitality).

At this time he worked as a newsagent's errand boy and a series of odd jobs – at a zinc works, with a hawker, at a livery stables, and on the London docks – carried him into early manhood. What was remarkable about Williams was the quality of his radicalism in the early 1870s. In addition to his Irish nationalism, he was an ardent advocate of republicanism and a supporter of the French Communards. He was active throughout the decade on behalf of the Irish Land League and like so many of his radical contemporaries he also supported populist movements such as the Magna Charta Association, established to forward the case of the Tichborne Claimant. He was also active in the work of the Commons Preservation Society.

Williams read widely, especially American Socialist journals, and in 1879 he joined the Rose Street Club, where he met many European Socialists, including ex-Communards. He became very friendly with Frank Kitz, but the greatest personal attachment he was to form was with H.M. Hyndman. Williams became a member of the Democratic Federation, later (1884) the Social Democratic Federation and throughout life remained utterly loyal to his leader, taking his side in the various splits which produced first the Socialist League and then later the Socialist Labour Party and the Socialist Party of Great Britain. He also followed Hyndman's lead in supporting the formation of the National Socialist Party in 1915. There was some truth in the sentiment of Frank Harris's assertion that Hyndman's later years were spent 'alone now with his arms about Jack Williams' neck' [Harris (1927) 328–9].

The occasion for the first contact with Hyndman was the Irish anti-coercion agitation and Ireland always remained important; but from the early 1880s Williams quickly became one of the leading propagandists of the early Socialist movement. When *Justice* was launched in 1884 he was indefatigable in its promotion for he believed fervently in the crucial importance of a Socialist press, and he was always to be found selling the papers and pamphlets of the SDF.

Inevitably Williams played a prominent part in the campaigns waged in the 1880s by London Radicals and Socialists for freedom of speech. In 1885 the SDF began to hold meetings in Dod Street in Limehouse. Despite the predominantly commercial nature of the area several of the speakers, including Williams, were arrested for obstruction. When he was charged he refused to pay his fine, serving a month in prison instead. An account of his grim experiences in Holloway gaol was published in the *Pall Mall Gazette*, 9 Oct 1885. In the following year he was convicted of a similar offence, this time in connection with SDF meetings in Bell Street off the Edgware Road. Once again he refused to pay his fine, and was sentenced to two months of a régime so severe that his health never fully recovered.

It was because he saw a chance to advertise Socialism that he agreed, at very short notice, to stand as an SDF candidate for Hampstead in the 1885 general election. He was unaware that the necessary money was part of the infamous 'Tory gold' provided by the Conservatives in the hope of splitting the Liberal vote. Although disturbed by the machinations which had produced the money he was quite unperturbed when he did discover its origin, as indeed he was by his paltry twenty-seven votes. He only fought at Hampstead, he said, 'to do as my friends thought best to make propaganda' [*Pall Mall Gazette*, 5 Dec 1885].

Despite his long membership of the SDF Williams only served on the executive in 1884, 1895 and 1896. His value was not in committee work but rather, as Hyndman pointed out, at street corner level. 'Never an agitation, never a strike, never an open-air debate in this metropolis, nor indeed anywhere throughout the country where his service could be useful but Jack Williams has been well to the fore' [Hyndman (1911) 344]. Williams had revealed considerable organising ability in arranging a demonstration against the Irish Coercion Bill in 1882, and the SDF executive was not slow to utilise this talent. When it was decided to launch a provincial recruiting drive Williams was chosen to lead the campaign, and in company with James Macdonald was responsible for establishing the first SDF branch outside London, in Blackburn in 1884. He represented the SDF at the Industrial Remuneration Conference in January 1885. In 1887 he helped to create the short-lived North of England Socialist Federation, while during the spread of trade unionism among unskilled workers at the end of the 1880s he was instrumental in establishing no less than thirteen branches of the National Federation of Labour Union. He assisted Annie Besant in the 1888 match girls' strike and he also helped to inaugurate the May Day demonstrations which became an important feature of London working-class life from 1890.

Tom Mann described Williams's appearance and platform manner in these terms:

> He was rather below medium height, round-shouldered, with one shoulder higher than the other. He spoke with a strong Cockney accent. On the platform, John was the picture of pugnacity. He had a fine command of language, was well-informed, and full of apt illustrations of the seamy side of a workman's life. He could hold an audience with the best, and was a most effective propagandist. He had a large family, and frequently had long spells out of work, but this never damped his ardour. In work or not, Jack was at his post taking his turn in any part of London, outdoors or in. He knew the East End particularly well, speaking its peculiar tongue, and using its characteristic phrases [Mann (1923) 42].

It was especially as an organiser of the unemployed that Williams made his mark. Along with Hyndman, Champion and Burns he was arrested for his part in the West End unemployment riots of February 1886. He was acquitted and continued to work among the unemployed for the next twenty-five years, his weekly meetings on Tower Hill becoming a regular feature of Socialist activity in pre-1914 London. Williams was a member of the London Central Workers' Committee established in 1905 to co-ordinate agitation in the capital; and he worked as its full-time organiser until the general election of 1906, when he unsuccessfully contested Northampton. The election was barely over, however, before he returned to the unemployed and the SDF's land settlement campaign. In this effort to encourage the unemployed to settle on unused land and cultivate it Williams was a leading figure, organising camps at Manchester and Plaistow. When unemployment reached abnormally high levels in the winter of 1908 to 1909 Williams acted as leader of several of the hunger marches organised by provincial Socialist groups. In 1907 he had been elected to the West Ham Board of Guardians on the SDF ticket.

Jack Williams's political activity cost him dearly. Apart from his prison sentences his reputation as an agitator made it hard for him to secure regular work, and his large family never knew much security. In the early 1880s he formed a window-cleaning company with James Macdonald and H.H. Champion, but it never really recovered from his absence in prison, and after a couple of years it collapsed. Thereafter, he became a house painter, but his ability to follow this trade was much restricted by a bad fall he sustained while working on a job at Holborn; and the rest of his working life was spent as a general handyman and mechanic although on his death certificate his occupation is given as house decorator. Casual labour of this type was punctuated with spells of paid activity on behalf of the SDF, although this was just as precarious financially, for the Federation was short of money. In the years 1904 to 1911 particularly, the columns of *Justice* were full of appeals for funds to support his work among the unemployed; but the response was generally poor, and in 1909 Williams was officially declared bankrupt. Three years later he was ostensibly pensioned off by the SDF with a testimonial fund, yet he continued his services, and undertook quite extensive tours until his health finally broke in 1914. The last years of his life he spent with his daughter Florence, still selling *Justice* and maintained by the SDF pension. He died on 4 November 1917 after a short illness which developed into bronchial pneumonia. He was buried on 10 November in Walthamstow Cemetery, and Hyndman, Tillett and James Macdonald spoke at the funeral. Letters from Lady Warwick and Herbert Burrows were also read. James Macdonald wrote in his obituary notice in *Justice*, 8 November 1917:

> Jack has gone, "Our Jack", to quote a phrase that I invariably used when speaking of Williams... Few, if any, in the wide world deserved better of his class than J.E. Williams... He was, indeed, a *noble man*, rugged and rough hewn, if you will, but as

bright and clear in character as the most polished intellect in the land . . . Others have given much to the movement: money, energy, brains, ability. But Jack gave his whole life and every living moment of it. Who could have done more? Of him, the entire movement can well say, "Well done, thou good and faithful servant!".

Writings: 'A Month in Holloway Gaol: an interview with John Williams', *Pall Mall Gazette*, 9 Oct 1885, 1–2; ibid., 5 Dec 1885 [letter to editor on his Hampstead contest] p. 6; Two speeches on behalf of the SDF reported in *Industrial Remuneration Conference. The Report of the Proceedings* . . . ([1885]; repr. with an Introduction by J. Saville, NY, 1968) 79–81 and 397–9; 'How I became a Socialist' [interview between J.E. Williams and H.Q. [Harry Quelch] repr. from *Justice*, 21 July 1894 in *How I became a Socialist: a series of biographical sketches*, no. 6 [1894] 34–41] [copy in Hutchinson Coll. 102, BLPES]; 'From the Past to the Present', *Justice*, 15 Jan 1914.

Sources: [SDF], *John E. Williams and the Early History of the SDF* (1886) 14 pp.; H.W. Lee, 'The Social-Democratic Federation', *Socialist Annual* (1906) 58–60; F. Knee, 'The Socialist Movement in Great Britain in 1907', ibid. (1908) 16; H.M. Hyndman, *Record of an Adventurous Life* (1911); J. Macdonald, 'Early Recollections of Jack Williams', *Justice*, 15 Nov 1917; M. Beer, *A History of British Socialism* (1919, later eds); T. Mann, *Memoirs* (1923; repr. 1967); F. Harris, *Latest Contemporary Portraits* (NY, 1927; repr. 1928); F.J. Gould, *Hyndman, Prophet of Socialism* (1928); G. Lansbury, *My Life* (1928); H. Lee and E. Archbold, *Social-Democracy in Britain* (1935); G.A. Aldred, *No Traitor's Gait* (Glasgow, 1955–7); C. Tsuzuki, *H. M. Hyndman and British Socialism* (Oxford, 1961); K.D. Brown, *Labour and Unemployment, 1900–1914* (Newton Abbot, 1971); biographical information: Dr R. Page Arnot, London. OBIT. *Call* and *Justice*, 8 Nov 1917; *Call*, 15 Nov 1917.

KENNETH D. BROWN

See also: †Annie BESANT; †John Elliott BURNS; †Ebenezer (Ebby) EDWARDS; *Henry Mayers HYNDMAN.

WILSON, Cecil Henry (1862–1945)

PACIFIST AND LABOUR MP

Cecil Wilson was born on 8 September 1862 in Mansfield Woodhouse, Notts, at Newlands Farm, of which his father, Henry Joseph, was at the time manager. His mother was Charlotte Cowan, daughter of Charles Cowan, Liberal MP for Edinburgh. Cecil Wilson was the eldest of five surviving children. In 1867 his father entered the family business, the Sheffield Smelting Company; this was a small works concerned with the smelting and refining of gold and silver from manufacturers' waste.

Cecil Wilson's family background deeply influenced his development. His father was Liberal MP for Holmfirth from 1885 to 1912, and was much involved in such causes as the anti-slavery movement, the temperance movement, Josephine Butler's campaign for the repeal of the Contagious Diseases Acts and the 'passive resistance' of Nonconformists to Forster's 1870 and Balfour's 1902 Education Acts. Members of the Wilson family, including Cecil, maintained until 1921 the refusal to pay a borough rate which might be used to finance church-endowed schools. Cecil's mother was prominent in Josephine Butler's campaign; she was also president of the Women's Total Abstinence Union.

Henry Joseph Wilson and his brother John Wycliffe Wilson were leading men in local Liberal politics: Henry Joseph founded a (short-lived) Sheffield Reform Association to promote the candidature of Joseph Chamberlain at the 1874 general election, and John Wycliffe was a city councillor, a member of the Board of Guardians and a magistrate; of Cecil Wilson's own generation, four became actively involved in public life and all the others were participants in religious or social work. Gertrude Lenwood, Cecil's sister, has provided a description of their upbringing in such a family:

> We were a *family*, and it was assumed that we should all be interested in the doings of the other members. Our father *depended* on this, and however busy in Parliament or on his missions to Ireland or India, he wrote vivid letters describing the people he met, unusual sights he saw, and the questions he was tackling. In local and national affairs we were encouraged to discuss and form our own judgement – but I have sometimes wondered what would have happened if any of us had broken away from the family tradition of public service and devotion to duty! [Fowler (1961) 7].

Cecil Wilson was educated at the Friends' School, Kendal, Wesley College, Sheffield, and Owen's College, Victoria University of Manchester, where he studied chemistry for two years. On leaving the university in 1881 he joined the staff of the family business as a chemist; he then became successively works manager, managing director and, in 1899, chairman, a position he held until he resigned in 1915. He remained on the board until 1922.

For two years, 1884 to 1886, he was president of the Friends' Adult School in Attercliffe. He then joined the Zion Congregational Church, Attercliffe, and was leader of the Men's Morning Bible Class from 1886 to 1919 and Sunday School Superintendent from 1919 to 1922. In later years he attended the Westminster Meeting House of the Society of Friends. Throughout his life Cecil Wilson was active in the cause of temperance. He was on the executive of the Workers' Temperance League. In 1898 he put up in his garden a board with the notice 'The Temperance Pledge may be signed here.' The board was many times vandalised, but Wilson persisted, and in eighteen years 2500 pledges were signed.

His political career began in 1903 when he was elected to Sheffield City Council as Liberal member for Darnall ward. He did his most important council work on the education, highways and watch committees. He was made a JP in 1907, and was for four years Overseer of the Poor for Brightside Bierlow Township. In 1914 he was offered the Lord Mayoralty, which he refused in favour of his brother Oliver.

During the Boer War both C.H. Wilson and his father were 'Little Englanders', Cecil Wilson becoming secretary of the Sheffield branch of the South Africa Conciliation Committee. This stance was so unpopular that in 1901 a mob surrounded his house and threatened to break windows. Soon after the outbreak of the First World War C.H. Wilson became a dedicated pacifist; he joined the Fellowship of Reconciliation in March 1915 and was president of the Sheffield branch from 1915 to 1930.

Pacifism had a profound effect on Wilson's political and business life. The Sheffield Smelting Company had early in 1915 begun to manufacture brass for the production of shells. In November of the same year, having failed to convince the other directors (his brother, cousins and uncle) of the moral case against arms manufacture, he resigned as company chairman, although he continued for two more years to manage the smelting and refining sections. His decision to resign the chairmanship was based on Christian conviction; he wrote to his uncle in 1915: 'I cannot love my enemies, do good to them that hate me and pray for those who abuse me and at the same time make something the object of which is to take their lives' [Sheffield Smelting Company papers, 20 Aug 1915]. He returned to the company in 1919, but his political activities had by then marred his relations with the directors, shareholders and employees. He ceased to be active in the company when he became Labour MP for Attercliffe in 1922; he retired from it finally in 1927.

Wilson's pacifist activities during the First World War brought him into contact with a number of like-minded men, including George Lansbury, whose *Herald* supported the conscientious objectors; and with members of the UDC, including Charles Trevelyan and Arthur Ponsonby. Many Radicals became wholly disillusioned with the Liberal Party during the years of the war, and after its end cast in their lot with Labour. Trevelyan, Ponsonby and Wilson joined the Labour Party, Wilson in late 1918; he also joined the ILP in that year as chairman of the Attercliffe branch. He regarded himself as a Christian Socialist. 'I have come into the Labour movement', he once stated, 'because to me it represents most nearly as a political faith the ethics of the New Testament' [*Sheffield Daily Telegraph*, 10 Nov 1945]. In 1919 he was reported as saying of the Liberal Party that 'Every principle for which his father had fought and suffered and which had been instilled into him [Cecil Wilson] had been given away.' He added: 'I am not sure I did leave the Party. It seems to me rather that the Party left me' [ibid., 23 Oct 1919]. A certain arrogance noticeable in that remark is present to a greater extent in an extraordinary comparison he is reported as making concerning his new Labour colleagues and himself: 'Jesus Christ gathered round him some people who were not quite desirable and I may hope to do some good to those I have joined' [*Sheffield Independent*, 26 Nov 1923 (quoted Barker (1973) 6)].

Wilson soon became prominent in the Sheffield Labour Party. He was leader of the Labour group on the City Council from 1919 to 1923. His 'betrayal' was bitterly resented by Liberal councillors whose colleague he had been; they refused several times to support his nomination as alderman by the Labour members. It was only after Labour achieved power on the Council in 1926 that Wilson was rewarded for more than twenty years of municipal service by being made a freeman of the City in 1929.

Wilson resigned from the Council after his election to Parliament for Attercliffe, a seat which he held from 1922 to 1931, when he lost it to a Conservative, and from 1935 to his resignation in 1944. In Parliament he worked particularly for pacifism and temperance. From 1929 to 1931 he was a member of the executive of the PLP and of the Selection Committee.

In 1936 Wilson convened the Parliamentary Pacifist Group, which campaigned for total disarmament, Free Trade, and a constructive programme of international relations. This group opposed the view of the majority of the Labour Party on the Munich appeasement policy. During the Second World War Wilson was the leader of a group of MPs who worked on behalf of conscientious objectors. He gave much support and aid to pacifists in his own constituency. His last years in Parliament were clouded by the unpopularity of his pacifist stand; he had to face hostility both in the Commons and in his constituency, where his eventual successor headed an executive unsympathetic to his views. Cecil Wilson was a reserved and rather austere-looking man. He had a Quakerly opinion of worldly honours and ostentation. When he seconded the address in reply to the King's Speech in 1929 he wore morning dress instead of the usual Court dress and in 1931 he refused to be considered for a knighthood. He was eighty-two when he resigned from Parliament in January 1944, and he lived only a year longer, dying on 7 November 1945 at 7 Vincent Square Mansions, London SW. His funeral was private. A memorial service was held at the Friends' Meeting House in St Martin's Lane, London, on 13 November. Cecil Wilson had married in 1890 Sarah Catherine Turner, a life-long member of the Zion Church in Attercliffe. They had one son, Henry Leonard (Harry), born in 1897. Sarah died during a visit to America in 1909. In 1912 Cecil married Mary Grace Annie, daughter of the Rev. W. Satchwell a Baptist minister of Nuneaton. His second wife and son survived him, and he left effects valued at £20,042.

Sources: (1) MS: H.J. Wilson Coll., MD 3983 A–B, Sheffield Univ. Library; Sheffield Smelting Company Coll., 461–2, Sheffield City Library. (2) Other: *Who's Who in Sheffield* (Sheffield, 1905); *Sheffield Daily Telegraph*, 23 and 25 Oct 1919, 28 Oct 1922, 26 Nov 1923, 19 Dec 1929; S.V. Bracher, *The Herald Book of Labour Members* (1923); *Dod* (1923); H.M. Wilson, *The Osgathorpe Family and its Descendants* [typescript for private circulation, 1937, in A.C. Wilson papers, Box C/1 Friends' House Library, London] 15 pp.; *LP Report* (1939); *WWW* (1941–50); A.C. Wilson, *Cecil Henry Wilson, 8 September 1862–7 November 1945* [private circulation,

1946; copies in Sheffield PL and *DLB* Coll.] 16 pp.; R.E. Wilson, *Two Hundred Precious Metal Years: a history of the Sheffield Smelting Company Ltd 1760–1960* (1960); W.S. Fowler, *A Study in Radicalism and Dissent; the life and times of Henry Joseph Wilson 1833–1914* (1961); M. Swartz, *The Union of Democratic Control in British Politics during the First World War* (Oxford, 1971); B. Barker, 'Anatomy of Reformism: the social and political ideas of the Labour leadership in Yorkshire', *Int. Rev. Social Hist. 18*, pt 1 (1973) 1–27; H. Mathers, 'Sheffield Municipal Politics 1893–1926: Parties, personalities and the rise of Labour' (Sheffield PhD, 1979); M. Ceadel, *Pacifism in Britain, 1914–1945* (Oxford, 1980); biographical information: the late T.A.K. Elliott, CMG; personal information: Dr J.W. Sterland, OBE, Sheffield. OBIT. *Sheffield Telegraph*, 9 Nov 1945; *Peace News*, 16 Nov 1945; *Bull. of Central Board for Conscientious Objectors* (Nov 1945).

HELEN MATHERS

Consolidated List of Names

Volumes I–VI

ABBOTTS, William (1873–1930) **I**
ABLETT, Noah (1883–1935) **III**
ABRAHAM, William (Mabon) (1842–1922) **I**
ACLAND, Alice Sophia (1849–1935) **I**
ACLAND, Sir Arthur Herbert Dyke (1847–1926) **I**
ADAIR, John (1872–1950) **II**
ADAMS, David (1871–1943) **IV**
ADAMS, Francis William Lauderdale (1862–93) **V**
ADAMS, John Jackson, 1st Baron Adams of Ennerdale (1890–1960) **I**
ADAMS, Mary Jane Bridges (1855–1939) **VI**
ADAMS, William Thomas (1884–1949) **I**
ADAMSON, Janet (Jennie) Laurel (1882–1962) **IV**
ADAMSON, William (Billy) Murdoch (1881–1945) **V**
ALDEN, Sir Percy (1865–1944) **III**
ALDERSON, Lilian (1885–1976) **V**
ALEXANDER, Albert Victor (Earl Alexander of Hillsborough) (1885–1965) **I**
ALLAN, William (1813–74) **I**
ALLEN, Reginald Clifford (Lord Allen of Hurtwood) (1889–1939) **II**
ALLEN, Robert (1827–77) **I**
ALLEN, Sir Thomas William (1864–1943) **I**
ALLINSON, John (1812/13–72) **II**
AMMON, Charles (Charlie) George (Lord Ammon of Camberwell) (1873–1960) **I**
ANDERSON, Frank (1889–1959) **I**
ANDERSON, William Crawford (1877–1919) **II**
APPLEGARTH, Robert (1834–1924) **II**
ARCH, Joseph (1826–1919) **I**
ARMSTRONG, William John (1870–1950) **V**
ARNOLD, Alice (1881–1955) **IV**
ARNOLD, Thomas George (1866–1944) **I**
ASHTON, Thomas (1884–1927) **I**
ASHTON, William (1806–77) **III**
ASHWORTH, Samuel (1825–71) **I**
ASKEW, Francis (1855–1940) **III**
ASPINWALL, Thomas (1846–1901) **I**
ATKINSON, Hinley (1891–1977) **VI**
AUCOTT, William (1830–1915) **II**
AYLES, Walter Henry (1879–1953) **V**

BAILEY, Sir John (Jack) (1898–1969) **II**
BAILEY, William (1851–96) **II**
BALFOUR, William Campbell (1919–73) **V**
BALLARD, William (1858–1928) **I**
BAMFORD, Samuel (1846–98) **I**
BARBER, Jonathan (1800–59) **IV**
BARBER, [Mark] Revis (1895–1965) **V**
BARBER, Walter (1864–1930) **V**
BARKER, George (1858–1936) **I**
BARKER, Henry Alfred (1858–1940) **VI**
BARMBY, Catherine Isabella (1817?–53) **VI**
BARMBY, John [Goodwin] Goodwyn (1820–81) **VI**
BARNES, George Nicoll (1859–1940) **IV**
BARNETT, William (1840–1909) **I**
BARRETT, Rowland (1877–1950) **IV**
BARROW, Harrison (1868–1953) **V**
BARTLEY, James (1850–1926) **III**
BARTON, Alfred (1868–1933) **VI**
BARTON, Eleanor (1872–1960) **I**
BASTON, Richard Charles (1880–1951) **V**
BATES, William (1833–1908) **I**
BATEY, John (1852–1925) **I**
BATEY, Joseph (1867–1949) **II**
BATTLEY, John Rose (1880–1952) **IV**
BAYLEY, Thomas (1813–74) **I**

BEATON, Neil Scobie (1880–1960) **I**
BECKETT, John [William] Warburton (1894–1964) **VI**
BELL, George (1874–1930) **II**
BELL, Richard (1859–1930) **II**
BENBOW, William (1784–?) **VI**
BENNISON, Thomas Mason (1882–1960) **V**
BENTHAM, Ethel (1861–1931) **IV**
BESANT, Annie (1847–1933) **IV**
BING, Frederick George (1870–1948) **III**
BIRD, Thomas Richard (1877–1965) **I**
BLAIR, William Richard (1874–1932) **I**
BLAND, Hubert (1855–1914) **V**
BLAND, Thomas (1825–1908) **I**
BLANDFORD, Thomas (1861–99) **I**
BLATCHFORD, Montagu John (1848–1910) **IV**
BLATCHFORD, Robert Peel Glanville (1851–1943) **IV**
BLYTH, Alexander (1835–85) **IV**
BOND, Frederick (1865–1951) **I**
BONDFIELD, Margaret Grace (1873–1953) **II**
BONNER, Arnold (1904–66) **I**
BOSWELL, James Edward Buchanan (1906–71) **III**
BOWER, Sir Percival (1880–1948) **VI**
BOWERMAN, Charles William (1851–1947) **V**
BOYES, Watson (1868–1929) **III**
BOYLE, Hugh (1850–1907) **I**
BOYNTON, Arthur John (1863–1922) **I**
BRACE, William (1865–1947) **I**
BRADBURN, George (1795–1862) **II**
BRAILSFORD, Henry Noel (1873–1958) **II**
BRANSON, Clive Ali Chimmo (1907–44) **II**
BRAUNTHAL, Julius (1891–1972) **V**
BRAY, John Francis (1809–97) **III**
BROADHEAD, Samuel (1818–97) **IV**
BROADHURST, Henry (1840–1911) **II**
BROCKLEHURST, Frederick (1866–1926) **VI**
BROOKE, Willie (1895/6?–1939) **IV**
BROWN, George (1906–37) **III**
BROWN, Herbert Runham (1879–1949) **II**
BROWN, James (1862–1939) **I**
BROWN, William Henry (1867/8–1950) **I**
BRUFF, Frank Herbert (1869–1931) **II**
BUGG, Frederick John (1830–1900) **I**
BURNETT, John (1842–1914) **II**
BURNS, Isaac (1869–1946) **IV**
BURNS, John Elliott (1858–1943) **V**
BURT, Thomas (1837–1922) **I**
BUTCHER, James Benjamin (1843–1933) **III**
BUTCHER, John (1833–1921) **I**
BUTCHER, John (1847–1936) **I**
BUTLER, Herbert William (1897–1971) **IV**
BUXTON, Charles Roden (1875–1942) **V**
BUXTON, Noel Edward (1st Baron Noel-Buxton of Aylsham) (1869–1948) **V**
BYRON, Anne Isabella, Lady Noel (1792–1860) **II**

CAIRNS, John (1859–1923) **II**
CAMPBELL, Alexander (1796–1870) **I**
CAMPBELL, George Lamb (1849–1906) **IV**
CANN, Thomas Henry (1858–1924) **I**
CANTWELL, Thomas Edward (1864–1906) **III**
CAPE, Thomas (1868–1947) **III**
CAPPER, James (1829–95) **II**
CARLILE, Richard (1790–1843) **VI**
CARPENTER, Edward (1844–1929) **II**
CARTER, Joseph (1818–61) **II**
CARTER, William (1862–1932) **I**
CASASOLA, Rowland (Roland) William (1893–1971) **IV**
CATCHPOLE, John (1843–1919) **I**
CHALLENER, John Ernest Stopford (1875–1906) **V**
CHANCE, John (1804–71) **VI**
CHARLTON, William Browell (1855/7?–1932) **IV**
CHARTER, Walter Thomas (1871–1932) **I**
CHATER, Daniel (Dan) (1870–1959) **IV**
CHEETHAM, Thomas (1828–1901) **I**
CHELMSFORD, 3rd Baron and 1st Viscount Chelmsford. *See* **THESIGER, Frederic John Napier V**
CHEW, Ada Nield (1870–1945) **V**
CIAPPESSONI, Francis Antonio (1859–1912) **I**
CLARK, Fred (1878–1947) **I**
CLARK, Gavin Brown (1846–1930) **IV**
CLARK, James (1853–1924) **IV**
CLARK, Thomas (1821?–57) **VI**
CLARKE, Andrew Bathgate (1868–1940) **I**
CLARKE, (Charles) Allen (1863–1935) **V**
CLARKE, John Smith (1885–1959) **V**
CLARKE, William (1852–1901) **II**
CLAY, Joseph (1826–1901) **I**
CLEAVE, John (1795?–1850) **VI**

CLUSE, William Sampson (1875–1955) **III**
COCHRANE, William (1872–1924) **I**
COLMAN, Grace Mary (1892–1971) **III**
COMBE, Abram (1785?–1827) **II**
COOK, Arthur James (1883–1931) **III**
COOK, Cecily Mary (1887/90?–1962) **II**
COOK, Samuel (1786–1861) **VI**
COOK, Samuel Quartus (1822–90) **VI**
COOMBES, Bert Lewis (Louis) (1893–1974) **IV**
COOPER, George (1824–95) **II**
COOPER, Robert (1819–68) **II**
COOPER, William (1822–68) **I**
COPPOCK, Sir Richard (1885–1971) **III**
CORMACK, William Sloan (1898–1973) **III**
COULTHARD, Samuel (1853–1931) **II**
COURT, Sir Josiah (1841–1938) **I**
COWEN, Joseph (1829–1900) **I**
COWEY, Edward (Ned) (1839–1903) **I**
CRABTREE, James (1831–1917) **I**
CRAIG, Edward Thomas (1804–94) **I**
CRANE, Walter (1845–1915) **VI**
CRAWFORD, William (1833–90) **I**
CREMER, Sir William Randal (1828–1908) **V**
CROOKS, William (1852–1921) **II**
CRUMP, James (1873–1960) **V**
CUFFAY, William (1788–1870) **VI**
CUMMINGS, David Charles (1861–1942) **VI**
CUNNINGHAME GRAHAM, Robert Bontine (1852–1936) **VI**
CURRAN, Peter (Pete) Francis (1860–1910) **IV**

DAGGAR, George (1879–1950) **III**
DALLAS, George (1878–1961) **IV**
DALLAWAY, William (1857–1939) **I**
DALY, James (?–1849) **I**
DARCH, Charles Thomas (1876–1934) **I**
DAVIES, Margaret Llewelyn (1861–1944) **I**
DAVIS, William John (1848–1934) **VI**
DAVISON, John (1846–1930) **I**
DEAKIN, Arthur (1890–1955) **II**
DEAKIN, Charles (1864–1941) **III**
DEAKIN, Jane (1869–1942) **III**
DEAKIN, Joseph Thomas (1858–1937) **III**
DEAN, Benjamin (1839–1910) **I**
DEAN, Frederick James (1868–1941) **II**
DEANS, James (1843/4?–1935) **I**
DEANS, Robert (1904–59) **I**
DENT, John James (1856–1936) **I**
DICKENSON, Sarah (1868–1954) **VI**
DILKE, Emily (Emilia) Francis Strong, Lady (1840–1904) **III**
DIXON, John (1828–76) **I**
DIXON, John (1850–1914) **IV**
DOCKER, Abraham (1788/91?–1857) **II**
DRAKE, Henry John (1878–1934) **I**
DREW, William Henry (Harry) (1854–1933) **IV**
DUDLEY, Sir William Edward (1868–1938) **I**
DUNCAN, Andrew (1898–1965) **II**
DUNCAN, Charles (1865–1933) **II**
DUNN, Edward (1880–1945) **III**
DUNNING, Thomas Joseph (1799–1873) **II**
DYE, Sidney (1900–58) **I**
DYSON, James (1822/3–1902) **I**

EADES, Arthur (1863–1933) **II**
EDWARDS, Alfred (1888–1958) **IV**
EDWARDS, Allen Clement (1869–1938) **III**
EDWARDS, Ebenezer (Ebby) (1884–1961) **V**
EDWARDS, Enoch (1852–1912) **I**
EDWARDS, John Charles (1833–81) **I**
EDWARDS, Wyndham Ivor (1878–1938) **I**
ELVIN, Herbert Henry (1874–1949) **VI**
ENFIELD, Alice Honora (1882–1935) **I**
EVANS, George (1842–93) **VI**
EVANS, Isaac (1847?–97) **I**
EVANS, Jonah (1826–1907) **I**
EWART, Richard (1904–53) **IV**

FAIRBOTHAM, Harold (1883–1968) **VI**
FALLOWS, John Arthur (1864–1935) **II**
FARMERY, George Edward (1883–1942) **V**
FENWICK, Charles (1850–1918) **I**
FINCH, John (1784–1857) **I**
FINLEY, Lawrence (Larry) (1909–74) **IV**
FINNEY, Samuel (1857–1935) **I**
FISHWICK, Jonathan (1832–1908) **I**
FLANAGAN, James Aloysius (1876–1935) **III**
FLANAGAN, James Desmond (1912–69) **IV**
FLEMING, Robert (1869–1939) **I**
FLYNN, Charles Richard (1883–1957) **III**
FORGAN, Robert (1891–1976) **VI**
FORMAN, John (1822/3–1900) **I**
FOSTER, William (1887–1947) **I**

FOULGER, Sydney (1863–1919) **I**
FOWE, Thomas (1832/3?–94) **I**
FOX, James Challinor (1837–77) **I**
FOX, Thomas (Tom) (1860–1934) **II**
FOX, Thomas (Tom) Samuel (1905–56) **V**
FOX, William (1890–1968) **V**
FRITH, John (1837–1904) **I**

GALBRAITH, Samuel (1853–1936) **I**
GALLAGHER, Patrick (Paddy the Cope) (1871–1966) **I**
GAMMAGE, Robert George (1820/1–88) **VI**
GANLEY, Caroline Selina (1879–1966) **I**
GEE, Allen (1852–1939) **III**
GIBBS, Charles (1843–1909) **II**
GIBSON, Arthur Lummis (1899–1959) **III**
GILL, Alfred Henry (1856–1914) **II**
GILLILAND, James (1866–1952) **IV**
GILLIS, William (1859–1929) **III**
GLOVER, Thomas (1852–1913) **I**
GLYDE, Charles Augustus (1869–1923) **VI**
GOLDSTONE, Sir Frank Walter (1870–1955) **V**
GOLIGHTLY, Alfred William (1857–1948) **I**
GOODALL, William Kenneth (1877–1963) **V**
GOODY, Joseph (1816/17–91) **I**
GOSLING, Harry (1861–1930) **IV**
GOSSLING, Archibald (Archie) George (1878–1950) **V**
GRAHAM, Duncan MacGregor (1867–1942) **I**
GRAHAM, Robert Bontine Cunninghame. *See* **CUNNINGHAME GRAHAM, VI**
GRAY, Jesse Clement (1854–1912) **I**
GRAY, John (1799–1883) **VI**
GREENALL, Thomas (1857–1937) **I**
GREENING, Edward Owen (1836–1923) **I**
GREENWOOD, Abraham (1824–1911) **I**
GREENWOOD, Joseph (1833–1924) **I**
GRIFFITHS, George Arthur (1878–1945) **III**
GROSER, St John Beverley (John) (1890–1966) **VI**
GROVES, Thomas Edward (1882–1958) **V**
GROVES, William Henry (1876–1933) **II**
GRUNDY, Thomas Walter (1864–1942) **III**
GUEST, John (1867–1931) **III**
GURNEY, Joseph (1814–93) **V**

HACKETT, Thomas (1869–1950) **II**
HADFIELD, Charles (1821–84) **II**
HALL, Frank (1861–1927) **I**
HALL, Fred (1855–1933) **II**
HALL, Fred (1878–1938) **I**
HALL, George Henry (1st Viscount Hall of Cynon Valley) (1881–1965) **II**
HALL, Joseph Arthur (Joe) (1887–1964) **II**
HALL, Thomas George (1858–1938) **II**
HALLAM, William (1856–1902) **I**
HALLAS, Eldred (1870–1926) **II**
HALLIDAY, Thomas (Tom) (1835–1919) **II**
HALSTEAD, Robert (1858–1930) **II**
HAMILTON, Mary Agnes (1882–1966) **V**
HAMPSON, Walter ('Casey') (1866?–1932) **VI**
HAMSON, Harry Tom (1868–1951) **V**
HANCOCK, John George (1857–1940) **II**
HANDS, Thomas (1858–1938) **II**
HARDERN, Francis (Frank) (1846–1913) **I**
HARES, Edward Charles (1897–1966) **I**
HARFORD, Edward (1837/8–98) **V**
HARRIS, Samuel (1855–1915) **III**
HARRISON, Frederic (1831–1923) **II**
HARRISON, James (1899–1959) **II**
HARTLEY, Edward Robertshaw (1855–1918) **III**
HARTSHORN, Vernon (1872–1931) **I**
HARVEY, William Edwin (1852–1914) **I**
HASLAM, James (1842–1913) **I**
HASLAM, James (1869–1937) **I**
HAWKINS, George (1844–1908) **I**
HAYHURST, George (1862–1936) **I**
HAYWARD, Sir Fred (1876–1944) **I**
HEADLAM, Stewart Duckworth (1847–1924) **II**
HEATH, David William (1827/8?–80) **V**
HEMM, William Peck (1820–89) **VI**
HENDERSON, Arthur (1863–1935) **I**
HENSHALL, Henry (Harry) (1865–1946) **VI**
HENSON, John (Jack) (1879–1969) **V**
HEPBURN, Thomas (1796–1864) **III**
HERRIOTTS, John (1874–1935) **III**
HETHERINGTON, Henry (1792–1849) **I**
HEYWOOD, Abel (1810–93) **VI**
HIBBERT, Charles (1828–1902) **I**
HICKEN, Henry (1882–1964) **I**
HICKS, Amelia (Amie) Jane (1839/40?–1917) **IV**
HILL, John (1862–1945) **III**

HILTON, James (1814–90) **I**
HINDEN, Rita (1909–71) **II**
HINES, George Lelly (1839–1914) **I**
HIRST, George Henry (1868–1933) **III**
HOBSON, John Atkinson (1858–1940) **I**
HODGE, John (1855–1937) **III**
HOLBERRY, Samuel (1814–42) **IV**
HOLE, James (1820–95) **II**
HOLLIDAY, Jessie (1884–1915) **III**
HOLWELL, Walter Charles (1885–1965) **V**
HOLYOAKE, Austin (1826–74) **I**
HOLYOAKE, George Jacob (1817–1906) **I**
HOOSON, Edward (1825–69) **I**
HOPKIN, Daniel (1886–1951) **IV**
HORNER, Arthur Lewis (1894–1968) **V**
HOSKIN, John (1862–1935) **IV**
HOUGH, Edward (1879–1952) **III**
HOUSE, William (1854–1917) **II**
HOWARTH, Charles (1814–68) **I**
HOWELL, George (1833–1910) **II**
HUCKER, Henry (1871–1954) **II**
HUDSON, Walter (1852–1935) **II**
HUGHES, Edward (1856–1925) **II**
HUGHES, Hugh (1878–1932) **I**
HUGHES, Will (1873–1938) **V**
HUMPHREYS, George Hubert (1878–1967) **VI**
HUTCHINGS, Harry (1864–1930) **II**

IRONSIDE, Isaac (1808–70) **II**

JACKSON, Henry (1840–1920) **I**
JACKSON, Thomas Alfred (1879–1955) **IV**
JARVIS, Henry (1839–1907) **I**
JENKINS, Hubert (1866–1943) **I**
JENKINS, John Hogan (1852–1936) **IV**
JEWSON, Dorothea (Dorothy) (1884–1964) **V**
JOHN, William (1878–1955) **I**
JOHNS, John Ernest (1855/6–1928) **II**
JOHNSON, Henry (1869–1939) **II**
JOHNSON, John (1850–1910) **I**
JOHNSON, William (1849–1919) **II**
JOHNSTON, James (1846–1928) **V**
JONES, Benjamin (1847–1942) **I**
JONES, Joseph (Joe) (1891–1948) **V**
JONES, Patrick Lloyd (1811–86) **I**
JUGGINS, Richard (1843–95) **I**
JUPP, Arthur Edward (1906–73) **IV**

KANE, John (1819–76) **III**
KELLEY, George Davy (1848–1911) **II**
KENDALL, George (1811–86) **VI**
KENYON, Barnet (1850–1930) **I**
KESSACK, James O'Connor (1879–1916) **VI**
KILLON, Thomas (1853–1931) **I**
KING, William (1786–1865) **I**
KNEE, Fred (1868–1914) **V**
KNIGHT, Robert (1833–1911) **VI**
KUMARAMANGALAM, Surendra Mohan (1916–73) **V**

LACEY, James Philip Durnford (1881–1974) **III**
LANG, James (1870–1966) **I**
LANSBURY, George (1859–1940) **II**
LAST, Robert (1829–?) **III**
LAW, Harriet Teresa (1831–97) **V**
LAWRENCE, Arabella Susan (1871–1947) **III**
LAWSON, John James (Lord Lawson of Beamish) (1881–1965) **II**
LEE, Frank (1867–1941) **I**
LEE, Peter (1864–1935) **II**
LEES, James (1806–91) **I**
LEICESTER, Joseph Lynn (1825–1903) **III**
LEWINGTON, William James (1862–1933) **VI**
LEWIS, Richard James (1900–66) **I**
LEWIS, Thomas (Tommy) (1873–1962) **I**
LEWIS, Walter Samuel (1894–1962) **III**
LIDDLE, Thomas (1863–1954) **I**
LINDGREN, George Samuel (Lord Lindgren of Welwyn Garden City) (1900–71) **II**
LINNEY, Joseph (1808–87) **VI**
LISTER, David Cook (1888–1961) **VI**
LITTLEWOOD, France (1863–1941) **VI**
LOCKEY, Walter Daglish (1891–1956) **V**
LOCKWOOD, Arthur (1883–1966) **II**
LONGDEN, Fred (1886–1952) **II**
LOVETT, Levi (1854–1929) **II**
LOVETT, William (1800–77) **VI**
LOWERY, Matthew Hedley (1858–1918) **I**
LOWERY, Robert (1809–63) **IV**
LUDLOW, John Malcolm Forbes (1821–1911) **II**
LUNN, William (Willie) (1872–1942) **II**

MABEN, William (1849–1901) **VI**
McADAM, John (1806–83) **V**
MACARTHUR, Mary (1880–1921) **II**

McBAIN, John McKenzie (1882–1941) **V**
MACDONALD, Alexander (1821–81) **I**
MacDONALD, James Ramsay (1866–1937) **I**
MacDONALD, Margaret Ethel Gladstone (1870–1911) **VI**
MACDONALD, Roderick (1840–94) **IV**
McELWEE, Andrew (1882–1968) **V**
McGHEE, Henry George (1898–1959) **I**
McGURK, John (1874–1944) **V**
McKEE, George William (1865–1949) **V**
MACPHERSON, John Thomas (1872–1921) **V**
McSHANE, Annie (1888–1962) **IV**
MADDISON, Fred (1856–1937) **IV**
MANN, Amos (1855–1939) **I**
MANN, Jean (1889–1964) **VI**
MARCROFT, William (1822–94) **I**
MARLOW, Arnold (1891–1939) **I**
MARTIN, Emma (1812–51) **VI**
MARTIN, James (1850–1933) **I**
MAXWELL, Sir William (1841–1929) **I**
MAY, Henry John (1867–1939) **I**
MELL, Robert (1872?–1941) **V**
MELLOR, William (1888–1942) **IV**
MERCER, Thomas William (1884–1947) **I**
MESSER, Sir Frederick (Fred) (1886–1971) **II**
MIDDLETON, Dora Miriam (1897–1972) **IV**
MIDDLETON, George Edward (1866–1931) **II**
MILLERCHIP, William (1863–1939) **I**
MILLIGAN, George Jardine (1868–1925) **V**
MILLINGTON, Joseph (1866–1952) **II**
MILLINGTON, William Greenwood (1850–1906) **III**
MITCHELL, John Thomas Whitehead (1828–95) **I**
MITCHISON, Gilbert Richard (Baron Mitchison of Carradale) (1890–1970) **II**
MOLESWORTH, William Nassau (1816–90) **I**
MOORHOUSE, Thomas Edwin (1854–1922) **I**
MORGAN, David (Dai o'r Nant) (1840–1900) **I**
MORGAN, David Watts (1867–1933) **I**
MORGAN, John Minter (1782–1854) **I**
MORLEY, Iris Vivienne (1910–53) **IV**
MOSLEY, Cynthia Blanche, Lady (1898–1933) **V**
MOTT, William Henry (1812–82) **VI**
MUDIE, George (1788?–?) **I**
MUGGERIDGE, Henry Thomas Benjamin (1864–1942) **V**
MURDOCH, Mary Charlotte (1864–1916) **V**
MURNIN, Hugh (1861–1932) **II**
MURRAY, Robert (1869–1950) **I**
MYCOCK, William Salter (1872–1950) **III**

NEALE, Edward Vansittart (1810–92) **I**
NEWCOMB, William Alfred (1849–1901) **III**
NEWTON, William (1822–76) **II**
NICHOLLS, George (1864–1943) **V**
NOEL, Conrad le Despenser Roden (1869–1942) **II**
NOEL-BUXTON, 1st Baron Noel-Buxton of Aylsham. *See* **BUXTON, Noel Edward V**
NOEL-BUXTON, Lucy Edith Pelham, Lady (1888–1960) **V**
NORMANSELL, John (1830–75) **I**
NUTTALL, William (1835–1905) **I**

OAKEY, Thomas (1887–1953) **IV**
O'GRADY, Sir James (1866–1934) **II**
OLIVER, John (1861–1942) **I**
O'NEILL, Arthur George (1819–96) **VI**
ONIONS, Alfred (1858–1921) **I**
ORAGE, [James] Alfred Richard (1873–1934) **VI**
OWEN, Robert (1771–1858) **VI**

PALIN, John Henry (1870–1934) **IV**
PARE, William (1805–73) **I**
PARKER, James (1863–1948) **II**
PARKINSON, John Allen (1870–1941) **II**
PARKINSON, Tom Bamford (1865–1939) **I**
PARROTT, William (1843–1905) **II**
PASSFIELD, 1st Baron Passfield of Passfield Corner. *See* **WEBB, Sidney James II**
PATERSON, Emma Anne (1848–86) **V**
PATTERSON, William Hammond (1847–96) **I**
PATTISON, Lewis (1873–1956) **I**
PEASE, Edward Reynolds (1857–1955) **II**

PEASE, Mary Gammell (Marjory) (1861–1950) **II**
PEET, George E. (1883–1967) **V**
PENNY, John (1870–1938) **I**
PERKINS, George Reynolds (1885–1961) **I**
PETCH, Arthur William (1886–1935) **IV**
PHILLIPS, Marion (1881–1932) **V**
PHIPPEN, William George (1889–1968) **V**
PICKARD, Benjamin (1842–1904) **I**
PICKARD, William (1821–87) **I**
PICTON-TURBERVILL, Edith (1872–1960) **IV**
PIGGOTT, Thomas (1836–87) **II**
PILLING, Richard (1799–1874) **VI**
PITMAN, Henry (1826–1909) **I**
PLUNKETT, Sir Horace Curzon (1854–1932) **V**
POINTER, Joseph (1875–1914) **II**
POLLARD, William (1832/3?–1909) **I**
POLLITT, James (1857–1935) **III**
POOLE, Stephen George (1862–1924) **IV**
POSTGATE, Daisy (1892–1971) **II**
POSTGATE, Raymond William (1896–1971) **II**
POTTER, George (1832–93) **VI**
POTTS, John Samuel (1861–1938) **II**
PRATT, Hodgson (1824–1907) **I**
PRICE, Gabriel (1879–1934) **III**
PRICE, Thomas William (1876–1945) **V**
PRINGLE, William Joseph Sommerville (1916–62) **II**
PRIOR, John Damrel (1840–1923) **VI**
PRYDE, David Johnstone (1890–1959) **II**
PURCELL, Albert Arthur (1872–1935) **I**

RAE, William Robert (1858–1936) **II**
RAMSAY, Thomas (Tommy) (1810/11–73) **I**
READE, Henry Musgrave (1860–?) **III**
REDFERN, Percy (1875–1958) **I**
REED, Richard Bagnall (1831–1908) **IV**
REEVES, Samuel (1862–1930) **I**
REEVES, William Pember (1857–1932) **II**
REYNOLDS, George William MacArthur (1814–79) **III**
RICHARDS, Thomas (1859–1931) **I**
RICHARDS, Thomas Frederick (Freddy) (1863–1942) **III**
RICHARDSON, Robert (1862–1943) **II**
RICHARDSON, Thomas (Tom) (1868–1928) **IV**
RICHARDSON, William Pallister (1873–1930) **III**
RITSON, Joshua (Josh) (1874–1955) **II**
ROBERTS, George Henry (1868–1928) **IV**
ROBINSON, Charles Leonard (1845–1911) **III**
ROBINSON, Richard (1879–1937) **I**
ROBSON, James (1860–1934) **II**
ROBSON, John (1862–1929) **II**
ROEBUCK, Samuel (1871–1924) **IV**
ROGERS, Frederick (1846–1915) **I**
ROGERSON, William Matts (1873–1940) **III**
ROWLANDS, James (1851–1920) **VI**
ROWLINSON, Ernest George (1882–1941) **VI**
ROWLINSON, George Henry (1852–1937) **I**
ROWSON, Guy (1883–1937) **II**
RUST, Henry (1831–1902) **II**
RUTHERFORD, John Hunter (1826–90) **I**

SAKLATVALA, Shapurji Dorabji (1874–1936) **VI**
SAMUELSON, James (1829–1918) **II**
SCHOFIELD, Thomas (1825–79) **II**
SCURR, John (1876–1932) **IV**
SEDDON, James Andrew (1868–1939) **II**
SEWELL, William (1852–1948) **I**
SHACKLETON, Sir David James (1863–1938) **II**
SHAFTOE, Samuel (1841–1911) **III**
SHALLARD, George (1877–1958) **I**
SHANN, George (1876–1919) **II**
SHARP, Andrew (1841–1919) **I**
SHAW, Fred (1881–1951) **IV**
SHEPPARD, Frank (1861–1956) **III**
SHIELD, George William (1876–1935) **III**
SHILLITO, John (1832–1915) **I**
SHORROCKS, Peter (1834–86) **VI**
SHURMER, Percy Lionel Edward (1888–1959) **II**
SIMPSON, Henry (1866–1937) **III**
SIMPSON, James (1826–95) **I**
SIMPSON, William Shaw (1829–83) **II**
SITCH, Charles Henry (1887–1960) **II**
SITCH, Thomas (1852–1923) **I**
SKEFFINGTON, Arthur Massey (1908–71) **V**
SKEVINGTON, John (1801–51) **I**
SKINNER, James Allen (1890–1974) **V**
SLOAN, Alexander (Sandy) (1879–1945) **II**

SMILLIE, Robert (1857–1940) **III**
SMITH, Albert (1867–1942) **III**
SMITH, Alfred (1877–1969) **III**
SMITH, Herbert (1862–1938) **II**
SMITHIES, James (1819–69) **I**
SOUTHALL, Joseph Edward (1861–1944) **V**
SPARKES, Malcolm (1881–1933) **II**
SPENCER, George Alfred (1873–1957) **I**
SPENCER, John Samuel (1868–1943) **I**
STANLEY, Albert (1862–1915) **I**
STANTON, Charles Butt (1873–1946) **I**
STEAD, Francis Herbert (1857–1928) **IV**
STEADMAN, William (Will) Charles (1851–1911) **V**
STEVENS, John Valentine (1852–1925) **II**
STEWART, Aaron (1845–1910) **I**
STOTT, Benjamin (1813–50) **IV**
STRAKER, William (1855–1941) **II**
STRINGER, Sidney (1889–1969) **V**
SULLIVAN, Joseph (1866–1935) **II**
SUMMERBELL, Thomas (1861–1910) **IV**
SUTHERLAND, Mary Elizabeth (1895–1972) **VI**
SUTHERS, Robert Bentley (1870–1950) **IV**
SUTTON, John Edward (Jack) (1862–1945) **III**
SWAN, John Edmund (1877–1956) **III**
SWANWICK, Helena Maria Lucy (1864–1939) **IV**
SWEET, James (1804/5?–79) **IV**
SWIFT, Fred (1874–1959) **II**
SWINGLER, Stephen Thomas (1915–69) **III**
SYLVESTER, George Oscar (1898–1961) **III**

TAYLOR, John Wilkinson (1855–1934) **I**
TAYLOR, Robert Arthur (1886–1934) **IV**
TEER, John (1809?–83?) **IV**
THESIGER, Frederic John Napier, 3rd Baron and 1st Viscount Chelmsford (1868–1933) **V**
THICKETT, Joseph (1865–1938) **II**
THORNE, William James (1857–1946) **I**
THORPE, George (1854–1945) **I**
TILLETT, Benjamin (Ben) (1860–1943) **IV**
TOOTILL, Robert (1850–1934) **II**
TOPHAM, Edward (1894–1966) **I**
TORKINGTON, James (1811–67) **II**
TOYN, Joseph (1838–1924) **II**
TRAVIS, Henry (1807–84) **I**
TREVOR, John (1855–1930) **VI**
TROTTER, Thomas Ernest Newlands (1871–1932) **III**
TROW, Edward (1833–99) **III**
TUCKWELL, Gertrude Mary (1861–1951) **VI**
TWEDDELL, Thomas (1839–1916) **I**
TWIGG, Herbert James Thomas (1900–57) **I**
TWIST, Henry (Harry) (1870–1934) **II**

VARLEY, Frank Bradley (1885–1929) **II**
VARLEY, Julia (1871–1952) **V**
VEITCH, Marian (1913–73) **III**
VINCENT, Henry (1813–78) **I**
VIVIAN, Henry Harvey (1868–1930) **I**

WADSWORTH, John (1850–1921) **I**
WALKDEN, Alexander George (1st Baron Walkden of Great Bookham) (1873–1951) **V**
WALKER, Benjamin (1803/4?–83) **I**
WALLAS, Graham (1858–1932) **V**
WALLHEAD, Richard [Christopher] Collingham (1869–1934) **III**
WALLWORK, Daniel (1824–1909) **VI**
WALSH, Stephen (1859–1929) **IV**
WALSHAM, Cornelius (1880–1958) **I**
WARD, John (1866–1934) **IV**
WARDLE, George James (1865–1947) **II**
WARNE, George Henry (1881–1928) **IV**
WARWICK, Frances Evelyn (Daisy), Countess of (1861–1938) **V**
WATKINS, William Henry (1862–1924) **I**
WATSON, William (1849–1901) **III**
WATSON, William Foster (1881–1943) **VI**
WATTS, John (1818–87) **I**
WEBB, Beatrice (1858–1943) **II**
WEBB, Catherine (1859–1947) **II**
WEBB, Sidney James (1st Baron Passfield of Passfield Corner) (1859–1947) **II**
WEBB, Simeon (1864–1929) **I**
WEBB, Thomas Edward (1829–96) **I**
WEIR, John (1851–1908) **I**
WEIR, William (1868–1926) **II**
WELLOCK, Wilfred (1879–1972) **V**
WELSH, James Carmichael (1880–1954) **II**
WESTWOOD, Joseph (1884–1948) **II**
WHEELER, Thomas Martin (1811–62) **VI**
WHITE, Arthur Daniel (1881–1961) **III**
WHITE, Charles Frederick (1891–1956) **V**
WHITEFIELD, William (1850–1926) **II**

WHITEHEAD, Alfred (1862–1945) **I**
WHITEHOUSE, Samuel Henry (1849–1919) **IV**
WHITELEY, William (1881–1955) **III**
WIGNALL, James (1856–1925) **III**
WILKIE, Alexander (1850–1928) **III**
WILLIAMS, Aneurin 1859–1924) **I**
WILLIAMS, David James (1897–1972) **IV**
WILLIAMS, Sir Edward John (Ted) (1890–1963) **III**
WILLIAMS, John (1861–1922) **I**
WILLIAMS, John (Jack) Edward (1854?–1917) **VI**
WILLIAMS, Ronald Watkins (1907–58) **II**
WILLIAMS, Thomas (Tom) (Lord Williams of Barnburgh) (1888–1967) **II**
WILLIAMS, Thomas Edward (Baron Williams of Ynyshir) (1892–1966) **III**
WILLIS, Frederick Ebenezer (1869–1953) **II**
WILSON, Cecil Henry (1862–1945) **VI**
WILSON, John (1837–1915) **I**
WILSON, John (1856–1918) **II**
WILSON, Joseph Havelock (1858–1929) **IV**
WILSON, William Tyson (1855–1921) **III**
WINSTONE, James (1863–1921) **I**
WINWOOD, Benjamin (1844–1913) **II**
WOODS, Samuel (1846–1915) **I**
WOOLF, Leonard Sidney (1880–1969) **V**
WORLEY, Joseph James (1876–1944) **I**
WRIGHT, Oliver Walter (1886–1938) **I**
WYLD, Albert (1888–1965) **II**

General Index

Compiled by Barbara Nield with assistance from V.J. Morris and G.D. Weston

Numbers in bold type refer to biographical entries and Special Notes. Roman numerals relate to items in the Additions and Corrections List

Aberdare Socialist Society, xxviii
Aberdeen, 112, 245; University of, 112, 245
Aberdeen Free Press, 245
Aberdeen, Lord (George Hamilton Gordon, 4th Earl), 212
Ablett, Noah, 2
Abraham, May (Mrs H.J. Tennant), 253, 254, 257
Accrington Express, 139
Action, 27, 112
Adams, Mary Jane Bridges, **1–7**
Adams, Walter Bridges, 1
Adams, William Bridges (1797–1872), 1
Adams, William Bridges (1889–1965), 1, 5
Adams, William Edwin, 116
Adamson, Janet (Jennie) Laurel, 246
Addison, Dr Christopher (*later* 1st Viscount Addison of Stallingborough), 263
Adin, Thomas Burgess, 149
Adler, Alfred, 203
Affleck, James, 47
Affleck, Robert, 47
Aflalo, Moussa, 87
Africa, British Imperialism in, 87, 232; Spilsbury expedition in, 87. *See also* South Africa
Agitator, 33
Agricultural labourers, Revolt of 1830, 49
Aitchison, Craigie Mason, 186
Aix-la-Chapelle Congress (1815), 209
Albert, Prince Consort, 123
Alcott House: *see* Ham Common Concordium
Alderley, Margaret, 103
All-India Trade Union Congress (AITUC) 1921, 238
Allen, John, 153
Allen, Marjory (Lady Allen of Hurtwood), xx
Allen, Reginald Clifford (*later* 1st Baron Allen of Hurtwood), 25, 26
Allen, William, 207
Allotments system, 207, 210, 234
Alvey, John, 147
Amalgamated Association of Operative Cotton Spinners and Twiners, 100
Amalgamated Engineering Union, 27, 105, 106, 265
Amalgamated Society of Carpenters and Joiners, 93, 135, 230, 231, 232, 233
Amalgamated Society of Engineers, xxi, 37, 100, 135, 146, 155, 244, 262, 263, 265; *Journal*, 263
Amalgamated Society of House Decorators and Painters, 19, 20
Amalgamated Society of Journeyman Tailors: *see* Amalgamated Society of Tailors
Amalgamated Society of Lithographic Printers, 243
Amalgamated Society of Railway Servants, 235
Amalgamated Society of Tailors, 138, 242, 243, 244
American Federation of Labor, 107
Anarchism, xxi, 19, 21, 22, 85; in Chicago, 19, 73; in Walsall, 21
Ancoats Brotherhood, 104
Ancoats Winders' Union, 102
Anderson, Adelaide, 254
Anderson, Richard, 180
Anderson, William Crawford, 24
Anglo-Russian Parliamentary Committee, 246
Annett, Peter, 48
Anti-Corn Law League, 55, 78, 172, 196, 217–18, 220, 266
Anti-persecution Union, 189
Anti-Semitism, 113, 203
Anti-Slavery League, 197
Apostle and Chronicle of the Communist Church, 13
Applegarth, Robert, 224, 225, 226, 227, 228, 231
Arbitration, international, 234
Argosy, 70
Arlen, Michael, 203
Armitage, Erasmus, 217
Armitage, Isaac, 217
Armitage, Isaac, Jr, 217
Armstrong, Dave, 263
Armstrong, Sir W.G., Mitchell & Co. Ltd, Elswick, 155
Army, corporal punishment in, 56
Arnot, Dr Robin Page, 5, 240
Art Workers' Guild, 71, 72
Arts and Crafts Exhibition Society, 72, 74

Ashcroft, Rev. Kenneth Fry, 126
Ashton Reporter, 216, 221, 222
Ashton-under-Lyne, 218, 219, 220, 222
Ashwell, Frances, 101
Asquith, Herbert Henry (*later* 1st Earl of Oxford and Asquith), 85, 186
Associated Blacksmiths' and Ironworkers' Society, 37
Associated Society of Shipwrights, 153
Association for the Relief of the Manufacturing and Labouring Poor, 208
Association of All Classes of All Nations, 211
Association of Cinematograph, Television and Allied Technicians, 108
Association of Education Committees, 236
Association of Municipal Corporations, 236
Association of Trade Union Officials: *see* Manchester and District Association of Trade Union Officials
Association of Working Men to Procure a Cheap and Honest Press, 168
Atkinson, H.A., 40
Atkinson, Harry, 252
Atkinson, Hinley, **8–10**
Attlee, Clement Richard (*later* 1st Earl Attlee), 9, 25
Attwood, Thomas, 60
Austin, Robert, 231
Australia, 182; Secularism in, 261
Austria, 173
Authors, influence of
Bacon, Francis, 14, 132; Bellamy, Edward, 132, 137, 181; Blake, William, 20, 199, 202, 203; Blatchford, Robert Peel Glanville, 132, 137, 139, 145; Campanella, Tommaso, 14; Carlyle, Thomas, 132; Carpenter, Edward, 199, 203; Comte, Auguste, 250; Darwin, Charles Robert, 70, 132; Davidson, John, 199; Dickens, Charles, 132; George, Henry, 250; Holbach, Paul Heinrich Dietrich, Baron d', 48; Huxley, Thomas Henry, 132; Jevons, William Stanley, 250; Kuenen, Abraham, 250; Loria, Achille, 132; McCulloch, John Ramsay, 123; Malthus, Thomas Robert, 123; Marx, Karl, 126, 132, 137, 199, 202; Maurice, John Frederick Denison, 126, 181; Mill, James, 123; Mill, John Stuart, 70, 202; More, Sir Thomas, 14, 132; Morris, William, 132, 137, 199, 203; Nietzsche, Friedrich Wilhelm, 199; Owen, Robert, 122, 171; Plato, 14, 199; Ruskin, John, 105, 199, 202, 203; Shakespeare, William, 20; Shaw, George Bernard, 8; Shelley, Percy Bysshe, 13, 14, 70; Smith, Adam, 123; Spencer, Herbert, 70; Spinoza, Benedict de, 14; Thackeray, William Makepeace, 132; Veblen, Thorstein Bunde, 202; Wells, Herbert George, 8; Whitman, Walt, 199. *See also Bible*
'Autolycus' (pseud.): *see* Burgess, Joseph
Aveling, Edward Bibbins, 18, 86, 89

Badger, Isaac, 66
Badger, Thomas, 65, 66
Baines, Mrs Jennie, 132
Baird, John, 85
Baldwin, Oliver Ridsdale (*later* 2nd Earl Baldwin of Bewdley), 112
Baldwin, Stanley (*later* 1st Earl Baldwin of Bewdley), 26
Balfour, Arthur James (*later* 1st Earl of Balfour), xxix
Bamford, Samuel, 30
Band of Hope Union: *see* Temperance Societies
Banner, Robert, 19
Barber, Jonathan, 192
Barker, Alfred, 20
Barker, Henry Alfred, **18–21**
Barker, Joseph, 261
Barker, Rose, 18
Barmby, Catherine Isabella, **10–18**
Barmby, John [Goodwin] Goodwyn, **10–18**
Barnes, George Nicoll, 22, 88, 100, 140
Barnes, Dr Thomas, 206
Barton, Alfred, xxi, **21–4**
Barton, Eleanor, 246
Bauer, Dr Stephen, 254
Bavaria, 1
Bax, Ernest Belfort, 72, 200
Bayley, Thomas, 135
Beale, Abigail, 13
Beales, Edmond, 116, 225
Bebel, Ferdinand August, 1
Bechhofer, Carl Eric (*later* Roberts, Carl Eric Bechhofer), 201, 202
Beckett, John [William] Warburton, **24–9**, 113
Beckett, Reginald, 251
Bedford, 12th Duke of (Hastings William Sackville Russell), 28
Bedstead Workmen's Association, 93
Bee-Hive, 224, 225, 226, 227, 228
Beer, Max, 31
Beerbohm, Max, 87
Belgium, 239
Bell, Andrew, 207
Bell, Richard, 82
Bellamy, Edward, 73
Bellew, Kyrle (Mrs John Beckett), 27
Belloc, Hilaire, 200
Benbow, John, 160
Benbow, William, **29–37**, 167, 168, 218
Benn, William Wedgwood (*later* 1st Viscount Stansgate), 239
Bennett, (Enoch) Arnold, 200

Bennett, Lily, 44
Benson, Thomas Duckworth, 164
Bentham, Jeremy, 207
Berry, Tom, 8
Besant, Annie, 18, 71, 75, 86, 137, 190, 238, 271
Besley's Devonshire Chronicle, 50
Best, Robert Hall, 96
Bevan, Aneurin, 9, 112, 187
Bevin, Ernest, 9, 107, 246
Bewick, George, 261
Bible, influence of, 105, 165, 188, 197, 274
Billington-Greig, Teresa [Theresa] Mary, xxix, 200
Bingham, John, 21
Binning, Thomas, 19
Bird, George, 11
Birkbeck Institute, 105
Birkenhead, 1st Earl of (*formerly* Sir Frederick Edwin Smith), 257
Birmingham, 8, 37–8, 55, 56, 92–3, 94, 96, 144–6, 170, 171, 194–5, 196, 197; Alliances, 93–4; Labour Association, 92, 93; Liberal and Radical Advance Group, 93; Municipal Technical School, 96; National Petition (1837/8), 169; People's Theatre Movement, 145; Political Union, 60, 170
Birmingham and West Midlands Employment Committee, 37
Birth control, 48, 51, 212
Bishop, Reg, 239
Black Dwarf, 46
Black, Clementina, 182
Black, Dr J. Roberts, 168, 169
Black, Joseph, 158
Blackshirt, 27
Blackwood's Edinburgh Magazine, 223
Blanc, Louis, 212
Blanketeers March (1817): *see* Demonstrations
Blatchford, Robert Peel Glanville, 100, 133, 138, 139, 140, 202, 250. *See also* Authors
Blunden, W., 43
Blunt, Rt Rev, Alfred Walter Frank (Bishop of Bradford), 129
Blunt, Wilfrid Scawen, 86, 87, 88
Board of Education, 236; Council of Advice on Art, 74
Board of Trade, Committee on Mercantile Marine, 100; Labour Correspondents, 82–3; Labour Department, 155; Unemployment Schemes, 182
Boards of Arbitration and Conciliation, xxviii, 92, 94, 95, 182, 243; Bedstead Makers, 93; Hosiery Industry, 148, 149; London, 20
Boards of Guardians
Bradford, 118; Dudley, 66; Epping, 107; Huddersfield, 164; Nottingham, St Mary's, 192; Poplar, xxviii, 126; Rochford, 107; Sheffield, 273; West Ham, 271
Boer War, attitudes to, 22, 41, 74, 75, 87, 94, 139, 183, 273
Boggart Hole Clough, 40, 139
Special Note on, **42–6**
Bogle, Alice, 66
Bolton Free Press, 50
Bombay, 237, 239
Bondfield, Margaret Grace, 184, 254
Bontine, Major William, 83
Booth, Eva Selina Gore, 101, 102, 103
Borradaile and Atkinson, 206
Boswell, Ruth, xxi
Bottom Dog, 120
Bourchier, Arthur, 27
Bower, Sir Percival, **37–9**
Braddock, (Bessie) Elizabeth Margaret, 247
Bradford, 39, 118–19
Bradford Labour Union, 118
Bradford Pioneer, 27
Bradford Socialist Vanguard, 119
Bradlaugh, Charles, 137
Bradley, John, 217
Brassworkers, Amalgamated Society of: *see* National Society of Amalgamated Brassworkers
Bridgeman, Reginald Francis Orlando, 239
Bridges-Adams, John Nicholas William, 5
Bridges-Adams, William: *see* Adams, William Bridges (1889–1965)
Brierley, Charles Henry, 43
Briggs, Henry, 15
Bright, James, 221
Bright, John, 233
Brindley, John, 212
Bristol, 188
Bristol Literary Magazine, 188
British and Foreign Consolidated Association of Industry, Humanity and Knowledge, 211
British and Foreign Philanthropic Society for the Permanent Relief of the Labouring Classes, 208–9
British and Foreign Unitarian Association, 15
British Association for Commercial and Industrial Education, 107
British Association for Promoting Co-operative Knowledge (BAPCK), 59, 60, 166
British Association for the Advancement of Science, 181
British Broadcasting Corporation, 187, 246
British Citizen and Empire Worker, 88, 94
British Council Against European Commitments, 28
British Council for Christian Settlement in Europe, 28
British Journal of Venereal Diseases, 113

British Legion, 25
British People's Party, 28
British Red Cross Society, 246
British Research Association for the Woollen and Worsted Industries (WIRA), 164
British Socialist Party, xxiii, xxiv, xxviii, 4, 22, 23, 88, 263
British Union of Fascists, 27, 113, 114
British Workers' League, 88
British Workers' National League: *see* British Workers' League
British Workers' Sports Association, 108
Broadhurst, Henry, 232
Broadhurst, Nathan, 167
Brocklehurst, Frederick, **39–46**, 251
Brockway, (Archibald) Fenner (*later* Baron [Life Peer]), 25, 26, 112
Broido, Eva, 246
Broido-Cohn, Vera, 246
Brotherhood Church, 20
Brotherhood Trust, 20
Brown, E.H., 237
Brown, Ivor, 200
Brown, William John, 100, 112
Browning, Rev. Archibald, 115
Buccleuch, 5th Duke of (Walter Francis Montagu-Douglas-Scott), 109
Buckley, James, 220
Bucknall, Rev. (Charles John) Jack, 126
Building Trades, Conference of, 224
Bulganin, Nikolai, 187
Bulgarian Atrocities (1876), 233
Bull, Rev. William, 120
Bulley, A.K., 103
Burdett, Sir Francis, 30, 32
Burgess, A.T., 18
Burgess, Joseph, 20, 138
Burma, English Government policy in, 85
Burns, Emile, 237
Burns, John Elliott, 72, 73, 85, 86, 156, 271
Burrows, Herbert, 271
Burt, Thomas, 1
Burton, James, 217
Burton, Sir Richard Francis, 87
Butler, Jesse, 43
Butler, Josephine Elizabeth, 272
Byron, George Gordon Noel, Lord, 31

Cabet, Étienne, 11, 212
Cabinet-Makers' Society, 166
Cabinet Newspaper, 65
Ca'canny, 96; **Special Note** on, **98–101**
Call, 4
Cambridge Art School, 199
Cambridge University, 107, 112; Queens' College, 39
Campaign for Nuclear Disarmament, 247
Campbell, Rev. Alexander, 188, 210
Campbell, Colin, 51
Campbell, Dame Janet, 257
Campbell, John, 267
Campbell, Sir John, 64
Campbell-Bannerman, Sir Henry, 82, 103
Campion, William, 48
Camrose, William Ewert Berry (*later* 1st Viscount Camrose of Hackwood Park), 27
Canada, 193
Candy, Henry, 159
Capital punishment, 56, 57, 160
Carlile, Alfred, 48, 50, 51
Carlile, Hypatia, 51
Carlile, Jane, 50, 51
Carlile, Julian, 51
Carlile, Mary Anne, 47
Carlile, Richard, 31, 34, **46–53,** 60, 142, 166, 167, 190, 212
Carlile, Richard, Jr., 51
Carlile, Theophila (Mrs Colin Campbell), 51
Carlile, Thomas Paine, 50, 51
Carlile's Political Register, 50
Carlyle, Thomas, 123
Caroline, Queen, 31
Carpenter, Edward, 139, 203
Carpenter, Rev. William, 59, 60, 61, 189
Carroll, Lewis (pseud.): *see* Dodgson, Charles Lutwidge
Carter, Huntley, 200
Cartwright, Major John, 30, 194, 266
Cash, W., 43
Castle, Barbara (Anne), 187
Castlereagh, Robert Stewart (2nd Marquess of Londonderry), 209
Catholic Crusade, 126, 127
Catholic Emancipation, 66
Cecil, Sir Evelyn, 37
Central Communist Propaganda Society, 11
Central Housing Advisory Committee, 129
Central Labour College, 2, 3, 4
Chain Trade Board: *see* Boards of Arbitration and Conciliation, xxviii
Chamberlain, Arthur, 92
Chamberlain, (Arthur) Neville, 9, 38, 128
Chamberlain, Joseph, 95, 100, 273
Champion, Henry Hyde, 86, 271
Chance, Charles, 53
Chance, James, 54
Chance, John, **53–4,** 66
Chandos Group, 203. *See also* Social Credit
Charity Organisation Society, 181
Charter, 170
Chartism, 10–15, 32, 33, 34, 50, 53–4, 55–8, 62, 70, 77–80, 115, 116, 118, 135, 136, 142, 143, 159–60, 168–73, 190, 192, 193–6, 212, 217–22, 224, 242, 266–8; and Irish Nationalism,

55, 62; and Temperance, 54, 57, 62, 67, 69, 136, 160, 193, 195, 260–1, (East London Chartist Total Abstinence and Mutual Instruction Association), 62; Birmingham and Midland Counties Chartist Association, 54; Central Registration and Election Committee, 78; Christian Chartist Church, 54, 194, 195, 196
Conferences:
1840, Birmingham, 194
1841, Ipswich, 11
1842, Birmingham, 34, 62
1843, Birmingham, 55, 267
1845, Manchester, 78
1846, Birmingham [Land], 78
1846, Leeds, 267
1847, Lowbands [Land], 160
1848, London [Land], 160
1849, London, 57
1850, London, 57
1851, Manchester, 58
1858, London, 54
Conventions:
1839, Newcastle, 11, 170, 217
1839, Scottish, 62, 193
1840, Manchester, 11, 194
1844, Manchester, 220–1
1845, London, 56
1846, Leeds, 56, 160, 221
1847, London, 56
1848, London, 56, 78, 160, 267
1851, London, 268
Democratic Committee for Poland's Regeneration, 56, 78, 267; East Suffolk and Yarmouth Chartist Council, 11; Fraternal Democrats, 267; Grand National Holiday, 31, 159, 168; Kennington Common, 56, 78; Labour Parliament, 115, 192; Land and Labour Bank, 58, 267; Land Company, 54, 55, 56, 58, 62, 65, 78, 160, 192, 221, 267, 268; Land Fund, 267; Local movements in: Ashton, 218, 219, 220, 221, 222; Bilston, 159, 160; Birmingham, 54, 55, 169, 170, 171, 194, 195, 196; Black Country, 53, 54, 159–60; Dewsbury, 15; Dudley, 53, 65, 69, 260; Edinburgh, 56; Ipswich, 11; Lancashire, 142, 218–19, 242; London, 34; Manchester, 34, 142; Newcastle upon Tyne, 115, 116; Nottingham, 135, 192; Sheffield, 56, 57; South Staffordshire, 53, 54, 65, 69, 159–60, 260; Stockport, 55, 56, 217, 218, 219, 220; Sutton-in-Ashfield, 147; Truro, 56; London Central Committee for Raising the National Rent, 61; Metropolitan Delegate Council, 77, 78, 267; Metropolitan Tailors' Chartist Association, 77; Midland Chartist Association, 55, 194; National Anti-Militia Association, 78; National Assembly (1848), 56, 221, 267; National Charter Association, 11, 54, 55, 56, 65, 115, 143, 171, 172, 192, 194, 196, 260, 266 (Executive of), 62, 78, 115, 143, 266, (Political and Scientific Institute of), 62; National Charter League, 57, 58; National Loan Society, 268; National Petition, 1st (1839), 170, 217; 2nd (1842), 172; 3rd (1848), 56, 192; Newport Rising, 55, 218, 267; People's Charter, 13, 34, 123, 169, 170, 172, 173, 196, 267, (Union), 173; Plug Plot (1842), 218–19, 220; Political Victims' Defence Fund, 192, 267, *see also* Veterans, Orphans and Victims' Relief Committee; Sacred Month, 62, 170; Universal Suffrage, Central Committee for Scotland, 193–4, Lanarkshire Association for, 194
Cheshire Daily Echo, 140
Cheshire Evening Echo, 139
Chesterton, Cecil Edward, 200
Chew, Ada Nield, 103
Chicherin, George, 3, 4, 5
Chichester, Sarah, 50
China, xx
China Campaign Committee, 108
Chinese Labour, in South Africa, 82, 234
Chorlton Twist Company, 206
Christian Aid, 129
Christian Arts Left, 127
Christian Evidence Society, 49
Christian Reconstruction in Europe: *see* Christian Aid
Christian Socialism, 105, 126–30, 202, 203, 253, 255, 274; Christian Social Union, 101, 255, Research Committee of, 255; Christian Socialist League, 127, 128, 130
Christian Warrior, 50
Church Congress (1911), 255
Church Disestablishment, 57, 85
Church Examiner, 60
Churches and religious groups
Baptist, 34, 60, 105, 196, 197, 235: Johnsonian, 249, Particular, 188; Church of England, 31, 39, 57, 66, 79, 101, 125, 126, 127, 129, 130, 134, 136, 141, 149, 157, 160, 162, 181, 188, 194, 256–7, Ellesmere College, 125, Men's Society, 126; Church of Scotland, 111, Scottish Foreign Mission Committee, 111; Communist Church, 13, 14; Congregational, 20, 64, 66, 69, 153, 227, 273; Council of Clergy and Ministers for Common Ownership, 129; Methodist, 31, 136, 165, 166, 205, 261: New Connexion, 260, Wesleyan, 8; New Church (Swedenborgian), 40; Our Father's Church (NZ), 252; Religion and Life Movement,

129; Roman Catholic, 28, 127, 134, 194, 196, 237; Salvation Army, 117, 118, 120; Society of Friends (Quakers), xxii, 40, 127, 273, 274: Shakers, 209, White Quakers, 13; Unitarian, 1, 14, 15, 137, 181, 206, 249, 250, 251–2: Band of Faith, 15, Congress (1891), 181, Manchester New College, 250; Zoroastrian, 236, 240. *See also* Chartism, Christian Chartist Church; Christian Socialism; Labour Church; Spiritualism; Theosophy
Churchill, Sir Winston Leonard Spencer, 132
Citrine, Walter (*later* 1st Baron Citrine of Wembley), 9
City of London College, 105
Clarion, 40, 43, 45, 74, 133, 139, 145, 150, 180, 202, 251
Clarion Movement, Cycling Club, 40, 145, 146; Scouts, xxix, xxx, 45; Sheffield Ramblers, xxvii; Vans, xxiv
Clark, Gavin Brown, 86
Clark, Thomas, **55–9,** 267, 268
Clarke, Joseph Finbar, 154
Clayton, Francis Corder, 93
Clayton, Joseph, 199, 200
Cleave, John, 33, **59–64,** 167, 168, 169, 170, 267
Clifton, Sir Robert, 192
Clynes, John Robert, 156
Coalition Government (1916–18), 4
Cobbett, Christopher, 43, 44
Cobbett, William, 30, 31, 43, 46, 48, 61, 194; Cobbett Club, 62
Cobden, Richard, 58, 172, 173
'Cogers', 58
Coit, Stanton, 250
Cold Bath Fields: *see* National Union of the Working Classes
Cole, George Douglas Howard, 98, 124, 201, 202
Cole, Margaret Isabel (*later* Dame), 5, 247
Collings, Jesse, 95
Collins, John, 143, 171, 194
Collison, William, 99
Colman, Grace Mary, 246
Colmore, Thomas Milnes, 95
Colne Valley, Labour Union, 163, 164; Socialist League, 163
Colquhoun, Patrick, 121
Combe, Abram, 122, 210
Commans, R.E., 106
Committee on Women in Industry (1919), 107, 256
Common Wealth (Party), 114
Commons Preservation Society, 270
Commonweal, 19, 21, 72, 74
Communism, attitudes towards, 9, 107, 128, 187, 202, 237, 238, 239, 246
Communist Chronicle, 13, 14
Communist Miscellany, 13
Communist Party of Great Britain, xxiii, xxviii, 4, 9, 23, 38, 107, 127, 128, 187, 202, 237, 238, 239, 240; Leeds Congress (1929), 239
Communitarianism: *see* Barmby, John [Goodwin] Goodwyn and Owen, Robert
Community of the Resurrection, Mirfield, 125, 131
Complete Suffrage Union, 78, 172, 173, 196; Birmingham Conference (1842), 55, 172, 192, 196, 267
Comrades of the Great War, 24
Conference of Amalgamated Trades, 224, 226, 228
Conley, James, 81, 82
Connolly, James, 134
Connolly, Thomas, 226
Conrad, Joseph (pseud.), 84, 88
Conscientious Objection: *see* First World War; *and* Second World War
Conscription, xxviii, 4, 96. *See also* First World War
Conservative Party, xxiv, 38, 41–2, 43, 115, 127, 140, 143, 246
Constitutional Association, 31
Contagious Diseases: *see* Parliamentary Acts
Contemporary Review, 228
Conybeare, Charles Augustus Vansittart, 86
Cook, Arthur James, 239
Cook, Frederick William, 69
Cook, Samuel, 53, 54, **64–8,** 69, 160, 260
Cook, Samuel Quartus, 64, **69,** 260
Cooper, Selina, 102, 103
Cooper, Thomas, 56, 62, 160, 161, 196
Co-operation, Owenite, 33, 209, 211
Co-operative Central Board, Midland Section of, 136
Co-operative Congresses: *Pre-Rochdale* 1832, London, 33, 123, 211; Liverpool, 123, 211
Co-operative Insurance Society, 235
Co-operative Movement, 2, 59–60, 135, 136, 231
Co-operative News, 135
Co-operative Party, 23
Co-operative Printing Society, 231
Co-operative Societies
Pre-Rochdale
Central Co-operative Association, 33; London, 122, 123; Westminster, 59–60
Post-Rochdale
Derby, 135; Dudley, 261; Honley, 165; Lenton and Nottingham, 135; Long Eaton, 136; Mansfield, 136; Medway, 158; Rochester, 158; Royal Arsenal, 1, 2; Thames, 158
Co-operative Union, 1
Co-operative Wholesale Society, 136
Co-operative Women's Guild: *see* Women's Co-

operative Guild
Co-operators
and Chartism, 135, 136; and education, 1; and Liberal Party, 136; and local government, 136; and religion, 136; and temperance, 136, 153, 157
Corfield, Joseph William, 213
Cotton Factory Times, 4, 5, 244
Cotton industry, Lancashire, 205–6; Scotland, 169, 206–7
Coulson, Edwin, 225
Council of Christians and Jews, 108
Court of Referees, 83
Cowan, Charles, 272
Cowen, Joseph, 116
Cradley Heath chain makers, 85
Crane, Anthony, 76
Crane, Thomas, 70
Crane, Walter, 2, **70–7**
Crawfurd, Helen, 237
Cremer, Sir William Randal, 231
Crimean War, 269
Cripps, Sir (Richard) Stafford, 9
Crisis, 211
Croft, Sir Henry Page, 140
Crooks, William, 254
Cuffay, William, **77–80,** 267, 268
Culham College, Abingdon, 199
Cummings, David Charles, **81–3,** 154
Cunninghame Graham, Robert Bontine, 72, 73, **83–91,** 98
Curran, Peter (Pete) Francis, 44, 100
Currency reform, 28, 123
Curzon, George Nathaniel (*later* 1st Marquess of Kedleston), 2

Daily Dispatch, 139
Daily Herald, 10, 26, 27, 202
Daily News, 57, 240, 255
Daily Star [Blackburn], 139
Daily Telegraph, 27, 71
Daines, Donald, 9
Dale, Ann Caroline (Mrs Robert Owen), 206
Dale, David, 94, 206, 207
Dalkeith, Lord (William Henry Walter Montagu-Douglas-Scott, *later* 6th Duke of Buccleuch), 109
Dallas, George, 247
Dalley, William Arthur, 96
Dalton, Edward Hugh John Neale (*later* Baron Dalton of Forest and Frith [Life Peer]), 25, 26
Dalton, John, 206
Davies, Charles, 217
Davies, Emily, 103
Davis, George, 78
Davis, William John, 65, **92–101,** 232, 256
Deakin, Arthur, 9
Deakin, Joseph, 21
Deist; or Moral Philosopher, 47
De la Balmondière, Gabrielle Marie (Mrs R.B. Cunninghame Graham), 84, 87
de Maeztu, Ramiro, 200, 203
Democratic Committee for Poland's Regeneration: *see* Chartism
Democratic Federation, 270
Democratic Friends of All Nations, 173
Democratic Review, 55, 58
Demonstrations
Blanketeers' March (1817), 30; Peterloo (1819), 47, 217; Reform (Bristol) (1831), 31; General Fast (London) (1832), 33, 60, 168; Tolpuddle Martyrs (Copenhagen Fields, London) (1834), 33, 61, 168, 211; Chartist (Birmingham) (1840), 194; Kennington Common (1848), 56, 78; Reform League (1866), 242; Reform (Brookfields, Birmingham) (1866–7), 161, 196; Trade unionists (Manchester) (1877), 143; Irish Coercion Bill (1882), 270; Unemployment (Hyde Park) (1886), 72, 271; Anti-coercion (London) (1887), 18, 85; 'Bloody Sunday' (Trafalgar Square) (13 Nov 1887), 19, 72, 85; May Day (London) (4 May 1890), 86, 271; International Socialist (London) (1896), 20; Unemployed (Manchester) (1905–8), xxix, 271; Unemployed Women (London) (1905), 182; Women's Suffrage (Trafalgar Square) (1906, 1908, 1910), 103. *See also* Hunger Marches
De Morgan, William, 72
Derby, 17th Earl of (formerly Lord Edward George Villiers Stanley), 4, 132–3
Despard, Charlotte, 108, 237
Detrosier, Rowland, 49, 62
De Valera, Eamon, 88
Devonshire Chronicle: see Besley's Devonshire Chronicle
Dickens, Charles, 62, 123. *See also* Authors
Dickenson, Sarah, **101–5**
Diefenbaker, John George, 187
Dilke, Emily (Emilia) Francis Strong, Lady (formerly Mrs Mark Pattison), 253, 254, 256
Dilke, Sir Charles, 255, 256, 258
Disarmament, 274; Geneva Conference on (1932), 5
Dixon, William, 58
Dobbs, Alfred James, 247
Dock, Wharf, Riverside and General Labourers' Union [Dockers' Union], xxviii, 100, 151, 157
Dockyard Labourers' Protection League, 157
Dodd, Frederick T. Lloyd, 100
Dodds, Ruth, xxiv

Dodgson, Charles Lutwidge, 71
Doherty, John, 31, 32, 211
Donald, A.K., 19
Doreck College, Bayswater, 181
Doughty, Charles Montagu, 87
Douglas, Major Clifford Hugh, 201–2
Doyle, Christopher, 56, 57, 58, 267
Dressmakers' Union, 150
Drew, William Henry (Harry), 20
Driberg, Thomas (Tom) Edward Neil (*later* Baron Bradwell juxta Mare, in the County of Essex [Life Peer]), 130
Drinkwater, Peter, 206
Dron, James George, 78, 267
Duckworth, Sir James, 140
Dudley, 53, 64, 66–7, 69, 160, 161, 195, 260–1; Mutual Improvement Society, 67, 260; Political Union, 64, 65; Working Men's Institute, 67, 69, 260. *See also* Mechanics' Institutes
Dudley, Lord (William Humble Ward, 10th Baron Dudley), 65
Duignan, William Henry, 161
Dummett, Mrs Elizabeth, 89
Duncan, Charles, 140
Duncan, Joseph, 245
Duncombe, Thomas Slingsby, 220
Dunning, Thomas, 228
Durham Chronicle, 50
Dutt, Rajani Palme, 4, 187, 237, 239
Dyke, Sir William Hart, 234
Dyson, Will, 200

East London Pioneer, 25
East Suffolk Working Men's Association, 11
Economy Committee (1931) [May Report], 127
Edinburgh, 122
Edinburgh and Leith Advertiser, 122
Edinburgh Freethinkers' Zetetic Society, 47
Edinburgh, Leith, Glasgow and North British Commercial and Literary Advertiser: see North British Advertiser
Education, 2, 5, 11–12, 18, 23, 85, 89, 149, 160, 162, 171, 181, 183, 188–9, 197, 207, 208, 209, 227, 235, 253, 272; Adult, 107; Experimental Schools, Hofwyl, Switzerland, 209; Half-time, 39, 137, 149, 253; Industrial (for women and girls), 183; Open-air Schools, 2; Medical inspection, 182
Educational Circular and Communist Apostle, 11, 12
Edward VII, 119
Edwards, John Passmore, 233
Egypt, 85, 239
Eight Hour Day Movement, 19, 85, 86, 89, 138, 157, 211, 226; in New South Wales, 261
Eight Hour League (Kent), 157
Elger, William, 106, 108
Eliot, Thomas Stearns, 130
Elliott, Dorothy (Mrs J.D. Jones), 246, 247, 248
Elvin, George, 108
Elvin, Harold, 108
Elvin, Herbert Henry, **105–9**
Elvin, Lionel, 108
Elvin, Mary, 108
Emmet, Robert, 115
Enfield, Honora, 23
Engels, Friedrich, 58, 86, 140, 214
Engineering and Shipbuilding Amalgamation Committee, 263. *See also* Metal, Engineering and Shipbuilding Amalgamation Committee
Engineering industry, amalgamation movement in, 263–4
English Chartist Circular and Temperance Record, 62
Epstein, Jacob (*later* Sir), 88, 89
Equal Pay, 247, 256
European Economic Community, 247
Evans, Edmund, 71
Evans, George, **109–10,** 138
Evans, Thomas, 30
Evans, Thomas Jr, 30
Excerpta Medica, 113

Fabian Essays in Socialism, 72, 181
Fabian Society, xxvii, 1, 8, 43, 72, 74, 118, 132, 137, 138, 139, 145, 146, 183, 200, 201; Arts Group, 200; Summer Schools, 145, 146; Women's Group, 247
Factory Inspectorate, 93, 232, 254
Factory reform, movement for, 205, 207, 208, 260. *See also* Eight Hour Day
Fagan, Hymie, 240
Fair Rents League, 19
Fairbotham, Harold, **111**
Farmery, George Edward, 162
Fascism, 127; attitudes to, 9, 107, 113, 203
Fascist Quarterly, 28
Fawcett, Mrs Millicent (*later* Dame), 102, 181, 183
Fay, Thomas, 79
Federal Council of Government Employees, 157
Federation of Engineering and Shipbuilding Trades, 155
Federation of Shop Workers and Clerks, 106
Federation of Women Workers [Manchester area], 102
Fellenberg, Philipp Emanuel von, 209
Fellowship of Reconciliation, 273
Fenwick, Charles, 1
Fielden, John, 211
Fine Art Society, 73
Finsbury Manhood Suffrage Association, 34

First World War, 1, 2, 3, 4, 24, 37, 104, 106, 107, 112, 126, 140, 151, 152, 165, 235, 238, 245, 256, 263; attitudes to, 4, 8, 20, 23, 75, 86, 88, 96, 106, 119, 133–4, 264, 273; Central Committee for Women's Training and Employment, 104, 256; conscientious objection, 8, 133–4, 274
Flag of Ireland, 269
Fleeming, Anne Elizabeth (Mrs William Bontine), 84
Fleeming, Charles Elphinstone, 84
Fleming, George Alexander, 211
Flower, Sarah, 1
Flynn, Terence, 244
Fordyce, W., 264
Forgan, Dr Robert, 27, 28, **111–14,** 187
Forman, John, 186
Forster, William Edward, 272
Forward [Glasgow], 150, 245
Forward [ILP], 131, 150, 186
Fourier, François Marie Charles, 11, 50
Fox, Alan, 154
Fox, F.A., 81
Fox, Rev. J., 189
Fox, Thomas, 45
Fox, William Johnson, 14
Foxwell, Herbert Somerton, 122, 124
Framework knitting industry, 147, 148, 149
France, 128; Revolution (1830), 66, (1848), 14, 66, 212, 221; Paris Commune (1871), 71, 270
Free Land League, 233. *See also* Land Law Reform Association
Free Speech, campaign for, 61; London (1880s), 18, 19; Ardwick Green (Nov 1893), xx; Manchester (1896): *see* Boggart Hole Clough
Free Trade, 234, 274
Freemasonry, 38, 42
Freethought, 47, 48, 49, 50, 70–1, 166, 173, 179, 188, 190, 209, 211–12, 234, 260–1
Friendly Societies, British Industry Association, 268; Friend-in-Need Life and Sick Assurance, 58, 268; Foresters, 83, 153, 156; Hearts of Oak, 37; Land and Building, 58; National Association of, 58; National Assurance, 58, 268; National Co-operative, 58; National Freehold Benefit Building, 58; Oddfellows, Manchester Unity, 230
Froebel, Friedrich Wilhelm August, 165
Frost, John, 55, 147, 196, 218, 221, 267
Frost, Thomas, 13–14, 78, 79
Fry, Henry, 11
Fulton, Robert, 206
Fun, 70

Gaitskell, Hugh Todd Naylor, 9
Gallacher, William, 239
Game Laws, 160, 173
Gammage, Robert George, 58, **114–17,** 147
Gammage, Thomas, 115, 116
Gandhi, Mahatma, 238–9
Garbett, Cyril Foster, Archbishop, 129
Garibaldi, Giuseppe, 66, 116
Garnett, Edward, 87
Gartmore, Perthshire, 84, 87
Gas Consumers' Protection League, 233
Gaskell, Daniel, 15
Gast, John, 169
Gateshead, xxiv, 25
Gauntlet, 50
Gazette [of Whittington Club], 13
Gee, Will, 133
General Convention of the Industrious Classes, 61
General Federation of Trade Unions, 82, 83, 94, 95, 100, 155
General Union of Operative Carpenters and Joiners, 231
Germany, xxii, 128, 203, 246–7; Munich Agreement (1938), 128, 274; Nazi Party in, 28
Gibraltar, 158
Gill, (Arthur) Eric (Rowton), 203
Gillies, William, 246, 247
Gillingham, 158
Gladstone, John Hall, 181
Gladstone, William Ewart, 109, 123, 181, 197, 224, 227, 228
Glasgow, 32, 150, 151, 169, 170, 180, 186, 190, 193, 217; Society of Trades in, 169; University, 88
Glasier, John Bruce, 44, 45, 72, 134
Glasier, Katharine Bruce, 45
Gleeson, Patrick, 44
Glyde, Charles Augustus, **117–21**
Glyde, Rev. Jonathan, 117
Goldman, Emma, xxv
Good Words, 70
Goodrich, Carter Lyman, 100
Gore, Canon Charles (*later* Bishop), 126, 255
Gosse, Edmund (*later* Sir), 72
Gossip, Alexander (Alex), 239
Goulden, Mary, 45
Graham, Sir James, 173
Graham, Robert, 87
Grand National Consolidated Trades Union, 77, 168, 211
Gray, James, 121, 122
Gray, John, **121–5**
Grayson, Albert Victor, xxix, 2, 133, 139, 163, 200
Great Northern Union, 169
Great Radical Association, 61
Greaves, James Pierrepoint, 12

Greenwood, Gertrude (Mrs Hubert Humphreys), 146
Grieve, Christopher Murray, 202, 203
Griffiths, James, 246
Groser, St John Beverley (John), **125–31**
Guild Socialism, 106–7, 200–3
Guile, Daniel, 224, 227, 228, 231
Gurdjieff, George Ivanovitch, 203
Gwynn, Stephen, 256

Haddow, William Martin, 2
Hadow Committee: *see* Health, Ministry of
Haemophilia Society, 187
Halifax, Lord (Edward Frederick Lindley Wood, 3rd Viscount, *later* 1st Earl of Halifax), 128
Hall, Abel, 166
Hall, James, 127, 252
Hall, William Knight, 110
Hall, (William) Leonard, 43, 44, 45
Ham Common Concordium, 12, 14
Hambly, Dr Edmund, 9
Hamilton, Archibald James, 210
Hamilton, Mary Agnes, 248
Hammond, John Lawrence Le Breton, 139
Hampden Clubs, Manchester, 30
Hampson, Walter ('Casey'), **131–5**
Hanson, Joseph, 212
Harcourt, Sir William George Granville Venables Vernon-, 232–3
Hardie, James Keir, xxviii, 20, 41, 44, 45, 85, 86, 88, 132, 163, 164
Harker, John, 43, 103, 139
Harker, Mary Helen, 44
Harmony Hall, 51
Harney, George Julian, 34, 55, 57, 58, 115, 116, 147, 169, 170
Harris, Frank, 87, 270
Harrison, Frederic, 73, 225, 226, 242
Harrison, George, 192
Harrow School, 84
Hart, Judith (Constance Mary) (*later* Dame), 187
Hartley, Edward Robertshaw, 118, 119
Hartwell, Robert, 60, 170, 224, 225, 226, 228
Haslam, James, 142
Hassell, Richard, 48
Hastings, Beatrice, 200, 201, 202
Hawkes, Thomas, 65
Hayden, Mrs, 213
Headlam, Francis John, 43
Headlam, Rev. Stewart Duckworth, 126
Health, Ministry of, 107; Advisory Committee to, 256; Departmental Committee on Qualifications, Recruitment, Training and Promotion of Local Government Officers (1930–4) [Hadow], 38
Heath, David William, 116, 136, 192
Heaton, Annie, 102
Heaviside, Thomas, 11
Hemm, William Peck, **135–6,** 192
Hempsall, John, 43
Henderson, Arthur, 2, 96, 239
Henley, William Ernest, 72
Henshall, Henry (Harry), 43, **137–41**
Herald of the Rights of Industry, 273
Herford, Charles Harold, 250
Hetherington, Henry, 14, 33, 34, 60, 61, 62, 115, 141, 167, 168, 169, 173, 190
Heywood, Abel, 50, 62, **141–4**
Heywood, Abel Jr, 143
Heywood, G.W., 143
Hibbert, Julian, 48, 49
Hicking, William, 231
Hicks, Amelia (Amie) Jane, 181
Hicks, William Joynson: *see* Joynson-Hicks, William
Higdon, Annie, 133
Higdon, Thomas, 133
Higgins, Timothy, 217
Hill, John, 82
Hill, Matthew Davenport, 61
Hill, W., 62
Hindley, Charles, 220
Hitler, Adolf, xxii. *See also* Germany
Hoare, Rev. James, 252
Hobson, John Atkinson, 202
Hobson, Samuel George, 40, 200, 201
Hodgkinson, Sam, 40
Hogg, Mrs F.C., 181
Holbach, Paul Heinrich Dietrich, Baron d', 48
Holmes, Isabella, 181
Holyoake, George Jacob, 58, 124, 173, 189, 190, 260
Home Colonisation Society, 211
Home Department, Departmental Committee on the Truck Acts (1906–8), 255; Departmental Committee on Dangers attendant on the Use of Lead in Potteries (1908–10), 254
Home Guard: *see* Second World War
Home Office: *see* Home Department
Home Work, 182
Hone, William, 46, 47
Honley, 163; Labour Club, 163
Hood, Jacomb, 72
Hornby v. *Close*, 225
Horrocks, William, 109, 110
Horton, Will, 96
House of Lords, abolition of, 19, 65, 85; reform of, 234
Houseworker Trust, 247
Housing, reform of, 186; working-class, 2, 18, 93, 128, 129, 180, 207, 235

Housing (Government Scheme) Advisory Council, 186, 236
Howard, George James (*later* 9th Earl of Carlile), 71
Howell, Denis, 146
Howell, George, 227, 232, 242
Howitt, William, 62
Howitt's Journal, 13, 14, 15
Hoxton and Haggerston Nursing Association, 181
Hoxton Labour Emancipation League, 18, 19
Huddersfield, 164, 165
Hudson, William Henry, 88, 89
Hughes, Fred, 107, 108
Hughes, Thomas, 225
Hull, 111, 151, 162, 190; University, 162
Hulme, Thomas Edward, 200, 203
Hulme Socialist Society, 180
Hume, Joseph, 62, 171, 173
Humphreys, George Hubert, **144–6**
Hunger Marches, 127, 271
Hunt, Henry, 30, 31, 47, 48, 49, 60, 167, 194, 195
Hunt, J., 264
Hunt, James Henry Leigh, 47
Hunt, Thornton, 34
Hurst, Ambrose, 58
Hyndman, Henry Mayers, 72, 74, 76, 85, 88, 132, 140, 270, 271. *See also* Authors

I.L.P. News, 41
Icarian Settlement, Texas, 14
Illustrated Weekly News, 19
Independent Labour Party, xxiii, xxiv, xxv, xxix, 1, 4, 8, 25, 27, 41, 81, 94, 102, 103, 112, 132, 133, 150, 164, 181, 235, 237, 251, 255
  Branches, Divisions and Federations: Birmingham, xxiii, 37, 145; Bradford, 118, 119; Burslem, xxiv; Clydebank, 150; Erith, 234; Glasgow, 150, 245; Hackney, 24; Honley, 163; Hull, 162; Hyde, 138; Kentish, 158; Lancashire, 40; Leeds, 199; Liverpool, xxi; London, 20, 237, and Southern Counties, 25; Manchester, xxix, xxx, 41, 42–5, 179, and Salford, xxix, 40, 43, 110, 138, 139, 180; Peckham, 26, 27; Rothesay, 186; Scottish, 238; Sheffield, 22, 23, 24, 45, 235, 274; Stockport, 139, 140; Yorkshire, 163, 238
  Conferences: 1893, Bradford, 20, 118; 1898, Birmingham, xxiv; 1899, Leeds, 41; 1900, Glasgow, 41; 1907, Derby, xxiv, xxx; 1908, Huddersfield, xxx; 1911, Birmingham, xxx; 1920, Glasgow, 237; 1921, Southport, 237; 1922, Nottingham, 25
  and Boer War, 22, 41, 74
  and Communism, 237
  and Labour Church, 250, 251
  and Socialist Federation in South Wales, xxviii–xxix
  Living Wage Policy, 202
  Manchester Fourth Clause, 140
  National Administrative Council of, 44, 163, 180, 237
  Scottish Council of, 186
  Song Book, 139
Independent Whig, 32
India, 26, 184, 236–9, 246, 273; Congress Party of, 238; Home Rule for, 74–5, 126, 127, 237, 238; Indian Mutiny, 75
Indian Home Rule League, 238
Indonesia, 239
Industrial Christian Fellowship, 105
Industrial Court, 83
Industrial Remuneration Conference (1885), 270
Industrial Review, 224, 227
Industrial Union of Employers and Employed (1895), 94
Industrial unionism, 150
Industrial Women's Organisations, Standing Joint Committee of, 246. *See also* Working Women's Organisations, National Joint Committee of
Industrial Workers of the World (Wobblies), 150
Inns of Court, Lincoln's Inn, 41
Institution of the Industrious Classes (1831), 210
Institution of the Working Classes, 31, 33
Inter-Parliamentary Union, 187; Congress, Washington (1925), 238
International, 237
International, First, 179, 228, 243
International, Second, Conferences: Paris (1889), 86; London (1896), 20
International, Third, 237, 239, 240; ECCI, 239; Sixth World Congress (1928), 239
International Arbitration League, 108
International Association for Labour Legislation, British section of, 254, 255
International Association for Social Progress, 108, 257; Committee of Enquiry on the Liberty of Trade Unions and Professional Associations (1936), 257
International Association for Workers' Leisure, 108
International Congress of Socialist Women, 184
International Council of Social-Democratic Women, 246, 247; *Bulletin* of, 247
International Federation of Landworkers, 245
International Federation of Ship, Dock and River Workers, 98, 99
International Labour Organisation, 108
International League, 14
International Socialist and Trade Union Congress, London (1896), 40, 74; Amsterdam (1904), 2. *See also* International, Second

International Working Men's Association: *see* International, First
Iraq, xxi
Ireland, 55, 58, 87, 134, 168, 196, 197, 208, 221, 273; Anti-coercion agitation, 18, 270; Anti-Union Association, 49; Civil War (1920–2) in, 88; Easter Rising (1916), 88; Fenian movement in, 269; Home Rule for, 19, 61, 62, 85, 86, 88, 89, 126, 221, 270; Socialist Party of, 134
Ireland, James, 158
Irish Democratic Federation, 62, 78
Irish Land League, 270
Irish Transport and General Workers' Union, 151
Irving, (David) Daniel, 132
Isis, 50
Italy, 14, 27, 113; Unification of, 66, 173

Jackson, Holbrook, 199, 200, 201
Jacob, Joshua, 13
James, John Angell, 64
January Club (1934), 113
Jenkins, John Hogan, 158
Jenkins, Roy Harris, 9
Jewish Machinists, Tailors and Pressers' Union, 102
Joint Industrial Councils, 106; Electricity supply, 111; Local Government, 106; Seed Crushing and Flour Milling, 162
Jones, Ben, 1
Jones, Ernest Charles, 56, 115, 116, 120, 123, 173, 192, 222, 260
Jones, Gale, 49, 166, 167
Jones, John, 205, 206
Jones, Patrick Lloyd, 212
Jones, Peter, 155
Jones, William, 55, 196, 218, 221, 267
Jose, J.H., 82
Jowett, Frederick William, 118, 120, 140, 163
Joyce, William, 27, 28
Joynson-Hicks, William (*later* 1st Viscount Brentford), 132
Judaism, 27, 82, 113, 203
Juggins, Richard, 93
'Junius Redivivus' (pseud.) *see*: Adams, William Bridges (1797–1872)
Junta, 224, 225, 226, 227, 228
Justice, 72, 74, 270, 271
Justices of the Peace, 41, 83, 95, 104, 111, 156, 162, 236, 257, 273; Lord Chancellor's committee for the selection of women justices: *see* Birkenhead, 1st Earl of

Kane, John, 226, 231, 232
Kelley, George Davy, 243
Kellogg, Frank Billings, 238
Kelmscott Press, 72
Kendall, George, **146–50**
Kennedy, John McFarland, 200
Kenney, Annie, 103
Kenney, Rowland, 202
Kessack, James O'Connor, **150–2**
Khrushchev, Nikita, 130, 187
Kimball, Janet, 124
Kime, Timothy, 264
King Alfred School, Hampstead, 251
King, Dr Horace, 186
King, Joseph, 4
Kingsley, Charles, 80, 181
Kitson, Arthur, 201
Kitz, Frank, 18, 270
Knight, James, 267
Knight, Robert, 81, **152–6,** 232
Knight, Thomas F., 263, 264
Knowlton, Charles, 62
Kossuth, Louis, 15
Kropotkin, Prince Peter Alexeivitch, 1, 85

Labour and Socialist International, Women's Committee of, 247
Labour Church, 2, 39–40, 101, 102, 110, 145, 163, 249–52
Labour Church Pioneers, 251
Labour Church Record, 250
Labour Church Settlement, 251
Labour Church Union, 40, 251
Labour Elector, 86
Labour Electoral Association, 110, 137, 138
Labour Exchanges (Owenite), 210–11
Labour Gazette, 96
Labour Governments: (1924), 238; (1929–31), 8, 26, 112, 186, 239; (1945–51), 247
Labour Laws campaign (1871–5), 227
Labour Leader, xxx, 4, 40, 41, 44, 45, 133, 134, 139, 199, 251
Labour, Ministry of, 83; Women's Consultative Committee (1941), 246, 247
Labour Party, 8–10, 23, 88, 89, 106, 108, 112, 113–14, 126, 127, 128, 130, 140, 164, 183, 184, 186, 187, 202, 234, 237, 239, 245, 247, 254, 256; Birmingham Proposals, 202; and Communism, 9, 237, 238, 239, 246; Constitution (1918), 94, 95; 'Fight for Freedom' Group, 247; International Department, 246–7; Labour Representation Committee, 22, 41, 82, 94, 133, 155; League of Youth, xxv; and Mosley Manifesto, 112; National Executive Committee, 186, 187, 237, 246; Parliamentary Labour Party, 186, 187, 200, 274; Peace Aims Group, xxvi, xxviii; Scottish Council, 86, 202; and Second World War, 9; and Social Credit, 202; and

TUC, 94, 95; Victory for Socialism campaign, xxvi; Women's Section, 246
Annual Conferences (LRC): 1900, London, 41; 1901, Manchester, 41; 1902, Birmingham, 94; 1904, Bradford, 102; (LP): 1924, London, 238; 1926, Margate, 265; 1960, Scarborough, 247; 1967, Scarborough, 146
Branches: Battersea, North, 237, 238; Birmingham, 37, 38, 145, 146; Erdington, 38; Gillingham, 158; Hassocks, 158; Hull, 111; Lewisham, East, 83; Peckham, 27; St Pancras, 238; Sheffield, 23, 235, 236, 274; Skipton, 8
Labour Pioneer [Bradford], 119. *See also Yorkshire Factory Times*
Labour Prophet, 40, 250, 251
Labour Representation League, 226, 231
Labour Research Department, xxvi
Labour Standard, 244
Labour Union, 19, 20, 153
Labour Woman, 246, 247
Lacey, William, 79
Ladies' Own Journal, 122
Lamartine, Alphonse Marie Louis de, 212
Lancashire and Cheshire Women Textile and Other Workers' Representation Committee, 102, 103
Lancaster, Joseph, 207
Land and Labour League, 228
Land Law Reform Association, 233, 234
Land Reform, 228, 233, 234, 253
Land Tenure Reform Association, 228
Lane, Joseph, 18, 19
Lang, Cosmo Gordon, Archbishop (*later* Baron Lang of Lambeth), 126, 128
Lansbury, George, xxvi, 9, 96, 126, 238, 239, 273
Lansbury's Weekly, 27
Larkin, James, 151
Lascelles, Henry (2nd Earl of Harewood), 208
Laski, Harold Joseph, 9
Latham, Charles, 106
Lavery, Sir John, 89
Law, Harriet, 190
Lawrence, Arabella Susan, 246
Lawson, Malcolm, 72
Laycock, Rev. William, 39
Leach, Joseph, 218
LeBlond, Robert, 34
League Against Imperialism, 239
League of Nations Union, 108
Leah, James, 217
Leasehold Enfranchisement Society, 233. *See also* Land Law Reform Association
Lee, R.E., 33, 168
Lee, William, 66
Leeds Art Club, 199–200
Leeds University, 125, 131, 162
Legal aid, 257
Lehmann, Dr., 1
Lenin, Vladimir Il'ich Ulyanov, 237, 264
Leno, John Bedford, 268
Lewington, William James, **156–9**
Lewis, Rev. Gomer, xxx
Lewis, (Percy) Wyndham, 203
Lewis, Walter Samuel, 38, 145
Lib-Labourism, 1, 22, 92, 94, 137, 155, 227, 228, 232, 234, 235, 243
Liberal Government (1892), 157; (1906), 82, 140
Liberal Party, 69, 85, 86, 88, 92–3, 107, 109, 118, 140, 149, 161, 163, 181, 222, 227, 228, 233, 234, 237, 272, 273, 274; in Birmingham, 92–3, 196, 197; Chatham, 157; Deptford, 81; Manchester, 44, 102, 143, 179, 180; Nottingham, 136, 192; Wakefield, 15; Women's Associations, 255
Liebknecht, Wilhelm, 20
Linnell, Alfred, 72
Linney, John Fisher, 217
Linney, Joseph, 53, 54, 66, 67, 69, **159–62,** 196
Linton, William James, 70, 267
Lion, 49
Lister, David Cook, **162–3**
Lister, John, 164
Littledale, Mr Justice, 171
Littlewood, France, 44, **163–5**
Liverpool, Lord (Robert Banks Jenkinson, 2nd Earl of Liverpool), 208
Lloyd, Edward, 62
Lloyd, Geoffrey William (*later* Baron Geoffrey-Lloyd), 145
Lloyd, James Henry, 106, 108
Lloyd George, David (*later* 1st Earl Lloyd George of Dwyfor), 132, 183, 256
Local Government Representation, 157; in: Birmingham, 37–38, 93, 145–6; Bradford, 118, 119; Gillingham, 158; Glasgow, 112, 186; Gourock 187; Hackney, 25; Honley, 163, 164; Hull, 111, 162; Leeds, 119; London [LCC], xxiii, xxvi, 9, 19, 81, 83, 128, 237, 263; Manchester, 40, 41, 43, 138, 139, 142, 143, 179–80; Middlesex, 108; Nottingham, 192; Poplar, xxvi, xxviii; Rickmansworth, 268; Rochester, 158; Rothesay, 186; Settle, 8; Sheffield, 22, 23, 235, 273, 274; Stockport, 217; Wakefield, 15
London, Central (Unemployed) Body, 182; Women's Work Committee of, 182; May Day Celebrations (1890), 86, 271; University, 1; King's College, 181
London Amalgamated Society of Carpenters and Joiners, 231
London Baptist Lay Preachers' Association, 105
London Building Trades Federation, 20

London Central Workers' Committee (1905), 271
London Co-operative Trading Association (Owenite), 122, 123, 166
London County Council, xxiii, xxvi, 1, 9, 19, 73, 81, 128; Technical Education Board, 183
London Democratic Association, 170, 172
London Dispatch, 61
London Labour Party, 8, 9
London Operative Tailors' Association, 242, 243
London School Board, 1, 181, 227, 228, 233, 253
London Trade Unionists' Committee, 133
London Trades' Combination Committee, 169
London Working Men's Association (1830s), 61, 168–70, 172
London Working Men's Association, 225, 226
Loughlin, Anne (*later* Dame), 246
Louis-Philippe, King of the French, 66
Lovett, William, 33, 60, 62, 122, **165–79,** 194
Lowell, James Russell, 250
Lowenthal, Esther, 124
Lowery, Robert, 190
Lush, Jennet, 257, 258
Lushington, Godfrey, 225
Lymington, Viscount (Gerard Vernon Wallop, *later* 9th Earl of Portsmouth), 28
Lynch, B.J., 100
Lyndhurst, Lord (John Singleton Copley, 1st Baron Lyndhurst), 141
Lyndon, William Smith, 65
Lytham Times, 139

Maben, William, **179–81**
M'Andrew, Philip, 44
Macarthur, Mary Reid, 92, 103, 106, 254, 255, 256, 257
M'Carthy, Charles, 78
McCarthy, Tom, 20
Macclesfield Courier, 39
MacDiarmid, Hugh (pseud.) *see* Grieve, Christopher Murray
Macdonald, James, 156, 270, 271
MacDonald, James Ramsay, xxvii, 8, 22, 25, 96, 164, 181, 182, 183, 184
MacDonald, Malcolm John, 184
MacDonald, Margaret Ethel Gladstone, **181–5,** 254
MacDonald, Samuel, 150
M'Douall, Peter Murray, 34, 115, 143, 217, 221, 267
McGhee, Richard, 98
M'Grath, Philip, 56, 58, 267
McHugh, Edward, 98
McKeown, Michael, 98
Mackinder, Halford John (*later* Sir), 150
Maclean, John, 4
Macnab, John, 28
Macpherson, Mrs Fenton, 183
McShane, Harry, 88
Magistrates' Association of Great Britain, 257
Magna Charta Association, 270
Maguire, Tom, 199
Mahon, John Lincoln, 19, 87
Mainwaring, Samuel, 19
Maisky, Ivan, 20, 246
Malthus, Thomas Robert, 123
Manchester, xxix, 30, 31, 35, 40, 41, 42–5, 101–3, 110, 132, 137–40, 141–3, 179–80, 206, 231, 242, 243, 250, 271; Academy, 206; Anarchist Group in, xxi, 21; Free Speech Association, xxi; May Day Demonstration (1892), 110, 138; School of Art, 74; Socialist movement in, xxix; University Extension Fund, 140; Victoria University of, 273
Manchester and District Association of Trade Union Officials, 231–2, 243–4
Manchester and Salford Association of Machine, Electrical and Other Women Workers, 102, 104
Manchester and Salford Women's Trade Union Council, 101, 102, 103, 104. *See also* Trades Councils, Manchester and Salford
Manchester and Salford Women's Trades and Labour Council, 103, 104. *See also* Trades Councils, Manchester and Salford
Manchester City News, 44
Manchester Courier, 143
Manchester Evening Chronicle, 139
Manchester Evening News, 40, 45
Manchester Guardian, 44, 221
Manchester Labour Press Society, 138, 139
Manchester New College: *see* Churches and Religious Groups, Unitarian
Manchester Political Union, 217
Manchester Press Club, 41
Manchester Radical Association, 179
Manchester, Salford and District Association of Power Loom Weavers, 102
Manchester Ship Canal, 110
Manchester Society of Journeyman Tailors, 242
Manchester Statistical Society, 41
Manchester Transvaal Committee, 41
Manchester Typographical Association, 138, 139
Mander, Ernest, 24
Mann, Jean, **186–8**
Mann, Tom, 44, 86, 117, 118, 163, 164, 199, 203, 263, 271
Mansbridge, Albert, 3
Mansfield, Katherine, 200
Marinetti, Emilio Filippo Tommaso, 203
Marles, Albert, 199
Marshall, Thomas, 116
Marsland, Samuel, 206
Martin, Emma, 51, **188–91**

Martyn, Caroline, 44
Marx, Eleanor, 86, 89
Marx, Karl, 124, 140, 199, 202. *See also* Authors
Marxism, 8, 126, 237
Mather, William (*later* Sir), 102
Maurice, John Frederick Denison: *see* Authors
Mawdsley, James, 100
Maxton, James, 26, 239
Maxwell, James Shaw, 20, 45, 86
May, George Ernest (*later* 1st Baron May of Weybridge): *see* Economy Committee (1931)
Mazzini, Joseph, 14, 173
Means Test, 127, 128
Mechanics' Institutes, 15, 53, 67, 141, 166, 242, 260
Medical Bulletin, 113
Medical News, 113
Medical Society for the Study of Venereal Diseases, 112
Medway Barge, Yacht and Boat-Building and Repairing Co-operative Society, 158
Melbourne, William Lamb (2nd Viscount Melbourne), 31
Mellor, Mary Ellen, 44
Mellor, William, 201, 202
Menger, Anton, 122
Metal, Engineering and Shipbuilding Amalgamation Committee, 263, 264
Metropolitan Political Union, 60
Miall, Edward, 173
Middleton, James Smith (Jim), 246
Middleton, Mary, 184
Midland Arbitration Union, 197
Midwifery, 17, 190
Mikardo, Ian, 187
Mill, James, 123
Mill, John Stuart, 124, 202
Millar, James Primrose Malcolm, xxvii
Millenarianism, 11, 14, 211
Millennial Gazette, 213
Millennialism, 49
Milligan, George, 151
Millington, Ernest Rogers, 114
Milton, John, 61
Miners' Unions
Local and Regional
South Staffs Coalminers' Association, 67
Mining
Colliery disasters: Round's Green (1846), 67; West Bromwich (1848), 67
Minimum Wage, 255
Missionary and Tract Society (Owenite), 211
Mitchel, John, 79
Mitchell, James, 217
Mitchell, Joseph, 30
Mitchell, Rosslyn, 186
Mitchison, Naomi, xxvii
Mitrinovic, Dmitri, 203
Mond, Sir Alfred Moritz (*later* 1st Viscount Melchett), 25–6
Montrose, James Graham (6th Duke of Montrose), 89
Moreville Communitorium, 12, 13
Morgan, John Minter, 122
Morley, Samuel, 192, 226, 227
Morning Post, xxiii
Morocco, 87
Morris, William, 1, 18, 19, 71, 72, 73, 76, 84, 85, 86, 134, 199, 200, 203
Morrison, Herbert, 8–9, 25, 114
Morrison, James, 211
Mortimer, James Edward, 154, 155
Morton, Howard, 58
Moscheles, Felix, 2
Mosely Industrial Commission, 82
Mosley Manifesto, 112
Mosley, Cynthia Blanche, Lady, 112, 113
Mosley, Michael, 113
Mosley, Oswald Ernald (*later* Sir), 27, 28, 112, 113, 127, 145, 202
Moss, Charles, 43
Mott, William Henry, 136, **192–3**
Moulson, Richard Percival, 206
Muir, Edwin, 200
Mundella, Anthony John, 45, 148
Munich Agreement (1938); *see* Germany
Municipal Employees' Association (*later* NUGMW), 111
Municipal Reform, 233; League, 234
Munitions, Ministry of, 96, 263
Münzenberg, Willi, 239
Murchie, James, 233
Murphy, John Thomas, 246, 263, 264
Musicians' Union, 95, 106, 132
Mussolini, Benito, 27, 113, 203

Napoleonic Wars, 208
Nation, 269
National Agricultural Labourers' Union, 227, 250
National Amalgamated Malleable Ironworkers' Association of Great Britain, 226, 232
National Anti-Sweating League, 254, 255
National Association for Promoting the Political and Social Improvement of the People, 62, 171, 172; National Hall of, 173
National Association for the Advancement of Art and its Application to Industry, 72
National Association for the Promotion of Social Science, 213
National Association of Probation Officers, 257
National Charter Association: *see* Chartism

National Community Friendly Society, 211. *See also* Owen, Robert
National Council of Labour Colleges, xxviii
National Emigration League, 227
National Federation of Labour Union, 271
National Federation of Women Workers, 256
National Free Labour Association, 99
National Government (1931), 27, 186
National Guilds League, 201
National Hall: *see* National Association for Promoting the Political and Social Improvement of the People
National Industrial and Professional Women's Suffrage Society, 102
National Industrial Association, 94, 156
National Institute for Housecraft, 247
National Institute of Houseworkers, 247. *See also* National Institute for Housecraft
National Labour Educational League, 1
National Parliamentary and Financial Reform Association, 57
National Party (1917), 140
National Party of Scotland, 88
National Peace Council, 108
National Playing Fields Association, 108
National Political Union, 60, 167, 268
National Reform League, 196
National Reform Union, 222, 226
National Reformer, 261
National Sailors' and Firemen's Union, 134
National Secular Society, 18, 179; Hall of Science, 18
National Service, 96
National Socialist League, 28
National Socialist Party (1915), 270
National Society for Women's Suffrage, 14
National Society of Amalgamated Brassworkers, 92, 93, 94, 100, 256
National Transport Workers' Federation, 152
National Trust for Scotland, 89
National Union of Clerks (*later* NUCAW), 105, 106, 107, 108, 237
National Union of Dock Labourers, 98, 151
National Union of Dressmakers' and Milliners' Assistants, 255
National Union of Ex-Servicemen (*later* British Legion), 24–5, 27
National Union of Gasworkers' and General Labourers (*later* National Union of General Workers), 2, 100, 119, 138
National Union of General and Municipal Workers, 111; Women Workers' Section, 256
National Union of General Workers, 119
National Union of Journalists, 139
National Union of Millers, 162; Technical Education Committee, 162
National Union of Railwaymen, 235
National Union of Shop Assistants, 22
National Union of the Working Classes, 31, 33, 49, 60, 61, 167, 168; Cold Bath Fields, 168
National Union of Women Workers, 103, 182–3, 255
National Union of Women's Suffrage Societies, 102, 103, 183
Nationalisation, 138; Electricity, 111; Land, 85, 138; Mines, 85
Navigation Acts, repeal of, 160
Needham, George William (*later* Sir), 41, 43, 44, 45
Nehru, Jawaharlal, 239
Nevinson, Henry Woodd, 88
New Age, 200, 201, 202, 203
New English Art Club, 72
New English Weekly, 203
New Europe, 203
New Harmony Community, 210, 212, 213
New Lanark, 206–8; Education Reforms, 207. *See also* Owenism
New Leader, 120
New Moral World, 11, 13, 51, 211, 213, 266
New Party: *see* Mosley, Sir Oswald Ernald
New Pioneer, 28
New South Wales, Australia, 261
New Statesman, 202
New Unionism, 99
New Zealand, 182; Socialist Church in, 252
Newbold, John Turner Walton, 237, 238
Newcastle Morning Telegraph [NSW], 261
Newcastle upon Tyne, 125; Committee for Watching the War, 116; Foreign Affairs Committee, 116; Garibaldi Committee, 116
Newcastle Weekly Chronicle, 114, 115, 116
Newman, Sir George, 257
Newspaper stamp duty, campaign for abolition of, 141–2, 143, 167, 168–9; Victim Fund for, 167
Newton, William, 34
Newtown, Montgomeryshire, 205, 213, 217
Nichols, John, 217
Nicoll, David, 21
Nicolson, Harold George (*later* Sir), 112, 113
Nietzsche, Friedrich Wilhelm, 199
Nine Hours Movement, 224
1917 Club, 145
No More War Movement, 25
Noel, Rev. Conrad le Despenser Roden, 43, 126, 139
Nonconformist, 196
Norman, Clarence Henry, 200, 237
Normanby, Lord (Constantine Henry Phipps, 1st Marquess of Normanby), 142
North British Advertiser, 122, 124
North British Daily Mail, 124
North of England Socialist Federation, 270

North of England Society for Women's Suffrage 102
Northern Reform Union, 116
Northern Star, 56, 57, 58, 62, 77, 79, 80, 143, 147, 148, 169, 170, 171, 172, 220, 221, 266, 267, 268
Northern Tribune, 116
Norwich Freedom Group, xxv
Notes and Queries, 35
Nottingham, 30, 135, 136, 192
Nottingham Review, 57
Nuffield Hospitals Trust, 236
Nuttall, Joseph, 43, 139

Oak, Rev. Edward W., 39
Oakeshott, Grace, 183
Oastler, Richard, 120
O'Brien, James Bronterre, 115, 116, 166, 170
Occult movement, 203
O'Connell, Daniel, 55, 61, 62, 169, 171
O'Connor, Feargus Edward, 54, 55, 56, 57, 58, 61, 62, 78, 115, 135, 147, 169, 170, 171, 172, 173, 195, 196, 220, 221, 267, 268
O'Connorville, 267, 268
Odger, George, 225, 228, 231
Officer Training Corps, 112
Old Age Pensions, 82, 95, 234, 255
Once a Week, 70
O'Neill, Arthur George, 65, 160, 161, **193–8**
Oppau Commission, 25
Orage, [James] Alfred Richard, **199–205**
Orbiston Community, Motherwell: *see* Owenite communities
Oregon boundary dispute, 212
Our Corner, 71–2
Ouspensky, P.D., 202
Owen, David Dale, 209, 213
Owen, Jane (Mrs R. Fauntleroy), 213
Owen, Richard, 209, 213
Owen, Robert, 11, 33, 121, 122, 123, 166, 169, 189, 190, **205–16.** *See also* Owenism
Owen, Robert Dale, 62, 209, 212, 213
Owen, William, 205, 209, 210, 213
Owenism, 10, 48, 53, 60, 122, 123, 166, 168, 173, 188–9, 190, 207–13, 266; Birmingham Congress (May 1839), 189; Halls of Science, 143, 170, 189
Owenite communities, 208, 209, 210, 211; Orbiston, 122, 210; Queenwood, East Tytherley, 11, 212
Oxford University, 2; Lincoln College, 253; New College, 253

Pacifism, 4, 8, 9, 23, 25, 57, 96, 106, 107, 145, 273, 274; Parliamentary Pacifist Group, xxvi, 274. *See also* First World War *and* Second World War, conscientious objection
Paine, Thomas, 30, 31, 47, 48, 51, 115, 194
Pall Mall Gazette, 270
Palmer, Elihu, 47
Pan-Anglican Congress (1908), 255. *See also* Christian Socialism
Pankhurst, Christabel, xxix, 44, 102, 103, 164
Pankhurst, Emmeline, 43, 44, 45, 164
Pankhurst, Estelle Sylvia, 44, 164, 264
Pankhurst, Dr Richard Marsden, 43, 45, 139, 164, 179
Pare, William, 123, 213
Parke, Ernest, 86
Parliamentary Acts
- 1798, Regulation of Printing and Publication of Newspapers, 141
- 1819, Regulation of Cotton Mills and Factories [Child Employment], 208
- 1829, Friendly Societies, 166
- 1832, Reform, 195
- 1834, Poor Law Amendment, 34, 61, 160, 195
- 1835, Regulation of Municipal Corporations, 142
- 1836, Newspaper and Advertisement Duties, 141
- 1848, Security of the Crown and Government [Gagging Act], 221
- 1851, Dissolution of the National Land Company, 58
- 1859, Combination of Workmen, 242
- 1866–9, Contagious Diseases, campaign for repeal of, 231, 272
- 1867, Representation of the People [Reform Act], xx
- 1870, Education, 197, 272
- 1895, Factory, 254
- 1901, Factory and Workshop, 254
- 1902, Education, 1, 272
- 1905, Unemployed Workmen, 182
- 1906, Trade Disputes, 95
- 1909, Cinematograph, 236
- 1909, Trade Boards, 255
- 1911, National Insurance, 183
- 1914, Defence of the Realm, 119, 264
- 1945, Emergency Laws (Transitional Provisions) [Rent of Furnished Houses Control (Scotland) section], 186
- 1946, National Health Service, 129

Parliamentary Bills
- 1815, Apprentices in Cotton Mills [Child Employment], 208
- 1818, Cotton Factories, 208
- 1832, Parliamentary Reform, 31, 53, 60, 64, 167, 217
- 1833, Suppression of Disturbances (Ireland), 61
- 1836, Stamp Duties, 168

1844, Masters and Servants, 34, 78, 220
1848, 'Gagging': *see* Parliamentary Acts, 1848
1864, Life Annuities and Life Assurances, 225
1882, Prevention of Crime (Ireland) [Irish Coercion], 270
1887, Coal Mines, Regulation, 85
1892, Eight Hour Day, 86
1897, Workmen (Compensation for Accidents), 255
1907, Unemployed Workmen ['Right to Work'], 140
1908–9, Licensing, 183
1927, Trade Disputes and Trade Unions, 26
1931, Unemployment Insurance (No. 3) ['Anomalies'], 27
Parliamentary Constituencies: Ayrshire, North, 86; Bath, 107; Battersea, North, 237; Belper, xxiv; Birmingham: Aston, 37, Bordesley, 95, Ladywood, 145, West, 95; Bolton, 40; Bradford: East, xxiv, West, 39; Chatham, 158; Chelmsford, 114; Cheltenham, 115; Coatbridge, 186; Cockermouth, xxix; Colne Valley, xxix, 133; Dartford, 234; Dewsbury, xxiv; Dudley, 65, 69, 160; Edinburgh, 272; Exeter, 115; Fife, West, 239; Finsbury, 115: East, 234; Fulham: East, 9, West, 9; Gateshead, 25; Glasgow: Blackfriars and Hutchesontown (*later* Gorbals), 40, Camlachie, 86, 150, Central, 186, Shettleston, 239, Springburn, 186; Hackney, 8; Hampstead, 270; Harwich, 23; Holmfirth, 272; Howdenshire, 8; Hyde, 40; Hythe, 28; Lanark, Selkirk, Peebles and Linlithgow [combined boroughs] 209; Lanarkshire: Mid, 86, North East, 150, North West, 85; Leicester, xxiv; Limehouse, 25; Lymington, 226; Manchester: East, xxix, Gorton, 102, 139, North, 102, North East, xxix, North West, 132, South West, 41; Marylebone, 212; Motherwell, 238; Newcastle upon Tyne, xxiv: East, 25, North, 25, West, 25; Newton, 265; Northampton, 271; Nottingham, 192; Oldham, 212; Paisley, 186; Peckham, 25, 27; Peterborough, 227; Preston, 227; Prestwich, 41; Pudsey, xxiv; Renfrewshire, West, 112, 113, 186; Rhondda, 239; Rossendale, 103; Scottish Universities, xxvii; Sheffield, 56, 57: Attercliffe, 22, 23, 24, 273–4, Park, 23; Shoreditch, 19; Skipton, 8; Spen Valley, 107; Stirlingshire and Clackmannan, West, 86, 88; Stockport, 140; Stoke-on-Trent, 226; Watford, 107; Westhoughton, 133; Whitechapel and St George's, 127; Wigan, 103; Wolverhampton, 65, 69
Parliamentary General Elections
1820, 209
1835, 65
1847, 56, 65, 69, 160, 212
1852, 115
1868, 226, 242
1874, 227, 273
1885, xxix, 85, 234, 270
1886, xxix, 85, 227, 234
1892, xxix, 86, 89, 95
1895, 40, 139, 234
1900, xxiv, 41
1906, xxiv, 2, 95, 103, 133, 158, 234, 251, 271
Jan 1910, xxiv, 103, 140, 150, 163, 234
Dec 1910, xxiv, 41, 150, 234
1918 'Coupon', 23, 86, 88, 234
1922, 25, 107, 237, 238, 273, 274
1923, 37, 238
1924, xxiv, 23, 25, 107, 186, 238
1929, 25, 107, 112, 186, 239
1931, 8, 25, 27, 107, 112, 186, 239, 274
1935, 145, 186, 239, 274
1945, xxvii, 9, 186
1950, 186
1959, 187
Parliamentary Labour Party: *see* Labour Party
Parliamentary Reform, 15, 19, 53, 54, 56, 57, 58, 60, 64, 85, 92, 116, 135, 138, 161, 166, 167, 172, 192, 195, 196, 217, 222, 226, 234, 260, 267
Parnell, Charles Stewart, 86
Parry, John Humffreys, 172, 173
Paterson, Emma Anne, 92
Paterson, Thomas, 189
Pattison, Mark, 253
'Peculiar People': *see* Manchester and District Association of Trade Union Officials
Peel, Sir Robert (1750–1830), 208
Peel, Sir Robert (1788–1850), 212
Peet, George, 264
Penny, Charles, 61
Penny, John, 164
Penny Papers, 60
Pensions, war, 104; widows, 256. *See also* Old Age Pensions
Pentrich Rising, 147
Penty, Arthur James, 199, 200, 201, 203
People's Journal, 15
People's League, 135, 173, 192
People's Palace, London, 105
People's Paper, 65, 268
People's Police Gazette, 61
People's Post, 28
People's Press, 98
Percival, Dr Thomas, 206
Perks, Charles, 96

Peterloo (1819): *see* Demonstrations
Petrie, George, 168
Petroff, Peter, 4
Philby, Harry St John Bridger, 28
Phillips, Marion, 245, 247
Phillpotts, Henry, 212
Pickard, Dolly, 133, 134
Pickard, W., 133
Pictet, Charles, 209
Pilling, Richard, **216–23**
Pilling, William, 216, 218, 220, 222
Pitter, Ruth, 200
Place, Francis, 1, 48, 60, 61, 62, 63, 166, 167, 168, 169, 171, 173, 212
Plant, Fred, 133
Platt, Sir Thomas Joshua (Baron of the Exchequer), 79
Plebs, 2
Plebs League, xxvii, xxviii, 2, 202
Plimsoll, Samuel, 155
Pointer, Joseph, 22, 23
Poland, 14, 56, 78, 267. *See also* Chartism
Police and Public : see Illustrated Weekly News
Political Letters, 60
Pollitt, Harry, 127, 239, 240, 264
Ponsonby, Arthur Augustus William Harry (1st Baron Ponsonby of Shulbrede), 274
Poor Laws, xxvi, 66, 117, 118; Pre-1850, 34, 57, 61, 120, 160, 195, 208
Poor Man's Guardian, 31, 48, 60, 141, 142
Poplar, xxvi, 126, 129, 182
Popp, Adelheid, 184
Popular Front, 9, 107
Postal Workers' Journal, 133
Postgate, Raymond William, 231
Postman's Gazette, 19
Postmen's Union, 19
Potter, George, **223–30**
Potter, Sir Thomas, 219
Potter-Wilson, J., 238
Potteries, lead poisoning in, 254
Pound, Ezra Loomis, 200, 202, 203
Powell, R., 158
Powell, Thomas, 78
Powys, Llewelyn, 200
Practical Socialist, 72
Pratt, Daniel, 226, 227
Pratt, Edwin A., 99
Pratt, Edward Loucestre, 263
Pratt, Jonathan, 197
Preston, 217
Preston, Thomas, 33
Priestman, Arthur, 164
Prior, John Damrel, 93, **230–3**
Progressive Society of Carpenters and Joiners, 223–4, 226
Promethean or Communitarian Apostle, 12
Prompter, 49
Pugh, Arthur (*later* Sir), 238
Punch, 70

Quaile, Mary, 104
Queenwood Community: *see* Owenite communities
Quelch, Harry, 20, 157
Quinn, James F., 138

Radical Reform Association, 49, 60, 166, 167
Railway Women's Guild, 183, 184
Rancliffe, George Augustus Parkyns (2nd Lord Rancliffe [Irish Peer]), 192
Randall, A.E., 200
Randall, Rev. T., 136
Rappites, 209–10
Rathbone, Eleanor, 256
Rational Quarterly Review, 213
Ravachol, François Claudius, 21
Raven, Rev. John, 66
Read, Herbert (*later* Sir), 200
Reading University College, 74
Reasoner, 58, 190, 260
Reckitt, Maurice Benington, 201, 202
Reddish, Sarah, 102, 103
Reform League, xx, 161, 225, 226, 242; in Ashton, 222; in Birmingham, 196; in Plymouth, 230
Reformer [Edinburgh], 226
Reformers' Monument, Kensal Green, 213
Register [Cobbett's], 30, 32
Reid, Andrew, 72
Rendall, Ellen, 1
Repeal Organisation: *see* O'Connell, Daniel
Republican, 47, 48
Republican Association, 33
Republicanism, 179, 228, 243, 270
Revolutions of 1848, 56, 66, 70. *See also* France
Reynolds, George William McArthur, 57, 62, 78, 80
Reynolds's News, 224
Reynolds's Political Instructor, 77, 268
Ricardo, David, 124
Richards, John, 196
Ricketts, Compton, 87
Rigby, James, 213
Ritchie, Joseph, 78
Rivera, Diego, 239
Robert Owen's Journal, 213
Roberts, David, 217
Roberts, William Prowting, 143, 267
Roebuck, Arthur, 193
Roebuck, John Arthur, 57, 60, 61, 171
Rogers, John, 193
Rogerson, George, 138
Roland, Marie Jeanne Philipon, 190

Roosevelt, (Anna) Eleanor, 187
Roper, Esther, 102, 103
Rosebery, Archibald Philip Primrose (5th Earl Rosebery), 73
Rosen, Tubby, 128
Rotary Club, 146
Rothenstein, Will, 76, 89
Rothermere, Lady (Mary Lilian Harmsworth), 202
Rothermere, Lord (Harold Sidney Harmsworth, 1st Viscount Rothermere of Hemsted), 113
Rowlands, James, **233–5**
Rowlinson, Ernest George, **235–6**
Royal Academy, 72
Royal Army Medical Corps, 112
Royal College of Art, 74
Royal College of Music, 165
Royal Commissions
  1845, Framework Knitters, 147
  1867–9, Trade Unions, 225–6, 242
  1871, Contagious Diseases Acts, 231
  1876, Factory and Workshops Acts, 92
  1884–5, Housing of the Working Classes, 18
  1886, Depression of Trade and Industry, 155
  1891–4, Labour, 153, 154, 155, 157
  1905–9, Poor Laws, 182
  1906, Trade Disputes and Trade Combinations, 82
  1926, National Health Insurance, 257
  1939–40, Distribution of the Industrial Population, 107
  1945–6, Equal Pay, 247
Royal Dockyards, 157, 234
Royal Institution, 181
Royal Maternity Charity, 190
Royal Society, 71
Royal Society for the Prevention of Accidents, 187
Royden, Maude, 20
Rudling, Alex., xxv
Rushton, Benjamin, 115
Ruskin, College, 96, 107, 108; Strike, 2
Ruskin, John, 70, 202, 203
Russell, John, 251
Russia, 3, 4, 20, 107, 127, 128, 202, 239, 246, 264; 'Hands off Russia' movement, 264; 1917 Revolution, February/March, 4, 237, October/November, 237
Russian Political Prisoners and Exiles' Relief Committee, 3, 4
Rylett, Rev. Harold, 200

St Katharine's, Royal Foundation of, 129, 130
St Martin's Hall Conference, 226, 230
St Simonism, 123
St Teresa, 84
Saklatvala, Beram Shapurji, 240
Saklatvala, Shapurji Dorabji, 20, **236–41**
Salisbury, Lord (Robert Arthur Talbot Gascoyne-Cecil, 3rd Marquess of Salisbury), 227
Salter, Dr Alfred, 133
Sand, George, 17
Satterfield, John, 205
Saturday Review, 87
Saville, John, 116
Saxton, James, 148
Scarth, Jonathan, 206
Schapper, Carl, 56
School Boards 1, 41, 81, 92, 110, 136, 149, 158, 181, 199, 227, 228, 233, 253
School children, employment of, 41, 207–8
Schwann, Charles Ernest (*later* Sir C.E. Swan), 102
Schwann, Mrs Elizabeth, 102
Scotland, Committee on Women in Agriculture (1920), 245; Home Rule for, 19, 85, 86, 88, 89
Scotland Yard, 264
Scots Observer, 72
Scots Town and County Councillor, 186
Scotsman, 122
Scott, Charles Prestwich, 102
Scottish Farm Servant, 245
Scottish Farm Servants' Union, 245, 248
Scottish Farmer, 245
Scottish Home Rule Association, 86, 88. *See also* National Party of Scotland, Scottish Labour Party (pre-1893), 86
Scottish Union of Dock Labourers, 151
Scouller, Robert Elder (Bob), 106
Scurr, John, xxvi
Seafaring, 98
Seamen's Christian Friend Society, 108
Seamen's Chronicle, 98, 99
Second World War (1939–45), 9, 28, 127, 128–9, 146, 246–7, 265, 274; Armistice manifesto, xxvi, xxviii; conscientious objection, 274; Information, Ministry of, 9; Local Defence Volunteers (*later* Home Guard), 28
Secularism, 137, 179, 260–1; Midlands Secular Union, 261
Seddon, James Andrew, 95
Select Committees
  1816, Employment of Children in U.K. Manufactories, 208
  1817, Poor Laws, 208
  1823, Employment of the Poor in Ireland, 208
  1851, Newspaper Stamps, 143
  1877, Employers' Liability, 155
  1899, Aged Deserving Poor, 255–6
  1907, Home Work, 182, 255
  1932–3, Local Expenditure (England and Wales) [Ray Committee], 38, 236

Senior, Nassau William, 81
Settle, Alfred, 138
Sexton, James, 95, 151
Shackleton, David James, 82
Shapiro, Michael, 128
Sharp, Clifford Dyce, 202
Sharples, Eliza, 49, 50, 51, 190
Shaw, Sir Charles, 142
Shaw, George Bernard, 8, 19, 74, 76, 85, 87, 133, 145, 200. *See also* Authors
Shaw, John, 268
Sheffield, xxvii, 22, 23, 24. 56, 57, 235, 236, 272, 273, 274
Sheffield, Lord (Edward Lyulph Stanley, 4th Baron Sheffield), 4
Sheffield Guardian, 22
Sheffield Independent, 57
Sheffield Reform Association, 272
Shelley, Percy Bysshe, 48, 143. *See also* Authors
Sherwin, William T., 46, 47
Sherwin's [Weekly] Political Register, 46, 47
Shipbuilding Federation, 83
Shop Assistants' Union: *see* National Union of Shop Assistants
Shop Stewards' Movement, 263
Shorrocks, Peter, **242–5**
Short, Rev. L.B., 252
Short Time Movement, 142
Sidmouth, Henry Addington (1st Viscount Sidmouth), 30
Simcox, Edith, 253
Simmons, John, 147
Simon, Sir John Allsebrook (*later* 1st Viscount Simon of Stackpole Elidor), 107
Sims, George, 2
Sinn Fein, 134. *See also* Ireland
Skene, George, 166
Slap at the Church, 60
Slaughter, Fred, 18
Slave Trade, 77, 173
Smalley, Agnes, 44
Smalley, S., 43
Smart, Hymen Russell, 41, 44, 138
Smethurst, Joseph, 222
Smillie, Robert, xxix, 150
Smith, Constance, 254, 255, 257
Smith, Edward James, 93
Smith, James Elishama (Shepherd), 211
Smith, Joseph, 200
Smith, Thorley, 103
Snowden, Philip (*later* 1st Viscount Snowden of Ickornshaw), 8, 133, 164
Snowden, Thomas, 8
Social Credit, 28, 202, 203; Council of Representatives, 203
Social-Democrat, 87
Social Democratic Federation, xxiv, 4, 18, 22, 71, 72, 73, 74, 75, 109, 110, 117, 119, 137, 138, 179, 180, 234, 270, 271. *See also* British Socialist Party
Social Democratic Party, xxiv, 1, 132
Socialist Labour Party, 150, 270
Socialist League (1885–94), 1, 18, 19, 21, 72, 75, 84, 270; (1932–7), 246
Socialist National Defence Committee, 88
Socialist Party of Great Britain, 270
Socialist Workers' Sports International, 108
Society for Promoting National Regeneration, 211
Society for Psychical Research, 199
Society for the Promotion of Permanent and Universal Peace, 197
Society for the Protection of Booksellers, 61
Society for the Suppression of Vice, 31, 47
Society for Women employed in the Bookbinding and Printing Trades, 102
Society of Arts, 230
Society of St Francis, 129
Solly, Rev. Henry, 226–7, 228
Soper, Rev. Donald Oliver (*later* Baron [Life Peer]), 130
South Africa, 82, 234, 273; Jameson Raid, 87
South America, 84, 87, 88, 89
South London Press, 124
South Place Institute, 213
South Side Labour Protection League, 157
South Wales Federation of Ship-Repairers, 81
Southey, Robert, 31
Southwell, Charles, 189
Soviet Union: *see* Russia
Spain, 84
Spanish-American War, 87
Spanish Civil War, xxv, 9, 127, 145; Basque children, 127
Spectator, 100
Spence, Thomas, 30, 32
Spencer, R., 244
Spiritualism, 213
Spottiswoode, Dr William, 71
Spurgeon, Charles, 135
Squire, Sir John, 113
Stacy, Enid, 45
Standard, 223
Stanley, Lord: *see* Derby, 17th Earl of
Star, 86
Star of Freedom, 34
Steadman, William Charles, 82
Stephens, Rev. John Rayner, 34, 170, 217
Stepney, 128, 129; Tenants' Defence League, 128
Stepniak, Sergei, 85
Stevenage Development Corporation, 10
Stevenson, J.J., 82
Stevenson, Robert Louis, 71

Stockport, 2, 132, 133, 137, 139, 140, 217, 218, 219, 220
Stockport Express, 134, 137, 139, 140
Stockport Herald, 133
Stockton, Herbert, 21
Storer, Thomas, 219
Strachey, (Evelyn) John (St Loe), 112, 202
Strang, William, 89, 258
Strathclyde University, 248
Strikes and Lockouts
  Brassworkers
    Birmingham (1874), 92
    Birmingham (1889–90), 93
  Builders
    London (1859–60), 224
    Birmingham (1864–5), 225
  Burston School (1914), 133
  Carpenters and Joiners
    Plymouth and Devonport (1864–5), 230
    Manchester (1877–8), 231
  Chain makers
    Brierley Hill (1859), 54
  Clerks
    Nobel Explosives Factory (1915), 106
  Cotton operatives
    Lancashire (1842), 218–19
    Ashton (1843), 220
  Derby (1833), 211
    Silkweavers at (1834–5), 61
  Docks
    London (1889), 86, 137
    Merseyside (1890), 151
    Hull (1893), 151
    Liverpool (1905), 151
    Belfast (1906), 151
  Engineers
    Bolton (1887), 117
    (1897), 155
    London (1907), 262
    London (1917), 263
  General Strike (1926), xxiv, 37–8, 107, 126, 164, 238
  Hosiery workers
    Nottinghamshire (1860), 148
  Leeds Corporation (1913), 119
  Manningham Mills, Bradford (1890–1), 118
  Match girls (1888), 86, 271
  Miners
    South Staffordshire (1842), 66, 160; (1858), 67; (1864), 161
    South Wales (1875), 232, 244; (1898), xxix
    Cambrian Combine (1910–11), 100
    (1926), 238
  Nailers
    Dudley and Lye (1826), 64
    Black Country (1850–2), 54
  Postmen
    London, Mount Pleasant (1890), 19
  Potteries (1842), 55
  Puddlers
    North Staffs (1865), 225
  Railways (1911), 103, 235
  Spinners
    Mossley and Stalybridge (1847), 220
  Tailors
    London (1834), 77
    Manchester (1865), 242; (1867), 242
  Textiles
    Stockport (1840), 218
    Preston (1853), 115
Student Christian Movement, 255
Sturge, Joseph, 62, 172, 195, 196
Summerskill, Dr Edith Clara (*later* Baroness Summerskill of Ken Wood [Life Peeress]), 9, 10
Sunday Chronicle, 133, 139
Sutherland, Alexander, 245, 248
Sutherland, Mary Elizabeth, **245–9**
Sutton, John Edward, 43
Swann, Joseph, 48, 142
Sweated Industries, 19, 106, 182, 244, 254, 255; Sweated Trades Exhibition (1906), 255
Swedish Social Democratic Women's League, 247; Congress of (1960), 247
Sweet, James, 136, 192
Swinnerton, James, 39
Switzerland, 187
Sykes, John, 221
Symons, Arthur, 87, 89
Syndicalism, 200–1, 263. *See also* Workers' Control

Taff Vale Case, 82, 99, 234
Tanner, Jack, 264
Tariff Reform, 100
Tariff Reform League, 140
Tasmania, 77, 79; Master and Servant Laws in, 79
Tata, Jamsetji Nasarwanji, 236
Tata, Sir Ratan J., 237
Taverner, Grace, 8
Tavistock, Marquess of: *see* Bedford, Duke of
Tawney, Richard Henry, 202
Taxation, reform of, 253
Taylor, Ida, 87
Taylor, Rev. Robert, 49, 50
Temperance Movement, 12, 83, 105, 108, 110, 153, 156, 157, 179, 261, 272, 273, 274. *See also* Chartism
Temperance Societies
    Band of Hope Union, 105, 180; Rechabites,

260; Sons of Temperance, 110, 261; United Kingdom Alliance, 67, 261; Workers' Temperance League, 105, 273
Temple Forum (Discussion Group), 58
Temple, William, Archbishop (of York), 126, 128, 129
Ten Hours Advocate, 260
Ten Hours Movement, in Lancashire, 217, 218, 260
Tennant, Harold John, 257
Tennyson, Alfred, Lord, 70
Theosophical Society, 199, 200; in Leeds, 199
Theosophy, 75, 200
Thistlewood, Arthur, 30, 33
Thomas, David Alfred (*later* 1st Viscount Rhondda), 100
Thomas, Dylan, 203
Thomas, James Henry, 96, 265
Thompson, Arthur Frederick, 154
Thompson, George, 217
Thompson, Thomas Perronet, 123
Thompson, William, 122, 123
Thorne, William James (Will), 20
Thornely, Thomas, 65
Tichborne Case, 270
Tilden-Smith, Richard, 240
Tillett, Benjamin (Ben), 39, 45, 86, 88, 100, 133, 181, 250
Time, 72
Times, 34, 51, 85, 99, 100, 123, 183
To-day, 72
Todd, Thomas, 15
Token coinage, 96
Tolpuddle Martyrs, 33, 61, 168, 211
Tong Pioneer of Social Reform, 119
Town and Country Planning Association (for Scotland), 186
Trade Unionist, 263
Trades Councils: Battersea, xxiii, 237; Birmingham, 37, 96, 145, 243; Bradford, 75, 119; Edinburgh, 226; London, 81, 224, 225; Long Eaton, 181; Manchester and Salford, 101, 103, 137, 138, 242, 243, Women's Group on, 101, 104; Medway District, 158; Sheffield, 22, 23, 235; Sheffield Federated, 22, 235; Southwark, 265; Stirling, 245; Woolwich and District, 2
Trades' Newspaper, 59
Trades Newspaper Co. Ltd, 224
Trades Union Congress, 83, 92, 93, 94, 96, 106, 108, 155, 228, 232, 238; Committee of Inquiry into Problems of Federation, 155; General Council, 107; and Labour Party, 94, 95; Parliamentary Committee, 1, 82, 94, 155, 227, 232, 243; and Social Credit, 202; Standing Orders Committee, 243; and workers' education, 1, 2
Annual Conferences:
1868, Manchester, 226, 242
1869, Birmingham, 92, 242, 243
1871, London, 227, 243
1875, Glasgow, 92
1876, Newcastle upon Tyne, 232
1877, Leicester, 92
1879, Edinburgh, 155
1880, Dublin, 243
1890, Liverpool, 98
1898, Bristol, 155
1902, London, 94
1906, Liverpool, 82
1908, Nottingham, 92
1909, Ipswich, 2, 92
1916, Birmingham, 94
1918, Derby, 95
1938, Blackpool, 107
Transport, Ministry of, 107
Transport and General Workers' Union, 152, 162
Travis, Henry, 213
Treasury, Departmental Committee on the Working of the Fair Wages Resolution (1907–8), 82
Trevelyan, Charles Philips (*later* Sir), 25, 274
Trevor, Hugh, 252
Trevor, John, 39, 40, 110, 138, **249–53**
Trevor, Stanley, 251
Tribune, 139
Tribune of the People, 33
Trotsky, Leon (Lev Davidovich Bronstein), 4
Troup, George, 224, 228
Truck system, 148, 160–1, 221, 255; Commission on (1871), 148
Tschiffely, Aimé Felix, 85
Tuckwell, Gertrude Mary, 2, **253–9**
Tuckwell, Rev. William, 253
Turner, Ben (*later* Sir), 119
Turner, William, 147
Tweedale, William, 43
Tweedsmuir, Lady (Priscilla Jean Fortescue Buchan, Baroness Tweedsmuir of Belhelvie), 186
Tytherley Community: *see* Owenite communities, Queenwood

Underwood, Florence, 108
Union of Democratic Control, 274
United Framework Knitters' Society, 148, 149
'United Front', 9, 145, 246
United Nations, Commission on the Status of Women, 247
United Society of Boilermakers and Iron and Steel Shipbuilders, 81, 82
United States of America, 30, 51, 73, 82, 84, 99, 182, 203, 210, 212, 213, 221, 249; Civil War,

213, 224, 225, 228; Valley Forge Community, 122
United Trades Association, 211
Universal Communitarian Association, 11
Universal Community Society of Rational Religionists, 211, 266
Universal Suffrage Club, 61
'Unstamped' Press, 47, 48, 60, 61, 62, 115, 141, 142, 167, 168

Vanity Fair, 89
Vansittart, Nicholas (1st Baron Bexley), 208
Vansittart, Robert Gilbert (1st Baron Vansittart of Denham), 247
Veerman, Leon, 132
Veterans, Orphans and Victims' Relief Committee, 56, 62
Victoria, Queen, 143, 218
Villiers, Charles Pelham, 65
Vincent, Henry, 54, 62, 115, 160, 173
Vowers, G., 43

Wade, John, 46
Wages Boards: *see* Boards of Arbitration and Conciliation
Wakefield, 15
Wakley, Thomas, 115
Waldegrave, A.J., 252
Wales, Home Rule for, 19
Walker, Benjamin, 135
Walker, Emery, 72
Walker, James, 247
Wallace, Rev. J. Bruce, 20
Wallace, Lewis, 200
Wallwork, Daniel, 65, **259–62**
Walmsley, Sir Joshua, 57, 58
Walpole, Spencer Horatio, 225
Walsall, 160–1. *See also* Anarchism
Ward, William George, 148
Wardle, George James, 140
Wareham, George, 217
Wareing, Alfred, 145
Warwick, Frances Evelyn (Daisy), Countess of, 2, 88, 132, 271
Watkin, William, 231
Watson, James, 33, 48, 60, 62, 166, 167, 168, 173
Watson, Dr James, 30, 47
Watson, William Foster, **262–6**
Watts, George Frederic, 75
Watts, Simon, 65
Weavers' Association, 217
Webb, Beatrice, 99, 145, 154, 228, 244, 257
Webb, Maurice, 8
Webb, Sidney (*later* 1st Baron Passfield of Passfield Corner), 99, 145, 154, 228, 244, 254
Weekly Free Press, 59
Weekly Police Gazette, 61, 62
Weitling, William, 11, 13, 14
Wells, Herbert George, 8, 87, 145
Wemyss, Col. Thomas James, 142
Westlake, Alice, 253
Westminster Gazette, 98
Westminster Review, 123
Wheatley, John, 26, 27
Wheeler, George, 268
Wheeler, Thomas Martin, 58, 78, 79, 80,**266–9**
White City Exhibition, 106
White collar unionism, 95, 105, 106, 107, 132, 139
White, George, 196
Whitley Councils, Local Government, 106
Wicksteed, Philip Henry, 250
Wilde, Oscar, 72
Wilderspin, Samuel, 15
Wilgar, Miss, 102
Wilkes, John, 169
Wilkie, Alexander, 94, 96
Wilkinson, William, 102
Wilks, Albert, 139
Willey, Octavius George, 8
Williams, John (Jack) Edward, **269–72**
Williams, Joseph B., 95, 106, 132
Williams, Morgan, 78
Williams, Samuel Norbury, 179, 180
Williams, Zephaniah, 55, 196, 218, 221, 267
Wilmot, John, 9
Wilson, Cecil Henry, **272–5**
Wilson, Henry Joseph, 272, 273, 274
Wilson, (James) Harold (*later* Sir), 187
Wilson, John Wycliffe, 272, 273
Wilson, Joseph Havelock, 95, 100, 134
Wilson, Mona, 257
Wilson, William Tyson, 133
Winnington-Ingram, Arthur Foley, Bishop, 126, 127
Wise, John Richard de Capel, 70
Wolfenden, Sir John, 129
Wolstonecraft, Mary, 17
Wolverhampton, 161, 195
Woman's Industrial Independence, **Special Note** on, 16–18
Women, rights of, xxviii, 10–15, 16–18, 51, 89, 92, 101–2, 104, 107, 173, 182–4, 189–90, 212, 218, 246, 247, 254–7. *See also* **Special Note** on Woman's Industrial Independence
Women Sanitary Inspectors' and Health Visitors' Association, 257
Women's Co-operative Guild, 2, 23, 101, 102, 103, 246
Women's Employment, Central Committee on: *see* Women's Training and Employment Central Committee.
Women's Freedom League, 108
Women's Industrial Council, 182, 183, 184, 254;

Home Industries Inquiry, 182; Industrial Training Conference, 183; Unemployment Conference, 182
Women's International Conference on Peace, The Hague (1915), 104
Women's Labour League, 183, 184
Women's Social and Political Union, xxix, 102
Women's Suffrage Movement, 102–3, 108, 132, 164, 183, 200, 246. *See also* Parliamentary Reform
Women's Total Abstinence Union, 272. *See also* Temperance
Women's Trade Union League, 2, 103, 106, 253, 254, 255, 256
Women's Trade Union Review, 254
Women's Training and Employment Central Committee, 104, 256
Women's Voluntary Service (WVS), 246
Wood, Mrs Henry, 70
Wood, William Henry, 242, 243
Woodcock, Patricia, 132
Woods, Fred, 108
Wooler, Thomas Jonathan, 46
Woolwich Arsenal, Trade Union Rights Committee, 263
Workers' Control, 264
Workers' Dreadnought, 264
Workers' Educational Association, 3, 107, 129
Workers' Temperance League: *see* Temperance Societies
Workers' Union, 139, 237
Workers' Weekly, 265
Workers' Welfare League (1916), 238
Working Man's Friend, 60, 61
Working Men's College, 107, 233
Working Men's Committee for Promoting the Separation of Church and State, 227
Working Women's Labour College, 3
Working Women's Organisations, National Joint Committee of, 246
Workman's Times, 81, 138
Workmen's Peace Association, 234
Wright, Carroll Davidson, 99
Wright, Frances, 190
Wright, John, 217

Yeats, John, 71
Yorkshire Electricity Board, 111
Yorkshire Factory Times, 4. *See also Labour Pioneer*
Young Men's Christian Association, 181
Young, Robert, 265

Zinoviev Letter, 238
Zschokke, Johann Heinrich Daniel, 71